John A. Kasson

JOHN A. KASSON

Politics and Diplomacy from Lincoln to McKinley

By EDWARD YOUNGER

STATE HISTORICAL SOCIETY OF IOWA
IOWA CITY 1955

PRINTED IN THE UNITED STATES OF AMERICA
BY THE TORCH PRESS, CEDAR RAPIDS, IOWA

To

BARBARA ELLEN
ELLEN BADGETT
WILLIAM RANDOLPH

Editor's Foreword

JOHN A. KASSON arrived in Iowa in 1857, the same year the capital was moved from Iowa City to Des Moines. Settling in the new capital, Kasson embarked on a political career that won him lasting renown for his "cumulative record as a constructive conservative" in American politics and diplomacy. He stands in the forefront of the galaxy of notable Iowans who served their state and nation between 1860 and 1900.

Born in Charlotte, Vermont, in 1822, Kasson graduated from the University of Vermont, tutored a slaveholder's family in Virginia, studied and practiced law in Massachusetts, and then came west to St. Louis in 1851 to practice law for six years before coming to Iowa. During his St. Louis sojourn he made warm friends who did much to shape his meteoric political career.

John Kasson was warmly received in Des Moines. He promptly identified himself with the newborn Republican party, and was named a delegate to the Chicago Convention that nominated Lincoln for president in 1860. Kasson, with Horace Greeley, Carl Schurz, Austin Blair, and William Jessup, drew up the difficult Republican platform of 1860 which Horace Greeley himself declared was "eminently due" to Kasson and which "reflected more fairly and fully" than ever before the "average convictions of a great National party."

When Lincoln became president, Kasson was appointed First Assistant Postmaster General. He represented the United States in the first International Postal Congress, taking the lead in its historic deliberations. His success at this conference paved the way for future diplomatic missions, a field in which the courtly, polished, well-trained Iowan excelled.

Kasson served three terms in the Iowa General Assembly, where he sponsored the appropriation to begin construction on the present-day state house. He also served six different terms in Congress, where his ability and constructive statesmanship stood him in good stead. A "brilliant orator, ready debater, and skilled parliamentarian," Kasson was always a "practical legislator" whether in the General Assembly or the halls of Congress, or negotiating with foreign nations in Paris, Vienna, Berlin, and Quebec.

Professor Edward Younger has written a scholarly, readable, understanding, and definitive biography of John A. Kasson. The book clearly portrays him as a man who was the "peer" of all his Iowa political contemporaries; it sheds much light on a host of notable Iowans who illumine the pages of Iowa political, economic, and social history prior to Kasson's death in 1910; and in a number of revealing chapters it gives a fresh treatment of American diplomacy from Lincoln to McKinley.

WILLIAM J. PETERSEN

OFFICE OF THE SUPERINTENDENT
STATE HISTORICAL SOCIETY OF IOWA
IOWA CITY, IOWA

Contents

Illustrations

John A. Kasson

Politics and Diplomacy from Lincoln to McKinley

☆ **I** ☆

At Lincoln's First Inauguration

On a raw, windy day in March, 1861, Chief Justice Taney tottered forward on a rickety platform in front of the nation's half-built capitol to swear in Abraham Lincoln as President of the United States. Curious and anxious people thronged about to observe the separation of a new order from the old under the threatening clouds of disunion and war. In the tense audience stood John A. Kasson, a rapidly rising Republican leader from Iowa. In the midst of a snowstorm he had left Des Moines by stagecoach to attend Lincoln's inauguration. While

1

in Washington, he was to receive an appointment of great significance to his future political and diplomatic career.

To bystanders Kasson presented a striking and commanding appearance on this eventful day. Aged thirty-nine, slightly under six feet, he was wiry, standing erect and walking with a lithe, positive step. In bearing he was proud, something about his carriage, manner, and dress giving him an air of self-confidence and determination. Always immaculately groomed, he did not look the picture of the typical rough westerner of his time. His chestnut hair was neatly parted and combed down, the ends curling up slightly over the ears; he wore a mustache which curved with his upper lip until it fell below the lower at the corners of his mouth and turned up; his chin and face were shaved, and his sideburns ran downward until they merged with a beard which grew under his chin from ear to ear like a furred chin strap. His nose was smoothly tapered, regular, and on the thin side; chin strong; eyes steely gray, with a slight, lynx-like droop of the lids; and face nicely proportioned, tapering smoothly from his forehead to his chin except for high cheek bones. He was austerely handsome, and his expression, which was to soften in later years, was intense, approaching severity. His intimates, however, knew him as a kindly, mannerly, urbane man, fond of forensics, society, and conversation.

Accompanying Kasson to Washington was Grenville M. Dodge, purposeful and positive engineer from Council Bluffs, Iowa. Dodge was soon to become a Civil War general, a capable builder of railroads, a skillful lobbyist, and, mixing politics with business, a substantial entrepreneur. His and John Adam Kasson's fates were to be closely intertwined for the next few years and their relations intimate, until the exigencies of politics and the soaring ambition of Dodge and his followers led to bitter animosity and Kasson's temporary disgrace and defeat in the critical and vulgar election of 1866.

In Washington, Kasson and Dodge were joined by William B. Allison, Herbert M. "Hub" Hoxie, and a few other Iowans to form a small coterie of men who held political powwows and, along with Iowa's congressional delegation, performed the functions of a placement committee for the state's share of federal patronage. Add Governor Samuel J. Kirkwood, and these men formed the core of the Iowa Republican organization. Allison, aged thirty-two, a broad-framed man of medium height, mild and dignified in manner and moderate in his views, had barely begun his political ascent. He was soon to enter Congress, where, first as Representative and then as Senator for five continuous terms, he became "The Republican Institution" as party conciliator and firm champion of the nation's expansive business urge. Indomitable "Hub" Hoxie, aged thirty-one, second-rate Des Moines lawyer, had just taken over the party reins from Kasson as chairman of the State Central Committee. Like Dodge, Hoxie hoped to find the main chance by mixing political influence with business. Only during the impending war was he to cut a large swath in politics. As a railroad lobbyist and intimate of Dodge he was to climb from the General Agency of the Union Pacific Railroad into the arms of Jay Gould as first vice-president of the Missouri Pacific before his untimely death in 1886.

This small group temporarily took a "half-house, with double parlors and five rooms upstairs," just back of the National Hotel, where they had their meals. There "everybody from Iowa" visited them. Their "parlors [were] always crowded," even the ladies "pressing the claims of their better halves" and importuning "everyone." Washington "bristled with bayonets,"[1] and old Winfield Scott, bleary-eyed, "the skin on his hands and face much discolored,"[2] was praised for his "great and excellent measures to keep the peace." "Such a rush and such a pulling I never saw before!" wrote Gren Dodge. "The Goths and Vandals from the Northwest take things by storm."[3] Fifty or sixty additional Iowans arrived, as the number from the Northwest swelled into the thousands. The Iowa crowd was received in the East Room by Mrs. Lincoln and Old Abe himself who paid close attention to one George May whose father he knew in Illinois; they called upon General Winfield Scott who received them in "a simple morning gown of some cheap material like calico";[4] and some of them attended the great inaugural ball in the rear of the City Hall in Judiciary Square, so crowded that thousands could not get in. There they probably saw short and heavily formed Stephen A. Douglas promenading with Mrs. Lincoln.

Mixed motives brought them to Washington. Some came out of curiosity, some to celebrate the great political victory: "Old Abe has never been inaugurated before . . . and the Northwest ought to be there to see it done."[5] Some came to give confidence and support to the new administration in the nation's greatest crisis. Some sought political rewards, and others hoped to cash in on the Republican victory by fat government contracts.

Dodge's main interest lay in the realm of railway legislation, and he was in Washington as a lobbyist. Hoxie, owing primarily to Kasson's backing, was already the unconfirmed United States Marshal for Iowa. Allison sought a federal appointment. All three of these men aimed to make money through political connections. By controlling an Indian Agency they might sell supplies to the Indians — or, in case of war, they might obtain lucrative war contracts. For such favors Dodge and Hoxie planned to lean heavily on Kasson's influence with two prominent St. Louisans, Edward Bates and Montgomery Blair, who were entering Lincoln's cabinet. Although these plans [6] were to go awry, they indicate that at the moment Kasson was the political superior of the coterie.

Kasson's rise to political promise had been meteoric. Only four years previously he had moved from St. Louis to Des Moines, unacquainted and without political connections in Iowa. Significant political changes were taking place. The Republican party, barely launched, had elected as governor, Ralph P. Lowe, and just as Kasson was settling in Des Moines the state capital was transferred there from Iowa City. Thus he found himself in the midst of intense and exciting political activity. In the short space of months he became Governor Lowe's unofficial adviser on matters of politics and statecraft. About the state it was jealously whispered that he was governor *de facto*. Two years later, in 1859, the party convention made him chairman of the State Republican Central Committee. In this position he energetically and astutely managed the gubernatorial campaign, electing Samuel J. Kirkwood, a rough-hewn ex-Ohioan, whose historical fame rests securely as Lincoln's war governor. Kasson next was sent as a delegate to the Chicago Republican Convention which nominated Lincoln. There he represented Iowa on the platform committee, became a member of the subcommittee of seven, and with Horace Greeley shared the major responsibility for drafting perhaps the most significant party platform of the nineteenth century. Following Lincoln's nomination, Kasson did yeoman work, and more, in achieving a Republican victory in Iowa.

Kasson's political long-headedness and his general competence attracted the attention of Senator James W. Grimes, Iowa's most powerful politician and founder of the Republican party in that state. During a six-year residence in St. Louis, Kasson had dabbled in politics, supporting the Blair brothers and B. Gratz Brown as they nurtured the Free Soil movement. There also as a lawyer he was associated with Edward Bates. Backed by men such as these, whose influence with Lincoln was great, there is little doubt that Kasson expected a political reward, though he may not have known that his abilities were to be recognized so generously. Kasson, interviewed in later years, remembered the incident of his appointment: Senator Grimes suddenly asked, "Kasson, do you want to be first assistant postmaster general?" This was the first intimation that Kasson was to be a factor in the Lincoln administration, and he did not answer at once. Grimes then said, "Let me know in an hour; you can have the place if you want it." [7] Still later, recalling the incident, Kasson said: "I was much surprised shortly after arriving to find that Montgomery Blair, later postmaster general, had asked President Lincoln to send my name to the Senate. It was the second nomination made by him." [8]

So, as Lincoln's First Assistant Postmaster General and in charge of the appointment office, Kasson began a public career that extended into the twentieth century. This important position put him on the inside of the Lincoln administration and provided a steppingstone for his entry into Congress and the diplomatic service.

Had John A. Kasson served only a few terms in Congress or on only a few diplomatic missions, he would perhaps not merit a biography. But his cumulative record over eighty-eight years spells out the need for a full-length biography. Local historians have encountered him at Charlotte and Burlington, Vermont; at Charlottesville, Virginia; at Worcester and New Bedford, Massachusetts; at St. Louis, Missouri; at Des Moines, Iowa; and in the District of Columbia. Political historians have encountered him in Congress, in the Iowa legislature, and as a delegate at the Buffalo Free Soil Convention of 1848, at the Memphis Commercial Convention of 1853, and at the Chicago Convention that nominated Lincoln in 1860. Diplomatic historians have encountered him in Paris, Vienna, Berlin, Bucharest, and Quebec in such varying positions as minister, postal commissioner, commercial agent, and as delegate at international conferences in Paris on postal matters and in Berlin on matters dealing with the Congo Valley and with Samoa.

During the forty years following Lincoln's first inauguration, Kasson served six terms in the House, three in the Iowa legislature, and represented the United States on nine diplomatic missions. During each Republican administration from Lincoln to Theodore Roosevelt he held positions of national importance. His service was a durable thread of competence running through the fabric of American domestic and foreign policy. A well-known politician and diplomat at the end of the nineteenth century, Kasson has gradually been forgotten until in the mid-twentieth century he is a shadowy, obscure figure even to professional historians. This book, therefore, seeks to illuminate more fully Kasson's life and those incidents and aspects of American history which he influenced and which influenced him.

Ancestry, Boyhood, and Education

IN 1722, exactly one century before the birth of John A. Kasson, his ancestors, Adam and Jane (Hall) Kasson, with nine children, arrived at Boston. They were in the van of a great Scotch-Irish, Presbyterian migration from Northern Ireland impelled to leave their homes because of economic frustration, immediate hard times, and religious discontent. In time Puritan inhospitality, thin soil, and land scarcity diverted the flow of this immigrant wave from New England to Pennsylvania and the Southern colonies. The Scotch-Irish, therefore, became

7

widely scattered, and their influence was to be felt in every colony. Their descendants, such as Andrew Jackson, John C. Calhoun, and Woodrow Wilson, have added luster to American politics. The Kassons, like the Jacksons some forty years later, came from Carrickfergus in County Antrim on the extreme northeastern coast of Ireland.[1]

From Boston, Adam Kasson, a spinning wheel maker and farmer, turned south and settled his flock in Windham County, Connecticut, at Voluntown (now Sterling) lying near the boundary of Rhode Island. Most of the unsettled lands of eastern Connecticut lay in Windham County, where the soil was thin, the terrain craggy, and the ownership of the land disputed by Rhode Islanders. The Kassons settled in northern Voluntown among a number of other Presbyterians from Northern Ireland. The early years were made difficult by harsh frost, drought, squabbles over land titles, and resentment from the older inhabitants, fearful of Popery and Presbyterianism alike. Adam Kasson and his sons were foremost among the leaders who shortly established a Presbyterian congregation; Adam served as one of the ten elders and in time became the deacon. One son married the preacher's daughter, and another administered the preacher's salary. In the great revival movement which swept Connecticut, the Kassons sided with the Old Lights, the less emotional, more conservative religious faction. As time went on the Kassons began to prosper, local resentment against Presbyterians died away, Presbyterians were swallowed up by the Congregationalists, and Presbyterians began to break through the Puritan monopoly over political affairs. Within a decade Adam Kasson and some of his sons had been granted the status of freemen and hence the right to participate in civil affairs. Soon thereafter a Kasson son was elected one of Voluntown's first two representatives to the General Assembly of the Colony.[2]

Despite their prosperity and growing influence in Voluntown, the Kassons soon had to face the fact that there was not enough land in eastern Connecticut for the fecund family. They had read the Mosaic command, "Be fruitful and Multiply, and replenish the earth; and they obeyed with cheerful alacrity." So spoke John A. Kasson a hundred years later. "The usual multiplication figure of my ancestral family," he explained, "was about eight. But the more zealous raised it to ten, eleven, and twelve; and one of them . . . was so anxious to reduce among his children the average of their inheritance of original sin that he increased the fruitful multiple to fourteen."

Within two generations Kassons fanned out over Connecticut, Massachusetts, New York, Pennsylvania, and Vermont. Later they turned up in Illinois, Wisconsin, Minnesota, Louisiana, Iowa, and faraway California. The craft of spinning wheel making and of wheelwrighting was passed down through the earlier generations. The old home at Voluntown meanwhile remained in Kasson hands until the latter half of the nineteenth century.

In 1742, amidst religious tumult and feverish land speculation, James Kasson (Adam's sixth son) pushed into the Housatonic Valley of western Connecticut and settled in the town of Woodbury. Among his neighbors in this town were the Grant and Sherman families, ancestors of Ulysses S. Grant and William Tecumseh Sherman. Two decades later James Kasson moved into the greener pastures of the "North Purchase," a part of Woodbury later incorporated as Bethlehem. Here he finished rearing a family of twelve. Two of James Kasson's brothers left Voluntown to swell the Kasson numbers in Bethlehem. As at Voluntown, they became leaders in the church and community as deacons and representatives in the General Assembly. Some served as privates in the French and Indian War; others, during the American Revolution, as Minute Men. At Woodbury, the recruiting center for western Connecticut, Kassons joined the Continental Army and marched under Washington's orders to defend New York. They served in the capacity of clerks, privates, corporals, and colonels; one became a brigadier general. Another, a wheelwright who had served in the French and Indian War, deserted when the Catholic French became American allies.[3]

Adam Kasson II, tenth child of James Kasson, was too young for soldiery but old enough to retain vivid memories of the Revolution. Like his grandfather Adam of Voluntown, he became a farmer and a wheelwright. At the age of twenty-one he married Honor Steele, a descendant of John Steele, one of the founders of the Hartford settlement. During Washington's first administration, Adam and Honor left Bethlehem, made their way southward along the rushing Housatonic River, and settled at Huntington, today swallowed up by industrial Shelton. Only recently incorporated, Huntington was a boom town, lying less than ten miles above Long Island Sound and nestling in a bend on the west side of the Housatonic. Across the river at the convergence of the Housatonic, the Naugatuck, and tidewater lay the thriving seaport of Derby. Here numerous sailing

vessels exchanged rum, molasses, and sugar for farm produce brought
from the interior by wagon trains a mile long.

Obviously Huntington was an attractive place for a wheelwright
as long as prosperity held up. Beginning with four acres in 1791,
Adam Kasson II increased his holdings to 100 acres in the lush 1790's.
Meanwhile four children arrived, but none was to survive to old age,
and only one was ever to be married. John Steele Kasson, Adam's second son, married Nancy Blackman, whose ancestor had led the Puritan band which first settled Stratford, Connecticut. At Huntington
two sons and two daughters were born to John Steele and Nancy
(Blackman) Kasson. The fifth child was born later in Vermont, an
area already populated with thousands of settlers from western Connecticut.[4]

Like quicksilver Connecticut settlers had flowed from the coastal and
river towns to the hinterland, zealously seeking freedom for religious
ferment, restlessly seeking new "lotts" upon which to build homes,
and ever building new towns along an old pattern. A half century
before Adam Kasson II and his son John Steele moved to Huntington,
settlers had been funneling up the longitudinal valley of the Housatonic and establishing a New Connecticut in the Green Mountains
of Vermont. From the beginning of the Revolution to the War of
1812 wave after wave swept into Ohio, Indiana, Illinois, and the
regions of the Upper Mississippi. This exciting movement of people
must have tempted Adam Kasson and his son, but the fact that they
remained at Huntington suggests that they were prosperous, socially
accepted, and personally contented.

In the lower Housatonic life was still homespun and lived in terms
of pewter, wood, and oxen. But in the realm of theology and ideas
a change was taking place. Speculative thought was shifting from
God to man, from heaven to earth, from theology to religion; religion
was becoming synonymous with the love of liberty and country; and
from the fertile soil of the Revolution political parties were springing
forth. In the Housatonic valley many people joined the party of
Thomas Jefferson, and some, like John Steele Kasson's family, eventually were to become Jacksonian Democrats.

The prosperity of the Huntington-Derby area was halted early in
the nineteenth century upon the completion of a turnpike which
channeled trade eastward to New Haven. Next came the Embargo
and the War of 1812 to end the remaining prosperity and to intensify

the already large-scale emigration. Huntington and Derby became ghost towns. Finally in 1816, amidst lonely streets, deserted warehouses, and rotting docks, Adam Kasson's flock loaded up their belongings and moved to Charlotte, Vermont. Among the family group were John Steele Kasson, his wife Nancy, and their four children. The fifth child, John A. Kasson, was yet unborn.[5]

Thus, for almost a century after the first Kasson landed in New England, his offspring had been moving gradually westward through Connecticut, building homes and churches, participating in local affairs, marrying Puritan maidens, and rearing large families. They were a deeply religious people, and, like the usual Scotch-Irish, they were tall and angular, their chins jutting, their countenances forceful, and their wills tenacious. They were self-reliant, serious Presbyterian folk, industrious and thrifty, with a natural zest and capacity for politics. From such materials then — hardy farmer-artisans, indoctrinated for a century with easy opportunity and Puritan habits — were molded the hereditary attributes of John A. Kasson. These, when combined with experience and training in Vermont and elsewhere, brought forth an ambitious, optimistic, competent man not fully understood even by his few intimates.

John A. Kasson (the A. standing for Adam) was born January 11, 1822, at Charlotte, Vermont, where summer's cool, gentle breezes from the Green and Adirondack mountains meet and caress the eastern shore of Lake Champlain. The next year President James Monroe in a memorable message to Congress warned Europe to keep hands off America. At Brandon, Vermont, young Stephen A. Douglas worked for his uncle and attended the district school. At West Haven young Horace Greeley cleared land and fulminated against the hardships of boyhood in Vermont. Thad Stevens of Peacham, nearing thirty years, had already emigrated to Pennsylvania. A few years later Chester A. Arthur was born at Fairfield and George Franklin Edmunds at Richmond. Sixteen years later the Territory of Iowa was created.

John A. Kasson was not born loaded with gold, but many Americans of even humbler origin have risen to prominence. Five years previously his grandfather Adam, patriarch of the migrating flock, had mustered half enough capital from his possessions in Huntington to purchase 100 acres of improved land in Charlotte. For the rest, he mortgaged the farm, and it took seven long years of toil and thrift to pay off the debt.[6] He was foresighted in choosing a place for his brood.

In the year of John's birth a canal connecting Lake Champlain with the Hudson River was completed. People in the Champlain Valley thereafter prospered, and Vermont for the first time became firmly attached to the Union. In the rest of the state the frontier boom ended, economic decline set in, and by the end of the next three decades almost half the restless population had surged westward. Towns like Charlotte, lying along the eastern shore of the Lake with easy access to the markets of the New York area, now grew at the expense of those inland.[7]

In the Champlain Valley of John Kasson's youth clearings had become farms, and forests, woodlots. Neat white story-and-a-half houses had replaced log cabins. Occasionally there arose a large square or rectangular white house like the Kasson's, imposing and at the same time simple with its doorways delicately carved and its mantels of native marble. Close in were barns and sheds surrounded by orchards, meadows, and pastures. Along the brooks were grist, saw, and cider mills, iron forges, tanneries, and distilleries.[8]

The Kassons lived in the southwestern part of the town near the Lake, in a village called Charlotte (or Baptist) Four Corners. Over the years the Lake had receded two miles, leaving a commanding elevation upon which rested the Kasson home, a former inn and tavern.[9] Below and rolling gently toward the Lake was the Kasson farm. To the west, north, and south young John could gaze upon a broad expanse of blue water ornamented with irregular small bays and trim little fleets of sloops and schooners. Beyond the Lake as far as his eyes could see were the picturesque Adirondack Mountains of New York. To the east, and nearer, were the rugged, irregular Green Mountains challenging his "youthful ambition to climb higher, to overcome obstacles, and giving him thoughts of a wider view of a wider world." Add sunsets and twilights, and the natural environment inspired the boy to "imagination and poetical sentiment." [10]

Some of his childhood memories he cherished, others he liked to forget. In later years it was a pleasure to recall the "whole view of the old garden, tall pear trees, blue plum trees, peach trees, berry bushes" and a profusion of flowers;[11] or the bird voices singing among the clump of beeches near the old schoolhouse where he used to swing;[12] or even the beet and onion beds which he had to weed till he doubted if nature's "fondness for weeds could be reconciled with her friendship for humanity." He enjoyed the winter evening spelling school which gave his "ambition a little scope"; and his "reckless indiscretion" at winter sports on snow and ice, in the absence of a father's supervision, led to many dangerous accidents. His best remembered friend was his intelligent Newfoundland dog Buck who carried notes to him at school, brought bottled beer to the field hands, and rescued his drowning brother. Kasson later recorded in his reminiscences that old Buck, ever constant, "of many virtues and no faults," taught him fidelity to friends.

Kasson did not recount all his boyhood experiences so fondly. The "bright and gay" [13] did not predominate in the life of a Vermont boy in the twenties and thirties. As experienced by Horace Greeley and many others, farm life borne by the younger children was "mindless, monotonous drudgery instead of an ennobling, liberalizing, intellectual pursuit"; and its "weary sense of routine futility" [14] drove from the state many young men, once their legal tie to the family ended at twenty-one. Young John Kasson, however, was more fortunate. His boyhood tasks were "slight, only incidental labor, light duties morning and evening with horses, cattle" and other chores, giving him time to read, wander in the woods, and get into mischief.[15] But duty, not pleasure, was the main theme, he observed, "till I pushed my boat of personal adventure from the shore." [16]

Charlotte was a town where common school, Sunday school, and the church were controlling influences. Following the revolutionary era of religious liberalism, successive waves of revivalism swept Vermont in Kasson's youth, creating general unrest and inspiring organizations for the salvation of the world, like the temperance crusade and the colonization society for Negroes. At the same time the Puritan atmosphere was re-established, with its restraint and coldness, its rigidity and strict morality.[17]

Although a church (probably Baptist) stood at Charlotte Four Corners, the "leading farmers" wended their way on Sundays about a mile eastward up the road through a gorge between two high hills to attend the orthodox Congregational Church and Sunday School. Here young Kasson spent a tedious day, attending long services in the morning and evening, with Sunday School in between; he listened to a preacher in a lofty pulpit elaborate upon doctrine and present Hell and Heaven as places of material punishment and reward; he heard bickering over theology, church practice, and the personal conduct of members; and he overheard the gossip at midday among the older people who found Sunday a relief from the monotony of weekday labors.

In retrospect Kasson thought the preacher was too aloof from his people. His sermons failed to emphasize "the active life of Christianity. Deeds of charity and kindness to a fellow man, sympathy with the unfortunate and unhappy, did not count. Faith in doctrine, not a loving Christian life, marked the road to Heaven. It was a cold, unattractive system of so-called religion, which made the people hardheaded and unsympathetic, but rigidly truthful, honest, and self-reliant." [18]

Vermonters revealed the brighter side of the Puritan spirit in their enthusiasm for education. Free common schools in every town, preparatory academies, female seminaries, and cheap tuition at the University provided a "democratic ladder" [19] up which bright, ambitious youths could climb. Circulating libraries, weekly newspapers and dailies from New York,[20] and later lyceums disseminated information and stimulated social ferment. In the twenties Charlotte itself, with a population of about 1,600, boasted of fourteen school districts and a female seminary along with its distillery and five taverns, "where liquor was a scourge of this town." [21] Several years before Kasson's birth, numerous young men of Charlotte were graduating from Middlebury College and the University of Vermont.[22] Families slaved and saved to send their brighter boys to college.

The responsibility of educating young John fell upon his mother Nancy (Blackman) Kasson. The early years in Charlotte, although relatively successful economically, were also distressing. Despite harsh weather and pestilence, old Adam Kasson and his wife Honor Maria, his unmarried son and daughter, and his married son John Steele, with his wife and five children, paid off the heavily mortgaged farm when young John was only two years old.[23]

They pursued the usual life of a Vermont farm family of the time, owning a span of oxen, a dozen cows, three or four horses,[24] a fine stallion, and by 1826 a flock of fifty sheep.[25] In distant markets they sold horses, cattle, sheep, and wool; locally they sold butter, oats, potatoes, fruit, and whatever gadgets they could think up. Men and boys still wore some homemade clothes with such "outward signs of economy as patches on coat and trousers." [26] Women and girls were "patterns of industry and economy" and took pride in the management of domestic affairs, though a local historian blushed at ordinary misses who aped the rich and attempted to heighten their charms "by excessive ornament in dress." [27] John Kasson remembered that a silk dress was a rare purchase, "expected to last a lifetime, and then be made over for the children." [28]

In a land and an era noted for disease in epidemic proportions, like typhus, dysentery, and tuberculosis,[29] the Kassons were becoming well established when death strode ruthlessly through the household. Before he was five John lost his father of whose influence there remained only the recollection of a cheerful face, bright laugh, and kindly disposition.[30] The next year old Adam, his grandfather, passed away, and three years later his father's surviving brother and sister died. The problem of his training and education now fell upon two widows, his grandmother Honor Steele, age sixty-four, and his mother Nancy Blackman, age thirty-seven. Both were considered "very intellectual women for their time and opportunities." In her early years in Connecticut, Honor Steele was "quite noted"; she possessed "unusual strength of character and sound judgment." [31] Nancy Kasson also must have been endowed with strong character and sound judgment. As remembered by her son John, she was "Calvinistic, rigid for truth telling . . . against Sabbath breaking and earnest for the education of her children." [32] Her photographs show a firm, alert, wise woman with an air of sobriety and determination, strength and command. To her management, counsel, and decision John Kasson owed much. The continued success of the farm, upon which the livelihood of all depended, and the successful education of her children attest to her ability.

As the years of the thirties wore "monotonously on," John finished common school with its three R's and the "stern rudiments of New England life." His two brothers and two sisters, all older, "felt bound" to supervise him, but he willfully refused to submit to any of them. He was strong, restless, insubordinate, with an excitable disposition. Headstrong as a youth, so he was as a man. His one great friend who never censored him was his dog Buck. But he always remembered the gentle kindness of his sister Mary Emeline [33] who was

patient when he was impatient, loving when he was perverse, understanding when he repented too late. To her, from whom he "tried to
learn virtue," he was to confide his inner thoughts during spells of
loneliness in later life.[34] As his older brother Charles De Forest ma-
tured and became a man of affairs, John admired and respected him
but did not always take his advice.

When he was twelve John was sent by his family to an academy for
boys about twelve miles away, where some of his uncles resided.
Finding there the same rigid orthodoxy, even sterner rules of living,
and fewer opportunities for "foolish adventures," he did not like it.
The next year (1835) his grandmother died, leaving Nancy Kasson
and her five children on their own resources. The family decided to
give John a university education. Soon they made ready to leave
Charlotte for a place with better educational and professional opportunities.[35]

Of all the lake towns, Burlington, a few miles north, was growing
fastest. Bustling with commerce and becoming one of the great lumber ports of America, it was the seat of the state university, a preparatory academy, and the center of a brisk law practice engaging some
of the most prominent lawyers of the state. Irish and French Canadians were trickling in to find jobs, say mass, and create religious
friction. Ambitious maidens were leaving the depleted hill farms
of Vermont to teach school or work in the cotton mills of Lowell,
Massachusetts, for board and two dollars a week. Mill towns were
spreading over the areas of Voluntown and Huntington. Economic
life in Charlotte was becoming static, while Burlington boomed.[36]

John Kasson's older brother Charles De Forest, age twenty-six, was
weary of farming and wanted to read law. Already he had gone
partly in debt to purchase a 100-acre farm adjacent to the Kasson
homestead, perhaps for speculative purposes.[37] John's younger brother Chester, nearing twenty-one, had departed for Troy, New York,
bent on a business career. His two sisters with their education partly
finished, perhaps at the Charlotte Female Seminary, were ready to
seek employment. John himself, age fifteen, must be given a college
education.

So in the fall of 1837, as a serious financial panic blighted the Republic, Nancy Kasson sold the old Charlotte homestead and moved
to Burlington. John Kasson never knew what became of his share of
the estate but thought the proceeds from the sale "probably became

a common fund out of which the children were clad and educated; and then went forth into the world expecting to make their own way in life . . . reared for a sturdy, honest and selfsustained manhood, independent and resolute, not accustomed to receive or bestow uncompensated favors." [38]

Burlington in the late thirties was a charming, busy little village spread neatly over the side of a hill which sloped off gradually into the Lake. From the University on the hilltop students could gaze out over the seven-acre College Green enclosed with a fine white fence and cedar posts; over dwellings, taverns, and stores to the distant horizon in New York. Etched in between was the cool face of the Lake freckled with slow-moving steamboats and picturesque islands.[39]

For a year John attended the Old Academy, a solitary two-story brick building standing midway between town and University. He studied Latin, Greek, and mathematics with the hope of passing the University entrance examinations the next summer.[40]

In the meantime, Chester continued to seek his fortune, which in the years to come he could never find without the brotherly guidance and assistance of John. Soon Mary, age twenty-five, would begin a teaching career which led to successful matrimony, and Maria, age twenty-two, would be enrolled at Mary Lyons' Mount Holyoke Seminary. Charles, either from keen judgment, recognized promise, or happy chance, joined the law firm of Lyman and Marsh and shortly was admitted to the bar. He became a senior partner in the firm, sold his Charlotte farm at a profit, and within a decade was considered a brilliant lawyer whose star in political and business affairs was rapidly ascending.[41]

Fortunately for both Charles and John, they attracted the favorable attention of Lyman's law partner, George Perkins Marsh, who at thirty-six was already famous as an erudite scholar, lawyer, and businessman. Marsh's personal dignity, punning humor, and fine library were the talk of the town and the object of John Kasson's boyish admiration. Early recognizing the influence of the frontier and religion in molding American character, Marsh extolled American nationalism, foresaw the need of conserving natural resources, and attributed everything good in the English tradition to Teutonic simplicity and virtue. As a Whig Congressman and later as a competent diplomat, he was to share freely his broad political and scholarly connections with the Kasson boys.[42]

The summer of 1838 saw young John complete his preparatory course at the Old Academy, pass his entrance examinations, and enter the University, where life was a vivid contrast to his earlier intellectual and religious experiences. Under the "presiding genius" of Professor James Marsh, a first cousin of George Perkins Marsh, the University was going through an era noted for its inspiring faculty, its educational innovations, and its intellectual stimulation. In the words of a responsible admirer, the air was filled with "a lofty intelligence floating sometimes in the cloudland of the Coleridgean philosophy and like the soaring thought of James Marsh lifting some to misty spaces and inspiring men young and old." [43]

The University of Vermont as John Kasson knew it was the product of James Marsh's study and imagination; his influence on his students and on general educational developments in America, though great, are yet to be adequately appraised. Like his cousin, George Perkins Marsh, he was a graduate of Dartmouth and was studious by nature and an omnivorous reader.

After Dartmouth and additional study at the Andover Theological Seminary, Marsh had found himself dissatisfied with the teachings of that center of orthodox Calvinism. Turning to German literature and the writings of Samuel Taylor Coleridge, he soon had a thorough mastery of all Coleridge's works in America and was searching for a new theology to satisfy "the heart in the head." In 1823 he accepted an invitation from a Southern friend, John Holt Rice, to become professor of languages and belles-lettres at Hampden-Sidney, a Presbyterian college in Virginia. Rice, a self-educated, dynamic divine with a national reputation, had rejected the presidency of Princeton, preferring a professorship in the new Hampden-Sidney Theological Seminary which he had promoted and organized. Owing to Rice's influence, the president of this Virginia college and most of its instructors were from Northern schools.[44]

While James Marsh pursued his work at Hampden-Sidney and John Kasson learned to walk and talk at Charlotte, inroads were being made upon the old classical curriculum and the patrician function of education. At Thomas Jefferson's youthful University of Virginia a layman faculty, hand-picked by Jefferson himself, experimented with the idea that higher education should be directly related to the life of a democracy and available to all talented young men, rich or poor; that the course of study should be less sectarian and more practical; and that students should govern themselves and elect to take whatever courses they desired. At Hampden-Sidney also, the authorities were said to be "secularizing." [45]

In this environment of educational flux, James Marsh taught classes, pondered the ideas of Coleridge, and translated the works of German writers. With Rice he organized literary societies aimed at assuring students "free and unrestrained feelings and habits" in their pursuit of excellence.

In 1826 Marsh returned to Vermont as president of the University. Finding a struggling, ineffectual college, lacking financial support and weakened by theological conflict, Marsh transformed it (ten years before John Kasson matriculated) into the "original center of academic idealistic philosophy," a "nursery of American Transcendentalism." All this took place long before the first meeting of the famous Transcendental Club at Concord in 1836.

Marsh's educational reforms were based on a combination of the ideas of Jefferson and Coleridge; his philosophy, on a combination of Neoplatonism, German Romanticism, and Kant's distinction between Reason and Understanding as interpreted in part by Coleridge. Aiming to break down the ancient barrier between a small learned class and an ill-informed public, Marsh reorganized the entire curriculum. Each course, he hoped, would be a progression toward the ultimate solution of man's worldly problems and his relation to the infinite. Education would still be grounded on Christianity. But Christianity was to be more than a mere philosophy or a religion; it was to be a way of life, the art of living well and happily. In support of his lofty aims, he replaced tutors with permanent professors, relaxed rules and regulations, and encouraged a genial, personal relationship between teachers and students. Instead of college distinctions, each student by doing his best would advance in accordance with his own capabilities. The art of writing and speaking for the public was emphasized, and public exhibitions were arranged to make the class appear as a whole in the best manner.

Five years before John Kasson enrolled, Marsh resigned the presidency in order to devote his full time to philosophy. As a teacher he inculcated his students with a spiritual philosophy which placed the individual squarely on his instincts, exalting man and finding infinite possibilities in human nature. He rejected Calvinistic theology because it ignored freedom of the will and the divine element in man. Like Coleridge he taught that Reason related to a consciousness beyond and above experience; that Reason transcended experience and dealt with spiritual objects; that Reason was intuitive. Christian belief was the perfection of human reasoning. Modern or romantic poetry was the inevitable result of Christianity, naturally serious and melancholy in tone, reaching out beyond the bounds of the known to the unknown. Man should turn his mind inward to unfold the deep foundations of truth abiding in his inner consciousness.

Thus, Marsh pumped into the minds of his students an optimistic philosophy which would permit the perfectibility of man and his democratic institutions. With divine reason in every man, the individual had merely to reach for the stars. Stiff and diffident in society but gentle and brilliant in conversation, Marsh emphasized by example hard work, calmness, moderation, and courage. His "philosophy" lingered long after his day and as late as the 1870's awakened in a young student named John Dewey a "distinctive philosophic interest."

John Kasson, who forever after included the works of Coleridge and Plato among his favorites, said students "reverenced" Marsh. Enthusiastic and optimistic graduates left the University confident of their superior instruction and abilities.[46]

☆　☆　☆

In addition to Marsh, John Kasson pursued his studies under three other professors. Succeeding Marsh as president was John Wheeler. Lincolnesque in appearance, affable, and well-to-do, he conducted morning and evening prayers in a cold, smoke-filled chapel, gave lectures in political economy and natural theology, and on Sundays sometimes preached "awful long" sermons on evidences of revealed religion. Wheeler also had a penchant for making money, and John Kasson thought the "old coon" wore a strong "smile of business." [47]

Joseph Torrey (solemn "Old Joe") occupied the chair of Latin and Greek. Known as the students' friend, he tried to reduce discipline by making every student "a law unto himself." He was reputed to teach more with fewer words than any other professor.

Ferrand N. Benedict, professor of mathematics, was a hunchback noted for his rigorous discipline and distaste for superficial methods. "Snappy as to eyes and walk," he pleased the boys with his one-sentence prayer: "May we all square our conduct with the Rule laid down in Thy word." He was supposed to be able to take the correct measure of every student, and those who did not pass mathematics found it hard to get a degree. He was known to most as "Little Ben," but John Kasson, who did poorly in mathematics, called him an old, hard-headed "evil genius." [48]

The power of this small faculty was said to be "like a running stream bearing down upon the students hour by hour." If plain living signifies high thinking, they lived in a cloudland of thought indeed. Annual expenses for no student exceeded $100. Since John stayed at home the first three years and did not have to pay board, his expenses, including tuition, seldom reached $40. The spare university plant consisted of three main buildings called North, South, and Middle College, all facing the Lake. Except for Middle College decorated with a cupola and bell they were barnlike structures of brick, three stories in height. In his senior year John occupied one of the limited number of rooms in North College or the Old Mill. With only one janitor for all the buildings, halls and stairways were often unclean. The rooms as remembered by one student were dreary and unkept, cluttered up with a bed, clothespress, washstand, tables, and chairs, and bursting with the winter's supply of wood, which had to be brought inside to keep classmates from stealing it.

The students themselves, ranging in numbers during John's four years from 99 to 110, were neither sons of millionaires nor of polite society, as one alumnus put it. Most of them were middle class farm boys, frequently self supporting. But according to another, these "young democrats" of the frugal depression years were "an aristocracy of brains." [49] At any rate, several of John Kasson's schoolmates made their mark.

A member of his freshman class was William A. Wheeler, a serious, simple-hearted lad from Malone, New York, who was later to become Vice President of the United States under Rutherford B. Hayes. Robert Safford Hale, another classmate, was to achieve fame as an educator and member of Congress. Two years ahead of John was diminutive, bright-eyed Henry J. Raymond, the sallow-faced son of a well-to-do farmer from Lima, New York. Before Raymond's habit

of overwork, developed in college, led him to an early grave, he was
to become a member of Congress and one of the nation's leading
journalists. James R. Spaulding, another classmate, also was to make
his mark in American journalism. As a junior, John Kasson became
acquainted with a freshman named Frederick Billings, but he probably
did not suspect that here was a budding railroad tycoon and educator.
Most of these students in later life, like Kasson, became conspicuous
for their optimism, hard work, and conservatism.[50]

Despite the moderated discipline at the University, John found
himself tied down to a strenuous daily program regulated by laws on
hours of study, religious exercises, and general deportment. The number of religious exercises in a single term ran to 374, and of literary,
to 240. Student activities were channelized into two literary societies
and the Society for Religious Inquiry upon which, it was claimed,
Congregationalism put few effectual checks. The literary societies,
Phi Sigma Nu and the University Institute, were designed to supplement the study of rhetoric. Membership was determined by lot, and
John probably considered himself lucky to be a member of Phi Sigma
Nu, the older society with a larger library and more important periodi-
cal literature. Each society was represented by a speaker at commencement, and politics for the offices were as lively for the students
as were the fall elections for the citizens. A prominent alumnus and
historian of the University claimed that no social fraternities ever
contributed so much toward making thinkers, writers, and speakers
as did these literary societies.[51]

Before the end of the first term, students usually classified themselves as conservative Blues or liberal Bloats, and John, whose brother
was a rising Democratic politician, was in all probability a Bloat.
Moreover there were literary programs and forensics, sailing and skating parties, visits in town, and political oratory. And on commencement day Burlington and the surrounding countryside was alive with
excitement, the roads dusty from numerous vehicles pouring in.[52]

John must have remembered vividly the commencement at the end
of his freshman year, when the famous Whig candidate, Henry Clay,
came to town. Clad in a black frock coat, white vest, and very wide
drilling pantaloons, Clay sat on the stage and graciously endured the
oppressive heat and the dull speeches. When Henry Raymond delivered an animated junior oration, Clay was heard to say, "That young
man will make his mark." John must also have had some interest in

the exciting hard cider campaign of the next year, when the Whigs carried Vermont and the nation for General William Henry Harrison. It is doubtful, however, that he paid much attention to the fact that the Liberty party candidate polled 319 votes in Vermont. For though protests against the proposed annexation of Texas were reaching the state legislature, and Vermont's Representative William Slade was crusading against slavery in Washington, slavery was not a burning political issue in Vermont. But it was on the verge of bursting forth, and within eight years both John and his brother were to bolt the Democratic for the Free Soil party.[53]

In college John seems to have had neither time nor inclination for excessive social and political activities. The attrition in his class from thirty-five freshmen to seventeen seniors indicates that the ordeal of mastering transcendental teachings was no light one. For the first three years John sat humped over his books in his room at home, eschewing company and conversation to his later regret. After moving to the Old Mill on the University campus in his senior year, he still "confined his thoughts and feelings to his college room" so much that he felt ill at ease in society, even though his "spirit always flowed freely." Moreover during the midwinter vacations of eight weeks he seems to have taught school in the countryside.[54]

His grades indicate hard study. In his freshman year only four students made a higher class average. As a sophomore he stood second. In his junior year he led the class in classical languages but dropped to sixth place in mathematics. Upon graduation he ranked first in Greek and second in the general class average in spite of a 35 per cent in trigonometry and a 45 per cent in calculus.[55]

During his first three years he aspired to be a poet, wrote several poems, and read one of them as his contribution to the Junior Class Exhibition. Believing, however, that he had no real talent as a poet, he turned to prose composition and read widely in history and English literature.[56]

His yellowed university essays and speeches,[57] with their long, stilted, and epigrammatic sentences, with a plethora of words and frequently a dearth of solid content, are a tribute to tireless efforts to achieve effect — to be exquisite — in the arrangement and choice of words. Here is evidence of the genesis of an indefatigable, hard driving perfectionist. They cover a wide range of subjects but fall roughly into three categories: art and philosophy; education; government and religion. And they are signed John A. Kasson as he always subsequently signed his name.

Such essays as "Poetic Enthusiasm," "A Philosophic Poetry and a Poetic Philosophy," "Relation of the Artist to his Age," and "The Realm of Common Sense" are testimonials of Professor Marsh's philosophy. The poet should not confine himself to the visible and tangible in nature, wrote young Kasson, but should seek the unseen power of life — an inward, moving power which is his real strength. Both poetry and philosophy were attempts of the soul to realize its destined freedom.

John regretted that in America, where only the "universal hum of gold-seeking men is heard," arts and letters found small favor. "Shall America never boast a bard worthy to sing of her discovery and deliverance?" he cried in a sophomore chapel piece. Before the literary society, he extolled modern German literature and exhorted his fellows to cast off their "old, shrivelled skins of sluggishness" and make the University a birthplace of literary abilities.

In a debate on whether learning is benefited in proportion as the number of colleges increases, he took the negative. In the absence of a permanent "intellectual high priesthood," he feared lowered standards, for until the great West was settled, few would devote their lives "to study *from a love of study*." Too many were "vomitted out of academic halls," their minds crammed "like a dung-cart," seeing "no beauty nor any enjoyment in the sublime energy of a determined spirit." He was critical of those who ran through a four-year course and considered their education finished.

His essays on government and religion were robustly patriotic, exalting the ideal of equality, freedom of the mind, the Constitution, and American nationalism. His sympathies ran strong for Democrat Thomas Wilson Dorr who then was waging a revolution against an outmoded colonial charter which restricted suffrage, lacked democratic guarantees, and kept Rhode Island under the minority control of conservative Whigs.

As to Americans whose numbers would increase in a few years from 18 to 100 million (he predicted), let them be Americans, he admonished his hearers:

As we are eminently a peculiar people, we should glory in having a peculiar character. . . . Did not we devise an original plan for the welfare of man?

Men who ape the old world in fashions and peculiarities will ere long want to ape them in their whole system of government. . . . Preserve fashion that is American; teach American doctrines, American sentiments, American philanthropy. . . . Walk like Americans, talk like Americans, think American thoughts; drink water, the American beverage, pure as Hellicon's fount; and marry American wives!

In another essay he sought the beautiful land of Idealism and found it, called Stephensis, to be an imaginary *Republic* in Central America.

As his senior year drew to a close, John must have grieved with the others at Professor Marsh's untimely death at the age of forty-eight. As he worked on his commencement piece, "The Heathen Philosopher and the Christian Fisherman," he may have had forebodings as to his graduation because of his poor mathematics grades. When August 2, 1842, brought Commencement Day, with a village full of life and gayety and a church literally jammed with people, John was there on the stage with his class, but only after the inevitable dressing-down by "little Ben," who, though passing young Kasson on, brought tears to his eyes and destroyed his happiness for that day. According to an eyewitness, however, the graduation of the class appeared well as a whole, some orations exhibiting research and clear thinking. And however deeply stung John may have been, he could comfort himself with the thought that the path to a new phase of his life now lay open.[58]

He could now pursue his own maxims set forth in his essays that "He, who possesses no spirit and neglects to enjoy what God bestows for his gratification and improvement, is in a situation of *being*, not *living*"; and that "To attain excellence in a pursuit, there must be vigour, determination, and constant zeal, a love of vocation, and a resolution to contest manfully for the highest success."

Yet John had not made up his mind as to the vocation he wanted to pursue. Surging within him was "an ambitious character irregularly forming under contradictory influences."[59] His independent, free flowing spirit conflicted with a cloistered, supervised life at home. Puritan virtues of intellectuality and the ideal of service, common in the Vermont of his youth, were in contrast to assertive individualism, shrewdness, and greed. The lofty, moderate tone of his university teachings was not in accord with religious zealotry and the boiling temperance and simmering antislavery crusades; but slavery itself was a practical denial of the cherished ideal of equality. "Vermonters were nothing if not contrary," says a careful historian of this era. And "all Vermont was restless."[60]

The flood of emigrants to the west continued unabated. In southern Ohio, Indiana, Illinois, and the future state of Iowa, upstanding Vermonters were coming in contact with easygoing Southerners, looking somewhat condescendingly at their poor schools and illiteracy, and being themselves suspiciously regarded as too righteous and thrifty. Educated young men were trickling into Boston and New York for professional and business careers. And, surprisingly, some continued to drift into the South where a few — a very few — settled down and "loved good liquor and went in for fun." [61] Most of those going south, however, were young men just out of college, many with consumptive tendencies, who combined temporary employment with recovery in a milder climate. Southerners were willing to employ the graduates of Northern schools in almost any educational capacity.

John's mother urged him to become a minister and teacher, perhaps following in the footsteps of Professor Marsh; his brother Charles offered the facilities of his office and urged a career in law. For a few weeks after graduation John seems to have read some law in Charles' office, but he was restless, and a career in hilly Vermont did not appeal to him. He had first, at least, "to push his boat of personal adventure from the shore" and see the world about which he had read and studied so diligently. The extensive acquaintances of the Marsh cousins would keep him from being a stranger in many parts of the land.[62]

☆ III ☆

Contrasts in Virginia and Massachusetts

IN THE EARLY autumn of 1842 as the chill winds descended from the North Pole twenty-year-old John A. Kasson shoved off from the Burlington docks. Like many other young Vermonters of his day he was headed south to tutor the children of a Virginia planter, if some more attractive job did not turn up en route. Self-confident and gregarious despite his somewhat cloistered and restricted life, this slender, sprightly young man with an independent spirit was filled with ambition, and as he charted his first fortune seeking course his thoughts eagerly anticipated a wider view of a wider world. Aglow with curiosity, he was determined to observe and learn as much as possible about people and things. Perhaps this voyage would dispel some of the clouds of doubt in his mind as to his choice of a career.

While John had composed transcendental poetry and extolled American nationality, the pall of the depression wore off. The time to go to school had been propitious, and now the time was opportune for a young college graduate to seek his fortune. For in America an old era had closed and the roaring forties rushed in a new one with illimitable opportunities but also staggering problems that would put to a severe test the democratic process he so loudly praised. In this decade youthful, self-conscious America swaggered westward across the continent toward horizons that never seemed to vanish. In rapid succession came the annexation of Texas, the Mexican War, the acquisition of California and Oregon, and the sizzling gold rush of '49, tingling patriotic pulses, releasing dynamic energy, and at the same time creating in the Republic uneven sectional growth, bitter sectional animosities, and splinter political parties in which ambitious young men might rise rapidly.

Power continued to fall from the hands of professionally select leaders into those of popularly elected representatives from the ranks. Great accumulations of wealth were being amassed through industry and finance. In the East, New York, Boston, Philadelphia, and Baltimore, to which young men were being lured, were becoming famous, great cities of wealth and opportunity, of prigs and prudes, of fashion and reputed iniquity. The swelling West was persistently demanding more attention to its needs and a greater voice in national affairs. And the fateful question of slavery was being projected more and more into the national limelight. There was talk of cotton lords in the South and wage slaves in the North. In the South, territorial and economic growth did not bring social ferment and sharp deviation in men's mode of living and thinking as in the East and Northwest. Here at least the ruling classes continued to cherish old institutions and to emphasize such personal values as men's honor and manners at the expense of the ideal of equality and public education. Slavery in Virginia, considered a curse by prominent leaders a decade before, was now believed to be a positive good.

In this era people read penny newspapers, listened to lectures on animal magnetism, had their heads examined by phrenologists, and swallowed tons of patent medicines. In political campaigns crowds of sixty thousand or more colorfully paraded and chanted in honor of their candidates. The rich dressed richly, and the social elite watered at Newport, Saratoga, and the Virginia Springs. As foreign observers journeyed from section to section they were impressed with the diverse nature of American society, where a great mass of people were in constant transition. They described a land of crudities, local jealousies, and paradoxes, but also of optimism and easy opportunity, where men by working hard could acquire wealth and position. However numerous the contradictions, the future held bright prospects for John A. Kasson and for his brother Charles as well.

On his journey southward, unworldly young John, impressed with his high university training, met George Perkins Marsh in New York. From him he received letters of recommendation, and there he negotiated for a job. And though he was unable to procure work, he saw enough of New York to consider it "the most corrupt, illiberal, and deceitful city in all North America." Passing on through Philadelphia, he was interviewed in Baltimore by the authorities of a private school, who wanted him to take charge of the whole French department for some eighty students. In spite of his vow in Burlington never to turn down a job "from want of an assumption of ability," he felt incompetent to handle so much French. Moreover he thought they really wanted a "jack-of-all-trades at a paltry salary" in this school, which for some reason he did "not deem one of the first order." In Baltimore, although black swine roamed the streets, the city was clean, and "whites, blacks, and pigs" were all "quite polite" in contrast to the selfish inhabitants of New York.

Going on to Washington, he found a quiet city and few attractions during the recess of Congress. Its few magnificent, self-conscious public buildings and isolated private houses were in sharp contrast to Baltimore's red brick and marble structures with their tinkling fountains. From "select circles" John picked up gossip concerning the Distribution Bill, and he learned that the old editor of the Burlington *Sentinel* had "quarters worth $1000" in the Post Office Department.

In the late days of September, John journeyed on down the Potomac to the Big Bend at Aquia Creek, the steamboat landing for Fredericksburg, Virginia, and made his way through this town of some 4,000 to Hagley, the home of John Taliaferro, Congressman and planter, whom Kasson came to idealize as personifying the admirable traits of a Virginia gentleman. Now John's ship had "been driven into a temporary harbor, the sails furled," and he began his "Notes on Virginia," which, he facetiously wrote, were "doubtless destined to rival those of Jefferson." [1] For the next nine months, in long, gossipy letters, responsive young Kasson kept his family posted on Virginians and incidentally revealed many of his own attitudes and aspirations. His "Notes" covered such widely varied subjects as Virginia gentlemen and ladies, slavery and agriculture, politics and mesmerism, religion and education, holidays and weddings, feminine laces and spencers, ice cream and "egg-&-ogg."

Although the Taliaferros received him warmly and hospitably, desiring him to remain with them, there were unsatisfactory aspects in the situation. Old John Taliaferro's two grandchildren were retarded, and the salary of $150, plus board and laundry, was not attractive. So John, using a letter from G. P. Marsh to George Tucker, a professor at the University of Virginia, found a tutoring position in Albemarle County paying $250 plus board and washing. Before his departure he wrote his brother to find another tutor for the Taliaferros. And he asked Charles to settle with Frederick Billings, the future railroad magnate, a small debt against him from the Society of Religious Inquiry.[2]

As cool nights and crisp autumn breezes sent tawny leaves fluttering to the ground in late November, Kasson traveled by rail and stage to Charlottesville, an easygoing little town sprawling in a deep intervale between wooded foothills of the Blue Ridge Mountains. As the aircraft flies, this was some sixty miles southwest of north-tidewater Fredericksburg and about the same distance straight north from Hampden-Sidney College, where Professor Marsh had spent profitable years.

Of all Kasson's adventures thus far he must have anticipated this one most eagerly. For Albemarle County in the Virginia Piedmont was noted for the University of Virginia, its great men, genial living, and salubrious climate. In Burlington, Dr. Marsh had told Kasson that it was "the most delightful section and temperature of Virginia, even the Union." Fredericksburg had been too near the river to suit Kasson, but at Charlottesville he expected a "mixture of salt-water and mountain air" to make "a proper medium temperature." [3]

John undoubtedly had heard much about the galaxy of distinguished leaders produced by this community in which he was now to make his temporary home. People of Albemarle could boast of their presidents, senators, congressmen, supreme court justices, governors, and diplomats. They could point with pride to their author of the Declaration of Independence; their father of the Constitution (who though from an adjacent county, had been so intimate with Jefferson and the University that they claimed him); their father of the Monroe Doctrine; their conqueror of the Old Northwest; and their trail blazers to the Pacific Ocean. The county reeked with history significant to state and nation, and the atmosphere was pervasive with the spirit of lustrous statesmen.[4]

When Kasson reached Charlottesville, fresh out of college himself, he immediately visited the University; a "most enchanting place," he described it, with its "beautiful sloping lawn" surrounded by professors' homes connected together by an arcade and set off at one end by a classical rotunda containing library and lecture rooms. All in one day he attended a few lectures, became acquainted with three or four professors, and visited at length with two of them.

Professor George Tucker invited him into his home, but John, hasty in his judgment at this age (as he was later to advise young men not to be), apparently did not enjoy the visit. Mrs. Tucker, he wrote his sister, was a "vain, affected, and deceitful woman . . . in possession of her fourth husband," while Professor Tucker, in possession of his third wife, was "vain and selfish." Although they "would like to entertain the rich and proud," Kasson thought they had "no genuine hospitality in a single vein" despite "their display of silver plate and fashion." Tucker was then widely known as a lawyer, author, and legislator. His urbanity, vivid imagination, sparkling sense of humor, and quick, emotional disposition were not always appreciated even by his faculty colleagues. It is not therefore surprising that sensitive young Kasson was unfavorably impressed with him. On the other hand, Judge Henry St. George Tucker, a distant relative and popular professor of law, impressed John as a "true gentleman" whose acquaintance he valued highly.[5]

Student life at the University of Virginia presented some sharp contrasts to Kasson's college days at the University of Vermont. In Jefferson's University, early experiments with mild student government, administered by student censors and foreign professors, had proved disappointing. When high-strung and fun loving youths from individualistic families of high social rank, where drinking and gaming were usual, found themselves in uniform and subjected to elaborate rules of discipline, they struck back; the ten years preceding Kasson's visit had been fraught with riots, duels, and violent pranks. One professor was horsewhipped and murdered before the honor system, initiated by Henry St. George Tucker the very session of Kasson's visit, solved the problem of discipline. Moreover, Jefferson's hope that the bright sons of indigent parents might enroll in numbers proved illusory. Instead, most of the students came from the social rank of the well-to-do in Virginia and the lower South, creating the popular impression that it was an institution of the socially inclined wealthy.[6]

John Kasson was shocked. "You never heard of such extravagance," he reported to Charles. "One [student] spent $1400.00 in 4 or 5 months; and a thousand per session (10 months) I believe is quite usual. A great many high-blood Southrons resort here from all the Southern States."[7] He probably did not know that officials of the University had been alarmed at its reputation as a "seminary of the wealthy" for fear among other reasons that taxpayers and the General Assembly would not support it.[8]

Promising to return to the University and get better acquainted with Judge Henry St. George Tucker, John then took the red dirt road which wound east and south through a steep gap separating Jefferson's Monticello on the left from Carter's Mountain on the right. A mile farther he passed Ashlawn, former home of James Monroe; turning south behind Carter's Mountain, he entered a cozy wooded community interspersed with small plantations three or four miles apart. One of these plantations, ten miles from Charlottesville, was Keelona, the home of Isaac White whose children Kasson was to tutor. From here he could see the low wooded summit of Green Mountain, the southwestern fringe of the Carter's Mountain neighborhood. Within the general vicinity were some half dozen other New England tutors.

For the next eight months Kasson lived here among slaveholders and broadened his background in a genteel society of easy comfort, leisurely living, and intellectual vigor — the sunset glow of a golden era of ante-bellum Albemarle social intercourse and private entertaining still influenced by Jefferson's cosmopolitan spirit. He came into contact with such people prominent in the affairs of the state and nation as the Carters of Redlands, the Coleses of Estouteville and

Enniscorthy, the Randolphs of Sharon, the Riveses of Sherwood, and the Stevensons later of Blenheim.[9] He was keenly interested in the mode of life of these people living in their famous ancestral homes. Sometimes critical, sometimes complimentary, he was always observant, and learned to mix well with them. In the end he found himself liking them. Though mildly critical of their institution of slavery, his views toward ameliorating the problem, even when his people were arrayed against these people in arms, were characterized by moderation. And impressionable young Kasson was plainly attracted to those personal and social attributes invariably associated with old Virginia gentlemen and statesmen. They were not only traits to be admired but also to be acquired.

At Keelona, John "fell into the embraces" of a "petulant . . . pack" of seven children, the tallest running up to six feet two. One was too young for school, but two others from a neighboring family made eight to be instructed. They were all "kind and clever" toward him, and two or three were "passably good scholars." The Whites were Baptists who once had lived at a more famous residence called Farmington. Keelona, which they now occupied, was an old log house enlarged and clapboarded. It was an unpretentious building, one and a half stories high, L-shaped, and low ceilinged. John occupied the attic space, where his head barely cleared the ridgepole and where cold wintry winds (even then considered unusual by Albemarlians) provided plenty of the fresh air so anxiously recommended by the family when he left Burlington. Old man White, who owned some forty slaves and farmed about 800 acres, was tall, lean, and "tight"; Mrs. White, who mended John's clothes, was fatter and hence more "liberal." [10]

Betty White, the oldest child, must have been a tantalizing student for a twenty-year-old masculine tutor. This popular and marriageable young lady with large black eyes and raven hair was "well bred and well disposed" as Kasson described her. An accomplished pianist, she played for him the "magnificent" *Soldier's Burial* and the "agreeably funny" *Lucy Long*. But however great her charms might have been, he seemed not unhappy when she told him to regard her as a sister or when later she was married. To her John spoke jestingly for his brother Charles but not for himself. Apparently at this stage of his life he was not wife hunting. He was content to describe meticulously for his brother Betty's attire as she departed for a dance dressed in a short-sleeved white satin gown covered richly with laces and tassels, a jewel on her breast and orange blossoms in her black hair.

She took him here and there in the neighborhood to dinner parties, where he realized his ambition to meet the leading families, politicians, and literary figures. As they trotted their horses over the countryside and chatted with neighbors, John's keen eye observed that times were shockingly hard. As on Vermont farms, the soil had grown thin and unproductive because of careless and wasteful agricultural practices. And the "niggers," although uniformly treated with kindness, "are as lazy as the land is lean," he informed his brother. Moreover, the slaves (called servants in Virginia) "consumed all that could be produced" from the prevailing crops of wheat, corn, and tobacco. Farmers therefore were leaving the county for the virgin soils of the West. There was an exodus to Missouri, where Isaac White, embarrassed at insufficient cash to pay Kasson till summer harvest, thought of going.[11]

Some families had already freed their slaves, and since the time of Jefferson there had been a strong antislavery feeling in the county. Some twenty years previously Edward Coles from a nearby plantation had loaded his household and slaves on wagons and emigrated to free-soil Illinois, emancipating his slaves and becoming the antislave governor of the state. Some still contemplated emancipation; others suspiciously regarded Yankee tutors as abolitionists. Kasson's friend, a young Yale graduate, was dismissed from a plantation a few miles away because he meddled with the slaves. John himself was apparently more circumspect, though he had remarked at dinner on the same plantation that he "could not but admire . . . a servant in the act of seeking its freedom." An attempt to escape for so noble an aspiration "could not be reprehensible." But John's observations of the slave system in Virginia did not make him a rabid antislavery man as was later claimed in Iowa and Vermont, for in time he himself was to own a slave.[12]

Kasson thought gossip was the main topic of conversation in Albemarle "higher society," where the "want of religious feeling and religious influence" betrayed itself. He also considered the colleges and high schools inferior. Then why, he wondered, had Virginians become in the past such sound men in public life? Setting himself to the task of answering this question, he revealed some of his own aspirations.

The genuine old Virginian with his "undeviating good sense" made no effort to display himself as young men frequently did in the North, according to John Kasson. Rather, he had a "natural air of kindness — not an air of patronism — but of truest civility" that made one feel completely at home. Into official relations he carried personal ease and the absence of uncertainty and excitement, making personal and political friends and waxing great with the occasion. These qualities, declared John, would hardly be termed "good common sense" in New England, but they were in reality "a sort of universal instinctive benevolence and intelligence, which made a Washington, Madison, and Jefferson." Gratefully responsive to the courtesy accorded him, Kasson resolved "that if Providence ever favors me with a roof large enough to cover two, the scriptural injunction to use hospitality shall be remembered among my most prominent virtues." And furthermore in the future he would lend a helping hand to aspiring young men who at "the beginning of the race" were "more ardent in their gratitude" and remembered kindness longer than at any other age. Old John Taliaferro of Hagley, who let him use his congressional frank when postage was high and who had lost thousands of dollars serving others, was Kasson's ideal, "worthy to be my example" as he put it. He was so deeply impressed with Taliaferro that a decade later, as a young lawyer from St. Louis, he paid him a call in Washington.

Virginians were more "epicurean" than in the North, where men's heads were filled "with business and nothing but business." The ladies demanded "ease and elegance in manner" which John thought he had sacrificed to hard study in college. Therefore, he informed his brother, he was applying himself to the "lesson of conversation" which he had "sturdily refused at home." Virginians also paid much attention to personal appearance, and soon Kasson was buying a new overcoat worth six dollars despite his scanty supply of cash. He ended his chapter "on the construction of great men in Virginia" with a statement significant in explaining the development of a man later noted for his urbanity and polite manners: ". . . there seems no place for learning *true* politeness like the society of the old-school Virginians, and if a year's residence could teach it to me beyond forgetfulness, I should secure to myself a valuable recompense for the time." [13] Certainly here was good training for a budding diplomat but more dubious was its value for the rough and tumble politics of the West, say Iowa, where unpolished personalities were often more popular.

John's preference for politics and law began to emerge during his Virginia sojourn. He showed a keen interest in his brother's political activities at home. He heard that Charles D. Kasson had become a colonel in the state militia, that he stood at the head "in business" of the largest bar in Vermont, and that he was contemplating the establishment of a newspaper in order to break up "old cliques" and break down "worthless newspapers." Both Charles and his law partner Lyman were deeply immersed in Vermont politics, and John kept abreast of national affairs from the New York *Evening Post,* which came to him from Burlington "like an old friend." [14]

An old acquaintance wrote John from Kentucky that he had given up a one-time fondly cherished theological career for law and had found the latter attractive. As John approached his twenty-first birthday he weighed carefully his own professional aptitudes. A theological career would perpetuate his "bilious temperament of mind," he explained to Charles, while law would have a contrary tendency. Moreover, his "cranial inclinations" were antagonistic to pastoral duties, which would bring him to his grave in ten years. If Conscience faintly whispered that Duty demanded the ministry, could not the influence and money acquired in a business life be expended "to produce results as beneficial as a direct appropriation of my person to the pulpit?" he queried. Charles still held open his offer to let him "dabble in a legal way" in his office, and John declared, "I do *know* that with God's blessing I could succeed in law." [15]

As the soft spring air of the Virginia Piedmont gave way to steaming hot sun in early July, 1843, John Kasson reluctantly bade farewell to the "pleasant" people around Keelona to whom he had become "quite attached." He was returning home now to commence his law studies, presumably in Charles' office. In New York he would meet his brother Chester, who had drifted on down from Albany, and perhaps his sister Mary, who expected to visit Chester. At home he could exchange stories with his sister Maria, who had just returned from Mary Lyons' Mount Holyoke Seminary.[16] In Burlington he would perhaps hear that young men continued to go West, and that a few of the more ambitious were turning their faces toward the East for careers in such cultural centers as Boston.

☆   ☆   ☆

To John Kasson, as he read law in his brother's office in the autumn of 1843, the lure of a more exciting life seemed irresistible. It was one thing to study law in Burlington, but to practice it there with Charles, as his family urged, was an entirely different matter. Instead of Vermont or the West, the cultural center of Boston beckoned him. When he laid bare his ambitions at home he met only opposition, and as winter approached he quietly slipped away without adieus. He had little money with him, and his ultimate destination was vague.

Still pondering his fate, he reached Boston, wandered aimlessly, and finally resolved to go to sea. Trodding from wharf to wharf, the gusty cold winds rushing in from the Atlantic, he could find employment only on an old schooner. As suspicious of the schooner's seaworthiness as the skipper was of Kasson's seamanship, he lost his ardor for a cruise, and as the New Year dawned he turned inland to Worcester, about forty miles to the west.[17]

Worcester, with its whitest of white buildings looking as if they had been painted that morning, was a "pretty New England town," according to Charles Dickens who visited there two years earlier. Rapidly becoming a railroad center, it was the second most famous town in the state for prominent lawyers. John carried with him a letter from Vermont's Secretary of State, who recommended Kasson as a "gentleman of pure character and of a reflective mind of much more than ordinary ability." If he had no letters from the Marsh cousins, he could still use their names.[18]

On the very day of his arrival, John entered the law office of Emory Washburn, "formerly an acquaintance of G. P. Marsh." Washburn, later governor and a revered professor of law at Harvard, had the largest law practice in Massachusetts west of Boston. With an even and sunny temper, he made young people feel that they were the special object of his solicitous interest. John Kasson aspired in vain to fall heir eventually to Washburn's wide law practice; in time it was inherited by another rising young lawyer named George F. Hoar.[19]

Hard pressed for cash, John appealed to his brother for long-term loans rather than accept funds from his mother's savings. His letters were "sad" and "depressed." Charles urged him to throw off "all such depressions" and promised funds, but only under certain stipulations that prompted John to fire back with an independence perhaps not surprising: ". . . one request for a favor without any legal obligation is enough for one man to make to another; and if declined there's an end of the matter with me. Take my bread but leave me the consciousness of well sustained sentiments of honor and it is bread enough." When he died, he declared, he wanted men to look upon his life stained by no "dishonorable act" nor "servile supplication." "And I ask you to watch me hereafter, when men begin to look at me, and mark if ever for the sake of place or prominence before the public . . . I am guilty of those things." He grumbled on: "That word money has with me been a bitter thing. It has depressed my mind, deprived me of privileges, narrowed my thoughts and qualifications, excluded me from society, and sent shame into my face."

Although he did not intend to use "that word" again, he was determined henceforth to make his own decisions. "Charles, I am weary, weary of opposition," he implored. He had always laid his plans before his family, but they had never met with concurrence. Now he had to have approbation or nothing at all. He wanted his mother to know that he was "not going to be lost" as one of her letters implied. "By blessing of God," he confidently affirmed, "I am going to succeed, as in 5 years from this time she will most joyously acknowledge, and perhaps in three."

John Kasson surveyed the possibilities for a legal career in Worcester and found them good. Judge Charles Allen, a rising free-soil politician, would soon resign from the bench and go into private practice, inheriting the clients of Washburn who, it was rumored, was to be promoted to a judgeship. Kasson, unduly optimistic, hoped to become Allen's partner. As a successful lawyer in Worcester he might in time move on to Boston, taking his clients with him. In any event he considered Massachusetts with its six state courts and numerous Boston courts to offer advantages superior to those of any other New England state.[20] He could be admitted to the bar upon completing three years' study; or better still, if he could pass a legal "inquisition . . . more or less severe" he could be admitted "as quick as Patrick Henry." It was an "impossible supposition," he informed his mother, that he would fail to pass the bar examination.

Rejecting a proffered partnership in Vermont with his brother, he disclosed his political ambitions and showed some insight as a political prophet.

. . . to me it seems heinous to settle down in that little hilly state, & simultaneously resign all hopes of progress and preferrment [*sic*]. To become a Whig I cannot, to surrender my democratic predilections I cannot; and I am unwilling to give up hopes of political advancement when the season shall come for it. Although this state is equally Whiggish, it will not be long before the third party will control matters here. There is a large class of first young men in Boston, & old men everywhere who are disconnected partially or totally from the Whig party, & entirely in favor of Abolition principles. And this Texas matter is making them spring up like toadstools in the rain. The Whigs are far more ready to act with the democrats than with themselves. . . . Now & then a little Ohio fever comes over me.[21]

Kasson made these statements three days after the first telegraph line had brought word to Washington that in Baltimore the Democrats had nominated expansionist James K. Polk. A year earlier John Tyler had initiated a treaty for the annexation of Texas, and, at the moment Kasson wrote, it was under attack in the Senate by Whigs and antislavery men generally. Polk's election in the fall, interpreted as a green light for annexation, and Tyler's forcing of the treaty through Congress the next spring by means of a joint resolution, stimulated in Massachusetts a closely-knit and aggressive antislavery faction in the Whig party. The leaders of this faction, joined by loco-foco Democrats, became the leaders of the later Free Soil and Republican parties.[22] There is no evidence that John Kasson at this time held radical antislavery views, but his "democratic predilections" if carried to a logical end would eventually put him in the antislavery ranks. At the age of twenty-two, however, he was primarily interested in his law studies, in the performance of eminent lawyers, in the doings around Boston, and in whatever opportunities might arise out of the prevailing political flux.

In Worcester, as the political storm gathered, Kasson undoubtedly became familiar with the activities of the "Learned Blacksmith," Elihu Burritt. As a young man in New Britain, Connecticut, Burritt shared his time at the anvil with study in mathematics and languages. Following the financial crash of 1837 he walked all the way to Boston, where he sought vainly a place to ply his trade and continue his studies. Turning to Worcester, he found ready employment as a blacksmith and easy access to the rare library of the Antiquarian Society. When Kasson reached Worcester, Burritt had become famous as a lecturer and reformer. He had already started a weekly paper devoted to peace, temperance, and cheap postage. Two years later he was to make an extended tour of England, advocating peace and a universal ocean penny post.[23]

John Kasson made a point of mixing in the local environment. In late May he requested a small bill from Charles for incidentals. He had just bought a coat, hat, pants, and umbrella, for he had been invited to membership in " 'the club,' a little select *conversation* of ladies and gentlemen" which met once a fortnight. Meanwhile, he buried himself deeply in his studies, and within five months he had read twenty-seven volumes in law and equity under Washburn's direction. With so large an acquisition of legal knowledge, John compared himself with the *Great Western* in dock at Bristol: ". . . there's no chance for her wheels to play, though her hold contains abundance of fuel. . . . Let me get into the ocean once, and fairly into deep water, & see if the spray does not fly!" [24]

The autumn of 1844 found John Kasson in deep water. In late summer he followed Washburn, now a judge, to Lowell and was there admitted to the bar in Washburn's court. In Boston, Rufus Choate advised him to establish in one of the smaller towns like New Bedford a clientele which might later follow him to Boston. In late September, Kasson exultantly informed his mother, "Didn't I tell you I *should* succeed." Three weeks earlier he had reached the whaling port of New Bedford, and in the interim he had found a job as an apprentice in a law office and had already collected his first legal fee.[25]

☆ IV ☆

Law and Politics in New Bedford

FOR THE NEXT five and a half years John A. Kasson participated in the colorful life of the old whaling town of New Bedford. Here he proved his competence as a lawyer, sharpened his spurs for politics, and disciplined himself in the ways of the world. During these years he passed from a delayed adolescence to manhood and finally wooed and won a wife.

New Bedford in the middle and late forties was a boom town of some 16,000 people lying along the western shore of a fine harbor where the Acushnet River enters Buzzards Bay. Expert tobacco chewers, for which the era was noted, could almost spit the distance to Boston. To some this town appeared turbulent and lusty; others found its daily life marked by a charming, Quakerlike simplicity; and Herman Melville in his *Moby Dick* described it as queer. Certainly it was a town of bustling commercial and legal activities.

Old Quaker families, the original settlers in the area, had for many years devoted themselves to personal simplicity and to the amassing of wealth. Back in the War of 1812 when they saw their carrying trade decline, they refitted their merchantmen as whalers, and by canny and persistent specialization in whaling — "hugging the oil casks" as Emerson called it — they made their town the first whaling port of America. Now they had become near-millionaires from the spoil of distant seas and the toil of beggarly seamen who not infrequently found themselves the victims of deceit, cruelty, and tightfisted extortion.

Kasson lived in this town during her golden age of whaling when she pushed Baltimore hard as the fourth shipping port in the United States. Day after day he saw coming into port "from the remotest secret drawers and lockers of the world" [1] whale-stuffed ships which if lined up would stretch out full ten miles. The town was a hive of business activity and buzzed with prosperity from this industry with its innumerable subsidiary interests such as shipyards, oil refineries, coopers' shops, tool works, marine insurance, banking, and law. New Bedford could boast the highest per capita wealth in the nation.

When Kasson arrived in September, 1844, he could see fine maples and horse chestnuts stretched out like avenues of green and gold. On high ground along the Old County Road princely mansions arose amid spacious lawns and luxurious gardens. In these homes, which Kasson vividly remembered ever after, lived the opulent shipowners and merchants — the Grinnells, Howlands, Rodmans, Rotches, and Delanos. On lower ground, in sharp contrast, were cheap boarding-houses, taverns, dance halls, and brothels. The business streets were alive with sailors of hodgepodge nationality — farm boys from New England and New York, Portuguese from the Azores and Cape Verde Islands, and Kanakas, Tongatabooars, and Filipinos from the Pacific.[2] Mixed in with the promiscuous population were at least 1,500 Negroes, Kasson noted.

With apparent ease, the first day following his arrival, John found a job as student apprentice in the law office of Timothy Coffin, an advocate especially prominent in marine practice. Called suddenly the next day to the police court, young Kasson succeeded in quashing an indictment of a group of Portuguese for riot. He had hardly strutted away with his first fee of three dollars and a swelling "heart of legality" when the same Portuguese were again arrested on a good warrant. This time Kasson cleared them "on the merits" and walked away with another fee of four dollars, his "bosom almost cracking." Coffin was generous with his student and let him keep all fees from police and justice business and from making out deeds and other legal papers.

Now with seven dollars of self-earned cash in his pocket, Kasson paid off his room rent at the costly Parker House downtown and moved out to a less expensive place on higher ground in the residential area. He was in good health, good spirits, and had a "passably good practice for a beginner," he informed his family. His weight of about 146 pounds had never been greater; "salt sea" bathing had invigorated him; his face was full, lungs sound, and chest thrown out; and his whiskers were growing.

Although he was joyous at the "good favors Providence" had bestowed, he was early critical of the new environment. New Bedford society was "rather jovial" and in many cases "dissolute," he thought. Unlike agricultural Vermont, where pennies were counted, here in a commercial region, where the acquisition of wealth was a "passion," dollars were thrown away. Diagnosing New Bedfordites, he concluded that large fortunes made from nothing begat a people with more "wealth than taste, more love of admiration than literature, and [more] attachment to fashion than to worth."

Soon, however, he found himself a participant in a whirl of activities befitting his age, training, and ambition. The town was filled with meeting houses of "all denominations," and John along with Coffin's family attended the South Trinitarian Congregational Church. His landlady's two "very pretty daughters" undoubtedly made life more pleasant for the young stranger. Coffin's two "sociable girls," whom John thought were not very "intellectual," called upon him and took him into their home and social set.[3]

Within a year John was revising his early appraisal of New Bedford society. "I find almost incessant calls upon my social feeling," he confided to his mother. There was hardly a night except Saturday and Sunday when he was not "outward bound." At Boston he had visited with Charles Sumner, a "clever" Harvard professor, and Judge Washburn. In New Bedford he had been elected a member of the "very Aristocratic Circle," the Bee, of which there was nothing higher, he affirmed. The Bee was a sewing circle of some fifteen young ladies who annually elected young men of their preference to have tea with them and escort them home at the end of an evening's sewing. Although in the main Unitarian, the Circle required that its members be "quite independent, and talk, walk, dance, waltz, play cards, or whatever else they like." Thus John strove to discipline himself in "good manners and some other solid accomplishments." [4] He was coming to enjoy fully the skating, sleighing, and bathing parties, and the fancy balls for which the town was famous. The doors of old and prominent families were being opened to him. [5]

By the middle of the decade he was writing his family that he was to be groomsman in a fashionable Washington wedding. En route John stopped in Baltimore, where his warm reception at church, dinners, and teas prompted him to write that he loved "the hearty unstudied sincerity of Southern women." In Washington he called on Dolly Madison, Congressman G. P. Marsh, and others. At the wedding, when foreign diplomats, senators, cabinet members, and other dignitaries arrived, John thought the company the most brilliant he had ever seen. The occasion was made the more impressive by the "mild, dignified, beneficent face of Mrs. Madison" looking cheerfully on. Following the wedding he remained for another round of gay affairs which, when described to his mother, caused her to write: "I think his nerves must have gained some strength to endure all the excitement and dissipation. . . ." [6]

John Kasson did not, however, devote all his leisure time and energy to purely social "discipline." There were other "solid accomplishments" to be acquired. In the South Trinitarian Church his abilities were soon recognized. In time he became the highly respected superintendent of the Sunday School and was remembered with appreciation by this congregation to his dying day. As one of the directors of the town's Benevolent Society he helped to administer charity. His years at New Bedford corresponded with the peak popularity of the lyceum movement, and he was called into its service. As a member of the program committee, he helped bring in such notables as Charles Sumner, Fanny Kemble, Richard Henry Dana, Jr., and his former schoolmate and rising New York journalist, Henry J. Raymond. John himself was developing a silver tongue as evidenced by repeated speaking engagements to large Fourth of July crowds, to Masonic orders, of one of which he was a member, and to other civic and patriotic groups. And all the while his law practice demanded long hours at the office and in court.[7]

The autumn of 1845 brought both professional advancement and good news from home. Having worked as student apprentice for a year, Kasson found an advantageous situation as the junior partner of Thomas Dawes Eliot, and as he warmed up to his new job, he heard that both his sisters Mary and Maria were getting married. "Glory to God in the highest," he shouted exuberantly in a letter home. Now the wrinkles would fall from his mother's brow and the stoop from Charles' shoulders.

Sister Mary, to whom John was closer all his life, had gone off to Malone, New York, to teach school and there had met her future husband, Samuel C. Wead, a lumber dealer who was later to establish a banding and paper industry. Soon John would hear that Wead's railroad stock was well spoken of in Boston. Sister Maria's husband was James A. Howe, hardware merchant of Troy, New York.[8] Brother Charles, who sometimes met John in Boston, remained a bachelor, but his activities in politics increased with the advent of a national Democratic administration. His law partner Lyman had been in Washington lobbying for an appointment soon after Polk's inauguration, and Charles kept writing to politicians, even to President Polk himself, promoting Lyman for the Collectorship of Vermont. To aid "Drooping Democracy" in his state, he urged removal of the incumbent whose official delinquencies were the gossip of the state.[9]

John's new law partner, Thomas Dawes Eliot, was fourteen years his senior and had been a scion of a leading Massachusetts family. Eliot's father, having suffered financial reverses in the War of 1812, had left New Bedford for employment in the Post Office Department at Washington, where he now lived. One of Eliot's younger brothers was building a reputation in distant St. Louis as a Unitarian minister and a dynamic man of great versatility. His youngest sister, an attractive brunette of fifteen years, was living with her father and mother in Washington.

Thomas Dawes Eliot was a Whig with antislavery views, a Unitarian of deep religious temperament, and one-time superintendent of the Unitarian Sunday School. In politics, he was to become a Free Soiler, a Republican, and finally a member of Congress for ten years during the Civil War period. Eliot specialized in marine insurance cases, and his family connections were an open avenue to the settlement of rich estates. As law partners, John A. Kasson and Thomas Dawes Eliot worked harmoniously. But there would come a time when, as fellow Congressmen, they would meet in the House of Representatives and turn away without speaking.[10]

When Kasson joined up with Eliot the firm took in between six and seven thousand dollars annually. Eliot's practice reached beyond New Bedford to Boston and into the federal courts of the entire state. With his reputation and connections, there was always the possibility that he might win high office or move to Boston, leaving to his junior partner his New Bedford practice and prestige. Aspiring young John was aware of this golden opportunity, and although he appreciated the advantages of the partnership he was not fully satisfied. In less than a year he was writing Mary that life was not opening for him as delightfully as he thought it would at his age; he was "discontented and too anxious about many things"; the "uneasiness" which had always clung to him still clung like "a thorn in the flesh"; his "nervous temperament" was still touchy and once touched "every wing and sting that the demon possesses is in full play." Eliot had been away for months in the state senate and courts, and the office confinement, said John, "has been closer than it will do for *me* to endure." [11]

This self-analysis was written in the spring of 1846 and was the last letter indicating anxiety or moodiness at New Bedford. His reports home also began to lose their color of adolescent exuberance: under the pressure of heavy professional responsibilities, he was maturing.

In midsummer of the next year growing New Bedford was incorporated, and the firm of Eliot and Kasson was retained as the new city's counsel. John participated in the colorful ceremonies celebrating the occasion, serving as toastmaster at banquets and delivering the principal address at the City Hall. Soon he was running for alderman. He tried cases between sailors and between sailors and their masters; he participated with Eliot in general mercantile and maritime practice while performing the functions of a justice of the peace; he helped

Eliot unsnarl the complications in the settlement of great estates; and in the interest of the firm he traveled widely — to Springfield, Boston, New York, Philadelphia, and elsewhere. Sometimes the firm was associated with top lawyers in Boston, as in the case of the eminent Rufus Choate whose "splatter-dash hieroglyphics" handwriting John could not always read.[12]

As the decade roared toward the end, John reported that in one week the firm had taken in twelve to fifteen hundred dollars. This however was an exceptional weekly intake, resulting primarily from the liquidation of a failing textile firm. In the peak year of the partnership, the firm grossed $10,000. Other lawyers, especially in Boston, had a more lucrative practice, but to young Kasson the proceeds of his own firm looked big, and he was able to save enough money from his share, which, when invested wisely, was to give him some freedom from financial worry.[13] And beginning with his New Bedford earnings, Kasson was always frugal and a shrewd investor.

As John plunged deeper into the practice of law, he began to recognize some of its defects. In June, 1849, he published an article on legal reform in Massachusetts which appeared in the *Law Reporter*. This article reflects both his training at the University of Vermont and the prevailing spirit of reform in Massachusetts. It shows Kasson to be a constructive thinker at this time, if not a reformer. And it is typical of his later reactions toward immediate problems which confronted him in a variety of public situations. He was unwilling to let matters drift. He sought to make improvements by diligently applying imagination and common sense to the administrative and social problems that came within the purview of his daily experience.

In this article he directed an attack against the cumbrous common law system. Painting a picture of utter confusion, he recommended the application of civil law practice to common law, the simplification of codes and pleadings, the partial disuse of juries, and the reduction of legal expenses.

Charles Sumner, a former contributor to the *Reporter*, who desired change on many fronts, read the article with enthusiasm and wrote John that in Germany, Thibaut, a master of law codification, had once told him that only "*the will* was wanted" for the reform of a "vicious" legal system. Now Kasson would share the honor in America of strengthening "that *will*." He hoped Massachusetts would have the wisdom to adopt Kasson's suggestions. As for the article itself, Sumner "admired the vivid style, the facility of practical illustration, and the complete mastery of the subject which it showed." [14]

While a law student at Worcester, John Kasson had predicted that ". . . it will not be long before the third party will control matters here." [15] He also forecast that with Whig disintegration his own political future might open. The hour of opportunity came sooner than he expected.

In early May, 1846, hardly two years after his prediction, he heard exciting and at the same time disturbing news. Scouts of General Zachary Taylor's army had clashed with Mexican soldiers on the Rio Grande, sixteen Americans had been killed, and a state of war between the United States and Mexico had been declared. In Burlington, Charles heard from Lyman (still in Washington seeking an appointment and attending the National Fair) that the city was full of "good stout spirited looking" volunteers on their way to the Rio Grande; that Polk had infuriated Northwestern Senators by not taking all the Oregon Territory instead of settling with Britain on the forty-ninth parallel; and that on the West Coast, where Britain was said to have a mortgage on California, there was fear of a clash between British and American fleets.[16]

James K. Polk had worked rapidly and directly since his inauguration in 1845. Unlike the array of presidents, from Jackson to Lincoln, who immediately preceded or followed him, Polk knew exactly what he wanted and how to get it. Tenacious in purpose, he construed his election to mean that the American people subscribed to rampaging territorial expansion. Specifically he wanted California, and while negotiating with Mexico over the boundary of Texas, which Tyler had already annexed, he sent Taylor's army into disputed territory where the inevitable clash with Mexico was hardly less than expected. Forthwith, he settled with the British on the forty-ninth parallel in the Oregon country.[17]

For the next sixteen months, while John Kasson practiced law, made speeches, and in numerous other ways brought his talents before the people of New Bedford, he also read about breath-taking, rapid victories in Mexico. In New England the atmosphere of reform of which John had breathed so much was reaching a condensation point.

In England, Elihu Burritt, the Learned Blacksmith, was urging an ocean penny post, especially for the Anglo-Saxon peoples, whom he predicted would number in a century and a half 880 million, with the United States constituting the "grand family center." [18] In Europe political unrest was coming to a boil. In New Bedford and throughout America a prolonged boom had set in. Cyrus Hall McCormick, the Virginian, was selling two hundred reapers a year in Chicago. Real estate values were soaring in St. Louis. Toward the West, railroads were spreading and Mormons were trekking. Long lines of covered wagons were inching toward Oregon.

In the autumn of 1847 John read thrilling news. Down in Mexico the starry American flag had been unfurled over the gleaming city of the Aztecs, and a treaty had been signed embodying Polk's chief aims. The American flag now waved over the entire Pacific Coast from Puget Sound to the Gulf of Lower California.

Yet this year of great victory brought neither laurels nor unity to the victorious Democratic party in power. Like a raging lion, slavery, around which was wrapped a dozen other sectional issues, stood in the path of political and national unity. The Democratic and the Whig parties both seemed on the verge of collapse, creating a dangerous political vacuum.

In the midst of war a year before, the main issue had been joined at Washington, when David Wilmot, a portly, baby-faced young Democratic Representative from northern Pennsylvania, proposed to debar slavery from all lands acquired in the war. To Northern antislavery men this proposal was a shimmering ray of hope; to Southerners, a danger signal of destruction. The Wilmot Proviso aroused controversy throughout the land and inspired a frantic, futile debate over the extension of slavery, which was to dominate American history until brothers were goaded to kill brothers and fathers, sons.

The antislavery movement which John Kasson had seen swell in Vermont and Massachusetts was reaching its peak, and when wedded to other sectional aspirations it was becoming North-wide. Over the Northwest, men grumbled that their interest in Oregon had been sacrificed to the slave power in the new Southwest. A powerful group of radical Northern Democrats and Whigs prepared to stand firm against the extension of slavery and to bolt their parties if their demands were not heeded. The approaching national nominating conventions were to be the tests.[19]

For party leaders and also for young John Kasson, 1848 was a year of political decision. Early in this year John wrote his brother that he was soon coming home for a visit. In Burlington, Charles may have told John that Vermont Democrats and Whigs were hopelessly divided over the Wilmot Proviso; that abolition was becoming a household precept among the voters; and that a group of young Democratic lawyers and politicians was planning to leave the party if it did not take a clear stand against the extension of slavery in the new territories. In all probability John also learned that brother Charles himself was a leading member of this small group of planners who observed with keen interest the Barnburner revolt in New York proclaimed with the glowing, radical slogan of "Free Trade, Free Labor, Free Soil, Free Speech, and Free Men." [20]

In May, the Democratic National Convention at Baltimore nominated aging Lewis Cass, who opposed the Wilmot Proviso. When a platitudinous platform, side-stepping the territorial question, was adopted, Free Soil delegates left the convention in a rebellious mood. The next month at Philadelphia the Whigs passed over Webster and Clay for General Zachary Taylor, a no-party man and a slaveholder with few if any political qualifications and principles — "an illiterate frontier colonel," sneered Webster. Free Soil Whigs, failing to commit the party to a platform prohibiting the extension of slavery, departed, angrily embittered. Charles Allen, the Worcester lawyer, declared the Whig party dissolved, and he and Henry Wilson, another Massachusetts delegate, stalked out of the convention hall. Handsome and intolerant Charles Sumner called Taylor's nomination an "unhallowed . . . conspiracy" between cotton planters and cotton spinners, between the "Lords of the Lash and the Lords of the Loom." [21]

Not long after the Whig Convention, John Kasson met Daniel Webster in a New Bedford home. Late in the evening, Webster stepped out on the back porch and stood there alone, gazing out toward the ocean, looking the picture of "solitude and despair" in his failure to realize the great hope of his life.[22] Massachusetts Whigs were deeply disappointed at Webster's failure as were certain Vermont Democrats at Cass's success.

At a Democratic Convention in Vermont, news of Cass's nomination initiated an outright revolt planned by Charles D. Kasson and L. E. Chittenden, a young lawyer of twenty-four years. When the state convention endorsed Cass, Charles Kasson, Chittenden, and four others walked out. Crossing the street to another hotel, they organized the Free Soil party of Vermont and launched the *Free Soil Courier,* a weekly newspaper to be published in Burlington.[23]

In late June, at Utica, New York Barnburners, led on by Preston King, Samuel J. Tilden, William Cullen Bryant, and others, nominated Martin Van Buren on a Free Soil platform. Simultaneous with the Utica meeting, a Free Soil Convention at Columbus, Ohio, called for a national convention and designated the place of meeting at Buffalo, New York, and the date, August 9, 1848. Chittenden, representing Vermont insurgents, participated in conferences with New York Barnburners to plan strategy for the Buffalo meeting. At Lindenwald, the home of Martin Van Buren, he heard the aging ex-President advise a small coterie of politicians to include in the new movement antislavery men of all stripes — Free Soil Democrats, Conscience Whigs, Liberty Party men, and fanatical abolitionists.[24]

Within less than a week after the Utica convention, John Kasson read of the dramatic launching at Worcester of the Massachusetts Free Soil party. Seven thousand enthusiastic people were said to have thronged in, selected delegates-at-large for the Buffalo convention, and endorsed the glittering slogan of free soil, free speech, and free men. The selection of district delegates to the Buffalo convention was left to the rapidly evolving party machinery in the districts.[25]

The wheels of the new movement rolled rapidly into the Democratic ranks of New Bedford and Bristol County. A call with John Kasson's name figuring prominently among the some 300 signers went forth to "Democrat citizens" for a "Free Soil and Free Labor" meeting at Taunton. On the last day of July the meeting took place, and although Kasson was not one of the temporary officers he addressed the delegates along with ex-Democratic Governor Marcus Morton. Two days later a convention at New Bedford chose Kasson as one of six delegates to represent the tenth district at Buffalo.[26]

For a young man of twenty-six, and only six years out of college, it was a real honor to be sent as delegate to a national political convention. To be selected from an old, well-established community, after less than four years residence in it, was a real personal achievement. It bespeaks Kasson's ability to mix well, to win friends and their confidence.

John Kasson, ever the enthusiastic traveler and ever eager to associ-

ate with the political and cultural elite, set out early, the morning
following his selection, on the great trip west "on the cars" via Boston,
Springfield, Pittsfield, and Albany. At Lenox, the resort town, he
visited with friends summering there, and picked up delicious gossip
about the actress, Fanny Kemble, whose vital presence lent color to
the literary group composed of Hawthorne, Longfellow, Holmes, and
others who frequented the area. At Albany, John left the train and
stopped overnight with his sister Maria at Troy. Soon Charles arrived from Burlington, bringing political news from home.[27]

At the end of a four-day journey from New Bedford, Kasson
reached Buffalo. For the next two days "it was Convention and
'nothin' else.' " At least 10,000 enthusiastic men (eventually screened
down to 465 voting delegates) of varying political hues and aspirations had thronged in from all the Northern and three border states —
Free Soil Democrats and Conscience Whigs, Liberty men and abolitionists, postal reformers and homestead men, hard money men and
rag currency men, free traders and high tariff men. Their dress was
as diverse as their political views and confirmed the general diversity
of American life. They wore squatty rimless hats, lofty bell crowns,
majestic sugar loaves, or insignificant tubs; their coats looked as if
"every tailor in the land had struck a new and original design"; their
pants ranged from short-legged, liberal baggy seats to long-legged,
scrimpy skin-tights.[28]

Protected from the sweltering sun by a mammoth tent, delegates
listened for two days to a succession of speakers who whipped up a
frenzy of enthusiasm. As the platform was read off screams and
shouts greeted such planks as cheap postage, river and harbor improvements, and free lands to actual settlers; thunderous applause greeted
the concluding slogan — free soil, free speech, free labor, and free
men. As planned by the New York Barnburners, Martin Van Buren
was nominated. Charles Francis Adams, who presided at the convention, was chosen his running mate.

To many delegates a lofty idealism approaching a religious fervor
animated the proceedings. These were breathless, dedicated days. In
John Kasson's opinion it was "the most solemn, imposing and numerous Convention" ever assembled since the Constitution; "attendance
was immense, the numbers incredible, the unity of spirit & harmony
of action miraculous." [29]

But as a young, inexperienced politician who seems to have done no more at the convention than look, listen, learn, and vote, he probably did not know that behind the scenes crafty Barnburners had manipulated the nomination of Van Buren in part as revenge against the regular Democrats; that Free Soilers like Adams and Bryant provided the reform-screen behind which certain Barnburners could seize political control in New York.

Although certain politically-wise Free Soilers had small hope of success, they zealously rushed into the campaign as if certain of victory. Stories of enthusiasm whipped up by Chase, Wilmot, Giddings, and Julian reached the East. John Kasson probably read that even the old Jacksonian, Frank Blair of Silver Springs, Maryland, was being converted, and that his brilliant and aggressive sons, Frank, Jr. and Montgomery, were organizing a Free Soil party out in St. Louis, Missouri.[30] John must have also noted the doings of a mass Whig meeting at nearby Worcester where a tall, gawky Whig Congressman from Illinois named Abraham Lincoln chided Free Soilers; they reminded him of a Yankee peddler who offered for sale a pair of pantaloons "large enough for any man, small enough for any boy." [31]

As Massachusetts Free Soilers got down to the serious business of organizing and campaigning, Kasson began to emerge as a substantial leader in his district. At a large mass meeting in New Bedford, early in September, he was placed on the committee of resolutions. Two days later he was chosen as member of the state central committee for the tenth district. In the month intervening before the district candidates were chosen, John also contributed his forensic talents to the cause.

On October 11, 1848, the district nominating convention, meeting at North Dartmouth, chose John A. Kasson on the second ballot to make the race for Congress.[32] This was a signal honor indeed, and Kasson at best could hardly have expected a greater one. It was a tempting political morsel that must have been hard to resist. But Kasson reflected upon the matter and rejected the nomination, apparently considering a race against the Whig incumbent as futile. Years later he wrote: "At that early age I had the practical sense to decline." [33]

In the general elections the next month, the Free Soil party split the Democratic vote in New York, and the Whigs carried that state and the nation for Taylor. In Massachusetts, Free Soilers led the Democrats and took second place. Although now defeated, their leaders, like

Adams, Sumner, Wilson, Dana, Hoar, and Andrew, were coming to the front; and although Kasson could not have defeated his Whig opponent, he passed up an excellent opportunity to build wider political connections in the state.

Out of the new movement Kasson got just about what he expected — political experience. If he considered Free Soilism as a burning moral cause his letters do not reflect it. And if he had so considered, he probably would have made the race despite inevitable defeat. Granted that he was opposed to the extension of slavery, he was still no rabid antislavery man. To court the friendship of men like Charles Sumner was one thing; to accept all their views was another. To Kasson the Free Soil party represented at least a breach in old established political parties through which young men without hereditary connections might enter into the land of political opportunity. If his prophecy of Whig disintegration, made four years previously, had not been completely fulfilled by '48, it was nevertheless the last national campaign the party was to win. And although the Democratic party was to hang together for another decade, the Free Soil revolt along purely sectional lines had made the chain binding together Northern and Southern Democrats precariously weak. Whether John Kasson then realized it or not, he could afford to await third party victory. Moreover, in the fall of '48 certain immediate personal interests may have crimped his enthusiasm to run for Congress.

☆   ☆   ☆

As the smoke cleared from the autumn political battles, John Kasson approached a year fraught with significance for his future. The year 1849 brought not only a peak in his law practice but also the necessity for important personal decisions. Ever since coming to New Bedford, John had shown a keen interest in girls and had been seriously considering matrimony. His letters home told of a Baltimore belle, a Philadelphia favorite, and a New York beauty. He was not in quest of a woman with wealth, but a prospective bride would have to have "considerable mental qualifications" and also looks.[34]

Caroline Eliot, the young sister of John's law partner, seemed to possess these qualifications. She and John had met on one of her frequent visits from Washington to New Bedford. Back in 1848 John had written that "no East Wind" would "deter him from the *Affair*" — a possible allusion to his courtship with Miss Eliot.[35]

Then, early in 1849, as winter's snow in "old Burlington style" blanketed New Bedford earth and heralded a gay sleighing season, Caroline Eliot returned. That John had more than a casual interest in her is shown in an outburst to his brother:

That charming sister of Eliot's who was here, as I wrote you, two years ago, is now again here, is 18 years old, full of vivacity, a little under medium size, irregular features, fine eyes of black, expressive mouth, quick temper, generous impulses, of a religion mixed up of Unitarianism, universalism, & elegant spices of charity; "a voice gentle, soft & low — an excellent thing in woman," splendid taste in singing, great power on the piano, & a beautiful handling of the guitar, and acquainted with the Italian & French; a pretty dancer, with a head of jet black hair, & a soft skin of a light brunette. For further description, inquire of the Painter. I have a strong penchant for her, so she says she has for me, & sudden visions of the *might-bes* has [sic] risen before me. But my heart & will are both excessively irresolute and timid on this subject. . . . I have a desperate inclination occasionally to plunge, & venture my life's stakes on the chances. But my blood after that point always runs cool.[36]

But the courtship went on, and as John's blood warmed up, he traveled over the country in the interest of the firm, completed his scholarly article on law reform, and continued to line up speakers for the New Bedford lyceum. Good news continued to arrive from home. Brother Charles had given up his law partnership with Lyman and was now sharing his legal activities with banking operations.[37]

Yet, scanning the future, John Kasson thought he saw obstacles ahead to a successful legal and political career at New Bedford. Before the coming of the new year, he had made his plans to settle in distant St. Louis, Missouri.

For one thing, New Bedford's great whaling boom seemed to be reaching a climax. While building a millrace on a baronial estate in faraway California, a keen-eyed mechanic had spaded up glittering yellow specks that turned out to be gold. By the end of 1848 the presence of the precious metal in fabulous amounts had been officially confirmed in Washington. In '49 the gold fever swept through Massachusetts. Farmers left their farms; clerks, their counting houses; and mechanics, their work benches. In New Bedford, where the Rotches and Delanos had organized an emigrant company, eight hundred men left for California. In the North Pacific and Arctic oceans sailors deserted, leaving whaling fleets only half manned.[38]

At the very beginning of the gold rush, John Kasson was showing concern. "A large no: of our people have gone, & are still going to

California," he complained to Charles. "The effect of all this distraction upon our regular course of business remains to be seen. I fear it will prove highly injurious. I am of Benton's opinion — the sooner this gold is exhausted the better for the country." John went on to tell how "little vials" of the yellow metal were arriving to stimulate the already feverish rush. He did not expect to have another year at law so prosperous as the present one.[39]

Almost sixty years later Kasson recalled that the whaling industry was "seen to be diminishing" in '49. Small cargoes were still arriving, but profitable ones were infrequent. Foresighted blubber barons had shrewdly begun to turn to new business outlets. Joseph Grinnell already had laid the base for a future commercial boom by launching the great Wamsutta cotton mills.[40]

For another reason also Kasson was beginning to doubt the wisdom of remaining in the East. Viewing the matter with hindsight, he explained that he had become dissatisfied with the "settled institutions and hereditary tendencies of the old eastern society." He had arrived at the "sorrowful knowledge" that in Massachusetts a "phalanx of old families, well intrenched in their profession, effectually shut out the younger men from early success." [41]

Still further explanatory of his decision to leave New Bedford was his ripening courtship with vivacious Caroline Eliot (called Cara by her intimates). John had overcome his timidity and now planned a partnership for life with his partner's sister. In the autumn Cara's dynamic brother from St. Louis, the ancestor of T. S. Eliot, the poet, came East on a speaking tour and preached at his old home town of New Bedford. From him it may be assumed John and Cara were briefed on St. Louis and its splendid legal opportunities.[42]

In the last month of '49 John received a touching letter from a committee representing the Sunday School of which he was superintendent. Children and teachers were saddened at his decision to remove "to a distant city far west." [43]

Early the next May, as the spring flowers burst out profusely over the nation's capital, "John A. Kasson, Esq., of St. Louis," was married to Caroline Eliot at her father's home in Washington. Her brother, Rev. William Greenleaf Eliot of St. Louis, read the vows.[44]

John Kasson was eight years older than Cara, who had just passed her twentieth birthday. John was the youngest child in a family of five; Cara the youngest in a family of six. Neither was the beneficiary of inherited wealth, but both were well educated, talented, and attractive. Both also were independent, high spirited, and ambitious.

As the bride and groom made ready for the long trip west, Congress then in session was on the point of finding a solution to the sectional deadlock which threatened to disrupt the Union. Having convened the preceding December, solons had been faced with free-soil California demanding admission to the Union. Acrimonious debate had since gone on, and the great oratorical giants in the Senate —Clay, Calhoun, and Webster — had given their swan-song speeches in behalf of section or Union. Mississippi had sent out a call for a meeting of slave state delegates at Nashville, but by the time the Kassons reached St. Louis this convention had petered out. Soon John learned that the great Compromise of 1850 between North and South had been passed in Washington. Disruption of the Union had at least been postponed. Many revolting Free Soilers now drifted back into Democratic or Whig ranks. The nation breathed easier, and men settled down to enjoy the prevailing prosperity of the fifties.

$\star$ V $\star$

Becoming Westernized in St. Louis

IN THE eighteen fifties the western region of the flatboat era was becoming the Middle West of productive farms, lusty business, and towering cities. Cincinnati, Cleveland, Chicago, and St. Louis rivaled each other for commercial supremacy. While one frontier surged west from the Mississippi, another moved more slowly east from the Pacific Coast. In St. Louis, as in the nation's capital, sectional interests of North, South, and West converged to churn up a political maelstrom from which discontents and frustrated aspirations produced kaleidoscopic changes. Slavery and abolitionism, immigration and Know-Nothingism, Pacific railroads and expansionism were vexing local problems as well as national issues.

St. Louis, like the nation, was going through the confusion of rapid growth. During the six fat years which John Kasson spent there the population doubled to nearly 160,000. Irish and German immigrants crowded in, producing social, religious, and political tensions. By 1860 more than half the population was foreign born. Although first flocking to the Democratic party, the Germans were soon to provide a solid vote for Free Soil politicians.

From Northern states business and professional men, preferring free labor, moved in to challenge the attitudes and supremacy of men of Southern backgrounds and to place slavery in a perilous situation. In the great sectional controversy which, four years after Kasson arrived, was to catch fire again, this metropolis was to remain steadfast to the Union, for its future lay more in western development than in association with New Orleans and the deep South.

St. Louis like other ambitious cities, especially in the Northeast and Northwest, was bubbling over with business and industrial activity. She had distinct urban characteristics, and her people called her the New York of the West. Occupying a crossroads position in the nation, she stood where the trade of the Mississippi, Ohio, Missouri, and Illinois rivers poured into her lap. The fur trade, the Mexican War, the gold rush, and the surge of settlers into the up-river country engendered a glowing optimism as well as a complacency in her ability to hold her trade against upstart Chicago.

By 1850 she was one of the world's greatest ports of exchange. Her merchants carried on an immense wholesale and jobbing trade throughout the entire region of the western waters. Produce packed in St. Louis made its way to Europe, and European wares were sold in St. Louis. Packets made regular sailings to New Orleans, Nashville, Cincinnati, Pittsburgh, Peoria, Dubuque, and St. Paul. Traders from the South, Southwest, and Northwest here gathered to buy and sell. Foreign and Yankee capital filtered in.

In the wake of destruction by disease, floods, and fire, business soared to new heights. Kasson trailed the "Great Fire" and the "frightful cholera scourge" by one year, merely to find that such calamities "spent themselves vainly against the prosperity of this city, like waves at the foot of an eternal sea-rock." [1] Reconstruction brought wider streets and massive private and business "palaces," built substantially but ornately in continuous blocks of stone, brick, and iron. The real estate business boomed, land owners feverishly divided their acres into small parcels, and the price of land per front foot increased tenfold in a few years. The rapid exchange of urban property was a real boon to lawyers to whose happy lot it fell to clear up complicated titles of French, Spanish, and American origin. So brisk and complex was this activity that the establishment of a Special Land Court was required.[2]

Moreover, the grandeur and romance of river steamboating around St. Louis flourished while John Kasson resided there. From the old courthouse where he spent long hours he could look down upon the river, six hundred yards away, at a mile-long expanse of boats smoking and throbbing. Along the levee motley crowds swarmed about — fur-traders, immigrants, and soldiers; merchants, land speculators, and politicians; reporters, peddlers, and hotel runners; tambourine girls, musical roustabouts, and Negro bands. In summer, moonlit excursions on the river gave relief from oppressive heat to the fun loving inhabitants. Floating palace showboats could accommodate more people than the second largest theater in America. Sometimes big freezes brought winter sport on the icy river.

With her wide-open saloons and suburban beer gardens, her houses of ill fame and Sunday night brass bands, her brawling Irish and election riots, St. Louis was no Puritan city. But this hurdy-gurdy was tempered by a tradition of conservatism, aristocracy, good living, and easygoing graciousness, emanating from surviving French influences and from old Southern slaveholding families who set the social tones.[3]

Swallowed up in this complex environment for only six years, John Kasson did not achieve great prominence. But here he continued the patterns of life begun in New Bedford, ever enriching his background for politics. As a talented young lawyer he worked tirelessly. Striking in appearance, well mannered, and becoming eloquent, he made frequent public appearances. With persisting faith in moderate Free Soilism, he performed a political lieutenant's work, while at the same time building up connections with men whose future power and influence were of inestimable value.

Kasson first formed a partnership with J. B. Crockett, of Virginia and Kentucky ancestry, and of local renown as a criminal lawyer, a Whig politician, and editor of the St. Louis *Intelligencer*. The lure of California, however, terminated this lucrative arrangement, by which Kasson received one half the proceeds of the firm. In less than two years Crockett pulled out for San Francisco, ostensibly for his health, but really, Kasson suspected, to speculate in California.[4]

John's next partner was B. Gratz Brown from Kentucky. Four years younger than Kasson, Brown had reached St. Louis one year before Kasson. A relative of the powerful Bentons, Blairs, and Breckinridges, he was rising rapidly within the political metamorphosis of Missouri. Kasson considered Brown a firm friend and an ardent Free Soiler with fine intellectual powers; but, apparently having more to gain from an independent practice, once he had become familiar with local problems, Kasson left Brown after a year and set up his own office at the northwest corner of Olive and Main streets.

In this area many of the city's 155 attorneys had offices. Nearby was the city hall, post office, newspaper offices, and the famous hotel, Planter's House. Around the post office, which lawyers visited daily, groups gathered to discuss public affairs.

A familiar scene was that of young Frank Blair in a dove-colored plug hat haranguing a cluster of men on the dangers of Calhoun Democracy. A dynamo of human energy, this tonguey Princeton graduate was, like Brown, a former Kentuckian with free-soil leanings. In 1852 Blair and Brown were to launch an aggressive newspaper called the *Missouri Democrat*, which, "like a mighty sea," would "hurl wave after wave of powerful propaganda against crumbling walls of conservatism." [5]

Frank Blair's older brother, Montgomery — a tall, genial West Point graduate — was also a St. Louis lawyer, a judge, and an important city politician. Soon he would move to Washington and live in the Blair House, just across the street from the White House. In a few years Justices of the Supreme Court would hear his thin fine voice crack out in behalf of a St. Louis Negro named Dred Scott.

The Blair brothers had settled in St. Louis, imbued with the spirit of Manifest Destiny. Investing heavily in real estate, they were vigorously urging rail connections with the East and Far West. From Washington, old Frank Blair, their father and a stalwart Jacksonian, sent sage business and political advice. The Blairs played politics with a passion, detested Calhoun's doctrine of secession, and were feverishly trying to prop up the sagging political fortunes of Thomas Hart Benton.[6]

Presiding over the Land Court at one time was Edward Bates, who, soon after the War of 1812, had arrived with "a good horse, a bag of clothing, and three dollars." Hailing from a Virginia plantation overlooking the James River, this short, swarthy young man had moved up steadily in Missouri politics as a Whig. In St. Louis he was noted for his winsome nature and his great interest in young lawyers. Bates, the Blair brothers, and Brown were all slaveholders soon to be grappling with the problems of emancipation and race readjustment.[7]

Among such men Kasson kept abreast of political currents and speedily gained a wide law practice, especially from merchants, boat captains, and mercantile incorporations.[8] He argued cases before the state supreme court, the circuit court, and the court of common pleas, spending long hours at the courthouse, watching the docket, and often taking work home at night.

Some of his clients were men of political and commercial importance. He became the agent of Elihu B. Washburne, an acquaintance of Cara's, who lived up the Mississippi at the thriving town of Galena, Illinois. A blunt, uncouth looking man, Washburne was using boundless energy and hard sense to forge ahead in Illinois politics.[9]

Another of Kasson's earliest and most steady clients was John J. Roe, a merchant prince originally from western New York. A slaveholder and commission merchant, Roe specialized in packing pork for the English market. But he also was connected with railroad, steamship, bridge, street car, coal, and insurance companies.[10]

Kasson's fees were often attractive, at least one amounting to $2,000.[11] Along with a lucrative practice were possibilities of investment and speculation. After eighteen months in St. Louis, he wrote Charles: "The best business here is the loaning of money. I have loaned some of my own and of others at 12 per cent, with ample personal and real estate security. Others loan at much higher rates." The wealthiest bankers, John continued, paid 4 per cent on current, and 6 on special deposits. Money for investment was coming in from England, Germany, and Scotland. Along the line of the "Pacific railroad,"[12] then crawling painfully from St. Louis, "some splendid speculations" had been made in land to which a good title never fell in price and usually advanced "at the rate of triple, or compound interest, and often at double that rate." If this struck Charles as speculation, John added apologetically, it was nevertheless "the simple statement of fact, of every day occurence [sic]."

He urged Charles to send him $10,000 to invest, and to come out in person and investigate "our business, resources, progress and facilities." Charles could leave his Burlington affairs part time in the hands of his new law partner, twenty-three-year-old George F. Edmunds, a future United States Senator.[13]

☆　☆　☆

In addition to his legal and business activities, John Kasson still found time to indulge his fondness for oratory. By the end of 1851 he had been invited, as an "accomplished scholar," to speak before the famous Mercantile Library Association whose roster of lecturers that year included such distinguished men as Emerson, E. D. Baker, and Edward Bates. Speaking on the subject of "St. Louis: Incidents in Its History and Its Prospects," Kasson informed Charles that he brought down a "handsome quantum of applause." A few days later he spoke impromptu at a bar dinner in the presence of Thomas Hart Benton and 150 other lawyers and politicians.[14]

On a more gala occasion, he served as toastmaster at a gigantic banquet of 600 guests given by St. Louis businessmen for the Illinois legislature, whose decisions on the terminal point of railroads running from the East could well be decisive in the contest between St. Louis and Chicago for commercial supremacy. Kasson presided over the ceremonies, and among the distinguished citizens with him at the head table were the Mayor, John A. Logan, Gustave Koerner of Illinois, and John's brother-in-law, the eminent Unitarian minister. Koerner, an intelligent and ambitious German politician, observed that Kasson, with his "winning manners," looked "quite young" and "very handsome" and was one of the best after-dinner speakers he had ever heard.[15]

Kasson's speech-making reached its climax upon the visit to St. Louis in 1852 of the noted Hungarian exile, Louis Kossuth. In the United States the nationalistic movement called Young America had sprung up, mostly among the younger politicians who wanted to quench sectional fires with an expansion of national power. Sometimes swaggeringly overconfident, these men advocated rapid settlement of the West, aggressive expansion in the Caribbean, and bold championship of oppressed democrats and radicals in Europe. Kossuth's extensive tour of America thus provided this group the occasion for much spread-eagle oratory.

It was a tribute to the oratorical powers of young John Kasson to be chosen to welcome the illustrious Hungarian patriot. On a stormy day in early March, Kasson, with Kossuth at his side, faced an audience of some 5,000 people gathered in Old Market Place on Lucas Street. Neither the "frowning elements of nature," nor "the frowns of despotic men and despotic principles, could . . . keep down the irrepressible energies of the people, roused in a good and glorious cause," he yelled out. Although Kasson's Young Americanism in this speech was not as rabid as that of many others who spoke in Kossuth's behalf, he could not resist the temptation to shout national glory and to hurl republican defiance at the crowned heads of Europe.[16] Moreover, his welcome of Kossuth identified him with the Free Soil political elements of St. Louis — a relationship which he had established almost on the eve of his arrival there.

In the nation the Free Soil party seemed dead in the years immediately following 1850. The popularity of the Great Compromise was demonstrated by enthusiastic gatherings all over the country and particularly in the border states, where support was most vocal. John Kasson had hardly settled down in St. Louis before he found himself in the midst of mass Union meetings favoring the Compromise. Soon he was joining with fifty-one other Union petitioners to invite Honorable T. A. Marshall, staunch Kentucky Unionist and descendant of the great Virginia Chief Justice, to give the Fourth of July oration on "The Union and Its Preservation." [17]

But the real core of free-soilism in St. Louis remained intact as a faction within the Democratic party. The bitter struggle of Thomas Hart Benton to hold his place in the United States Senate and to maintain his supremacy in the Democratic party of Missouri provided the opportunity for Free Soilers to act as a political unit.

For thirty years a Senator, a stalwart Jacksonian, and a nationalist, Benton had ridden roughshod over the growing proslavery opposition within the Missouri Democracy led by Missouri's other Senator, explosive, hard hitting David R. Atchison. During the six years that Kasson lived in St. Louis, Benton and Atchison made Missouri the storm center of factional and sectional politics. The Old Roman, vowing to exterminate Calhounism, was himself hunted down and eventually exterminated.

Revolving around this titanic struggle were a multiplicity of political issues and factions which, cutting across old party lines, soon crystallized into a contest between the slave and free-soil powers. Out of the hardened core of Benton's free-soil supporters arose young political leaders to be reckoned with. Quick to come to his rescue was the Kentucky clique in St. Louis led by Kasson's one-time law partner, B. Gratz Brown, and by the Blair brothers — Frank and Montgomery. John Kasson here found for himself a political situation made to order. By jumping with his law associates into the fight for Benton he was merely transferring his free-soil activities from New Bedford to St. Louis.[18]

Leaders of Benton Democrats in St. Louis were not radical anti-slavery men in the early fifties. The Blairs and Brown were Southerners and slaveholders; and John Kasson, within a year after reaching St. Louis, had acquired one or more slaves.[19] Although considering themselves Unionists first of all, these men were also practical politicians, at once reaching for political power and representing Western and metropolitan interests.

As spokesmen for metropolitanism, they considered free labor superior to slave labor. One German immigrant, it was claimed, knocked out three slaves. Acutely sensing the problem of race readjustment, however, they advocated gradual emancipation. As Westerners and metropolitans, they demanded rapid development of the Republic's potential wealth, voicing the desires of the surging businessman and promoter interested in real estate speculation, railroads, banking, and manufacturing. Eager to use the power and resources of the federal government to build railroads and improve river transportation, they anticipated the early opening of the territories. At heart they were nationalists and expansionists.[20]

Despite Benton's defeat for the Senate in 1851, at the hands of proslavery Democrats and Whigs, the Blair-Brown faction supported Pierce in the national election of 1852 and seemed reconciled with the new Democratic administration in its early stages.[21] But in Missouri the factional war raged on furiously and was finally transferred to the arena of national politics at Washington in connection with the fateful issue of a Pacific railroad and the territorial organization of Kansas and Nebraska.

For years Benton had been an ardent champion of a central railroad connecting St. Louis with San Francisco. Glamorously calling it the

Route to the Orient, he aroused eager hopes among Southerners and Westerners interested in the markets of the Orient's teeming millions.[22] While he rode the Pacific railroad hard as a political issue in Missouri, the opportunity arose for Kasson to give his support in one of the famous Southern commercial conventions. In June, 1853, some 500 delegates from the South and West swarmed into Memphis, Tennessee, to discuss common commercial problems, to overcome the trade disparity between their regions and the Northeast, and in part to cement rapidly breaking commercial ties between the South and the Upper Mississippi Valley.

John Kasson and Frank Blair, Jr., were among Missouri's twenty-seven delegates. And, to judge from the convention proceedings, Kasson and Blair were there primarily to support Benton's "Central National Highway." They worked closely together, consistently backing each other's proposals. As was characteristic of Kasson at such meetings, he arose frequently to express his views — more frequently than most of his Missouri colleagues.

All delegates were vociferous in their demands for a Pacific railroad, "the Aaron rod that swallowed up" all other discussion. But the matter of location and means of construction brought sharp disagreement. Both Blair and Kasson supported the central route and urged that it be constructed under the auspices of the federal government. Kasson "in a very able manner" fought in vain a pet project of New Orleans to support a railroad across the Isthmus of Tehuantepec in Mexico.[23] On the other hand, the convention accepted unanimously Kasson's less controversial proposal that each state set up a bureau of statistics under a competent statistician to inform each session of the legislature on the state's wealth, industry, arts, capacity for production, and population.[24] Other resolutions which Kasson saw approved touched almost every economic need and ambition of the South and West. Delegates denied that the convention was sectional in a political sense. Businessmen and their spokesmen predominated, and the tone was politically conservative and economically visionary, despite an occasional undertone from radical sectional elements. There is no evidence that Kasson objected to a resolution recommending the education of Southern children at home by Southern teachers using Southern textbooks. He was there to represent the economic interests of St. Louis and the political interests of Benton, not the interests of North against South or South against North.[25]

Returning to St. Louis, Kasson found Benton and Atchison engaged in a furious and vituperative campaign in which the ever-popular Pacific railroad was becoming the main issue. By boldly urging the immediate organization of the Nebraska territory as indispensable to the success of the road, Benton was whetting the land-hungry appetites of western Missourians and forcing Atchison into an extreme position. On the stump in Missouri, face to face with his proslavery constituents, Atchison declared that he favored the organization of Nebraska, indeed, but he would prefer to let it "sink in hell" than become free soil. In short, he favored it only if the hoary Missouri Compromise, barring slavery from it, were repealed.[26]

John Kasson and his free-soil friends steadfastly supported Benton on this issue. At a county mass meeting of "the friends of Nebraska" in St. Louis, Kasson, Blair, Brown, and several others — the "confidential friends and mouthpieces" of Benton, according to Atchison — made speeches. At the end of the meeting they passed a strong resolution favoring territorial government for Nebraska and accusing all who opposed it "upon *whatever pretext,* as hostile to the best interests of the State." Thus Kasson was playing a small role in a great drama, which, perhaps unforeseen by him, was to unleash once more fierce sectional hatreds on a national scale.[27]

In the closing weeks of 1853 Benton and Atchison returned to Washington, both committed to the organization of Nebraska: Benton, without slavery under the Missouri Compromise; Atchison, with slavery and the repeal of the Missouri Compromise.

Unlike Missouri, the political situation in the nation seemed serene under the sectional truce and heady prosperity. But in the spring of 1854 John Kasson read startling news which charged the political atmosphere with passion. Congress had passed legislation to organize Nebraska on Atchison's terms, not Benton's. The former Vermonter, Senator Stephen A. Douglas of Illinois, pressed hard by Atchison and other Southern Senators and motivated by a number of other factors, had impulsively pushed through the Kansas-Nebraska Bill,[28] repealing the slavery restrictions provided by the Missouri Compromise, transferring the power to decide on slavery expansion from Congress to the people in the territory, and indirectly instigating a prolonged era of bloody civil strife on the plains of Kansas.

This measure acted as a catalytic agent crystallizing political parties into new forms. Anti-Nebraska groups sprouted up throughout the

North, simultaneously and spontaneously, calling themselves "Republicans." Even in Washington shortly after its passage, thirty Representatives met in the boardinghouse rooms of Congressman T. D. Eliot, Kasson's brother-in-law and former law partner, to lay plans for a third party to be called Republican. In Missouri, Frank Blair worked desperately to put Benton back in the Senate in 1855. But the bitterly deadlocked Missouri legislature, unable to agree upon either Benton or Atchison, left the state with only one Senator for the next two years. With Benton almost completely destroyed as a political power in Missouri, and with the life blood ebbing away from the Whig party, Blair vigorously struck out to organize anti-Nebraska men — free-soil Whigs, Democrats, Know-Nothings, and German-Americans — against the proslavery Democrats. At one time called the Free Democracy of St. Louis, Blair's organization was to be the nucleus of the Republican party in Missouri.[29]

The Nebraska Bill acted also as an agent to speed up the gradual emancipation movement in St. Louis. Kasson's brother-in-law, the "Unitarian Bishop of the West," began to write discreet antislavery letters to the newspapers, signing them "Ergon" and subtly playing up the advantages of free labor. Frank Blair, having spearheaded the emancipation movement, commenced to free his slaves gradually. So did B. Gratz Brown, Edward Bates, and many others. Near the end of the decade a less prominent St. Louisan, shabbily dressed in an old slouch hat and a fading blue army overcoat, made his way to court and emancipated his slave, Willie. This was private citizen Ulysses S. Grant, then a failing farmer and real estate agent.[30]

As the sparks of civil war along the Missouri-Kansas border continued to sputter in December, 1855, John A. Kasson also appeared before the circuit court and signed a significant document which read: "I do emancipate and set free my slave Lydia, about thirty, dark, rather thin, middle height, quiet manner and rather cracked voice . . . the wife of Stephen Woodley . . . and commend her as strictly honest and worthy of protection and favor." [31]

The rosy glow of prosperity was not enough to keep calm and satisfied the restless spirit of John Kasson. With political stalemate and increasing violence in Missouri, a number of other factors combined to make life unpleasant if not uncertain. Hard work, an enervating climate, the fear of "deteriorating" health, his wife's unhappiness, and distressing news from home diluted the satisfaction derived from a growing law practice.

In the busy season, with practice in "four or five courts" at the same time, he would come home completely exhausted, although still required to be ready for "every emergency." This constant and anxious attention to business made him want to turn farmer on a small scale, he informed his mother. In the harsh and unhealthful climate of St. Louis he sighed for the New Bedford breezes "like a prisoner for his freedom." He longed to have a glimpse of Charlotte, his old birthplace, now vivified with a depot and the whistles of locomotives. There he would like to stretch his legs, as in youth, in the "big orchard," the "little orchard," the "great woods," and the "little meadow." [32] To sister Mary he declared: "If the Lord would teach me how to keep a clear conscience and make $25000, how quick I'd show St. Louis a clean pair of heels & the East a dusty face." Yet every "calling" had its "burdens and joys," he philosophized. How to make the best of it was the "nice question," rather than how to change it. With God's blessing, patience, and a "brazen front" he would probably make more than $25,000. [33]

Neither John nor Cara found everyday home life in St. Louis to be fully satisfying. First boarding out at "not a very good table," as Cara described it, they later rented a house. But John regretted that he did not own a handsome home like sister Mary's in Malone, New York. Cara visited frequently with her brother's family, and on festal occasions, such as New Year's, received her callers at the Eliot's or at the home of the famous pioneer physiologist, Dr. William Beaumont.

But John's lovely wife was frequently homesick and unhappy. "I sometimes wish we had never come here," she wrote. [34] "Cara is not happy here and that gives me much regret, as my fortunes seem plainly to be hers," John confided to Mary. [35]

Cara despaired of her husband's overwork, feared for his and her health, and pined for the companionship of her aging parents. Her letters to John's family show lonesomeness and inexplicable emotional struggles, the source of which perhaps only she and her husband understood.

In this decade of feverish reform movements and religious extravagances, Cara's reading was "pretty much of a religious nature." She, and perhaps her husband, attended Spiritualist seances. It was not a long step from Transcendentalism to Spiritualism, which caught on most strongly in Massachusetts among upper class intellectuals and rapidly spread as far as St. Louis. Cara wrote to John's brother tolerantly if not approvingly of the new religion: "We have had a great deal of excitement in St. Louis about the Spiritual Rappings . . . our experiences . . . are very wonderful and impressive. . . . It is so wrong to laugh at anything because it is strange that I hope you are not one of the scoffers, dear Brother."

Cara's reluctant decision to join her husband's Congregational Church aroused emotions so deep that she temporarily lost her zest to live, she tearfully informed Charles Kasson. It filled her with "anxieties" so to "grieve" her friends, old parents, and brother. "But I shall make *John* happy, and I would die to do that," she affirmed. John was good to her, making her laugh when she was sad and bringing a "gentle voice and kind word" when she needed to be "cheered up dreadfully." [36] When John's sister and Cara's niece announced the arrival of babies, Cara responded with enthusiastic approbation and emphatically added: "Well, if *baby having* were catching, I should have had the disease long ago, for all my friends are in the blissful state, and give ample promise for the coming months!" [37]

Not all the letters from the East carried tidings so thrilling as the birth of children. In 1852 Cara wrote of her old father's "pecuniary losses." The next year brought saddening news from both Burlington and Washington. In the summer a fatal brain tumor cut short the life of Charles Kasson, who, in his prime at forty-two, gave promise of a brilliant political career, as free-soil forces in Vermont gathered momentum. Only a few months later Cara's father passed away.[38]

John's other brother, Chester, was frequently in trouble. He used "profane language," "drank sometimes to excess," shifted about from place to place without steady employment, and found it difficult to provide for his family. To his brother's "misfortune and fault" John responded with admirable generosity and tolerance, sending money, seeking employment, and writing him, "hinting [at] his bad habits . . . in a quiet, sincere, & gentle tone, free from all offense." "Why . . . should I over judge any one, least of all a Brother?" [39]

As the humid days of late spring in St. Louis crept toward the dog days of hot sultry summer, John's spirits sagged in the absence of clients during this dull season. Nearly every summer, therefore, saw

John and Cara headed east to visit with relatives and friends in Washington, New Bedford, Boston, and Malone, and sometimes to vacation with the elite at Saratoga and Newport. On one trip, John and Cara returned home along the St. Lawrence, among the Thousand Islands, via Niagara Falls, Buffalo, Detroit, and Chicago. From Detroit to Chicago they were stowed away like cattle in cars pulled by a "weak sister" locomotive.[40]

Along this northern railroad route more and more people were traveling and shipping their goods. The Upper Mississippi Valley was being tied to the industrial Northeast, while the agricultural South fell deeper into a colonial status. Swaggering Chicago was fast becoming the crossroads recipient of this east-west traffic. Her horn-blowing business leaders were winning the race for railroads to the East, and eventual commercial supremacy, against their less aggressive competitors in St. Louis.

A discerning, ambitious young lawyer with a New England background must have pondered these significant developments and their impact on politics, business, and the law profession. The surge of settlers of Northern antecedents into the Upper Mississippi Valley, spontaneously generating a fluid society, a new political party, and easy opportunity with their bustle and enterprise, made this region a happy contrast to the whirlpool of violent sectional discord which Missouri was becoming.

As clouds of dark foreboding hovered over Kansas early in 1856, John Kasson packed up his bags and left St. Louis, thus beginning a year of "comparative idleness" apparently devoted to recuperation, travel, and contemplation as to where next to settle. He later ascribed his departure to "deteriorating health under the influence of a miserable climate," the tense feeling engendered by the slavery question, and distaste for "the controlling pro-slavery elements in Missouri."[41]

While Kasson traveled over the country, visiting, vacationing, and scouting for a new location, violence flared up in Kansas and Washington. The sacking of Lawrence in Kansas, the caning of Charles Sumner in the Senate chamber, and the massacre led by John Brown on Pottawatomie Creek followed fast and furiously on the heels of each other in May.

The drift toward civil strife was ominous as the Democratic National Convention met in June and nominated James Buchanan, a proslavery man. Young Frank Blair's "Black Republican" delegation, among whom was B. Gratz Brown, were denied entrance to the convention hall. They clubbed down the doorkeepers and entered anyway, only to be later ejected.

Already the Republicans had held a preliminary convention at Pittsburgh. At this meeting old Frank Blair, "the lion among the delegates," had served as permanent chairman, and Henry J. Raymond had written the resolutions summoning the national convention to be held in Philadelphia.[42] At this convention the Republicans selected John C. Fremont, Benton's son-in-law and a man groomed for the presidency in part by the Blairs. The moribund Whig party was unable to put a candidate in the field.

During the summer campaigns early in August, 1856, John Kasson read that St. Louis Free Soilers had elected young Frank Blair to Congress. "Hurrah and handclapping. . . . I congratulate you, Frank, from my heart!" he wrote from New Bedford. The movement for Fremont was "wonderful," he added.[43]

In the November elections the national Democratic party precariously hung together long enough to win by a slender margin. But the combined popular vote of Fremont and Fillmore, the American party candidate, exceeded that of Buchanan. With the American party marked for practical extinction by its poor showing, the sectional Republican party, even in defeat, was defiantly unchastened. It was left in a strong position to sweep the dividing Democrats from power in 1860.

Meanwhile, John A. Kasson departed for "a tour in Europe," [44] the purpose of which still remains a mystery. Was it a pleasure and recuperative trip? Kasson was always an enthusiastic tourist, and according to his own testimony his health had deteriorated. Was it a trip already planned in anticipation of a diplomatic appointment? A yellowed notebook[45] of St. Louis days, in his own handwriting, contains elaborate figures on the salary and expenses of diplomatic officers. Or was it a business trip to buy and sell for his merchant clients like John J. Roe, the pork producer? His forwarding address was Woodruff and Company of New York City.[46]

Returning to St. Louis in 1857, John received long letters from a young Iowan named S. V. White, who had studied law in Kasson's office but had now returned to the straggling frontier village of Des Moines. White painted an optimistic picture of Iowa's future and of opportunity in growing Des Moines. Already a rapidly coalescing

Republican party had swept this state for Fremont and had won a majority of the legislature.

In the midsummer John heard significant, final news which had long been in the discussion stage: the state capital of Iowa was immediately to be transferred from Iowa City to centrally-located Des Moines.[47] That fall John Kasson plotted a course away from strife-torn Missouri and bleeding Kansas and headed straight for Des Moines, where political opportunity beckoned.

☆ VI ☆

Winning Republican Spurs in Iowa

AT NO OTHER period in his life span of four score and eight years did John A. Kasson rise so rapidly as in Iowa during the four years immediately preceding the Civil War. Arriving at Des Moines in the late months of 1857, he was an unknown lawyer without influential acquaintances. Within a few months he was the governor's confidential adviser; within a year, state chairman of the committee directing a young and vigorous Republican party; within three years, a useful delegate to the national convention that nominated Lincoln; and within four years, one of the half dozen most prominent politicians in the state and a vital influence in the national administration at Washington.

Over the years the New England granite in Kasson's personality had been softened. He was "polished in speech and manners," "conservative in his instincts, of fine genial ways," and urbane. His urbanity was the trait to be repeatedly ascribed to him in Iowa and a trait which was to do him no good among many of the minor politicians. He was a "finished" public speaker. His "eloquence rang out over the Iowa prairies and brought strength to the party and credit to himself." Among the many newcomers who would contest with him for position and power, he was "the mightiest, most stately of all." He was "colorful." He possessed "remarkable constructive capacities." [1] He also possessed an independence of spirit and action which in time was to become a political liability.

But despite his undoubted intelligence, diligence, competence, and refinement, his swift political ascent must be attributed also in part to significant political and economic developments taking place particularly in Des Moines and generally in the state of Iowa and the nation.

Until 1850 Iowa's population, institutions, and government had been predominantly Southern. Until 1854 she had been a Democratic stronghold. But in the decade of the fifties railroads, land companies, and Eastern newspapers advertised the fertile prairie soil so well that Iowa became a household word. As railroads reached the eastern river towns, connecting the trans-Mississippi West with the Old Northwest and the East, wave after wave of immigrants rolled in, mostly from Northern states and Europe.

By 1857 the frontier line had been pushed back so far that only the northwestern third of Iowa remained a raw, unsettled prairie. The thickest settlements were in the eastern third. In the southern half, along the Missouri border, and in some of the southwestern and western counties of the interior, men with Southern backgrounds prevailed. Northerners tended to gravitate to the northern and eastern counties, inhabiting the fast growing towns and cities along the Mississippi.

This "Great Migration" of the fifties did not make Iowa a pro-Northern state. Nor had the predominance of Southerners prior to 1850 made her pro-Southern. But the Great Migration did create a climate favorable to rapid political change. And the impact of Northerner with Southerner produced a society first of all Western. Western predominance in national affairs will surely come, predicted an Iowa editor as he watched the tide of immigrants swell.

The emerging ruling class of the fifties in Iowa — lawyers, editors, businessmen — was energetic, dynamic, and aggressive. They demanded free homesteads, home industries, better transportation to the East, South, and Far West, and a greater voice in the national government so vital to the realization of their aspirations. They were nationalists and could readily identify their interests with those of the nation. They would cast aside either Easterner or Southerner, whichever stood in their way or in the way of national development. The Democratic party had been preferred until the mid-fifties in part because it seemed national.

Southerners, whether from the South or from the southern half of the Old Northwest, were tolerant of slavery and detested abolitionists and Negro equality. But the influential opposed the extension of slavery. Some of the Northerners were indifferent to slavery, many mildly disliked it, but only a few violently opposed it in any form, anywhere. Most were content to let it alone where it was, but opposed its spread beyond the Missouri Compromise line. Whether from the North or South, a potent group could be welded together against slavery extension.[2]

Iowans had supported the Mexican War enthusiastically, had remained steadfastly Democratic in the sectional crisis of '48, and both Whigs and Democrats had accepted the Compromise of 1850. In 1852 Whig defeat had been so overwhelming that this party seemed about to disintegrate and leave a number of competent and potentially powerful leaders stranded without a party. The Democracy then seemed firmly intrenched. But two years later Douglas' Kansas-Nebraska Bill, for which both of Iowa's Democratic Senators voted, produced, perhaps unexpectedly, a sudden political and moral reaction. Antislavery Whigs took a new lease on life under the able management of James W. Grimes, a well-to-do lawyer and owner of real estate from the Mississippi River town of Burlington.

Grimes was a native of New Hampshire and a graduate of Dartmouth. He had been a consistent Whig since youth, and, for a decade, a conspicuous and forceful Whig leader in Iowa as a member of the legislature, a champion of railroad development, and an outspoken opponent of slavery extension. Possessing great natural ability, he was courageous, a good judge of men, and above all an astute politician.[3]

At the Whig state convention in 1854, antislavery elements seized the initiative, nominated Grimes for governor, and put through a strong resolution condemning the extension of slavery. In an aggressive campaign Grimes struck out to consolidate all antislavery groups, to absorb the Know-Nothings without their principles, to detach the German vote from the Democrats, and to win new recruits through a broad appeal to local and Western interests.

Grimes's close victory can be attributed to his own energy and astuteness, to Democratic overconfidence and lethargy, to the German vote, the temperance vote, and to his clever appeal to every economic interest in the state. Although slavery as a moral issue was secondary, the issue of its extension had been squarely met. His victory in a state considered a hotbed of "dough faces" was a national surprise and elicited congratulations from leading Republicans such as Chase of Ohio. Grimes became a national figure.

As governor, he extended the power of government into many fields. Under his administration a new constitution was adopted, repealing measures restricting corporations. A state banking system was established, educational reforms effected, railroad construction encouraged, and long-sought railroad grants obtained from the federal government.

At the same time, the governor kept up a running correspondence with politicians, both old and new comers, in almost every county in the state. As violence flared up in Kansas, as sectional passions hardened in Washington, as one disquieting state election followed another in Iowa, sometimes two and three a year, more and more antislavery radicalism began to work, although practical politics required that it be kept submerged. Know-Nothings, making little headway under their own steam but centering their attack on the Democrats, gravitated toward the fusionists.

Early in 1856 a mass of delegates assembled in Iowa City and formally organized the Republican party. James Harlan, James F. Wilson, and Samuel J. Kirkwood should share with Grimes the laurels of fathering the party.[4]

Harlan, hailing from Indiana, a prominent educator and Methodist, combined a strong moral earnestness with practical politics. Already, in 1855, he had been chosen United States Senator.[5] Wilson, a newcomer from Ohio, clean-cut and handsome now at the age of twenty-eight, was in the words of Grimes "a 'singed cat' . . . prudent, cautious, sagacious and if he has a mind that way, can be eloquent . . . a good politician." [6] Kirkwood, another newcomer from Ohio, a friend of Salmon P. Chase and suffused with Republicanism in John Sherman's home town of Mansfield, possessed a wagon full of homespun virtues and was good at rough and tumble debate.[7]

The delicate task of welding together Old Whigs, temperance men, Know-Nothings, German-Americans, Free Soilers, and anti-Nebraska Democrats was accomplished under a single platform dedicated to preventing the extension of slavery. In the summer elections the young, aggressive party won victory after victory by impressive majorities, electing their state ticket, winning control of the legislature, capturing the two congressional seats, and carrying the state for Fremont in the presidential contest.

But during the year 1857, the year of Kasson's arrival, Republican majorities were whittled down, and resurging Democrats won back some of the state offices. As the Dred Scott decision failed to catch on as a political issue, the conviction grew that Kansas was bleeding only for the benefit of Republican politicians! The Iowa City platform, devoted exclusively to slavery, and the Fremont platform, two-thirds of which concerned the same issue, were too radical for Iowa voters. In the April elections for minor state offices, the Democrats won two out of three contests. In the October elections the Republican-sponsored new state constitution, providing for a state banking system and fewer restrictions on corporations, carried by a small majority, but the voters emphatically rejected, 6 to 1, a clause providing for Negro suffrage.[8]

In the governor's race shaping up for October — the third election of this year — Republican leaders showed anxiety. To keep the party "consolidated" Grimes repeatedly urged systematic organization. Though condemning the Dred Scott decision and the events in Kansas, Republicans campaigned on a platform broader than that of '56 and vigorously defended the economic legislation of the Grimes administration. As a candidate for governor they nominated Ralph P. Lowe, a mild mannered, moderate ex-Whig and ex-Ohioan from Keokuk.

The campaign showed a tendency toward personal scandal-mongering and revealed among public officials a highly dangerous laxity of morals, such as defalcation and bribery. Lowe was charged with being a spiritualist and with having consorted with the Know-Nothings at Keokuk. Although Lowe and his running mate won, and the Republicans increased their control of the legislature, several local areas, like Grimes's home town of Burlington, fell to the Democrats. Primarily Lowe had won because the Democrats could not get out their vote.

Thus, when John A. Kasson appeared on the scene late in 1857, there was still much consolidating and organizing to be done before Iowa could be made *safely* Republican. But the mounting tensions in the land were to make such work easier. In October, Iowans read that at the Lecompton convention in Kansas intensely proslavery men had rammed through a constitution making slavery a permanent institution in an area becoming daily more intensely antislavery. This news, coming at a time when the speculative bubble was yielding to an aggravating depression and heralding the coming of a great revival in religion, infused an increasing moral element into politics.[9] Young and positive Republican leaders, motivated by a combination of morals, economics, and the desire for political power, and representing the aggressive demands arising from the nation's rapid growth, stood ready to cast aside what they considered the negative rule of the Democracy, as this party showed dangerous signs of splitting into two wings — Southern and Northern.

Des Moines in 1857 was a shabby town of less than 4,000 people, located in south-central Iowa between the Mississippi and Missouri rivers, and associated politically with the southwestern third of the state. It straddled the Des Moines River near the junction of the inflowing Raccoon River. In territorial days a sleepy frontier military outpost, it had become, after statehood in 1846, a county seat and, in the early fifties, a trading center for emigrants bound for California and for settlers pouring into the surrounding territory. It was severely isolated by bad roads and hazardous shallow-draft steamboating on the Des Moines River, which provided an uncertain outlet through Keokuk to the Mississippi and St. Louis.

Kasson, for instance, on the last leg of his journey from St. Louis, had to travel for "two days and nights" over muddy roads and swollen streams in a "mud wagon" built especially with large wheels and broad tires for quagmire tracks. When the "mudder" became stalled

in Skunk Bottom a few miles east of Des Moines, he had to slog
through mire to higher ground, carrying in his arms an old lady
passenger. Two miles east of town the wagon broke down, and Kasson
trudged on in tediously through the mud.[10]

Inside the town men hurried here and there with their trousers
"tucked in boots and boots generally tucked in mud." Across the
river in East Des Moines, "all [was] rude, with stumps of trees,
perilous ravines, and walks made of coal slack. . . . Boarding houses
on streets were indicated by surveyors' stakes, or by a path through
mud of various consistency." [11]

But what Des Moines lacked in improvements she balanced off
with a soaring ambition. And despite the depression then hovering
over the land, her residents had good cause for optimism. In the
August elections the new Republican-sponsored state constitution had
been adopted, fixing the capital in their midst. And even as Kasson
settled down into new quarters, ten oxen hitched to two bobsleds
were dragging the state safe and other valuables from Iowa City, the
old capital in the eastern part of the state one hundred twenty miles
away.

The new state capital was preparing for the inauguration of a new
Republican governor and the installation of a Republican legislature.
Building was rampant, and the noise of hammer and saw waked people
early at morning and late at night as commercial buildings and
shanties went up by the dozens. Real estate men on the east side of the
Des Moines River, having won the bitter and scandalous contest
against West Siders for the capitol site, were rushing up at their own
expense a new capitol building. Things whirled fast, and men were
dizzy with schemes as railroad promoters, land seekers, town-lot speculators, settlers, and politicians crowded into town.[12]

While the center of political gravity shifted to this small town,
the scepter of political power was falling from the hands of the old
into the hands of the new. A new order was supplanting the old —
a new order in which as yet there were no serious factions and few
controlling leaders. An individualistic, free-for-all competition was
shaping up in which aspiring leaders, many of them newcomers like
Kasson, and most of them young men, united with each other for
common cause and victory and vied with each other for respect, position, power, and wealth. Out of this competition were to arise future
leaders of state and nation.

Kasson identified himself with the interests and problems of Des Moines, made friends easily, and immediately was recognized as a talented civic leader and speaker. He had hardly scraped the mud from his boots when the newly organized Literary Institute invited him to give the first lecture of the season. He was put on a committee of West Siders to set up a reading room and library. On patriotic occasions, becoming ever more popular as emotions from the sectional crisis welled up, he quickened the pulses of a people strongly devoted to the Union.

After two months orientation, Kasson's reputation was sufficient to give him a place of prominence in the welcome this busy little town extended to the new state government. In early January, 1858, Des Moines citizens and a multitude of strangers celebrated the coming of the new state officers with a grand Inaugural Festival, "western in style." Eight hundred guests crowded into the new Representative Hall to hear toasts and to be served refreshments by Des Moines ladies. Of the thirteen regular toasts, Kasson responded to one given to "The Patriots of the Revolution." Eventually the guests spilled out into the Senate Chamber, the promenade room, for music and dancing. At a late hour omnibuses, "four-wheeled and four-horse," just recently arrived from Dubuque, bore the tired merrymakers home. A little later, Kasson no doubt was present at the grand reception given by Grimes to the state legislature and other notables in appreciation of his election to the United States Senate.[13]

The next month at the "brilliant" Washington's Birthday Banquet, Kasson presided "in the most happy and dignified manner." The band played patriotic music, and Kasson, from the head of the center table, "in an admirable style," read out popular toasts, expressing thoughts foremost in the minds of his listeners: "The West: Today the Frontier, Tomorrow the Center! — Old Settlers of Iowa: May They Live to See the Buffalo Tracks Obliterated by Railroad Tracks! — Railroads: The Iron Wedlock of Agriculture and Commerce! — Union of the States: A Few Matrimonial Dissensions Don't Justify Divorce!" At the end of the banquet, pretty ladies joined solemn legislators in a half-hour promenade in which newcomers met old comers. Dancing then followed until three in the morning.[14]

In the pulsing life of the new capital Kasson also won quick standing as a competent lawyer. During his first year's practice the Iowa *Reports* show him appearing before the state supreme court as frequently as the other leaders of the mushrooming Des Moines bar. In a majority of the cases appealed, he was the victor.[15] By the middle of his second year, his practice extended as far northwest as Sioux City, where he successfully defended Woodbury County's refusal to honor the issue of certain bogus warrants. An appreciative Democratic editor of Sioux City thought Kasson's "high toned and gentlemanly character" combined with his "able and successful" management before the court won him a "host of admiring friends" and established for him an "enviable reputation" as a lawyer.[16] In his third year of Des Moines residence, Kasson was one of the half dozen lawyers, including the governor and attorney general, chosen to speak before the state supreme court upon the death of one of its members. His brief speech is somewhat in contrast with the others because of its fine polish, breadth of legal view, and humanness. Law, which "too often strengthens intellect at the expense of the heart," should combine "broad justice in a natural sense" with "justice according to law," he admonished the attentive bar members.[17]

When hard working farmer clients, destitute of money during the depression years, came to Kasson, he won their lasting friendship by accepting their farm produce as fees. He employed young law students in his office, drafted a child adoption law for a client and the legislature, defended an unpopular judge for appropriating money for an expensive county courthouse, and, at a railroad meeting, favored the Mississippi & Missouri Railroad.[18]

And he was in the favorable position of having brought from St. Louis, during this period when money was so scarce, enough cash to lend out at a lucrative interest rate. F. M. Mills, a young Indiana shoemaker, turning printer upon reaching Des Moines, borrowed the money from Kasson with which to construct his publishing house, presumably at the "standard rate" of 40 per cent. The first book Mills published was one edited by Kasson — *The Civil Code of Iowa*. Kasson in turn prepared many of the young printer's blank forms to be used in the county and state offices.[19]

It was altogether fitting that Republican politicians would become interested in this striking and energetic young stranger, and Governor Lowe was one of the first to become attracted to him. The inaugural ceremonies were barely over when the governor found his and Grimes's preceding administration faced with a number of embarrassing scandals, such as bribery in the location of the capitol site, defalcation of school funds, and expensive, haphazard administration of the state government. Both the governor and the Republican legislature, which Grimes described as the "most *investigating*" [20] one he had ever seen, were put on the defensive.

The capitol site investigation grew out of the fierce struggle between East Siders and West Siders for the capitol building. Before Kasson reached Des Moines, the five commissioners appointed to select the exact site had decided in favor of East Siders. Enraged West Siders, claiming to have offered the state more land and money, hired Kasson as their attorney, filed a protest with the legislature, and demanded an investigation. The legislature responded with a special committee, whose majority report, based upon investigation, found the commissioners guilty of not having acted "in strict regard with the interests of the entire state." Although committee members lamented their lack of power to bring out all the testimony, they unanimously condemned one commissioner, Benjamin Pegram of Council Bluffs, for accepting a bribe.[21]

While this scandal was coming to a head the state superintendent of public instruction had been dismissed for defalcation of funds. This discredited official had loaned out school funds indiscriminately, some for personal speculation and some to certain East Siders who had obligated themselves to erect the capitol building at their own expense. The amount of the arrears remained undetermined upon Lowe's inauguration.

Confronted with obvious laxity, decreasing revenues, and mounting expenses, the legislature empowered the governor to appoint a committee of three to investigate the state executive offices and to recommend reforms. Lowe responded immediately by making Kasson chairman — a position of unusual importance and responsibility for one who had been in the state less than a year.

Kasson's committee made a searching investigation of the methods, files, and accounts of the several state offices. The report, reading as if Kasson wrote it, was thorough, systematic, and extensive. Account books of the lax state superintendent were found to be completely unreliable, filled with alterations and erasures. In order to recover the shortage of more than $70,000, the report recommended an immediate suit against the guilty official and his bondsmen, who were circulating petitions to relieve themselves from obligation.

In the rest of the state offices (the important auditor and treasury offices, for instance), the committee found only a few poorly-kept records, even of incoming revenues and disbursements. From the governor's office on down, no archival system existed for the preservation of official records. The committee's recommendations are said to have "worked a revolution" eventually in methods of accounting and the preservation of official documents.[22]

Thus Kasson played the role of a "specialist" in government administration a half century before the term was to become familiar in American history. And thus he found himself in a position to be constructive while at the same time becoming, through his activities as an investigator, a real power in the Republican party of Iowa.

Early in 1858 light snow flurries and soft autumn air gave way to wintry blasts and sub-zero temperature reminiscent of Kasson's boyhood in Vermont.[23] Governor Grimes in a farewell address, as he stepped down from office, gave the voters a "*blizzard*" on Dred Scott, Kansas, and the "Centralizing influence of the central government." In his inaugural address Governor Lowe excoriated the Buchanan administration. In the legislature Senator Kirkwood helped press through a resolution condemning the Dred Scott decision. In the spring, incessant wet weather and cold nights brought on disastrous crop failures, extending over two-thirds of the state and aggravating the economic distress already prevailing from the depression.[24]

Having won the senatorship and returned to Burlington, Grimes grew alarmed at Republican prospects. In the "investigating" legislature, with "too much loquacity" and "too many *great* men," Republicans would be driven to inactivity by the Democrats, he feared. Passage of the Lecompton Bill in Washington "will be the only thing that can save our party," he apprehensively wrote Kirkwood.[25]

Meanwhile the political pots boiled briskly in Des Moines as plans were laid for the state convention to be held in Iowa City in early summer. With the state government now located in Des Moines, some of her citizens, many of them newcomers, were in a favorable position to become real political forces in the state. Governor Lowe, seeking to steady and direct his administration, found himself relying heavily on local talent. In addition to Kasson, whose influence was growing phenomenally, the governor, for instance, chose as his private secretary twenty-five-year-old Thomas Withrow, a Virginian

Miss Caroline Ives, St. Louis

CAROLINE ELIOT KASSON

Frederick W. Wead

JOHN A. KASSON

VIEW OF DES MOINES IN 1857

from Kanawha County, who had spent two years in Wisconsin before turning up in Des Moines to practice law.[26] Withrow and other young politicians to appear later in this story saw in Kasson a rising star and champion whom for several reasons they could accept and promote, at least temporarily. Kasson in turn, as yet unwary and not lacking in ambition himself, became an eager recipient of such support. When the state convention adjourned in Iowa City, many Republicans must have expressed surprise at the name of a rank stranger — John A. Kasson — who had been made chairman of the state central committee to conduct the critical elections of the next year.

Two other members of the seven-man committee — Thomas Seeley and H. M. Hoxie — came from the Des Moines area. Seeley, Kasson's colleague on the three-man committee set up by Governor Lowe to investigate the state offices, was from Guthrie County, a few miles west of Des Moines. Hoxie, who like Withrow was to become a significant influence in Kasson's career, was from Des Moines.[27]

As committee chairman, Kasson would have to assume the principal burden of planning and directing the crucial summer and fall campaigns of 1859, in which the important offices of governor, lieutenant governor, and three supreme court justices would be at stake. His duties would bring him into intimate contact with party leaders, and would involve extensive conferences, correspondence, and public speaking. He would become apprised of the ambitions of various politicians and factions, and party success could well depend upon the chairman's ability to harmonize internal conflicts. In this position Kasson could serve the party and at the same time achieve experience, recognition, and contacts so vital to his own future political success.

While he awaited the assumption of his duties, the old committee, headed by Grimes's right-hand man, Samuel J. Kirkwood, conducted the summer and fall contests of 1858 for minor state offices and Iowa's two congressional seats. These campaigns lacked the enthusiasm and excitement previously demonstrated by the Republicans. Kansas lost ground as a rallying issue; Dred Scott was poor political bait. For his lack of organization and activity Kirkwood was later criticized. And though the Republican slate won, the contests were dangerously close. Majorities for some offices were reduced from previous years, despite a great increase in the number of immigrant voters from Northern states and Europe. Worse still, Republican control of the state legislature was gradually being whittled down. Even the famous Lincoln-

Douglas debates in neighboring Illinois elicited only languid interest in Iowa, although both Lincoln and Douglas made speeches at Burlington.[28]

Early in 1859, when the new committee took over, Democrats had a number of reasons to be confident and Republicans to be anxious. From Washington came news that harmony was being restored between the Buchanan and Douglas factions. Iowa Republicans heard rumors of vast sums of money to be spent in behalf of Democratic candidates. Democratic managers hoped to capitalize upon Republican scandals and financial embarrassments in the state administration, while Republicans, finding themselves on the defensive, feared public apathy and party indifference. A reaction against Republicanism appeared to have set in; a lull in public indignation over the slavery issue prevailed; commercial interests were opposing further agitation; and the churches were balking at an extreme position.

Moreover, Iowa's foreign-born voters were questioning Republican policies both at home and in other states. Already as a concession to beer drinking Germans and Irish, Republicans had modified their own "prohibitory liquor law," and in so doing had aroused mutterings from temperance minded churchmen. German leaders distrusted the Know-Nothing element in the Republican party, and especially feared suffrage restrictions. When the Massachusetts legislature, firmly in the hands of Republicans, proposed to limit electoral privileges of aliens, Iowa Germans became belligerent and prepared for a showdown on this issue.[29]

The importance of the approaching elections, as seen by Republican managers, was succinctly expressed by Elijah Sells, secretary of state: "If we succeed in 1859 we shall be triumphant in 1860, and so the Democracy understand it, and hence they mean to make a desperate strike for power. . . ." [30]

Kasson was fortunate to be chairman at a time when party leaders were thoroughly alarmed and eager to cooperate in a hard driving campaign. The party was fortunate also to have at the managerial helm a man of Kasson's ability, experience, and political insights. From the outset he seized the initiative and waged a campaign noted for its aggressiveness and efficient organization.

A prerequisite to success was the selection of a strong gubernatorial candidate, for it was known that the Democratic choice would be Augustus Caesar Dodge, distinguished ex-Senator and diplomat, popular campaigner, "wise in the experience of long years in the public service," and "honest and upright in his private life." [31]

Governor Lowe desired a second term and during the first four months of 1859 received the loyal support of Kasson and his Des Moines following. But as sentiment crystallized, especially among eastern party leaders, Lowe was found wanting. In the words of the ex-Englishman, W. W. Hamilton, a leading contestant for lieutenant governor from Dubuque, Lowe was "said to be a very good man; but a man may be too good and too soft, just as pure gold may require a little alloy to harden it for the world's commerce." The same writer predicated these remarks upon some political gossip at Dubuque: "They think he is influenced and even governed by others; and some say that a Mr. Kasson is governor de facto." [32] Earlier, a Davenport politician had written: "I see Kasson the Chairman of the State Committee has become State Director so we go." [33]

If Lowe lacked the independence and toughness for a hard slugging campaign, then who most nearly possessed these qualities? Senator Grimes in his quest for "common sense" leaders had long since spotted the man — the plain miller-farmer of Iowa City, Samuel J. Kirkwood, who for some time had been diligently lining up his own support. This man, simple in manner and careless in dress, an adroit canvasser and seasoned in politics from experience in both Ohio and Iowa, could be expected to "use up" the aristocratic Dodge on the stump before farmer audiences. A man of more than moderate means, he was a large landowner and a businessman becoming banker and railroad promoter. As a firm supporter of public education and eleemosynary institutions, he was "progressive." As a former Marylander and Democrat, he perhaps could be made palatable to voters in southern Iowa. Fundamentally a moderate, he could be radical on the slavery issue as the occasion demanded. After the Nebraska Act, he had firmly opposed slavery extension.[34]

Since 1857 Grimes had been grooming the willing Kirkwood for high office, and there are indications to support the rumor that the governorship was to be a steppingstone to Harlan's place in the United States Senate. [35] A Grimes-Kirkwood axis was forming to become the real core of the Iowa Republican organization. But it must not be assumed that Grimes's support was altogether personal, nor that Grimes alone backed him. Kirkwood, because of his peculiar qualifications, was the candidate most likely to beat Dodge, and by

May this fact was conceded by a majority of the Republican leaders in the state.

For the sake of party harmony and victory, Kasson himself was quick to subordinate his own preference. From his "personal intercourse and correspondence," and after a trip into western Iowa, he reported to Kirkwood that the voters, though finding no fault with Lowe, preferred a man with "more zeal, strength, and other elements of success." In central Iowa, Kirkwood support was "sincere and hearty." And the Democratic element, he advised — "which I understand you represent as well as my humble self" — would welcome Kirkwood's nomination. The Whigs, who had predominated thus far in state and national offices, should "neither be ignored nor too prominent." Referring to a previous meeting between himself and Kirkwood, Kasson suggested an easy way out for his friend, the governor: Lowe would settle for the state supreme court bench. Hence, the coming state convention could "reconcile conflicting purposes as I suggested to you at Iowa City in Feby." [36]

Two weeks later (about mid-May) Kasson again wrote Kirkwood. He had just received a letter from Lowe, whose tone assured "good feeling." Kasson had replied to Lowe that Kirkwood, having been drawn out as a candidate by his friends, meant no disrespect to the governor and his administration. And now, confided Kasson to Kirkwood, Lowe's name would *not* be withdrawn until near the convention date. "At that time if his friends choose to do so, he can be named for a place on the supreme bench. . . . The canvass must be preserved from bitterness." He warned Kirkwood against any impression of "contract." [37]

Two months later, when the nominating convention convened in Des Moines, it was no surprise that the dilemma of conflicting ambitions had been solved. Even before an informal ballot could be completed, a friend of Lowe's arose and dramatically withdrew the governor's name in order not to compromise "harmony of the party." Kirkwood's selection by acclamation was quickly followed by the nomination of Lowe for supreme court justice. [38] The choice of Caleb Baldwin of Council Bluffs as one of the other two nominees for the supreme court was a sign of the growing importance of southwestern Iowa, or the Missouri Slope, in state politics. And Baldwin, like Hoxie and Withrow, would be an important factor in the political future of John A. Kasson.

After presiding over an immense ratification meeting immediately following the convention, the state chairman, now having played a major role in making up the party slate, threw himself into the canvass with indefatigable energy, procuring and distributing campaign documents, advising candidates and planning itineraries, lining up speakers and taking the stump himself before the "sovereigns." [39] In the manner of the Lincoln-Douglas debates of the preceding year, the central committee arranged for joint discussions which put Kirkwood face to face with Dodge in almost every town in the state.

Kasson anxiously planned Kirkwood's itinerary in the southern counties, showing a fine appreciation of campaign details and a full understanding of political cleavages in the state. He advised the candidate as to the best places to spend the night, and the time of day when farmers would most likely attend rallies. Kirkwood should have good reliable horses, a man along to attend them, save their strength, and keep the carriage in readiness. And further, "If your companion should happen to be good at giving instruction on political organization," he should do so while the debates went on. Strong, good men for the legislature should be lined up and supported.[40]

Throughout the campaign, Kasson expressed an anxiety over the southern tier of counties sharply in contrast with the feeling of Senator Grimes who was now taking a consistently rosy view of the election outcome. In these counties, Kasson warned, people from Kentucky, Tennessee, Maryland, and southern Indiana, Illinois, and Ohio were "scared" at abolitionism. Therefore, Kirkwood should stress his Maryland birth, make the Democrats the real agitators of the slavery question, and portray Republicans as upholding the tradition of Jackson, Clay, and Webster. Slavery within the states should be let alone. Kirkwood, while speaking, should be constantly on guard against drunken, insulting interruptions. In each of these doubtful counties, Kasson promised to have a friend on hand to give advice.

As the canvass gathered steam, Kasson kept Kirkwood informed of its progress. Following a trip to Sioux City he reported cheering news, though northern Republicans were not sufficiently aroused. In general, Republican editors were jubilant, though few knew how "to keep the tone, the esprit of the party." Here and there dissension over personal ambition threatened the loss of a county. In Warren a disappointed Republican was "raising the devil. . . . Drunk, hungry, fickle, and inflated" with self-importance, he had been bought off.

The chairman and a couple of other party trouble-shooters were going to Warren County to patch up this difficulty.[41]

From late July to early October, while Kirkwood and Dodge sniped at each other from stump after stump, the central committee and other party managers turned loose upon the state a galaxy of effective speakers which today reads like a Who's Who of Iowa political leaders for the next half century. New political personalities, men like Grenville M. Dodge, Frank W. Palmer, and William Boyd Allison, won their spurs in this campaign. In a surprise visit to Council Bluffs, a visit then unheralded but of later great significance, Abraham Lincoln spoke for Kirkwood and against slavery. Sixty-two Republican newspapers, with additional ones sprouting up daily, poured vituperation upon the Democratic slate, especially Augustus C. Dodge. It was the most vigorous campaign up to that time in Iowa Republican history.[42]

The cardinal principles of the Republican platform embraced opposition to slavery extension, support of liberal naturalization laws, and the demand for free homesteads, but the campaign dealt equally as much, if not more, in personalities. Grimes's advice to Kirkwood provides a good clue to its tone: "Be sure to always get Dodge mad. Show him always to be a fool, as he is." And again, "Keep him on the defensive . . . stired [sic] up all the time . . . lead him to abuse Harlan and myself."

Earlier Grimes had sketched a picture of Dodge which became a stereotype in this campaign and for many subsequent years. The Democratic nominee was a "great vain pompous blockhead," indefatigable in shaking hands, incapable of statesmanship — a wooden political god, who, during nineteen years of officeholding in Iowa, had drawn $105,000 from the public treasury, but who had never been known "to aid in building up any village or city in the state or to give to any charity, unless it be the catholic church of which his family are members. . . ."[43]

In turn, Democratic attacks upon Kirkwood were equally as vehement, picturing him as filthy in dress and crude in manners, as an ignorant blackguard and a consummate demagogue. But Republican campaigners, cleverly exploiting such attacks, produced their own stereotype of Kirkwood — the plain, unambitious farmer, careless in dress and toilet, who, fresh from the people, reluctantly left his wheat harvest to save party, state, and nation.[44]

It was a jubilant state chairman who on October 12, 1859, sat down to write Kirkwood of Republican victory in Des Moines and Polk County. Final returns showed that the entire Republican ticket had squeezed by, and that the Republican majority in the legislature had been increased. In most of the southern counties Kirkwood had trailed Dodge, true to Kasson's fears which Grimes had discounted.[45]

One historian of this campaign has emphasized the connection between Republican victory and the German vote, attracted in part by the candidate for lieutenant governor, Nicholas Rusch, a German.[46] But much credit must go to Kirkwood, the shrewd and tireless campaigner, and to Kasson, the shrewd and tireless manager. In the words of another historian, "Never before and seldom since was the Republican party so thoroughly organized. . . ." The campaign had barely got under way when a former state chairman, A. J. Stevens, reported: "The Central Comte are doing glorious work and their efforts will tell." C. C. Cole, prominent Democratic candidate for supreme court justice, attributed his defeat to Kasson's "influence" and "masterful manner" in handling the campaign. Even the political master, Grimes himself, wrote to Kirkwood in approving terms of the chairman's labors. And Kasson later took much pride in Grimes's commendation of his effective work in organizing the party.[47]

But running among expressions of approval was a slight undertone of disapproval. Know-Nothing elements complained of the committee's catering to the German vote. John Edwards, passed over for lieutenant governor, took temporary umbrage at "Lowe's friends." John Teesdale, the newspaperman from Iowa City — English-born and schooled in politics in Ohio — having previously been sent to Des Moines by Grimes and Kirkwood to become state printer and editor of a Republican journal, zealously guarded Kirkwood's candidacy and kept a critical eye on the chairman. A full month after Kasson had gone over to Kirkwood, Teesdale reported that Lowe and his friends were still "active." "You [Kirkwood] were mistaken, I apprehend, as to the position of Kasson, who having given up all views of his own, is now regarded as a Lowe man." Later, as the committee laid plans for the joint canvass, Teesdale blurted out: "I do not know what our committee are about. Kasson is the committee and thinks he knows it all . . . he would do better to take advice occasionally, instead of giving it all the time."

Teesdale was irked at Kasson because he "talked a Committee Campaign Paper," which, if established, would by-pass the editor's own Des Moines *Citizen*. "I have offered to furnish them a campaign *Citizen* to which they may contribute . . . at 25 cents per copy for the campaign," he explained.[48]

More serious, in the light of future developments, was the criticism of J. C. Savery, New York-born businessman, politician, and builder-proprietor of a leading Des Moines hotel. Early in the campaign he informed Kirkwood: "I have no confidence in the management of the 'Chairman' in pecuniary matters connected with politics, not however as applying to his motives, but want of judgment. He is energetic and efficient in his peculiar way, but knows nothing of the things that impart vitality to the political heart." Savery, not unamenable himself to an appointment, wanted Elijah Sells, then a strong Kirkwood man, to handle Republican money. He had already made arrangements for five hundred to a thousand dollars to go into the hands of Sells. He also urged that supreme court nominees should contribute. A few weeks later Sells wrote Kirkwood that "Kasson knows no way by which he can raise sufficient funds." Could not Kirkwood's milling company, through the candidate's partner and brother-in-law, send two hundred dollars? Grimes would contact "other companies." [49]

Almost fifty years later Kasson, mellowed and in a reminiscent mood, gave his version of campaign expenses: "Our resources were limited. There was little money for campaign purposes, less than four hundred dollars altogether. Senator Grimes sent me a check for one hundred dollars — a handsome contribution in those days — with the remark that this [Kasson's committee activities] was the first effective and systematic work done for the party in Iowa." [50]

Kasson's alleged inability in "pecuniary matters" was not Savery's only complaint. More than a month after the election, he warned the governor-elect not to reappoint Lowe's private secretary, Thomas Withrow, who had made himself obnoxious to Kirkwood's friends. "I regard the gentleman devoid of good sense, and a school Boy in political management, a fit tool for his ambitious & aspiring principal (Kasson) whose servant he is." "We do look with distrust," Savery continued, "upon a class of new politicians here . . . who gives early promise of a regency." [51]

Despite slight ripples of distrust, motivated by the chairman's independence and by the fear of a rival faction led by him, Mr. Kasson had become Mr. Importance in high Republican circles, and his name could be written right after those of Grimes, Harlan, and Kirkwood. His tenure as chairman was extended, and additional party leaders were put on the committee. He would help plan strategy for the all-important year, 1860, and he well knew, as did many of his colleagues, that the new party could not stand the shock of deep factional squabbles.

For Iowa was not yet *safely* Republican. Kirkwood's majority, despite herculean efforts, had been less than 3,000, or a margin of only 2.6 per cent of the total vote. Grimes's edge, five years previously, had been 4.1 per cent. To be successful in 1860, Republicans in Iowa, and in the nation, would have to find a means of welding together their disparate elements. Their program would need to have greater universal appeal. The antislavery radicalism of the Fremont campaign would have to be trimmed.[52]

☆ VII ☆

In the First Lincoln Campaign

THE YEAR 1860 dawned bright for Republicans. But the mistakes of '56 would have to be avoided. The conservative reaction appeared still to be in full swing. In the Northwest, conservatism demanded support of the region's material interests. Farmer, laborer, merchant, railroad promoter, and budding manufacturer, in the depression years, looked to government for relief. Radicalism on the single issue of slavery meant defeat. Conservatism, with its broadened material base as to issues and availability as to candidates, meant victory.

Horace Greeley, whose New York *Tribune* was widely read in Iowa, caught the temper of the time after an extensive tour of the West late in 1859. The country was "not Anti-Slavery"; it was willing to swallow only "a little Anti-slavery in a great deal of sweetening"; an anti-slavery man could not "*per se* be elected"; but, predicted Greeley, "a Tariff, River and Harbor, Pacific Railroad, Free Homestead man may succeed although he is anti-slavery." [1]

Although the campaigns of '58 and '59, marking essential conquest, had not confirmed possession, they had suggested the strategy of victory. The presidential election would require a candidate and program with broad appeal to doubtful groups and doubtful states. Radical antislavery hotspurs would have to be throttled, sectionalism and antislavery agitation identified with the Democracy, and Republicans made to appear as champions of the Union and the material needs of the nation. [2] On the local level, tactics would require that party organizations be perfected, divergent views reconciled, and conflicting ambitions harmonized by passing around as many political honors as possible.

John A. Kasson, by conviction a moderate, was among the vanguard of Iowa politicians who considered a conservative candidate and conservative platform indispensable to victory; who would contain the "indiscreet" radicals but retain their support; who approached the campaign warily, confident of victory but cautiously groping for openings and guarding against blunders; who keenly sensed that 1860 was the main political chance, which, if lost, might be the last; but who little suspected that if won it would be the signal for the disruption of the Union. In the Des Moines preliminaries and in the Chicago semifinals, Kasson's work of balancing and broadening was to be a strong thread in the finished fabric of Republican victory. In the finals, Kasson was to plan tactics and campaign vigorously for Lincoln.

Enthusiasm engendered by Kirkwood's election in October, 1859, was not permitted to cool off before the central committee called a party council to choose delegates to the national nominating convention. Early in December, Chairman Kasson sent out the call, "in accordance with expression of public sentiment"; place, Des Moines; date, mid-January. [3] Two weeks later Chicago and mid-May were designated as place and time for the national convention. The selection of Chicago was a salute to the growing West. All signs pointed

to a Western show in which Western men might predominate, and
Chicago's proximity would undoubtedly increase the zeal of Iowa
Republicans to attend as delegates.

Kasson's call, issued so many months ahead of the national convention, put Iowa among the first states to choose delegates. The state
committee had timed the conclave to take place shortly following
Kirkwood's inauguration and the organization of the legislature that
would elect a United States Senator to fill Harlan's expiring term.
It was a splendid opportunity for a large turnout of local politicians,
since many of the delegates could combine their participation in these
exciting events with convention activities. Moreover, disappointed
patronage seekers might be mollified with a trip to Chicago as delegates.

By January 9, 1860, the lobbies of Des Moines hotels swarmed
with political managers, legislators, candidates, and office seekers.[4]
News from Washington within the past month — John Brown's raid
and hanging, the deadlock over the speakership in the national House
of Representatives, and the fiery speeches of Southerners — was sufficient to supercharge the atmosphere with excitement and anxiety. But
it is doubtful that these threatening events made up the chief topics
of conversation among the lobbies and caucuses. Brown's raid was
embarrassing to a party striving to take on the garb of conservatism.
Republican leaders and newspapers roundly condemned it, although
a few approved of Brown's aims and admired his courage. In his
inaugural address Kirkwood branded the raid as unlawful, wrong,
reprehensible, and destructive, but charged the Democrats with its
responsibility through their Kansas policies.[5]

At this Des Moines gathering local issues vied with the fascinating
game of politics for first place in the minds of men. It was not a mass
meeting expressing moral indignation at slavery nor fear that the
Union was on the point of disruption. It was a gathering of practical
men, impelled by the scent of victory, more concerned with close-at-
hand questions. Who was to be Senator, state printer, or delegate to
Chicago? How could temperance men and German beer drinkers, old
Whigs and Democrats, Know-Nothings and the foreign-born be kept
reconciled? What would be the political effect of delinquent taxes,
depleted treasuries, and the popular suspicion of railroad corporations and the new banking system?

The problem of political geography had also to be considered.

Northern Iowans around Dubuque laid claim to the senatorship, since both Grimes and Harlan hailed from the east and southeast. Through the Council Bluffs *Nonpareil* the southwest also, with its portentous growing strength, had mildly warned that Senator Harlan had no valid claim to succeed himself. Harlan supporters for months had been watching potential rival candidates. At one time they had apprehensively observed a Kasson movement that, failing to catch on, "blew up." "K[asson] & his friends," Elijah Sells reported, "begin to see the effect that this movement will have upon his future, and they now deny having had any such intentions." [6]

All anti-Harlan booms were weak and abortive, however, and the party caucus quickly dispatched this business with his unanimous renomination. Northern Iowa won the coveted state printership in the person of Frank W. Palmer, editor of the Dubuque *Times*. This former member of the New York legislature and a newcomer of two years in Iowa must be added to the expanding group, including Thomas Withrow, H. M. Hoxie, and Caleb Baldwin, whose activities and aspirations were to be vital influences in Kasson's future. John Teesdale, incumbent state printer, could now devote his full talents to his newspaper that, dressed up with a new name — the *Iowa State Register* — was in time to become the most powerful Republican organ in the state.

With the governor inaugurated, the legislature organized, the Senator elected, and much of the patronage dispensed, the central committee could proceed with the state convention. At two o'clock in the afternoon of January 18, 1860, some four hundred men crowded into Sherman Hall for the sole purpose of choosing delegates to the national convention. It was the largest Republican convention held thus far in Iowa and had the widest distribution, with seventy-eight of the ninety-seven counties then organized represented. Kasson called the meeting to order and, without speech or fanfare, appointed a Quaker — an Underground Railroad operator from eastern Iowa — as temporary chairman, balancing off this appointment with a man from conservative southern Iowa as secretary pro tem. Without the usual keynoting of issues, the temporary chairman chose committees on credentials and permanent organization. While these committees deliberated, the convention for the next two hours was entertained with light ex tempore speeches from party chiefs including Kasson.

The committee on organization chose as permanent chairman W. W.

Hamilton of Dubuque, the unsuccessful candidate for lieutenant
governor the previous spring. The other losing contestant for this
office, John Edwards, had already been elected speaker of the state
house of representatives. The committee then proceeded to scatter
around ten vice-presidencies and six secretaryships, among which
the foreign-born and men from Dubuque were conspicuous in
number.

As the convention next proceeded to choose Chicago delegates, one
of Seward's radical supporters provoked animated discussion which
went on till dark when he proposed the selection of only eight delegates, the exact number of votes to which the state was entitled in
the national convention. Such niggardliness in passing out honors
ran counter to the popular desire to broaden the base. Senator Grimes,
with a firm grip on the convention, had sagely advised: ". . . select
a goodly number to cast the vote of Iowa . . . have them divided
fairly between old whigs & old democrats, & entirely uncommitted
. . . — men who will try to nominate for the good of the party &
not for the benefit of themselves." [7] Another party leader reported
that "Everybody is a candidate for delegate to the Chicago Convention";[8] and another that there were "over five hundred candidates
for the places." [9]

Eventually the motion was amended to include five delegates-at-
large, and two from each of the eleven judicial districts, making a
total of twenty-seven. The balloting which then began gave some
clue to the importance and popularity of the political managers.
Kasson received scattered votes on the informal and the first two
formal ballots. On the third formal vote he was elected, giving him
the rank of number three among the delegates-at-large. After the
five delegates-at-large had been chosen, there still remained a number
of disappointed, strategic men unrewarded, and a motion was carried
to elect unanimously four more delegates-at-large, running the total
to thirty-one. Delegates from the judicial districts were then chosen,
and the convention adjourned until an "after supper session." Since
the essential purpose of the convention had now been fulfilled, this
session was evidently called to give party oratory full rein and to whip
up enthusiasm.

But the recess stimulated a desire to send even more men, and
upon reassembling, the convention selected two additional delegates-
at-large, a Dutch newspaper editor and a fiery hunter-trapper who

would appeal to the "old pioneer" vote. The selection of these additional delegates, and an alternate who was to participate in the Chicago deliberations, ran the total to thirty-four. Each delegate would have less than one-fourth of a vote. This zeal to spread around the honors caused John Teesdale to quip, "If the hall [at Chicago] is large enough, the delegates will probably be admitted." [10]

Of the thirty-four delegates, the average age was thirty-eight. Kasson had passed his thirty-eighth birthday by five days. The average years of residence in Iowa was twelve. Kasson had been in the state for about two years. In numbers, men from Ohio and New York predominated, but there were more from the South than from New England. At least four were foreign-born. In education, personal polish, and breadth of background, Kasson was easily the most outstanding. Along occupational lines there were one banker, two preachers, four merchants, and twenty-three lawyers. In this strictly agrarian state, only five farmers were chosen; and lawyer, farmer, preacher was often also banker, merchant, realtor, town and railroad speculator. Eight were then considered abolitionists or radicals, but the political exigencies required at least temporary acquiescence to conservatism.

Nineteen were soon to go into the army. One-third were to have noteworthy careers in the national government; three were to become United States Senators; and seven, members of the House. Conspicuously absent from the list of delegates were the governor, the Senators and Congressmen, and other "top-flight office holders, who already possessed their rewards and whose diligent work in the approaching canvass could be counted upon."

With all delegates chosen, the evening session was converted into a "mass ratification." Kasson and eight others made speeches, said to be "spicy, full of marrow," blowing up enthusiasm. [11] Appraising the entire proceedings, one reporter found it the "noisiest, most uproarious, confused, good-natured, hardworking and enthusiastic convention ever witnessed in Iowa . . ."; they were "all aspiring politicians, very wary" and difficult to sound out as to the presidency. [12] Another was struck by the number of "official and unofficial" office seekers attending the convention. "Never since the northern barbarians overran . . . Italy," he predicted, "has there been such an irruption as there will be in Washington with a change in dynasty." [13]

In the evening session there was really nothing to ratify except the

Chicago delegates, for the convention had been conspicuously reluctant to commit the party to men and issues. A motion requiring the delegates to vote as a unit had been quickly defeated. Tactics of victory required that they go to Chicago uninstructed, with complete freedom to support the man and program of the hour. Throughout, there had been keen appreciation of the necessity of carrying the doubtful states of Pennsylvania, New Jersey, Illinois, and Indiana, and it was understood that the Iowa delegation would work with men from these states for candidates and measures leading to victory.

Perhaps a majority of Iowa Republicans favored Seward. Chase also had a large following. But there was an undercurrent of fear that neither, because of his radical stand on slavery, could carry the doubtful states, including Iowa.[14] And no matter how radical an Iowa delegate might be, he was prepared to acquiesce in the choice of the national convention. A more available candidate would do — say, Bates, Lincoln, or Cameron, each of whom also had an Iowa following.

Kasson was leader of the Iowa boom for his old St. Louis friend, Edward Bates, who was being promoted by Greeley, the Blairs, and B. Gratz Brown. Not only did Bates's moderate views appeal to Kasson, but his St. Louis ties of friendship were potentially powerful. Young Frank Blair now was the head of Republicanism in Missouri; Brown was the heart, and, like Kasson, had moved up to the chairmanship of the state central committee. Old Frank Blair and his other son, Montgomery, were leading the movement in Maryland. In Missouri, Republican emancipationists had gained control of St. Louis, but Blair, Bates, and Brown, instead of pressing the slavery issue, were demanding free homesteads, a Pacific railroad, and improved overland mail service to California. Although the Bates balloon in Iowa was soon to be almost punctured by Davenport Germans, suspicious of the St. Louisan's Know-Nothing leanings, Kasson remained firm in his support.[15]

In late March the state chairman called another convention "pursuant to the majority vote of the central committee." [16] This assembly, to meet in Iowa City one week following the Chicago convention, was to nominate certain state officers and presidential electors. Moreover, it was to be a giant ratification of the national candidates and platform.

As convention time approached, Kasson grew "more than ever

KASSON IN LONDON, 1863, ENROUTE TO
PARIS POSTAL CONFERENCE

MEMBERS OF THE PARIS POSTAL CONFERENCE, 1863

anxious" about the nominations. "I regard it as absolutely necessary," he wrote to Governor Kirkwood, "that we secure the so-
called conservative vote of the free states, by offering to that element
a moderate man, reserving to ourselves a thoroughly republican administration. Pray be at Chicago to aid and influence the indiscreet
by your counsel." The "territorial issue" would never again be so
"potential." Republican defeat would make the next contest "more
than ever sectional." Democratic victory might secure for the South
"Cuba and secession." Kasson was going to Chicago early, "the last
of the week previous to the convention," and he hoped to meet Kirkwood there.[17]

Heading for Chicago a few days later, Kasson, according to legend,
stopped overnight in Cedar Falls and there drafted the national platform. Though this legend cannot be confirmed, there is every reason
to believe that he was giving serious attention to the platform as he
journeyed along.[18]

In sharp contrast to the wrangling Democratic Convention at
Charleston, where cotton-state delegates had angrily walked out,
Republican delegates descended upon Chicago in high spirits. John
A. Kasson watched thousands of enthusiastic men roll into this mushrooming prairie city on iron rails which now connected East with
Northwest; he must have been reminded of the excitement which
had prevailed twelve years earlier when as a young delegate he had
attended the Free Soil Convention at Buffalo. The same diverse
groups remained to be welded together, although after several years
of trial and error they were finding common ground in the expanding interest of the East and Northwest. The same carnival spirit prevailed, although the present scene was more typical of the rough,
exuberant outlook of the West; it was greater in size, in noise, in wire-
pulling, and in lust for office. Some of the same idealistic fervor prevailed, though at Chicago radical antislavery men and reformers were
to yield to practical politicians organized for victory, spoils, and
greater freedom to exploit the nation's potential wealth. Facing a
divided enemy, the men at Chicago were more confident of victory;
but they tempered their confidence with caution; there must be no
blunder on candidate and platform. The dividing Democrats might
yet reunite before election time.

At noon on Wednesday, May 16, a thousand delegates and ten thousand spectators crowded into the Wigwam, an immense auditorium thrown up a few weeks previously by aggressive Chicagoans. In the sea of expectant faces, Kasson could see many acquaintances from widely scattered areas over the country. Outside, crowds milled about, choking up the streets and calling for speeches. Chicago hotels, filled to overflowing, hummed with activity.[19]

Resisting the animated response to oratory, with every word eliciting cheers, the convention proceeded to organize. Only three organizational committees had been appointed before Horace Greeley popped up prematurely and demanded a committee on platform. Several delegates objected because permanent organization had not been completed, and the convention soon adjourned. Almost immediately upon reassembling at five that evening, it set up the committee on platform, and each delegation answered a roll call by designating its platform committee member.[20] The choice of Kasson by the Iowa delegation was perhaps no on-the-spot decision. The importance he attached to the platform, his conservative views, his ability to write, and his knack of reconciling conflicts were well known.

This unwieldy committee of twenty-seven members, significantly headed by Judge William Jessup from strategic and tariff-loving Pennsylvania, at once met in the parlor of the nearby Tremont Hotel. Until 11 o'clock at night men labored spiritedly over a flood of resolutions upon every possible topic of political agitation, and they seemed to be getting nowhere. At this point, Kasson, who the day before had anticipated some such confusion in the committee, moved that a subcommittee be appointed to iron out differences, put the resolutions into final form, and report back to the general committee at nine the next morning.[21]

Kasson's motion carried. And for the rest of the night, the subcommittee of eight [22] carefully-selected members forged out a platform designed to attract low tariff Democrats and high tariff Whigs; men opposed only to the extension of slavery, but also abolitionists; men who desired homesteads, railroads, and river and harbor improvements from the federal government, but also state rights men; and finally Know-Nothings who wanted to restrict alien rights, but also the foreign-born who demanded liberal alien rights. Kasson and Greeley, appointed to the subcommittee, took the lead that night.

The most heated debate arose over the tariff. Greeley was an ardent defender of a high tariff but no more so than the delegates from Pennsylvania and New Jersey, who came to Chicago boastfully determined to win protection for their ironmongers. The tariff had become only recently important in Republican circles. The early party had shown little interest in protection — a party that had been spontaneously spawned in 1854 basically from the common man's resistance to the extension of slavery over the free lands of the West. Doctrinaire Whigs within the party had been checkmated by low tariff Democrats. The trend of the previous three decades toward free trade had culminated in the low tariff of 1857 which satisfied New England textile manufacturers as well as Southern and Western Democrats. But with the panic of 1857, iron interests had inspired a political movement which, opportunistically combining protection with opposition to Democratic policies in Kansas, had evolved eventually into the Republican party of Pennsylvania.

Without Pennsylvania, Republicans could not win in 1860, and as early as 1858 party leaders in Congress had veered to the support of a higher tariff in an effort to win this key state. Pennsylvania delegates therefore had arrived in Chicago cocksure and almost insolent. Their price was a platform plank and a presidential nominee favorable to protection. Lincoln, a former Henry Clay Whig, having been previously sounded out, was considered satisfactory on this issue, although the Railsplitter would have preferred to let it alone in 1860.[23]

But the Pennsylvanians faced unexpected opposition in Chicago. Western members did not want to mention the tariff. In the general platform committee, a New Jersey delegate close to the Pennsylvanians and an ardent apostle of Henry C. Carey, the Philadelphia propagandist of protection, made threats: if his colleagues did not adopt a tariff they would be compelled to fight it out on the convention floor the next day. "Feeling ran high," remembered Kasson. "This was the vital question to be bridged . . . if the party was to be held together." The general committee promised some sort of tariff resolution.[24]

In the subcommittee Greeley insisted on "extreme protection." Austin Blair, a leading Seward man from Michigan, took "more moderate ground" and Kasson "still more conservative ground." With both Pennsylvania and the Northwest in mind, Kasson "personally undertook to reduce from the various contradictory propositions a conciliatory resolution." "I finally drew," he later explained, "from the first tariff act passed by congress, and using the language of the preamble . . ., framed a plank that was satisfactory to both parties." This was Article 12 of the platform as adopted.[25] At the moment Kasson was probably not aware of the extent to which he had helped elevate the pet dogma of Pennsylvania to national significance. In time he would come to regret the shading which manufacturers and their political lieutenants were to give this resolution.

Kasson and Greeley also disagreed on the expression of their anti-slavery position. All members were united on a plank opposing the extension of slavery, but Greeley insisted on a resolution embodying the Wilmot Proviso doctrine, now out-of-date since the free-soil victory in Kansas. Again, Kasson took more conservative ground. The subcommittee, he later wrote, "accepted my views as necessary to the nationalization of the Republican Party." The plank, as finally adopted, declared that "the normal condition of all Territories was freedom" and that legislation to maintain it was to be passed only when necessary. The radical, insulting platform phrase of '56, that slavery and polygamy were the "twin relics of barbarism," was dropped.[26]

On other issues, such as a daily overland mail, river and harbor improvement, a Pacific railroad, free homesteads, and concessions to the foreign-born, there was apparently little disagreement. Both Kasson and Greeley claimed credit for the homestead plank providing free land for the actual settler rather than unlimited sale to all applicants for revenue. The two important German members of the subcommittee, Carl Schurz and Gustave Koerner, had little difficulty in procuring the famous "Dutch planks," which, in vigorous tones, assailed any effort to take away rights of citizenship previously accorded the alien-born. It was here necessary, Kasson recalled, "to stand up in a square fight with the Native American element." [27]

By two o'clock on the morning of May 17 most controversial points had been settled by the subcommittee. One after another, members withdrew until only Kasson and Greeley remained. It had been understood that Kasson would put the platform into orderly arrangement as a whole. At sunrise Greeley departed to wire his New York *Tribune* of convention activities. A little later, his work of revision completed, Kasson went to his room in the Tremont, doused his sleepy head in cold water, and ate breakfast. At nine he met with the general committee, where, after careful reading, not a single amendment was added. There was enough discussion, however, to indicate that minor changes might be made on the convention floor.

Late in the afternoon of the same day the platform was read as a whole before the convention. Each resolution "drew bursts of applause — the most enthusiastic and long continued being given the tariff and homestead clauses." [28] The Pennsylvania delegation greeted the tariff resolution with "spasms of joy," rising in mass, swinging their hats and canes, and applauding lustily.[29] But in reality they were disappointed because of its mildness.

Although the committee had "spotted" men over the convention hall to urge acceptance of the whole platform without debate, and thus control the "indiscreet," two points drew fire.[30] Some delegates wanted a stronger state rights plank. And the old irrepressible abolitionist, Joshua Giddings, almost created a storm when he stalked out of the hall after his amendment, to insert certain phrases of the Declaration of Independence, had been voted down. Quick work on the part of two or three delegates, however, brought the old radical back and provided one of the most dramatic incidents of the convention, when his amendment was accepted almost simultaneously with the adoption of the entire platform.[31]

A roaring shout of applause went up, renewed again and again for fifteen minutes; the vast audience of ten thousand sprang to its feet.[32] For generations to come, participants were to retell this thrilling incident until it became a part of the legendary lore of the party. Kasson could retell his role with personal pride, for, next to Greeley, he had been the chief architect in building one of the most significant party platforms of the nineteenth century — a platform through which a revolution was to take place and modern America to emerge.

Greeley himself gave Kasson much of the credit and, incidentally, national prestige as a rising political leader. Five days later, in a lengthy editorial on the platform, Greeley concluded: "That the platform presented is so generally satisfactory . . . is eminently due to John A. Kasson of Iowa, whose efforts to reconcile differences and secure the largest liberty of sentiment consistent with fidelity to Republican principles, were most effective and untiring." The following fall, while campaigning in western New York for Lincoln, the busy editor is reliably reported to have said: "Kasson was right about the slavery and tariff planks. We should have been 'dished' if I had had my way." [33]

Kasson and his colleagues had shown themselves to be superb political trimmers. In their efforts to broaden the party base, to "nationalize" Republicanism, as Kasson liked to say, they had produced a program broad enough to include all groups except Southern slaveholders. But the platform was at the same time boldly constructive; antislavery idealism had yielded to economic realism; the party had been steered into the deeper currents of American life; Whiggery now was coursing through the Republican body very strongly. Unfortunately, however, this program was not national. Although the aspirations of the East and Northwest had been successfully wedded, the Chicago platform makers had not taken into consideration the passionate fears and growing resentments of the deep South. Merely to denounce threats of disunion was not enough to reassure a minority region accustomed to power and daily being reduced to a colonial status.[34]

The next day, as the convention proceeded to the nominations, John Kasson at first backed his former St. Louis associate, Edward Bates. Standing midway between the radical and conservative wings of the party, Bates had recently been losing ground. The Constitutional Union convention of May 9 had chosen a conservative candidate on a platform almost certain to sweep away much of his support among the broad belt of border state people. Moreover, declarations by German leaders at Chicago cast serious doubts that he could carry the foreign-born vote, then considered necessary for victory.

Nonetheless, Kasson stayed with Bates on the first ballot and probably carried along with him H. M. Hoxie, T. B. Seeley, and Nicholas Rusch, all three of whom had been closely associated with Kasson in Des Moines. In any event, Bates received one Iowa vote, the equivalent of support from four delegates. On the second ballot these men probably followed the popular trend toward Lincoln; and on the third ballot, as the convention went over to Lincoln, so did a majority of the Iowa delegates.[35]

Seward had been the candidate most likely to win, as delegates streamed into Chicago. But in the scramble for votes, Lincoln managers had shrewdly settled upon Pennsylvania, New Jersey, and Indiana as vital. By playing up the undercurrent of fear that Seward could not carry the doubtful states, by promising political rewards, and by using effectively the support of the railroad men, they won over these states. With this block of votes, and by packing the excited

Wigwam crowd with the greatest number of shouters, they stampeded the Railsplitter to victory on the third ballot.[36] Underlying the success of Lincoln managers was also the fact that the convention collectively had conducted a process of eliminating more prominent men for one reason or another. Lincoln had been settled upon because he had fewer enemies and would appeal to a greater number of divergent interests.

In drafting the platform and in choosing the standard-bearer, expediency and availability — so familiar to national conventions — had triumphed. But expediency in this case was to prove broadly constructive and the candidate surprisingly strong. Much of the future story of remarkable Republican successes lies in the work of the Chicago convention. And John Kasson's part had been of such calibre as to warrant careful consideration by politicians, local and national, as they laid their plans for final victory and power.

In an exultant mood, Kasson and his colleagues hurried away from Chicago. Over the week end, final preparations would have to be laid for the grand ratifying convention which he had already called to meet at Iowa City the following Wednesday. The enthusiastic gathering, called to order by Kasson, the outgoing state chairman, was the opening shot in the Iowa canvass for Lincoln. It also revealed that the Grimes-Kirkwood wing controlled the state offices. The Chicago platform and candidate were unreservedly endorsed, and all state incumbents were renominated except one.[37]

C. C. Nourse, a Kirkwood man from Des Moines, beat Kasson for attorney general. This witty, outspoken ex-Marylander was a popular speaker, but, considered sometimes erratic, he already had enemies in the party. His rivalry with Kasson was to lead to a breach that was never completely healed.

A few weeks later Kasson lost again. This time he was supported for a supreme court judgeship vacated by the death of L. D. Stockton. In the end, however, his friends yielded to the organization's choice of George G. Wright; Kasson could wait; he would "be all right next year."

Western Iowa, on the other hand, was recognized by the selection of Kasson's admirer, H. M. Hoxie, as the new state chairman.[38] Party headquarters would still remain in Des Moines, and, through Hoxie,

Kasson would exert much influence in the canvass; but unfortunately he would also become enmeshed in an intrigue for spoils which would do him no credit and from which he would have prolonged difficulty in extricating himself.

Through September and October, Republican orators fired away from Iowa stumps. Grimes, Harlan, Kirkwood, Kasson, and Curtis were the long guns to appear before unprecedentedly large crowds. Slavery and economic issues were the bone and sinews of the campaign, but the lust for spoils, as men hurried onto the Lincoln bandwagon, provided the lifeblood. The bare facts of Lincoln's life had wide appeal to the common folk of Iowa. With telling effect, campaign orators emphasized his humble beginnings, his rugged honesty, and his conservatism. Moreover, he was a Western man, a homestead man, a railroad man, and a friend of the Germans. In short, he was the human embodiment of the Chicago platform. The tariff elicited little discussion. Iowans were content to let the Pennsylvanians campaign at home on this issue. Party leaders stood consistently firm against the extension of slavery, and, though they tried to keep the abolitionist element under control,[39] there was sufficient antislavery radicalism to reveal a sharp division within the ranks.

The campaign was noted for its emotional appeals and pageantry. At gigantic rallies thousands of young men, wearing colorful glazed capes and smart military caps, well disciplined and drilled, marched in solid columns to the blare of brass bands and cadenced cheering. These were the famous Wide-Awakes who unsuspectingly were soon to be marching to the crack of the rifle and the roar of the cannon.

At the little village of Cedar Falls, Kasson spoke to an audience so large as to empty the entire Cedar valley. Wagon trains from fifty miles away arrived with impressive floats; Wide-Awakes marched; a bevy of twenty-three girls surrounded their Goddess in a Liberty Car and 100 "older belles" fell in behind; crowds chanted, "Land for the landless, not niggers for the niggerless." At the "Grand Outpouring" at Keokuk, Kasson addressed a mass of people from Iowa and Illinois estimated at 25,000. Among other orators were Senator Grimes, Samuel Freeman Miller, later Associate Justice of the United States Supreme Court, and Orville Browning, Lincoln's friend from Quincy, Illinois. Twenty-six companies of Wide-Awakes paraded; oratory spouted from grandstands in every picnic grove; and, "along with irrationalities," there was solid talk about homestead legislation, free labor, and federal aid for internal improvements. At Fairfield, proclaimed "the greatest meeting in Iowa," Kasson, Grimes, Kirkwood, and several other speakers watched a procession five miles in length. From Agency City came a company of women, wearing white dresses, blue waist-sashes, jaunty red caps trimmed with red ribbon, and carrying Lincoln-Hamlin banners attached to long spears. Printed slogans called for free homes and free territories. Three speaking stands were in constant use. Among the multiplicity of motivations behind these gigantic rallies was an immediate economic one. Budding newspaper editors and businessmen, with a booster spirit in the rising towns, saw a temporary revival of business in one of the worst of the depression years.[40] As the canvass entered its final stages blind optimism prevailed. There was little recognition of the peril that hung over the nation.

Although Lincoln's election seemed certain, Democrat C. C. Cole of Des Moines was giving Samuel Ryan Curtis, Republican candidate for re-election to Congress, a close race in southern Iowa. To Curtis' rescue promptly came Hoxie, Kasson, and a number of railroad men. At the suggestion of Kasson, Hoxie contacted Grenville M. Dodge, a young railroad engineer from Council Bluffs. Thereupon Dodge and Hoxie, operating through certain railroad contractors, "hired off" an undetermined number of Democratic Irish railroad workers in Van Buren and Wapello counties. This meant that the Irish were hired off from one railroad company inside Curtis' district and employed on another railroad company outside the district, at least until after the election. Apparently railroad officials of both companies cooperated because they felt that a Republican victory was a victory for railroad interests generally. For this service, Hoxie was sure that Curtis would owe his election to young Dodge, who provided some of the money.[41]

In the November elections, Iowa went Republican by a comfortable majority. Lincoln beat Douglas by more than 15,000 votes, while Bell and Breckinridge together polled a bare 3,000. Curtis was re-elected by a majority of 3,696. Hiring off the Irish votes had helped, but it was perhaps not decisive.[42]

For twelve years John Kasson had dabbled in third party politics, had participated in many a close fight, sometimes winning, sometimes losing, and now the movement had blossomed into a positive institution with a firm grip on his home state. Republican possession of Iowa was temporarily confirmed. A civil war and reconstruction, and the simultaneous adoption of the platform of 1860, were to establish permanent possession for many years to come, so permanent that the men of '60 came to identify their party and their sectional aims and battles of the fifties with national patriotism. The more realistic political and economic aspects of the campaign have often been obscured by emotions stimulated by a subsequent war. The campaign had not been fought in an atmosphere impregnated with the immediacy of secession but with the immediacy of hard times and the hope for remedial free lands, cheap transportation, general economic and political uplift, and, not the least important, the spoils of victory.

In solid American political tradition, Iowans by the hundreds, high and low, began to present their bills, keeping the road hot to Washington and Springfield. Some wanted jobs; some, appropriations for pet projects; and some, fat government contracts. Appetite for perquisites seemed insatiable.

Victory celebrations had gone on scarcely a week before a group of purposeful men began to consolidate around Kasson to combine patronage, business, and railroad promotion into vague, shifting plans for personal advancement. Kasson was to be the front man, the man of high political influence to procure contracts and concessions in Washington. His reward apparently was to be the political backing of those who received the perquisites. Kasson, ever eager for such political backing, was a degree more cautious than those pushing him. Cooperating willingly in the early stages of "The Plans," he grew more reluctant, and, in time, impatiently tried to wash his hands of them.

The initial "Plans" included Kasson and H. M. Hoxie of Des Moines, Grenville M. Dodge and Caleb Baldwin of Council Bluffs, Peter R. Reed of Moline, Illinois (an employee of the Rock Island Railroad), and a few others in the lower echelon. As Kasson gradually faded from "The Plans," W. B. Allison of Dubuque stepped in. So important are some of these men in the Kasson story that they must be more fully introduced.

Twenty-nine-year-old Grenville M. Dodge was rapidly becoming the most powerful Republican in southwestern Iowa. Born in Massachusetts of a poor, Democratic family, he had been educated in civil engineering and soldiery at Norwich University, Vermont, where enthusiasm for railroad expansion was at a fever pitch. In conservative Norwich, he carried no torch for abolitionists and once dashed a dish of oysters into the face of a Negro whose independence he considered insulting. Although aggressive and rebellious in college, Dodge graduated in 1851, well disciplined and trained to command. Following friends to Illinois, and to great railway projects, cheap lands, and attractive jobs for young civil engineers, Dodge was eventually employed by the Chicago & Rock Island. The builders of this road, the first to reach the Mississippi from Chicago, planned an extension on west through Iowa to the Missouri River, and for this purpose had organized the Mississippi & Missouri (the M. & M.) to connect Davenport, Iowa City, Des Moines, and Council Bluffs. This might be the link in the magic chain to the Pacific.

Dodge had his first contact with Iowa when put to work surveying this line in the spring of 1853. With "wonderful energy," he helped push the survey westward; noted the frenzy with which railroad promoters sought to reach the Missouri first and thus connect with a "route to the Orient"; observed the eagerness with which some settlers, faced with falling commodity prices, supported almost any scheme for cheaper transportation; and made the acquaintance of railroad promoters and politicians everywhere.

As an engineer, and with purpose, Dodge recognized the little village of Council Bluffs, where "the Missouri river sprawled out on the flood plains like a great chocolate-colored worm," [43] as the strategic point of departure for the road to the Pacific. Here he bought real estate; and here, during the lull of the railroad boom punctured by the panic of 1854, he married, staked out land claims across the river near Omaha, Nebraska, for himself, his father, and brother, and settled down to farming and trading.

Two years later, the giddy railroad boom was renewed when the federal government contributed some three and one-half million acres of lands to four east-west lines, one of which was the M. & M. Dodge rejoined the road; an infant "Crédit Mobilier" construction company was devised for laying and grading; rivalries between towns and counties were pushed, the one voting the largest bond to get the road; railroad lobbies badgered the legislature for state aid; and Democrats and Republicans vied with each other for the honor of being the railroad party. Dodge became liaison man between Republicans and the promoters.

The panic of 1857 again checked the boom. Railroad men grew desperate as work ground to a halt and as popular resentment swelled up from broken pledges and unfulfilled contracts. Dodge reported that only bribes could get bonds voted in his home county.[44]

Through his railroad interests Dodge was building high prestige and great potential power. He had moved over into the Republican party because it was the party most likely to favor railroads, especially a Pacific railroad. During the gubernatorial campaign of 1859, Dodge and Lincoln, the railroad attorney, discussed railroads and politics at Council Bluffs. Dodge was summoned to the Chicago convention by N. B. Judd, Lincoln's manager and also a railroad attorney. There, with other railroad promoters, he worked for Lincoln and a plank in the platform committing the federal government unreservedly to a Pacific line.

Dodge was a dynamic doer, a natural leader, capable of demanding and receiving loyalty. As a railroad engineer, he could always count on the support of those for whom he procured jobs and from those in areas in which he might locate a road. It is little wonder that Kasson, reaching out for high office, would solicit the influence of a man like this. As a politician, Dodge was to develop the knack of hiding his real aims under a disarming cloak of pontifical crusading. Behind the scenes, he was at ease among the boys and could operate with amazing effectiveness. As an engineer, he was constructive; as a businessman, acquisitive.

During the railroad slack, beginning in 1857, Dodge, his father, and his brother were engaged in a multiplicity of business activities stretching from Denver to Davenport — banking, milling, contracting, real estate, freighting, and selling supplies to the Indians on the frontier. Associated with him were John T. Baldwin and a man named Pegram — the same Pegram condemned by a special committee of the legislature for accepting a bribe in connection with the locating of the new state capitol.[45] As the depression wore on, Dodge's enterprises teetered on the verge of bankruptcy.

An intimate political associate in Council Bluffs was Caleb ("Cale") Baldwin, a 430-pound justice of the state supreme court. Born in Pennsylvania, Baldwin had attended Washington College with James G. Blaine. As described by an admirer, he was timid and modest in personality despite his great size; in politics, there was nothing credulous about him; he took nothing for granted; he grasped the main questions and took no time with nonessentials; on occasions, he could be "bold as a lion" in defiance of opposition. Baldwin, as he traveled his court circuit over the state, helped distribute the patronage and kept Dodge informed of politics, business, and men. Dodge, on the other hand, pressured his friend Cale to "shade" court cases in behalf of railroad interests.[46]

H. M. Hoxie had lived in Des Moines since the age of seven, when his father arrived with the family from New York. Now thirty years old he was becoming familiarly known as "Indomitable Hub." An admiring friend and subsequent "Republican Regent" of Iowa was to describe him as the "most stirring or stirring-up man" in Iowa politics. But a leading gubernatorial aspirant characterized him in 1861 as "suspicious, treacherous, and corrupt as the devil wants him to be." Three years later Kasson recommended him as "intelligent, writes well, talks well, and has popular manners among the people. He is not polished, cares little about dress, can keep secrets, can talk, can mould conventions, remembers much more than he forgets, and possesses indomitable energy."

Hoxie had gone to California during the gold rush; had returned and married into a family which kept an Underground Railroad station near Des Moines; he was considered a radical antislavery man. But his interest in overground railroads and other material matters was eventually to become dominant. Said never to have possessed an income greater than $800 before the Civil War, he was in time to visit his home town in his own palace car.[47]

Kasson and Hoxie had served together on the Republican state committee and as delegates at Chicago. But when, where, and how Kasson and Dodge became acquainted has not been ascertained. Kasson is reported to have been attorney for the M. & M. before 1860 and to have hobnobbed with the railroad promoters at Chicago. No documentary proof of such facts has been found, though this may be a reasonable assumption. At a railroad meeting of Des Moines citizens in the summer of 1858, Kasson had shown his preference for the M. & M. From Dodge he received railroad passes during the Lincoln campaign. And, according to Hoxie, he then knew Dodge well enough to recommend him as the man to handle the Irish workers in the Curtis campaign.[48]

"The Plans" can be unfolded from letters of the participants to Dodge. On November 12, Peter R. Reed wrote: "Now Lincoln is elected, I think you and I should be together and see if there can be anything done under the new administration *to make us comfortable.*" [49] Four days later, Hoxie went into great detail. While attending to the Irish matter, he had conferred with L. Williams, contractor on the M. & M., who thought "influences" could be used to procure "contracts that would pay without much means invested." Hoxie had received letters from Williams and Reed proposing to form a company, to include Dodge, Hoxie, Reed, and Williams, to handle contracts "of the various public works of the U. S." Hoxie was "willing and ready to go at anything that will make money" though he could raise only a "few hundred, maybe better, thousand dollars."

Hoxie had told Williams that he believed he could get the support of the Iowa congressional delegation. And "with the aid of our friend Kasson," he explained, "I could secure the services of Mr. F. P. Blair, Jr. and of Mr. Edward Bates of Mo. one of whom will certainly be in the cabinet. Mr. Kasson advises me to go in provided you [Dodge] are one of the partners." But, cautioned Hoxie, "I do not wish to do anything that will prevent me from being of service to Mr. Kasson politically. Rather than loose [*sic*] my influence for him in the state, I would try to live along at this place. . . . K's future is bright — he should have the best office in the gift of the people. He has worked hard and is deserving. Could Mr. Lincoln give him the right place I would be satisfied to work in the rear rank." [50]

Three days later, Reed wrote from Grinnell, where he was desperately trying to sell some town lots to pay his taxes: "We want to begin early in the Republican administration to see if we can do something. Mr. Hoxie, Mr. Williams, Mr. Henry and myself . . . all want *you* [Dodge] in . . . the idea is to get some government supplies to furnish Indian agency & transportation, etc. . . . say nothing to outsiders." [51]

Next, Hoxie wrote to Dodge: "Kasson and myself would like to have a general understanding with you about our future aspirations. I am at Sea without a chart & willing to do most anything that is honorable for a living." Some of Hoxie's "friends" wanted to send him to the new territory to get him out of politics! But, said Hoxie, he was "in for the next year" as state chairman. He preferred to remain at Des Moines, for "The Legislature to be chosen must be Republican. . . . It will have to apportion the state into Congressional

Dists. & Senatorial & Representative dists. — the Senators elected next year will help select a United States Senator, and other matters of importance both for the party and *for individuals and corporations* will come before them for action." Hoxie, besieged with job seekers in every mail, concluded with innocent disgust: "I did suppose that we had some men working for principle and not for pay, and I find that I am mistaken." [52]

Meantime, Judge Baldwin, writing from Des Moines, advised Dodge on the distribution of the patronage. Baldwin recommended for United States Marshal, Stewart Goodrell — "A good fellow, poor as a snake." For this appointment, Baldwin wanted Dodge to enlist the backing of a few Council Bluffs Republicans but not that of Pegram who might connect Goodrell with the capitol scandal. Instead of Kirkwood's candidate, Baldwin supported Joseph H. D. Street for federal land register: "1st he is sound, it may do him good; 2d it puts him out of the ring for other matters; 3d it does not amount to much and will dry him up." Baldwin was looking to the future: "Within 4 years we will have Representatives, Senators, District Judges, perhaps a congressman and if [Street] don't get the Registership, he will be pitching in all the time bringing up old sores." Baldwin cautioned Dodge, in his conversations with Street, not to say anything against Fitz Henry Warren to whom Street reported. Some Iowa Republicans were pushing Warren, a party founding father of '56, for a cabinet place. As an anti-Grimes-Kirkwood man, and considered erratic and hard to control, he was a thorny problem. Baldwin had a solution: "Can't you [Dodge] through Judd [Lincoln's Chicago manager] cut off all Fitz's chances for a cabinet office. I want him to have some good subordinate position in some of the departments but it will never do for him to be where he can control appointments." [53]

On December 14, Reed opened up again. He had been to Chicago, had returned by way of Springfield, and had seen Lincoln. "I told him," Reed wrote Dodge, "I had intended to call his attention to the wants of the people of Nebraska and the Western Slope of Iowa. I said to him our interests had been badly neglected. . . . I expected some men from Council Bluffs in regard to this matter and that you was [sic] one of them. He said his sympathies were with border peoples as he was a border man himself. I think we are all right with Mr. Lincoln as we have N. B. Judd with us and Mr. Hoxie of Iowa." [54]

On January 3 Kasson wrote to Dodge: "Can't you come to Des Moines before the 25th instant. . . . Privately, Hoxie will probably leave about the 25th for Washington and both he and I would like to consult with you about sundry matters before he goes." [55] Two days later Hoxie advised that he had been looking for Dodge on every stage. "I must get to Hdgs. [in Washington] early before the slate is made up," he explained. "Things look now as if 'Old Poultice' [Buchanan] was going to give up Washington to the traitors. . . . I suppose that two of the cabinet offices have been selected, Messrs. Bates and Wilmot. Judge Bates is a warm personal friend of Kasson's. K. will therefore be on the right side and can aid his friends." [56]

Kasson replied to a letter from Dodge on January 10. Kasson wanted Hoxie to remain in Des Moines rather than become Indian agent, as apparently had been planned; he wanted Hoxie to hang onto the party chairmanship: "Hoxie is the only man in Central Iowa for that place. We are better organized than ever before, but we must look out for the reaction this year. Nor will it do to send the [Iowa Republican] Headquarters East again. Once do it and we shall probably have trouble to get it again." Therefore, Kasson had in mind another undisclosed place for Hoxie. As for the St. Louis influence about which Dodge had spoken, Kasson advised: "I have easy access to it all. It seems to me the main spoke in your wheel should be the Commissioner of Indian Affairs at Washington. The right man there will secure all proper results." [57]

While these men devoted their attention to the pragmatic aspects of Lincoln's victory, they did not fully realize that during these fateful days American institutions were falling apart. Wheat prices were dropping, stocks falling, and a banking crisis impending. Northerners generally regarded Southern threats to secede with cool indifference. But after South Carolina seceded in mid-December, Northern opinion began to stiffen. During the first feverish weeks of the new year thousands of communities were the scenes of excited meetings, patriotic speeches, and stern resolutions. On January 8 Hoxie called a mass meeting in Des Moines. Kasson and a dozen others made speeches. Kasson, Kirkwood, and Teesdale, on the committee of resolutions, declared that any laws in any state, absolutely in conflict with the Constitution, should be repealed; but there would be no other compromise with the South. Consecutively, on the next three days, Mississippi, Florida, and Alabama seceded.[58]

By the end of January, with aroused public opinion in the North somewhat cooled, Kasson believed that Virginia might hold the border states in the Union. "With them remaining," he wrote, "we can win the Gulf states back . . . if we want them. If they all go out nothing remains but a peaceable separation and division of property; and this . . . is not so dreadful for free state interests as their perpetual liability to southern panics and browbeating insults." [59]

By February 8 the Montgomery convention had in reality created a Southern Confederacy and was on the point of choosing Jefferson Davis as president. On this day Kasson wrote Dodge that he would depart for Washington on the 18th or 20th by way of St. Louis, where he would see Blair, Brown, and perhaps Bates. He urged Dodge to accompany him. Hoxie had already reached Washington. [60]

Dodge arrived at Des Moines on February 17, having been swamped a "hundred times" in snow storms. He had passed women and children "half clothed and half fed." Hard times pinched many he "had hardly dreamed of." Crowds of people were awaiting the eastern stage for departure for Washington, where Dodge was also headed. "K. will go with me," he wrote his wife, "and today I have had lots of callers. They think my prospects at Washington are splendid. I find letters here from all the leading men . . . to have me go on." [61]

So Kasson and Dodge departed for Washington. They did not yet realize that the gravity of the national crisis would require postponing at least some of "The Plans."

☆ VIII ☆

Politics and Patronage Under Lincoln

From the capitol grounds in Washington in late February, 1861, yellow crocuses peeped out to enjoy the bright beams and soft air of balmy spring days. At six in the morning of February 23, Abraham Lincoln, already looking worn and weary, quietly slipped into the city. Tipped off as to the President-elect's secret arrival, five Iowans, including H. M. Hoxie, were on hand to see his train pull in. The next day John A. Kasson was reported to be in town. Washington was filling up with strangers. General Winfield Scott was collecting marines and organizing volunteers for local defense. At once Lincoln was engulfed by an endless stream of pushing office seekers.[1]

H. M. Hoxie had "done it up brown." For Iowa Republican headquarters, he had rented a half house at 854 C Street, just back of the National Hotel. This was the clearing house for Iowa's share of the federal patronage and perquisite. Here came politicians by the scores to divide the spoils. Here came Senators Grimes and Harlan, Congressmen Curtis and Vandever, Governor Kirkwood, and dozens of minor political managers yet to be rewarded. Here also came Grenville M. Dodge, Henry Farnam, and other railroad promoters seeking government contracts, legislation providing for a Pacific railroad, the appointment of their men as governors of the territories through which the road might run, and a federal armory to be located where the Rock Island crossed the Mississippi. Here Dodge developed a friendship with a young office seeker from Dubuque, William Boyd Allison, who was soon showing interest in "The Plans" for government contracts and easy money.[2]

Lincoln's inauguration of March 4 took place with unexpected quietness. John Kasson and his wife attended the ceremony in company with Senator Grimes. That night Grenville M. Dodge wrote home: "Old Abe delivered the greatest speech of the age. The Sermon on the Mount only excells it. It is backbone all over; and Washington with its one hundred thousand Republicans is very very high." Dodge went on to say that "all our friends were in favor of Mr. John A. Kasson for [First] Assistant Postmaster General and succeeded in having him appointed."[3] A few days later, he added: "They all give me credit of it." But Kasson gave the credit to Senator Grimes and Montgomery Blair, Lincoln's Postmaster General.[4]

H. M. Hoxie was appointed United States Marshal for Iowa, a position which would enable him to do important work for "The Plans," the party, and the nation.[5] Meanwhile, Dodge had already made a quick trip to New York, where he met railroad promoters Henry Farnam and Thomas C. ("Doc") Durant, who returned with him to the Iowa headquarters in Washington. Other railroad men arrived to help lobby for a Pacific road from Council Bluffs along the Platte River Valley. After the inauguration, Dodge optimistically ("it looks as though we can get all our measures through") hastened back to New York for another conference; thence to the Washington "political whirlpool," where he and two other railroad men talked matters over with Lincoln; thence to New York for three days of conferences with Rock Island promoters; and finally to Council Bluffs. In the East he had carried all his "points except one."

Returning home via St. Louis and the Missouri River, Dodge learned that secession military companies, then forming in northwestern Missouri, planned to capture at St. Joseph certain federal troops as they moved from the Nebraska country to the East. Dodge notified Kasson, who contacted the War Department, and the troop movement was deflected at Council Bluffs through Iowa.[6]

At Washington in early April, Kasson found himself swamped with the tasks of his new job in the Post Office Department. The secession movement in the Upper South was gaining ground. Amidst rumors that Fort Sumter was to be evacuated, Lincoln was gingerly (but not blindly, as was then believed) taking over the reins of the government. Kasson's immediate superior, Montgomery Blair, was demanding at Cabinet meetings that Fort Sumter be held. And Lincoln was on the point of sending reinforcements, fully aware of the risks of open resistance from South Carolina. In the West, merchants, bankers, and river-boat operators were experiencing the blight of commercial panic.[7]

At Council Bluffs, Dodge found letters pouring in from his business friends. W. B. Allison, now back home and a director of the Dubuque branch of the state bank, wired him: "Will let Bluffs branch have $5000 to loan you."[8] On April 12, H. M. Hoxie, sick from rheumatism at Dubuque, inquired, "What is the next stroke for our programme?"[9] On the same morning, a little before daylight, people in Charleston, South Carolina, heard a dull, heavy rumble. Confederate guns had opened on Fort Sumter, and the war had come. Three days later Lincoln called for 75,000 volunteers. Four days later Hoxie wrote Dodge: "Now is the time for war contracts . . . write Kasson at once. . . . We ought to supply the Northwest Forts."[10] Next, Allison, who had been conferring with Hoxie, wrote: "Can't we manage together to make something out of this rebellion or war?"[11] Next, Hoxie, still at Dubuque: "There must be money in this war some place and we ought to have our share. . . . Don't you [Dodge] enlist or take command of a company. There will be plenty of men that will want to go. Keep clear of that."[12]

Meanwhile, new factors and a new personality were brought into play: Judge Baldwin, writing from Davenport, disliked the fact that the Council Bluffs *Nonpareil* was not supporting Governor Kirkwood's political aspirations. "Kirkwood is a noble fellow," wrote Baldwin, "and is ready to do all he can for us. . . . I know and have influence with him and can use it to our favor when required." Baldwin then thanked Dodge for his and Judge Lowe's season passes over the M. & M.[13]

Governor Kirkwood responded to Lincoln's call for volunteers with alacrity and appointed men in various sections to recruit and organize companies. On May 7, Peter R. Reed, also writing from Davenport, informed Dodge that Kirkwood had given Baldwin "full discretion" to muster troops "in the river counties"; Reed suggested that their subsistence might be left to Dodge. Reed too was interested in army contracts; moreover, he wanted pressure brought on the Iowa congressional delegation to divide the Indian superintendency into two districts.[14] Dodge became Judge Baldwin's "acting adjutant" and helped organize a number of skeleton companies in the southwest.[15]

By early June, thousands of tents nestled among the fine old trees of Washington, bursts of martial music responded from every street, and the city bristled with bayonets. John Kasson, buried deep in the details of the Post Office Department, besieged by office seekers on every hand, and looking thinner, now began to recognize the immediacy of national danger and the urgent need to put aside "The Plans." In this frame of mind, an undertone of impatience crept into his reply to Dodge's request for information "re war contracts." Kasson had repeatedly tried to get information at the War Department: "But I have been overwhelmed with business myself." He had learned that McClellan's commissary at Cincinnati would advertise for contracts: "Make offers to him and obtain information from him"; he had not found out how troops in Kansas and Nebraska were to be supplied: "You can learn that from officers in that region . . . such matters need personal and particular attention from those interested to insure success." On a note of sharp inquiry, Kasson closed with: "What are you doing in a military way?"[16]

Dodge had been trained in military science at Norwich University. At Peru, Illinois, he had helped organize a crack artillery squad which the governor had effectively used to quell a labor riot; and as early as 1856 he had organized the Council Bluffs Guard. In the light of his training and peacetime interest in military matters, it was only natural for men to expect him to enter the service.[17] Undoubtedly

Dodge had pondered the idea also, and before he received Kasson's letter he was on his way again to Washington to apply to the highest authorities for a commission. On the same mission Governor Kirkwood authorized him to procure arms and supplies for the soldiers of Iowa.[18]

In Washington, Dodge saw Lincoln and Secretary of War Simon Cameron. Sixty thousand soldiers were encamped in and around the town. Troops were moving to Harper's Ferry, and people were "painfully on the tiptoe of expectation." Dodge and Mrs. Kasson drove out across Long Bridge to view the camps in Virginia. At Arlington, Colonel Robert E. Lee's mansion had been turned into army headquarters. On this drive, Mrs. Kasson said to Dodge: "Tell Mrs. D., though I am not acquainted with her, that she ought to give her consent [to Dodge's joining the army]." Dodge wrote this to his wife and commented: "Her husband is a member of a volunteer company here."[19]

Cameron offered Dodge a captaincy in the regular army, but Dodge declined. Lincoln and Cameron urged him to take a reserve colonelcy in an Iowa regiment. Again he declined, probably waiting to be offered a commission as brigadier general. Then one night John Kasson and Judge John W. Rankin came to see him. He wrote his wife immediately afterward: ". . . both attacked me, so I gave in and have accepted. Could not refuse without disgracing myself." He was to be colonel of the Fourth Iowa Regiment to be stationed at Council Bluffs for service in Missouri. Dodge wrote his mother: "I go into the war on principle — pecuniarily it will ruin me."

Dodge hastened off to New York to procure supplies for Iowa soldiers, to borrow money for his hard pressed business at home, and to discuss business plans, which now obviously would have to be revised or postponed. Back at Council Bluffs, he received a letter from T. C. Durant, Rock Island promoter: "I am sorry you left [New York] when you did . . . we could have made something out of war contracts." There "has been and will still be good pickings." If the war lasts "two years it will pay us to spend some time in Washington."[20] Doc Durant had not given up.

Desperately needing guns as he whipped his regiment into shape, Dodge appealed to Kasson. At old Fort Kearny on the Platte River were six idle howitzers. In response to a telegram, Kasson took the matter up "personally" with the Secretary of War, and, from "old lion-headed" General Scott he received in person an order for the guns to be transferred to Dodge's regiment. Kasson wrote: "God bless you, Colonel!" [21]

As the first summer of the Civil War, with its confusion and frustration, stretched into autumn, Dodge moved his regiment to Rolla, Missouri. The campaign for the control of Missouri would in time get under way. And, in the meantime, though the campaign for "The Plans" apparently had been shelved, Kasson began the campaign for Dodge's promotions, which was to last until the guns thundered victoriously around Atlanta.

John and Cara Kasson had rented a suite of rooms at Rugby House on F Street. A few blocks west were Judiciary Square, City Hall, City Hospital, and the county jail. Still farther west, at F and Seventh Street in the principal business district, was the General Post Office, where John was to do some of the most constructive work of his life. [22]

The half-finished, rambling Southern town so familiar to Cara's childhood days had suddenly become a strange maelstrom of frenzied military, political, and social activities. With time to spare, John Kasson's attractive and restless wife, now thirty years old, threw herself into this whirl of events, and, for the next four years, she "exulted, mourned, and moralized" in long letters published in the Des Moines *Register* under the pen name of "Miriam." Ubiquitous, she gossiped flippantly to Iowans about the President's levees, and about Cabinet calls, picnics, extravagant entertainment, and women's fashions.

She poured out word-streams of exhilaration and depression as the tides of battle ebbed and flowed. In victory she jubilated, in defeat she wailed and prayed as she watched the wounded and dead returning from Virginia battlefields in never ending wagon trains. Proud and arrogant, she lashed out with fighting words at the "Chivalry," the "F.F.V.'s," the "sacred soil" of Virginia, and Rebel girls swinging tauntingly down the streets of Washington.

In defeat and victory, strange moodiness, deep religion, and burning patriotism welled up; religion and nationalism blended together to approach fanaticism. Cara Kasson bled her emotions white; to bleed profusely was ennobling. To read her letters one suspects that she was disappointed that her husband was not fighting and bleeding on the field of battle. She became boastfully devoted to "her Western men" whom she considered to be bearing the brunt of fighting.

She chided and became disillusioned with the "great ones of our land," who, when "the summit of ambition" was attained, "cast aside the Cross and worshipped alone the world"; she shamed idle officers, "glaring in tinsel on the streets" of Washington while battles raged at the front. Denying any knowledge of politics, she nevertheless gossiped discerningly on the strong currents of factionalism as men fiercely haggled over policy, power, and prestige. As the war mercilessly dragged on, daily bringing doubts and frustrations, she became converted to radical aims. (And so did her brothers, Reverend Dr. W. G. Eliot of St. Louis and Congressman T. D. Eliot of New Bedford.) One "might as well give peppermint to a dying whale," she wrote, as to try "to still the throes of this tempest-tossed nation with sops of compromise." But she steadfastly maintained her faith in Lincoln: "We have a long-headed president; he takes time to move but his foot tells when he puts it down."

Inveighing against the frivolities of Washington, Cara Kasson grew "heart sick and weary with the glare of gay crowds." She nevertheless became a leading participant in them. "Experience has taught me," she rationalized, "that those who talked loudest of their abstinence from scenes of entertainment are the first to yield to the pressure of actual temptation. . . . I dare not prate of others' dissipations, for what I see in Washington has taught me distrust and Charity. The better acquainted one becomes with the great men of Washington, the more seeming their greatness proves a myth."

The Cara Kasson revealed in her letters was a strange paradox — moody and gay, flippant and sober, worldly and deeply religious, practical and mystical. Torn by what she wanted to happen and what was really happening, disturbed at what she thought she ought to be and what she really was, she was a frustrated woman, but a woman fanatically devoted to a Cause; and Victory and Union during the war years were The Cause.[23]

John and Cara Kasson were soon given a foretaste of the cost of Union. Late in May, 1861, when the Federals moved against Alexandria, Lincoln's former private secretary, Elmer Ellsworth, now of the New York Fire Zouaves, was shot and killed as he tore down a Confederate flag from an Alexandria hotel. Lincoln grieved his loss like a son; his funeral was held in the White House, and crowds gathered mourning his death as a personal loss. A day or two later Kasson called on Lincoln, and as they stood talking at a south window of the Executive Mansion, Kasson remarked that the view of Virginia looked better now that the Confederate flag no longer waved over Alexandria. Tears came to the President's eyes, and he said, "Yes, but at what a cost!" Reminiscing over the incident forty-six years later, Kasson did not believe the President then "comprehended the terrible state of political sentiment or the seriousness of his own responsibility." [24]

In early July, Washington was in a "painful state of expectancy"; the Radical clamor for military action was too strong for Lincoln to resist, and he ordered General Irvin McDowell to attack the Confederates near Manassas; the "romance of war" was about to be punctured. As McDowell moved his green, uniformed civilians south, Kasson, Judge Rankin, another Iowan who called himself "Charley," and Colonel Middleton of the District militia took a carriage for the advance post of the main army. From the Postmaster General they procured "passes and a basket well-filled with bread and ham and certain bottles in which we carried water, etc."; they hid their revolvers under their carriage cushions.

Driving out from Long Bridge, they saw farmers gathering crops at Falls Church; they slept that night at Vienna on the floor of a farm house where officers of certain New Jersey regiments were quartered; they heard nervous sentinels outside banging away at each other. Up at five the next morning, the party drove to Fairfax Courthouse and saw pictures of pretty South Carolina girls left behind by the "retreating Chivalry"; soon overtook an army food train of 104 well-filled wagons belatedly making its way to the front; picked up a girl from Maine, jauntily uniformed and headed for Centreville; and finally overtook the main army within a half mile of Centreville. There they saw General Daniel Tyler and his staff gallop down the road to take command of a flanking movement. Straight ahead across a winding creek called Bull Run the Confederate army waited. Hearing that the major engagement would take place within the next day or two, Kasson and his friends confidently returned to Washington, carrying away souvenir cannon balls and grapeshot.

This trip took place on Thursday and Friday, July 18 and 19. On Friday and Saturday, word circulated in Washington that the big battle would take place on Sunday. Cara Kasson observed that "Every man has been, or is going into Virginia. Carriages, horses, and all kinds of conveyances are in demand. . . . Mr. Cameron has gone over and many members of Congress." By Sunday, carriages, like spectators at a race, had drawn up at Centreville on a hill overlooking Bull Run. On Sunday afternoon Cara learned from Dorothea Dix, the nurse, that the Confederates were completely routed. With the sound of "Washington's March, pealing from a brass band" outside, she contentedly went to bed.

In the meantime, John, hearing that the engagement was taking place, had driven rapidly toward the front. Across Long Bridge he began to meet returning noncombatants. As night came on he found it almost impossible to buck the tumbling torrent of smashing carriages, army wagons, and fleeing soldiers. It was a rout, and frightened people were running for their lives! Kasson pulled up at a place called Goodwin's Tavern, abandoned his carriage, mounted a musket, and commandeered and made camp with a group of weary soldiers. General Ambrose Burnside galloped by, bareheaded, weary and mud-splashed, with disaster written on his face.

The next morning before sunrise, Kasson returned to the humiliated capital. Cara was awakened by "low, sad voices in the house." On the streets "bright and joyous" Washington was desolate. Footsore soldiers and horses stiffened from work dragged wearily along. From her window, as heavy rain fell that day, she saw wagons and ambulances bearing the groaning wounded to hospitals. Over on 12th Street, between E and F, Dorothea Dix had opened up a hospital in a carpenter's shop to take care of the overflow. "We walk in a fevered dream," Cara wrote, and "bow to God's mysterious decree." But spiritedly she added, "We shall rally! We shall conquer!" [25]

Within a few months, dashing George B. McClellan drilled into existence a magnificent army and restored confidence to the capital. A tranquil Christmas season opened. Washington ladies kept open house on Christmas Day, and Cara found their rich chocolate and strong coffee a delicious contrast to boardinghouse fare. On New Years Day "everybody went to see everybody"; and on this day, twenty-three Iowans, in a body, called on the Kasson's at the Rugby House.

Lurton D. Ingersoll, treasury employee and writer, led the party, and as they entered the Kasson home he made a three-minute speech, praising Iowa soldiers and John Kasson, "public-spirited civil servant." Kasson responded with warm-hearted, happy remarks, and the party partook of "edibles and drinkables." In the center of a table in a back parlor was a great cake emblazoned with the word,

"Iowa." Hanging between the two parlors was a graceful American flag to which every man had to bow as he passed to the table for refreshments.[26]

In the early months of the new year, the Federals captured Fort Henry, Roanoke Island, and Fort Donelson; the Confederates abandoned Nashville. The small Army of the Southwest, commanded by ex-Congressman Samuel Ryan Curtis, cut loose from Rolla, Missouri. In command of a brigade was Colonel Grenville M. Dodge.

Through the past summer, autumn, and winter the mails had been heavy with Kasson-Dodge correspondence. Kasson had been Dodge's personal emissary before the powers in Washington, procuring supplies, supporting the Colonel's recommendations for officers, sutlers, and office seekers, and backing to the hilt Dodge's own campaign for a brigadier-generalship.

This campaign for Dodge's promotion had begun in earnest in early November. The drive had been started off by Frank W. Palmer, state printer and now editor of the Des Moines *Register*; by Thomas Withrow and H. M. Hoxie of Des Moines; by Judge Caleb Baldwin of Council Bluffs; and by Captain M. P. Small, Chief Commissary and Quartermaster at Rolla. The aid of Governor Kirkwood and the entire Iowa congressional delegation had also been enlisted. By November 13, Kasson, loaded with letters, had pressed the matter upon Lincoln and Cameron in person. The President himself promised to consider all testimonials. "I mean to succeed, Dodge. God bless you," Kasson declared. But soon he had withdrawn all Dodge's papers and sent them to Senator Grimes. The President would not move "without the approval of Senators."

In mid-December, Kasson conferred with the congressional delegation, who recommended Dodge, along with three other Iowa officers, for brigadier general. Senator Harlan and Congressman James F. Wilson, Curtis' successor, took the recommendations to Lincoln, but there were no immediate results; Kasson again called on the President, but Grimes was holding back until sure of Senate confirmation. There the matter rested for a while, with Kasson promising to confer with Lincoln a third time for merely "one" promotion.[27]

On March 9, 1862, John and Cara heard glorious news from two widely separated fronts. Curtis' army had turned back a superior Confederate force at Pea Ridge, Arkansas; down in Hampton Roads, the Confederate ironclad *Merrimac*, having played havoc with Union vessels, had been forced to retire by a curious low-strung ironclad *Monitor*. Missouri was saved for the Union, and Federal forces, their Kentucky flank no longer exposed, could plunge through Tennessee and pierce the heart of the deep South. More monitors would be built, and a strangling blockade of the Confederacy maintained.

In the thick of action at Pea Ridge, Colonel Dodge had led a brigade, had been wounded, and was to be furloughed for two months. This was the action which Kasson thought he needed to clinch Dodge's promotion. In the Washington papers he ran news items on Dodge "which everybody read, and which prepared Senators to know and recognize" the Colonel's name. By June, Kasson could at last announce Dodge's promotion "with all hearty congratulations." [28] Cara wrote to Dodge:

> For my part I felt sure of your courage and promotion long before the first had been proved in battle, or the last accomplished. . . . You are wounded, but that in my eyes is only the seal set to your daring. Should you safely recover I could congratulate you more for the wound . . . than for aught else. When the first report came that although three horses had been shot from under you, you were unhurt, I felt a sense of disappointment! . . . I wanted you should have had just hurt *enough* to have really given some drops of blood for our dear flag, and I knew this would cheer you, when in your old age, and approve to the world that you fought in very deed. I believe I should feel this way were my nearest and dearest concerned. But a strange spirit actuates me in this strife. I count it glory to *suffer* for the cause, and so I doubt not do you.[29]

Shortly after the Hampton Roads engagement, John Kasson, "with a Congressional party," visited the *Monitor* at Fortress Monroe. The party also sailed out to observe the *Congress* and *Cumberland*, sunken victims of the *Merrimac*. Flushed with excitement from the scene, Kasson returned to Washington and wrote a vivid description of the sinking of the *Cumberland*:

> After the iron "Merrimac" had passed the "Cumberland," and received her iron hail as so many peas from a pop gun, she hailed her and demanded a surrender. Morris, her gallant commander, replied "No never." The "Merrimac" gave her a broadside, tearing the timbers of the Cumberland with terrific force, and receiving a tremendous, but almost harmless fire in return. Again the enemy demanded a surrender. Morris again replied "No never." The "Merrimac" then drew off and plunged into the broadside of the Cumberland with her iron prow, breaking her in two, and leaving her rapidly sinking. Still her gallant crew fired gun after gun, as the water rose upon them, and as the last gun was about to be covered, — the men standing in the water, — it was

fired at the assailing monster just as our ship disappeared in the sea. Thus the Cumberland sank beneath the waves, with many wounded, many dead, many living, on board, and, thank God, with her flag still flying in the face of the foe.

Just one week after this victory of metallic impenetrability over magnificent gallantry, I visited the scene, and sailed around the Cumberland. Her three top-masts were above the water, and at the fore we saw, with intense emotion, the glorious flag still floating upon the wind, over a waste of waters, as if the hundred souls below, sea buried, still challenged the dastard rebels to renew the combat, for that unconquered and unconquerable flag.

Such valor, wrote Kasson to Whittier and Longfellow, demanded from the poet "an Epic, or a Lyric to inspire the Navy with the brilliant memory of this defense and of the dead who made it." And in his letters to these poets he enclosed the above description.

From Whittier came "I thank thee for thy striking description. . . . I read it with deep emotion. I presume my fd. Dr. Holmes will make the event the theme of one of his stirring Lyrics." From Longfellow: "That whole affair is so complete a poem in itself, that I am not sure it can be improved by rhyme. But I thank you for the hint." [30] The next December, Longfellow's poem "The Cumberland" appeared in the *Atlantic Monthly*.

While these thrilling but sobering events took place, John Kasson found himself "overwhelmed" in the Post Office Department. The mass of marble housing the Department was, like the Republic, only partly finished and in a very insecure condition. A leaky roof, poor lighting, scant equipment, insufficient room, and a meager staff added to the enormity of the tasks, and soon both Kasson and his chief were reported to be ill.[31]

Never before had the Department faced so many problems. The confusion created by the war and the advent of a new party was sufficient to tax the skill of the best of administrators; moreover, Blair and Kasson inherited the harvest of American lethargy in postal development. The United States lagged far behind England and the European nations. Postal rates were high and without uniformity; there were no free deliveries in the cities, no railway mail cars, no system for the safe transmission of money, and no international postal union; the franking privilege was the source of abuse; mail contracts had become the object of corruptionists; and financially for several years the Department had been running in the red.[32]

Instead of "the cabinet politician," Montgomery Blair preferred to consider himself an efficiency expert and a postal reformer.[33] He and his first assistant, John Kasson, performed all these functions with marked success. Within three years the Department under Blair is said to have made more improvements than had previously been made since the days of Benjamin Franklin. By introducing expert management and efficient methods, Blair reduced the normal tendency toward deficits and at the same time increased the number of post offices and added many other services. By strict supervision of contracts, especially extortionate railroad contracts, he reversed the trend toward corruption. Among the innovations and improvements was the establishment of the postal money order system, railway or traveling post offices, free delivery in cities, and the initiation of an international postal union. There was also legislation codifying the scattered postal laws, making uniform postal rates throughout the country, classifying postmasters and establishing their salaries, and prohibiting postmasters and their friends from franking the mail. In addition Blair and Kasson used the postal service to ferret out and suppress disloyalty and to herd together in the Lincoln camp the faction-ridden Republican party. Although often blunt and tactless as a politician, the Postmaster General's honesty of purpose and straightforwardness in the Department endeared him to his subordinates. Blair inspired them with the spirit of hard work, gave them free rein to originate improvements, and was quick to appreciate their merits.[34]

Exactly where Blair left off and Kasson took up is difficult to determine. As Blair's first assistant, Kasson had much to do with the administration of the entire Department. During the former's frequent absences he served as Acting Postmaster General, and, according to his own testimony, sometimes attended Cabinet meetings. He supervised the discontinuance and establishment of post offices; looked after the distribution of blanks, stamps, furniture, and other supplies; had charge of pay clerks and special agents; and was responsible for interpreting and enforcing regulations affecting postmasters. In cooperation with Blair, he devised and administered an army postal system, as the Union forces moved into the South. He prepared a systematic code of postal laws that had formerly been scattered through the federal statutes. He helped draft the legislation which

provided for uniform domestic postal rates.[35] His interest and labor
in behalf of a uniform and cheap international postal system turned
out to be one of the most enduring achievements of his life and gave
him a pleasant foretaste of a diplomatic career.

Reports on Kasson and his work struck common notes of praise.
He possessed business aptitude and administrative tact in dealing with
vexatious details and applications; he had a comprehensive knowledge
of complicated postal affairs; and he was prepossessing in appearance
and polished in manners. "There was no more efficient, laborious, and
valuable public officer at Washington," and the Post Office Department owed much of its "efficiency" to him. Albert G. Riddle, Ohio
Congressman, was impressed with "the judicial mind of young Kasson
. . . [who] began his very useful and brilliant public career as Assistant Postmaster General. He was a man whom I liked." [36]

In later years Kasson informed college students that Montgomery
Blair, against great political pressure, administered the Department's
patronage on "principle." "[Blair] said to me: 'The Postmaster is
especially the people's agent. . . . Find out who is most satisfactory
to the largest body of responsible patrons. . . . Let him have the post.
In case of doubt, the member of congress can decide for he is more
than any other their legal agent. But he must not be allowed to over-
rule the people's evident wish.' " Principle, Kasson advised young
Americans, was the only "shield against calumny," and, to discuss
public issues without it, merely engendered "prejudice and passion,
the rubbish heaps in the road of human progress." [37]

Kasson's mellowed idealization of this episode should not obscure
the deep currents of political realism which motivated himself, the
Postmaster General, and the President. Abraham Lincoln, having
grown up with the spoils system, put few restraints on the expected
"clean sweep" of federal officeholders. As an astute politician and a
wise statesman, he subtly used the patronage to beat down venomous
factions and maintain his own control.

With more jobs to let than any other Cabinet member, Blair was
"run to death" by office seekers. Applications for 15,000 postmaster-
ships had poured into the Department before the inauguration.

Blair was perhaps more instrumental than any other department
head in using the patronage to build up the powerful Republican
machine that was in a large measure responsible for Lincoln's renomination. Many a Radical was hatched out as much from the fear of

not sharing the patronage and perquisite as from war and reconstruction policies.

Under Blair there were more removals than ever before in history. Congressional dictation of postmaster appointments was "regularized and universally recognized," with one important exception. If a majority of "our friends" favored some other person than that recommended by the Congressman, "the majority wins," Blair insisted. By "our friends" he meant Republicans. And he made special efforts to reward newspaper editors who would support the party and the Union.[38]

"I took the head off every man," said Kasson, "whose position was not absolutely for the Union."[39] He could have said with as much truth also that he took the head off every Democrat. Civil appointments in most cases went to Republicans only; loyal Democrats received military rewards.

Although party institutional development had not yet reached the point where the Postmaster General yielded his function of "cabinet politician" to his first assistant, John Kasson at the head of the appointment office was a more powerful party man than has hitherto been indicated.[40] High party leaders and lowly job hunters directly approached him. Iowans in droves solicited him, and he appears to have handled the bulk of postal patronage in his home state. For Iowa's share of appointments in other departments and in the military services, he sat in on the councils of the Iowa congressional delegation. Through Attorney General Bates, he could perhaps exert influence in the appointment of federal judges, attorneys, and marshals. Through Blair's intimacy and power with Lincoln, he had an inside track to the White House, and he frequently conferred with the President on appointments. Records also reveal his hands in the patronage affairs of the Interior Department. So successful was he in securing commissions and promotions for army friends that he aroused the resentment of Governor Kirkwood.[41]

Consequently it began to be whispered in Iowa political circles that Kasson had more influence with Lincoln than any other Iowan. Kasson's popularity among Iowa officeholders in Washington was demonstrated through group entertainments and flattering newsletters from the capital appearing in Iowa papers. For Iowa politicians holding, or aspiring to, high office, here was a man to be watched as a potential rival.

As Assistant Postmaster General, Kasson was a hard working man of vision, unwilling to use his office as a political sinecure. He was also a hard working politician, and his use of patronage was to be an important factor in his election to Congress, before the end of his second year in the Department.

Exultation from Union victories in the West was short lived in the spring of 1862. McClellan's grand movement upon Richmond was "like putting salt on a pigeon's tail," Cara Kasson observed anxiously in mid-March. By July 3, with this magnificent army retreating toward the James River, she could see only "discord" in the North. McClellan's repulse had created a stronger reaction than had Manassas the summer before. She prayed for the presence in the East of strong Western soldiers and strong Western preachers.[42]

Throughout the North confidence gave way to utter confusion. Military failures increased the general impression of incompetence in Washington. Factionalism within the Republican party ran dangerously on the rampage. Conservatives denounced Lincoln's arbitrary arrests and summary methods, while on the other hand a groundswell of vindictive radicalism threatened to push the President toward further extremes. Hostility to Lincoln's administration had never before been so intense.[43] Into this atmosphere John Kasson went forth to defend the President and to seek a higher office during the crucial mid-term elections of 1862.

The census of 1860 had opened up a new, fertile field for the Assistant Postmaster General. So great had been the population increase in Iowa that the number of congressional districts could be enlarged from two to six. In April, 1862, the Republican legislature had obligingly redistricted the state so that strong Democratic areas were made at least "doubtful." Des Moines had been put into the Fifth District of twenty-three counties covering the southwest one-fourth of the state. From the outset Republicans considered the Fifth a tough district; a mere party hack could not win it.[44]

In late July news reached Washington that Kasson had been nominated for Congress on the third ballot. Nomination had required no hard campaigning. He had become well known in the district as a speaker and party manager. His control of postal patronage had brought some support perhaps from every county. He had, moreover, the backing of such men as H. M. Hoxie, Frank W. Palmer, and Caleb Baldwin. Ubiquitous Hoxie, though having relinquished the chairmanship of the state central committee, had been effectively combining politics with his duties as federal marshal. Palmer, in the pages of the *Register,* had given flattering attention to Kasson's activities in the Post Office Department. But he had neither openly supported him for the congressional nomination nor given more attention to him in his paper than to other Iowa political leaders in Washington. Baldwin had at first supported another candidate but eventually came over to Kasson. General Dodge had returned to his command two or three months before the convention met, and his letters do not show active work for Kasson's nomination. However, Dodge's army friend, Colonel M. M. Crocker, presided over the convention.

The balloting does not indicate that the convention was stacked, but rather that Kasson, somewhat stronger than his closest competitor on the first ballot, picked up enough votes to win, as three weaker candidates fell out. The runner-up, Thomas Hart Benton, Jr., held on to most of his first-ballot votes but could not pick up additional ones.[45]

Benton, a nephew of "Old Bullion" whom Kasson had loyally supported in St. Louis, was only a lukewarm Republican. Previously the holder of several offices in the Democratic party, he had not made the transition to Republicanism until after the war had begun. A resident of Democratic Pottawattamie, home county of Baldwin and Dodge, he had the backing of Judge Baldwin until Kasson announced his candidacy. Benton was later rewarded with a colonelcy in the army; but after the war, unable to accept Radical Republican domination, he returned to the Democratic fold.[46]

Of the five candidates placed before the convention, Kasson, on his own merits, was the strongest. Basically moderate in his views, a former Democrat hailing from Missouri, he could be expected to win in a former Democratic stronghold inhabited by many people of Southern origin. As a persuasive speaker, he could appear radical enough to please the growing demand for more backbone in the prosecution of the war. Fresh from the inner circle at Washington, and a strong Lincoln supporter, he would appeal to the plain man who had not forsaken Old Abe.

In celebration of Kasson's nomination, thirty or more Iowa officeholders in Washington gave him a farewell party at Brown's Hotel.

Senator Harlan presided. "Affable and capable in the highest sense," Kasson "is popular with all classes here," an observer reported.[47]

On August 2, 1862, Kasson wrote a warm letter to Lincoln. "With every appearance of fidelity to the President and his principles," he was about to depart for his Iowa campaign. "Owing to the request of the Post Master General that he should return, after the canvass, to aid in the preparation for the next session [of congress]," he had left his resignation "in the hands of Judge Blair, to be presented in his discretion."[48]

In Des Moines a few days later, John and Cara found Iowans seething with dissension. Military disasters had produced hysterical fear, doubt, and divided counsels. The recruiting system, abandoned during the wave of optimism in the spring, had been re-established. Secretary Stanton had issued a blanket order for the arrest of anyone seeking to discourage enlistments, giving aid or comfort to the enemy, or, through writing, speech, or act, engaging in any disloyal practice. Ever equal to the occasion, the indomitable federal marshal, H. M. Hoxie, now threw out his net for Peace Democrats, stigmatized as Copperheads. Not without political design, Hoxie snared Dennis Mahony, editor of the Dubuque *Herald*, bold critic of the war, and strong potential Democratic candidate for Congress against W. B. Allison. Arrested without warrant, Mahony was shuttled off to the Old Capitol prison in Washington, there to be nominated and to make the race in absentia while Allison, vigorously campaigning at home, won the office.

Meanwhile, Union forces for a second time, in late August, were sent reeling back from Manassas to Washington. To this news Governor Kirkwood responded with a special session of the legislature, ostensibly to provide bounties for volunteers, but, equally important, to give the soldiers in the field the right to vote in the pending critical elections. Faced with the issues of military failures, apparent administrative inefficiency, suppression of civil liberties, threats of conscription, and fears of Negro immigration, Republicans were taking no chances. Democrats, blind to their vulnerability from the exigencies of war and economics, were confident.[49]

In Daniel O. Finch of Des Moines, Kasson had a respected opponent whose loyalty was beyond question. A former law associate of Kasson's, he had moved from New York to Wisconsin, to Cedar Rapids, and finally to Des Moines in 1853. Personally popular, he had been one of the most conspicuous Democratic leaders in Iowa. Republican respect for his strength as a candidate was attested by the willingness of some of them to buy him off with a lieutenant-colonelcy.[50] Whether Finch was offered, and rejected, the lieutenant-colonelcy cannot be ascertained, but the plan fell through.[51]

The postponed joint canvass got under way September 1 and continued up to the eve of the election on October 12. Kasson and Finch, friendly and courteous, sometimes riding together over the country in the same carriage, visited every county in the district and spoke to audiences in more than thirty towns and villages. For the better part of a week Grimes joined Kasson, and the two traveled thirty miles a day, speaking every day except Sunday. "Infamous traitors," Grimes wrote confidentially to a friend, had concentrated their efforts to win two congressional districts — "Kasson's and another"; as "very much a rebble rousie," he had been brought in to help.

In the middle of the canvass, Lincoln, pressed by radicals and playing for European public opinion, issued his preliminary announcement of the Emancipation Proclamation. This, Grimes thought, "suited our people exactly." [52] But Kasson, though strongly defending emancipation, took pains to make it clear that it was a "war measure" designed to bring quick victory and thus save the Union; it was not "the object of war"; let Lincoln use it "in his discretion"; if Congress could take away sons at eighteen, then it could also take slaves away from rebels who were killing those sons. He dismissed as a "scarecrow" Finch's persistent argument that emancipation would inundate Iowa with free Negroes. Slavery had been the impelling force to emigration from the South. And he pointed out that a state law forbade the immigration of free Negroes and mulattoes into Iowa.

Kasson also defended confiscation of Confederate private property and Lincoln's suspension of the writ of habeas corpus. He upheld Hoxie's arbitrary arrests on the grounds that they were made upon "sworn complaints" of disloyal practices and that Marshal Hoxie was merely carrying out the orders of his superior — Secretary of War Stanton, a "loyal Democrat."

Finch's claims to loyalty were questionable, Kasson argued, because he assailed the President, Congress, and the armed forces at a time of peril, when any strong opposition cheered the rebels to greater effort. Kasson consistently connected Finch with the Peace Democrats and their "Mahony platform." The loyal must rally around Lincoln, who had called loyal Democrats into his administration and who always abided by the "clear expression of public will."

Thus, Kasson was turning the spotlight on the dilemma of an opposition party in wartime; to criticize and oppose was disloyal; there could be only one loyal party. For almost a half century thereafter, Republican orators were to use this line of argument so effectively that, when combined with other issues, they were able to maintain one-party control of Iowa and of the nation most of the time.

Kasson did not neglect to emphasize Republican economic achievements under the platform of 1860: the act declaring the territories "forever free to the white man without competition with slave labor"; the act securing "free homesteads to the actual settler, instead of the speculator"; and the act, passed only two months previously, providing for the "certain construction of the Pacific Railroad, with one of its two great branches" leading to Iowa. He supported the administration's tax measures but did not mention the tariff.

On the stump Kasson made a favorable impression. Dignified but also witty, he established a reputation as a man of superior ability. His carefully prepared speeches, sprinkled liberally with historical references, were orderly, meaty, and fluent. While drawing laughter from the audience at the expense of his opponent, he could also whip up a fighting mood for the Union. Although avoiding extremes, he managed to appear radical enough to please those desiring a tougher policy toward the South. He was not in sympathy with "kid-glove warfare." [53]

But oratory in this campaign was not considered enough. Party leaders frantically solicited the soldiers, who had been given the right to vote from the field by the recent special session of the legislature. In reply to a letter from General Dodge, Kasson urged the former to work on "friends of the right stamp in the regiments." Kasson was anxious as to the influence of Colonel John A. Williamson commanding the Iowa Fourth at Helena, Arkansas. Williamson, a former Democrat and personal friend of Finch, shortly showed up in Des Moines to watch the "disgusting struggle for office." Returning to Helena, he informed Dodge that he would work for the right man "so far as consistent with his duty as an officer." Although the vote for Kasson might not be unanimous, there was no need for fear. Williamson, deserting Finch because the latter "virtually" justified rebellion, was making the transition to Republicanism.[54]

From Camp Burnside came word that another Democrat was joining Republican ranks. This was George C. Tichenor of Des Moines, former secretary of the Democratic central committee. Soon to become General Dodge's adjutant, he must be mentioned here because of his future importance in the story of Kasson's life.[55]

Actually, the soldier vote, when the returns came in, was not as decisive in Kasson's district as had been expected. Kasson carried the home vote by a little over 1,000. His more impressive soldier-vote majority of near 2,000 gave him a total margin of about 3,000. On the home vote alone, according to the *Register,* his majority was equal to Lincoln's in 1860. With his soldier support he exceeded any vote ever before given a Republican in the counties of the Fifth. In other congressional districts, the Republican vote failed to reach the standard of '60. The soldier vote was decisive for Josiah B. Grinnell, who squeezed by with a little over 1,000 majority. "Mr. Kasson has achieved a triumph which stands alone among free state elections of 1862," the *Register* boasted.[56]

While Iowa maintained a solid Republican front, the administration suffered humiliating defeats in Pennsylvania, New York, Ohio, Indiana, and even Illinois, Lincoln's home state. Only by the barest majority could Republicans control the new Congress. Therefore, victory in Iowa was doubly appreciated and would assure to the Hawkeye Republican leaders great influence and high rewards.

Although Kasson's victory exceeded all expectations, there appeared on the horizon a fleck of criticism which might swell up into a storm cloud. On the eve of the election Kasson had recommended a man named Everett from Council Bluffs for a vacant collectorship. General Dodge's brother, Nathan, was pulling strings for the same position, and Judge Baldwin had rushed off to Davenport to press his claim. Nathan Dodge was surprised that Kasson would make the appointment without talking to Baldwin or other prominent Republicans at Council Bluffs. Everett, he wrote, was the most unpopular man on the "Slope." From Davenport, where Baldwin learned that Everett had been appointed, he wrote General Dodge: "Kasson has made a bad mistake. . . . They say that is his weakness. He exercises poor judgment in his appointments . . . the party must be careful. There is weakness in our strength unless we watch closely." Baldwin added that Governor Kirkwood disliked Kasson, although he had nothing against Judge Baldwin and General Dodge.[57]

Apprised of the matter at Columbus, Kentucky, General Dodge dispatched a message to Kasson. But it was too late, Kasson replied apologetically. News of Everett's appointment had already reached the press. Kasson belittled the job. There was not enough in it to be "pecuniarily" attractive, anyway: pay small, responsibility large, and a bond of $100,000 required.[58]

Kasson hurried back to Washington. While waiting thirteen months to take his seat in Congress, he was assigned to important work in the Post Office Department. His resignation as Assistant Postmaster General was made effective October 22, and on the same day he was appointed special agent.[59] In this position he helped Blair prepare reports and legislation for the next session of Congress, laid plans for an important international postal congress, and all the while campaigned for the promotion of General Dodge and his friends.

General Dodge had resumed his campaign for further promotion immediately after the election. Its objectives included a major-generalship for himself, a brigadier-generalship for Colonel M. M. Crocker, and the advancement of a few minor officers. H. M. Hoxie and Judge Baldwin protected the rear in Iowa, while Kasson made frontal attacks on Lincoln, Stanton, and Halleck in Washington. Grimes, Harlan, and Wilson were enlisted, but Grimes was the strong defender of the Washington flanks. Harlan was reported to be "non-committal." [60] Kasson fired the first shot at Halleck but returned from an interview discouraged and doubting Dodge's immediate promotion; Dodge would have to send all memorials and testimonials through Halleck; recommendations from Grant, Rosecrans, and Curtis would strengthen the case; also, "some brilliant victory . . . would help greatly." [61]

Dodge wrote Kasson a long letter in which he praised the Emancipation Proclamation, pointing out its military advantages and urging that it be "faithfully and earnestly carried out." Kasson gave this part of the letter to the President, writing Dodge: "I always keep the public men posted about you." Lincoln afterwards said he "had read it twice and could put his hands on it any moment." At this point Kasson "took occasion to say" that Dodge was the "next man from Iowa for major general." [62]

The New Year brought no confirmed promotions. In early February, 1863, Kasson replied to a letter from General Dodge, who had criticized the administration. Kasson said he was "powerless"; the administration "undoubtedly" lacked efficiency; Stanton was "not adequate to the War Department," but Lincoln would not remove him; there was "great dissatisfaction with Halleck." But the "party reactionary movement" in the North was transient, Kasson optimistically predicted.[63]

In mid-February, Kasson wrote Lincoln, urging the promotion of Dodge so that Dodge would not be outranked by Brigadier General Francis J. Herron, who was being promoted because of his hard fighting at Prairie Grove, Arkansas. "I pray you, Mr. President, not to mortify one of the best officers in your service," Kasson pleaded.

On March 2 Kasson wrote Dodge: "So long as the two California lawyers, Stanton and Halleck, are at the head of Military Affairs, let us put our trust in God." Kasson had called on Stanton, urging Dodge's promotion to match Herron's. And Stanton said, "Herron has been so fortunate as to distinguish himself more than Dodge; we may make mistakes, but this is *settled* now." Crocker's promotion was confirmed, and, a little later, Crocker wrote Dodge that Herron's "glory" in the Southwest was a "damned humbug." [64]

On March 4, 1863, Kasson's salary as special agent for the Post Office Department was discontinued "at his request." Already the clerks in the appointment office had given him a warm farewell party and, "for his kindness and courtesy to them" had presented him with a "magnificent gold headed cane." Now he was headed for Connecticut "to play a western hand" in the congressional elections there. His reputation as an orator was spreading, and the Connecticut central committee had invited him to demonstrate his prowess.[65]

Returning to Washington two weeks later Kasson made final preparations for a trip abroad. In a half-grown, divided, and isolated nation, amidst the roar of cannon and the confusion of politics, Kasson and Blair, a quarter century ahead of the times, had initiated a movement for a world-wide postal union. Kasson was to sail on April 4 to represent the United States at an international conference in Paris.

On the eve of his departure he was entertained again by "a house full of [Iowa] beauty, accomplishment, and brains." And he took time, before leaving for Paris, to recommend H. M. Hoxie to Secretary Chase as the man to supervise "internal revenue officers and frauds upon the Treasury currency." [66]

IX

A Venture in International Cooperation

As FIRST Assistant Postmaster General, Kasson had inherited the important function of supervising the operations of the international postal system. Here he found disorganization, a deplorable lack of uniformity, and an unnecessary waste of time, energy, and money.

International postal relations were then regulated on the diplomatic theory of national interest — by conventions between individual countries. Where no treaties existed between countries, there was no official mail service. The aim of treaties was not so much to improve the mail service for the population as to make the foreigner pay the bill. Postal treaties were complex and the rates ridiculously nonuniform and high. A letter mailed in the United States with a foreign destination bore four charges — the American domestic rate, the sea postage for maritime transport, the overland transit rate assessed by each country through which it passed, and the domestic rate collected by the country of destination. For ocean transit there were almost as many different rates as there were steamship companies carrying the mail.

Charges on an item to Vienna varied from fifteen to thirty to forty-two cents per half ounce, depending on whether it passed respectively through Bremen, Hamburg, or some French port. One sending a letter to Australia had a choice of six different routes requiring postage ranging from five cents to $1.02 per half ounce. On the same routes different rates prevailed for open and closed mails.

The scale of progression by which rates advanced in accordance with weight was both diverse and complex. In England and the United States the scale was by the half ounce, in France by the ten grams, in Germany and Austria by the *loth,* and in Denmark, three-fourths of a *loth.*

Some countries fixed the maximum weight of letters at 250 grams; others recognized no limits. Some restricted the thickness of letters; others the width and length. In Denmark, the maximum thickness was two and five-eights centimeters; in England the maximum length, two feet, the maximum width or thickness, one foot.

The system of accounts in each nation was therefore extremely complex. Accompanying each piece of mail was a letter bill upon which the postmaster was required to enter minute details of accounts. Each country was given credit in all other countries through which an item passed for its portion of the sum prepaid on the item. Since accounts were kept by the standard weight and rate of the creditor country, credit on a single letter might require reckoning by the English ounce, the French gram, or the German *loth.*[1]

As John Kasson characteristically came to grips with these complex problems, he discovered that balances on international mails payable in gold were annually accumulating against the United States at the very time when the war had put gold at a greater-than-usual premium. He discovered also that it had been an old story for the Post Office Department to run in the red as the vast new territories in the

West were filling up with settlers demanding improved postal communications. For the past eleven years the department records had shown an unbroken series of annual deficits rising in 1859 to more than seven million dollars. Each year the deficit for foreign mails had been proportionally greater than the total for all other mails. And now, in the midst of war, domestic revenues desperately needed by the hard pressed government had to be used to pay in gold the balances due foreign postal departments.[2]

Here was a problem on the one hand immediate, practical, and national; on the other, remote, idealistic, and international. Kasson was peculiarly fitted to grapple with it. He had the drive and the technical knowledge to master its complexities. He had the breadth of background to understand the idealistic and international aspects of it.

He was thoroughly familiar with the surge in America and abroad for postal reforms. Some twenty years previously he had lived in Worcester, Massachusetts, where Elihu Burritt, the "Learned Blacksmith," had launched his famous campaign for a uniform and cheap international postal system. By 1846 Kasson had settled in nearby New Bedford to practice law. And here, week after week, he read in the newspapers about Burritt's speechmaking junket in England, where the Learned Blacksmith, traveling through the countryside, made 150 addresses pleading for an ocean penny post. Burritt's activities were widely acclaimed in both Britain and America. Kasson undoubtedly took note of the fact that prominent political leaders of the vicinity where he then resided heartily endorsed Burritt's plans, that among such advocates were Charles Sumner, Edward Everett, and Joshua Leavitt.

Two years later, as delegate at the Buffalo Free Soil Convention, Kasson had seen thousands of men wildly acclaim the mention of cheap postage as a party platform plank. Later, in St. Louis, Iowa, and Washington, he had had ample opportunity to become familiar with memorials and petitions from settlers, immigrants, and importers — all urging the federal government to improve the postal system, both domestic and foreign. Such demands were the natural consequence of the Republic's rapid growth and the surging democratic movement.

Early in 1861, moreover, through negotiations with Britain for a more liberal postal convention, Kasson had come in contact with the work of England's famous postal reformer, Sir Rowland Hill. Kasson was also impressed with the ease by which postal communication between the United States and Canada was maintained under liberal treaty arrangements.[3]

If all nations could be brought to endorse certain general principles in their postal relations, could not the log jam be broken thereafter through bilateral treaties incorporating such principles in detailed arrangements? Clearly the problem could best be approached through a concert of nations. The time seemed ripe for a beginning. Accordingly, some time in the spring of 1862, Kasson proposed that the United States call a conference. Postmaster General Blair, who had already sent a postal observer to England, heartily agreed.

Kasson then drafted a circular letter, which, sent through the Department of State on August 4, invited to a conference all countries with which the United States carried on diplomatic relations. In this letter he pointed up the serious embarrassments resulting from mistakes, delays, and diversity of rates. Specifically, he singled out fourteen points suitable for conference deliberations, but he wisely limited conference powers to "discussion and recommendation of measures" for adoption by respective postal administrations. He recommended that postal experts from postal departments — not diplomats — should be sent as delegates. The time and place of meeting would be set by the United States on the basis of replies to the invitations.

While awaiting replies, Kasson, it will be remembered, returned to Iowa and conducted his campaign for Congress. Following the election, Blair turned in Kasson's resignation as Assistant Postmaster General but appointed him a special agent. In this position, at an annual salary of $1,600 plus $2.00 per diem for subsistence and travel, Kasson continued to lay plans for the conference.

Responses were cordial and in some cases enthusiastic. By the end of December, 1862, all the leading powers of Europe and several small countries had accepted. Delegates of the German-Austrian Postal Union, having already scheduled a bilateral meeting in early summer, wanted the general conference held in the spring in order to consider its conclusions at the German meeting. Accordingly, Blair and Kasson set May 11, 1863, as the opening date. As a gesture to France, with whom they probably anticipated difficulties, they designated Paris as the place of meeting.

With preliminary arrangements completed, Kasson resigned as

special agent on March 4 before participating in the political campaign in Connecticut. Meanwhile he was appointed commissioner
to the Paris Postal Conference at a salary of $12.00 per day for travel-
ing and current expenses. But the appointment was not to take effect
until March 30. The next week he departed for Paris.[4]

☆   ☆   ☆

On the morning of April 22 the "most noted" among the stream
of visitors at the American Legation in London was John A. Kasson.
Benjamin Moran, morose legation secretary, who deflated thousands
of personalities in his "Journal," sized Kasson up and bluntly recorded: "He is an intellectual middle aged man, but has too good
an opinion of himself." This was Moran's first impression, which a
few months later he was to modify somewhat.[5]

Kasson had reached London at a time when Northern diplomatic
fortunes were sagging. In British shipyards the famous Laird Rams,
designed to break the blockade of Southern ports, were ominously
nearing completion, and the British government had made no move
to detain them. Across the Channel, Napoleon III was conniving
with Confederate agents for the construction in France of several
powerful commerce destroyers. A huge Confederate bond issue had
recently been floated in Europe, and Southern partisans in Britain
and France were oversubscribing. To Unionists in Europe, prospects
for the recognition of Southern independence by Britain and France
momentarily seemed bright.

To destroy public confidence in Southern bonds, Robert J. Walker, former governor of "bleeding Kansas," appeared on the scene
almost simultaneously with Kasson. Walker, seeking to connect Jefferson Davis with bond repudiation in Mississippi and Arkansas following the panic of 1837, called on Kasson for help. Nowhere in the
legation could adequate evidence be found to prove Davis a repudiator of state debts. Kasson rushed off to Blair an urgent request for
files of the *Congressional Globe* and certified copies of Davis' speeches.
By midsummer Walker was producing a series of newspaper stories
and tracts allegedly showing Davis to be indeed a debt repudiator and
likely to swindle British bondholders out of their money.[6]

Meanwhile, Kasson busied himself with postal matters, meeting
British postal officials and gathering postal data for Blair. He found
Sir Rowland Hill, oldest of British postal reformers, "egotistical and

obstinate" but generous with his vast store of postal information. From Hill, Kasson gathered information on the free delivery system in cities.

Blair was planning to establish the city delivery system in America and had instructed Kasson to check on the desirability of appointing one Pliny Miles as special agent to organize city post services. Miles, a lawyer, teacher, traveler, lecturer, and newspaper correspondent, had been in London for the past ten years. Both in America and England he had been a consistent publicist for postal reforms.

On shipboard to Europe, Kasson had already drafted regulations to govern city carriers, providing for carrier uniforms and a system of promotions based on time in service. Checking on Miles in London, he sent back an unfavorable report. Miles would not "work either smoothly or safely in official harness," Kasson wrote; he lacked "comprehension and prudence," had more "speed than bottom," was not "well-enough ballasted for an administration involving discretion," was "too impatient both in judgment and action," and would not pay his debts. Kasson's appraisal of Miles was backed up by legation secretary Moran who sprinkled twelve years of his "Journal" with unflattering remarks about "Yahoo" Miles, the "human shrimp tramp." Miles did not return to the Post Office Department in Washington, but died two years later at Malta, en route to report the opening of the Suez Canal.[7]

By May 1 Kasson had moved on to Paris, meeting the French foreign minister, gossiping with Americans, and conferring with gathering postal delegates. Northern diplomats were "in tribulation" over Hooker's retreat at Fredericksburg, and Kasson feared trouble at home from enforcement of conscription unless someone in the War Department had more knowledge of the people and their emotions. Stanton and Halleck, he informed Blair, should be removed. France was having financial difficulties which restrained her from intervention in behalf of the South; the Mexican Affair, regarded as a "waste of money and blood," was unpopular. The United States, Kasson reported, lagged far behind European postal departments in "sagacity and foresight, and in comprehension." At the head of the foreign divisions they had men of "experience and decided ability." In his "Journal," which he was sending to Blair in installments, Kasson promised to record a detailed appraisal of various postal delegates with whom the United States might be negotiating in the future.[8]

Delegates from fifteen nations assembled for conference at the Hotel des Postes on the morning of May 11. All major powers except Russia were represented. Although a few of the delegates had had previous diplomatic experience, most of them were postal experts who possessed a detailed knowledge of international postal communication. The absence of diplomatic maneuvering was conspicuous, and a remarkable spirit of cooperation and harmony prevailed. Only France presented a serious obstacle to the deliberate efforts to attain unanimity on all major decisions.[9]

No one delegate dominated conference proceedings, though much deference was naturally paid to Kasson as the representative of the nation that had initiated the conference. And Kasson throughout the conference showed a keen appreciation of the gossamer thread spun around national interest and international matters. Although consistently supporting advanced proposals, he recognized the limitations of the conference and was willing to compromise for the sake of harmony. Striving for the unanimous acceptance of general principles only, he would make haste slowly and let time and patient negotiations work out the details.

Where discord prevailed, Kasson often let delegates who shared his views do the talking. Particularly he received tactful and effective support from Kern, the Swiss delegate. Behind the scenes in committee, Kasson and Kern worked out the answers to the most knotty problems. In the conference, Kern usually defended committee decisions.

In the opening address, Vandal, French Counsellor of State and Director General of the Posts, paid glowing tribute to the spirit of fusion then permeating international relations. But his definition of conference objectives was disappointingly narrow. The purpose was merely to proclaim certain principles or "speculative doctrines" in the interest of the public and of the "treasuries" of the several countries. "Physical facts belonging to the domain of negotiation" were not to be discussed. Decisions would be binding on no one. To exclude the consideration of "physical facts" would, of course, make it impossible to arrive at acceptable general principles.

At the moment, no one challenged this limitation, and Vandal, upon Kasson's nomination, was made president of the conference. The French delegation then presented thirty specific questions for consideration, including those enumerated by Kasson in his letter of invitation, a list submitted by the British delegate Sir Frederick Hill, and several suggestions from other delegates. To these, Kasson added two additional proposals which in the end were approved by the conference. The first proposed a geographical division of the world into postal zones, each to include the greatest number of countries practicable and each to be assigned a uniform rate of postage. Of all proposals made, this was the most significant and was later to become the core of the Universal Postal Union. Kasson's second proposal called for free official postal communications between the several postal administrations.[10]

During the second session, it became evident that a point by point approach to the agenda in conference as a whole would lead to superfluous and endless discussion. Closely related questions elicited simultaneous comment; delegates jumped from the immediate proposition to questions of special concern farther down the list; and the president could not keep attention focused on a single issue. Consequently early in the third session, the British delegate successfully proposed a subcommittee to formulate decisions for conference discussion. Thereafter answers were reported singly, debated, and voted upon without delay. Kasson was made chairman of this committee of which Kern of Switzerland, Hill of England, Metzner of Prussia, and Maurin of France were members.

All other questions were secondary to the three main problems — uniformity of weight, uniformity of rate, and the simplification or suppression of accounts. Once agreement was reached on these, the others could be easily settled.

On the conference floor, Kasson managed the question of uniform weight. Maintaining that the same scale of weight should indeed be adopted, he proposed the decimal metrical system as the best scale. He described the advantages of this system in detail and criticized his own government for not having adopted it as a national standard of weights and measures. The delegates readily accepted the metric system as a uniform scale of weight, but the selection of a specific rate of progression drew considerable debate. In the committee Kasson had favored a rate of fifteen grams, which, after considerable French opposition, was approved in conference.

The major problem of establishing a uniform rate for overland and ocean transit engendered animated discussion. No such rate could be established without at least temporary financial loss to some postal department. Through France, the favorite entrepôt to Europe, more foreign mail passed in transit than through any other country, and unlike other postal systems, the French postal department was subordinated to the treasury department. The touchy nature of this problem had caused frequent postponement, until finally at the fifth session the Italian delegate boldly proposed to abolish all transit charges accruing to intermediate offices. The favored geographical position of a nation, he declared, should no longer be an obstacle to the direct exchange of closed mail, the reduction of rates, and the increase of correspondence the world over.

At this point the committee came up with a compromise solution. The overland transit rate within a nation should never be higher than one-half its domestic rate; small nations should charge even less. For ocean transportation the cost claimed by one nation from another should never be higher than the rate charged upon its own correspondence for similar conveyance. In committee, the French delegate declared himself "incompetent to discuss" this problem. On the floor, he insisted that it was beyond the power of the conference; it could be handled only as a matter of reciprocity in bilateral treaties; no government would consent to pecuniary sacrifices without a *quid pro quo*.

French objections were answered by Kern, Kasson, and the Italian delegate. Kern declared the conference competent to deal with the matter, quoting from Kasson's letter of invitation that transit charges "overland and on the sea ought to be established on a uniform basis." Kasson maintained that the transit rate was inseparable from the problem of the suppression of accounts and that the committee meant to establish only a maximum rate, not an absolute one. He dismissed as impracticable the Italian proposal to abolish both intermediate transit rates and accounts.[11] In the end the committee proposal was accepted, but only after the Swiss delegate had replaced Vandal in the chair in order to put the matter to vote. The proposal to suppress accounts also met French opposition and also ended with a compromise — a pledge that accounts should be simplified as much as possible.

By June 8, after a total of nine sessions, thirty-four specific issues had been discussed and accord reached upon thirty-one. At the final session, devoted in the main to oratory extolling the importance of the conference, Kasson made a felicitous address of thanks on behalf of the United States. Nine-tenths of the commerce and nineteen-twentieths of the correspondence of the world had been represented at the conference, he declared. Conference recommendations, if adopted by the respective states, would increase foreign correspondence, augment foreign and national trade, and sustain merchant marines. The improvement of international postal facilities was a precursor of international peace and prosperity, he predicted. The Swiss delegate officially closed the conference with praise of Kasson's "liberal and conciliatory spirit constantly shown." [12]

The thirty-one articles approved were not binding upon the participating powers; they were merely general principles recommended for approval by various postal departments. Concrete results depended wholly upon their future incorporation in treaties.

Blair was enthusiastic over the outcome and instructed Kasson to open negotiations for postal conventions based on conference recommendations. Kasson immediately approached the French government but encountered evasion and delay. While awaiting a reply, he met the Italian Director General of the Posts at Turin, where they easily worked out a treaty embodying generally the conference principles. Back in Paris early in July, Kasson submitted to the French government a treaty project through the American minister, William L. Dayton. Along with the project, Kasson informed Dayton that he did not believe the French were disposed to accept fundamental changes for improvement. Unfortunately, Dayton transmitted both Kasson's project and letter to the French foreign minister, who denied that the French were unwilling to negotiate along liberal lines. Vandal, he declared, had put Kasson off while engaged in negotiating with Switzerland and Denmark.[13]

But Kasson, eager to return home, did not follow up the French treaty. In Paris he found Unionists rejoicing. On July 4, Vicksburg had fallen, and Lee's army had been sent reeling back from Gettysburg. Now, Kasson wanted to hurry home to build political fences and share in turning the political tide for the Lincoln administration.

Heading for Washington early in August, Kasson again passed through the American legation in London. Again Secretary Moran appraised him. Kasson had been "much improved by his trip, having lost a great deal of his unpleasant and forward manner." Moran, in the meantime, had been to Paris and had dined with Kasson and the Union preacher-propagandist, Henry Ward Beecher, at the American legation.[14]

☆ ☆ ☆

The Paris Postal Conference was the Universal Postal Union in swaddling clothes. Formally established eleven years later, the Universal Postal Union has been one of the most successful and enduring experiments in international cooperation.

For the United States, isolationist and torn by political strife and war, to initiate and participate in this conference was at the same time a startling innovation in our foreign policy and a harbinger of our fast developing new relationship to the rest of the world. International conferences not concerned with the results of war were without numerous precedents in 1863, and the United States had yet to participate officially in such a conference.[15]

Although the currents of internationalism surged strongly in Europe in the sixties, America pursued an official policy of hands off, refusing to adhere either to an international code of merchant marine signals or a sanitary Red Cross convention. It was unwise, according to an official pronouncement, for us to become a party to instruments to which there were "too many other parties." [16] The Paris Conference was, therefore, a fissure in this hard-shell attitude of isolation, which four years later was opened a little wider by our participation in another Paris conference, this time assembled to standardize the system of weights, measures, and coinage. Again Kasson was to be a key figure behind this conference. In Congress, he was to launch a House committee on weights, measures, and coinage, to become its chairman, and to help push through an appropriation to finance a delegate to Paris. Within a quarter century our participation in nonpolitical international conferences would become commonplace.

In 1874, twenty nations assembled at Berne, Switzerland, to confirm in a general treaty the postal principles recommended at Paris. During the intervening years, Kasson had returned to Europe on another postal mission and had worked out a number of postal conventions embodying the Paris recommendations. But at the Berne Conference, the German postal reformer, Heinrich von Stefan, was clearly the dominating figure. Having promoted a second conference for many years, von Stefan arrived with a detailed project for a world union, which was adopted as the basis of the Universal Postal Union.

The general treaty carried Kasson's recommendation to divide the world into postal zones much further than he had anticipated. Today all contracting nations form a single postal territory over which mail may be dispatched at a low and uniform rate. Not only is the rate of transit uniform; transit is guaranteed throughout the Union, and the cost is borne by the country of origin. Each postal administration keeps the total sum it collects, and there is no necessity for a complicated system of accounts.[17]

Heinrich von Stefan is recognized by posterity as the father of the Universal Postal Union. In the general accounts of the origin of the Union, Kasson's name is seldom mentioned. First honors for the Paris Conference have usually been accorded to Postmaster General Blair, who himself gave full credit to Kasson. "I deem it proper," Blair wrote, "to make known the fact that the public owes the suggestion to invite this international conference to the Honorable John A. Kasson, who represented our government in it with such zeal and ability as to command the thanks and warm approval of his associates."[18] Neither in Iowa nor in the rest of the nation did Kasson's postal activities command much attention. They were submerged by war news, little appreciated, and soon forgotten.

Von Stefan himself modestly summed up the Union's origin: "Ideas are not originated by any single individual. They float in the atmosphere for a whole epoch, at first vaguely, then in a more distinct form, until they condense and precipitate into taking body and life."[19] He might have added, nevertheless, that certain individuals often speed up the process of precipitation. Kasson and von Stefan took the lead in giving the idea "body and life."

It was characteristic of Kasson, when confronted with a problem, to seek its solution. It was his duty to be constructive, and Kasson was by instinct and training duty bound. Three years before his death, in summing up his career, Kasson considered the Paris Conference one of his "proudest achievements."[20] In his long life, plagued with many disappointments and frustrations, this little-heralded conference was indeed one of his most foresighted, satisfying, and fruitful experiences.

A Lincoln Moderate in Congress

POLITICAL WORK hastened John Kasson to Des Moines immediately upon his return from Paris. Iowa Republicans were beginning a campaign in which the governorship, the legislature, and other state offices were at stake. Vicksburg and Gettysburg had brightened party prospects, but a new element, the returning soldier, now actively seeking office, produced an atmosphere of uncertainty.

The nominations for the governorship of Col. William M. Stone (Republican) and Gen. James M. Tuttle (Democrat) were harbingers of the returning soldiers' growing power in Iowa politics. From the first day of the war, officer and politician had been synonymous, but from this point on for a generation the soldiers' claims would have to receive first consideration. Few men could win in a campaign without championing their demands. These were political realities which John A. Kasson, without military experience, would have to face.

Kasson reached Des Moines in late August, just as the canvass got under way. In company with Frank Palmer, he concentrated his efforts in his own congressional district, covering county after county in a buggy, stirring up support for the state ticket, the national administration, and the Union, and participating in a brand of pageantry which left no doubt as to the patriotic sentiments of his constituents nor of his own popularity among them.

In the strong Democratic counties of Decatur and Wayne on the Missouri border, he was accorded a most enthusiastic reception. At Decatur City, 200 mounted ladies, nattily uniformed in red, white, and blue and divided into feminine-officered companies, escorted Kasson to the speaker's rostrum. At Corydon "a beautiful procession of ladies and gentlemen" advanced to meet his carriage; a lovely young lady dressed to represent the flag of union led the procession into town. Behind her rode three other ladies, one dressed in white, one in red, and one in blue; a throng of people fell in behind the carriage, the women among them dressed in patriotic and military motifs. Palmer's *Register* purred with contentment over Kasson's enthusiastic receptions and his "able, logical and convincing" speeches.[1]

Grimes, Harlan, and Kirkwood joined the canvass. Furloughed soldiers took to the stump — Curtis, Chipman, and General Dodge's adjutant, George Tichenor. Even General Dodge, on his way to New York to discuss railroad matters, showed up in Council Bluffs and Des Moines. Hoxie and Withrow concentrated on the soldier vote in the field.[2]

At Council Bluffs, Kasson invaded a Secesh stronghold and there met General Dodge's sister. At Dubuque, at the opposite end of the state, he attended the State Fair and made a two and one-half hour speech at Union League Hall on national affairs, "exciting his hearers to the utmost pitch of enthusiasm." [3]

In the middle of the campaign, Kasson wrote Postmaster General Blair about the canvass (and also about General Dodge). Kasson complained of "badly diminished vigor"; "three years hard service with mind and hand" had begun to tell on him. But his labors had not been in vain; whereas in '62 he had made an "uphill" fight for the President, now he found the people's faith in Lincoln "complete, strong, and deeper than in any man"; the President needed only to "use his powers with utmost vigor" to hold his followers. In the canvass, Kasson was advocating a vigorous war policy, he told Blair. But on the delicate problem of reconstruction, he was veering toward a relatively moderate program under executive leadership.[4]

The election returns in November exceeded the most optimistic expectations. The Republican slate won by majorities ranging above 30,000. Stone's lead doubled that of Kirkwood's two years previously. Year after year the attrition from war issues was whittling away Democratic underpinnings, and Republican possession of Iowa was being confirmed. This election, wrote Kasson, elevated "noble" Iowa "on the pinnacle of glorious states."[5] In all other Northern states, except New Jersey, Republicans victoriously avenged their losses of '62.

While John Kasson campaigned effectively for an unwavering home front for Lincoln, Union, and party, he also continued his activities in behalf of General Dodge, whose aspirations now included not only military but also railroad promotion. Both Hoxie and Mrs. Kasson had reassured Dodge during a lull in Kasson's efforts while he was in Paris: ". . . if we can wait until Kasson comes home," advised Hoxie, "we know we can succeed. Mr. Kasson has more influence with the President than any other member." Upon Hoxie's urging, Cara wrote and poignantly unburdened her grief on the death of her youngest brother at Chancellorsville. "I cannot feel easy until your shoulder wears another star," she also reassured Dodge.[6]

When Kasson reached Des Moines to begin the canvass, a letter from Dodge awaited him. The General was on his way home to recuperate from illness.[7] The time of Dodge's furlough, when all leading politicians would come home for the canvass, was opportune, for both his military and railroad interests could be pushed in person. Chiefly through Rock Island promoters, Dodge had been kept posted on the Pacific railroad developments from the day he had entered the army. In the spring of 1862 he had promised P. R. Reed that, if the pending Pacific railroad bill passed Congress, he would resign from the army and identify himself with that road.[8]

In July, 1862, the long-heralded measure had passed Congress, chartering a Union Pacific Railroad Company and providing it with princely subsidies of federal lands and loans. Four branch lines were to be built from the Missouri River to connect with the main line in central Nebraska. One section of the act authorized the Union Pacific Company to construct a branch line from the western boundary of Iowa to the main line, the starting point to be designated by the President of the United States.[9] Dodge and his Rock Island associates immediately began a campaign to make this Iowa branch the first and main line. The M. & M. eastward through Iowa would thus become a link in the main chain. With real estate and business interests at Council Bluffs, Dodge devoted his energies to having his home town designated as the starting point.

In September, 1862, Judge Baldwin and General Curtis had been on hand in Chicago to see the Union Pacific formally organized. During the following year, the unscrupulous "Doc" Durant of the Rock Island gradually emerged as the most dominant promoter of the company. Stock subscriptions came in slowly because investments were more attractive in other fields, and because company officials were holding out for more favorable terms from the federal government. By the end of the summer in 1863, Durant was ready to launch his program. Union Pacific commissioners were to meet soon in New York; the Iowa terminal point would have to be designated, an engineer hired to start construction, and a lobby turned loose upon the next Congress to work for greater federal subsidies.[10]

When General Dodge reached Council Bluffs in early September to recuperate, he had in his pocket an offer from Durant to become chief engineer for the Union Pacific at $5,000 per year. Within three weeks John Kasson dispatched two important letters to Washington. One urged Lincoln to appoint Judge Caleb Baldwin as a "Presidential Director" of the Pacific railroad; the other (already quoted in part above) urged Postmaster General Blair to persuade Lincoln to order Dodge to Washington for a conference. "I want you to see him and I want the President to talk with him." Kasson did not suggest that the objective of the proposed mission was to be railroad matters. Rather, Dodge's "sound judgment and great experience" would throw light on civil and military affairs in the South. Kasson explained that Dodge had come North "for the first time to restore his shattered health"; Dodge's next address would be the Rock Island office in New York City.[11]

Near the end of September, Kasson, at Council Bluffs for a campaign speech, learned of Dodge's offer from the Union Pacific and of his recent departure for Chicago and New York. After talking with Dodge's brother and friends, Kasson advised the General to stay in the army. "The service of the country is the highest service and I should reluctantly see you leave it until the country is safe," he wrote. But Kasson promised to use the offer to wrest from Lincoln a brigadier-generalship in the regular army.[12]

Dodge went on to New York, conferred with Durant, and returned to his command in mid-October. Another Iowan, Peter A. Dey, received the appointment as engineer on the Union Pacific. Meanwhile, Kasson heard from Blair, who wanted to see Dodge and "would try to have" him ordered to Washington.[13]

In late October, when the Union Pacific stockholders met in New York, Rock Island men took control. Durant, the real power, was made vice-president and general manager. On November 17, Lincoln designated Council Bluffs as the starting point for the Iowa branch. Early in December, cheering crowds from Council Bluffs and Omaha saluted the first spadefuls of earth as the stormy history of Union Pacific construction began. In Washington, Durant's lobbyists with hats in hand were awaiting the arrival of the Congressmen.[14]

The day before Kasson entered his first session of Congress, he wrote Dodge that he was "down in the mouth." Stanton had told him that there were no vacant major-generalships and that General George H. Thomas, the "Rock of Chickamauga," had been given the only vacant brigadiership in the regular army. Kasson promised to see Grimes and Halleck. "I never forget you a single day of my life," he concluded. And as a postscript, Kasson added again: "Hub Hoxie has wanted me to get the place of counsellor to the Pacific R. R. Co. Do you think it worthwhile?"[15]

☆　☆　☆

Cara Kasson, with a "froth of ideas," surveyed the Washington scene as John took his seat in the Thirty-eighth Congress. The "shoddy" new-rich from war speculation now roamed the streets. Ladies' styles were "so capricious," with dresses and cloaks trimmed with epaulettes; the Glengary hat with wings instead of feathers; curls, all the rage; Russian leather muffs and belts; gold and silver butterflies in the hair; while hoops were "beautifully less." Some ladies were introducing the strange custom of leading around "little wretched curly poodles."

In the midst of gaudy richness, salaried people caught by inflation were "cramped in meeting their expenses." But Cara was not complaining. Shoddiness was a necessary concomitant of the "grand revolution." In "new soil many weeds must flourish." Soon Cara was engulfed in the whirl of activities — lectures, concerts, callings, and drives. She and John attended a party given by the officers of the Russian fleet, tasting "marvels of food," and swirling to "intoxicating, bewildering music." Cara also listened to angry debates in Congress over slavery and reconstruction. "The leaven of right is leavening the whole Congress, the country, and the world," she exulted. "That which was once called politics, has become principle, religion!" She was a thorough, idealistic Radical.[16]

When John Kasson took his oath in the Hall of Representatives on December 7, 1863, he perhaps little suspected the difficulty of decision which lay ahead. As a friend of the Blairs, who were fanatically loyal to Lincoln, he was a marked man from the beginning. A great bloc of his constituents was conservative, but Republican leaders in Iowa, his Iowa colleagues in Congress, and the soldiers soon to return would be blown into the Radical camp by the shifting winds of events, policy, and party power. Kasson's wife, his brother-in-law in Congress, and his politically powerful brother-in-law in St. Louis were all more Radical than he. In the House, Kasson was soon to find it difficult to be half-Radical, half-conservative, to work harmoniously with both factions, and to support the mild reconstruction measures of the President. And his efforts to stay in both camps dot his record with spotty inconsistency. Like many other moderates of the time, he was to waver before the whiplash of party discipline wielded by dour old Thad Stevens.

Radical Jacobins considered the autumn elections as a mandate for their policies, and, with swaggering confidence, grimly took their seats to force through their reconstruction measures. The crisis of the war had been passed; Vicksburg and Gettysburg had assured eventual triumph of the Union; old sores would now erupt as problems of restoration were pushed to the top. Behind most activities in this Congress also lurked the presidential nomination coming up the next spring.

Despite the defeats in the congressional elections of '62, the Republicans mustered sufficient strength to organize the House. Schuyler Colfax was elected Speaker. Kasson drew a seat next to another new member, James A. Garfield. Young James G. Blaine also took his seat for the first time. Among old members who monopolized the important committees were Elihu Washburne of Illinois, Kasson's friend of former days; J. S. Morrill of Vermont; H. L. Dawes and T. D. Eliot of Massachusetts; General Robert Schenck of Ohio; and James F. Wilson of Iowa.

Across the aisle sat a group of hard hitting, unterrified Democrats who would see to it that yeas and nays were recorded on nearly every important measure — D. W. Voorhees and W. S. Holman of Indiana; S. J. Randall of Pennsylvania; George Pendleton and S. S. Cox of Ohio; Fernando Wood and James Brooks of New York.

In the van of the Radicals stood fiery young Henry Winter Davis of Maryland, but glowering above all was cynical Thad Stevens, who, with sarcastic invective and great parliamentary skill, was tightening his dictatorship of the House. With unsurpassed ruthlessness, Stevens would combine hatred for the South, idealistic fervor for the Negro, and generous handouts to Northern industrialists into a single program designed to maintain Republican politicians and their allies in power.[17] Woe to the man who dared to oppose him!

John Kasson was assigned to the powerful, first-ranking Ways and Means Committee. But even so, he was number eight in a membership of nine, and he could be watched by Chairman Stevens, who used this committee, loaded with Radicals, to control the House. Kasson was not assigned to the committee on postal affairs, where his rich experience and technical knowledge might have been used with real effect. Nor was he placed on any of the committees dealing with war, reconstruction, the freedmen, or railroads. Early in the session he introduced a resolution providing for a standing committee on national and international coinage, weights, and measures. His experience and interest qualified him for this committee, and he was made chairman. In time he prepared and carried through worth-while legislation legalizing a uniform decimal system of weights and measures. But this committee was not of first importance and did not correspond with Kasson's prominence as an administration leader. In the middle of the session he was put on a select committee to study the feasibility of giving Cabinet members a seat in the House. But the fact that a Democrat, George H. Pendleton, was chairman and Stevens the second ranking member indicates the hollowness of the proposal.[18] Imagine Stevens offering Blair or Seward a House seat!

Kasson was a strong administration man, although he sometimes climbed on the fence before Radical onslaughts. He went to bat for recommendations from Lincoln's department heads — Blair, Seward, and Chase. But in backing Chase's monetary policies, he made it clear on the floor that he was "no political or personal partisan" of the ambitious Secretary whom the Radicals were booming for the presidency. He resisted efforts from both Democrats and Radicals to censure the administration, voted against all resolutions for peace negotiations, and opposed resolutions requiring a definition of war aims. He voted for the Thirteenth Amendment which put Lincoln's Emancipation Proclamation into the Constitution; for the Freedmen's Bureau bill; for the organization of Montana Territory restricting suffrage to whites; for the enlargement of the confiscation act; and he argued for the drafting of free Negroes and slaves as well as white men. He presented to the House a resolution of the Iowa legislature urging equal pay for Negro soldiers and veterans' preference for federal jobs. The Post Office Department had already instituted the practice of veterans' preferences. He protested delay in processing soldiers' claims.[19]

Kasson introduced a resolution for information on a military road from the Platte River to Virginia City in Idaho Territory. He also introduced bills to revise and codify the postal laws, to dispose of captured cotton, to punish counterfeiting, to authorize Chase to sell surplus gold in order to prevent a "corner" from the New York "dens of speculation in which hooked noses, bushy eyebrows and long beards prevailed," and to permit Des Moines to mine coal beds under the Des Moines River.[20] He supported Morrill's tariff measures but grumbled that consumer interests were being neglected. When accused by Brooks of being a Whig, he replied: "No, Sir, I was never a Whig. I was raised a Jackson and Benton Democrat, and hold myself still a reliable exponent of their principles." [21]

He contributed running comments on bills originating from the Ways and Means Committee and managed a few of them on the floor. He bucked Thad Stevens' bill to compensate Pennsylvania for losses (including Stevens' own iron works) incurred from Lee's invasion, until certain Iowa war losses were recognized. He supported a tax on whisky but did not want committee activities to leak to whisky manufacturers who might use the anticipated tax increase as an excuse to raise prices. Stevens accused Kasson of starting a story that Stevens himself was "interested" in whisky and had been tipping off whisky dealers. And Stevens called it a "slander." Over the opposition of Stevens, Kasson put through legislation providing for the coining of one and two cent pieces from copper. He provoked Stevens' sarcasm while managing Seward's diplomatic and consular bill.[22]

Undoubtedly, Kasson would have considered himself a party regular. But Lincoln's proclamation of amnesty and reconstruction which greeted the convening Congress was a dangerous political touchstone as the Radicals, intent on seizing power, joined the issue.

When young Frank Blair stormed into the House, excoriating Chase, lashing Missouri Radicals, and rebuking Iowa delegates for opposing General John M. Schofield, Kasson arose neither on attack nor defense. When the Radicals with their Wade-Davis bill struck out to take over eventually the Southern states as conquered provinces, Kasson did not join in the debates which raged from early March through April, 1864; nor did many other new members. But when time came for the all-important test vote, Kasson wavered, voted for the preamble, and then, on the main bill, climbed up on the nonvoting fence. Two of his Iowa colleagues — Hubbard and Grinnell — also squirmed; when they voted for the final bill "under protest," vindictive Old Thad chided, "I suppose I ought to say that I refused to vote under protest." The bill was not yet strong enough for Stevens.[23]

The attitude of Iowa Republicans toward Lincoln during this session is filled with interest. Indications are that Lincoln's mild reconstruction plan when proclaimed on December 8, 1863, was then heartily accepted. Grimes endorsed it; so did both the incoming and outgoing governors. At the grass roots in Iowa the President's popularity was unquestioned. But the Wade-Davis vote foreshadowed a gradual shift among party leaders. Senators Harlan and Grimes and Congressmen Wilson, Allison, and Price voted for the measure apparently without qualms. And, prior to Lincoln's surprising, smashing re-election the following fall both Grimes and Allison were to take an undercover anti-Lincoln stand.[24] Allison, in the House, voted more consistently Radical than any of his colleagues. Although other factors may lurk behind the shift, the fierce lash of Radical party discipline on Capitol Hill was almost irresistible. Kasson might as well have voted against the Wade-Davis bill; his failure to vote for it was enough to cause the Radicals to whet the scalping knife. But so long as the President and the Postmaster General remained in power, Kasson was safe.

In this session, Kasson delivered no maiden speech. Among his Iowa colleagues he was overshadowed by James F. Wilson, who, with seniority and great natural ability, was chairman of the powerful Judiciary Committee. But in intellectual ability and breadth of knowledge on varied legislation, Kasson stood above all his Iowa fellow House members. He could be a ready debater, possessing the talent "to think clearly and continuously on his feet"; he spoke tersely "with sustained nervous fluency and with a voice whose volume and cut . . . filled all parts of the hall." Legislation was a "business with him," and he worked indefatigably on the committees.[25] He clearly belonged to the moderate wing of his party; his Iowa colleagues were clearly veering toward the Radical wing.

Contrary to what one might have expected, Kasson played no leading part in railroad legislation. He voted against the Stevens-sponsored subsidies for the Northern Pacific, the rival of the Union Pacific.[26] But in the struggle to amend the Pacific Railway Act of 1862 and increase the subsidies for the Union Pacific, he was cautious. Early in the session, a select committee on the Pacific railroad was set up with Stevens as chairman. Hiram Price, a railroader of long standing, not Kasson, was Iowa's member on this committee; a man named Oakes Ames represented Massachusetts. At this time, it will be remembered, "Doc" Durant's construction crew was breaking first ground at Council Bluffs.

But while the committee worked on a bill, Dodge was stunned to learn from his brother that Cedar Rapids interests were trying to change the M. & M. so as to miss Council Bluffs and Des Moines. Could Durant be trusted? At once W. B. Allison introduced a bill requiring the connecting route to run through these two towns. Dodge, in the dark as to why Allison instead of Kasson sponsored the measure, wrote Kasson for an explanation. H. M. Hoxie, always closer to Dodge than was Kasson on railroad matters, was at that time in the East; Kasson let him answer Dodge's letter. Allison introduced the bill, explained Hoxie, because he was on "the land committee and we want to commit him to its [the bill's] provisions." A week earlier, James F. Wilson had advised Judge Baldwin "to rest easy": "under no circumstances will we permit the M. & M. to leave Council Bluffs." Thus, the ubiquitous Hoxie, though admitting that railroad matters were "mixed up," had lined up two additional Iowa Congressmen behind Dodge's interests. Hoxie also assured Dodge that Council Bluffs would be protected.

Earlier, Hoxie had informed Dodge that he had written Durant to learn what "the Doctor" wanted "done with the Iowa legislature." Durant was so busy "making money on the curbstone in Wall Street" that he had ignored the legislature and the governor. If Durant was negligent of lobby work in Iowa, Dodge was not. Dodge's adjutant, Lieutenant George Tichenor, was in Des Moines, and reported that the legislature then in session was under control; it had taken no action against the M. & M.[27]

When Allison's bill came to a vote, Kasson pushed through an amendment denying the company any lands unless twenty miles had been constructed within a year. The M. & M. had been notoriously slow in building the road from Iowa City to Des Moines. The amendment passed and so did the bill, in late April, 1864.[28]

Meanwhile, in March, Durant had begun negotiations for the charter rights of a Pennsylvania construction company called the Crédit Mobilier. In April, H. M. Hoxie, who had returned to Des Moines, showed up again in New York and Washington.[29]

In mid-June, Stevens reported the Pacific Railway Act of 1864. The "Great Barbecue" was well under way. Never before had the federal government been so generous to a private corporation. The staggering land grant of '62 was doubled. Old loan features were maintained, but nonrailroad bonds and government loans were to be secured by second mortgages on railroad property, not first mortgages as had been provided in '62. Kasson's friend, Washburne of Illinois, and Democrat Holman of Indiana, attacked the bill as needlessly extravagant. Washburne bluntly stated that "one individual" controlled the Union Pacific; the "real management" was in the hands of "wall street jobbers." He called out the names of some of the lobbyists. At an evening session, when final vote on the bill was expected, "an excited and animated scene" greeted the House. The lobby was mustered in full force; galleries were packed with people, "male and female," interested in the measure; corridors were filled; "shysters and adventurers" crowded into the seats of members on the House floor, according to Washburne.

Kasson was present at this session and voted against Holman's

amendment to require the company to transport government troops
and supplies free. But when the main bill passed by an overwhelming
majority a few days later, he did not vote. From early June until the
end of the session on July 2 Kasson was repeatedly reported to be sick.
But Washburne's attack and the frenzied lobby activities may have
made him wary of the whole thing. Hoxie, not Kasson, had assumed
major responsibility for Dodge's railroad promotion.[30]

But throughout the session Kasson unrelentingly jabbed away at
Dodge's military promotion, writing and calling on Lincoln and
Halleck, watching for vacancies in the army, and enlisting the aid of
Grimes, Blair, and Grant. Hoxie kept Dodge posted: "Kasson has
been indefatigable, worked every day, and he is a tower of strength.
He is about the only Lincoln man in our [congressional] delegation
and could therefore do more than all else."

Finally, Lincoln's close friend, General Richard J. Oglesby, the
man who had dramatically launched Lincoln before the country as
the Railsplitter, was pulled in. Oglesby journeyed to Washington,
"became acquainted with Grimes and Mr. and Mrs. Kasson," talked
the matter over "freely" with Lincoln, and later vowed (according to
Hoxie) that he would resign if Dodge were not promoted.

In early June, Kasson wrote joyfully to Dodge: "Thanks to Dick
Oglesby . . . you are fully and fairly nominated major general. . . .
My dear friend, God save you and keep you. . . . I often want an
hour's talk with you to regain courage and confidence in myself." [31]

Major General Dodge now stood triumphantly on the top rung of
the military ladder. He could go no further without a special act of
Congress. His later boasts that he never once sought his own promotion must be dismissed as Gilded Age false pretension and Dodge pon-
tification. Not by chance had success smiled benignantly upon him.

Although Kasson realistically depended upon Dodge's political support and implicitly trusted Dodge's political loyalty, his unswerving
and effective activities in behalf of Dodge's military advancement
cannot be dismissed as purely political. In Kasson's letters there is a
ring of sincerity, of appreciation, and of patriotic fervor which also
must be considered when assessing the Dodge-Kasson relationship.

In the meantime, General Dodge had found the key to financial
success also. In February, he announced newly found wealth to his
brother Nathan, who cautioned Dodge to keep the good news within
the family; the General should neither build a new home nor other-

wise make an ostentatious display of his wealth. Nathan went about bailing from debt the Dodge business firm and, in the same month, wrote for $5,000 to invest in the name of the General's wife.[32] The source of this new wealth is a mystery and a problem worthy of challenge to a badly needed Dodge biographer.

Kasson's hand in the renomination of Lincoln, although by no means crystal clear, is more discernible than that of his reticent Iowa congressional colleagues. If the matter had been left to the Republican majority in Congress, perhaps Chase, zealously using his treasury patronage for himself, would have been chosen. But political managers in the states, closer to the rank and file and many of them owing their federal jobs to the administration, stood between Lincoln and the Radicals. Lincoln men were quietly at work early in 1864. Obviously their best strategy was to use the powerful federal patronage to line up delegates to the state conventions. Here at the grass roots, in defiance of Radical plans, resolutions endorsing the President could start the band wagon rolling. Here delegates to the national nominating convention could be pledged.

Day after day, with these aims in mind and with implacable hate for Chase and the Radicals, Montgomery Blair contacted his loyal postmasters. It is not too much to suspect that Kasson, a popular and frequent visitor at the Post Office Department, was a party to Blair's operations. In the House, Kasson put himself on public record as opposed to Chase. In Iowa he was in a position to be effective: Marshal Hoxie was a member of the national committee; Thomas Withrow was chairman of the state committee.[33]

In mid-January, Kasson told Hoxie to postpone until February his trip to Washington, anticipated earlier. Apparently there was more work for Hoxie in Iowa. On February 2 Withrow called the state convention to choose national delegates. On February 14 Polk County instructed its delegates to the state convention to support Lincoln.[34] On February 22 the state convention at Des Moines endorsed Lincoln's war policies and measures, chose national delegates, and instructed them to vote as a unit for Lincoln; on the same day a Republican convention in Blair's Maryland duplicated the Iowa performance; and also on the same day the Union National (Republican) committee, Marshal Hoxie now participating in its deliberations, met in Washington and endorsed Lincoln four to one. The facts leading to these dramatic endorsements of the Railsplitter, all falling on Washington's birthday, suggest that there was more than coincidence behind them and in Kasson's connection with them. Certainly the Lincoln band wagon rolled faster over frustrated Radical ambitions; one state convention after another climbed on behind the President.[35]

Kasson hardly let the ink dry on the Iowa convention resolutions before he presented them to Lincoln with his compliments. And a little later, "for the benefit" of his district, he courteously asked the privilege of appointing two federal officers usually "disposed of by the President." "If public service and friendship for the President and some reputation as a supporter of the Republican organization, afford any claim to recognition," he pleaded, "I trust this request will prove agreeable." [36]

En route to the national convention, the Iowa delegates stopped in Washington. The entire congressional delegation, now having swung into line, joined them in a love call upon the President. Arriving at Baltimore, the delegates found that their fellow member, "Hub" Hoxie, had arranged "tip-top" accommodations for them at the Eutaw House — abundant proof of Kasson's previous recommendation that Hoxie was a good convention man. At the Eutaw House also was the powerful New York delegation, already committed to Lincoln and headed by Henry J. Raymond, Kasson's former schoolmate at the University of Vermont. Now editor of the New York *Times* and official biographer of Lincoln, Raymond was becoming Lincoln's "political lieutenant general." Hoxie had put his men up at the right place.[37]

The convention opened June 7, 1864. Angry Congressmen swarmed around, most of them opposed to Lincoln, or, at least, to "that kite with the Blair family for the tail." There is no evidence that John Kasson was present but much evidence that he was then confined to his rooms in Washington by illness. Iowa delegates were in "good spirits," agreeing that "a radical programme and Mr. Lincoln" would win.[38]

Henry J. Raymond, the leading member of the resolutions committee, dished up a platform with political trimming reminiscent of Kasson's cookery at Chicago four years previously. It "had something for everybody." It had Radical flavor but was fundamentally conservative, and it avoided the explosive issue of reconstruction.

Raymond led the Lincoln forces on the floor, and he shrewdly maneuvered the nomination of Andrew Johnson (Lincoln's man) for the vice-presidency. Governor Stone of Iowa conspicuously jumped up several times to press the unanimous selection of Lincoln and Johnson. In the end, popular enthusiasm for the sagacious, wily man in the White House was too emphatic, and his control of the convention through federal patronage too tight, for the Radicals to resist.[39]

The President's renomination had never been seriously threatened, but re-election was another matter. His ability to overcome the handicaps of military stalemate and war weariness, and to win the election over Radical Fremont and War Democrat McClellan, was so doubtful as to inspire the most vigorous efforts from loyal Lincoln men.[40]

During the spring and early summer, while John Kasson remained in Washington, Montgomery Blair prepared to convert the Post Office Department into a vast agency for the distribution of campaign literature, especially among the soldiers. In early July, Iowa officeholders in Washington organized the Iowa Association for the main purpose of disseminating campaign documents. H. M. Hoxie's brother, probably a Kasson appointee, held the position as a clerk in the Post Office Department. Again, it is not too much to suggest that Kasson probably had a hand in these arrangements despite his illness.[41]

Throughout June, Kasson received favorable reports on his own renomination for Congress as counties chose delegates pledged to him. General M. M. Crocker, suffering from a fatal illness in Des Moines, predicted Kasson's success "without a dissenting voice"; A. J. Bell of Council Bluffs, half-owner of three newspapers, and a possible future rival, advised the retention of Kasson until he could be put into the Senate. Bell, however, doubted that Lincoln could carry Pottawattamie County. H. M. Hoxie foresaw Kasson's nomination "by acclamation," despite a "little envy" in Washington from Harlan and Wilson with their eyes on the next senatorial election.[42]

At Winterset on July 5, 1864, the congressional convention unanimously renominated Kasson without a "murmur." General Crocker presided, and the committee on resolutions, with Marshal Hoxie as the chairman, heartily endorsed Kasson's course in Congress. There was no evidence that his equivocation on the Wade-Davis bill had injured him. Iowans at home were not yet as Radical as Iowans in Washington.

A Union (Republican) state convention at Des Moines two days later nominated minor state candidates and chose Hoxie to succeed Withrow as chairman of the state central committee.[48] Kasson men in the second Lincoln campaign were riding high. His schoolmate of yesteryear, Henry J. Raymond, was head of the Union National (Republican) Committee.

While Hoxie prepared for a "hard" canvass, Kasson pressed Lincoln to promote General Dodge's friend, Colonel John A. Williamson. "If satisfied with his military deserts, I beg to assure the President that [Colonel Williamson's promotion] will be most beneficial to us in Iowa." [44]

Early in August, a few weeks before the canvass commenced, Kasson reached Des Moines; he was still "not well." By late August he had recovered sufficiently to witness the nomination of General George B. McClellan by the Democrats in Chicago. At a great Union meeting there following, Kasson made one of the principal speeches on the theme that "Peace now is disunion forever." A week later, at a Union meeting in St. Louis, he admonished bitter Missouri factions to bury the hatchet and support Lincoln. B. R. Pegram, Dodge's former business associate, heard the "big speech" and observed: "He talks well but I hardly think his man [Lincoln] will win this time." A few days later, Kasson was back at Davenport, conferring with General Dodge and probably with Senator Grimes.[45]

About July 1 General Dodge had written his father: ". . . I think that I shall quit military life. I have struggled up about as high as I can go, against ill-health and with but few influential friends." But Sherman's army, of which his corps was a part, had drawn up before Atlanta a few weeks later, and Dodge had been wounded in the head while peeping at the enemy through a hole in a log fortification. Now he was returning home to convalesce. At Davenport he pressed certain Iowa politicians to do something for him. Hoxie wrote: "Grimes, Kasson, and Allison all promised to look after the matter and I believe Grimes is in earnest. Kasson will do everything in his power for you. Allison also — but he don't amount to much in that way." The first week in October, Dodge headed for New York to confer with "Doc" Durant.[46]

In midsummer H. M. Hoxie had also gone to New York to see Durant at a Saratoga meeting of Union Pacific managers. In August, Hoxie had been granted a contract by the Union Pacific to lay the first hundred miles of track west from Omaha. And before Dodge left for New York, Hoxie had turned over his contract, with the number of miles to be constructed increased, to "Doc" Durant and the Crédit Mobilier of America. In return he was to receive $5,000 cash and $10,000 stock in the Union Pacific. The Hoxie contract provided the handsome sum of $50,000 for each mile of railroad constructed. The upright Peter A. Dey of Iowa City, who thought it could be done for $20,000 a mile, soon submitted his resignation as Union Pacific engineer — "the best position in my profession this country has ever offered to any man." Under Durant, the Union Pacific Railroad Company and the Crédit Mobilier Construction Company had become one and the same. By voting themselves lucrative construction contracts, stockholders of the former could realize dividends from the latter staggering to the imagination. In time it was to be revealed that Mrs. Grenville M. Dodge, not her husband, possessed a hundred shares of stock in the Crédit Mobilier.[47]

Meanwhile, Kasson returned to Des Moines, and from mid-September to the November elections, he canvassed his district and other parts of the state as he had done in '62 and '63. His Democratic adversary, D. M. McHenry, a former Kentucky judge, lacked the strength exhibited by D. O. Finch two years previously. From all accounts, he was no match for Kasson on the stump. Their speeches grew personal near the end of the canvass; each accused the other of having been a slaveowner. When Kasson maintained that he had bought a slave girl in St. Louis in order to set her free, McHenry wired the clerk of the court for a record of manumission, which could not be located. Kasson then also wired; the deed was found and published in Iowa newspapers. But Kasson did not prove that he had bought her merely to free her.[48]

The election in Iowa proved to be a Union (Republican) landslide. Kasson rolled up a lead of more than 6,000 over McHenry. All his Iowa colleagues were returned to Congress by wide margins, and Lincoln carried the state by almost 40,000.[49]

In September the fall of Atlanta, Farragut's victory at Mobile, and the sacrifice of Montgomery Blair to the Radicals for Fremont's withdrawal had helped swing the tide to Lincoln.[50] With Blair out of the Cabinet, Kasson had lost powerful influence; but the President's position seemed supreme as Kasson returned to take his seat in the second session of the Thirty-eighth Congress. Yet the crack of a pistol, the

tearing thud of a bullet would remove this last great barrier from
the long frustrated, hate ridden, hard charging Radicals.

Cara Kasson found Washington more wicked than ever during the
winter of 1864-1865. She heard of "opium eating, of arsenic eating,
of whiskey drinking." In the "air of intense fashions," ladies' styles
were "dashing," "extravagant." Half-dressed, penniless Negroes clustered in nearby Judiciary Square. Congress was "crazed with work
. . . night sessions, Sunday committee meetings — everything that can
possibly wear and tear a poor Representative's head to pieces." Cara's
calls upon Cabinet ladies had become an "unmitigated bore." Her
heart grew sick from the "hot house intensity of the moral atmosphere." [51]

John Kasson perhaps found this session of Congress more to his
liking than the preceding one. Everywhere the Southern Confederacy
was disintegrating. Lee's army was tightly contained around Richmond and Petersburg, and Sherman was racing through Georgia. One
more campaign each from Grant, from Sherman, and from Thomas
bade fair to end the war.

Moreover, there were surface signs that the Radicals had been chastened by Lincoln's great victory. The opening of Congress resembled
a remarriage feast, with Radicals pretending that the President was
now the best of all Radicals. They congratulated themselves that in
the fall election they had saved him from the Copperheads. Stevens,
still the power behind the Republicans in the House, was less inclined
to crack the lash of party discipline.

Lincoln now threw his decisive strength behind the Thirteenth
Amendment, which in the preceding session had cleared the Senate
but had fallen short of the requisite two-thirds majority in the
House.[52] Through January, 1865, debates on this measure occupied
the House and attracted excited galleries. Now John Kasson on January 10 threw himself into the debates in a "maiden" and "record"
speech. Despite heavy rainfall, the gallery was filled as he arose to
talk. His speech having been previously announced, many Iowans
were among the spectators. He countered charges that administration
pressure had been exerted on members by pointing to the amendment's
endorsement in the Baltimore platform. In joint debate, it had been
discussed on the stump the previous fall "in every one of the twenty-

three counties" of his own district; and so throughout the loyal states. Citing expressions from Jefferson, Madison, Washington, Patrick Henry, and Edmund Randolph, Kasson cogently defended the emancipation amendment on the grounds that it was both constitutional and sound public policy. The speech was carefully prepared and closely argued. Kasson parried thrusts from Democrats Mallory and Cox with skill. By both contemporaries and historians, this speech has been described as noteworthy, strong, and effective. When he sat down, congratulating House members crowded around him. For publicity purposes, nearly 9,000 copies of the short speech were separately printed. The next day, Kasson's brother-in-law, Rev. W. G. Eliot, gave "thanks to Almighty God" before a Missouri state convention which passed a resolution urging emancipation. Three weeks later, federal emancipation, considered a Radical measure in '61, passed the House.[53]

With Lincoln giving ground, the Radicals charged in to write their own reconstruction bill along Wade-Davis lines; and, in order to guarantee permanent Republican control, they planned to slip in Negro suffrage to boot. The bill would have undone the President's restoration work under his moderate "ten percent plan," already maturing in Arkansas, Tennessee, and Louisiana; it would have taken reconstruction out of the hands of the President and put it into the hands of Congress. Against this Radical thrust for power John Kasson unequivocally stood up and let himself be counted. All his Iowa colleagues supported it. James F. Wilson and T. D. Eliot (Eliot, it will be remembered, was Cara's brother and John's former law partner at New Bedford) took leading roles in managing the bill on the floor.[54]

On the other hand, Kasson voted for Eliot's bill to enlarge the functions of the Freedmen's Bureau. He supported Eliot's motion to table a resolution referring to Wilson's Judiciary Committee the question of seating the Louisiana representatives then knocking at the House door. He hotly denied the charge of Wilson and Price that, during Stevens' absence, the Ways and Means Committee, in recommending appropriations, had fallen under the domination of Lincoln's department heads. He voted against a resolution by Davis of Maryland that Congress should have concurrent power in the recognition of foreign nations. He did not vote on Davis' resolution to abrogate the Canadian reciprocity treaty of 1854.[55]

At one time Kasson seems to have served the purposes of the Radical committee on the conduct of the war by presenting a memorial from a New York *Tribune* correspondent charging that General Grant had suppressed three letters covering the dismissal from the James River command of a Radical favorite, General Ben Butler. But more probably, Kasson was merely responding to a request from an acquaintance, Samuel Wilkeson, the memorialist.[56]

There were no clashes with Stevens on the floor as in the past session, although Frank Palmer's *Register* grumbled that Kasson had been elbowed off the Ways and Means subcommittee on appropriations, which, dominated by Stevens and Morrill, gave the "Great West little part in shaping financial measures and currency medium." [57]

But Kasson did clash with the Radical Secretary of War, Edwin M. Stanton, over the promotion of Colonel J. A. Williamson of the Fourth Iowa Regiment. It has been seen above that Kasson had pressed Williamson's case upon the President prior to the fall elections. He had made it clear that favorable action from Lincoln would probably beget favorable political action in Iowa. In time, with an order from Lincoln for Williamson's promotion, Kasson called on Stanton, who seized the order, angrily refused to execute it, and kept it. Kasson departed, promising himself to open up on Stanton some day in the House forum. A few days later Lincoln gave Kasson another order which was processed at the War Department during Stanton's absence, and Williamson's promotion was duly confirmed by the Senate.

Finally, one morning, Kasson walked into the House to find Stanton under fire for his arbitrary confinement of prisoners in the Old Capitol prison. With Thad Stevens defending Stanton, Kasson jumped into the fray, denouncing the Secretary's "arbitrary frame of mind," his "tyrannical course," his disobedience to the President, and his disrespect for "a representative of the people." By an overwhelming vote the House passed a resolution to investigate Stanton's arbitrary imprisonments, as one member after another blasted away at the unpopular Secretary then visiting fallen Savannah. Kasson received congratulatory letters for helping dramatize Stanton's "outrages." But Joseph Medill, fiery Radical editor of the Chicago *Tribune,* who had called Montgomery Blair "a d—d old wind-broken mule" in comparison with "full blooded courser" Chase, attacked Kasson so severely that Frank Palmer had to come to his rescue in the pages of the *Register.*[58]

At the Executive Mansion, Kasson was accorded more favorable receptions. The next time he saw Lincoln, the President (according to Kasson many years later) "showed his gratification in his peculiar and familiar manner, by his twinkling eyes, and by his slapping me on the thigh, as I thought quite unnecessarily." [59]

Kasson had attended a White House levee, taking along two of his constituents, Captains James H. Knox and Lewis Todhunter, both from Warren County near Des Moines. Knox, a former Baltimorean, was also editor of the Indianola *Weekly Iowa Visitor*. At the Winterset convention he had moved Kasson's unanimous renomination for Congress. When Kasson introduced Todhunter, Lincoln replied that he once knew some Todhunters in Illinois. Knox's quick observation, that Lincoln had once been a "Todd-hunter" (Todd was the maiden name of Mrs. Lincoln), brought "hearty laughter" from the President. Kasson then introduced Knox as the first man to hoist Lincoln's name on the masthead of his paper for re-election, and the President asked his name a second time so that he would not forget it. That night "Old Abe" wore a claw-hammer coat and white kid gloves. To an Iowa observer, he "looked about as awkward as a Pottawatomie in a meeting house." [60]

Prior to his brush-off from Stanton, Kasson early in the session had called at the War Department in behalf of General Dodge. Kasson was "astonished and gratified" when Stanton greeted him with "Dodge is ordered to take the Department of Missouri in the place of Rosecrans." This was essentially what Kasson had previously proposed, but he attributed the change to Grant. [61]

To have a command in the West beyond the Mississippi, where railroads were to be built through unexploited country, had been an ambition of Dodge almost as old as the war itself. In the spring and summer of 1862, following the battle of Pea Ridge, he had shown interest in a Kansas assignment, and Kasson had pulled wires for him in Washington. [62]

In the early autumn of 1864, it will be remembered, Dodge had returned to Iowa, and at Davenport had pressed Kasson and Grimes for a political favor. While convalescing from a wound, he had gone to New York for a conference with Thomas C. Durant. Fresh from this conference, Dodge had visited with Grant for a week at City Point, Virginia; next he was in Washington conferring with Lincoln; then he journeyed to Nashville and there awaited further orders. These conferences had taken place while Kasson campaigned in Iowa.

Early in December, as the short session of the Thirty-eighth Congress opened, Stanton and Kasson informed Dodge of his new command over the Department of Missouri. Dodge's visits to Grant and Lincoln had not been social calls. The Department of Kansas was now merged with the Department of Missouri, and Dodge moved his headquarters to Fort Leavenworth.[63] From this point he could use federal troops and scouting parties to explore the western country and to clear it of hostile Indians in preparation for the building of the Union Pacific.

When Kasson learned of Dodge's new command, he immediately wrote Hoxie, who was in Washington for the opening of Congress. Hoxie showed Kasson's letter to Durant, who said, "Dodge can help me now." Durant was running into competition from the Kansas branch of the Pacific railroad.[64]

Missouri Radicals in Congress, including Senator B. Gratz Brown, now descended upon Kasson. Believing him to be responsible for Dodge's new post, they urged him to line Dodge up behind their Radical program including Negro suffrage. Kasson told them that Dodge would "seek to pacify Missouri, suppress guerillas, and restore order"; Dodge "would work for the country, not for the newspapers"; Dodge "would not touch negro suffrage"; it was a "local question" to be decided by Missourians. All this was indirect advice to the new commander of Missouri, but Kasson proceeded to give more. Rosecrans had been too "Jesuitical," talking to both factions "as their respective adherent"; Rosecrans had "loved pleasure and society more than he loved work, and loved flattery more than either." "The true policy" was "to hear all parties without talk . . . to let acts talk."

Kasson recommended to Dodge's consideration the advice of "two honest men in St. Louis — well informed and of true patriotism, and without flattery and uncontrolled by any personal schemes." The first was Kasson's brother-in-law, Rev. Dr. W. G. Eliot, who was "thoughtful and prudent and knew how to keep counsel." The other was James E. Yeatman, humanitarian president of the Western Sanitary Commission.[65] Erroneously, Kasson believed Eliot a moderate, and, through him, hoped in vain to steer Dodge on a moderate course through the stormy crags of Missouri politics. Hoxie took a different tack: "Let the Missouri Radicals have no cause for complaint against you and all will be well." [66]

Dodge proceeded to pacify Missouri with military dispatch, and within a month angry remonstrances against his alleged repressive

measures reached Washington. Kasson took one of Dodge's explanatory letters to Lincoln. He urged the President not to counteract
Dodge without hearing Dodge's own side of controversies. "If you
see trouble ahead," Kasson wrote Dodge, "let Grimes or me know in
advance." Kasson promised to "keep straight" the editor of the
Missouri Democrat. He wrote Dodge to send his aide, George Tichenor, to see "an old Iowan," now editor of the German *Missouri Radical,*
and also another Iowan who worked in the office of the *Evening
News.*[67]

A person using the pen name of "Mack" wrote from St. Louis to
the Des Moines *Register* that Kasson was "a great favorite in St. Louis."
"Mack" also lauded Dr. Eliot as a "quiet, modest, and a sensible abolitionist" whose influence was powerfully exerted in the St. Louis social,
religious, and political world. He wielded "powerful influence" and
helped "shape the course of our best and soundest politicians." [68]

While Missouri seethed with factional hatred in late February, 1865,
John Kasson as a member of the inaugural committee busied himself
with the details of Lincoln's second inauguration. Washington was
filling up with spectators and office seekers. Rumors flew around that
Senator Harlan was to join Lincoln's cabinet as Secretary of the Interior, that C. C. Nourse was to become federal attorney for Iowa, and
that Peter Melendy was to succeed H. M. Hoxie as federal marshal.

Hoxie, in Washington looking after railroad interests, found
"bussle [*sic*] and confusion" as the session of Congress ended. Durant
was putting pressure on him to leave politics. Hoxie informed Dodge
that Kasson stood "in the eyes of the departments and all members
ahead of all others in the lower House. Allison told me he could not
get a place, that Grimes and Kasson carried off the things if they
wanted to. . . . Hubbard and Price are in the same fix." [69]

A slow drizzle greeted the capital on the morning of March 4. By
nine, Cara Kasson stood among the rain drenched spectators on Capitol Hill, and at eleven she pushed her way into the Senate gallery to a
"splendid front seat." Thousands of "jabbering ladies" crowded
around her. While the Senate, the President, the Supreme Court, and
the diplomatic corps nervously awaited, handsome Charles Sumner
pointed his finger "gravely and rigidly" at the twittering ladies, in a
vain effort to silence them. Andrew Johnson dramatically arose and
took the oath as Vice President of the United States. Cara did not
comment on Johnson's speech, which, though in good sense, was so

badly out of taste that it caused dignitaries to cover their faces in embarrassment. Convalescent from illness and a wearing trip from Tennessee, Johnson had taken too much whisky. But he was neither a drunkard nor intemperate.

Lincoln was then escorted to the East Portico, and, as he faced the expectant crowd, the sun burst forth in a "clear strong light." Pale and quiet, he spoke a "few clear sentences, with a modesty and self-forgetfulness unparalleled." In his address he showed no signs of yielding to the Radicals.[70]

With the President's words, "malice toward none and charity for all," ringing in their ears, John and Cara Kasson a few days later started home by the way of St. Louis. Cara had written her last "Miriam" letter.

* XI *

Johnsonized, Scandalized, Defeated

JOHN KASSON appeared to be a happy man as he traveled leisurely along from St. Louis to Des Moines in early April, 1865. During the last ten days the telegraph had hummed out the thrilling news of Sherman's triumphant march into North Carolina, of the fall of Richmond, and of final Confederate collapse at Appomattox. Political matters also appeared promising. He had apparently clinched the powerful Dodge-Baldwin political influence; his voice had recently been decisive in the appointment of Judge Baldwin as federal attorney.

177

Simultaneously, Senator Harlan had stepped into Lincoln's cabinet, and Kasson, one of the most outstanding Lincoln men in Iowa and with what appeared to be a strong party organization, might well step into Harlan's shoes. Governor Stone might appoint him to fill Harlan's unexpired term, or the legislature might nominate him the next January for a full term.

Yet Kasson was not altogether happy. He was weary from hard work, harassed from political demands, and deeply troubled from personal problems. He had made tentative arrangements to accompany General Dodge on a trip across the Great Plains in order to escape from private and public vexations and, at the same time, to familiarize himself with Indian, mining, and railroad issues which were almost certain to come up at the next session of Congress.

Homeward bound, Kasson stopped at Davenport. The fateful evening of Friday, April 14, came on, and he boarded an M. & M. train for Des Moines. As the train pulled out someone yelled from the platform that President Lincoln had been assassinated! The train gathered momentum and sped on into the night. Hours of intense anxiety, station after station, were passed without further news. When the train reached the end of the M. & M. tracks, Kasson boarded a stagecoach, still without news. Finally in the dead of night the coach stopped at Newton to change horses. Here a dazed, sleepy crowd of villagers hovered around a small telegraph office. Here Kasson listened to the details of the shocking event — the distress signal of a turning point in the lives of millions, including his own.

The next morning, Kasson reached Des Moines. The mayor had called a public meeting for Sunday, and he invited Kasson to deliver the President's funeral oration. Both Kasson and Frank Palmer spoke that Sunday morning. As Kasson eulogized the dead President and gave details of the assassination, he also eulogized the living President, Andrew Johnson, and reassured his hearers of Johnson's sobriety and character. In the grief and shock of the moment, Kasson probably did not have patronage motives in mind. To laud the new President was the obvious thing to do before an apprehensive audience. Moreover, Kasson, when Assistant Postmaster General, had found Johnson's work as war governor of Tennessee deserving of praise. Nor was it then known that Johnson would be other than fully acceptable to all Republicans.[1]

While a stunned people paid final tribute to Abraham Lincoln,

Jefferson Davis fled southward from Richmond. His capture symbolized the end of power of a restraining, agrarian aristocracy in America. Lincoln's passing removed the last effective check on vindictive Radicals and symbolized the end of power of a restraining, agrarian democracy. Out of the confusion created from the scars of war and from the demise of hoary agrarian restraints, business-industrial America was to swagger in under the cloak of the platform of 1860 and Radical Reconstruction. Ephemerally, hate and revenge would run rampant, tarnishing reputations, sweeping away moderate men, and pushing to the top many who had not even expected political leadership a few years before.

For John Kasson the immediacy of events probably obscured the significance of Lincoln's assassination. There was no reason to believe that Andrew Johnson would not follow in Lincoln's footsteps, harmonizing and controlling party factions while restoring the Southern states with dispatch. Early in May, Kasson wrote Johnson: "You have known from our former acquaintance, and from the action of my state in the national convention [1864], how sincerely I tender you the assurances of my cordial and earnest support, in congress and out of it." He hoped the President could initiate Southern state governments by "loyal men" in the interest of "the masses" without further contention over slavery.[2]

In Iowa, the contest for Harlan's Senate seat and the apprehension over Johnson's distribution of the patronage focused a spotlight upon Kasson's every word and deed. In the spring of 1865, Kasson and Kirkwood were the two leading aspirants for the Senate. Kirkwood had the larger following, but fear that Kasson might line up the governor or the legislature runs strongly through Kirkwood's correspondence.

Closely connected with rivalry for the senatorship was rivalry for patronage — rivalry which had built up a host of powerful Kasson enemies including Kirkwood and most of the congressional delegation. Kasson's independent action and success during the war years had engendered jealousy and envy. His "superior intelligence and grand manners" evoked derision. His independence was translated as slipperiness.

Kasson was personally popular among his rank and file constituents. But dignified and somewhat aloof in his relations with political managers on the state level, he was never popular among them and could hold their support only so long as his power and influence at the top were unchallengeable. With Lincoln and Blair gone, much of his influence was gone, unless President Johnson's relation with the party and Kasson's relation with Johnson remained strong.

Shortly before Lincoln's death, Kasson's decisive backing of Dodge's man, Judge Baldwin, for federal attorney had revealed strong opposition and, moreover, weak structure in the Dodge-Baldwin cornerstone of his own organization. Judge Charley Nourse, a Kirkwood man and an old Kasson adversary, had been an applicant for the same office. The congressional delegation had deadlocked 4 to 4 for Nourse and Baldwin, and since both applicants were from Kasson's district, they let him make the choice. Kasson proposed to nominate Nourse if he would "bury the hatchet"; Nourse refused to do so, and Baldwin got the job. But Baldwin, though out of a job, cagily shied away from this stick of political dynamite. It might blast a gap between the Dodge-Baldwin and the Kirkwood wings.

Dodge's military and political aide, George Tichenor, reported from Des Moines that Kasson was in a "devil of trouble" over the matter. "If Old Caleb don't accept the devil will be to pay." H. M. Hoxie added that Baldwin lacked "the courage to go into a fight." "Put some starch on Cale's backbone if you get a chance," he urged Dodge. The General apparently provided the starch, for Baldwin reluctantly accepted the position. But a few weeks later Dodge's brother reported that Cale was "sick of his office"; it was not as "lucrative as represented"; it was "a trick of Kasson's to serve his revenge on [James F.] Wilson." [3]

The cleavage among the congressional delegation on this appointment was roughly a harbinger of the cleavage on Reconstruction issues. Harlan, Price, Wilson, and Allison had backed Nourse. Grimes, Kasson, Grinnell, and Hubbard had supported Baldwin.

The scramble for the Senate, and the Baldwin appointment, brought to a head long welled-up anti-Kasson feeling. Jacob Rich, a Kirkwood man, reported that Hubbard, Allison, Grinnell, and Wilson were "all terribly down on Kasson" for using "some system of chicanery" in behalf of Baldwin. In a rage, Charley Nourse began to solicit support for his own election as chairman of the central committee at the next state convention. "This would be a good pill," he wrote Kirkwood, for that "political mountebank" Kasson, "the dapper gentleman of one gut and no conscience." [4]

Through May and early June, 1865, Iowa Republicans laid plans for their June state convention. Governor Stone confidentially promised to appoint Kirkwood to the Senate in return for Kirkwood's support of Stone's renomination for governor. Soldiers began to return in great numbers. There was an air of political uncertainty as men watched Andrew Johnson's first moves toward reconstruction, economic, and patronage policies.

John Kasson, leaving convention work for his trusted lieutenants, Hoxie, Palmer, and Withrow, struck out for Washington, probably to ascertain the drift of the new administration. By correspondence en route he continued to make arrangements to accompany General Dodge across the Plains. To go along with them, he invited moderate Secretary of State Seward, then convalescing from the wounds of the would-be assassin. In Washington, Kasson learned that Grant was considering Dodge for a commission in the regular army. He also got a close-up view of the impending struggle between the administration and the Radicals.[5]

For a few fleeting days following Lincoln's assassination, Radicals had purred contentedly around Andrew Johnson. The new President was one of them: he talked of harsh treatment for rebels. But by the time Kasson reached Washington in late May, Johnson had unmistakably shown his hand; he was following Lincoln's moderate reconstruction policies. Not only had he recognized Lincoln's reconstructed governments in Arkansas, Louisiana, and Tennessee, but in a sweeping proclamation of pardon and amnesty he had laid down simple procedures for the restoration of all other Confederate states. When Kasson conferred with Seward or Montgomery Blair, he was undoubtedly assured of the President's sobriety and wisdom. Moreover, if he sampled public opinion that summer, he would find Johnson's policy popular among the people. But the Radicals, sparked by Stevens, Sumner, Schurz, and Phillips, joined the issue and immediately proceeded to educate the public.[6]

By mid-June, Kasson was back in Des Moines. He had been gone only three weeks, but much had happened. In the state convention, adjourned a day or two before his return, a marked deference had been shown to the numerous soldier delegates. A rising temper of Radicalism had been revealed. Despite the efforts of a resolutions committee to bury the issue of suffrage, Radicals on the floor had pushed through a proposal committing the party to an amendment to the state constitution allowing Negro suffrage. Hiram Price, Kasson's congressional colleague, had been a leader in the floor fight for this resolution. The long suppressed Radicals in Iowa, those whom Kasson in 1860 had considered "indiscreet," were at last pushing to the top.

According to Hub Hoxie's brother, a Washington postal clerk on hand to observe the convention, four classes of men were in attendance: "those holding office, a good sprinkling; those wanting to hold office, an immense throng; genuine peoples who imagined (poor incredulous souls) they were nominating the officers, a fair number; those having convention on the brain, standing, chronic delegates." Governor Stone was renominated. Charley Nourse was put on the central committee and despite his "general cussedness" sought to land the chairmanship. But a more diligent worker, J. F. Tracy, another Kirkwood man, won this honor. Nourse was dumbfounded, and people in Des Moines grinned. Young Hoxie predicted that the suffrage question would keep Kasson busy in his district.[7]

But Kasson awaited the distillation of opinion (including his own), made preparations for the Plains trip, and in the meantime accepted an invitation to campaign in Kentucky for the Thirteenth Amendment to abolish slavery. Before departing he made a "happy address" and solicited contributions at an educational meeting launching the University of Des Moines. His old Democratic friend, P. M. Casady, was a leader in this project.

To an audience in Covington, Kentucky, in late June, Kasson was introduced as a "friend of Kentucky who had done all he could to prevent her from the ruin of secession — a good and true man." He appealed to "Old Kentucky and the Old Democracy in which he grew up" to accept emancipation. While "charmingly extemporaneous," he was also systematic and used "scholarly diction."

At Lexington, Kentucky, Kasson and Frank Blair addressed a large Union mass meeting. When fiery Blair attacked Chase, Stanton, and other Radicals, Kasson, who had spoken first, was called back. He regretted his old friend's personal attacks on members of the government, he said. As for the Negro franchise: "You, Gentlemen, will do as you please about the right of suffrage in your state."

Kasson followed his speaking tour in Kentucky with an observation tour into the deep South as far as Atlanta, Georgia. He was preparing to commit himself to his constituents on the Southern question. On his return to Des Moines he wrote General Dodge that he would be ready for the Plains trip at the appointed time. "I cannot get away from vexations, except by leaving . . . and I am worn out." [8] In Des Moines he carefully drafted for the newspapers a long letter on public policy, which appeared in the Des Moines *Register* after he had departed with Dodge on the trip. For those in the dark as to his views, here was abundant clarification. It was a long letter, filling nearly five columns with a thorough discussion of national issues. In dignity, reasonableness, and practicableness it was masterful. The manner in which Kasson cut the passion and political claptrap and bared the real issues was refreshing. It remains one of the most statesmanlike expositions of his entire career.

The real issues, Kasson maintained, were economic ones — public credit, taxes, tariff, monetary standards, and foreign trade balances. Sound statesmanship and Northern self-interest alike dictated the speedy restoration of Southern government, labor, and productive capacity. From his own observations in the South, he painted a graphic picture of destitution. From Nashville to Atlanta he had seen little but ruin and desolation. Hunger could be staved off only by a successful corn and cotton crop. But the disposition of freedmen to roam about and subsist from government rations endangered the crops. Until a reliable system of free labor could be established, there was danger of starvation.

As to political feeling in the South, Kasson declared that the vast majority honestly accepted Union and emancipation as "the inevitable results of war." Although not in love with their conquerors, they accepted their fate "as disappointed litigants accept the decision of the courts." This group included "all the common sense of the South, all its enterprise and most of its self-interest." From the "law of self-interest" they were ready to cooperate.

The Negro had been assured his "natural rights" by the Thirteenth Amendment. "Conventional rights" which led to political and social equality would be granted when merited. States in the Union had long exercised the power to safeguard the ballot box by restricting suffrage. To grant universal suffrage to the Negro would enable "base politicians" to pander to "ignorance and incapacity"; the race as a whole would be unfit to exercise the voting privilege for a generation. Kasson was willing to grant only limited suffrage based on literacy or military service. "Suppose we adopt, at first," he pleaded, "the proposition of that lamented, great, and wonderfully wise man, that slow but sure reformer, Abraham Lincoln. . . . Let us make haste so slowly and deliberately, so surely, that like our great leader, Lincoln, we shall be obliged to take no steps backward."

Kasson handled delicately the recent action of the Iowa Republican convention advocating Negro suffrage. The resolution had been incorporated in the platform as "the basis of discussion" prior to its consideration by the people; there was ample time for maturity of thinking, for it would take three or four years to amend the state constitution. In the meantime he pleaded that one's stand on this issue be not made the test of party allegiance. The "interest of the whole country" required "tolerance of minor differences of opinion." Frank Palmer, whose habit had been to heap profuse praise upon Kasson's words, published this letter without comment.[9]

The fateful Plains trip about to begin was in part an army-financed expedition for the Union Pacific Railroad. General Dodge, soon to accept from Thomas C. Durant the position of chief engineer, hoped to clear out hostile Indians and find a suitable pass through the first ranges of the Rocky Mountains before he took off his uniform. For more than a year Plains Indians, pushed relentlessly from their hunting grounds by miners, immigrants, and railroaders, had been on the warpath. The previous winter Dodge had organized a campaign against them, restoring communications and securing settlements and immigrant trains. Backed by Grant and Sherman, Dodge had planned to drive the Indians far from the probable railroad route. But Johnson's administration, groping for more peaceful remedies, was bucking the army's plan of pacification by force. This trip was one of reconnaissance in anticipation of a favorable decision in Washington. Practical wisdom had dictated an invitation to Dodge's Congressman to go along.[10]

The Plains party included Dodge, Kasson, Dodge's brother Nathan, General John A. Williamson, a cook, a surgeon, servants, two companies of cavalry from the Army of the Potomac, twelve four-mule wagons, and two ambulances. The party took the stage from Council Bluffs to old Fort Kearny and there rendezvoused with the cavalry. On August 17 John Kasson mounted the saddle and headed his horse out for the Rocky Mountains.

Within a week the party reached Julesburg in Colorado Territory and then headed for Fort Laramie in the Wyoming Black Hills. Near

Fort Laramie, Kasson saw great herds of antelope roaming over the Platte valley and the surrounding sandy hills. The party was entertained at an Indian feast, where choice wines flowed freely. Kasson and some of his companions partook ravenously of the main dish, a large pot of steaming stew in the center of the council-tepee, until the discovery of a dog's paw in it cut short the delicious meal.

During the first two weeks of September the party probed deeply into hostile Indian country on the Powder River some 150 miles northwest of Fort Laramie. Kasson saw Indian smoke signals and prairie fires and almost froze from the cold of higher altitudes. Dodge, appraising the terrain and the Indian menace, concluded that the best railroad route lay to the south of Fort Laramie, and to Fort Laramie the party returned.

In mid-September they turned south toward Denver. Threading their way upward through the Cheyenne Pass to the summit of the Wyoming Black Hills, they followed the divide southward until Dodge at last located the pass through which to build the Union Pacific.

During the last week of September the party was serenaded and banqueted by enthusiastic citizens of Denver and Central City. In a number of appearances, Kasson was reported to have charmed his audiences with his wit and elegance and his advocacy of federal aid for the development of the Mountain West. For a whole day Kasson and Dodge explored the mines, some of them 500 feet deep. On another day they rode up to the top of a snowy mountain range; Kasson's horse fell and slid rapidly down the slope, momentarily endangering horse and rider, until the horse stopped on a rocky edge of the slope.

In early October the party headed east for Leavenworth, Kansas, following approximately the Smoky Hill route over which Missourians and Kansans sought to build the Kansas branch of the Pacific railroad. One day the party traveled through thousands of buffalo grazing in every direction, and a small group fanned out to hunt them. When night came, Kasson failed to show up. The next day Dodge sent out search parties; early in the afternoon they found Kasson in a camp of forage trains. He had been up all night firing his revolver to keep the buffalo from running over him.

The party reached Leavenworth in mid-October to find General Sherman, direct from Washington, awaiting them. Kasson and Dodge's brother struck out for home and arrived at Council Bluffs on October 20.[11] Kasson had been gone seventy days and had traveled on stage and horse some 1,600 miles.

He was "strong and black" from so many hours in the saddle. He was rested, but deep trouble lay ahead. Politically the trip had been a serious mistake. In letters to the Des Moines *Register* and to Andrew Johnson, Kasson had loyally defended Dodge's interests. But Kasson's friends in Iowa had not defended their Congressman as he obviously expected them to do during his absence. In Iowa, Governor Kirkwood campaigned furiously on a Radical platform, as Radicalism caught on full fire, and Tichenor, Palmer, Withrow, Hoxie, and Baldwin made ready to hitch on to the Kirkwood faction.[12] And there is reason to believe that these former friends were busy stirring up marital difficulties between Kasson and his wife Cara, who was then residing in Des Moines. Whether Kasson's undeviating support of Dodge's interests during the trip would retain the General's political loyalty remained to be seen.

On the eve of the state elections, as Kasson reached Des Moines, Judge Nourse informed Kirkwood that Kasson would not be an open candidate for the Senate but would "play Mr. McCawber" in case of a deadlock in the legislature. "His wife is here for several weeks past," Nourse wittily warned, "but she *has not called on me yet.* She is to remain during the winter. Tell Mrs. Kirkwood she must come over next winter and bring all the parisian style she can put on, for it isn't fair to have *you fight crinoline.* She must take care of Mrs. John in this fight. If she don't, why she will have to go to Denmark instead of to Washington." Nourse's guess was completely wrong. Cara Kasson had not come to Des Moines for the purpose of supporting her husband's political ambitions.[13]

The elections, showing a clear postwar reaction against the party in power, alarmed Iowa Republicans. George Tichenor wrote Kirkwood of his deep "regret and humiliation" at seeing the Republican majority whittled down in one year from 40,000 to 14,000. To keep "Copperheads, traitors, and slave propaganda" from winning control, Tichenor declared that "we must keep within our group every state, congressional District, county, township, city ward, and school district . . . unite policy, yes, strategy with principle" in future political plans. He blamed Thomas F. Withrow and his kind for having called the state convention before the return of the soldiers. "A new race of leaders is needed," he declared.[14]

In reality the victory was comfortable. Significantly, it was also a Radical victory. Although advocacy of Negro suffrage had reduced the majority, this issue had been met squarely and won. Although not fully recognized at the moment, the victory was a signal for moderate Republicans either to desert the party, swallow the Radical program, or suffer defeat. Frightened at the Democratic upsurge, Radical leaders were in no mood to tolerate differences of opinion within the ranks. There was therefore a scramble among party managers, officeholders, and office seekers to catch on to the Radical band wagon and enforce political conformity. Political expediency led men to talk like Radicals whether or not they believed in Radicalism.

To hold his managers in line, John Kasson would have to trim fast his political sails to Radical winds. Behind his back, his "bosom friends" were laying plans to desert him. Yet in Iowa in the fall of 1865 he made no attempt to "correct" his stand on Negro suffrage. Rather, he ignored the issue in his only public appearance. In Des Moines, with "unequaled fluency and elegance," he spoke on "The Plains and Mountains," advocating speedy construction of the Pacific railroad and a new Indian policy based upon firm treatment. He censured the rapacity of white agents and traders among the Indians, and he lauded General Dodge as a "master mind" in Indian and railroad matters. In reply to a letter from Dodge, he promised to support the General's interests in Washington. Dodge not only wanted favorable railroad legislation, but he also wanted to hang on to his major-generalship for a while longer.[15] In late November, Kasson departed for the coming session of the Thirty-ninth Congress. Cara remained in Des Moines.

At this time, despite his stand on the suffrage question, Kasson was still conceded to be the third man in the Senate race. Kirkwood and Harlan easily stood ahead of him. Although his chance was slim, fear that he might win was deep seated and persistent. There was no doubt of his strength in his own district, and, with this solid bloc, he might combine with some other faction and slip in. He had hardly had time to reach Washington before defection in his own ranks began. George Tichenor sparked the movement.

Tichenor, still in uniform and attached to Dodge's Fort Leavenworth command, had spent much of his time in Des Moines since Lincoln's assassination, dabbling in politics and trying to find himself a place in civil life. Unrestrained Tichenor was stepping into irrepressible Hoxie's shoes as Dodge's Iowa political lieutenant. This former Kentuckian and Democrat, nosey, gossipy, and loquacious, was emerging as a powerful influence. Because of his meddling in company elections as the war came on, James M. Tuttle (later a general) had described him as "an infernal fool." Tossed up by the political flux of war and reconstruction, Tichenor was a spoilsman and no more. He lacked the depth to wear well, and he would pass ephemerally from the scene, leaving as his imprint tarnished reputations and a political vocabulary earthy-rich in the vernacular. But for almost a decade he was to deal out a barrel of misery to John A. Kasson.[16]

During the war Kasson had tried and failed to secure for Tichenor a position in an army corps as assistant judge advocate general. In May of 1865 Tichenor demanded the Des Moines post office and brought heavy pressure on Kasson to throw out the incumbent, "old Teesdale, a d—d old 'Pub Funk' and infernal old Iscariot."[17] But Kasson could not toss out John Teesdale, party stalwart and former newspaper editor, and Tichenor laid plans to organize the soldier vote.

As Kasson traveled toward Washington, Tichenor promised Dodge: "I'll do all in my power against Kasson. He treated me shabbily and I shall pay him off at all hazards." And Tichenor had his own candidate for the Senate — General Dodge. "The Legislature will be controlled by Army men," he wrote Dodge, "and with them there is a firm determination to give political control to Army men." The leading politicians, "as a means of keeping the Union [Republican] strength united," would acquiesce.

Two days after Tichenor declared war on Kasson, Nathan Dodge reported that Judge Baldwin was also working for General Dodge's election to the Senate. If the General would not run, Baldwin would support Kirkwood. Baldwin was "sore" at Kasson for saddling him with appointment as federal attorney![18]

Meanwhile, Kasson reached Washington, immediately conferred with President Johnson, and wrote George G. Wright as follows: "I have renewed faith in his [Johnson's] wisdom, statesmanship, and loyalty. His message [to Congress] is prepared, and will, I judge, justify his course before the tribunal of national intelligence and national conscience." This private letter, although probably not written for public consumption, appeared forthwith in Palmer's *Register*. Almost simultaneously, a long letter, signed "G.G.W." [George G. Wright?], appeared in the Chicago *Times*, advocating Dodge's candidacy.[19] The General's campaign was well launched, although he was later to deny that he ever had political ambitions.

At twelve noon, December 4, 1865, John Kasson heard the Speaker's gavel rap out the opening of the Thirty-ninth Congress. Outside, the Washington weather was balmy as on a May day. Inside, the Hall of Representatives was resplendent from redecoration. A brilliant and fashionable crowd thronged the galleries — diplomats, men high in government, and society leaders — all sensing the drama in the tragic struggle about to begin for control in the rebuilding of a divided nation.

Thad Stevens, cool, grim, and confident, sat ready to "spring the drop" on Southern Congressmen, on President Johnson, and on moderate Republicans who stood in his way. With malice toward the defeated and with charity toward Negroes, railroad entrepreneurs, and industrialists, this cynical old man had some carefully laid plans for the perpetual ascendancy of the Republican party.

During the summer and autumn Andrew Johnson had quietly "reanimated" the "suspended vitality" of the Confederate states. On terms even more liberal than Lincoln had anticipated, he had restored all these states except Texas and Florida. Senators and Representatives from the restored states had arrived in Washington to take their seats. The matter of Negro suffrage, Johnson had left to each state.

Johnson was taking seriously the idea of a Union party which had elected him. His would be a party of the center with Northern Radicals on the extreme left and Southern irreconcilables on the extreme right. His plan, if allowed to mature, would bring Western and Southern men (with certain Eastern allies) into a combination to rule the Republic. Such rule, agrarian in nature, might mean loss of power for Republicans; and it would almost certainly dilute or reverse wartime tariff, railroad, and monetary policies so lucrative to the expansive business, financial, and industrial interests. Much more was at stake than the fate of the emancipated Negro and the defeated white. Many people, of course, genuinely feared that return of Southerners to Congress would mean renewal of the old ante-bellum issues which had led to disunion. But financiers, ironmasters, and railroad entrepreneurs had as much to lose from an unfavorable economic policy as did Radical politicians from a Reconstruction policy which might bring loss of power and patronage. In the looming struggle between Johnson and the Radicals, ties between Radicalism and patronage, Indian affairs, railroads, and iron were real and strong.

Stevens had laid plans to blot out Johnson's work by slamming the doors of Congress to Southern representatives. Through the clerk of the House, his own appointee, he would keep their names off the roll until a resolution could be pushed through declaring that there were no Southern states to be represented. Meanwhile, a special committee would deal with the admission of Southern members and would take complete charge of drafting a new program of Reconstruction. To bind the Senate to the plan, the committee was to be a joint one, and neither branch of Congress could admit members which the other refused to recognize.

At the Republican caucus held on December 2, the party surrendered the leadership to Stevens. Making most of the important motions, storming and threatening, he browbeat the members into accepting his program. The Ways and Means Committee was divided into three parts, and Old Thad headed the most important one — appropriations. As number four on this same committee, Kasson could be kept under control.

Two days later, at the opening session, the House clerk, according to plans, refused to recognize Southern members, and with a wave of the hand and a sarcastic jab, Stevens dismissed those who protested the clerk's action. Next, Old Thad introduced his resolution for a Joint Committee of Fifteen on Reconstruction, stifled debate, and, under suspended rules, saw the measure pass, 139 to 35. The "Directory" of the Radical dictatorship was now established. The *coup d'etat* was complete, and Johnson's restoration was to be undone. Amid Radical rejoicing, Southern members began returning home.

John Kasson fell in behind Stevens' leadership in the party caucus and voted to set up the Joint Committee on Reconstruction. Henry J. Raymond and Robert S. Hale, his former schoolmates at the University of Vermont, both moderate, distinguished, and able men, did likewise. At this early stage, moderates little suspected the fate that awaited them. They were soon to be put on trial in Washington and at home. Radical discipline would tolerate no deviation from its program.[20]

In Iowa, patronage, railroad matters, and Negro suffrage were creating deep fissures in Republican ranks. General Dodge and the forces consolidating around him were intently watching John Kasson's every movement. Kasson would have to get more Radical and vote "right" on economic legislation to retain their support. If the aspirations of this group required the sacrifice of Kasson, George Tichenor was ready to "move heaven and earth against him." Shrouding his plan in mystery, Tichenor informed Dodge: *"And I know where and how to strike effectively."* [21]

But Kasson, sometimes surprisingly independent, liked the idea of a Union party, too. Deep down, he respected Andrew Johnson and believed sincerely that the President was following a wise course in his restoration policy. Kasson wanted to make his Iowa constituents less Radical, but to do so would require a ferocious battle with Radical leaders in Congress and with party lieutenants in Iowa. It would mean complete political slaughter. Therefore, he undertook to ride in both the Johnson and Radical wagons until the hot passions of the war had cooled off. When the Radical vehicle became a band wagon, he sought to apply the brakes down the more precipitous grades. But, like other moderates in this Congress, he gave ground under Radical pressure, voted with them in party caucuses, and joined them, after barbed protests, to push measures over the head of the President. At the same time, he kept certain Iowa politicians in a state of jitters from the fear that he could control the patronage through the President and his department heads. Kasson frequently demonstrated the courage to tangle with the undisputed master of the House, Thad Stevens. But ultimately he would retreat in deference to party regularity and to his own political future, seriously menaced by backstage maneuvering at home.

In Washington, also, Kasson's conduct was closely scrutinized. His five colleagues in the House made the transition to Radicalism completely and with alacrity, and on important Reconstruction measures arrayed themselves solidly against him. Two of them — Hiram Price and Josiah B. Grinnell — derided Kasson on the floor, capitalizing on his alleged high-flown manners, broad knowledge, and issue straddling. Even so, Kasson was the most prominent Iowan in the House except James F. Wilson, chairman of the powerful Judiciary Committee, who ranked high among Radical strategists.

As a member of the important Appropriations Committee, Kasson demonstrated expert knowledge and admirable skill on the floor. But as a spokesman for appropriations for the executive departments, he was the victim of Stevens' sardonic wit and of jibes from other Radical "economizers," including Iowans, in no mood to support Andrew Johnson's budget requests. On more than one occasion, while guiding the appropriations bill through the House, Kasson found himself defending items for a wider distribution of mail in the destitute South and for the dilapidated navy yards at Norfolk and Pensacola. In each case he drew Radical fire and saw the appropriations slashed to the bone. With the next election in mind, Radicals had settled on the opportune strategy of identifying moderates with Johnson, the South, and therefore the Democrats. Kasson parried Radical sarcasm with sarcasm, and his obvious scorn for their vindictiveness, their lack of knowledge and foresight was not calculated to increase his popularity with them. For vindication of his course, he would rely on his constituents in Iowa.

Kasson was assigned to two other committees, both of minor importance. He was permitted to continue his chairmanship of the harmless committee on coinage, weights, and measures. As a member of the select committee to do honors to the Lincolns, he again incurred Radical wrath. The dead President's wife, scandalously abused from the day she entered the White House, was now accused of taking away government furniture. When Kasson, after investigating the matter, arose to defend her, Stevens sarcastically informed the House that Kasson spoke only for himself and not for any committee.[22]

More serious was Kasson's stand on the admission of Southern Congressmen. Representatives from Tennessee and Arkansas lingered in Washington hoping to be seated. One of these, Horace Maynard of Tennessee, had served as postal agent under Kasson and had been a staunch Unionist since the war began. Even Stevens admitted the loyalty of such men, but he refused to seat them on the ground that they were from disloyal and defunct states. Kasson favored admitting Tennessee representatives without question and those from all other states if loyal to the Union. Power in the disorganized states, he insisted, adhered to the loyal people therein, not to Congress. He voted against a resolution declaring it the duty of Congress to lay down a program of Reconstruction. And when James F. Wilson introduced a resolution designed to smother the issue in the Joint Committee, Kasson answered with an emphatic nay; his Iowa colleagues and a House majority, yea.[23]

Moreover, Kasson took a firm stand against unlimited Negro suffrage in the District of Columbia. He elicited a savage attack from Hiram Price and other Radicals, and the debates degenerated into a crossfire eventually involving Iowa personalities and politics. Over the protest of Stevens in a party caucus, it had been agreed to limit suffrage to those, whether white or black, who could pass an educational test. On the floor Kasson challenged the constitutional arguments of William D. Kelley, Pennsylvania iron manufacturer, once a furious Democrat but now a fiery Radical, who patronizingly attacked President Johnson and demanded unlimited Negro suffrage. Kasson's grasp of the constitutional issue was superior to Kelley's, and he was cutting Kelley's argument to pieces when Price, claiming ignorance of constitutional issues, demanded to know whether the voters of Iowa favored Negro suffrage. Kasson's reply that the issue had reduced seriously the party majority in Iowa brought from Price the rejoinder that men like Kasson were so constituted "by education or by nature" that they could not move straight to a given point. Kasson, who was "trimming his course to suit Southern slaveholders," represented neither the people of his state nor of his district!

On this measure, despite Radical ire, Kasson voted for limited, and against unlimited, suffrage. But the Radicals, despite the caucus agreement, pushed through unlimited Negro suffrage, all other Iowans voting yea. Later in the session, however, Kasson voted with the Radicals for an enlarged version of the Freedmen's Bureau providing sweeping jurisdiction and power under which Radical agents could operate in the South. He was willing to support relief measures for the freedmen but thought it dangerous to give them all the vote.

With candor that irritated, Kasson suggested that Radicals, who designed to deprive the states of their right to control voter qualifications, should preface their speeches with Wordsworth's famous maxim of:

> The good old rule, the simple plan
> That they should take who have the power
> And they should keep who can.

As to amendments to the Constitution, Kasson wanted only those which looked "to the great future of the country and the safety of all parts, rather than to the embarrassment and encumbrance of a particular portion of it." A measure then passed against the South in a spirit of vengeance might be used later against the North. For,

Kasson prophetically warned, "manufacturing, commercial, and agricultural interests move to and fro in different sections of this Union; majorities change from year to year; the opinions of men change." He urged the Representatives to resist the Madison-styled "occasional impetuosities" of the House. "Better submit to some ills that we know than rush into others that we know not of." [24]

On economic matters, early in the session, Kasson advocated measures in behalf of consumers, small landowners, and the Union Pacific Railroad. He favored state tax discrimination against nonresident land speculators, proposed to exempt the real property of homesteaders from bankrupt proceedings, and submitted petitions from the Free Trade League of New York. Probably as a result of his recent visit in the Mountain West, he submitted a politically ingenious mining act, providing that any man, no matter how poor, could "homestead" the minerals. The title to mineral lands was to remain perpetually with the United States, but funds from an income tax on the net mining returns were to be applied to the payment of interest on United States bonds issued in aid of the Union Pacific. Thus, miners would help pay for the railroads which would open up the West to greater mining development. [25]

Kasson opposed further appropriations for destitute Indians until reports of fraud through previous use of such funds could be investigated. This was a touchy problem for it involved Secretary of Interior Harlan, his subordinates Elijah Sells and D. N. Cooley, and the Senate race in Iowa. Harlan, at first a loyal supporter of Johnson, had made the transition to Radicalism by the opening of Congress. Planning to leave the Cabinet, he was now an active candidate for the Senate. Rumors of mismanagement and fraud in the Indian Bureau kept circulating in Washington and Iowa. Because of his opposition to the appropriation, Grinnell accused Kasson of impeaching candidate Harlan's character. Asahel Hubbard vigorously supported the appropriation, and all Iowans, save Kasson, voted for it. [26]

Kasson was having no more success at pleasing General Dodge than he had at pleasing his colleagues in the House. But the General still pressed his Congressman for personal service, and Kasson obliged. Early in January, 1866, Dodge suddenly received his muster-out order from the army. Immediately he contacted Kasson and several other men of importance, and the order was revoked. But Dodge was dissatisfied with Kasson's railroad activities. Kasson distrusted T. C.

Durant and was reported to be supporting a rival group in Des
Moines among whom were prominent Democrats and old friends of
Kasson — Casady and Tuttle. This group planned to run a line west
to connect with the Union Pacific, since the M. & M. had completely
bogged down. Kasson replied to a complaint from Dodge that he
was "wearied of groundless suspicions." [27]

All the while, since Kasson's departure from Iowa, George Tichenor had kept up a running correspondence with Dodge concerning
the Senate race. Tichenor was still trying to land the Des Moines post
office, but he had many other lines out. Kasson was dead politically,
Tichenor kept arguing. "Palmer, Hoxie and others agree. . . .
Kasson like a fool made all appointments here [Des Moines] with
reference to Palmer's interest; now neither Palmer or his backers will
do one thing for Kasson." The ebullient Tichenor wanted to put
Dodge "squarely on the track" for the Senate, hoping for a deadlock
between Kirkwood and Harlan. If Kasson gave trouble, he knew how
to take care of him. But Hoxie, in a letter to Thomas C. Durant,
who for obvious reasons was much interested in the Iowa Senate race,
reported that Kasson could carry his own district and that he had
"strength outside his district." Other correspondents agreed with
Hoxie. And Kasson himself in late December, 1865, thought that he
might slip around deadlocked Harlan and Kirkwood.[28]

But on the very last day of 1865 Tichenor wrote Dodge that he was
pleased that the General was beginning to see the senatorial contest
"in the proper light." Neither Kirkwood nor Harlan would have a
majority, Tichenor predicted. And gleefully he advised: "Make
Hoxie and Baldwin get in the harness and come here a few days before the legislature meets. Send Generals Rice, Carpenter, Weaver,
Howard and other army men here." [29]

Now, at the beginning of the year 1866, Kasson had become a liability, and Dodge had dropped him; moreover, the General had con-
sented to have his own hat tossed into the ring in case of a deadlock
between the two leading contenders. Soon he dispatched letters
to Kasson and Kirkwood. He censured Kasson for voting against
James F. Wilson's resolution to bury in the Joint Committee the
matter of seating Southern Representatives until Congress "admitted"
into the Union the states they were supposed to represent. No officer,
he said, in command in the South would advise that the region "was
fit to resume the reign of government." The Negro should be given

suffrage and the South "put in such a position that she can never regain control . . . and thus undo gains of Civil War." To Kirkwood, Dodge pledged his own support and advised that other Kasson men on "the slope" would turn to the former governor.[30]

Before Kasson had time to reply, men began to gather in Des Moines for the opening of the state legislature. On January 11, 1866, Caleb Baldwin wrote Dodge's brother that a caucus of the Fifth District had decided not to present Kasson's name. His course in Congress had "cooled the ardor of his friends." Baldwin was hoping for an impasse from which Dodge would emerge the victor.

The next day in Washington, Kasson penned a cool letter to Dodge:

> I am not a candidate for Senator since Jan. 1st. From the moment you were announced, I foresaw no success from the west with a divided front.
>
> If our party does not moderate its tone, as against the President, we become divided, and our supremacy is lost for years to come. My action has been to the best interest of party and country, as the future will show.
>
> I have no railroad news beyond what you probably know.[31]

While this letter made its way westward, the party caucus in Des Moines chose Harlan for the long Senate term and Kirkwood for the short. In the caucus balloting, Dodge received one vote for the short term, but the expected impasse did not materialize.

In a rage, George Tichenor charged Dodge's failure to Kasson, who kept Dodge "off track and himself on" until "the very hour of the caucus." Tichenor was sure that Kasson was ruined; he had "distributed all his patronage to his enemies" and had acted "in violence to the sentiments" of his district and state. "Kasson ought to have given me this P. O. He has treated me badly," declared Tichenor, "and I intend that he *shall be beaten* for Congressman." And Dodge was the man to do it, beamed Tichenor.

Tichenor went on to say that in the distribution of the state patronage, Frank Palmer had managed to hold on to the state printership, and that Senator-elect Kirkwood (who disliked Kasson) had departed for Washington saying that he "loved" Dodge and was at the General's command "in all things at all times." By February 9, Dodge was writing Kirkwood that "Cale [Baldwin] would be strong if he would consent to run" for Congress.[32]

As John Kasson pondered the political situation he must have suspected that he was falling from grace. Yet he continued to oppose Negro suffrage and other Radical measures. Perhaps his popularity in

Historical Dept., Des Moines

GEORGE C. TICHENOR

Historical Society, Iowa City

GRENVILLE M. DODGE

Historical Society, Iowa City

CALEB BALDWIN

Historical Dept., Des Moines

HERBERT M. HOXIE

FRANK W. PALMER

JAMES S. CLARKSON

JAMES C. SAVERY

CHARLES C. NOURSE

his district would save him. Up to this point his personal life had been spared from attack. Yet within a month after the senatorial election, even this wall began to crumble and fall away. A story began to circulate in Iowa and Washington that John Kasson's wife was now deserting him. She was suing for divorce on grounds which impeached the character of her husband. The charge was infidelity!

☆   ☆   ☆

J. N. Dewey, Des Moines businessman and politico, who had kept Kasson under surveillance for Kirkwood since the early war years, broke the news to his mentor. In a letter dated February 16, 1866, overflowing with mirthful satisfaction, Dewey informed Senator Kirkwood that he had just been talking with Mrs. Kasson's attorney, none other than Thomas Withrow, who was preparing a petition for divorce. The ground, said Dewey, was "————, well adultery they call it here. I don't know what name it goes by at Washington. The other party in the 'crime case' I understand to be an ex-w. [wife or worker?] in the P. O. Dept. Help Johnny ere he sinks." Dewey thought Kasson might as well join the Democrats to whom he had always belonged.[33]

Within a few days the Kasson divorce had become a national scandal, one of the first of the great scandals peculiar to the dawning Gilded Age. Newspapers seized upon it and took sides — the Dubuque *Herald*, Davenport *Gazette*, Cincinnati *Gazette*, St. Louis *Democrat*, Des Moines *Statesman*, and many others. But Frank Palmer, the editor who probably knew most about the affair, imposed a long and conspicuous silence upon it in his Des Moines *Register*. Wild stories appeared with strangely garbled facts. The Cincinnati *Gazette* reported gossip from Chicago that at New Bedford, Kasson had been Miss Eliot's French teacher, and against the wishes of her parents and friends the couple had eloped, only to be reconciled with the Eliot family later. Other stories made Kasson a native Southerner, an Alabamian, who had been an official delegate to the secession convention held at Nashville in 1852.[34] Kasson, the Vermonter, proud of his New England ancestry, must have been surprised to learn these "facts" about himself!

On February 19, 1866, Kasson ceased speaking and voting on measures in the House. Radical Congressmen were then frothy from anger. Andrew Johnson had vetoed the Freedmen's Bureau Bill, and they were contemplating passing it over his head. Johnson was on the point of making a speech directly attacking Radical leaders. Kasson was reported to be running away to avoid the controversy.

But on March 3, just before noon, John Kasson appeared before the district court at Indianola in Warren County, Iowa, to participate in a humiliating drama. Before Judge C. C. Nourse, his bitter political enemy, he had to answer Cara's petition for divorce pled by his erstwhile political friend, Thomas Withrow. The petition stated that Caroline Kasson had ceased to cohabit with John Kasson on February 18, 1865, because on that date John Kasson had cohabited "with some other person or persons . . . unknown to the plaintiff." The application for divorce was not being made "from any fear or restraint." The petition was in Withrow's hand and notarized by R. G. Orwig, then under suspicion for fraud involving swamp land funds.

Kasson's reply was brief but left room for doubt as to the allegations: "After six years of domestic difficulty which Defendant has in vain endeavored to remedy, *I take the responsibility of admitting the charges in this petition so far as essential to this suit*, and concur in asking for a decree of divorce." [35]

The decree was granted, and Kasson and Withrow returned to Des Moines. Amid rumors that Kasson would resign from Congress and refuse to run for another term, opinion was sharply divided on the merits of the Kasson case and the causes behind it. That it had its roots deep in the hate ridden politics of the era is obvious. The first reaction was favorable to Kasson. R. S. Finkbine, member of the legislature then in session, a Kirkwood partisan with a large reputation for integrity and sound judgment, had a talk with Cara's attorney before the decree was granted. Withrow admitted to Finkbine that he could not "make defense for proof conclusive," but it would be settled "with as little scandal as possible." Dodge's sister in Council Bluffs expressed sympathy for "poor Mr. Kasson" and criticized Mrs. Kasson for letting her name be brought before the public in such a manner. [36]

The Radical *Missouri Democrat* (March 13), drawing from the Democratic Dubuque *Herald*, reported that the lady with whom Kasson was alleged to have had illicit relations was indiscreet enough to let one of her letters fall into Mrs. Kasson's hands. The letter "contained many things a friendly epistle should not contain." But

Kasson's friends maintained that his enemies in his own party, "jealous of his power and popularity . . . operated on Mrs. Kasson . . . magnified slight indiscretions to great wrongs . . . and goaded her on" to seek divorce. The *Democrat* further speculated that the absense of children from the union was "remotely or directly no small part of the trouble." And here indeed this editor may have pointed up one aspect of the problem, for Cara and John had adopted a child named Emma Snyder whose further identity is still a mystery.

Even George Tichenor thought the "weight of opinion and sympathy [was] settling down decidedly in favor of Kasson. Notwithstanding Withrow, Palmer, and Hoxie [were] with Mrs. Kasson." At tea, Kasson told Tichenor that "he was not afraid of the popular verdict" and that he intended to run for Congress again. Hub Hoxie from Quincy, Illinois, where he was lining up contracts for the Crédit Mobilier, did not comment on the merits of the case but urged Dodge to run if Kasson resigned. Cale Baldwin from Des Moines reported that "sympathy here is with him," despite Withrow and Palmer. But Cale urged Dodge to take up residence at Council Bluffs in order to run for Congress. "Don't write any letters till I see you," he warned. Dodge's brother also urged the General to settle at Council Bluffs upon leaving the army, "for many reasons"; one of them: "Kasson's term is up soon." [37]

The Democratic Des Moines *Statesman* bluntly blurted out that "a more deliberate and rascally conspiracy to destroy a man was never set on foot." Motive: "political and pecuniary"; "at bottom" a $3,000 fee.[38]

By mid-March, Kasson was back in his House seat. He had left Des Moines confident of a favorable public verdict; he expected renomination at the district party convention to be held in June. This would be his vindication. But such an optimistic outcome did not take into account the extent to which his alleged misdeeds could be expanded, and public opinion changed, under the climate of hysteria being whipped up by the Radicals. The Vindictives were riding in on the crest of a storm in large measure precipitated by themselves. Throughout the land in the pending critical congressional elections of 1866, Radicals seized every opportunity to proscribe moderates. Iowa was no exception. In politics as in war all was fair.

In Congress, Kasson began to bow to political expediency. Although still demonstrating some independence, he was not going to permit himself to become identified with President Johnson and the Democrats, all of whom the Radicals were now calling Copperheads.

He spoke for the immediate sale of land-grant college lands in order to prevent their being held for speculation. In Iowa, he said, many counties were "half depopulated because Congress has tied up lands by grants to railroads and other corporations who refuse to sell them." He sought to reduce by one-third an appropriation for the Freedmen's Bureau sponsored by Stevens and Thomas Dawes Eliot, until recently Kasson's brother-in-law. He considered this appropriation extravagant, unnecessary, and susceptible of fraud, or in other words a political slush fund for Radicals. But he favored admitting Colorado to the Union despite an amendment to strike from the constitution the word "white" as a voting qualification.[39]

On the important Civil Rights Bill, Kasson yielded to the Radicals and voted to pass it over Johnson's veto. He used this vote to convince Dodge that he was, after all, not "slewing after Andy." He wrote Dodge: "We have just passed the Civil Rights Bill . . . over the veto — with cheers, etc. . . . it will have a good effect on the Pres. and show him the deep feeling we of the north have in respect to protection of white and black unionists in the south." He also sent Dodge a copy of Rules on the Conduct of War. It was his last personal service for Dodge.[40]

For the General had unmistakably ditched the Congressman. From the moment Kasson left Des Moines, Withrow, Nourse, Palmer, Hoxie, Baldwin, and Tichenor kept laying pressure on Dodge to run for Kasson's seat in the House. Dodge had other plans and did not want to run. He wanted his own man in Congress, all right, but was there any other man in the district who stood a better chance of beating Kasson than himself? His sponsors thought not.

Dodge was the "only man" who could beat the "apostate whoremaster Kasson" who had gone over to "his apostate majesty, drunken Andy," wrote Tichenor. As a preliminary, Tichenor wangled through the state legislature a joint resolution thanking Dodge for his war services and operations against the Indians. Cale Baldwin, said Tichenor, lacked the courage to submit the resolution.[41]

Baldwin wrote that the Fortieth Congress would be an important one, and it would be a year and a half before Dodge would have to go to Washington — plenty of time for the Union Pacific in the interim. And besides, urged Baldwin, "Kasson will not run against you . . . he might run against any other man." [42]

Dodge sought the advice of Hub Hoxie, who had fitted up a new office for the Union Pacific at Hoxie's Landing, St. Joseph, Missouri. Hoxie replied that Kasson "only looked after your interests when I made him. I had to push him to make him do it. Some things he did himself, but sometimes grumbled when I made him work." Hoxie said he had received a letter from Frank Palmer who was "alarmed." And, added Hoxie, "I don't know but justly," for Kasson was hard at work.[43]

Kasson like Palmer was alarmed, and on April 18, 1866, he dispatched a frank and pragmatic letter straight to the fount of danger.

My dear General:
I have a letter from home saying that you are likely to be a candidate against me for nomination to Congress. Now, my friend, I have never asked a service of you yet. I do so now. You know whether I have stood like a rock here for all your interests for five years. A few men, who ought to be willing to acknowledge that I had essentially served them, it is said, have gone back on me. Now, when outsiders have assailed me most maliciously and in most respects *falsely*, I must call on my friends to assist me in repelling their attacks. I have sustained the two bills which the Pres. vetoed, working hard to keep the Civil Rights bill over his head, and have in other respects differed from the President. Yet, because I could not also write in as denunciating policy which at one time threatened, & still threatens to lose us some states, they have tried to make me out unfaithful to the party, and so get me out of the way. It is all false. My every vote has been with the party caucus, whereon it has acted, and in full accord always with the Republican platform and principles. Under these circumstances you will readily see that I am unwilling to be overslaughed on the grounds they speak of. I am as thoroughly radical today as I ever was and follow no man against our party action.
I wish you would write me frankly on the question, and let me know if I may count on your assistance.[44]

While pondering a reply to this direct approach, Dodge, a week later, conferred with T. C. Durant at St. Joseph on becoming chief engineer for the Union Pacific. He was offered $10,000 a year and stock in the Crédit Mobilier. Moreover, the Union Pacific would be glad to have him run for Congress in order to have somebody "thoroughly posted." Durant was then under fire for squandering company funds through construction contracts. Someone had made much money on the first forty miles of rusty, insecure rails laid between

Council Bluffs and Elkhorn, Nebraska. The day following this conference, Frank Palmer wrote Hub Hoxie that Cale Baldwin said
Dodge would run against Kasson.[45]

Early in May, Dodge replied to Kasson, secured leave from his
command at Fort Leavenworth, and moved to Council Bluffs to take
over his engineering job. Pontifically, Dodge wrote Kasson that he
certainly would not advise him to run if it meant a split in the party.
If Kasson's old friends were deserting him, it was because they thought
the election too important to risk. As for his own role in the campaign, said Dodge: "I shall take no part in the contest . . . if the party
considered it necessary that I should run, I would accept if nominated." [46]

In sharp candor, Kasson concluded the correspondence on May 12:

Dear Sir: I regret my appeal to you. For it has dissipated the opinion I had
formed of you. After serving your interests here for five long years with
constant fidelity, I had supposed you incapable of forgetting it under the
influence of a clamor unfounded in reason and in fact. Friendship that cannot back its object, and cannot remember benefits beyond the point at which
ambition or self-interest intervenes, is hardly what I had reason to expect
from you. With a high salary in the past, and to be continued in the future,
I could not believe you would wish to take bread away from me.[47]

Shortly after this letter reached Dodge, Palmer's *Register*, goaded
by the Democratic press for ignoring Kasson, broke its long silence.
"That Mr. Kasson should be singled out for championship by the
Copperhead press," declared Palmer, "will be cause for alarm to the
Republican Party of this district." Other Radical papers over the
state took up the same theme: Kasson was a tool of the "cops." [48]

Between letters to Dodge, Kasson struck off a long one to Samuel
C. Wead, businessman in Malone, New York, and the husband of his
favorite sister Mary. Wead had previously written, wanting information on the state of the nation and on how the South was to be handled. Kasson's analysis, written for private eyes and safe from political adversaries in Washington and Iowa, must be accepted as expressing his real views.

One large group, he said, cried justice and vengeance in the same
breath and sought political servitude of Southern whites to the North.
This group "is still carrying on the war," "has not laid down the
bayonet, and is willing to spend any amount of money to keep up
the warfare, high tariff, and high prices." The middle group, to which

Kasson obviously belonged, did not believe in "pacification cemented in blood," but in "leading examples of the administration of justice, enough to justify the constitution, and not too much to merit the approbation of History." This group was not "bloody-minded . . . believing that true statesmanship after civil war to be in extinguishing, not fanning, the fires of party hatred." It was seeking "future fidelity of the South through proper guarantees." The third group, which he dismissed lightly, was willing to yield to the South without guarantees and would "trust a traitor as quick as a Unionist."

Andrew Johnson belonged to the middle group, said Kasson. The President was patriotic, "perfectly sober," did not "touch liquor in any form," and worked "from early morning to near midnight." His manners in private were "quiet and gentlemanly toward all." The President had "no wish for personal vengeance," but he had been too prompt in extending pardons before reorganization. "The error was in time rather than in fact, or numbers." He was a "badly abused man," and although his policy deserved some "criticism and opposition," he did "not deserve the denunciation put on him." [49]

Kasson did not make a single reference to his own personal difficulties. But Radicals in Iowa were not going to let any skeletons be locked up. Even additional ones might be dragged out.

☆ ☆ ☆

Now that the Radicals in the Fifth District had found a champion, they nevertheless developed acute jitters as convention time approached. There was serious doubt that the mighty General himself could beat the "pernicious scamp." Reports coming in from the counties produced cold fear. "Kasson is a wiry man [and] . . . may defeat you"; "Kasson suits us in all circumstances . . . and we shall go for him"; "Kasson as an orator and talented man . . . makes a very fine showing"; Kasson's "strength is increasing every day"; "Kasson seems to be carrying Polk, Dallas, and Guthrie counties." Even the distinguished associate justice of the United States Supreme Court, Samuel Freeman Miller, a native Iowan, was working for Kasson, it was reported.[50]

On May 30 Kasson arrived in Des Moines. He "is using money freely," Tichenor shrilled out to Dodge. "Bring Cale, Sapp and Ross. Hooker and his stages [stagecoaches] are free for your use." But the "golden opportunity" had passed, Tichenor lamented. "Have constantly urged a bitter and open denunciation . . . but our folks have been weak kneed. Had they commenced at the time I advised them to, Kasson never would have dared to show his face in this district." Palmer and Withrow, he said, were preparing and distributing certain mysterious "necessary documents," but it might be too late. Almost hysterical, he urged Dodge again and again to hasten to Des Moines. *"No consideration must keep you from the convention.* YOU MUST COME. . . . Hoxie must be here." Tichenor also advised Dodge that he had received "the circulars" from Nate, the General's brother, and had made "good use of them." Tichenor said he had still other material "for use at the convention." [51]

Frank Palmer was scared, too, and urged Dodge to bring all his military friends and be on hand at the convention. Kasson had put to work assessors and postmasters "without number." But, confided Palmer, "as a last result there will be a way to match Kasson's own delegates, which you can guess, and which would be warrantable, considering the means Kasson himself is using." [52]

Hub Hoxie was downright gloomy. Withrow, Palmer, and Tichenor had not "fixed" the county conventions, wrote Hoxie to Dodge; Kasson had "packed them" and would carry Polk, Harrison, and Dallas. Hoxie "firmly" believed that Kasson would be nominated. It was too late for him to go to Des Moines, as Dodge was urging.[53]

But the indomitable "Hub" had not been sitting idly by. He had helped initiate a plan which was having more desirable results than his pessimism warranted. From St. Joseph it was easy for Hoxie to contact Cara's brother in St. Louis, the Rev. Dr. William Greenleaf Eliot, with whom she was residing. This Hoxie had done. This distinguished and powerful gentleman was also a Radical, and the people in Missouri as in Iowa were seething with dissension.

A few weeks before the divorce scandal broke, Rev. Eliot had made a trip to Washington and had conferred with his brother, Congressman Thomas Dawes Eliot, and with a relative, Dr. Johnson Eliot. Although advised by his brother to keep out of the affair, he returned to St. Louis glowering with rage, ready to make "war to the knife" against that "double twisted villain," Kasson.

With Eliot in this mood, Hoxie easily worked out with him a plan which involved men widely scattered from Washington and New Bedford to St. Louis, Council Bluffs, Des Moines, and every county in Kasson's district. Dr. Eliot provided the "necessary documents," including alleged private letters written by Kasson to his former wife. Some of the documents were merely to be shown to wavering delegates; others to be printed as circulars and distributed. Chief distributors were Hoxie, Baldwin, Nate Dodge, Withrow, Palmer, and Tichenor. Many years later, General Dodge piously wrote that he had vainly tried to keep the campaign on a high level and prevent the "circular" attack on Kasson. But this is not the case. Not only did Eliot unfold the plan to Dodge, but the General was also a "distributor." [54]

One of the extant circulars, allegedly authored in the main by Baldwin, summarized the proceedings of a "Convention of Republicans of Pottawattamie" (Dodge's home county), which soundly condemned Kasson for his "moral defection and political declension." The time had come when the Republican party would have to put forward "its purest and wisest men." The circular also carried a letter from Dr. Eliot. It spared no details. Kasson was *a diseased man from dissipation* so that it was not safe for any decent woman to live with him," Eliot charged! Two doctors had said so — one at New Bedford and the other, his relative at Washington. Moreover, continued the letter, Kasson "had had criminal connection with three different women," and Dr. Eliot, in this circular, vowed that he could produce Kasson's "own written admission of the fact." But Dr. Eliot hoped that Cara's "name would not come into the controversy."

In early June, as convention time approached, Dr. Eliot's wrath mounted. He besieged Dodge with letters and kept feeding "necessary documents" to the proper persons. Under his pen, Kasson's misdeeds grew and grew. Dodge was given some kind of damaging information allegedly provided by Kasson's former slave Lydia and her husband Steven. To Dodge he said, "You must scatter it *far and wide*." Palmer had put it "in type" but was holding it back until "Convention meets." It would appear in the St. Louis papers, Eliot promised. He predicted that a strong protest against Kasson's nomination would come from "leading men in Washington." Finally, to cap off all these activities, Eliot decided to appear at the convention himself to show and circulate letters written by the "cold-blooded scoundrel." "*You* and *Hoxie* will be there of course," he wrote Dodge. "Spare neither expense nor effort." [55]

The stage was now set for what the Radicals hoped to be the final act. The convention opened Monday, June 18, in an atmosphere

charged with tenseness and uncertainty. Dodge was on hand. So
was Eliot, busy showing documents. Kasson had departed for Washington, inspiring the accusation that he did not have the courage to
face his brother-in-law.

Two other candidates besides Dodge and Kasson were in the
field — J. A. Harvey of Fremont County and M. L. McPherson of
Madison County. Harvey was soon to fall out, but McPherson commanded a small bloc of votes which might determine the winner.
This former North Carolina Quaker, abolitionist, and agent for the
Underground Railroad had already been pressured by Dodge for support. Even Senator Kirkwood had been put to work on him.

The balloting was prolonged and bitter. For three days and for
eighty ballots or more Kasson led Dodge by three to ten votes most
of the time, but short of the number required for nomination. When
Harvey's name was withdrawn, Kasson's lead increased. On the second day Taylor County went over to Kasson, running his total to 64,
or 6½ votes short of the required 70½. Three other counties, instructed to support Kasson whenever McPherson's chances looked hopeless,
were ready to switch and nominate Kasson on the next ballot. At this
point the Dodge and McPherson men maneuvered an adjournment
until the next morning. That night McPherson and Dodge met at
the Savery Hotel. Said McPherson, "I agreed to turn my back on
friends who had stood by me for seventy-seven ballots and would
stand there seventy-seven more. . . . I made an arrangement with
Dodge."

The next morning, after a few ballots, McPherson's Madison
County went over to Dodge, and the vote stood, Dodge 76, Kasson
64. The victorious General was then called to the convention hall,
and he made a speech to prove that he was thoroughly Radical.[56]

As the denouement in the drama, several letters were soon posted.
With the event fresh on his mind, McPherson immediately gave Kirkwood elaborate details as to how he threw the nomination to Dodge.
He wanted "the matter explained" to the Iowa congressional delegation. A few days later he wrote Dodge: "Previous to our interview
at which we finally arranged matters I understood you to intimate
that a position or positions on the U. P. were at your disposal and
also that you could give me a situation at Des Moines." McPherson
wanted to know how to turn his "defeat into profit." His friends had
told him that he could have commanded thousands from Kasson.[57]

J. N. Dewey wrote Kirkwood: "Kasson died hard if indeed he is dead yet. I am glad you wrote McPherson just as you did. . . . His defection would have nominated Kasson any time." Dewey hoped that McPherson and others would be remembered in the future. As for Kasson, said Dewey, "If the snake is only scotched and not killed, I trust you will not refuse a few more licks, when called upon, as you will be shortly, to rid the state of his presence." [58]

Dodge, now facing the Democratic candidate, General James M. Tuttle, wrote Kirkwood that the fight had been "bitter and moving." Some "sore heads" remained and some "dirty work" would be done.[59] Dodge also wrote Rev. Eliot. The campaign had been costly, and the General wanted a contribution. With a mixture of indignation and apprehension Dr. Eliot replied:

I scarcely know what to say in answer to yours, 25th, for I am not at all sure that my part of the "fight" is over. From Wash. I learn that Kasson is evidently contemplating *some* movement. . . . It looks a little as if he means to sue me for libel, and *the shape in which my letter was put in the Circular may give color to such proceedings.* I can prove the facts alleged from his own letters and from other evidence, but *they were somewhat harshly stated.* . . .

If Dodge "had *failed*," continued Dr. Eliot, "he would feel like bearing half the burden, though from an empty purse." He had entered the campaign believing that political parties paid their own expenses. His brother had not concurred with his course of action, but his temperament was "*hotter.*" He did not have the means to contribute anything else.[60]

A week earlier Dr. Eliot had similarly revealed both a sense of uneasiness about his course and a disgust with Iowa politicians. For the record, he had left a sworn statement of the Kasson case with Dodge, "*not* to be published but to show to anyone who needs to be convinced." He hoped the whole affair would be laid to rest. Then he blandly stated: "Thus far *I* have published nothing, and my sister's cause is sufficiently vindicated by Kasson's defeat. If I should be compelled to publish anything, it would be to defend myself and you, *not her!*" And, concluded Dr. Eliot, "If we ever have another fight, I hope we shall have bolder men . . . than those in Des Moines!" [61]

In early July, Cara wrote Mrs. Dodge a letter. She congratulated General Dodge but warned him that he was "going to a far more trying scene of strife than the battle scene." Yet Cara was ambitious to brave this scene again herself. "My friends in Washington want to see my face again," she said. "Perhaps you and General Dodge will take me in charge for a week or two. I may go under your wing two winters hence." As for her former husband, she predicted that "policy and scheming" would prompt him to stump Iowa for the General.[62]

As an echo to the affair, in after years General Dodge insisted innocently that he had never asked for public preferment and that he had tried to keep the scandal out of the campaign. Tichenor, he said, could never comprehend "why I did not ask for anything; why I would not write a letter asking anyone to aid in my promotion and refusing absolutely to *touch politics!*" The scandal did Kasson more good than harm in the race, he affirmed. General Dodge's own private correspondence shows all these statements to be false. As for the scandal, there are letters from county politicians sufficient in number to show that the circulars turned away from Kasson enough delegates to defeat him. Without the "necessary documents" John Kasson probably would have won on the first ballot.[63]

If John Kasson ever discussed the affair, no such record coming directly from him has been found. Other than his qualified concession to the allegations for purposes of the divorce, he neither admitted nor denied the accusations. He naturally pursued the course of letting time bury the skeleton.

Kasson was a spirited, ambitious man. He thought well of himself and his opinions. He was meticulous in his habits and drove himself hard. It is difficult to think of him as a "whoremaster." It is doubtful that, burdened so seriously with social diseases before medical science had mastered them, he could have lived to be an octogenarian. It is likely that his moral delinquencies were grossly exaggerated. But he may not have been a good companion in marriage; he may have been hard to live with.

Cara Kasson was also ambitious and spirited. The youngest child in an old, proud, and aristocratic family, she was well educated, talented, and thought well of herself and her activities. In one sense this lady was a strait-laced Puritan; in another, a woman of the world. A contemporary many years later declared that Kasson's divorce "resulted from the jealousy of his wife who was a high-toned cultured handsome woman." Today in Des Moines there persists a legend, handed down from Kasson's intimate friends, that Cara was "insanely jealous." [64] And as the war years dragged to an end, Cara and John found themselves differing fundamentally in their politics. Cara was probably also hard to live with.

That there were incompatibilities in this union there is little doubt. Nor is it to be doubted that the existing difficulties were discovered in 1866 by men who considered Kasson no longer useful, and who seized upon, agitated, and magnified these difficulties for their own selfish ends. Because of his independence and his support of Andrew Johnson, Kasson had committed political heresy. The scandal presented an opportune means for excommunication by the Radical hierarchy.

The consequences were not as serious for Cara's future as for John's. Within three years she had married a very wealthy banker-manufacturer of St. Louis, who could indulge her tastes far more fully than John had been able to do. There, in a stately old mansion, she lived out her long life happily as a civic and society leader among women. To her is given the credit for having inaugurated the first society department in the *Globe-Democrat* for the young ladies of the first families of St. Louis.[65]

But of all the participants in the drama, General Dodge was riding highest. Through railroad entrepreneurship, great wealth awaited his command; through politics, great power. A whole flock of political lieutenants, many of them former military lieutenants, stood ready to fly over the land and represent the General's interests in Iowa, Washington, the South, and the West. Moreover, he was the intimate of Grant and Sherman and could rely on the backing of Senator Kirkwood and Congressmen Wilson and Allison. In the realignment of party factions in Iowa, Dodge was emerging as political boss of the state and as a powerful influence in national affairs. John Kasson had been no small factor in the General's rapid ascent.

From the campaign of 1866, John Kasson received the severest setback. Politics had become his career, the main force in his life, the chief means of his livelihood. Now there was serious doubt that he could ever piece together the shattered fragments of this career and rise again. Although his conduct in Congress had been geared to political expediency all along, he imposed some restraint upon the Radicals and demonstrated some foresight as the nation plunged headlong into the new postwar era. More men of his type were needed in the Congress to moderate the excesses of the coming debacle called Reconstruction.

* XII *

Political Retreat and Foreign Mission

WHILE RADICALS in Iowa anxiously tried to guess John Kasson's future action, he continued his duties in the House from mid-June to late July, 1866, as the first session of the Thirty-ninth Congress drew to an end. His harassing experiences had not blunted his diligence nor his thrusts at the Radicals. As usual, however, on crucial Reconstruction issues between the President and the Radicals he yielded to party discipline, contrary to his obviously natural inclinations.

He put the finishing touches to his elaborate and technical report advocating a uniform metric system of weights and measures, having previously submitted this constructive report with a bill making the metric system legally permissive throughout the land. At the same time he introduced a resolution to appoint a uniform coinage commissioner to attend the Paris Industrial Exposition to be held the next year. Only Wilson of the Iowa delegation supported these foresighted measures long advocated by such men as Jefferson, Madison, and John Adams.[1] Apparently behind the proposals they suspected a trip abroad for Kasson.

On problems of Reconstruction, Stevens' committee continued to grind out propaganda for the looming, critical campaign and harsh legislation for the Southern states. During Kasson's absence the Fourteenth Amendment had been passed, and now the Radicals were preparing to force the Freedmen's Bureau Bill over Johnson's veto. Kasson voted to table Stevens' resolution to make ratification of the amendment a requirement for the restoration of the Southern states, but he readily supported the seating of Tennessee's delegation in Congress after that state had quickly ratified it. On the Freedmen's Bill, he followed the Radicals in passing it over the President's veto.[2]

As railroaders and manufacturers pressed in to consolidate their war victories under the aegis of the Radicals, who were economic conservatives, Kasson courageously took the side of the consumer. Aware of the desperate need for transportation in the West, he consistently supported local, state, and federal subsidies for railroads, but he also warily demanded safeguards against excessive rates and profits, and against the failure of companies to live up to their agreements.

As matter of course, he had always backed the Iowa branch of the Union Pacific. In the House he took credit for a conference with Lincoln that had been instrumental in locating the eastern terminal at Council Bluffs. But he was unwilling for the Chicago-Iowa interest to make this branch line the only branch line. Therefore, he backed the St. Louis-Kansas group for liberal terms to extend a branch westward up the Smoky Hill valley to Denver, rather than following the northerly Republican River valley to the main line several hundred miles to the east. Durant and Dodge obviously wished to push the junction of the Kansas branch as far east as possible, and in the House they were loyally supported by Wilson, Allison, and Price.

Despite future political consequences in Iowa, Kasson stuck to the

Kansas group. Referring to his trip west over the Omaha route and his return by the Smoky Hill route, he prophetically declared that it was of the "utmost importance to the country . . . for some competition in transportation . . . across the plains to the Rocky Mountains." Without competition, the benefit of "this great Pacific railroad to the people . . . would be diminished by one half." He favored liberality to both the Iowa and Missouri branches. But there must be no "great railroad monopoly of freight and passenger service." Let the miners and farmers have the benefit of competition, he warned. For the same reason, he demanded for Des Moines an outlet to St. Louis as well as Chicago and supported the "general right" of all railroad companies (rather than the specific right of one or more) to erect bridges across the Mississippi River.[3]

On the Morrill Tariff Act, Kasson found common ground with his Iowa colleagues. This measure, upping the tariff on a variety of products from 10 to 600 per cent, was bending beyond recognition the tariff plank of '60, which Kasson had helped author in order to win Pennsylvania and New Jersey. During the war, the plank had been seriously bent from the weight of tariff for badly needed revenue. Now Pennsylvanians with strong allies from New England and elsewhere were pressing in on Congress for even higher rates.

The tariff had not yet become the test of party allegiance, and Westerners were demanding a general reduction of duties. Pennsylvanians and New Englanders, it was rumored, were agitating the Southern question in order to forestall tariff revision. In the West, the war's end was bringing forth a resurgence of agrarian distrust against corporations, monopolies, and tariffs. In New York, the Free Trade League, led by William Cullen Bryant, was scattering propaganda against high tariffs far and wide.

John Kasson, reared in a home of Jacksonian Democracy, a reader as a young man of Bryant's *Evening Post*, and a former Free Soil and Benton Democrat, could well understand the rising protest, and he was sympathetic to it. The Morrill Act, he protested, made every "prominent necessity of life" more expensive to the consumer, particularly lumber, nails, salt, and iron rails so necessary to western farmers. Even the duty on boys' pocket knives, he reported, had been increased 600 per cent. The title of the bill, he declared, should be changed to "A bill to prevent the diffused blessings of divine Providence from being enjoyed by the people of the United States."

When Our Johnny was a Copperhead—In Bed with Andy Johnson in 1866, Opposing the Republican Policy of Reconstruction in Congress, and Making Speeches Against Negro Suffrage in Kentucky.

Not Meant for Anybody that It Don't Fit—And Not Fit For Anybody that It Don't Mean.

Anti-Kasson Cartoons from Des Moines "Register,"
August 28 and September 6, 1874

THE CAPITOL BUILDING IN DES MOINES

Stevens dubbed recalcitrant Westerners as free traders willing to debase free labor in order to defend a Southern dogma. He specifically charged Kasson with being a manager of the Free Trade League. Kasson replied that there were two extremes — free traders who would close all customs houses, and protectionists who would cut off all trade. Stevens' Pennsylvania colleague and friend William D. (Pig-Iron) Kelley, Kasson sarcastically charged, had promised to build up a "Chinese Wall" between the United States and the rest of the world.

Kasson denied belonging to either extreme. The "fundamental error" of the Morrill Act was that it rested on no "fixed policy or principle," he argued. To yield to the pressure of "this interest and that interest" would merely lead to yielding everywhere in order to equalize benefits, and eventually this would lead to a gigantic system of bounties. It was the means of making one group of Americans rich at the expense of another; it was the case of thousands of organized lobbyists against millions of unorganized consumers; it was "absurd" for some to insist that farmers would profit from protected rails, as badly in need of transportation as they were.

Still pressed on the floor to reveal his connection with the Free Trade League, Kasson finally admitted that he was a "council-elect" to it, but reiterated that he was not an extremist. Apparently he preferred to stand on the platform of 1860: a tariff for revenue with only "incidental protection." [4]

In late July a nervous Congress finally adjourned, contrary to the wishes of Stevens. The critical elections had to be faced. In Iowa a strong War Democrat, General James Tuttle, seriously challenged Dodge, and Kasson's reticence about his plans aroused anxiety.

Early in August, Kasson arrived in Des Moines. Cara had predicted correctly; he was not planning to bolt the party. In the nominating convention the preceding June, Kasson men had backed a movement to invite him to campaign for the entire state ticket, including Dodge. The district executive committee of eighteen members had forthwith issued an invitation. Balloting in the convention, wrote the committee, "fully established" that no man had "warmer, truer, and more tenacious friends" and "a stronger hold upon the affections of the people." In response to this flattering invitation, Kasson was now ready to take the stump.[5]

His arrival created excitement. A bonfire, a club of serenading German singers, and a crowd of loyal supporters greeted him at his hotel. He was host and speaker at what J. N. Dewey called a "glorification supper"; speaker at a ground-breaking celebration for the Keokuk, Fort Des Moines & Minnesota Railroad; and main speaker, "in his happiest vein," at an elaborate welcoming ceremony as the first train of that railroad pulled into town. He had come to Des Moines also with a congressional appropriation in his pocket for a new post office and custom house. Keeping this matter to himself to prevent speculation, he quietly purchased for the federal government an entire block for the building.[6]

Dodge men from the beginning had dreaded the return of the "venerial gentleman," as Frank Palmer called him. Dodge did not think it "good policy" for Kasson to participate in the canvass. Palmer then suggested that Kasson's stumping activities could be cut off through the chairman of the state central committee, M. E. Cutts. And now George Tichenor warned Dodge: "I tell you it won't do to allow this damned scoundrel to go on the stump . . . if he goes on . . . he must be followed, watched, and met on all occasions." Tichenor, who feared that Tuttle might beat Dodge, urged the General "to get every vote possible" from the "N. W. and U. P. railroads." He referred of course to the Irish laborers.[7]

J. N. Dewey was plainly exasperated at public demonstrations for Kasson. Never, he growled, until Kasson "got the class and partook of the holy sacriment" did people "think it necessary to so honor him."[8] Frank Palmer warned that "Andy" was using federal patronage actively to defeat Iowa Republicans; and Thomas Withrow wrote Dodge that Cutts declared "he would *not* put Kasson on the stump." Withrow added: "I hope that snake is scotched."[9]

But Chairman Cutts was finding it difficult to "scotch the snake." Cutts wrote Dodge: "Kasson's friends are importuning me every day to put him on the stump. . . . It is a strange fact that men will become so infatuated over and about that man and that they have gotten so that they consider him . . . higher than humanity. . . . His faults, defects, and shortcomings seem to be commendable virtues."[10]

In the end Kasson's friends did put him on the stump, but he made only two speeches, both in Des Moines. In the first, at a "complimentary" banquet, he lauded Radicals, Conservatives, the President, and even some Democrats; he admitted that he had favored the admission of Southern representatives to Congress from the beginning and that the admission of Tennessee delegates at the end of the session had proved his wisdom.

Kasson neither defended the Radical Congress nor condemned the President, screamed the *Register*. He was trying to array the loyal West against the loyal East in behalf of the disloyal South, Palmer affirmed. He is "bound straight into the Johnson camp, is delaying merely to do mischief," growled Dewey; "sugar-coated Andrew Johnsonism," declared Withrow.[11]

For Kasson's next appearance, planned by the central committee, this time three weeks in advance, he was to speak from the same platform with Senator Grimes. But Dodge men had other plans. Palmer simply "neglected" to publicize the Grimes-Kasson rally. Instead the *Register* carried "flaming notice" of another meeting, scheduled for an earlier date, at which Grimes, unaware of previous plans, appeared before an "imposing demonstration" — alone! Kasson had to make his speech later — and alone. But "notwithstanding the large and beautiful court room" was filled and overflowing.

A few days later the *Register* gleefully reported: "The Republican ranks are now solidified, and they will proudly sweep the field." John Kasson had declared in his courtroom speech that he was "an unconditional supporter of the Republican Platform and of the Republican candidates, General Grenville M. Dodge" included! [12]

The Dubuque *Herald* had earlier reviewed the background of the "bad box" in which Kasson was incased. In the early days of the war he had given John Teesdale the Des Moines post office so that Frank Palmer could have the *Register*; he had helped make Thomas Withrow supreme court reporter and had also transferred his law practice to Withrow; he had made Hub Hoxie, first, chairman of the central committee, next, federal marshal, and finally had procured him a lucrative job with the Union Pacific; he had made Baldwin federal attorney against the wishes of some members of the congressional delegation; he had supported the "wise policy" of Andrew Johnson.

But at this point, said the *Herald*, the "Des Moines clique" of "titsuckers" turned upon him, "entered his own house and stirred up his own wife against him," imported a "mendicant priest . . . his wife's own brother," who brought along "all Kasson's letters to his wife written under the sacred seal of marriage," and "hawked them about the street" while "pot-house politicians and bar-room loafers begged to read them." All this, charged the *Herald*, despite the fact that Kasson "made over" to his wife "nearly every dollars worth of property he possessed." In spite of these past services, Baldwin did not deny authoring scandalous circulars; "magnanimous" Hoxie came all the way from Omaha to help defeat Kasson; and the clique used Dodge to beat him. And now, continued the *Herald*, "poor Kasson," once a conservative, had "concluded" that the Radicals would win, and that "concluded him"; he was now Radical.[13]

A full month before Kasson made his alleged Radical speech, he had forecast his course in a letter to his old friend, Montgomery Blair, who was out campaigning for Andrew Johnson. Kasson also confirmed the worst of Radical fears — the fear that he still had a pipeline to the federal patronage.

As to his own course, Kasson explained: "My honor holds me to the party that elected me. Our fundamental principle [1864 platform] was the Union without slavery. I for one will not abandon the first clause of that principle any more than the last." He was ready "to preach the old Republican faith."

This letter was a carefully worded effort by Kasson to tell Blair tactfully that he wished Johnson well but that he would not go along with him. Political expediency demanded his sticking to a party, the dominant wing of which was trying to get rid of him. But at the same time it would do moderates, including the President, more harm than good to muddy the waters with a patronage scramble. Therefore, he requested, let me continue to hold my patronage.

Blair transmitted the letter to Johnson, but long before it could have had its desired effect, the *Register* had reported falling heads. Attorney Baldwin, whom Kasson considered expendable, had "resigned" and Marshal Peter Melendy, against whose dismissal Kasson had warned, had been "succeeded." Johnson had already taken matters into his own hands.

The "Simon Pure Copperhead State Central Committee" had taken over federal patronage, cried the *Register*, and the "Kangaroo Committee, with Johnny Kasson at its head" had "no part, nor lot, nor hope." Yet this rejoicing was premature, for later reports were to renew old fears that Kasson still had a hold on the patronage.[14]

On the other hand Radical fears of defeat at the polls in Iowa proved ungrounded. In each of the six congressional districts Republicans, who called themselves Radicals, won by comfortable margins. Only Kasson and Grinnell of the old House delegation would not return to the Fortieth Congress. Although professing extreme radicalism, Grinnell had shown signs of weakening, and like Kasson he was given the "holy sacriment"; he was cut down in the nominating convention.

It is doubtful that General Dodge, far away in the Rockies, forgot the election day, as he later claimed. George Tichenor spattered down ink to Dodge over the "glorious" results and ended his letter with "gloriously yours." "Every appliance," he shouted, "that treachery, meanness, Hell and David could invent was used against us but we met the scoundrels and fought over every inch of the ground and have given you" a majority. And now, he implored, "I want you to go to Washington and make friends with Johnson for the purpose of turning every d—d scoundrel that voted [against us], out of office." Tichenor did not refer to the scandals used to beat Tuttle — scandals almost as unsavory as those used to beat Kasson.[15]

Throughout the North, as in Iowa, Radicals won smashing victories. Congressional propaganda, campaign smears, claptrap discussions, and the evasion of fundamental issues had won over presidental patronage and blundering. Neither the Congress nor the President nor the South had been wise. In the North the people had been deceived into believing that the Radicals had a plan for orderly restoration and the competence to put it into operation. But in reality they had a plan which, burdened with the spirit of vengeance, was designed to achieve little more than their own temporary supremacy. They had no program designed to achieve reasonable and enduring solutions. The Union had been saved, but in the wake of the war the rising leaders were showing the lack of foresight and wisdom to grapple with the problems of the new order. The end result for a generation was to be a "shoddy aristocracy" in the North, destitution in the South, and a low level of political morality in the nation.[16]

The time had come for consolidation of Radical control. John Kasson, a lame duck, without a wife, almost without a party, but still trying to hang on, returned to Washington to finish out an episode of a frustrating experience in Congress.

☆   ☆   ☆

In the late elections the Radicals finally had brought the people in the North around to their way of thinking. As the short session of the

Thirty-ninth Congress opened, only a handful of Democrats and fewer moderate Republicans stood in their way. Faced with Radical discipline and the election results, moderates would either fall in line or fall out of politics. John Kasson, harshly disciplined and somewhat chastened, fell in line — with reservations milder than usual. Defeated and retreating, he was spared the usual Radical barbs, dripping with sarcasm. Nor was he the target of his Iowa colleagues as before, now that he was harmless. Still active as a member of the Appropriations Committee, he managed several bills with skill. But he put no serious obstacle in the way of Stevens' machine.

Old Thad and his satellites on the Joint Committee were grinding out measures to deprive Johnson of the federal patronage and control of the army, and to vest these functions in the hands of Congress. And at the first party caucus Stevens rebuked Republicans who in the late campaign had assured their constituents that the Fourteenth Amendment alone was an adequate condition for the restoration of the "conquered provinces." [17]

In order to obstruct Johnson's activities during the recess between the Thirty-ninth and Fortieth Congresses, the Radicals hurried through a resolution providing that the Fortieth Congress would convene immediately the following March, when the current session closed; Kasson voted yea. Next, a measure to shear away the President's pardoning power; Kasson, yea. And within a month, a resolution instructing the Judiciary Committee (James F. Wilson, chairman) to investigate Johnson's conduct for probable impeachment; Kasson, yea.

But Kasson spoke out to moderate the severe Military Reconstruction and Tenure of Office Acts. He was willing for Congress to establish military law where insurrection existed in fact, and he admitted that in "small areas" of the South insurrection did exist. But he denied the right of Congress to govern by military power and martial law any territory where peace prevailed and civil law could be applied. He offered his own amendments to the Reconstruction Act and voted consistently for milder Senate amendments. But when the President vetoed the amended act, Kasson followed the Radicals in passing it over the veto.

Kasson took the floor more than once in favor of having Cabinet members and their first assistants exempted from the Tenure of Office Act. This was a radical change of the Constitution, he declared. Department heads were "ministerial adjuncts" of the presidency and wholly responsible to him. To make them independent of him would leave him only a "sounding title" in the government.

His efforts to amend the bill failed, but he helped pass it over the President's head anyway. He also helped vote down Johnson's veto of the District of Columbia Franchise Bill, despite his previous fight against it. And as if to remind his colleagues that consistency required even further suffrage extension, he voted with the Democrats to give women the ballot!

In this session, revision of wartime economic legislation had been pushed into the background by Reconstruction matters. However, when, through Morrill, industrialists quietly slipped in a bill to revise the tariff upward by 20 per cent, Kasson voted no. But he introduced no petitions from Bryant's Free Trade League, as he had done before the elections.[18]

On March 2, 1867, a nasty sleet and snow storm greeted the end of the Thirty-ninth Congress. The next day Kasson watched the Fortieth Congress file in. Among the crowded galleries was a "lobby composed of unscrupulous thieves . . . and pretty women with flashing diamonds." Thomas D. Eliot and a group of other Radicals clustered around a new member, General Grenville M. Dodge, fresh from the Great Plains, where he had been engineering the building of the Union Pacific. Kasson gazed on fixedly but kept his distance. Little had he suspected, back during the war years, that his congressional career would be closed out by a scene in which his former brother-in-law and law partner would be congratulating his former protégé for taking his seat in Congress.[19]

In his congressional career now ending, Kasson had demonstrated ability, expert knowledge, streaks of courage, and flashes of foresight. In his campaigns he had not indulged in scandalmongering; he had stuck to the issues, although he had trimmed them severely. He could put country above passion and vindictiveness, but he would not, when faced with acid tests of party discipline, put all his professed principles above party. To bolt the party would have been futile, he must have reasoned; neither country nor himself would gain from desertion. Reaction to Radical excesses would come anon, and in the same party in which he had fallen he might be able to rise again.

Congressman Dodge and his lieutenants in Iowa were still worried about what Kasson might do. Dodge had brought Cale Baldwin, his candidate for the next governor, along with him to help divide the spoils. But to find Kasson still hanging around was irritating. He "is here to keep us from doing anything," muttered Dodge; he has "played some very sharp tricks"; is here to "watch and block . . . to see that I don't get any of his pets out of office"; and "has the inside track with all the Depts. and Andy, etc. and gets pretty much what he wants." [20]

Tichenor, Palmer, Withrow, Dewey, McPherson, Nourse, and several others were now pressing in for the pay-off. They were all still trying to "scotch the snake" but were somewhat in the dark as to his next movements. Would Kasson be able to keep his men in office? Would he run for governor in the summer? Or would he wait and oppose Dodge in 1868? In any event, would he be stumping around at random over the Fifth District? While asking for their rewards on the one hand, these gentlemen kept reminding Dodge on the other that it was all in the interest of keeping Kasson down. Using a variety of devices, they first of all blocked off Kasson's control over the building of the new post office.

Tichenor, his lumber business in Des Moines now failing, still wanted the post office, but he would settle for almost anything else — an Indian superintendency, a pensions agency, a collectorship farther west, or even an "outside" job as lumber dealer which would put him "inside the ring of combined railroad influence" so that he could control lucrative lumber shipments to and from Council Bluffs. What is more, Tichenor struck out to silence the voices of Withrow, Palmer, and Dewey in dividing the spoils and to exercise complete authority himself. These men were neither competent nor trustworthy political managers, he informed Dodge. Withrow and Dewey worked only for themselves! Palmer meant well but yielded "too readily to Withrow." "As God lives," Tichenor declared, "I believe their game is to kill Kasson and then you [Dodge]." Not given to modesty, Tichenor averred that he could do more in one year to "kill Kasson" than these gentlemen would do in "1000 years." But Kasson "must be *used* a while longer in some manners [*sic*]."

The rift between allies arose over who was to become the Des Moines postmaster. In the campaign to block Kasson's nomination, Tichenor, Palmer, and Withrow had promised the office to Isaac Brandt if he would desert Kasson and back Dodge. Now, Brandt was demanding his office, and Palmer and Withrow were writing that it would be a "breach of faith" to give it to Tichenor.

For a while Tichenor looked elsewhere. He urged Dodge to oust Peter Myers, a Kasson man, from the Des Moines pensions agency. It was "indecent intermeddling," he said, for Kasson, "the sneak . . . to want anything." Moreover, old Pete Myers was a "dirty dog . . . incompetent . . . vulgar . . . obscene" and spent "his Sundays playing cards." "For Gods sake," Tichenor yelled, "I want the Pup thrown out — and want the place for myself"!

Exasperated at the delay, Tichenor headed out for Washington but became sick and had to return home. Next, posing as a War Democrat, he dispatched Colonel N. P. Chipman, a friend of Johnson's private secretary, to "play a trick" on Andy, and procure the office. Meanwhile, he began to play Kasson men off against Palmer and Withrow. He convinced Dodge that the best way to keep down Kasson was to woo Kassen men with kindness — to give them some of the offices.[21]

From another source also Dodge was asked to pay off. McPherson, who had delivered Madison County to Dodge in the nominating convention, would not let him forget their arrangement. McPherson demanded a good position, "not a sinecure." He wanted Dodge to be the "wheel horse" in procuring for him an Indian superintendency. Johnson had the appointment on his desk, but Kasson was reported to be holding it up.

When Dodge finally recommended McPherson, Palmer was "glad." But he added: McPherson "played the damned scoundrel with Withrow and Nourse but after a fashion he kept his promise with you." Yet for some unknown reason McPherson was not appointed, and the next winter he was still wanting "any job that would pay $2000 or over."[22]

Tichenor fared better. Kasson's influence with the administration had been somewhat exaggerated, and Dodge shortly was to become master not only of patronage in his own district but also of some of the spoils in the South. He was rooming at the famous Wormley Hotel with Wilson and Allison, both influential among the Radical hierarchy and both becoming strongly attached to Dodge and his interests; he had access to the Grant-Stanton influence; and he was a man sought after by the numerous railroad Congressmen like himself. In the Fortieth Congress a man named Oakes Ames was distributing Union Pacific stock left and right. Dodge received full cooperation from the entire Iowa delegation, who joined him to put through Tichenor's appointment to the Des Moines post office.

Tichenor's enthusiasm gushed out over pages of stationery. His right hand was "dislocated" from congratulatory handshakes, he cried. It followed naturally that he would have to placate Withrow, Palmer, and Brandt. But "no concession," he affirmed. "They must come to me." In time, however, he smoothed out affairs, and Brandt had to settle temporarily for a recommendation of his son to the Naval Academy. Next Tichenor launched his program to buy up Kasson men with jobs. The President, he reassured Dodge, had gone back on Kasson after all; now, the snake was "essentially dead everywhere." [23]

All along, Tichenor had been urging Dodge to procure a register-ship of bankruptcy in Alabama for George E. Spencer, an old army crony. Spencer had once speculated in lands and dabbled in politics in Iowa. During the war he had been a sutler, a hotelkeeper behind the lines, assistant adjutant to General Dodge, and eventually a colonel of a regiment which he had helped recruit in northern Alabama. He had been an eager witness before Stevens' Joint Committee on Re-construction. Through Tichenor and Dodge he was eventually awarded his land registership, which reportedly paid $20,000. In this position, with Tichenor's aid, he would play off Negro against Scala-wag, Scalawag against Carpetbagger, and conservative white against Negro, Scalawag, and Carpetbagger until he became United States Senator from Alabama.[24] General Dodge's influence was indeed ex-panding.

Early in April, 1867, when fears at what Kasson might do were highest, he returned to Des Moines. This time there was no fanfare. But the feeling persisted among his adversaries that a great many people believed that the "snake's" fangs were not as poisonous as they had been represented to be. Kasson was still a popular man around Des Moines.

He tarried at home just long enough to make personal arrangements for a trip abroad. His old friend, A. W. Randall of Wisconsin, who had succeeded Kasson as Assistant Postmaster General in 1863 and whom Kasson had initiated into his new duties, had moved up to become Johnson's Postmaster General. Randall had appointed Kas-son Special Commissioner to negotiate postal conventions with a number of European nations. In one sense, this appointment may have been a last desperate thrust by Kasson to hang on to some connection with the government. In another, it was a case of the postal service's immediate need for a man of Kasson's peculiar ability and experience.

Since 1864 no further postal treaties had been concluded, incorporating the broad principles laid down by the Paris Conference of 1863. Negotiations by correspondence had been involved, complicated, and endless. Now, in the spring of 1867, Britain had terminated her convention, requesting an entirely new one on a more liberal basis; and the treaty with France had become outmoded, failing to secure public benefits for which it was intended. Randall had notified France of the necessity for a new treaty, and she had responded favorably, requesting a special delegate with full powers to negotiate.

Perhaps no one in America was better qualified than Kasson for such a mission. Randall recommended his appointment "because of his knowledge of postal details obtained during his connection with the department, and particularly on account of his familiarity with the postal questions to be dealt with, which were fully discussed at the Paris conference, in which he took a prominent part." His mission was to extend to Britain, France, Prussia, and Belgium, and was later expanded to include the Netherlands, Switzerland, and Italy. Kasson was instructed to follow the principles of the Paris Conference, or in general to reduce and establish uniform postage rates.[25]

The appointment was not lucrative, with "compensation" at eight dollars, and "expenses" at eight dollars, per day. But Kasson was glad to receive it; lest backstage finagling block it, he rushed to New York for embarkation — and got there barely in time. For, the evening before his departure, he received a note from Randall: the President had revoked his commission.

Why? Kasson must have pondered. Was his consistent vote to pass measures over Johnson's veto catching up with him? Were post office funds running short? These indeed may have been factors. But also, George Tichenor's relations, through Chipman, with the President's private secretary, may have been effective.

Kasson was "astounded . . . mortified." He had his bags packed; his mission had been announced in "all the papers"; so the next morning he boarded the *City of Antwerp* anyway, for Queenstown, Ireland, gambling that Johnson would withdraw his revocation. Two days later a message from Randall followed, upping his expense allowance to ten dollars a day and leaving the matter of compensation for "future consideration and adjustment." Kasson was still officially the Commissioner, but with a cut in pay of six dollars a day.

On the ship, Kasson ran into Senator John Sherman, whose moderating amendments to Stevens' Reconstruction Act he had recently supported. In Des Moines two of Sherman's brothers were Kasson men, though Tichenor was trying to win them over with jobs. Another brother, General William Tecumseh Sherman, was a close friend of Dodge. Sherman found Kasson "physically sound" and a "good companion." He had "the military air and step of a soldier." For firing a pistol at birds hovering around the ship, Kasson was suspected by British officers of being an Irish Fenian agitator, and had his luggage inspected and his pistol taken away. From Queenstown, Kasson and Sherman toured Ireland, kissed the Blarney Stone, and went on to London.[26]

From May to August, Kasson hurried back and forth between London, Paris, and Brussels, negotiating, sightseeing, socializing, and writing long letters to his sisters, letters filled with minute observations on people, their institutions, and society. To his sisters he confided restlessness, loneliness, and the longing for home life. The adjustment to bachelorhood was not coming easy.

In London, which he preferred to Paris, he was cordially received officially and socially. Here negotiations proceeded rapidly and successfully. Here he dined with the American Minister, Charles Francis Adams, and was introduced to Lady Strangford, with whom a long and warm friendship developed. This cosmopolitan viscountess invited him to her houses in Paris and London; provided for his honorary membership in the Atheneum Club; took him to the House of Commons to hear Bright, Disraeli, and Gladstone debate the Reform Bill; and introduced him into old English society, until he became so well "posted in aristocratic ways" that he felt at home.

Kasson spent week ends at Fryston Hall, the country estate of Lord Houghton (Monckton Milnes), staunch partisan of the North during the Civil War. Here at a round of social affairs Kasson conversed with such British notables as Robert Browning, the poet; the Earl, John Russell, former Minister of Foreign Affairs; and Sir Morton Peto, investor in American railroads. From here he visited industrial

Sheffield, kennels stocked with 200 sleek hounds, and Scrooby, the church of William Bradford and the Pilgrims. Lord Houghton took him to the Mechanics' Institute at Castleford where Kasson made a speech entitled, "Education of the Masses." Throughout, the audience applauded every reference to the United States. At the end they "cheered him to the echo . . . as in the West." He enjoyed the leisurely country life, but the "bird voices" at Fryston Hall infected him with nostalgia for his boyhood days long ago at Charlotte, Vermont. He found full dress for dinner a "pleasant habit," and was impressed by England's intellectual, "handsome, well dressed women."

In Paris, he observed all manner of Americans, thronging to see the Industrial Exposition and the gathering of Europe's "glittering royalty." Senators, Representatives, governors, generals, and the *nouveaux riches* were arriving with their wives, expecting courtesies from diplomats and private audiences with the Emperor. According to the former American Minister, John Bigelow, they were "an intolerable lot . . . easily impressed, easily rebuffed, shrewd, boasting, with an insatiable thirst for recognition."

Kasson found the French unwilling to give ground in negotiations; the weather was cold and wet; he suffered from a "benumbed feeling" in his leg which was diagnosed as sciatica and which did not respond well to a new electric treatment. Time dragged, life grew monotonous, and in a fit of "ennui" he confided to his sister that "some kind of home life" was "essential" to his comfort.

The Industrial Exposition was interesting but "tiresome." The many "things beautiful in art and utility created a desire for enough money to indulge one's taste." He noted that Maximilian's execution before a firing squad in Mexico "shocked public sentiment in Europe." In deference to such feeling in Paris, Kasson and several other Americans postponed their anticipated Fourth of July celebration.

Bright spots in Paris were the open doors to the homes of General John A. Dix and Henry S. Sanford, United States Ministers respectively to France and Belgium. He considered Dix a "good American representative" abroad. Finding the family "kind and friendly," he spent many gratifying hours at their home. Sanford, who kept a house in Paris and a castle in Brussels, was a "good friend," whose friendship dated back at least to Kasson's Paris mission of 1863. Kasson found him well informed, speaking several languages, "social and hospitable," a "good Minister," with "a beautiful wife, a beautiful house, and fond of the show that his private fortune" enabled him to make. When Kasson moved on to Brussels, he frequently accepted their "standing invitation" to dine with them and meet diplomatic dignitaries.

In Belgium he bought lace for his sisters and observed that the Belgian government owned and made money on railroads, express companies, and the post office. He thought the Crown Princess of Belgium showed "great resolution" in caring for her insane sister-in-law, Carlotta of Mexico.

In a long letter to his sisters' children, he told them dogs were used for horses in Antwerp. Walking along the street studying the dogs' faces, he concluded that they "might get up a society for dogs' rights, demand universal suffrage and occasionally strike for higher wages." But if he were a dog, Kasson continued, he would prefer a woman to a little boy for a master. Little boys were cruel to animals, but "a woman wouldn't beat me . . . would give me some water and a bone as soon as I got home."

To his sisters' sons ready for college he gave sound advice: pray, study, play; hold up shoulders; avoid gloom; beware of quick romances — "girls are as thick as whortleberries . . . no hurry to pick them"; "work not for merit marks but complete mastery" of subject; no secret conduct — "face up to consequences" of shortcomings; "don't be a hypocrite, which is one of the worst of all faults and sins, and clouds the whole character"; and don't gossip.[27]

While thus philosophizing and undoubtedly probing deep into his own life for wisdom, and in some measure summarizing his own conduct in his divorce scandal, Kasson at the same time traveled to other capitals and spent long hours on technical aspects of postal negotiations. By late November he had signed treaties with Britain, Belgium, the Netherlands, the North German Union, the Swiss Confederation, and Italy.

But French officials adamantly resisted any fundamental change. Between trips from Paris to other countries, Kasson kept up steady pressure. But subordinate postal officials refused to discuss any reduction of postal rates and transit charges, which Kasson considered a *sine qua non* to a treaty. He undertook to deal with higher officers but ran into red tape, evasion, and delay. The foreign minister skipped two appointments and went calling. Subordinates at the foreign office referred Kasson to the Chief-of-Cabinet who referred him to the

Director who referred him to the Under Director who referred him to the Head of the Posts who postponed negotiations until certain information could arrive from the British office. Later, after negotiations were opened, the Head of Posts deferred the discussions because of the absence of the minister of finance to whom he was subordinate. Kasson reported to Randall: "It is hard to work here"; the French were "too . . . fond of being waited on"; they were "negligent and dilatory"; it is "a mere waste of time to argue questions of equity with subordinates who travel only in old ruts."

The practical minded French well understood the advantageous location of their country over which a huge volume of mail passed in transit to other points in Europe. They were unimpressed by Kasson's arguments that the whole world was moving out of old ruts in the direction of removing postal restrictions. Finance was the key to the matter. The French Administration, Kasson was informed, "is not unaware in what measure the reduction of its transit charges will favor its financial interest."

Finally, Kasson advised Randall to shear away some of the revenue France was taking in from American mails in transit. Terminate the old treaty with France. Direct continental closed mails through Dover to Ostend so that the American public could enjoy the lower rates under the British and Belgian treaties just negotiated.

Early in November, Kasson returned to Paris from Florence where he had concluded a treaty with Italy. Again he prevailed upon the French to use his treaties with the other countries as models; they refused, and at last he gave up "the disagreeable task." [28]

Others were to encounter similar difficulties with France. Although the old treaty was in time terminated as Kasson had advised, negotiations dragged on until the eve of the international postal conference at Berne in 1874, which established the famous and enduring Universal Postal Union.

Even so, Kasson had done well, and he fully merited Randall's warm congratulations. His treaties were practical achievements and another important solid rung up the ladder to the Universal Postal Union. Yet his mission drew fire from Congress. Under what authority had John Kasson been touring around Europe without Senate confirmation, queried a House Resolution. But it was not difficult for the Postmaster General to cite abundant statutory authority and precedent for such negotiations by executive agents.[29]

Kasson left London in early December as cold weather came on. He was anxious to reach Des Moines, buy a lot, build a house, and re-establish a home. He had never liked boarding out. Moreover, he still had many loyal friends there. During his absence, he had received the surprising news that he had been chosen to represent Polk County in the Iowa House of Representatives.

It was something of a surprise to George Tichenor also. This political manager and his allies were still trying to "scotch the snake." Hoyt Sherman and other Kasson men were now accepting or begging favors from Dodge. George Spencer, with his registership in bankruptcy in Alabama, was making money and urging Tichenor to come down and be made a Congressman.

But Tichenor was too busy in Des Moines scotching the snake. And he was hard put to explain the nomination of Kasson, who, Tichenor affirmed, wrote no one and had nothing to do with it. "It is *no victory*," screamed Tichenor to Dodge, who was now railroading in Cheyenne; "*It will prove the last stroke of final and eternal defeat and political ruin to him and his friends!*" All the leading papers in the state were "pitching into" Kasson. In the legislature he would be "tied hand and foot, spit upon and scourged. . . . All his old friends here wish him in Hell." Tichenor averred that Kasson's enemies duped his friends into nominating him.

But Kasson won in the general election with ease. Dodge's home county (Pottawattamie) almost went Democratic. Republican majorities in Iowa, New York, Ohio, and Pennsylvania were cut down. Money was becoming tight and there was agitation in the West for more of it. In Des Moines, Tichenor reported business failures. Had the reaction against the Radicals begun so soon? [30]

A public demonstration greeted Kasson's arrival in Des Moines. People had a job laid out for him. He was considered to be the one man, who, in the legislature, could keep the state capital at Des Moines in face of vigorous efforts on the part of other towns to take it away. He had been nominated primarily for the purpose of pushing through an appropriation for a new state capitol building, which, once erected, would keep the capital of the state in Des Moines forever, it was hoped. Whether Kasson at the moment knew it or not, his membership in the legislature was to be the base for his fight back.

☆ XIII ☆

The Fight Back: In the Iowa Legislature

CONTRARY TO George Tichenor's prediction, John Kasson was not scourged but warmly received in the Iowa legislature. If not one of the two "most notable" House members, as one historian of Iowa has stated,[1] Kasson was from the beginning at least one of the half dozen most active members. Before retiring from the House he was to secure a firm place for himself in Iowa legislative history on the basis mostly of his work in connection with the new state capitol appropriation, the revision of the Iowa Code, and railroad legislation.

229

More important to Kasson's political career, however, was the fact
that he could use his House seat as a springboard in his fight back for
a place in the Republican party. During the next five years he was
engaged in a bitter struggle with the Dodge forces, who used every
device at their disposal to block him off from all places of importance
and to expel him from the party. But for three successive terms, Des
Moines and Polk County sent him to the legislature, despite the diligence of Dodge's "secret service" men directed by George Tichenor.
With these exceptions, Tichenor was so effective that Kasson at one
time seriously considered leading an independent movement, but when
golden opportunities presented themselves for a bolt in 1872 and
1873, he turned them down. He was first of all a party regular, and
by that time his prospects within the party were brighter.

With strong committee assignments in the Twelfth General Assembly, Kasson managed to blunt some of the sharper resolutions censur-
ing Andrew Johnson. But he failed to vote on resolutions approving
Johnson's impeachment and Negro suffrage in Iowa. On railroad
legislation, Kasson voted to reserve to the legislature the right to regulate rates, and he was accused by Tichenor of writing anti-railroad
articles for the *Register*. In the struggle for appropriations for a new
state capitol, Kasson had to settle for a weak measure, which merely
provided for a study of plans to be submitted to the next Assembly.[2]

The fight for the new state capitol had barely begun when the
Twelfth Assembly closed, and there was serious doubt that Kasson
would be returned to the legislature to renew it. For, during 1868,
General Dodge, through George Tichenor's "secret service" kept "spies
on his tracks all the time." Palmer, Withrow, and Nourse from Des
Moines and Allison, Wilson, and Price of the congressional delegation
also helped keep tab on "the late urbane Johnny K." Consequently
Kasson was blocked off from the county convention in March, which
urged the nomination of Grant for president; from the district convention in May, which unanimously nominated General Dodge's hand-
picked candidate, Frank Palmer, for Congress; from the state convention in May, which fiercely censured the falling Grimes for voting
against Andrew Johnson's impeachment; and from the national convention, which nominated Grant and Colfax. Despite Tichenor's
efforts to keep him off the stump in the presidential canvass, Kasson
spoke before a "ten-acre" Republican rally in Des Moines. His "trip-
hammer" words brought a "storm of enthusiastic greeting," it was

reported. But Kasson found a warmer reception from New York politicians, who invited him to that state to campaign. Greeley's *Tribune* paid glowing tribute to his "ringing eloquence."

With the election of Grant and Palmer in the fall of 1868, Dodge men prepared to distribute "the jewels." Only the "old guard . . . the honest and reliable men" should become Grant's advisers, Tichenor warned. Isaac Brandt's claim on the Des Moines post office was brushed aside by General Dodge himself. Kasson was headed off from a federal appointment by Dodge and Hiram Price, who warned Grant that Kasson, lacking "political and moral character," was not acceptable by "our people."

During the winter following Grant's election, Tichenor carefully laid plans to defeat Kasson for the legislature, but in June, 1869, Kasson broke through and won renomination. Tichenor had been able to control the Des Moines delegates, but the rural townships put Kasson over.

This victory revived new fears among Dodge men, who hoped to pick the successor for Senator Grimes, now broken in health and convalescing in Paris. Kasson himself might form a combination with Senator Harlan and Governor Samuel Merrill and win the Senate seat. Dodge men preferred James F. Wilson, but after Wilson accepted one of the directorships of the Union Pacific, Dodge settled upon William B. Allison. Kasson's renomination to the Iowa House caused Tichenor to lose confidence in Allison's ability to win. Why not ditch Allison and run Wilson, or better still, run yourself, he urged Dodge. Let Allison have the short term. Undoubtedly it was the implorings of Tichenor and Palmer that brought Dodge to Des Moines to assume personal generalship of Allison's forces in the senatorial contest.[3]

Several days before the Thirteenth General Assembly convened in January, 1870, General Dodge and his Fifth District lieutenants were swarming over Des Moines. Each train brought fresh delegations of Allison men who were conspicuous for their "sheer force of bluster" and their apparent confidence of certain victory. There was much truth in the rumor flying about that this faction had the support of the railroad forces and of a majority of the federal officeholders.[4]

On January 10 at 2:00 p. m., John Kasson called the House to order. Three days later at the party caucus George G. Wright, on the first ballot, was chosen Senator for the long term by a thumping majority. Allison stood second and Merrill, third. James B. Howell of Keokuk was awarded Grimes's unexpired term. The Harlan-Merill-Kasson combination had either evaporated or had never been so strong as Tichenor, Palmer, and Allison had led Dodge to believe. The thrust of Dodge, through his man Allison, to take over Grimes's former powerful position in the party machine had failed. New recruits would have to be lined up and Harlan's reputation destroyed before the Dodge-Wilson-Allison faction could become supreme.

Although Merrill's light vote showed that Kasson was somewhat powerless, he would still have to be blocked on all avenues. Such statements as the one from the Dubuque *Times* that Kasson was the "leading member" in the new House did not inspire confidence that he was completely hemmed in.

In the Thirteenth Assembly, Kasson was in a strong position to push through the capitol appropriation. Since spring he had been lining up legislators behind this measure, and very probably George Tichenor had mistaken some of these activities as senatorial electioneering. Moreover, Senator-elect Wright had thrown his influence behind the bill. Under these circumstances, George Tichenor, with the "wolves" growling at his door for the Des Moines post office, adopted the strategy first of defeating the capitol appropriation. Should it succeed, Kasson must not receive credit for its passage, no matter what the cost to Des Moines. Prominent citizens were openly predicting that the next congressional contest in the Fifth District would depend in a large measure upon the fate of the capitol bill. Its final triumph or defeat "by common consent" rested upon Kasson. Not only would its defeat hold Kasson down, but Tichenor could use it as a "leverage to crush old Wright and his friends" who were trying to get him out of the post office.

Several days before the bill was even reported, Tichenor advised Dodge to join Wilson and Allison and "form a ring" with the "different asylums" expecting appropriations, in order to defeat the "capitol swindle." Tichenor thought he could control about twenty votes in the legislature. When apprised of Tichenor's plans, Dodge appreciated "the existing status of the capitol matter fully" and apparently cooperated. But Tichenor's strategy would have to be executed quietly, else Palmer and his friends be charged with the responsibility for the bill's defeat.

If the strategy of defeat or postponement failed, Tichenor had a line of retreat worked out. He would saddle the bill with a rider enabling Dodge to control the booty in the actual construction of the building; he would pack the building commission with Dodge lieutenants. Kasson, although he might secure the appropriation against cunning opposition, would thus have no part in approving plans, awarding contracts, procuring materials, and employing personnel.[5]

Kasson was not fully aware of the nature of this opposition as he assumed the leadership of the measure in the early days of the session, for the building committees were packed with men favorable to the appropriation. Representatives from widely scattered state institutions guarding their own appropriations, and delegates eager to transfer the capital to their areas, composed an obvious bloc of opposition. But more serious, Kasson thought, were the numerous timid delegates who conscientiously favored the measure but would vote against any new expenditures to be on the safe side. One-fourth of the House membership, he estimated, was guided by their fears rather than by their "deliberate judgment." From "personal conversation" Kasson was convinced that a large majority, from "honest convictions," were favorable to a fine new capitol.

Since in the Twelfth Assembly the bill had been passed easily in the House but had been "mutilated and slaughtered" in the Senate, it was now decided to report it first in the Senate where Kasson's friend, George E. Griffith of Warren County, was chairman of the building committee. Accordingly, the bill easily passed the Senate early in February with only minor changes. Evidently, the real challenge was to be made in the House.[6]

The ease with which the measure cleared the Senate brought Tichenor around to his plan of retreat. "You can be made Capitol Commissioner," he informed Dodge as the measure reached the House, by making Representatives John Beresheim and George H. McGavren "stand by you and *make them for the Bill contingent upon your appointment.* . . . We can hold 20 votes for or against the bill." Kasson was "working like a Beaver," Tichenor warned. "We must beat him . . . must not sleep, for he is making strength. We should be better organized in this district than we are." Two days later, in a reply to Dodge, Tichenor wrote: "We are forming a most powerful Allison, Dodge, Wilson organization." [7]

In the House, the "Ajax" of the now well-organized opposition was a new member, Marsena E. Cutts of Mahaska, the same gentleman who as chairman of the state committee in 1866 had joined up with Dodge men to keep Kasson off the stump. Argumentative, witty, sarcastic, and persistent, Cutts "far more loved to attack than defend any cause," according to Kasson. It was his "special province . . . to terrorize the representatives . . . by predictions of excessive taxation and poverty as a consequence of building a new Capitol."

When the bill came down from the Senate, Cutts and his allies sought vigorously to postpone its consideration indefinitely, but Kasson, managing it on the floor, finally had it made the special order for March 8. This day was the climax in the contest, and long remembered by the men and women of Des Moines who thronged in for the showdown between Kasson and Cutts. Throughout the day and well into the night the most exciting debates of the entire long struggle went on. In a speech "of artful adaptation" mingled with "wit, vaporing, and argument," Cutts appealed to every element that might create timidity among members and excite their prejudices against further expenditures. In his reply, Kasson did not dare trust "sentimental arguments," he later wrote. He kept his "feet on solid ground" by trying to prove that the old building was completely inadequate for a growing state, that the appropriation could be made without increased taxation and harm to other state institutions, that the state was obligated to the people of Polk County for the sacrifices they had already made, and that members should by all means vote according to their "honest convictions."

When Kasson maneuvered to bring the issue to a vote, he found the opposition dangerously strong. His motion for the previous question won by a mere two votes (47-45) and the main question of engrossment by only one vote (49-48). Since fifty-one votes were required for passage, he immediately moved with success for adjournment, until at least two more votes could be drummed up.

For four weeks, Kasson recalled, "we did not dare call it up for a third reading," until "at last it was certified to us that if we would admit a couple of riders . . . we could secure the additional votes." So critical was the situation, said Kasson, that he reluctantly accepted the riders, and the log jam was apparently broken.

The crucial day to vote arrived on April 13. Kasson, on the prowl for possible absentees, learned early in the morning that a friendly delegate, James Dunne of Jackson County, had been drugged with whisky by the opposition and had disappeared. Kasson immediately enlisted the aid of his old friend Father Brazil, who found the drunken Irish member on a log on Coon River. Shortly before the voting began, the man came reeling in, the accommodating priest hard on his heels.

Halls and galleries were crowded to overflowing, and the silence was intense that morning as the clerk monotonously called out the ayes and noes. When the official count was announced, the immense audience almost brought down "the frail walls" of the old building. The bill had passed by "one solitary vote." [8]

In Des Moines, John Kasson became the hero of the hour. Three days later he described the scene to his sister Mary, who, with her husband, was planning to visit him in Des Moines. He had won "the great victory"; "all our people" were "rejoiced." The fierce, bitter fight had been the "grand struggle" of the session. The evening after passage of the bill an immense crowd — men, women, children led by a band of German musicians — gathered in front of his "cabin," filled his rooms, blocked up the street, tramped down his grass, and presented him with a gold-headed cane. They credited him with "the best speech he ever made in the Old Capitol."

In the years that followed, as men reminisced about this exciting contest and repeated the details, they invariably considered it a personal victory for Kasson. Charles Aldrich, clerk of the House and an anti-Kassonite at the time he called the roll on final passage, later wrote that the capitol appropriation resulted from Kasson's "able, persistent, unremitting efforts." "Ninety-nine hundreds of its friends had given up in despair," declared the Dubuque *Times*, when Kasson with "indomitable energy and untiring perseverance" pushed the bill through.

Kasson himself considered it the "longest continued and bitterest parliamentary battle" he ever fought. Although he gave credit to his many colleagues who ably assisted him, he was proud of his own role in it. A state, like an individual, he said, should present a "decent exterior to the world" in "her outer garments." A "grand building" with "noble lines" and "elegant architecture" would improve the taste of the people and would be an inspiration and a stabilizing influence.

It is perhaps fitting that in the background of Kasson's portrait for the Iowa Hall of Fame, the new state capitol in all its splendor was etched in, and that the gold-headed cane was presented to the state historical museum at Des Moines, where it still remains. His capitol fight has become a classic in the historical lore of Iowa.[9]

Now that Kasson had won the battle, and the field could be cleared for building operations, the question immediately arose as to who had won the mopping-up fruits of perquisite and political prestige — Dodge or Kasson? Tichenor, Hoxie, and Palmer all congratulated Dodge for his "great victory achieved for Dodge, Wilson, Allison interests in the selection of the Capitol commission." The bill provided for a nine-member commission to supervise building operations. All the members were Republicans. The selection, according to Kasson, "was not left, as it should have been, to the responsibility of the Governor, nor even to the earnest friends of the new Capitol. . . . my earnest request for a non-partisan board was not granted." The choice of members was dictated by "partisan and personal considerations."

The governor was ex officio president. Six members were chosen in joint legislative convention. Significantly, two members were "forced" on the Commission by one of the riders which Kasson said he had "reluctantly" accepted as the price of the bill's passage. This rider was obviously the work of George Tichenor. The "forced" members were of course General Dodge and Congressman Wilson. Tichenor was jubilant. Kasson's victory could be cashed in on. "Now we must stand firm and gather the fruits," he cried. Commissioners Dodge, Wilson, J. N. Dewey, James Dawson, James O. Crosby, and William L. Joy would "cooperate heartily." C. Dudley and S. G. Stein could be "managed." Kassonites and others "must work with us or suffer the consequences. We have the purse and can hold its strings."

Tichenor's imagination soared to Olympian heights as he pondered the possibilities. Dodge could "delay or push the work," erect a five or a fifteen-million-dollar building, "secure or defeat additional appropriations," or "make or break the whole damned thing." "Another thing," Tichenor continued, "you must be our next governor. . . . Another thing, we must have a soldier ticket this fall."

And still another thing — John Kasson was not down yet. Tichenor was busy preparing "a careful article" for the newspapers in order to blast Kasson's "entire record" in the legislature. Kasson, the sneak, had had the audacity to oppose the gerrymandering of "Copperhead Dubuque" over into a new Republican senatorial district! If Kasson

failed to beat Frank Palmer for Congress in the next Republican
nominating convention, he would run "independent on a peoples'
ticket!" [10]

Tichenor evidently had not weighed fully the fact that those who
controlled the "fruits" of the capitol bill would also have to assume
responsibility to the public for their use, that mismanagement or mistakes of judgment might boomerang into the faces of those in control.
Indeed the "fruits" were to prove bitter, and John Kasson's capitol
fight was not yet over.

More immediate, however, as the Thirteenth Assembly adjourned
in April, 1870, was the looming contest between Kasson and Palmer.
From the capitol encounter, Kasson's star was again rising rapidly. In
the Fifth District his popularity was "immense" and growing every
day. To make matters worse, Thomas Withrow informed Dodge,
Kasson was galloping over the country taking "the fight to the people
. . . from the bottom up."

To head him off, time, money, and campaign propaganda were of
the essence. Withrow, Tichenor, Palmer, Dodge, and his Council
Bluffs strategists all arose to the exigencies of the moment. In order
to "disarrange Kasson's plans" and cut short his booming campaign,
they quietly managed to call the convention two weeks early — and
at Council Bluffs. General Dodge gave financial assistance and bar-
tered for some of Kasson's supporters; Withrow prepared items for
the newspapers on Kasson's "suffrage and Johnson record"; Palmer
and Dodge brought out from Council Bluffs an old "Colored Preacher" to appear at the county conventions which chose district delegates;
and Kasson's divorce scandal was re-opened. These tactics elicited a
hard hitting circular from Kassonites, charging the Dodge "ring" with
the use of chicanery, trickery, bribery, and fraud in the fashion of
the "Tammany ring." The convention was called early in order to
inconvenience the people's delegates, and the number of delegates had
been reduced in order to "diminish popular representation."

But Kasson was too late with too little. On June 3, at Council
Bluffs, Dodge men easily put Palmer over for a second term. After
the convention, Tichenor summed up for Dodge. He wanted to make
Palmer concede that Dodge was "the central figure in victory"; he
was aware that Dodge had spent a "considerable amount of money"
and that had to be "arranged"; he himself had spent $800; he wanted
Palmer to cut "square off" the heads of several officeholders who were

his enemies, but Palmer lacked "pluck"; he wanted Dodge to help him with the "President and Senate" to hold the Des Moines post office because Wright, Palmer, Withrow, and Nourse were ditching him on this matter; and finally, Kasson had not been put down but rather had thrown down "the gauntlet for battle two years from now." [11]

The summer of 1870 wore on, with Tichenor trying desperately to hang on to the post office; Dodge was involved in a fight over a railroad bridge at Council Bluffs, while Kassonites made a "h—l of a breeze" over the matter. Wilson, Palmer, and Allison were working for Dodge's railroad interests and receiving stock market tips in return. The Capitol Commission laid plans and procured materials for the new building. Farm prices declined and protests swelled up against railroad discrimination and high rates. Men like Isaac Brandt and William Peters Hepburn, the latter something of a newcomer to Iowa politics, were moving over into Kasson's camp.

John Kasson, again without a political job, apparently considered the time ripe for a long vacation abroad. So on September 27 he boarded a ship for Europe, pondering the possibility of launching an independent party movement.[12]

☆   ☆   ☆

For a whole year, Kasson toured Europe and Asia Minor, cramming notebooks with his observations and writing long letters to his sisters. Landing on the Irish coast, he toured his way to Paris, for several days roaming over the battlefields of the Franco-Prussian War. From Paris he went on to Italy and settled down for the winter months at a suburb of Naples in the home of two English sisters, both "highly educated," and one a "titled lady" whom he "had known for 3 or 4 years." This was probably Lady Strangford whose husband had died two years previously. Naples, "the most picturesque city in the world," he thought, merited the proverb, "See Naples and then die." From here he journeyed with General Philip Sheridan to see the King's triumphal entry into Rome, and joined with a group of other Americans there to give a dinner in the King's honor.

With the coming of spring, Kasson made an extensive tour of Egypt and the Holy Land. On this trip, he humorously informed his sister, he had tried to steer clear of Yankees because he did not like their "loud, self-asserting voices, nor nasal tones." But soon after his departure, he realized that he was in the company of a Mrs. Dogget, wife of a Chicago merchant and a Vermonter because she had a "strong will, any quantity of self-assertion, and when excited she left her throat and went straight into her nose." Near the end of the journey he was surprised to learn that she was Kate Newell, a boyhood playmate formerly of Charlotte, Vermont. And, concluded Kasson, "She was of course, being a Vermonter, intelligent, clearheaded, and, whenever there was special occasion for it, a good Christian, as they all are." [13]

Back in Florence in late June, 1871, Kasson was apparently still drifting, with no clear-cut political plans. Politics in America did "not appear inviting." On June 30, 1871, he confided to Mary's husband, S. C. Wead:

There is a bad odor in [Republican politics] which will yet drive off good men and leave the administration to the Democrats. I have no wish to return home until after the Fall elections, and no wish to be in politics again till the people become disgusted with the dominion of cliques, and caucuses and selfishness. I am half inclined to go home and try to create a third party — of patriots — who shall hold the balance of power at least in some parts of the country, and who will boldly *bolt* the corrupt nominations of either party and go only for men who are personally fit for their places. But how I should be abused! [14]

Thus a whole year before the Liberal Republican revolt was to reach its fullest flowering, Kasson was toying with the idea of an independent movement. One can only imagine the rejoicing which would have taken place among Kasson's adversaries in Iowa to learn that he was entertaining such a thought. To force him out of the party was exactly what they had been trying to do for five years. But the march of political events was to deprive them of this pleasure, for John Kasson soon received good news from Des Moines. For the third time, Polk County Republicans had nominated him to the Iowa House of Representatives — for the same purpose as they had nominated him four years previously when he had been abroad, then also drifting without political anchor.

During Kasson's absence, General Dodge and his Capitol Commissioners, while enjoying the sweet fruits of perquisite, were also learning something about the bitter fruits of responsibility. While Kasson was pondering the wisdom of a third party movement, these gentlemen were bringing down upon themselves a heavy charge of criticism from the newspapers for their choice of foundation stones which, it was rumored, were likely to crumble to bits. Public condemnation of the Commissioners forecast a stiff fight in the next legislature for additional appropriations, and therefore John Kasson was renominated to lead the struggle.[15]

Meanwhile, despite the faint rumbling from the crumbling capitol foundation, General Dodge and his men had quietly settled upon the next governor and were perfecting their plans for Allison's defeat of Harlan for the Senate at the next session of the legislature. For governor they had fixed upon young, conscientious Colonel Cyrus Clay Carpenter of Fort Dodge, a former army commissary and George Tichenor's colleague on General Dodge's staff. Carpenter's nomination brought from General Dodge the proud and fatherly remark that he could almost "drum together" a whole staff from governors and other high officials who had served under him and watched his "struggles for success in the war." [16]

George Tichenor, now relieved of the Des Moines post office, had been made chairman of the state central committee. James S. ("Ret") Clarkson, a newcomer in this story, had stepped out of the state committee chairmanship and into Tichenor's shoes as postmaster.

"Ret" Clarkson, with his father and brother, had moved from Grundy County to Des Moines in 1866, the year of Kasson's divorce. In Brookfield, Indiana, before the Civil War, the Clarksons had edited a Whig newspaper. They had been abolitionists and were now Radicals. In 1870, they had bought the *Register* from Kasson's friend, Frank M. Mills. Talented writers, hard fighters, and inveterate politicians, they were highly regarded by the Republican hierarchy. "Ret," now editor of the *Register* and Des Moines postmaster, needed only the state printership to put him in position to become the head of the "Des Moines Regency" precariously maintained by Tichenor, Withrow, Palmer, and others.[17]

George Tichenor, though busy as party chairman and at seeking another job, in the summer of 1871 was still trying to head off Kasson. Whereas in previous years, he had tried to keep Kasson off the stump, now he was trying to smoke the "sneak" out of Europe. How loyal a Republican was this man, a candidate for the legislature, who, instead of "stirring the stumps" in Iowa for the state ticket, was off vacationing in Europe?

On July 26, 1871, Tichenor magnanimously invited Kasson to join the canvass! Kasson's carefully worded answer from Basle, Switzerland, appeared in the Dubuque *Times*. It did not, of course, mention the "bad odor" in Republican politics nor a contemplated party bolt. Distance and "unfinished" business would keep him away from the fall canvass; he could not conceive that the people would desire to change the Republican character of Iowa government. It would be "folly to change the engineer who keeps the machine in perfect order"; he had no news indicating other than the "usual Republican victory."

That fall Republicans carried the state with ease. But in Polk County, General James M. Tuttle, a Democrat, was chosen to be Kasson's House colleague in the anticipated fight for additional capitol appropriations.[18]

During the summer and fall, the Capitol Commissioners had pushed the construction work rapidly. By November, two-thirds of the cellar had been finished, and, as Kasson returned from Europe, plans were under way for an elaborate program to celebrate the laying of the cornerstone upon which, for posterity to read, the names of the Commissioners were neatly carved. Nowhere was Kasson's part acknowledged. Nor was he to have the privilege of participating in the cornerstone ceremonies if J. N. Dewey, a member of the Commission, could prevent it. Dewey would "not feel hurt" at any trick which would exclude "Johnny and some of his satellites . . . from the show."

But when the program opened, "amid a cold, raw, sleety storm" on November 23, 1871, Kasson was on the rostrum with other state dignitaries. James F. Wilson gave the introductory address; Governor Merrill read an historical paper; and J. B. Grinnell, a poem. Kasson spoke briefly as he presented to the governor a silver trowel and mallet from the architects and the superintendent of construction. For a short time, rumors of cracking foundation stones died down, only to rise again after the legislature convened in January, 1872.

As the year 1871 ended and Kasson awaited the next session of the legislature, he gave a "descriptive lecture" on his travels in Egypt and was master of ceremonies at a banquet feting Yankees.[19]

☆ ☆ ☆

Political events in Iowa moved fast and with increasing bitterness in 1872. In this year, the victors from the fierce intraparty contests were to establish their supremacy for the rest of the century.

The convening of the legislature in January filled Des Moines hotels with the senatorial lobby. Since Wright's election in 1870, General Dodge and his men had been grooming William B. Allison to beat Harlan. In Washington they had set one Hawkins Taylor to work to destroy Harlan's reputation, already blemished by persistent rumors. Taylor had been one of the founders of the Republican party in Iowa and an original Lincoln man. As a government clerk, lobbyist, and newspaper writer in Washington since the early 1860's, he had accumulated a wealth of information. Reviving old scandals about Harlan's management of Indian affairs as Johnson's Secretary of the Interior, Taylor fed a steady stream of damning information for Dodge-Allison use in the newspapers. Taylor in this phase of the campaign was ably assisted by J. N. Dewey, who had departed for Washington a few days before the laying of the capitol building cornerstone in November. Could a soothsayer have read John Kasson's future in 1872, he would have said: "Beware of Hawkins Taylor who has become so adept at digging up nuggets of smear." Kasson probably did not know that in 1866 Taylor had helped Dewey plan strategy and glean "data" for Dodge.

To clinch Allison's victory, Dodge men in late 1871 had finally won over to their side the *Register* and "Ret" Clarkson who helped process Hawkins Taylor's data. The party legislative caucus brought quick victory to Allison and the end of Harlan's political career. James F. Wilson, third man in this race, had missed his great opportunity when, two years previously, Dodge and Tichenor had dangled the senatorship before him and he had not snapped it up; he moved back into the Dodge camp.

Kasson and Harlan had now been rendered powerless, and in the party organization, William Boyd Allison assumed the front once occupied by Grimes. "Ret" Clarkson came out of the Senate race with the state printership, and was now the undisputed master of the Des Moines Regency. Behind the cooperative Allison and somewhat in the background stood General Dodge, the expert wirepuller and at the moment the head of the Dodge-Allison-Clarkson wing which was to dominate Iowa politics until 1908. Republican politics in Iowa had become in large measure the politics of railroads and other business.

Though John Kasson could expect cold comfort from such a combination, he might fight up to his old place on the periphery of power, at least. His work in the Fourteenth Assembly was to be the final test.[20] As the legislature settled down to work less exciting than electing a Senator, Kasson emerged as perhaps the most active member in the House. From his close friend, Speaker James Wilson from Tama County (later famous in Washington as Secretary of Agriculture under three presidents), he received strong committee appointments and hearty cooperation. He was made chairman of both the powerful ways and means, and the rules committees, and high ranking member of the committees on federal relations, the State University, and congressional districts. He was also chairman of the party caucus which chose Wilson speaker; he was later chairman of the committee of the whole.[21]

Legislation to regulate railroads consumed much time in the Fourteenth Assembly. Kasson had watched sentiment build up against railroads until now it was reaching a breaking point. In 1868, as has been noted above, maximum rate bills had been introduced but failed to reach the voting stage; instead, the legislature, in making re-grants of public lands resumed from defunct companies, stipulated the right of the state to prescribe "rules, regulations, and rates of tariff." Kasson had supported this measure, and the railroads had failed in their efforts to force Governor Merrill to call a special session to repeal it.

In 1870, in the Thirteenth Assembly, three bills, designed to regulate freight and passenger rates and to set up a railroad commission, had passed the House. Kasson supported these measures also, but they were blocked in the Senate by close votes. From this time on, farm prices continued to sag, while railroads jauntily imposed high and discriminatory rates. The "third house," the railroad lobby at Des Moines ("the sharpest, shrewdest men," "perfect gentlemen" in high standing, paid by the year to defeat railroad legislation), had become a commonplace. By 1872 most areas in Iowa had access to railroads, and the fear that regulation would frighten away capital was no longer a serious barrier to rate control. Therefore, during the Fourteenth Assembly, a half dozen regulatory bills were introduced, one of which, the O'Donnell Bill, passed the House. Kasson also voted for this bill, which again failed in the Senate, where the influence of Lieutenant Governor H. C. Bulis may have been decisive in the close vote. At any rate when, the year before, George Tichenor and General Dodge were lining up their slate of state officers, including Governor Carpenter, Tichenor had warned Dodge: "We *must* fix on

a *good* man for Lieut. Gov. one who will give us the Committees."
Bulis, who as state senator in 1870 had fought regulation, was the man
"fixed on" and elected. In connection with another railroad bill,
Kasson vigorously fought an amendment which exempted railroads
from township and municipal taxation. It was contrary to a recent
Supreme Court decision, he declared, and to the state constitution
which provided that property of "corporations shall be subject to
taxation, the same as that of individuals." [22]

The failure of the legislature to act was the signal for a storm of
protest the next year as the aggravating economic depression spread
over the land and farmers proceeded to elect farmers to the legislature. Though Kasson had consistently supported rate regulation, his
railroad record was to attract close scrutiny in the years to come.

The anticipated stiff fight in the legislature for increased capitol
appropriations did not materialize. General Dodge's Capitol Commission had made Kasson's work easier. Amidst persistent rumors that
the foundation stones were faulty, the legislature set up an investigating committee that found that a great many of the stones were indeed
cracking wide open. The unwieldy and partisan Capitol Commission,
now sick of the "fruits," recommended a smaller bipartisan Commission; and, in the House, Kasson moved that the names of "John G.
Foote of Burlington, Maturin L. Fisher of Clayton county, Robert S.
Finkbine and Peter A. Dey of Johnson county, two Democrats and
two Republicans, all of whom bore the highest character," be inserted
as commissioners in a new bill. The measure passed, and the old Commission was thus disposed of. After a brisk fight with representatives
from the institutional counties and those who sought to emasculate
the measure with amendments, Kasson by a close vote pushed through
a provision providing for a permanent annual appropriation and instructing the Commission to keep in mind a total cost of $1,500,000.

In time the crumbling stones were removed at a cost of $52,343.76
to the state, and a new foundation was built. Though the old commissioners were under bond, they were not required to make up this
amount. But the next year, at an adjourned session, the Fourteenth
Assembly provided that their names be removed from the cornerstone
and replaced with the words, "Iowa, 1873." Why perpetuate their
failures in the marble of the cornerstone?

Twelve years later, when Kasson delivered the address dedicating
the new building before a distinguished audience, he glowingly de-

scribed the work of the *new* Commission as "a source of profound gratification." "Not one act of speculation or spoliation, not one coin wasted or vainly spent, has defaced the bright record of their administration," he cried out. The vast and durable walls had been laid "in the cement of honesty, and built by the rule of fidelity." [23] Old Capitol Commissioners in the audience must have winced as these fine-feathered darts struck their ears.

More immediately, in 1872, the capitol fight ended with Kasson's popularity soaring and his adversaries on the defensive. To make prospects even brighter, a bill emerged, redistricting the state into new congressional districts. The census of 1870 had revealed startling population growth, entitling Iowa to two more national representatives. Politicians had awaited a decision from the legislature with impatience. In response to a rumor that two congressmen-at-large would be provided, George Tichenor had fixed upon either Dodge, Wilson, or Allison. But now, in the Fourteenth Assembly, a Senate bill providing for two new districts came down to the House and was promptly passed. It could have pleased no one more than John Kasson. The old Fifth District of twenty-three counties was divided, and Kasson's new Seventh District embraced ten counties, six clustering around Des Moines and four cutting on south through the southern tier to the Missouri border. The Missouri Slope, including General Dodge and his Council Bluffs crowd, was cut off into another district! Whether Kasson played a gerrymandering hand in the arrangement, as alleged, is not clear. If so, he received cooperation from men on the Slope, who sat on the redistricting committees and voted for the measure on the floor. Kasson was "excused or absent" from the House vote. [24]

For the first time since 1868, the odds were now against Frank Palmer, with Kasson's prestige rising in a new district where he had always been strong, with General Dodge's territory cut out, and with Dodge men somewhat discredited because of the capitol affair. Angry farmers accused Palmer of being a "railroad congressman."

In this session of the legislature, about to adjourn following passage of the redistricting bill, Kasson successfully led a movement to reduce the cost of printing state laws in newspapers, and as a result was accused by Clarkson's *Register* of calling Iowa newspapers "barnacles on the ship of state." Kasson also played a strong and constructive role in the elaborate revision of the Iowa Code, which, to complete, was to require an adjourned session of the legislature in January, 1873.[25]

When the legislature adjourned in late April, 1872, John Kasson squared away for a showdown with Frank Palmer, who had returned from Washington "spoiling for a fight." Now there was no setting of the convention date early and far away. The campaign sped on remorselessly through the spring and summer, Kasson and Palmer fighting it out for delegates at the county conventions. "Ret" Clarkson and the powerful *Register*, having joined the Dodge-Allison forces in the Senate contest, logically assumed Tichenor's role of keeping Kasson at bay, though Tichenor, still in Des Moines, kept charging in. Clarkson appealed to Hawkins Taylor and James F. Wilson in Washington for Kasson "intelligence," and Taylor, who could later boast that he had in his possession "500 letters" from people requesting information about their enemies, responded with "desired data" that Kasson had kept his nephew, while in college, on the government payroll; and Clarkson had replied, "Place me under great obligation to you. Anything I can do for you please call on me." [26] How Kasson could have kept a nephew on a government payroll is not clear, since he had not been connected with the federal government while his nephews were in college.

The Des Moines *Daily Republican* took up the battle for Kasson and gave full approval to the Avoca *Delta's* charge that Palmer pandered to railroad rings, worked for monopolists, "dispossessed honest men of the hard earned fruits of their labor," and was a "fawning, sneaking, dirty reptile who crawled in the mire at the bidding of his masters." "People of the 7th., go for Kasson if you don't want to be sold out." [27]

Meanwhile, Iowa Republicans in convention at Des Moines had chosen delegates to the national convention and had endorsed James F. Wilson for Vice President and called for the renomination of Grant. Kasson was not one of the delegates selected. A howling mass of independents had met at Davenport, demanding the end of government hand-outs to business, amnesty for the South, and reform in the administration of public affairs, and choosing 150 delegates to the national Liberal Republican convention to be held at Cincinnati. Grant and Henry Wilson of Massachusetts were nominated at Philadelphia; Democrats and Liberal Republicans combined to nominate two of Kasson's old friends, Horace Greeley and B. Gratz Brown.

The "bad odor" in Republican politics had driven away some of the most distinguished men in the country as Kasson, in Europe the year before, had predicted. But Kasson, though he may have momentarily flirted with the Greeley forces, held back, still busy drumming up delegates in his bitter contest with Palmer. Finally, in mid-August, full two months later than usual, the Seventh District convention assembled in Des Moines, packed with Kasson men, to nominate a Congressman. So strong were Kasson forces that Palmer's name was not even presented. Instead, his delegates threw their 24 votes to Kasson's ally, William Maxwell of Guthrie County, who had remained loyal to Kasson throughout from the beginning of the divorce scandal and who had chastized General Dodge two years before for trying to buy his vote. On the first ballot Kasson was nominated, 50-24. In his acceptance speech he committed himself strongly to Grant and Wilson and promised to join the canvass in behalf of the national ticket.

No longer was there a struggle to keep him off the stump. That fall he was reported to be giving "eloquent, elegant, polished, convincing, and pleasing" speeches before Republican rallies at Davenport, Clinton, Cedar Falls, and Dubuque. A reporter described the Clinton speech as "free of rant" and charming because of its choice of words, its pure diction, and its easy flow. As an orator, Kasson stood up to the "altitude of the best in the land."

In early November, Kasson revealed his exuberance in a note to his sister Mary. In the general election, the voters in his district had given him a 7,000 majority over his Democratic opponent. In Polk County he had received 1,000 votes more than Grant. He was ready to spend Thanksgiving Day with her.[28]

In January, Kasson was back in Des Moines for the adjourned session of the Fourteenth Assembly to complete revision of the Iowa Code. He was made chairman of the committee of the whole and a member of the five-man joint committee to put the Code in final form. A reporter for the Sioux City *Journal*, looking in on this hard working session, observed that Kasson pushed House business "in a manner peculiar to the man." Quiet and unassuming on the floor, he sprang to decisive action when the House resolved itself into committee. He was not popular, like Speaker "Tama Jim" Wilson, the reporter added, but he always commanded respect. He was prepossessing and affable upon first meeting people, but then assumed a "cold, rigid," businesslike exterior. "Shrewd, sagacious, hard-working," he was "always in a hurry — always thinking," and he never lost an opportunity to "spot an enemy or reward a friend." Previously, another reporter had referred to Kasson's polished "hyar" and "ni-ther" as a peculiarity of his speech — European airs, the reporter suggested.[29]

While the legislature put the finishing touches to the revised Code in the winter of 1873, twelve hundred depressed agrarians thronged into Des Moines to attend a state Grange convention. Since 1868, in the wake of decreasing farm prices and high profits for railroad and other corporations, the Grange had spread like wildfire in Iowa. Now, angry farmers demanded immediate legislation to regulate railroads. When the legislature failed to respond, the convention broke up, but farmers returned home talking menacingly of a third party movement. Early in June, Polk County farmers in convention called an Anti-Monopoly state convention and created a state committee of five members. Soon afterward, Republican politicians, in state convention at Des Moines, endorsed a strong resolution calling for railroad regulation and condemning the Crédit Mobilier scandal which, having recently been revealed in Washington, involved General Dodge, Hub Hoxie, and several other Iowa Republicans. In August the state Anti-Monopoly convention, called by Polk County delegates, met in Des Moines and nominated a slate of candidates for state offices. The next month, the failure of Jay Cooke's banking house ushered in a staggering financial panic which degenerated into a long, aggravating depression.[30]

That summer, George Tichenor and Frank Palmer bade farewell to Iowa and moved to Chicago, both going into business. Although never to reside in Iowa again, they were still to help the Dodge-Clarkson-Allison wing plan political strategy and keep down Kasson, and they were to receive rewards for their work. Both failed in their Chicago ventures and fell back upon the spoils of politics. Tichenor was to try business again in Philadelphia, to fail again, to land a political appointment in New York, and finally to show up in Washington serving the party and the corporations as tariff expert. Palmer, from time to time almost destitute, was also to appear in Washington near the turn of the century as the public printer of the United States, only to be dismissed by President Theodore Roosevelt because of his handling of the perquisite and patronage of his own bureau.[31]

"Ret" Clarkson had now inherited from these gentlemen the principal burden of "scotching the snake," and in the summer of 1873 he may have been trying to herd together and turn against Kasson the irate Anti-Monopoly men in Polk County. Inconclusive evidence suggests that behind the Polk County convention, the first strictly Anti-Monopoly convention to be held in Iowa, had been the strong hand of "Ret" and his allies. On the other hand, Kasson had friends among the Anti-Monopoly followers and no doubt hoped to use them to maintain his own supremacy.[32]

John Kasson at last had fought his way back. Strong in the Seventh District, he could be returned to Congress almost at will, although another bitter contest was yet in the offing. But whether he could ever live down the scandal about himself, break through the Dodge-Clarkson net, get beyond the periphery of power in the party, and reach the Senate, the governorship, or the Cabinet, only the future could tell. One thing was certain: as an orator and campaigner, he was an adornment to the party and too valuable to expel, now that the reaction against Grantism had set in.

In Des Moines his commodious two-story brick home on the west side of Seventh Street between Grand Avenue and High Street had now been completed. On the south side of the building Kasson occupied a one-story "cabin" wing, which, "elegantly" furnished, became the "mecca of politicians." The main building was occupied by his close personal friend, Colonel J. M. Griffiths, and his family.

Upon his renomination to Congress in 1872, Kasson was described as weighing 160 pounds and standing five feet eleven inches in a strong, muscular frame. His brain was "tough and active" and well disciplined; he was "determined but not stubborn," "full of life, and companionable"; he had "large ideality, full caution, firm hope, moderate acquisitiveness."[33] As he closed up his cabin late in 1873 to take his seat in the Forty-third Congress, he was six months past fifty-one years of age. Six vital years of his life had been occupied with his fight back. What sort of welcome would he receive from those in Congress who had worn the badge of Radicalism during the days of Andrew Johnson?

☆ XIV ☆

Half Way with Grant: In Congress, 1873-1877

THE CIVIL WAR had severed the Southern checks on the exploitation of natural resources, had supplanted an old, experienced ruling class for a new, inexperienced one, had released the dynamic energies of the nation, and had ushered in the Era of Manipulation. Under President Grant, pliant and politically naive, the government had fallen into the hands of dishonest and incapable men. While Kasson had served in the Iowa legislature, politics under the cloak of Radicalism more and more had become indentified with manipulation for

250

economic favor. Hordes of lobbyists and speculators had swarmed over the land, seeking railroad subsidies, mining concessions, and thousands of other government handouts.

The West was being plundered by railroad and mining corporations, the South by Carpetbaggers and Scalawags. The cities and the state legislatures, in North and South alike, were infested with rings, lobbyists, bribegivers, and bribetakers. Even the national Congress had become a tool of predatory business interests. Machine politics, firmly founded on patronage, economic privilege, the bloody shirt, and the soldier vote, prevailed everywhere. The new ruling classes, flushed with prosperity, had lost their sense of responsibility, and corruption had kept pace with the upward swing of the business cycle. Political morality had sunk to its lowest level in American history.

But now in December, 1873, when John Kasson returned to Washington, the Manipulators, large and small, had temporarily overreached themselves. Like a gigantic tidal wave, hard times were halting the easygoing, rollicking mood of the era. In Iowa, corn was selling at fifteen cents a bushel — not enough to pay the railway freight to Chicago. Radical Republicanism was losing its grip, Southern carpetbag governments were falling apart, and power was passing back into the hands of native whites. An outraged public demanded an end to scandals.

Kasson had seen deep resentment well up and blow out in Iowa as the Anti-Monopolists increased their power in the state legislature, and as the Republican machine gave ground to their demands. In the House in Washington he was confronted with a chastened group of men, anxious to conform to the temper of the day. Headed off for six years by forces temporarily in retreat, Kasson was now all primed to express the will of his constituents.

In the House there was no Thad Stevens to beat down recalcitrant members. Instead, Grant's self-styled floor leader, audacious old Ben Butler, was rapidly losing ground. Since Kasson's last appearance James G. Blaine, Speaker of the House, and James A. Garfield, chairman of the Appropriations Committee, had become powerful leaders. At the head of the Ways and Means Committee was Henry L. Dawes of Massachusetts. "Pig Iron" Kelley of Pennsylvania still relentlessly drove on for higher and higher tariffs. New faces, and old ones, from the South had appeared — Alexander H. Stephens, former Vice President of the Confederacy; Lucius Q. C. Lamar of Mississippi; and R. Q. Mills of Texas. William S. Holman of Indiana, Samuel J. Randall of Pennsylvania, and James G. Beck of Kentucky led a strong, resurging Democratic minority. From Iowa, George W. McCrary, a favorite of the dominant Republican faction, matched Kasson in intelligence and competence.

Speaker Blaine treated Kasson as a newcomer in the distribution of committee assignments. Placed on Ways and Means, Kasson ranked number six in twelve. But since this committee was to conduct several investigations, it turned out to be an important assignment.

Kasson immediately began pursuing a line of action which won him a reputation as an economizer, a reformer, and a "renegade" Republican. In the early days of the session he conspicuously joined the Democrats in slashing attacks against the Grant administration. His first opportunity arose in connection with salary readjustment of high government officials. In the closing days of the last Congress, Ben Butler and a few others had slipped through a measure increasing the salaries of the President, members of Congress, and other high officials. Tacked onto the unpopular measure was a retroactive feature which in effect gave each member a $500 bonus for his services the past two years.

Popular reaction against this "salary grab" was so strong that Republicans in their first caucus voted to set up a select committee to report a repeal bill. Kasson and a Democratic colleague, as members of this committee, submitted a minority report criticizing the majority for not reducing the President's salary also. There had been a tendency during his absence from the House, Kasson declared, toward "a certain element of personal Government, of aggrandizement of executive authority, irresponsible in a great degree to the legislative branch of the government." To reduce the salaries of Congressmen and not that of the President would censure and degrade the people's representatives. He also urged that the repeal be made retroactive so that many officials would have to pay back to the government the "bonuses" already received. For these efforts he drew sarcastic remarks from several members. A newcomer and a confidant of Blaine, witty William Walter Phelps from New Jersey, called the move of his "experienced friend" Kasson a "conspicuous sacrifice — a splendid self-exaltation." Let Kasson yield up a part of his own salary if he desired, but why require it of all? [1]

On several other occasions Kasson criticized the President and some of the executive heads, especially the inept and corrupt Secretary of the Treasury, W. A. Richardson. Because of "the influences which surrounded Grant," Kasson kept away from the White House until the last year or two of Grant's term. By then some of the influences had been curbed, and moreover political exigencies were to require cooperation between the President and his critics. Through the influence of the upright, sagacious Secretary of State, Hamilton Fish, Kasson in time began to view the administration in a better light. Before this session ended, he singled out the State Department for a ringing commendation. Speaking in behalf of appropriations for additional consular clerks, he declared that he had done "his share of grumbling against extravagant expenditures in other Departments" but against the State Department not one single piece of extravagance would be charged; its administration was "perfectly honest and perfectly honorable." [2]

Kasson opposed further extension of congressional as well as executive powers. In debate against a bill to establish a national education fund from land sales, he declared it unconstitutional and a greater assumption of federal power than anything done during the war, when dangerous but necessary powers had been assumed. Although favoring public education, he did not want the federal government to exercise control over the educational system, as the measure provided. It was time to put the brakes on expenditures and the extension and centralization of federal powers. Let the states manage their own educational system. Warmed by a round of applause coming mostly from Democrats, he declared that the Education Bill contemplated the continued sale of public lands to the speculator. He painted a graphic picture of the poor and homeless roaming over the West looking for good lands, which Eastern corporations and speculators had acquired by manipulating the homestead and pre-emption laws. He urged the Committee on Commerce to release his "reform bill," which would close the public lands to all except men who tilled them. George F. Hoar of Massachusetts, author of the Education Bill, replied that Kasson's speech was meant for some "distant audience" — not for the House; and a Democratic member taunted him for taking a state rights stand now that the Northern states had already carved up the public domain.[3]

Throughout the session, Kasson kept in mind the farmers in "distant lands." In addition to his bill to stop the raids on the public lands, he introduced or supported legislation to prevent extortion in the use of patent rights, to conserve the natural resources, to regulate and tightly control railroad rates and practices, to increase the supply of money, and to lower the tariff on commodities needed in the West.

As a conservationist far ahead of his times, he introduced and saw passed bills to prevent the wanton extermination of the buffalo then taking place in the West, and of fur-bearing animals in Alaska. He opposed a measure disposing of placer mining lands because it contained pre-emption features of which speculators could take advantage. He wanted a guarantee that the mining lands would go to the men who mined them and then back to the government when the mines were discontinued.

On the matter of railroad regulation, which the Anti-Monopoly legislature in Iowa was taking into its own hands, Kasson introduced a rigid control bill which anticipated the effective railroad laws of the early twentieth century, going beyond the Interstate Commerce Act of 1887. When his bill failed to clear the Committee on Commerce, he voted for the McCrary Bill, a milder measure designed to establish a railroad board which could determine fair and reasonable rates. But this bill did not go far enough, he protested. Later he demanded that land-grant railroads discharge their obligations to the federal government without further delay. On the important so-called "Inflation Bill" to fix the maximum amount of legal tender notes (greenbacks) at $400,000,000, Kasson voted with the majority to pass, but in the same session he spoke in behalf of the resumption of specie payments, and he probably was pleased with Grant's veto of the "Inflation Bill."

Though hedging somewhat in the tariff debates, he took a moderate stand. He opposed raising the duties on low qualities of steel, but he would approach the tariff cautiously, keeping in mind both industry and the consumer. Duties should not be so high as to be prohibitive and thus create American monopoly, nor so low as to destroy American industry and permit foreign monopoly. The tariff should be so delicately adjusted that competition was always promoted, not destroyed.[4]

As a member of Ways and Means, Kasson helped to conduct the investigation of the notorious Sanborn contracts by which one of Ben Butler's henchmen, under a friendly nod from the Secretary of the

Treasury, enriched himself with lucrative fees for the collection of taxes due the federal government. In strong, precise language Kasson defended a bill, which the committee proposed, to prevent such scandals in the future.[5]

In a floor fight against the franking privilege, Kasson flushed up hostility from one of his colleagues, which at the moment no doubt was a great surprise. James N. Tyner of Peru, Indiana, was managing a franking bill when Kasson attacked the measure as merely a restoration of the old system which the Forty-second Congress had sought to change. Several Democrats joined the attack, and Kasson obligingly yielded much of his time to them. When his thirty minutes were up, Tyner refused to extend Kasson's time and sharply rebuked him for not being able "to hold the floor." When Kasson provoked great laughter and disorder by introducing six basketfuls of petitions against the franking privilege, Tyner was not amused. If given more time, he growled, Kasson would merely "farm it out." Later in the session these two were to have another sharp exchange over postal appropriations, but it would be midsummer before Kasson was to learn fully what was behind Tyner's hostility.[6]

On the closing day of the session, June 23, 1874, self-congratulatory speeches from committee chairmen Dawes and Garfield drew criticism from Democrats who considered the speeches campaign oratory. When Kasson jumped to the defense of these Republican House leaders, one Democrat wanted to know why he had now joined the Republicans after having "served with the Democratic side for the first several weeks." Kasson replied that the Democrats at the last moment were merely trying to steal credit for "my reforms." [7]

Though Kasson in this session had tried to make himself appear a greater reformer than he really was, he had clearly identified himself with the anti-Grant elements of the party.

☆   ☆   ☆

While Kasson was attacking corruption, cooperating with Democrats, and in the end defending Republican achievements in Congress, the old Dodge-Palmer faction, now led by hard hitting Ret Clarkson, was spinning a web from which their renegade Congressman, they believed, could never escape.

James S. Clarkson and John A. Kasson had naturally become rivals. Clarkson had taken up residence in Des Moines in 1866, the year in which the Dodge forces believed they had finished off Kasson's political career for good. Clarkson, a hard driving, ambitious young man, readily fell in with the Dodge crowd. Within three years he had become chairman of the Republican state central committee, and in 1869 he had the usual difficulties with keeping Kasson off the stump in the state canvass. At the beginning of 1870 Frank Palmer had urged Clarkson to remain in Des Moines rather than accept a possible position in Kansas City. "Power," argued Palmer, was more important than capital. Ret would get the capital through his "friends and power," Palmer promised.[8] Later in 1870 Clarkson had become the editor of the *Register*; in 1871, Des Moines postmaster and state printer. Obviously he could not have fallen heir to these positions, which brought him power, prestige, and wealth, without the aid of the dominant Dodge influence. Obviously he inherited the keep-down-Kasson responsibility as well as the leadership of the Des Moines Regency, when George Tichenor and Frank Palmer left the state.

Kasson's nomination in 1872 over Frank Palmer had been a bitter blow, and there is reason to believe that Clarkson and the *Register* merely feigned support for the party nominee in the general election. Significantly, another man named Palmer had emerged to run against Kasson on the Liberal Republican-Democratic ticket — a ticket in part engineered by the wealthy speculator-hotel proprietor, James C. Savery, who back in 1859 had fallen out with Kasson over the conduct of the Kirkwood gubernatorial campaign. In 1872, however, the combined Liberal Republican, Democratic, and disgruntled regular Republican combination had failed to keep Kasson from winning, even against a man bearing the same name as Kasson's party convention adversary. Actually Kasson seemed to be popular among grass-roots Liberal Republicans and no doubt had received many of their votes in 1872. During this campaign, the Indianola *Leader*, a Kasson supporter, had accused Clarkson of drawing two salaries from the federal government at the same time — for two months as a temporary clerk in Washington while receiving pay as Des Moines postmaster. Smarting from this accusation, which he found hard to refute, Ret resolved to give Kasson the same medicine.

Now in 1874 Kasson remained a serious threat. There was always the possibility that he might eventually establish control over the state legislature, become himself a United States Senator, put a new man in as Des Moines postmaster and state printer, and launch a powerful newspaper as a rival to the *Register*. In 1873, for instance, the Des Moines nominee for the state senate was a Kasson Republican whom Clarkson bolted and succeeded in defeating. Although the post office and state printership remained secure in Clarkson's hands, the dominant faction, as of old, could not depend on Kasson's obeisance in matters of patronage and legislation.[9]

The fight shaping up in the Seventh District promised to be a lively one. Clarkson was bold, a hard hater, a prolific writer, and a straight-down-the-road Radical Grant Republican. Behind him stood the old Dodge crowd — the railroad gang — the state machine, and most of the state's newspapers. Kasson had a large following among the citizenry of Des Moines and among the disgruntled farmers. Lacking Clarkson's punch in a fierce frontal attack, Kasson usually veered off around the flanks and struck from behind the lines in a surprise attack. For failing to strike back in face to face combat, to use the same kind of weapons hurled against him, Kasson's enemies called him a moral coward, always running away in a crisis; his friends replied that he was a cultured gentleman who would not compromise his dignity by stooping so low. Kasson was more at home on the stump before a crowd than among machine politicians. He had an appetite for political independency which he could never quite satisfy because of the rigid demands of his day for party regularity. As an adversary, however, Kasson made up for his alleged apostasy, political trimming, and lack of nerve by a perseverance which often left his opponents gasping in futile desperation and resignation.

As early as the winter of 1873, Clarkson had begun spinning his web for Kasson. J. N. Dewey, a Kirkwood man and a Kasson hater of old, was then in Washington as a place holder. Writing to Clarkson in a trembling hand for eleven pages, this taciturn gentleman sputtered down venom on Kasson — "the d—d treacherous cold-blooded cuss," "forenst" whom he had devoted, with no regrets, an eleven-year "labor of love." Grimes and Kirkwood in 1863, declared Dewey, had urged him on "to drive the pins and tie the grass" in Kasson's path. But of the whole pack who had in the past fought Kasson — Dodge, Hoxie, Withrow, Allison, James F. Wilson, and Palmer — nobody was willing to carry on except Palmer. Therefore Ret and Frank Palmer, now editor of the Chicago *Inter-Ocean*, would have "to strike straight from the shoulders." [10]

Late in 1873, while Kasson was getting his bearings in the Forty-third Congress, Frank Palmer and Thomas Withrow, the latter also residing in Chicago as general solicitor of the Rock Island Railroad, began to feed information to Ret, who as Mr. Kasson's "Postmaster" now became Mr. Kasson's "Historian," declaring that he would get the full story of Kasson's life if it took sixty years. Withrow volunteered the information that Kasson had been a member of the Buffalo Free Soil Convention and had run for Congress on the Free Soil ticket. He added the misinformation that Kasson, a disgusted, defeated candidate, had then moved to St. Louis, joined up with the proslavery elements of the Democratic party, had been nominated to office on a proslavery ticket, but because of a Free Soil speech made at Buffalo had had to give up the nomination. Then, added Withrow, Kasson had bought a residence in New York City, engaged in stock operations on Wall Street, got "scortched," and then settled down in Des Moines.

In another letter Withrow volunteered the "original affidavits," obtained in 1866 from the Reverend Dr. Eliot, Kasson's former brother-in-law, showing that Kasson had purchased a slave woman in St. Louis for $500, had hired her out from 1850 to 1855, until she and her husband could buy her freedom for $650 after her health had broken down. All this was to show that Kasson's story that he had bought the slave in order to keep her from being sold down South was false. Withrow promised to get additional information from St. Louis if necessary.[11]

Meanwhile, Kasson Republicans and Anti-Monopolists in the seventh district were feeling out Kasson for his plans, and in late April, 1874, he replied to an inquiry. "I decline *to be a candidate* for renomination," he said. He would leave it to his constituents to find some other candidate, who, "devoted to reform," would "abolish abuses, restrain monopolies," whether "within or without his party." A candidate's only compensation for the burden of the office, he went on, "must be the consciousness that *the office has sought him, not he the office.* . . . I must withdraw my name unreservedly."

Somewhat taken to task for his party irregularity by Andy Felt, editor of the Waterloo *Courier*, Kasson elaborated upon this statement. He lamented the hard work of overcoming falsehoods in campaigns and of having to serve in a Congress generally classified as "a corrupt Congress, Salary Grab Congress, Credit Mobilier Ring, a Party of Corruptionists." Because of his reform efforts, the "*railroad and postoffice* organs" of Iowa were shouting "party infidelity!" Of this he was proud; he had nothing to take back.

On the other hand, he had neither said "farewell to one party nor hail to another." He could not aid reform by accepting nomination from the Anti-Monopoly caucus. "I have simply *declined a candidacy* in order to leave my friends and opponents both *free to choose as they would!*" [12] In effect, Kasson was saying that he was not going to get out and stir the stumps for the nomination. But he did not say that he would not accept the nomination if offered him. These letters were of course clever appeals for a draft-Kasson movement and for the support of the reform element in all parties.

Nobody recognized this maneuver better than Ret Clarkson and Frank Palmer, and these two newspaper editors immediately threw their political and printing machines into high gear. A whole host of men, high and low, most of them already familiar to this story, were tapped for help — J. N. Dewey, Charley Nourse, Thomas Withrow, Grenville M. Dodge, Hub Hoxie, James F. Wilson, Hiram Price, B. F. Allen, J. C. Savery, Ralph G. Orwig, James C. Tyner, and most of the Republican newspaper editors in the state. Against Kasson these gentlemen hurled all the muck they could dig up — and more.

High strategy called for submerging Kasson with charges coming one after another so fast that before he could fend off one he would be faced with half a dozen more. But the basic lines of attack can be boiled down to his party treason, his slaveholding, his previous divorce scandal, his "office poligamy," and his involvement in three railroad deals. In addition he was pictured as a foreigner, an aristocrat, and a rich man who kept his money in Wall Street and California banks.

J. N. Dewey and Frank Palmer flushed the railroad deals; Thomas Withrow provided inside information; the Crédit Mobilier gentlemen, Dodge, Hoxie, and Wilson, gave encouragement but little basic information. Dodge was too busy traveling here and there, from Washington to St. Louis, to Marshall, Texas, to San Diego, although during the campaign he did show up in Council Bluffs. Wilson had cold feet and felt that there should be a halt to attacks on men in public life. And Hoxie contributed only hearsay.

B. F. Allen, former Des Moines banker, whose Cook County Bank in Chicago was on the point of failure, tried to find out where Kasson

kept his money, but failed. Ralph G. Orwig, tramp printer, and
J. C. Savery, along with Clarkson and Palmer, made frontal attacks
in the newspaper.

Savery, a Greeley man in '72, who backed Palmer, the Liberal
Republican-Democrat against Kasson, revealed that he had dickered
with Kasson to run on the Greeley ticket. And as the campaign of
1874 moved along, Savery emerged as one of the managers of the
Polk County Anti-Monopoly party, whose candidate received the
backing of the *Register*. This candidate was J. D. Whitman, a former
Democrat, a carpenter who had helped build the Savery House, had
turned farmer, and now lived in Dallas County. Savery, the Des
Moines businessman, a confidant of Clarkson, was a prominent leader
in the farmer, Anti-Monopoly convention which chose Whitman.
All this makes more credible the innocent statement in the reminiscences of William H. Fleming, long-time private secretary to Iowa
governors, that Clarkson cultivated the Anti-Monopoly movement
locally for the purpose of using it to defeat Kasson.[13]

For Kasson's "poligamy in office," Clarkson and Palmer, both
former Indianians, enlisted the aid of a third Indianian. This was
James N. Tyner, member of the House committee on post offices
and post roads. Clarkson and Tyner both had been born at Brook-
ville, Indiana, and probably had been boyhood friends. Sometime
in April, probably immediately following Kasson's letter of "declination," Palmer wrote Tyner to check Kasson's former record in the
Post Office Department for evidence of double office holding. By the
end of May, conniving with a clerk in the Post Office Department,
Tyner had marshalled the evidence and brought it to his House desk,
but, in the rush to get away as the session closed in June, failed to
take it with him to Indiana.[14]

Early in July when Kasson arrived in Des Moines, two or three
counties had already instructed their delegates to support him in
the nominating convention, and Polk County was holding precinct
primaries to choose delegates. It looked like a draft movement had
begun.

Already the *Register* was well launched in its campaign, and for
the next four months one charge after another was hurled at Kasson.
In those days the four-page *Register* was twenty-eight inches long
and eighteen inches wide, and each page carried nine columns of
small print. Seldom a day passed without some reference to Kasson

— sometimes a half column, sometimes two full columns, and often one or two full pages. Editorials, news items, letters to the editor, soldier petitions, poems, and cartoons, all were brought to bear on the victim.

From random selections taken from the *Register* one gets the machine's portrait of Kasson. He was Kunning Kasson, Massa Kasson, Oily Gammon Kasson, Mr. Salary Grab Kasson, spruce proud fixey Kasson, the elegant boarder of the Aborn House, the slippery, arrant demagogue and political trickster, the Political Flea hopping back and forth from the Anti-Monopoly Maiden to the Republican Lady, a demagogue of demagogues, a cowardly poltroon, Kasson of barnacle notoriety, Johnny Hoist By His Own Petard, Kasson of Blue Blood and Foreign Accent — the French Gentleman, John Arnold Kasson who slept with Andrew Johnson and conspired with Jeff Davis to defeat the fruits of the war. And, yelled J. C. Savery to the Anti-Monopoly convention, from Aaron Burr to John A. Kasson the greatest rogues in American politics have been the smooth-tongued polished rogues!

In a fourteen-stanza poem entitled "Johnny to Andy Felt Again" the *Register* on August 28 portrayed the many charges against Kasson. Two stanzas pointing up alleged party slipperiness and social disease help reveal the tone of the attack:

> These Anti-Monops and other "dear friends"
> Crying out for reforms and other good ends
> Can't see how it is that I am their man
> And be regular still with my old party clan. . . .
>
> And my health isn't good, you know I'm afflicted
> With — no matter what — and the doctor predicted
> That sudden exposure or any reverse
> Must surely result in my getting worse. . . .

Throughout all this there ran the refrain that Kasson had ability — "admitted ability." But the important economic issues of the time were neglected.

At the "Black Flag" Polk County Convention held July 25, Kasson received sixty-one of the sixty-eight votes cast. The next day Clarkson's attack in the *Register* contained "more real bitterness" than anything Governor C. C. Carpenter had ever read. A few days later Clarkson warned his readers that he would, before the district convention met on August 5, print documents to prove that Kasson drew a double salary — nay, triple — as a member of Congress and employee of the Post Office Department. Both Palmer and Clarkson wrote Tyner in Peru, Indiana, to hurry up the documents. But Tyner, having left them in his desk in the Hall of Representatives in Washington, did not want to add another confidant to the scheme by wiring the House doorman. Tyner did not want to "belittle" himself by having his name connected with the affair. He enjoined Palmer and Clarkson with the "closest secrecy," for Kasson "never did me an injury." Yet Kasson should be beaten, Tyner went on. If nominated, "it would be safe to elect his competitor." Kasson could never be relied on for "party fealty"; no one else seemed to enjoy an attack on the party so much. In the House, Kasson sat right behind Holman, the Democratic "watch dog of the treasury," and egged him on to attack the administration. Tyner had taken the documents to the House, intending to "clip Kasson's sails." But Kasson would not "swallow the bait" Tyner threw out as provocation.

In one of his letters Tyner made known that he too had "declined" the renomination in his district because of criticism for his having taken "back salary" in the Forty-second Congress. He had control of matters, however, and would return to Congress two years hence. Would Ret and Palmer please run a little story in the *Register* and *Inter-Ocean* in reference to his magnanimous declination? And they did, but Tyner never did return to Congress.

As district convention time approached, and Tyner still had not sent the documents to Clarkson and Palmer, they sprang the charges anyway and promised to produce the documents later. They accused Kasson of campaigning in 1862 while drawing a salary as Assistant Postmaster General (this he did); of drawing a salary as special agent in late 1862 and early 1863 while doing nothing (he was engaged in the Department gathering data for a postal mission to Europe); and finally of drawing a salary as Congressman, special agent, and foreign postal commissioner all at the same time (on the contrary, these salaries did not run concurrently). Kasson was here being falsely scandalized in connection with some of the most constructive achievements of his career.[15]

On August 5 the district convention at Des Moines renominated Kasson on the first ballot by a vote of 47-22, and passed resolutions condemning Ret Clarkson among other things for "willfully and maliciously libeling" Kasson and for conspiring with enemies of the Republican party to defeat its candidates. Governor Carpenter, a party regular, was shocked at the choice of Kasson despite "bitter opposition" for years and "vulnerable points" in his character. Previously, Carpenter had confided to his diary: "Kasson himself will not spend money but his admirers will give freely in his behalf." Now the Governor considered Kasson like "a child of star-eyed destiny." But, even so, his success would have to be attributed to his "brain and industry." [16]

Clarkson, denying that he had a candidate in the field, now began to build up John D. Whitman of Dallas County as a plain dirt farmer, pitted against a smooth-tongued, double talking, former slaveholding aristocrat. On August 12 at Indianola, Whitman was nominated on the Anti-Monopoly-Democratic ticket. James C. Savery opened this convention, made a speech against "Grantism, Kassonized, Johnsonized Republicanism," and served as chairman of the committee on permanent organization.

Savery was soon publishing in the *Register* vitriolic attacks against Kasson. Joining in the attack was the *State Record*, a Republican paper of Des Moines, edited by R. G. Orwig, who had been accused of embezzlement of state funds while Governor Stone's private secretary and who had been involved in the infamous swamp land scandals. The Democratic paper of Des Moines, the *Leader*, also repeated the charges thrown out by Savery and Clarkson.[17]

Of all the charges, Savery's were the most serious. They would be devastating if proved. They appeared in three long letters to the *Register* and were republished on the eve of the general election. Briefly, they accused Kasson, while a member of Congress in 1866, (1) of selling his vote to the St. Louis railroad interests who were competing with Iowa for the main line of the Union Pacific east of the 100th meridian; (2) of hoodwinking the entire Iowa legislature into exempting the Des Moines Valley Railroad company from the Doud amendment, which retained to the state the right to regulate rates; (3) of exacting a bribe from the Rock Island Railroad for services never rendered while a member of the Iowa legislature. In the first two charges, Savery also either said directly or inferred that Kasson received money.

As the charges were piled up, Clarkson and Savery urged and dared Kasson to deny them face to face with his enemies on the ros-

trum or to vindicate himself in a libel action. Wisely, Kasson refrained from facing his accusers with their wild, irresponsible accusations before a mass of people. But during the closing days he turned
on them in a witty, forceful speech in the Opera House of Des Moines
in the presence of Senator Allison. This speech was immediately
published and circularized over the district. Kasson did not try to
meet all the charges in detail; to have done so would have taken
weeks. He did question the credibility of Savery and Orwig, merely
touched upon the best defense of the more serious charges, but he
ended up by waving the bloody shirt.[18]

In the last minutes of the campaign, rumors flew around Des Moines
that Kasson was filing a petition for libel against Savery and the
Clarkson brothers — a rumor which Ret dismissed as pure bun-
combe.

Finally, when the election returns were added up in early November, Kasson led Whitman by more than 2,000 votes. This was a greater
lead than had been amassed by George W. McCrary, the idol of the
machine, who had also "declined" to be nominated. In the third
district, the Anti-Monopoly-Democrats for the first time since 1856
broke the solid Republican ranks and elected Lucien Ainsworth.
Throughout the land, the Republicans had lost ground, and for the
first time since 1860 the Democrats secured a majority in the national
House of Representatives.[19]

Kasson's victory, against great odds, was a surprising achievement
and an indication of the high regard his constituents held for him.
But was it a real victory? For Kasson in the last hours of the campaign had permitted himself to be goaded into a libel suit against the
Clarkson brothers and Savery. Now he would have to face his
adversaries in a court of law before a jury of twelve men and the jury
of public opinion in the state. The burden of proof in such an action
was upon him. The possibility of finding twelve men without pre-
conceptions of this bitter feud was slim; and before the jury of public opinion Clarkson with his satellite newspapers had by far the
greater advantage.

☆   ☆   ☆

One of Kasson's first moves in Washington, as the short session
of Congress opened in December, was to procure the "double salary"
documents from James N. Tyner. In Iowa during the campaign he

had traced them to Tyner's hands, and had coldly written Tyner to learn to whom the certificates impeaching his "uncompensated service" had been delivered. No answer. In Washington, Kasson met Tyner but refused to speak to him. Instead, he wrote Tyner, "demanding" the original certificates of the "sinister transaction." Tyner of course did not deliver up the documents, but in an insulting letter lectured Kasson on the "indelicacy of *demanding* from a peer." To Clarkson's father, in Washington on a tour which would take him through the South and on to California, Tyner read this exchange and sent a copy to Ret for his "amusement."

Kasson's "style and habit, you know," added Tyner, "are to express his contempt by refusing to recognize anyone who opposes him and to air his dignity by assuming to be more respectable than others." Perhaps "King John borrowed his habits of pouting in the midst of love quarrels during his late married life." Tyner promised to "dissect" him in the House if Kasson "opened the door." But Ret was soon announcing that Tyner had been appointed Second Assistant Postmaster General. In this Department for the next few years, Tyner was to win the reputation as one of the nation's leading spoilsmen.[20]

Some 150 other lame-duck members showed up in the House during this anti-Grant session. Kasson, with at least a two-year lease on his place, found himself huddling closer and closer with his Republican colleagues, hard pressed to control a rampaging Democratic minority awaiting to take over the Forty-fourth Congress. Radical power in the South continued to crumble under Democratic, or native, assaults. Only five Southern states now remained under Negro-Republican domination.

Under these circumstances and in part as a gesture to the deceased Charles Sumner, a Civil Rights bill to protect the Negro and maintain Republican supremacy emerged, only to be vigorously opposed by the Democrats who day after day by parliamentary maneuver and dilatory tactics seriously threatened to obstruct passage. Kasson threw himself fully into this fight, cooperated effectively with Garfield in procuring a rules change to avert dilatory tactics, and played a key role in the maneuvers which eventually led to the measure's passage. But he refused to support Ben Butler's Force Act giving Grant the right to suspend the writ of habeas corpus in several of the Southern states.

Clarkson's *Register* and Palmer's *Inter-Ocean* misrepresented Kasson's *maneuvers for* the Civil Rights bill *as filibustering against* it. "The Frog A-Wooing Gone," ran a *Register* headline. When Kasson spoke out against the Force Act in party caucus and then voted against it, despite a majority vote for it in caucus, Clarkson sternly rebuked him for failing to help protect "Republicans and colored men" in the South in spite of his "moist blubbering" for Southern Republicans in the recent campaign. And when Kasson voted for the resumption of specie payments and introduced a supplementary measure to regulate the volume of greenbacks until the Resumption Bill should take effect, Clarkson growled that Kasson and his "Wall Street" friends were trying to make themselves the assignees of a bankrupt nation.[21]

Furthermore, Ret was not pleased with the part Kasson played in the investigation of the notorious Pacific Mail Subsidy; nor with his opposition to the Texas & Pacific Railroad subsidy, which Ret favored and General Dodge was promoting; nor with his support of an amendment to limit the president to one term of six years — a Democratic measure aimed at Grant's alleged third term aspirations.

In the Pacific Mail investigation it was revealed that Schuyler R. Ingham, once of Des Moines, had received $10,000 as lobbyist in Washington. During the war, Ingham and J. C. Savery as intimates had been reported at one time as "flourishing like Green Bay trees" in stock operations on Wall Street. When the Chicago *Tribune* tied Ingham's lobbying stipend with Frank Palmer and the *Inter-Ocean*, Ret arose to Palmer's defense and at the same time accused Kasson of trying to cover up for former Senator Harlan, whose name also had become involved in the scandal. The Chicago *Tribune*, engaged in a war against both Palmer and the Grant administration, now accused the *Register* of having a "small interest in the Credit Mobilier, the Pacific Mail, the Whiskey Ring, Indian Ring, B. F. Allen's broken bank, and Reverend Harlan." Finally, when the Kasson-authored report called merely for a judicial investigation and the enactment of measures to cope with the "enormous evil," Clarkson called it a whitewash under a headline entitled, "Our Mis-Representative and Mis-Report." [22]

When this short, anti-Grant session ended in early March, Clarkson branded it as filled with too many "flickering, faltering Republicans ... too much timidity, half-wayism."

That winter and summer many events stole the headlines from the Clarkson-Kasson feud. B. F. Allen's Cook County Bank failed, mob violence flared up in the Pennsylvania coal regions, the Henry Ward Beecher adultery case droned on in New York, Mrs. Abraham Lincoln was declared insane by a Chicago court, and Frank Blair and Andrew Johnson died.

From Washington, Kasson went to Connecticut and participated in the spring canvass, as a result of which, Ret Clarkson declared, the Republican candidates lost votes. By May, Kasson was back in Des Moines, urging the Baltimore & Ohio Railroad to build competitive lines in the West to relieve the farmers from the "tyranny of combination" then taking place, and making speeches in Burlington and Davenport. In July, Ret Clarkson, party regulars, and the railroad influences maneuvered James B. Weaver out of the governorship race and old Governor Kirkwood in.[23]

☆ ☆ ☆

In November, 1875, John A. Kasson's petition for $50,000 libel against the Clarkson brothers and J. C. Savery finally emerged from the district court docket of Polk County. It was the burden of Kasson and his counsel to prove that the defendants "wickedly and maliciously" contrived and intended to injure him, to bring him into public scandal and disgrace, to expose him to public hatred and contempt, and to deprive him of the benefit of public confidence. The action was based only on the three railroad charges authored by Savery and published successively in the *Register*.[24]

The trial lasted two full weeks. A total of seven lawyers participated, two for Kasson and five for the defendants. Thirty-two prospective jurors were examined in settling upon twelve. Large crowds attended, particularly after Kasson made his belated appearance. The case was turned over to a jury on November 24, and while Des Moines speculated, a hung jury dragged its deliberations over the Thanksgiving holidays. They could not agree on the facts. Finally, after three days of indecision, the judge discharged them. No decision, of course, meant no libel and a defeat for Kasson unless he pressed for a re-trial sometime in the future.

Throughout, Kasson's counsellors seemed to present the weakest case possible. They did not use fully the abundant evidence in the *Register* of malice, nor seldom did they question the credibility of an array of defense witnesses whose hatred for Kasson was of public knowledge. On the other hand, the defense was well prepared, alert, and generally on the offensive. Charley Nourse, one of the two leading defense lawyers, quoted Scripture, appealed to public opinion, and at last displayed publicly the deep hatred he so long had held for Kasson.

The charge that Kasson had been bribed in 1866 to vote in Congress to subsidize the Great Smoky Branch of the Union Pacific Railroad, and thus betray the Iowa or Chicago interests, was admitted by the defense to be weak, based almost altogether on hearsay, suspicion, and personal prejudice. Actually Kasson did not vote to subsidize this Kansas Branch of the Union Pacific. The subsidy had been provided in the Pacific Railway Acts of 1862 and 1864. Kasson merely voted to extend the time by which the Kansas Branch could meet certain technical requirements in the acts. In the brief House debates on the matter Kasson had justified his vote on the ground that the Kansas Branch would provide a competing line against the Union Pacific — a point which the dissatisfied farmers in 1875 could well appreciate. Also at the time of his vote, the success of the Union Pacific was reasonably assured; hence he was not selling out Iowa. Behind Kasson's vote were also two other motivations. From Hoxie he had learned enough of Doc Durant's manipulations to become wary of the whole Union Pacific-Crédit Mobilier scheme, and, moreover, at the very time of his vote, Dodge and his railroad crowd were on the point of throwing Kasson out of their circle. His surprising independence on this matter merely confirmed their suspicions that Kasson could not be dictated to on railroad legislation.[25]

On the charge that Kasson in 1869 slipped through the Iowa legislature an amended bill which exempted the Des Moines Valley Railroad from state regulation as provided by the Doud amendment, the defense seemed more successful. They did not prove that Kasson accepted money to do so, as Savery had charged in the campaign, but they did show that such an exception had been made for the Des Moines Valley line and that Kasson had had a hand in the matter. It seems incredible, however, that he could have tricked the whole legislature by interpolating into the law a clause which defeated the law. A better answer is that there was no serious objection to such an exemption for this much favored road.

But on the third charge the defense struck pay dirt. From Kasson's own deposition, they showed that he had accepted a fee of $500 from the Rock Island Railroad. They maintained that it was a bribe which Kasson squeezed from an agent of the road *after* he had voted for a measure to permit the company to resume its land grant subject to the Doud amendment. Kasson maintained that he took the money, *after* the legislative session had ended, as a lawyer's fee for assistance in future important Rock Island litigation then looming up. Although defense witnesses, including banker B. F. Allen, were contradictory in some of their testimony, the evidence was damaging. By his own admission Kasson *had accepted money from a railroad company* whose interest had been a concern of the state legislature of which he had been a member.

Equally as damaging was the fact that Kasson relied upon his own deposition rather than taking the stand personally to vindicate himself. To both the "Smaller Jury" of the court and the "Greater Jury" of public opinion (as Clarkson put it), this must have looked like an indirect confession of guilt and an act of cowardice.

Actually it worked out in this case that Kasson the plaintiff became the defendant in a political trial in which it was intended that public opinion would indeed be the greater jury. Kasson had played into the hands of his opponents; he had won the election, but in the war to eject him from Iowa politics, which had been going on for some thirteen years, Ret Clarkson had won a crushing personal battle. As Kasson returned to Washington in late 1875, there was serious doubt that he could extend his political career beyond the next two sessions of the Forty-fourth Congress.

The first session of the Forty-fourth Congress was devoted primarily to making political ammunition for the next presidential election; the second session to determining who was to be president after the election was over. For the first time in sixteen years, Democrats organized the House. To many Republicans it looked as if the "old Southern Rule was returning with a vengeance"; of the thirty-four most important committee chairmen, twenty-one were from late slave states. For the first time in his congressional career, Kasson found himself a member of the minority. So great had been the Republican fatalities in '74 that he also found himself now a member of the smaller inner-core Republican leadership in the House. Men like Garfield were more than eager to use every bit of talent that Kasson possessed, and these two men became close personal friends.

Democrats capitalized fully on past Grant scandals and set in motion a number of investigations to uncover more. Kasson went along with a resolution to limit the presidency to two terms, but thereafter he moved to the defense of Grant and made the transition to a leading partisan of the House.

This was easier for him to do because Grant himself had been moving in the direction of cleaning up his administration with the appointment to the cabinet of such men as Benjamin Bristow as Attorney General and William Jewell as Postmaster General. With Bristow, as with Hamilton Fish, Kasson worked up an acquaintance which was more than casual. The next spring, three months prior to the Republican national convention, Kasson was predicting that Bristow would receive the nomination; and Bristow was discussing the possibility of Kasson's succeeding him in Grant's cabinet.[26]

Meanwhile, Kasson defended Grant and Fish with alacrity, yielding to no one first honors in resurrecting the Civil War in order to discredit Democrats. He supported Grant's hard money policies, defended the President personally, and tied up Democratic investigations whenever possible. Kasson's first "special personal acquaintance with Grant" originated from the investigation of Grant's Secretary of War, General W. W. Belknap, Kasson's fellow Iowan and casual acquaintance.

One morning in early March, 1876, Kasson at the capitol met his Democratic friend Heister Clymer of Pennsylvania, who headed a committee which had been investigating the War Department. Clymer was hurrying along, noticeably excited, and Kasson learned from him that a resolution to impeach Belknap was to be introduced in the House. Belknap's pretty wife, with her husband's full knowledge, had been selling Indian post traderships. Kasson hurried to the White House and informed Grant. But the President had already been informed by Belknap himself and had accepted his Secretary's resignation. Shortly, the Republicans of the Iowa delegation proceeded to Belknap's home at the Secretary's request, and thereafter they stood behind the disgraced Secretary through the impeachment proceedings, Kasson on the House floor seeking to delay the resolution to impeach.[27]

The Belknap scandal was still blowing hot when national convention time arrived. The Iowa convention delegates, all under the tight control of Ret Clarkson, were determined to nominate James G. Blaine.[28] The choice of untainted Rutherford B. Hayes, who talked in terms of civil service and of leniency toward the South, was a bitter disappointment to those stalwarts who still considered themselves Radicals. Next to Bristow, Hayes was Kasson's second choice. His third choice was William A. Wheeler, former schoolmate at the University of Vermont, now chosen as Hayes's running mate.

The Democrats also nominated a strong candidate, Samuel J. Tilden — shrewd New York attorney whose work in connection with the overthrow of the Tweed Ring gave him national standing.

In the ensuing campaign Democrats hammered away on Republican scandals, harsh Reconstruction, and the lingering hard times. On the defensive, Republicans waved the bloody shirt and harped on Tilden's alleged "copperhead" war record. The House in Washington shortly became the hall of vituperative electioneering. Kasson fiercely joined the chorus and in a major speech branded Tilden as a secessionist, a war obstructor, and a party to the Tweed and Crédit Mobilier rings. So partisan and radical was Kasson becoming that even Ret Clarkson approvingly declared: "Our Johnny has been doing so many good things lately that we are all getting proud of him." And Hiram Price's Davenport *Gazette* suggested that Kasson would be a worthy successor to Blaine as Speaker of the House.

All this was like showering the unwanted, departing guest with bouquets, for Kasson had neither renewed the libel suit nor stood for re-election that spring; and the nomination of his successor, Colonel H. J. B. Cummings, had prompted the *Register* to declare that the old fight was "practically dead and buried. As it has gone to its grave, let us give it over to forgetfulness." In short, Kasson was no longer a threat for position, power, and perquisite *in Iowa*.[29]

With Congress adjourned, Kasson in October, 1876, made campaign speeches in Vermont, Maine, West Virginia, Ohio, Indiana, and finally at the Opera House in Des Moines. Ret was present to hear Kasson, and he printed the speech in full. Although Clarkson praised the speech, it was a mediocre one pleading for "sound money" and waving the bloody shirt at rebels in Congress and at the "Solid South." [30]

Three weeks later, on election day, first reports indicated that Tilden had won a sweeping victory. But Republican managers learned that both Republicans and Democrats were claiming victory in three Southern states — Louisiana, South Carolina, and Florida. Perceiving that if Republicans could hold these states, Hayes would win, they appealed to Grant to send "eminent Republicans" at once. Grant, still smarting from the criticism of his Southern policy, chose party "visiting statesmen," who had not been closely identified with his own faction. He called Kasson in and sent him to Louisiana, but, upon arrival, Kasson found New Orleans swarming with Republican politicians.

Not needed there, he was sent on to Tallahassee, Florida, where for two weeks he worked with a half dozen other "visiting statesmen," advising and supervising the Republican counting board, taking affidavits, throwing out Democratic votes, counting in Republican votes, and in general participating in a shabby, pettifogging affair. Whether Kasson knew it or not, James Tyner's postal agents were swarming about offering bribes and taking affidavits. In the election both parties indulged in fraud. In the scramble over who won, both sides used money. But even so, the evidence leans in favor of a Tilden victory in Florida.

Back in Washington for the opening of Congress in December, Kasson was interviewed by a reporter, and his report published in the newspapers. He insisted that the Republican returning board in Florida was honest and that Florida had gone for Hayes. Louisiana was more doubtful, but the solution to the deadlocks lay in the law (i. e. in the law vesting the power of decision in returning boards, which then were Republican). Significantly, in Florida, Kasson reported, the people were less inclined to violence than in the North and West and more interested in control of Florida than in the election of Tilden.[31]

With the arrival in time of two or more sets of returns from each of the disputed states — at least one each for Hayes and Tilden — a deadlock was reached, for the constitution did not make it clear whether the Democratic House or the Republican Senate should count the electoral votes. Kasson vigorously opposed setting up extralegal devices to break the log jam, and he voted against the Electoral Commission Bill, in part fathered by his Iowa colleague George W. McCrary, which provided the machinery for a solution. Since this bill was a Democratic measure in its early stages, Kasson feared that Tilden would win. He believed that without such a measure the Senate would in time count the votes and declare Hayes elected. In the House, Republicans stood a good chance to take advantage of a division between Northern and Southern Democrats to head off any move there to declare Tilden elected and thus obstruct the Senate count.

All along, Kasson sensed the "indisposition" of Southerners to become embroiled in "national disorder." More than Tilden, they wanted "intelligent white rule in the South." Therefore, he urged Hayes on December 17, 1876, to send to Washington someone who could "keep counsel," foster a Democratic split, and give "an orderly and peaceful alternative" to the discontent among Southern Congressmen. Such an observer might also indicate the "provable spirit . . . if not the policy" of Hayes's administration toward the South. Kasson advised that Benjamin Bristow, Grant's former reforming Attorney General and exposer of the Whiskey Scandal, would be a good Hayes spokesman in Washington.

When Hayes cautiously eschewed commitments, Kasson replied that he had not contemplated "agreements for mutual considerations" and that he had seen "no disposition for what is called bargaining." Instead, explained Kasson, "My desire was for the presence of a trusty friend, whose ears would be more open than his mouth, and whose candor would induce frankness of expression in response to questioning suggestions. . . . It is rather inquiry into probable future action, not involving pledges."

Hayes, two weeks later, thought that he "ought to leave Washington well alone." He already had friends there who could "speak confidently" of his "ways of thinking and acting." He was glad to get Kasson's reports, nevertheless, and would appreciate additional information.[32]

In the weeks that followed, legislation establishing the Electoral Commission was passed, but the independent member of the Commission, on whom the Democrats counted, resigned and was succeeded by a Republican. This unexpected turn of events gave the Republicans a majority of one on the Commission. Faced therefore with almost certain defeat, the Democratic majority in the House dangerously threatened by dilatory and filibustering tactics to prevent the completion of the electoral count before March 4, 1877.

From coast to coast excitement and apprehension prevailed. There might be serious bloodshed, even another war, if the matter were not worked out amicably. Would Democrats, convinced almost to a man that Tilden had been legally elected, assist in the seating of Hayes despite the fact that in the filibuster they had the means to prevent it and perhaps throw the decision into the House?

The idea of splitting Democratic ranks and of wooing Southern members had struck several other Republicans at about the same time that Kasson had suggested the possibility to Hayes. And with full knowledge on the part of Hayes there was unfolding a fantastic Compromise, until recently unknown,[33] which would open the way for a peaceful inauguration of the Republican nominee.

Confronted with the loss of the presidency and the cold fact that Carpetbaggers had become a political liability, practical Republican politicians discovered from the forgotten history of the South that ante-bellum Whigs had once spoken for the same type of economic interests as post-bellum Republicans — business enterprises with federal subsidies. Observing the contemporary scene, they discerned that most of the Southern leaders in Congress were Democrats of the conservative brand or former old-line Whigs, who were vigorously demanding federal internal improvements. Southwestern Democrats had already revived the ante-bellum dream of a Southern railroad to the Pacific, and some members of Congress were officers in the re-organized Texas & Pacific Railroad company, whose lobbyists were then pressing Congress for liberal aid.

Happily aware of this resurgence of Whiggery in the South, Republican planners at the same time observed that Northern Democrats were displeasing their Southern colleagues by firmly opposing federal internal improvements now unpopular in the North because of railroad malpractices and the scandal and corruption involving railroad subsidies. Having arrived tardily at the Great Barbecue, Southerners were now growing impatient with the niggardly and pious attitude of the Northern Democracy. To a small group of Republicans, the time seemed ripe to split the Democrats, throw the Carpetbaggers overboard, and rebuild the Republican party under the leadership of conservative whites in the South.

With these objectives in mind, Republican managers evolved the Scott plan, which enlisted the aid of Thomas A. Scott, Napoleonic railroad empire builder, owner of the Pennsylvania and the Texas & Pacific systems. Chief negotiators were the officials and agents of the Western Associated Press led by William Henry Smith, Hayes's closest friend, and Andrew J. Kellar, editor of the Memphis *Avalanche*.

The contact man with the railroad interest was Henry Van Ness Boynton, Union general, newspaperman, and exposer of the scandals under Grant. Boynton in turn worked through that railroad lobbyist par excellence of the Gilded Age, General Grenville M. Dodge. Scott and Dodge put their army of agents to work on Southern Congressmen who were led to believe that Hayes would support Southern internal improvements, especially the Texas & Pacific Railroad. There were other aspects of the Compromise, but the heart of the scheme was the Texas & Pacific.

Thus it happened that late in February, Southern opposition in the House to the Electoral Commission mysteriously collapsed to the chagrin of Northern Democrats, and Hayes was inaugurated. In a large measure his road to the White House had been paved by railroad lobbyists.

Though Kasson had seen the possibility of a compromise with the South, he had not been a party to the Great Compromise involving the Texas & Pacific. He had anticipated, and had been indirectly a party to, the better-known Wormley Bargain, which conceded home rule in the unredeemed Southern states. But the Wormley Bargain was merely a side show occurring *after* the Great Compromise had taken place in the main tent. Throughout the Forty-fourth Congress, Kasson had vigorously opposed subsidies for the Texas & Pacific and, as a member of the Texas Pacific Railroad committee, he took credit for defeating the lobbyists. General Dodge, as he set about to capture this committee, warned Scott that he could not handle Kasson, who was watching his every movement. On the other hand Dodge could control Platt of New York through Jay Gould, and he could "overwhelm Garfield" with petitions from his own district.[34]

During the hearings on Florida, Kasson and McCrary appeared before the Electoral Commission. Kasson spoke "clearly and forcibly," wrote James A. Garfield, despite "a certain air of affectation which detracts from the impressiveness of his speech — an effort to be exquisite." Kasson argued that the Commission could not go *behind* the certified electoral return in Florida to determine whether there was fraud. The Commission could begin only where state authority concluded — the *counting* of the electoral vote.[35]

Hence, throughout the election — as campaigner, as partisan on the House floor, as "visiting statesman" in Florida, and as spokesman before the Electoral Commission — Kasson had landed solid blows for the party. Now, in the spring of 1877 he was definitely a leading member of the Hayes circle in Congress. It was not altogether a case of leaping on the Hayes band wagon, for he had been pushing for the kind of man Hayes professed, and was to prove, to be. But now what was to be his reward for strenuous party work?

There was rumor that he was slated for a Cabinet position. John A. Hubbell of Iowa urged Kasson for a cabinet post. He had a "cool head & cool judgment," Hubbell wrote Hayes. His appointment would be "a just recognition of that class of able and incorruptible men who have given and received hard blows in behalf of the party."

But Kasson's colleague McCrary, also a strong Hayes man, had the support of the dominant faction in Iowa. Charles E. Perkins of the Chicago, Burlington & Quincy Railroad, who was supporting Mc-Crary, wrote Hayes's friend, General Manning F. Force, that Kasson was a "shrewd politician but an unscrupulous one . . . accused of bribery as a member of Congress." But Perkins did not inform Hayes that in the recent Congress, Kasson had opposed legislation favorable to railroads. When General Force transmitted the letter, he wrote Hayes: "My impression of Mr. Kasson was different . . . have heard . . . scandal about his wife, but gathered much of it was rumor. . . . Otherwise, I have heard him well spoken of." Frank Palmer, who called on Hayes, probably also put in a few words for McCrary and against Kasson. The lingering depression had forced Palmer to give up the *Inter-Ocean,* and in the closing days of the Grant administration he had been appointed postmaster of Chicago, subsequent to the appointment of his Indiana friend, James N. Tyner as Second Assistant Postmaster General. Tyner, meanwhile, in the last days of Grant's administration was made Postmaster General in time to throw his department into the campaign of '76.[36]

McCrary went in as Secretary of War, and Kasson got a foreign mission, as did many other "visiting statesmen." Without Kasson's knowledge, six Senators, including Allison, and most of Iowa's Congressmen recommended Kasson, who wanted the post at Vienna. But Hayes and the new Secretary of State, William M. Evarts, first assigned him to Spain. When Kasson, however, learned that the author, James Russell Lowell, had turned down the Austrian mission because of the harsh climate, he offered to exchange Madrid for Vienna. Evarts and Lowell approved the suggestion, and the switch was made.

Kasson's appointment caused a friend of Allison to congratulate the Senator for having disposed of McCrary and Kasson as rivals in the next senatorial election. Ret Clarkson did not refer to Kasson's appointment in the *Register*, though he ran headlines on Tyner's and Palmer's.[37]

In Iowa, the Clarkson-Allison-Kirkwood faction reigned supreme as Reconstruction came to an end and John Kasson moved off to Vienna. General Dodge still controlled much Iowa patronage but was too busy with railroad lobbying and building to direct affairs. Ret Clarkson had taken his place.

Although Hayes liberally rewarded his "visiting statesmen," his diplomatic appointments were definitely superior to those of Grant. Some of the "visiting statesmen" were the highest type of politicians in both parties. Kasson, with quasi-diplomatic experience, some grasp of German, and conversational facility in French, was better qualified than the usual politician of his day for a diplomatic mission at the court of the Hapsburgs.

Hayes's Minister to Austria-Hungary

BY THE END of June, 1877, Kasson had completed a business trip to California, had returned to Des Moines and made final arrangements for his long absence, and was back in New York. Here he spent a Fourth of July week end with Hamilton Fish but failed to find at home another friend, George William Curtis, civil service reformer and editor of *Harper's Weekly*.[1]

In London a few weeks later Kasson headed straight for the "tradesman, tailor, and hosier." The "distance from the tree-climbing,

HAYES'S MINISTER TO AUSTRIA-HUNGARY

fence-jumping school boy of Charlotte, Vermont, to the Envoy Extraordinary and Minister Plenipotentiary at the most etiquettish court of Europe" was very great, he wrote his sister. He had to buy at least "a new suit of clothes." With feigned modesty he went on, "You know how careless I have always been about dress where dress was of little account." But now where great importance was attached to dress, he would have to conform in order to escape the "reputation of a barbarian."

By August 1, with a full wardrobe, Kasson was at the court of the Hapsburgs. Almost thirty years before in St. Louis, as a young orator, while making a flowery speech in honor of Louis Kossuth, the revolutionary, he had excoriated the Hapsburgs. Now at the age of fifty-five he was to fall in with their ways. His first call upon the Emperor in his palace was a pleasant experience. The Emperor was particularly interested in President Hayes's Southern policy and civil service reform. He also expressed his desire to see trade between the two countries promoted and increased — a desire which pleased both Hayes and his Secretary of State Evarts.

With preliminaries over, Kasson started house hunting. It was up to the Minister to make either a "fitting, or unbecoming, representation of his country"; the old legation quarters were not fitting. So Kasson rented a large house — "perfectly plain on the exterior," he modestly wrote a friend in Des Moines, "while within it satisfies the sense of comfort, will bear any criticism of good taste, accommodates a hospitable disposition, and is full of objects of interest." He did not tell his friend that this house was the spacious Putzen Palace.[2]

Kasson realized the close alliance between political and social functions in Vienna, and he made every effort to give the United States legation a high position in Vienna society. As a foreign diplomat, he had access to the high court society, into which the only other passport was ancestry. In this society, dominated by the Austrian nobility, he moved at ease, entertaining and being entertained as the demands arose. He liked the natural simplicity of Austrian society, where the "grossness of materialism was softly veiled" and "personal ostentation an offense to good manners." Vienna women were, however, more pleasing in manners than brilliant in conversation, he wrote.[3]

He was amused at the royal stag hunts, one of which he early attended near Pest, the Hungarian capital. The British ambassador lent him a horse, and he ordered his red coat and white breeches from London. In the party were the Emperor and about thirty-five other huntsmen, including two ladies. Kasson enjoyed the scenery, costumes, and company, but the chase was "almost painful." To an American accustomed to hunting wild animals, it seemed artificial to take a deer in a wagon to the hunting grounds and then to have "whippers-in" beat off the dogs when the animal was at bay.

Kasson kept his sisters informed of his social life and his daily routines. He could not "get ready for sleep at the Austrian hour of ten in evening," he wrote Maria.

I am usually reading an hour or two later and of course quite alone. Rise at eight in the morning, coffee, bread, and grapes at nine. Read the papers and my mail, take a short walk, write and attend to Legation business, till about two, breakfasting with fork at one. The carriage arrives at two, and usually a drive for a couple of hours, or cards left if calls are to be made. Dine at six, and about twice a week at the opera, for the evening, closing at ten. Other evenings, sometimes a visit, sometimes French conversation, and sometimes books. The days are monotonous 'and evenings at home somewhat lonely.[4]

Kasson varied his diligent official reporting with letters to friends in America and to American friends in Europe. Men like Hamilton Fish, James A. Garfield, and John Sherman kept him abreast of inside politics in America. In Europe he got valuable information on how to act as a diplomat from George Perkins Marsh, long-time minister to Italy and benefactor of Kasson during the latter's boyhood at Burlington, Vermont. Edward F. Noyes at Paris and E. H. Stoughton at St. Petersburg, both personal friends, had been "visiting statesmen" with Kasson in Louisiana and Florida in 1876.[5]

Twice Kasson returned to the United States on leave, once upon the illness and death of his sister Maria at the age of sixty. Frequently he visited the American colony in Paris, and each summer he vacationed at such watering places as Carlsbad, Gastein, and Ischl.

The climax of entertaining at the American legation took place in the summer of 1878 upon the visit of General Grant during his famous around-the-world trip. For eight days Grant lived at Kasson's house, where the diplomatic set and Austria's social upper crust were entertained. Kasson also made arrangements for Grant to meet Bismarck and the German Emperor at Gastein, accompanied the General there, and helped serve as interpreter. During long conver-

sations with Grant at Putzen Palace, Kasson, like so many of his contemporaries, fell under the simple charm of the General and became
earnestly convinced that Grant, if given a third term, would this
time make a good president.[6]

John Kasson was never too busy with social events to neglect the
real business of the legation. His administration, according to John
Hay, Assistant Secretary in the State Department, was noted for its
"industry and activity." Kasson seemed to "enjoy work," and the
busy personnel in the legation at Vienna, wrote Hay, "belong to a
new race who have arisen since my time, who knew not Joseph."
Hay inferred that Kasson had been a good choice to help President
Hayes in his "gallant fight" to get the right kind of people into the
diplomatic and consular service.[7]

Kasson's mission stretched over the first four years of a decade
characterized as the doldrums in American diplomacy. Americans,
lustily engaged in exploiting their own natural resources, in building
railroads and cities, and in playing the exciting game of internal
politics, were indifferent to what went on in the rest of the world.
Separated from Europe and Asia by broad oceans, they felt secure
from the ambitions and broils of those lands. A feeling of apathy
toward foreign affairs prevailed, despite an enormous increase in
commerce; and the American foreign service was considered an expensive luxury which should be dispensed with. "Abolish our foreign
ministers! Recall our farcical diplomats!" cried one newspaper; while
another declared, "It [the foreign service] is a costly humbug and
sham. It is a nurse of snobs. It spoils a few Americans every year,
and does no good to anybody. Instead of making ambassadors, Congress should wipe out the whole service."

James Tyner, the Post Office spoilsman, expressed a popular view
among politicians late in 1888. As for filling the State Department,
he wrote:

. . . we will have no trouble. Any man well up in social etiquette, with
capacity to employ diplomatic language (which means high sounding phrases
full of polite expressions), with enough judgment to consult the President
and Secretary of the Treasury about any commercial questions that may
arise, and with an ample fortune to furnish terrapin and champaign at diplomatic dinners, will answer our purposes. That Department is the dress

parade part of the Govt. Real diplomacy, involving the application of international principles and the enforcement of international law, will soon be obsolete with us for the whole world is anxious to be at peace with us, nobody wants to fight us.

The Post Office in my judgment is next to the Treasury in importance. It is the Keeper of Administration politics. Think of it! eighty odd thousand appointments, scattered everywhere, the walking representatives of the dominant party constantly within the gaze of the people.[8]

In Vienna, Kasson encountered no pressing diplomatic dispute until the eve of his final departure in 1881. He therefore directed his energies to keeping Washington informed of the drift of international politics. Residing in a center of European diplomatic gossip and in daily contact with some of Europe's leading diplomats, he sensed trends which he thought dangerous to the future security of the United States. While European nations girded themselves for a struggle for territories, markets, and raw materials, America slept. In dispatch after dispatch, Kasson poured warnings into the State Department. We were not prepared to grapple with the diplomatic problems which lay ahead, he kept insisting.

The strong American navy of the Civil War era had rapidly rotted away, until it was said to be merely "an alphabet of floating washtubs" — "worn out, slow in speed, feeble in offensive power, even in the power of running away from danger." [9]

Like the navy, the American merchant marine had also rapidly declined during and following the Civil War. By 1880 it was carrying only 23 per cent of our mounting foreign trade. Although our export trade had increased more than 200 per cent by 1880, William Maxwell Evarts, Hayes's Secretary of State in 1877, made the further expansion of overseas commerce the cornerstone of his foreign policy. Hayes and Evarts moreover instructed their diplomats to submit suggestions for the reform of the foreign service.

The expansion of foreign trade would expedite economic recovery and absorb growing surpluses, especially agricultural products, the disposition of which was causing anxiety to men of vision. Beyond these goals, however, Secretary Evarts laid down no far-reaching policy. Now in the declining years of a brilliant legal career, he took long vacations, awaited diplomatic disputes rather than trying to head them off, and left the routine of the Department in the hands of subordinates. On trade expansion, let it be repeated, he was persistently explicit, exhorting his diplomats and consuls in a number of private and circular instructions to provide statistical information and to keep alert for every opening.

John Kasson, foreseeing tremendous economic development at home and aware of his country's immediate power, showed chronic irritation with the American attitudes toward foreign affairs and with the low estate into which the foreign and consular services had fallen. Under Grant, the spoils system had reached a low-water mark in those services which in a large measure had become the storage vault for undesirable office seekers. Salaries were low, upkeep on the legations lacking, and the personnel often inefficient or inadequate in numbers to handle the expanding business of the country.

At Vienna, Kasson received $12,000 per year, while the British Minister in Washington received £6,000 annually. For clerical help Kasson was allowed but a single secretary; for legation upkeep a contingent fund of $700 a year. The legation was "unfit" for official purposes and "unbecoming" to the country it represented, even drawing criticism from American travelers, he complained. Consequently when he moved the legation into more "becoming" quarters, he managed also to get the contingent fund increased to $1,000 annually.

For four years Kasson peppered his official reports with criticism of the foreign service and with suggestions for improving it. These suggestions boil down to a plea for better trained personnel who knew the country and could speak its language. Near the end of his mission he submitted concrete proposals for reform, based on his study of the Oriental Academy, originally devoted to training Austrian consuls for the Orient. This Academy, established during the reign of Maria Theresa, offered a five-year training course in law, history, government, and languages for highly screened students. Impressed with the thoroughness and rigidity of the program, Kasson became acquainted with the director of the school, studied the system in detail, and included his findings in his broader report to Washington on the Austrian diplomatic and consular system.

The Secretary of State had personally enjoined him to report all means of increasing American commerce abroad. Kasson concluded that, first of all, the foreign services would have to be improved and geared to the rising needs of the expanding nation. No longer could the American government "proceed on the theory that a consul, like a poet, *nascitur non fit.*" For, he continued,

We have few native-born Consuls who are really masters of any other language than the English. Even after a few years of employment, when they have picked up shreds of a foreign language, they are often transferred to posts where the language and usages are wholly unknown to them. . . . As a rule such agents content themselves with mere routine, and for ordinary intercourse depend upon some poorly paid interpreter of foreign origin, of whom the English language becomes in turn the victim. The same is true of some of our Legations. The real interpreter of our interests becomes at last an irresponsible and partially educated foreigner. . . . The United States should escape from this condition of inferiority.[10]

In the looming struggle for influence and trade in Asia, the Indies, and South America, the United States, despite her splendid geographical position, was ill prepared. How many native Americans could speak, or write an order in, Japanese, Chinese, or Spanish? The time had come for the establishment of a foreign service school in Washington, he urged. Perhaps the Smithsonian Institution, for which he had high admiration, would make room for the classes.

In these recommendations Kasson was almost a half century ahead of the American government and almost a full century ahead of the thinking of the American people.

An improved merchant marine was but the next logical step along the road toward increasing America's overseas trade. A great part of Kasson's voluminous correspondence is therefore concerned with this problem. To improve the foreign service was only the first of a number of recommendations which he submitted.

In connection with the Russo-Turkish war, and an anticipated war between Russia and Britain, Kasson advocated a reckless plan as a means of restoring the American merchant marine to the status it had occupied prior to the Civil War. Kasson's plan in brief would have opened American territorial waters for the belligerent use of Russian ships and would permit Russian officials to issue letters of marque to privateers that would operate against British shipping from American coasts and harbors. Thus the British merchant marine would be destroyed; the American merchant marine would be supreme. Before Kasson reached Vienna the Russo-Turkish war had broken out. In five months Russia crushed the Turks and imposed upon them the humiliating Treaty of San Stefano, which made Russia the dominant power in the Balkans. At once Britain and Austria-

Hungary, their vital Near Eastern interests threatened, forced Russia to submit the Turkish question to a European Congress, which met at Berlin during the summer of 1878.

Prior to this Congress, and during its session, diplomatic circles in Vienna expected a war between Russia and Britain. Meanwhile Russia was making elaborate plans for the use of American ports and private vessels against British shipping. Kasson, after frequent discussions with the Russian and British ambassadors, also concluded that war was inevitable. Consequently he plunged into a background study of the whole complex problem — conventions, treaties, neutrality laws, and customs; wrote his friend, former Secretary of State Hamilton Fish, for advice; and showered Evarts with long dispatches on the subject. The American people, he declared, still held Great Britain responsible for the Civil War destruction of their merchant fleet; nor had they forgotten that Russia was their friend during that struggle. In order to embarrass British commerce and recover their own they would be willing to go to the "extreme of international law." In Europe it was expected that the United States would seize this opportunity. In the event of such a war Kasson was positive that

Our flag will surely be insulted if our Navy shall be either unprepared, or unobservant. It is always necessary to remember — all her history shows it — that Great Britain when her blood is up, does not hesitate to hit an unwary neutral in the face; and that in a fight, she has too often been known to strike "below the belt" of international right. There is but one path of safety for a neutral, when England is belligerent. It lies in complete preparation, constant vigilance and a recognized courage to "strike back." [11]

As a lawyer, Kasson looked up loopholes in America's existing treaties and neutrality legislation in order to permit Russian use of our coasts and the issuing of letters of marque to privateers. But Secretary Evarts calmly poured cold water on any such plans when he warned the Russians against unneutral use of American territory.

The Anglo-Russian war did not break out. Instead, at the Berlin Congress, Russia was forced to yield her Balkan supremacy in an elaborate compromise. Among the territorial changes, Rumania and Serbia were recognized as independent states. Kasson had failed to grasp the importance of Austrian influence in this Congress, and he was sanguine as to Russia's attitude toward the North during the Civil War. He did not know that, back in 1863, when he and Cara were so royally entertained by the Russian fleet, the Russians were merely trying to protect their fleet in American waters in case of war with Britain.[12]

Moreover, Kasson's proposals were a step backward in international law, and contrary to the due diligence articles in the Treaty of Washington between Britain and the United States and to American practice until the eve of the Second World War. Though he reflected the strong anti-British feeling of this era in the North, he had historical precedent to back such statements as: "The British conscience is always cloudy where the British mind is intent on its worried commerce"; or "when a strong nation like England goes to war the neutral has no safety except in complete preparation to strike back." [13]

In the newly created independent states of the Balkans, and in Persia, Kasson next pressed for trade expansion. That these areas offered potential fertile markets was evidenced by the struggle he observed going on between European powers for commercial treaties with them. When Austria-Hungary sent a minister to Persia in July, 1878, Kasson warned Evarts that the United States should negotiate a commercial treaty at once. Although Russia, Britain, and France had already worked out favorable commercial arrangements, it was not too late to find there a promising outlet for American cotton goods and firearms.

But nearer at hand, in Rumania, Serbia, and Montenegro, greater opportunities awaited. As soon as Kasson learned that the Berlin Congress was to grant Rumania and Serbia quasi-independence, he launched a campaign to induce Evarts to open diplomatic relations with them. Interspersed with the commercial motive, there runs through his dispatches a strong desire to secure political and religious equality for the Jews. While the Berlin Congress was in session, he proposed initiating a plan among the powers for a guarantee of religious toleration in Rumania. Evarts considered the proposal as one "eminently deserving consideration," but he showed no willingness to have any connection with the meeting at Berlin.

Kasson for the rest of the year turned his attention to the representatives of the Danubian countries in Vienna, exploring trade possibilities and investigating the attitude of their governments on the Jewish question. In the summer of 1879, while in Washington on vacation, he conferred with Evarts and, because of Kasson's "lively appreciation" of the matter, he returned to Vienna with formal instructions to open up diplomatic relations with Rumania and Serbia.

Already in the summer of 1878 Evarts had sent a commercial agent to Bucharest. But the Rumanians, sensitive in their new independence, demanded a full fledged diplomatic officer — not a consular agent. Faced with a cut in his appropriations, Evarts could not appoint a minister, and there the matter rested until Kasson returned to Vienna in 1879. Late that summer Kasson unexpectedly encountered the Rumanian foreign minister at a watering place in Austria, presented his treaty projects, and obtained a pledge that Rumania would not hold out any longer for a diplomatic officer but would now settle for an American consul.

While the Rumanian government considered his treaty projects, Kasson hastened to Belgrade where he was enthusiastically received. Significantly, in his first interview, the Serbian Prince humorously reminded him that American pork products, even in the absence of commercial treaties, were already seriously competing with Serbian pork. A commercial treaty nevertheless was concluded without difficulty, but the sudden illness of the foreign minister postponed completion of all details for a consular treaty. Without full powers to sign the commercial treaty, Kasson returned to Vienna and finished the consular treaty through diplomatic correspondence.

Meanwhile Rumania had renewed her demands for full American diplomatic representation. Serbia thereupon renewed her demands also, and as Kasson continued negotiations for another year, he learned that Austria, under an article of the Berlin agreement, was holding up the Serbo-American treaty. The Kasson treaties remained unsigned until after Kasson had left Vienna for good. In 1882 the United States accredited Eugene Schuyler, a friend of Kasson, as charge d'affaires and consul general to the courts of Greece, Rumania, and Serbia. Under this title he was formally received and concluded the treaties begun by Kasson.

During these negotiations, Kasson made an unofficial trip to Montenegro which had no significance other than a careful report which analyzed the trade possibilities there.[14]

☆ ☆ ☆

Another aspect of trade expansion upon which Kasson submitted reports was the influence of the American tariff policy. Through his own observations of trade relations in Austria, he committed himself more fully than ever before to protectionism and to a "sound money," resumption of specie, gold standard policy. He attributed the sagging economy of Austria to the silver standard with its fluctuating monetary values, but more especially to an unfavorable, low-tariff trade treaty with Bismarck's Germany.

All Europe, he declared, was entering upon an era of "national selfishness," both commercial and political. In the rapid industrial expansion of the sixties and seventies, European nations had been blinded to the fact that production was exceeding "legitimate demands." Discovering this fact only after 1873, they began to lay plans for the protection of their markets at home and their extension abroad. Austria, Germany, and many other governments were now feverishly revising their commercial treaties for self-protection.

The United States, Kasson indirectly admitted, had been in part responsible for the looming trade war. European leaders had already taken note of America's surprising trade balance against their countries, and of the widespread fears of their farmers, who dreaded the competition of American agricultural products. They had therefore begun to appreciate the "visible results" of the American policy of protection and were on the point of striking back.

What was the answer? Continued protection, tempered with reciprocity treaties and a specialized tariff board, advised Kasson. America would be in a "dangerous and anomalous" position, he declared, if she revised her tariff downward as Europeans revised theirs upward. The tariff should always be high enough to prevent flooding of the home market that was so essential to "national independence." But for "special relations with certain countries," reciprocity treaties, free from the jurisdiction of most-favored-nation considerations, were preferable.

But Kasson found among American merchants a "defective knowledge" of tariffs and commercial treaties. Therefore he recommended in America the creation of a commission of representatives from "well-informed trading interests" to study the effect of constant treaty transformations. The commission could be set up under the Treasury Department, but it should be wholly free from political affiliations. Such a board of competent men, ever alert to the complicated and shifting nature of international trade, could advise legislators in their efforts at tariff revision; more important, it could advise commercial interests how best to meet the retaliatory tariffs which Europe was certain to employ soon.[15]

Thus Kasson at an early date was advocating reciprocity and a tariff commission as devices to soften American protection and to control the flagrant, logrolling abuses connected with tariff legislation in the American Congress. For the rest of his life, however, these devices were to be little more than smoke screens behind which high protectionists hid.

While the United States kept edging her tariff ever upward following the Civil War, her agriculture products swelled in volume and spilled out over Europe. By the late seventies, American pork products had captured the market in England; on the continent home producers were pushed hard to stay in the field. Native producers pressed for relief, and European leaders squirmed in their official positions to find the means to meet American competition.

Shortly after reaching Vienna, Kasson warned Evarts that the importation of American pork was likely to be restricted or banned. In the spring of 1878 Vienna newspapers began to print stories from German publications, warning that American meat was infected with trichinae. Only one German ham out of every 2,500 contained trichinae, it was alleged, while five to ten American hams out of the same number were infected. Circulating also in the European press was the rumor that the frequency of the parasite in American products naturally resulted from unsanitary feeding and packing practices. Trichinosis was propagated by the "great slaughtering houses" which fed their hogs refuse. These reports were particularly damaging in Central Europe where meat was frequently eaten uncooked.

Though Kasson vigorously denied the accuracy of such reports, he was unable to get his version before the Austrian public. Hence the reports continued to circulate, damaging American sales. About a year later Kasson opened a Vienna newspaper to read that from a shipment of American hams locally examined, seventy or eighty were condemned as containing trichinae. To counteract such adverse publicity, Kasson proposed the setting up of an *impartial* committee to examine hams of American and Austrian origin for comparative figures on the presence of the parasite. But when he offered his proposition to three leading Vienna newspapers, each turned it down.

In the spring of 1881 the matter finally came to a head, following a report from an English consul stationed at Philadelphia. The report, confusing mortality of swine from hog cholera with danger to human life from eating trichinae-infected meat, was published in England in February, 1881. Immediately it reached the newspapers, and almost overnight panic struck the European public. At once France, Germany, Italy, and several smaller nations prohibited further American pork importations. In the United States packers and importers pressed the Department of State for help in allaying public fears abroad and in removing restrictions.

Kasson took up the matter with dispatch and vigor. When news of French and German action reached him, he tried to find out in advance what the Vienna government would do. From a minor official in the foreign office he picked up the information that the Austrian government had already prepared a decree for exclusion and had transmitted it to Hungary for her concurrence. Kasson telegraphed this information to Secretary Evarts, who wired back that he was to protest to the foreign minister at once. If the decree took effect without an interval of notice and for reasons other than public health, it would be regarded in Washington as "intolerable and oppressive."

In an interview with the Austrian foreign minister Kasson declared that rival interests in Europe were using "unscrupulous means" to discredit American pork products. There was less likelihood of trichinae in pork from the United States, where hogs were fattened on Indian corn, a pure food, than from Europe where hogs were fed garbage, carcasses, and even rats. It would be an injustice to exclude American products alone on "mere suspicion," even though European pork was to be more strongly suspected. The Austrian foreign minister, citing the decrees in France and Germany, frankly admitted that protection of home production was an influential factor in the contemplated ban.

Meanwhile, reports, probably inspired by rival pork producers, as to the danger of the American products kept circulating in the newspapers. Kasson's repeated denials of the authenticity of such reports were received with courtesy at the Austrian foreign office, but they had no effect in changing the course the government had charted. The long-expected decree appeared in the *Wiener Zeitung* on March 16, 1881. Published simultaneously in Austria and in Hungary, it was naked exclusion, not based on grounds of health. It became effective immediately upon publication.

Again Kasson protested. In a sharp note he declared that for the decree to be acceptable actual disease resulting from the eating of American pork would have to be proved. Moreover, the same treatment would have to be applied to all nations, without discrimination, as provided by an old and binding treaty between the United States and Austria. The Austrian foreign minister then merely replied that the ban was issued solely out of regard for public health. The United States, he said, had failed to take the necessary precautionary measures to prevent the spread of trichinosis.

A week before the decree was published, Kasson analyzed the controversy in a long dispatch and admitted the weakness of the American case. He doubted that the United States had done her share in removing "every just cause of complaint." Three steps should be taken before we were "without fault for the alarm" existing in Europe: (1) The causes of hog cholera should be officially determined and publicized. (2) Official inspection of pork products for trichinae should be conducted either at slaughterhouses, depots, or ports of exportation. (3) Official investigation should establish definitely whether salting, smoking, drying, or other curative processes destroyed the dangerous parasites. Once the United States had established a system of meat inspection, Kasson then recommended the providing of an economic weapon of retaliation for American diplomats. The European sense of international justice, he wrote,

... is largely influenced by the widespread fears among their people of the effect of the recent development of the industry of the United States and of the resulting competition in European markets. . . . These considerations are pressed upon the Governments. It is more than likely that they will lead to injustice and inequality toward the United States in the near future. Hence the question whether Congress ought not to arm the Executive with the power to impose temporarily a percentage of discriminating duties on the products of the soil and of the industry of those nations which apply discriminating duties or regulations against the products of the soil or industry of the United States.[16]

This was Kasson's last dispatch as Minister to Austria. With a change of administration in Washington, Kasson's successor had been appointed and was en route to Vienna. Though failing to get the decree revoked, Kasson had been energetic in his efforts. He had used the strongest arguments possible, and in his recommendations to the State Department he had provided the basis for an eventual settlement of the dispute. But until the United States government required her packers or exporters to inspect and guarantee the safety of their products, American diplomats could make little headway in Europe. Moreover, to succeed in getting the bans removed, they would have to have either a reduction of American tariffs or legislation discriminating against European goods.

In the mid-twentieth century it seems incredible that in the early eighties the United States government had not taken steps to protect both home and foreign consumers against contaminated meat products. But even so, to protect public health was not the main force behind the Austrian decree. This was merely a pretext to hide the economic motive, for the truth of the matter was, as Kasson had pointed out, European pork contained more trichinae than American.

In the near past Austria had been a great exporter of pork products herself and possessed good markets, particularly in England, France, and Germany. But in recent years her exports had gradually been pushed out by those of the United States. Now, American products had captured the British market and were competing heavily in Germany and France. Great Hungarian pork producers faced ruin. Hence when France and Germany clamped down on American imports, they were knocking out one of Austria's strongest competitors. Naturally the Vienna government followed with a similar decree, and it was too much to expect that she would repeal it so long as Germany and France pursued their course of discriminating against American meat. Resentful of the American system of protection, neither of these powers would yield in the absence of tariff revision and meat inspection by the United States.[17] The key that would unlock the closed door was tucked away in the desk of Germany's Iron Chancellor.

There the matter rested in the spring of 1881; the story of John Kasson's role in pork diplomacy had only begun.

The final steps in Kasson's program for commercial expansion called for a new interpretation and use of the Monroe Doctrine, the building of a strong navy, and the acquisition of overseas territories. Vienna was a splendid vantage point for observing the direction of European ambitions. He discerned at once the rising surge toward imperialism, caught the fever of expansionism himself, and urged

JOHN A. KASSON IN VIENNA, 1877

KASSON AND UNIDENTIFIED FRIEND IN BERLIN, 1884

the United States to throw herself into the competition. In short, America should contain the dangers from Old World imperialism by becoming imperialistic herself.

Although Kasson repeatedly emphasized these themes throughout the years of his sojourn in Austria-Hungary, his dispatches on the subject grew shrill as he read about the efforts of the great French engineer Ferdinand de Lesseps to build a canal across the Isthmus of Panama. In America, the press and Congress expressed hostility to this project, and by the spring of 1880 both Hayes and Evarts had gone on record as favoring an exclusively American-controlled canal. Moreover, they had interpreted the Monroe Doctrine to mean that the United States had paramount interests in hemispheric affairs. In a report to Congress on the canal affair, Evarts, however, did not mention de Lesseps nor did he recommend a policy of preparedness and expansion as a safeguard against foreign threats.

When Kasson read an abstract of Hayes's message, and Evarts' report to Congress, he at once sent his congratulations along with a long dispatch airing his views on the Monroe Doctrine, the canal, and world politics. The de Lesseps concession in Central America would lead Panama to the same fate as his activities had led Egypt — to the administration by some foreign power. In Europe, Kasson warned, there was "a general revival of the lust of conquest, of territorial acquisition." Powerful navies, the thrust to expand commerce, and the animation for colonies among the people were irresistible forces with which the United States would have to reckon. America had most to fear from England, France, and Germany, although Germany had only begun to enter the race for insular possessions. Since Africa would only partly satisfy these nations, they would next move into Central and South America and the islands of the Pacific unless obstructed by the "earlier intervention" of a strong American navy at the exposed points. Therefore, Kasson declared, the following conclusions were evident:

1st, the unequivocal assertion of the "Monroe Doctrine" recently made, is timely and demands the concurrence of all branches of our government and the hearty support of the American people; and ought (perhaps) to be fortified by a treaty *ad hoc* between the United States and each of the existing continental governments of both American continents. 2nd, the naval power of the United States should be sufficiently augmented and strengthened to demonstrate our ability to enforce the principle asserted in the "Monroe Doctrine." Right, separated from might, has in the last ten years greatly lost its force with all the great nationalities of Europe. 3d, If there are Islands in the Pacific Ocean, as there are, which will be of importance to our national commerce and national power, in the coming enlargement of communications and trade, it is of serious importance that the United States should be first on the ground, and prompt to establish their control.[18]

A few weeks later, when he learned that the mighty Bismarck was supporting a government subsidy for a German private corporation operating in distant Samoa, he again forecast a Reich hungry for overseas crumbs. The time has come, he emphatically declared, when

. . . American statesmen must contemplate a change in our extra-territorial policy. . . . Our naval and commercial power will not be secured, nor sufficiently prepared for the future, without a controlling and unconditional possession in the West Indies, another looking to the immediate command of the Isthmus-transit, and others on the great lines of navigation leading from California to China, and from Panama and California to the new Australian world so rapidly advancing in commercial and international importance. It is to our discredit that the first century of our Statesmanship has developed but one formula of Foreign Policy, and that the plagiarism of the "Monroe Doctrine." [19]

In America the de Lesseps affair inspired a surprising wave of nationalism. At once in the spring of 1881, the press took up the canal question and its relationship to the Monroe Doctrine. The discussion waxed warmest in the fall of 1881. With enthusiasm Kasson joined the discussion through two articles published in the *North American Review*. The first, a fairly accurate historical treatment of the Monroe Doctrine, laid down the background for the second in which he discussed the applicability of the Doctrine to an isthmian canal. The underlying motive of Monroe's original declaration, he maintained, was to secure American "material interests" against European encroachments. The unrestrained spread of foreign trade in the New World would inevitably lead to foreign intervention into the affairs of weaker nations to protect such trade. Economic domination would eventually lead to political control. Consequently, Kasson demanded, the Doctrine as a device to protect our "material interests" should be used to forestall armed force by any European power in the New World. In short, the United States, as in the later days of Roosevelt and Taft, should become an international policeman. To uphold the Doctrine, Kasson next demanded an isthmian canal under American control. To defend the canal and maintain the Doctrine, moreover, he logically demanded strategic outlying possessions and a strong navy. The trend of the times, he declared, demanded

. . . a change of our passive policy into one of action. . . . The tradition against the policy of outlying possessions, is at this stage of our history, simply imbecile. It belongs to a country of few resources, timid and trembling in the presence of some great naval power. We have passed that stage of our existence. We are rapidly utilizing the whole of our continental territory. We must turn our eyes abroad, or they will soon look inward upon discontent. Touching the two great oceans which divide the world, this Republic should, like the Roman Janus, have two faces, regarding both Europe and Asia, and the islands interposed. It is the duty alike of her political interests and her wealth, to connect the waters of the two seas which embrace her coasts, and then to keep the connecting waters bright with her passing keels.[20]

Thus, during the years when America had no consistent foreign policy nor the military power to support one, Kasson had advocated a complete and vigorous program built around the fact of our tremendous economic expansion at home — an expansion which called for commercial expansion abroad. As Kasson worked it out from experience and observation in Vienna, commercial expansion required (1) a foreign service revitalized with highly trained personnel who knew the way of the foreigner and could speak his language; (2) a commission of experts sitting in Washington who understood the complications of foreign trade relationships and could manipulate the tariff for national advantage; (3) the speedy opening up of diplomatic and commercial relations with new governments and peoples as the opportunities arose. Lastly, and more broadly, Kasson kept emphasizing the cyclical foreign policy which was to become commonplace by 1900. Commercial expansion required merchant marine expansion which required naval expansion which required territorial expansion. All these requirements could moreover be better met by using the Monroe Doctrine to justify the exclusive control of an isthmian canal and to head off further European economic expansion in the Western Hemisphere.

Kasson then, as Minister at Vienna, was helping lay the intellectual foundation for a vigorous foreign policy and providing the expansionists of the nineties with the rationalizations so vital to their program.[21]

XVI

All the Way with Arthur: In Congress, 1881-1883

DURING KASSON'S sojourn in Austria-Hungary the shifting sands of politics covered over old fissures and smoothed out a path for his return to a position he had not held in the party since the assassination of Lincoln. Hard-pressed Republicans in Iowa and in the nation needed his service *inside* the country, as the party's grip on national power continued to weaken during the Hayes administration.

Once inaugurated in the spring of 1877, President Hayes immediately set about to put into effect the Great Compromise designed to split Southern Democrats and rebuild the Republican party in the South on a more solid conservative-white foundation. He appointed a Southern man to his Cabinet, distributed patronage to Southern Democrats, and withdrew the remaining troops from the South.

Other phases of the compromise could not be carried out. The first breach took place in the fall of 1877 when Southern Democrats in Congress failed to bolt their party as expected and join with Republicans to elect James A. Garfield Speaker of the House. The second and major breach was Hayes's failure to support Southern internal improvements, especially the Texas & Pacific Railroad.

Although General Dodge and his assistant lobbyists continued to badger Congressmen and to mobilize the press and public opinion for a federal subsidy, Hayes grew cold on the project. Meantime, while Dodge and Tom Scott won converts in Congress, their arch rival Collis P. Huntington was laying rails eastward through Arizona — without a subsidy. Dodge and Scott were never able to get their bill through. In 1880 Scott sold his Texas & Pacific holdings to Jay Gould, and the next year the Gould line from the east made a junction near El Paso with the Huntington line from the west. Thus the South got her road without a federal subsidy.

Hayes's Whiggish coalition was still further undermined by a renewed upsurge of radical agrarianism in the South and West. Instead of railroad subsidies, long suffering debtor-farmers demanded railroad regulation; they wished to crush monopolies, not foster them; instead of "sound money," they wanted greenbacks or free silver; and they called for a political alliance between the agrarian West and South. In 1877-1878 these two sections joined up in the House to pass measures increasing the circulation of silver and repealing the law for the resumption of specie payments. For a while the agrarian groundswell threatened the elaborate structure of economic legislation favorable to business and industry, of which the Republican party had become the guardian.

The Southern policy of the President split his own party, not the Democrats. The Republican oligarchy in the Senate, led by Blaine, Conkling, Cameron, and their carpetbagger friends, still calling themselves Radicals, engaged in fierce attacks upon the administration. In the House, Democrats, completely ignoring the Compromise, turned to investigating the 1876 elections in Louisiana, South Carolina, and Florida. Now faced with a "Solid South" instead of a Republican

South, Republicans continued to stress the politics of the "bloody shirt" as a form of obscurantism in order to corral the Western agrarians in an alliance with the moneyed East.[1]

Meanwhile, the party split into three factions—Stalwarts, followers of Grant, nominally led by Roscoe Conkling; Half Breeds, followers of Blaine and led by him; Mugwumps, the reform element. On issues, there was little difference between Stalwarts and Half Breeds. They were mere factions, each struggling for power.

In Iowa, party regulars caviled against the soft Southern policy of "Missy" Hayes and "Aunty" Evarts. They longed for a return of the Old Guard under Grant, Blaine, or Morton. In the seventh district, Ret Clarkson, having blocked off Kasson, lost complete control over the obstreperous agrarians who successfully stormed this Republican fortress in 1878 under the banner of the Greenback party fused with some of the Democrats in the district.

Kasson's Republican successor in 1876, Colonel H. J. B. Cummings, had distinguished himself in Congress mostly for supporting veterans' pension legislation. This was not enough to suit disgruntled farmers, who in '78 turned to the able Edward H. Gillette, living in East Des Moines under the shadow of the partly finished new state capitol. From Ret's *Register*, Gillette immediately emerged as a "coupon clipper," a "slacker," a "millionaire communist," a corruptionist, a coward, and "an elegant gentleman of which Iowa has not produced many." On the other hand Colonel Cummings was the "Candidate of National Honor and Iowa Honesty" who would not drive capital from the state as "corrupt Greenback leaders" were doing. Gillette, however, surprisingly beat out Cummings by less than 1,000 votes. In the sixth district, Greenbacker General James B. Weaver won by more than 2,000 votes.[2]

Reverberations from these events rumbled all the way to Vienna. James A. Garfield early in 1878 wrote Kasson that the country had gone "clean daft" over silver. The times were "very dark"; Hayes's Southern policy was wrecking the party; the people were crazy. Garfield longed for Kasson's help in the House in fighting "our old foes" (Democrats) and the new ones, "inflationists and silver lunatics."

Hamilton Fish wrote that reconciliation was flourishing "as smooth as oil on a bombshell connected with a galvanic battery." At the White House there was "weakness and vacillation"; in Congress, "demagogery and narrow rancor." The President had conciliated the South but had lost the North, gloomily sighed Fish.

Stung by Democratic investigations of fraud in the election of 1876, Edward F. Noyes, American Minister at Paris and "visiting statesman" in Florida, wrote Kasson: "You will remember how honestly we conducted ourselves during that Florida fight — that we who went over from Louisiana all the time insisted that nothing should be done which was liable to criticism. If there were frauds . . . on the Republican side, certainly they were concealed from us." Noyes was particularly irked at the publication in the American press of a Democratic letter urging Kasson and Noyes "to resign at once and come home to share the fate of their confederates in the crimes." Noyes quite correctly concluded that a "thorough inquiry into all the facts" would not help the Democrats.

From such letters as these, from reading American newspapers, from his personal impressions of Grant during the latter's long stop in Vienna, Kasson was becoming convinced that the General was the only man who could lead the party to victory in 1880.

Kasson regretted the lack of political "savoir-faire" in Washington. But Garfield's fight for "sound money and political honor" gave him "strong hope still for 1880." "I am trying to do my duty here, and there is more to do than I expected," he wrote Garfield. But he was not at all fascinated with life in Vienna. The "free and healthy air" of his own country was more appealing.[3]

In June, 1879, when Kasson returned home for a vacation, he undoubtedly was gratified and perhaps surprised at the exuberant reception accorded him in Des Moines. The Union League and a half dozen other organizations staged a gigantic torch parade and mass meeting to welcome him. Ret Clarkson's rising young partner in the Des Moines Regency and state party chairman, John S. Runnells, rode in the same parade carriage with Kasson and introduced him to the audience. Kasson made a brief speech lauding particularly the Republican policy of "sound money." Neither nihilists nor communists nor capitalists nor laborers in Europe desired a depreciable currency, he declared. Clarkson's *Register* gave two full columns to the "glorious, inspiring demonstration." Ret's "most modest calculation" placed the crowd at five to seven thousand people. Kasson's speech was "as sound as live-oak timber" and Kasson himself "a most powerful leader."

That summer Ret yielded the Des Moines post office to another man, and his brother Richard gave up the state printership to Frank M. Mills, an old Kasson friend. Despite Ret's hope that Kasson would participate in the fall canvass, Kasson shortly returned to Vienna.

No evidence has been found to indicate that Ret and Kasson had struck a bargain. On the contrary, Ret's brother opposed "burying the hatchet," and there is much evidence in the *Register* showing that Ret was yielding to a popular demand for Kasson and to the cold reality that Kasson was the best bet to beat Greenbacker Gillette.[4]

The next spring (1880), in response to a query from Adair County Republicans, Kasson replied that he would come home and make the canvass for Congress if nominated. In March, when Adair County instructed its delegates for Kasson, he understandably sent sister Mary "surprising accounts from the Iowa newspapers of the unanimity" with which "people and papers" hailed his running again. "Even my old enemies are swelling the tide," he confided, including the *Register*, which "still loves a fling at me." "After my long persistence in the fight," Kasson continued, "you will easily understand how these things move me, and impress me. I suppose their defeats two years ago have something to do with it. It seems to be a spontaneous movement, beyond the management of politicians. The steady attachment of the people to me makes me feel toward them as to kindred." [5]

By mid-April enough counties had instructed for Kasson to assure his nomination, and several weeks *before* the convention he wrote out his acceptance speech and sent it to his old friend James C. Jordan to be read. In response to a request for biographical data, Kasson cautioned another old friend, S. J. Loughran, to keep the source of his "recollections in close personal confidence." He explained:

I say in confidence because I have never blown my own horn and I do not like to do it now. I had rather be under-praised than over-praised always. I have worked and I am willing that should be known. I have not done as well as I ought to have done, and I know it. Reflection shows many faults. We must learn by experience to correct them, all of us. I hope in the future to do better.[6]

By convention time, June 20, 1880, all counties had unanimously instructed for Kasson, and although the convention at Chariton in the southern part of the district was a mere formality, it was a rousing one. Special trains were run to accommodate the enthusiastic delegates and crowd. Kasson's acceptance speech called for a sound financial policy, a national committee of public works to allocate an annual fund for internal improvements, a foreign policy designed to compete with our European commercial rivals, and (sensitive to the criticism of his role as "visiting statesman") a nonpolitical tribunal to settle disputed federal elections.

In analyzing Kasson's easy victory, Clarkson bluntly stated that someone who could unite all elements in the party was required. Several prospective candidates, including Colonel Cummings and Charley Nourse, might have won the nomination but not the election. Kasson neither "wanted the nomination nor agreed to take it" till convinced that he had the support of all factions. A majority of the voters were Kasson's "devoted friends and admirers." Therefore, said Ret of himself and others, the "robust minority" acquiesced in order not to involve the whole district in turmoil. Running through Ret's rationalizations is the point that Kasson was not his personal choice but a strong candidate who could win the election and that is what counted when the party had its back to the wall.[7]

Meanwhile, twenty days before Kasson received official news of his nomination, he read in the Vienna newspapers that James A. Garfield had been nominated for the presidency. "It has come four years sooner than I expected," Kasson congratulated Garfield. "My old colleague in many parliamentary battles, God bless you!" Chester A. Arthur, Conkling Stalwart and machine politician of New York, was chosen Garfield's running mate.

With these preliminaries over, Kasson applied to the State Department for leave "for public reasons" and arranged passage to America for August 12. After a full month's delay and a telegram from Kasson, Evarts wired that if Kasson was returning "for the canvass," rather than to "rest in the country or cut up in the city," he had better resign. This was carrying civil service reform too far to suit Kasson. Foreign ministers should have the same right as home ministers "to speak on the question of a *revolution* of the government," he wrote Garfield. Besides, his ship was to sail before he could pack up all of his things. Therefore, he set sail for New York with the expectation of having "a full understanding with Evarts" in Washington.[8]

Early in September, Kasson was in Des Moines to launch his campaign before "the largest gathering since Blaine spoke here in the fall of 1878." For the next six or seven weeks he stumped his district, defending the resumption of specie payments, supporting a protective tariff "intelligently adjusted," trotting out the old bogey of Southern war claims, and capitalizing fully on returning prosperity under Republican rule. He refrained from personal attacks upon his opponents. In the closing days of the canvass the Democratic nominee withdrew, throwing his support to Gillette, the Greenbacker.

When Kasson's opponents began to circulate published supplements on the old charges of '66 and '74 against him, Ret Clarkson defended him. Specifically, Ret denied that Kasson had interpolated an amendment to the Rock Island land grant resumption act so as to defeat the will of the legislature. "Further investigation" since the libel trial, declared Ret, had convinced him that Kasson did not do it. The next day following Ret's denial, the Democratic Des Moines *Leader* published a letter from J. C. Savery to Gillette stating that Kasson had withdrawn the libel suit and paid the costs. Savery did not say when Kasson withdrew the case.[9]

In the general election of November 2, 1880, Kasson beat Gillette by more than 2,000 votes. In the sixth district, where two years before Greenbacker J. B. Weaver had won, M. E. Cutts beat out another Greenback candidate by about 100 votes. Iowa now was back in the solid Republican ranks, giving Garfield a 40,000 majority. With returning prosperity and the rise of the clamor for free silver, the Greenback movement was on the downswing. In the nation Garfield squeezed through with a 10,000-vote popular lead. General J. B. Weaver polled 308,000 for the presidency on the Greenback ticket. In this campaign Republicans purchased floater votes in New York and Indiana and took on the name of the Grand Old Party (G.O.P.).

John Kasson was gratified with his own election and also with the election of a Republican House that he would help organize. But a letter from Ret Clarkson three days later was the climax in this satisfying campaign:

My dear sir,

In a more personal manner and feeling than as an editor I wish to congratulate you on your success, which I know must be very grateful to you personally as well as politically. For you have the consciousness that it is a personal as well as a political and party victory.

In view of the circumstances of the past the only thing that can add to the pleasure of a triumph so complete is the knowledge that it is a pleasure shared by those who formerly opposed you. This knowledge you now have.

For no one more sincerely rejoices over your election, & the sweeping manner of it, than those who were not with you in your campaigns & ambitions in the past.

Mr. Runnells was called yesterday to New Hampshire to the bedside of a dying sister. He tells me of conversation had with you as to the Speakership. It will be a pleasure to me to aid you in that matter, & I have already been looking after it in certain quarters. I go to New York Sunday or Monday, to meet Runnells there on Wednesday or Thursday. If we can be of service to you there, we have only to know what to do.

Very truly yours
J. S. Clarkson [10]

This letter brought down the curtain on a fifteen-year struggle to drive Kasson from his home district and Iowa politics. Now his supremacy in the Seventh District was admitted to be unchallengeable by his former adversaries. He was not, however, a member of the inner core of the state organization. It remained to be seen whether he would push on to the center of power and land a senatorship or a Cabinet position. During the long and bitter fight the years had run along fast, and he was now fifty-eight. As a national legislator he had lost vital years during which seniority could have been built up. The fight had circulated damaging rumors and gossip which, quietly behind the scenes, could be dragged out again. Battle-scarred, he was still game; and his political prospects in the autumn of 1880 seemed rather bright. In the new President-elect he had a close personal friend. Several newspapers were booming him for Speaker of the House, and a few more mentioning him for the United States Senate.

☆ ☆ ☆

Kasson hurried away to New York on a party conciliation mission for Garfield, apparently at the request of the President-elect, anxious to heal the breach between Stalwarts and Half Breeds. In Newark, New Jersey, he dined with Frederick T. Frelinghuysen; in New York he conferred with Hamilton Fish. Both these men were Stalwart followers of Grant and were the very highest type of men in either faction. Both were personal friends of Kasson, and both, according to Kasson, "entertained the most loyal sentiment" toward Garfield. Unexpectedly Kasson ran into Roscoe Conkling at the Fifth Avenue Hotel, rendezvous of politicians in New York. From Conkling's conversation, Kasson got the impression that the Grant champions wanted "to control the political gateway for 1884."

In order to avert such a possibility and to avoid another embittered factional struggle, Kasson advised Garfield to choose for his Cabinet two or three older men who were on excellent terms with Grant and Conkling. These men should be "perfectly honorable and perfectly loyal" to Garfield and should have the confidence of the "best men in the country," whom even the radical reformer George William Curtis would approve. In the three powerful departments, Treasury, Interior, and Post Office, Kasson emphasized,

. . . there ought to be unquestionable men in respect to executive ability, integrity, and *personal devotion to yourself*. I hope there will be no candidate for the presidency in either place. Both you and I know men who represent differing elements of the party, but who will at once work harmoniously and be loyal to the President. You can continue a pure administration and make it a powerful and *representative Republican* administration without slighting either great interest in the party. This appears to me to be the portrait of the *ideal* next cabinet.

Kasson went on to say that he was soon to be "far away"; but he added, "I beg to remind you of my offer, when any advice of mine can be useful to you, to return at once on receiving letter or telegram." [11]

Kasson was here not only giving sound advice to the head of a faction-ridden party; but in painting a portrait of the ideal Cabinet member he was also painting a self-portrait.

From New York, Kasson went to Washington and waited a week before getting to see Secretary Evarts. Several newspapers kept advocating Kasson's candidacy for Speaker of the House. Clarkson's *Register* fully approved the movement and averred that Kasson "would look good" in the Cabinet but for the Speaker's race.

Finally, in late November, Kasson sailed for Vienna. Evidently, he had been persuasive with Evarts in settling the problem of his having taken leave for the canvass. For several days the ship bucked a storm, smashing up furniture and hurling passengers against the bulkheads. Kasson was tossed across the companionway and down two steps. Coming up with a gash across his throat and the ligaments of his short ribs injured, he was under a surgeon's care for two days.[12]

In Vienna by Christmas, for the next five months he wrote long dispatches to Evarts on the rising tide of imperialism in Europe, urged the United States to adopt a more aggressive policy in Latin America and the Pacific, and gathered material for magazine articles dealing with the Monroe Doctrine and an American isthmian canal. He corresponded with the new diplomatic officer accorded to Rumania and Serbia by the United States, and gave aid in the negotiations to conclude his commercial treaties with Rumania and Serbia. In March he sailed along the Adriatic coast and made a trip to the capital of Montenegro, where American sewing machines and reapers were yet unknown, and was received at the palace of the Montenegrin Prince.

Before Kasson returned to America in early April, 1881, Garfield had already been inaugurated. The new President in choosing his Cabinet and handling the New York patronage had infuriated Roscoe Conkling, haughty champion of the Grant Stalwarts. The rift between factions had been widened — not sealed. Conkling's arch-enemy, James G. Blaine, had gone in as Secretary of State. Conkling and his New York senatorial colleague, Thomas C. Platt, had dramatically withdrawn from the Senate in protest to Garfield's appointment of an anti-Conkling man as head of the New York Customs House.

Garfield had probably never seriously considered Kasson for a Cabinet post. Even if he had, there were strong reasons for not taking him in. Kasson's stand on the tariff had not been consistently and strongly protectionist, and Garfield was leaning over backward not to offend the industrialists. More serious was the fact that the Iowa inner circle — Allison, Clarkson, Kirkwood, and James F. Wilson — had their own plans for the Cabinet — plans which called for the future control of the Iowa senatorship as well. Allison was a much closer friend of Garfield than Kasson. Twice he was offered the Treasury and once the Interior. Astutely, he turned them down and used Iowa's claim to a Cabinet post to clear the path of obstacles to the senatorship for his friend James F. Wilson and for his own re-election. Old Governor Kirkwood, always a serious threat for the Senate, was promoted up into the Cabinet as Secretary of Interior. The Senate was reserved for Allison and Wilson.

With this turn of affairs Kasson was keenly disappointed and utterly disgusted. Back in Des Moines by early June, he wrote his sister that he was "extremely busy with gardening, cleaning, repairing and painting my cabin." Des Moines was "wonderfully growing"; everybody was talking of the boom, especially in manufacturing and railroad enterprises. "But all this, and all political talk" was tedious, he wearily complained. "I want peace and a quiet life, which cannot be had here, nor in political life." He was disgusted with the early opening of the feud with Conkling, which "so properly could have been avoided," and which would lose the party two New York Senators. Then Kasson proceeded to pick to pieces Garfield's cabinet and party leadership in general.

> There is not one prudent, just, wise, longheaded man in the administration. Garfield is an oratorical schoolboy, Blaine a mere manager of a rival Theatre in Politics. Windom a well-disposed country man who will not spill his milkpail — till somebody jostles him. The War & Navy secretaries will draw their salaries with promptitude & fidelity — & obey the orders of Sherman and Porter. Kirkwood is honest, & old without a bit of executive ability, and with much dislike of labor. McVeagh is young, bright, a good lawyer, an agreeable talker, resolute, but don't understand politics — and James is an excellent post office manager, but is nothing at the Cabinet table, and would be utterly lost in a cabinet of full grown men.
>
> There is my grumble — only for family ears. I am afraid the Lord will not much longer take care of the Republican party. Its blunders come too often, that is to say the blunders of its leaders. And now Conkling must put on the fools cap and pose before the country as an ass, refusing oats because he couldn't have wheat. I am tired of it all, & wish I could hide somewhere.
>
> You wouldn't think it, perhaps, but I am really well, & have had no bilious attack! My love to the nephews & nieces seen & unseen.[13]

In less than one month after Kasson wrote this letter he received the shocking news that a brutal, disappointed office seeker had shot down President Garfield, while crying out, "I am a Stalwart of Stalwarts . . . Arthur is President now!" Kasson wired Garfield, "I thank God you are saved!" and rushed to Washington. Through the long hot weeks of July and August, Garfield's strength rose and ebbed until finally in mid-September he passed away. All the while the government drifted, rudderless, while wild rumors flew over the country from premature fear of what would happen under the rule of the Stalwart machine politician, Chester A. Arthur.[14]

Kasson, neither a Half Breed nor a Stalwart, knew Arthur at least casually and probably had no such fears. Arthur's prudence and caution soon restored public confidence, although some of his Stalwart followers desired, and Half Breeds fully expected, a clean sweep of officeholders. And for the first few months many changes in personnel, and some hasty reversals in policy, did take place. Among the Cabinet changes, Kasson's personal friend, Frederick T. Frelinghuysen took Blaine's place as Secretary of State. As the time for the opening of the new Congress approached, however, it was clear that

Roscoe Conkling was not to be the premier of the new administration as generally feared.

Kasson, meanwhile, rented a house at 1512 H Street, N. W., and settled down to watch developments in the Speaker's race. Ever since his election more than a year before, press opinion had run strongly in his favor. Ret Clarkson reprinted newspaper stories on the race and rose to Kasson's defense whenever certain eastern newspapers, especially the protectionist Boston *Traveller*, accused him of being an "advanced free trader." John S. Runnells met Greenbackers and Independents in Chicago in an attempt to throw these elements behind him. Following one such conference, General J. B. Weaver was reported to be Kasson's close friend and great admirer.

It was now the West's time, and Kasson was the ideal claimant, ran the discussion. From the newspaper comment on his candidacy, there emerged a Kasson portrait which became and remained the traditional one. His "eminent fitness" for the place was almost unanimously conceded. He was a "scholar, a dialectician, a diplomat . . . cultivated, travelled, polished, acute"; "affable, yet cool, ambitious, bright-eyed . . . a credit to any parliament"; a polished man of the world, externally cold as an iceberg but warm-hearted, "keen as a razor, courtly as Chesterfield," "rather a stately creature, elegant and quiet . . . unlike the typical western man . . . resembles a Southerner . . . say from Maryland"; "a brilliant orator, ready debater and skilled parliamentarian with commanding influence in both parties"; a "practical legislator," knowing the House rules and possessing intellectual stature, personal aplomb, self-control, and easy address.[15]

During the last days of November, 1881, Kasson was said to be hourly gaining. The race had narrowed down so that he faced only two serious contenders — Frank Hiscock of New York and J. Warren Keifer of Ohio. Keifer had served two terms in the House; Hiscock two; Kasson, four. On the eve of the party caucus it was reported that Senator Don Cameron had gone to New York for a conference with Roscoe Conkling, had returned to Washington, and was closeted in frequent meetings with the Pennsylvania delegation. Reports kept circulating that Kasson was a free trader and Blaine's candidate for the speakership. He repeatedly denied that he was a free trader. In an interview, he declared that he was "an adherent of the protective principle *in the adjustment of the tariff,* and always would be." Then he paused ("always" was a long time), and added, "I will be as long as the industries of the country require it." [16]

During the last twenty-four hours preceding the caucus, it was rumored that Keifer was gaining and that Kasson and Hiscock had made arrangements to combine their votes for one or the other, if necessary. At the caucus on December 3, Keifer led from the first and on the sixteenth ballot was nominated. In the balloting Hiscock maintained second place. Kasson held third place on most ballots but, on the sixteenth, dropped to fourth. He at no time received enough votes to be a serious competitor. [17]

Except for the politicians in Washington, Keifer's nomination was a surprise indeed. Joseph Medill's Chicago *Tribune* screamed in a headline: Roscoe Conkling So Willed It and Cameron It So Executed — A Stalwart Love Feast Over the Ashes of Garfield! [18]

Kasson lost, first and foremost, because his candidacy had been smashed between the jaws of Stalwart and Half Breed factions struggling for supremacy in New York and in Congress. Hiscock, representing the Blaine faction in New York, was the primary target. Stalwart strategy had been worked out during Senator Don Cameron's visit in New York. To win the powerful Ohio delegation the planners settled upon easygoing 200-pound Keifer, at that time a nonentity in politics and undistinguished as a House leader. With Keifer peddling chairmanships of committees, Cameron and his Stalwart colleagues in the Senate finally won over the Pennsylvania delegation. Next Wisconsin and New Jersey were pledged. Rotund George M. Robeson of New Jersey, Grant's former Secretary of the Navy, was settled upon as floor leader. It is not clear whether President Arthur entered actively into the plan, though he may have given his nod. It is clear that it was conceived and executed by Senate Stalwarts led by Don Cameron.

Several other factors accounted for Kasson's poor showing. The *rumor* that he was Blaine's candidate and the *fact* that he was from Iowa, where the machine had been consistently strong for Blaine, made him ineligible for Stalwart support in Congress. There is some inconclusive evidence that Garfield and Blaine had settled upon Kasson as their candidate, but after Garfield's death such plans, if made, were apparently dropped. Thereafter, it is probable that Kasson's favorable newspaper publicity was conveniently used as a

Library of Congress

HENRY S. SANFORD

Harper's Weekly, 1883

HENRY M. STANLEY

Harper's Weekly, 1885

FREDERICK T. FRELINGHUYSEN

Harper's Weekly, 1883

JOHN TYLER MORGAN

Supreme Court Justice Samuel F. Miller Addressing Constitutional Centennial, 1889
(Kasson is fifth from right in second row. Note Rutherford B. Hayes with beard in center front row; Grover Cleveland in chair)

screen behind which the two factions consolidated their forces for Hiscock and Keifer.

The persistent allegation that Kasson was a free trader obviously weakened him in the eyes of many high tariff representatives, especially the Pennsylvania delegation representing ironmongers whose millions made from the tariff were commonplace talk in the land. Old "Pig Iron" Kelley of Pennsylvania, Nestor of the House, could remember how fifteen years before he had chided Kasson for being a member of the Free Trade League and how Kasson, perhaps more strongly than any other member of the House, had resisted the efforts of Kelley and Thad Stevens to raise the tariff.

Ret Clarkson, who went to Washington to find out what had taken place and why, thought Kasson's absence in Vienna and lack of personal acquaintance with many of the members hurt him. But next in importance to the Stalwart and Half Breed feud, Ret declared frankly and bluntly, "the powerful lobby element" distrusted Kasson. This element, "actively aided by star route people and *others higher in past places* . . . did not want a speaker who would take no hints in appointing appropriation and investigating committees." In the same letter Ret told how he had gone to the Ebbitt House in Washington and there found fifty Iowans. Gath (George Alfred Townshend), the discerning free-lance journalist, *bête noir* of lobbyists, and one who kept a close track on Iowans, stated that Kasson was defeated partly by "the treachery and jealousy of his own people." Whether Gath meant Kasson's "own people" in Congress or in the lobby or both he did not make clear.

Rumors that Kasson was passed over for Speaker because he could not be spared as floor leader proved false when, upon the opening of Congress, Robeson assumed this function. Both Keifer and Robeson were weak leaders and party liabilities. Keifer lacked knowledge, experience, prestige, and forcefulness. Robeson was a bungler already discredited by his flagrant mismanagement of the Navy Department under Grant. In time they fell under the domination of the aggressive, able Thomas B. (later "Czar") Reed in the rules committee, and Reed emerged as the real leader in the House.

Kasson was the "martyr of the majority," cried the Chicago *Times*. Ret Clarkson declared that his candidacy was "peculiar" because it was "dignified and unbegging." Another newspaper claimed that his personal strength proved to be his main weakness; another, that the next three years under Arthur would be "pre-whitewashed Grant-ism." [19]

On the basis of experience and ability John Kasson undoubtedly deserved more recognition as he began the third and last phase of his congressional career. Had he been from one of the more powerful states and diligent in making pre-caucus deals he probably would have won. Or had he been a zealous partisan of either faction he might have fared better. But characteristically he had been trying all along to keep on good terms with both factions and play the role of party harmonizer — a role which he continued to essay in the coming sessions of Congress.

Within a month after Congress opened he was also eliminated in the Iowa senatorial race. In the state legislature he had the solid backing of the Seventh District. But against James F. Wilson, the "singed cat" of Civil War and Reconstruction and one of the Iowa machine's Big Four, Kasson never stood a chance; nor did he actively campaign for the position. With Wilson's victory the senatorship was secured for Allison and Wilson for the rest of their lives. Old Governor Kirkwood, having lost his Cabinet post in the Stalwart succession, was now safely on the shelf. [20] Kasson took these disappointments with calm indifference. He still had the Seventh District to fall back on.

Great were the demands upon the Forty-seventh Congress. Business still suffered from stock market stagnation brought on in part by Garfield's lingering prostration. Poor crops and railroad wars in the West increased the tempo of the silver crusade and other agrarian demands for relief. Tariff and civil service reform, the disposal of an increasing government surplus, the strengthening of a decaying national defense, and the clarification of confused foreign relations — all these problems called for a smooth working, efficient Congress for which Republicans in the House were ill prepared.

Lacking a comfortable working majority, faced with an extraordinary array of strong Democrats, and burdened with fumbling leadership, House business drifted, and Congress failed to cooperate with the Arthur administration, which soon settled upon a course calculated to produce party harmony and good clean government, if not strong executive leadership.

One clue to Keifer's selection as Speaker became evident when he began to pass out committee chairmanships liberally to Pennsylvania, New York, Ohio, and Wisconsin, the four states whose Stalwart delegates had banded together to choose the Speaker. Pennsylvania got seven chairmanships and placed three ranking members on the important Ways and Means Committee, "Pig Iron" Kelley at the head. Kasson, for all his experience, received no chairmanships. He was made number two on Ways and Means, and three on Foreign Affairs, of which from interest and experience he would have made an excellent chairman. Later he was placed on a select committee to eulogize Garfield and number two on select civil service. The Washington *Post* called Kasson's treatment "cold and unprecedented"; Ret Clarkson declared that Kasson received no chairmanships because he would "not condescend to beg" for them.

In disgust, Godlove Orth of Indiana, third in House seniority and also a candidate for the speakership, resigned from some of his weak committee assignments and introduced a resolution providing for the selection of committees by an elective board of eleven members. To counter this proposal and placate disgruntled members, Robeson, would-be floor leader, proposed enlarging and reshuffling committee membership. The clamor and disorder which followed suddenly halted when Kasson took the floor. Democrats moved over to the Republican side and filled the aisles to listen. If they expected irreconcilable blasts at the majority leadership, they were disappointed. Though wittily and sarcastically chastising Keifer and Robeson, Kasson wove in a thread of harmony for the benefit of warring Republican factions. "The induce to bribery" by promising committee places for Speaker votes was regrettable. But "we have no complaints to make," he added. "The Speaker did as he thought wise on the counsel of persons he thought wise." Robeson's proposal, however, was so clumsily drafted that it would actually "extinguish" a number of committees. To enlarge committees, moreover, would merely infringe upon the "dignity of the Speaker" and create greater inefficiency. To soften his criticism in the end he gave the proposal a partisan twist: it was a stratagem of the Democrats to secure better places! [21]

It soon became apparent that Kasson might as well have been the lowest ranking member on Ways and Means. All eyes were on this committee, which was charged with the responsibility of revising the tariff downward. Since 1870 most tariff legislation had been dictated by the elaborately organized Industrial League of Pennsylvania. But

by 1882 several tariff reform leagues led by able men had sprung up
to channelize and publicize the popular demand for reduction. Even
manufacturers admitted the need for revision, and a majority in Congress favored it. But "Pig Iron" Kelley had no intention of permitting
a general revision bill to clear his committee. Instead of Kasson for
his right-hand man, he turned to the fanatical protectionist, Dudley
C. Haskell of Kansas.

To stall off reduction until the demand cooled, Kelley and Haskell
seized upon the tariff commission plan which was favored by the
administration, several tariff reformers, and many businessmen. Four
years previously in Vienna, Kasson had recommended such a fact-
finding commission composed of businessmen as the remedy for the
disgraceful logrolling tariff sessions in Congress. Therefore, Kelley
let Kasson, the moderate protectionist, introduce the bill. Kasson
made two short, strong speeches for the measure, which passed both
houses and was signed by the President. Thus the businessman took
charge of tariff reform. It remained to be seen in the next session
what the outcome would be. Many in Congress, and out, considered
the measure a mere dodge.[22]

Civil service reform fared even less well. In the Senate, the Democratic Pendleton bill was tied up in committee. In the House, Chairman Orth was ill, and the other members took no initiative. On the
floor, Kasson advocated impeaching any public official making political assessments upon officeholders, but he defended the right of the
latter to make "voluntary contributions."

Instead of revenue and tariff reform, Congress settled upon a
"pork barrel" rivers and harbors bill as a means to relieve the federal
treasury of its surplus. To Kasson's credit, he voted against this measure and would not follow his colleagues who passed it over the President's veto.[23]

In the field of foreign affairs Kasson assumed House leadership,
defended the Arthur administration, and undertook to harmonize the
early, stumbling policy reversals of Secretary Frelinghuysen with the
spirited policy launched by Blaine during the latter's nine-month
tenure as Garfield's Secretary of State.

Blaine had read Kasson's long, imperialistic dispatches from Vienna
in March, 1881, demanding an aggressive foreign policy in Europe,
Latin America, and the Orient. Blaine also demanded an aggressive
policy in these areas, particularly in Latin America and the Orient;

and with shocking suddenness he embarked on a policy in Latin America designed to throw an American canal across the isthmus, to integrate the trade of American nations through reciprocity treaties, to dislodge European trade competition, and to herd Latin American republics into the orbit of Washington under the banner of Pan-Americanism. Unfortunate in the choices of his diplomats and too swaggering and dogmatic in his demands, he was soon in deep trouble with Chile and Great Britain particularly. In a sincere effort to mediate the War of the Pacific, in which Chile was arrayed against Bolivia and Peru in a brutal struggle for rich nitrate beds, Blaine was plagued by his quarreling Civil War political-generals who had been accorded to these nations as diplomats. With greater promise on the other hand, he had planned a Pan-American conference in Washington and had received cordial responses to the invitations already sent out. But in his efforts to clear the way for an American canal he had failed to talk the British into modifying the old Clayton-Bulwer treaty which forbade the unilateral construction of a canal by either the United States or Britain.

Blaine's flashing strokes and temporary setbacks had frightened Stalwart conservatives like Hamilton Fish and had made him an easy prey for his Democratic, Stalwart, and Mugwump critics, who called him "Jingo Jim" and his policy "meddling and muddling."

On the other hand, Frelinghuysen was considered an easygoing, stay-at-home, non-entanglist who thought the American eagle a "mere hen past middle age." Without diplomatic experience, he probably had no clearly defined policies as he took over Blaine's duties. Prompted by Fish and J. C. Bancroft Davis, Fish's former understudy in the State Department, he reversed Blaine's policies with careless haste — without full consultation with Arthur, without proper study and appreciation of Blaine's diplomacy, and without awareness of its popularity in the climate of a rising new nationalism in the United States.[24]

Blaine adherents, Democrats, and nationalists among all groups immediately showered the administration with a round of criticism for its weak-kneed policies. The attack was launched with a forceful speech in the House by a Democratic expansionist from Tennessee. At this point Kasson joined the issue as the leading administration spokesman, but also as a party harmonizer. He admired Blaine's policies and undertook to placate Half Breeds by showing that Frelinghuysen was merely feeling his way — not reversing former policies. Identified as a "friend of Arthur," Kasson declared in an interview that there had been no change from Blaine's policies — only a change in "tone and method." "A demand was made a request; a threatening query, a polite question." On the House floor he conspicuously defended Frelinghuysen but did not criticize Blaine, claiming that the Secretary had merely halted Blaine's policy for further study; there was no change "in the mind of the President as to the great objects to be accomplished." Blaine's proposed mediation of Latin American disputes and plans for a Pan-American conference would be renewed, he predicted. He applauded Frelinghuysen's plans for bilateral, reciprocity treaties with Latin American nations, and as an adjunct to this method of expanding commerce, he hailed the creation of a large navy, which, he declared, would bring the United States to the position "where the great future demands." Let "the whole moral force" of Congress be brought to bear against the "idle traditions and prejudices of the past," he implored.[25]

On the bill to regulate Chinese immigration, Kasson either anticipated the administration's stand or gave it support in accordance with prearranged plans. As a gesture to Californians, the Senate cleared a bill to prohibit Chinese immigration for twenty years under the authority of a recently revised treaty. In an eloquent and admirable speech, showing elaborate historical study and preparation, Kasson attacked the bill as going beyond the bounds of the treaty and as hostile to America's traditional dealings with foreigners. He defended the Chinese civilization — its religion, civil service, culture, pacifism — declaring that its "higher authorities" were the "peers of European and American statesmen." If his colleagues would not yield to the "principle of justness, fairness, and right," he begged, "yield then to . . . your own commercial interests as against . . . the Old World." Among Kasson's several amendments to bring the bill into line with the treaty, he proposed to reduce the time of immigrant prohibition from twenty to ten years. When the House passed the bill anyway, Arthur vetoed it and also advised reducing the time to ten years. The veto sustained, Congress then settled for the ten-year suspension.[26]

On the question of an isthmian canal, also, Kasson either anticipated the administration or cooperated with it in formulating policy. Hardly had the House been organized before he demanded a special canal committee. Failing in this, his Foreign Relations Committee took up the matter, listened to technical lectures on the engineering problem, studied data poured in by conflicting canal interests, and conducted extensive hearings. In the end Kasson produced a majority report, strongly advocating a bill for federal incorporation of a private American company to construct a canal across Nicaragua. This company had been organized a few years previously by a group in New York with General Grant as head. Two other private companies, de Lesseps' and J. B. Eads's ship railway scheme, had powerful lobbies in Washington, badgering Congressmen for federal aid of one kind or another, each with members of Congress on its payroll through shares of stock or retainers. Kasson's preference for the Nicaraguan company was also the preference of the administration, and Kasson's repeated warnings that unless the federal government aided the company it would turn to foreign capital may have prompted the administration to later drastic action.[27]

Thus Kasson had helped smooth the way for Frelinghuysen to reverse his own foreign policy reversals. The American eagle would soon be soaring again, though not screaming so loudly as under Blaine. Gradually and somewhat reluctantly, Frelinghuysen would yield to pressures and events until he became more interventionist than Blaine.

Before this session closed Kasson was reported to be "intimate" with Frelinghuysen. He was seen frequently at the State Department and at Frelinghuysen's home, the social center of the very social Arthur administration, where the Cabinet members and Arthur's closest friends gathered to be entertained by Frelinghuysen's attractive daughters. Kasson was repeatedly reported to be in the company of the charming Lucy Frelinghuysen. He also was occasionally invited into the literary-reform social circle led by Henry Adams and his wife Marian, who took delight in analyzing and criticizing American politicians of the Gilded Age.[28]

When Congress adjourned in August, 1882, Kasson was still not a member of the Stalwart faction, but he was an administration stalwart. Arthur had settled down to be the president of all factions. The administration had made a better record than the Congress.

In the mid-term elections of 1882, voters expressed their emphatic disapproval of Congress — its bungling leadership, its pork barrel legislation, and its failure to come to grips with civil service and tariff reform. In a landslide, Democrats swept out seventy-one Republicans, including thirty-four committee chairmen. For the next six years, Democrats would control the House.

Kasson fared better than many of his colleagues. At the congressional convention in July he had been renominated by acclamation; in the general election he won by a comfortable margin. In a letter thanking Ret Clarkson for his support, Kasson apologized for his long absence from home and complained that the long, hard session in Congress, the hot days and nights in humid Washington, had "shaken his whole nervous system." [29]

The short lame duck session of the Forty-seventh Congress, which returned to Washington in December, 1882, was like "a bunch of whipped boys," each side snarling at the other. Civil service and revenue reform immediately became popular. Early in the session Kasson informed the House that although Chairman Orth was ill, the Civil Service Committee would go ahead and draft a bill anyway. Serving as acting chairman, a few days later he reported the Kasson bill. The product of compromises within the committee, and hastily drafted in order to head off the Democratic Pendleton bill which the Senate had released, Kasson's measure fell short of the expectations of reformers. By failing to require competitive examinations it would not control the personal and political influence behind appointments, and by providing a fixed tenure rather than basing tenure upon good behavior, it was an open invitation for wholesale removal at the end of each fixed period. Such civil service reformers as George William Curtis, Dorman B. Eaton, and Andrew D. White warned Kasson that the bill would be considered a trick or an evasion and urged him to let the Pendleton bill go through. Curtis wrote that he did "not presume" Kasson to be the author of the "thoroughly wrong" measure. White, who honored Kasson for "long and faithful public service . . . for statesmanship" advised that anything short of the Pendleton bill would be considered "an evasion, a trick, a juggle."

Kasson nevertheless prepared to introduce his own bill but was forced to yield to a House motion to let the Pendleton bill go through. That night at a reception given by Frelinghuysen, Kasson angrily burst out to Mrs. Henry Adams, "Well, we've passed your *Boston* bill," meaning the Pendleton bill which a Boston reform group was backing. When Mrs. Adams made some "allusions to the wings which were sprouting on Congressional shoulders since the November elections," Kasson sputtered out something "about grasping Bostonians." Marian Adams thought Kasson had visions of "floating into the White House" on his bill but that no one else shared his belief in himself. Henry Adams "howled with delight" at Kasson's temper.[30]

On tariff reform also Kasson was disappointed. At the opening party caucus he attributed recent Republican "disasters" to failure to reduce taxation and revise the tariff and he declared that he favored "a thorough revision . . . a general reduction." The "strength and vigor" of the party in the West demanded it. He also declared that he favored the abolition of all internal revenue taxation — a statement which elicited a warning from Joseph Medill that "Pig Iron" Kelley and other tariff extortionists were trying to hide behind the repeal of these taxes.

The businessmen's tariff commission had made extensive hearings over the country and now recommended a general 20 per cent reduction. In the House the protectionist minority led by Kelley and Haskell on Ways and Means had no intention of clearing a bill with substantial reduction. Instead they came up with a measure which provided little beyond the *appearance* of reduction. Meanwhile the Senate picked up an old revenue bill that, in the last session, had come over from the House, and tacked on an assortment of amendments, actually reducing the tariff below the commission's recommendations. By the time Kelley's bill reached the House floor the Senate bill lay on the House table. Though defending the Kelley bill as better than nothing, Kasson preferred the Senate bill and undertook to change the rules in order to get it off the table. But Kelley and Haskell, working through Speaker Keifer and T. B. Reed on the Rules Committee, managed to throw the Senate bill into a conference committee stacked with protectionists. At this point hungry duty-hunters descended upon the conference committee in numbers and intensity such as were never known before. Even members of the tariff commission now joined the hordes of lobbyists to defeat their own recommendations. The conference committee was a mere screen for a "game of grab played on a large scale." The result was the "Mongrel Tariff" in which manufacturers got what they wanted. In the closing days of the session the bill was rushed through both houses, Kasson voting for it, and Arthur signing it. The businessmen's commission had failed largely because businessmen had rushed in at the last minute to undo what they had recommended.

Under pressure from public opinion demanding some kind of bill, many members voted for the Mongrel Tariff without full understanding of its contents. At the moment Kasson considered it a party victory. As Congress adjourned on March 4, 1883, he wrote his sister that he had been in session all night. "But my long labors for tax and tariff reduction are at last crowned with success," he exulted. "Victory! not for me alone, but for the Republican party as well. I opened and closed the battle for the Tariff Commission — the first step; and closed the fight yesterday for the bill, the last step." Kasson, like many others that day, mistook the mere passage of a bill as a party victory. It was victory only in the sense that the party had obediently served the corporations.[31]

Having been a member of the platform committee in 1860, Kasson ought to have known how demanding Pennsylvanians could be on tariff matters; in 1883, they were merely collecting installments and interest for going over to the Republicans in 1860.

☆   ☆   ☆

During the next ten months Kasson was busy. He made an excursion trip to Portland, Oregon, with the nation's political and business elite as a guest of the recently completed Great Northern Railway, addressing at Portland a great promenade of richly dressed men and women. He presided over the Republican state convention in Des Moines and approved the party's stand for prohibition. At the new Iowa state capitol dedication, he made a thoughtful, terse address, pointing up the national problems inherent in the great accumulations of wealth on the one hand and the growth of poverty on the other, and emphasizing the dangers inherent in reckless political demagogy, political libellers, and irresponsible newspapers. He also published an article on "Municipal Reform," offering as a solution for municipal extravagance and corruption only the restricting of suffrage to those who pay taxes.[32]

Back in Washington in December for the Forty-eighth Congress, Kasson for the second time in his congressional career watched the Democrats organize the House. With some muttering and protest, the Republican minority gave the unpopular Keifer its complimentary vote for Speaker. The Democrats elected as Speaker the brilliant and able tariff reformer, John S. Carlisle of Kentucky. Of this event, Kasson wrote his nephew: "The Rebels have won the Speaker, and I am glad of that. He is a good fellow." In the same letter Kasson revealed that two weeks before he had told his constituents to count him out of the next contest for Congress.

In this Congress, Kasson served as number ten on the Ways and Means Committee, just below Kelley. He supported an appropriation for the civil service commission under the Pendleton Act, voted with the Democrats to repeal the old Radical Tenure of Office Act, and enthusiastically backed the 1884 naval appropriation bill — the beginnings of the Great White Fleet. Though his bill to incorporate the Nicaraguan Canal Company had been defeated in the last session, he had the satisfaction of knowing that Frelinghuysen had a scheme under way which if approved would put the United States government into the business of canal building despite the Clayton-Bulwer treaty. On tariff legislation, he helped obstruct the Democrats, defended the Mongrel Tariff while at the same time squirming, and made a speech against free trade, using arguments of professional protectionists with such skill that they were published as protectionist propaganda.[33]

With Congress in session less than two months, Kasson informed Ret Clarkson that he did not plan to run again: "I am too thoroughly wearied with work which often occupies me till after midnight and has nearly worn out my eyes. . . . I would fain save up my strength a little after this time of life." (He was sixty-two.)

But he was not retiring from politics: "I may be wanted in some other service less confining if we win the next battle." More immediately, he aspired to be delegate-at-large to the national convention at Chicago — to help nominate Chester A. Arthur. The President was the strongest prospect, argued Kasson, because of his fidelity to the whole party, his abolition of machine politics, his prudence, fairness, and sense of justice, and because businessmen felt safe under his straightforward, simple administration. He urged that the Iowa nominating delegates be sent to the convention without instructions to support any given candidate. The coming national election would be close, he predicted, but voters would not permit "Southern domination of Northern interests unless the North itself again becomes base and craven."

The Iowa organization remained strong for Blaine, and at the state convention instructed the delegation for the Plumed Knight, despite Kasson's opposition on the floor. Ret Clarkson headed the delegation; Kasson was not chosen as a delegate. At the convention which nominated Blaine, two Iowa delegates close to Kasson broke loose and voted for Arthur, for which they were strongly censured by Clarkson's *Register*. The Democrats nominated the ruggedly honest mayor of New York, Grover Cleveland. Soon several leading Republican Mugwumps and newspapers were ominously moving over into the Cleveland camp.[34]

In Washington, meanwhile, "some other service less confining" was looming up for Kasson in connection with seriously strained German-American relations. The American Minister at Berlin and the House of Representatives had pushed Secretary Frelinghuysen into deep trouble with the proud, illustrious German Chancellor Otto von Bismarck. At the bottom of the trouble was trade rivalry agitated by militant German nationalism and growing American nationalism, and immediately aggravated by tension in distant Samoa and a flare-up of the pork controversy. Since Kasson's Vienna mission, the State Department under Blaine and the neutral Belgian government each had conducted elaborate investigations and concluded that less danger existed from trichinae in American meat than in European meat. Yet no move was made in Germany to repeal the import prohibitions against American products. On this issue all other nations deferred to Germany to take the lead. Germany was the key to a solution of the issue.

In 1882, Arthur had appointed Aaron A. Sargent, peppery machine politician from California, as Minister to Berlin, and Frelinghuysen instructed him to renew the pork controversy. Sargent needed no urging. Accustomed to the bombast and political intrigue of American Gilded Age politics, he conducted his diplomacy in the same spirit, conspiring with Bismarck's political opponents, stirring up political controversy in German newspapers, and in general ignoring or bypassing the proud Chancellor. Bismarck's reply to all this was an emphatic, *total* exclusion of all American pork on unsanitary grounds. Belligerently, Sargent accused the Chancellor of having other motives and directly threatened to take economic reprisals against Germany. When Bismarck sharply demanded to know whether Sargent had been instructed to threaten retaliation, Frelinghuysen had to say no and rebuke his Minister. The American press and the House of Representatives, weathercocks of public opinion, jumped into the fray; several resolutions calling for retaliation were introduced.

Dramatically at this point Edward Lasker, Bismarck's bitter political enemy, Jewish left-wing leader of the German Liberal Nationalists and a former leader of the opposition in the German legislature, appeared on the American scene as a tourist. On a lecture tour in the pig-raising Middle West, where many German-Americans resided, Lasker vigorously criticized Bismarck's new program of economic nationalism, for which he received enthusiastic applause. When in the middle of the lecture tour Lasker suddenly died, the House of Representatives innocently passed a resolution expressing to the German Reichstag deep regret upon the loss of a great German statesman whose "liberal ideas" had advanced the "social, political, and economic conditions of the German people." Frelinghuysen, in accordance with a House request, innocently transmitted the resolution to Sargent to be submitted to the Reichstag through the German Foreign Office.

Upon its arrival Bismarck feigned indignation and refused to receive it. Why had Sargent not found out whether it would be received before presenting it? Resentful of Lasker's popularity in America and beset by political enemies at home, Bismarck converted the Lasker resolution into an opportunity to get rid of Sargent, put the brakes on American efforts to remove the pork discriminations, denounce his political enemies, and fire up his nationalist followers. By his own admission, however, he recognized the resolution as a friendly and perfectly innocent gesture toward the German people.

In the House all the while, Kasson joined with his Republican colleague, William Walter Phelps, to head off reckless counter resolutions and to moderate belligerent discussion. Let the matter cool off and let the State Department deal with it, he advised. At the same time Kasson seems to have been helping Frelinghuysen handle the situation, a Washington correspondent reporting that he had seen the rough draft of Frelinghuysen's note to Bismarck on the Lasker resolution, and it was in Kasson's handwriting.[35]

When Sargent, seeing that his time was limited, resigned in April, 1884, Kasson was right on hand and the obvious choice as his successor. Perhaps nobody else in the party was so available and so peculiarly well qualified for this mission. The appointment came through in time for him to resign from the House on July 4, 1884; and the bells that rang in the nation's 109th anniversary rang out forever John Kasson's congressional career.

☆ XVII ☆

Arthur's Minister to Germany: The Congo

WORLD DIPLOMACY swirled hectically around the mighty Bismarck in the middle eighties as all eyes were cast upon the fierce scramble for empire in the Pacific, in the Middle East, and especially in the heart of Africa. Bold was the diplomat in Berlin who did not court the Chancellor's favor, ponder his personal motives, and humor his whims. Kasson approached the Iron Chancellor with caution and deference, buttered him up at every opportunity, soft-pedaled the economic disputes, and awaited a more favorable opening.

En route to Berlin in late August, 1884, Kasson had been given a thirteen-gun salute by an American warship anchored at Southampton, and had stopped in London to buy clothes and to visit with Minister James Russell Lowell and Legation Secretary Henry White. In Brussels he also visited his friend Nicholas Fish, son of the former Secretary of State and now American Minister in Belgium. Kasson was warmly greeted at court by the Belgian monarch, Leopold II, and spent a night at the "Chateau de Gingelom," the country estate of the American, Henry S. Sanford, former Minister to Belgium and a confidant of the Belgian King. Since his appointment, Kasson had received congratulatory letters and invitations from members of the American diplomatic corps in Europe, who considered his presence in Berlin an asset to the foreign service.

In Berlin he was received cordially by the Emperor and Empress but not immediately by Bismarck. The aging Emperor's strength had failed fast since Kasson last met him five years before at Gastein, and the Empress was confined to an invalid's chair. With Bismarck, Kasson merely exchanged cards and awaited the latter's pleasure for a formal interview or a reception. In the meantime he established close relations with the officials about the Chancellor, particularly the personnel of the German Foreign Office. But even with these gentlemen, remembering Sargent's experience, he did not bring up the pork controversy.[1]

To John Kasson the race for empire had greater personal appeal and more importance to the United States than bogged-down disputes over pigs, trichinosis, and tariffs. He had arrived at Berlin at the very moment when great decisions were to be made as to the future disposition of vast territory and illimitable trade (it was believed) in Central Africa. Already diplomacy, sparked by Germany and France, had reached the point of calling an international conference of all powers interested in Africa to meet in Berlin. Already Secretary Frelinghuysen had deeply committed his government to the future fate of Africa. Already three other Americans — would-be empire builders, dreamers, restless promoters, market seekers — had focused American attention, public and official, upon the Dark Continent.[2]

Back in the early seventies, Americans had glowed with pride as they read newspaper stories about the exploits in Africa of their fellow citizen, Henry M. Stanley. Reading like an American success story so familiar to the Gilded Age, suffused with hardship and adventure staggering to the imagination, this man's life and his explorations were thrilling; they tingled nationalistic pulses which throbbed faster and faster as the years ran along. Orphaned, kicked about from one relative to another, and inured to bestial hardship as a boy in England, John Rowlands ran away to New Orleans, where a planter-merchant, Henry Morton Stanley, picked him up and gave him his name. In 1860 the adopted young Henry M. Stanley was running a country store in Arkansas. The next year he joined the Confederate Grays, he was captured at Shiloh, lay for a while in a federal prison, and before the war was over served in both the Union Army and Navy. In the postwar years, as a free-lance reporter of the Mountain West and Indian fighting, he caught the attention of the New York *Herald,* and young James Gordon Bennett assigned Stanley the wide, wide world as a territory from which to report dramatic events wherever they loomed up. From Abyssinia, Crete, Spain, Suez, Persia, Bombay, Zanzibar, Stanley eventually moved into Central Africa, where in 1871 he startled the Western World by tracking down and finding on the upper waters of the Congo the famous Scottish missionary David Livingstone, long given up as lost. After a lecture tour in the United States, Stanley returned to Africa in 1874 and during the next three years made a series of brilliant discoveries momentous in their geographical, commercial, and political results. In 1877 he followed the Congo from its headwaters to its mouth, proving that the Lualaba was the upper Congo, not the upper Nile, and that this great valley was rich in rubber, ivory, and other products. He had opened up the interior of Africa to man's gaze.

News of Stanley's discoveries had preceded him, and when his ship docked at Marseilles, France, agents of the Belgian King were on hand to welcome him and to make him propositions. One of these agents was the American, Henry S. Sanford.

Leopold II of Belgium had caught a vision of Central Africa painted in rich commercial colors against a vapory humanitarian background. Stanley, however, hurried on to London to offer his empire in embryo to the British. At this time, as Minister at Vienna, John Kasson, reading about Stanley's explorations with deep pride, informed Washington of the keen interest Austrians showed in the matter. In other dispatches from Vienna, Kasson made it clear that he did not think American foreign policy and diplomacy measured up to the energy and promise of imaginative American citizens.

Unable to arouse British interest in Central Africa, Stanley in 1878 turned to the eager Leopold II. This monarch, a year before Stanley's landing at Marseilles, had demonstrated intense interest in Africa by calling an international meeting in Brussels of the Western World's eminent explorers, geographers, and philanthropists; here the African International Association was organized, ostensibly to sponsor humanitarian and scientific aims. An International Commission was set up to support the organization, an Executive Committee with Leopold as its head was created to manage the Association, and national committees were organized in all leading countries, including the United States. At a meeting of the International Commission in 1877, a few months before Stanley's return from Africa, Henry S. Sanford was chosen as one of the four members of the Executive Committee; a blue flag with a gold star in the center was adopted for the Association. Within a year after this meeting, the African International Association passed into the hands of Leopold II, and its affairs were directed by his personal envoys, Henry S. Sanford and a Belgian, Colonel Strauch. By 1883 the name had been changed to the International Association of the Congo, although it had ceased to have an international character; the name was a mere front.

Stanley, meanwhile, apparently not recognizing the private character of his employer, returned to Africa on another famous expedition and for the next five years made treaties with native chieftains who ceded lands to the Association and placed themselves under the protection and patronage of Leopold II. Altogether he established some twenty-two stations on the Congo and its tributaries, each flying the flag with a blue background and a gold star in the center.[3]

Stanley's dynamic activities in the name of the Association excited the fears of France and Portugal, who also had claims on the Congo. For centuries Portugal had claimed the territory in West Africa around the mouth of the Congo River, but she had had no effective sanctions for these claims. Now, in 1882 she began to press Britain hard to recognize her claims by formal treaty. The British, awakened by French activities in Africa and fearful of French exclusive trade policies in whatever territory staked out, were lending attentive ears to Portuguese entreaties.

British recognition of Portuguese claims, amounting to a veiled British protectorate, would cut off Leopold's stations from the sea. He therefore began to cast about for some means to give the Association international backing. Henry S. Sanford and Colonel Strauch came up with a plan which if then fully understood in America would have seemed fantastic. Let the United States redress the balance in Africa, they suggested. They knew Stanley was exceedingly popular in the United States; that humanitarian motives had led to a virtual American protectorate over Liberia and a kind of gateway to the trade in Africa; that many Americans were still sincerely hoping to solve the race problem by sending Negroes to Africa; that recent American policy had been strongly devoted to trade expansion everywhere and freedom of commerce in Africa; and that there could be blown up certain sentimental analogies between the Association's stations and the American colonies in their struggle for recognition by other powers. If the United States could be talked into recognizing Leopold's domains, then other powers might follow suit.

Only someone thoroughly acquainted with American character and history would have conceived such a plan in the first place, and in the second place could have put it into effect once conceived. Big, bluff, pompous Henry S. Sanford was the man. Like Stanley, Sanford was restless and energetic, a dreamer. Unlike Stanley, he was rich — the son of a wealthy Connecticut manufacturer. Well-educated in America and at the University of Heidelberg, he had entered the diplomatic service before the Civil War. During the war, as Lincoln's Minister to Belgium, and in charge of a large discretionary fund, he was very successful as the leading Union propagandist and purchaser on the Continent. After the war he continued as Minister at Brussels until 1869, or a total of eight and a half years. A court favorite, he entertained lavishly and became an intimate of Leopold II. Hopping from Europe to America in the seventies, he combined politics and business in large-scale operations as campaigner, lobbyist, speculator, entrepreneur. In the early seventies he purchased large tracts in Florida on the St. Johns River and promoted citrus fruit growing and railroad building. After arousing native white hostility by his use of Negro labor, he planted a colony of Swedish immigrants at nearby New Upsala, Florida. On the St. Johns he built a magnificent estate, "Belair," which became the mecca of high public officials, including Presidents Grant, Arthur, and Cleveland. The town of Sanford, Florida, which he founded, is today a tribute to his restless energy.

With a home in Washington as well as in Brussels, Sanford, keeping up his political contacts, had a host of friends among the officialdom of the Garfield-Arthur administration. As early as June, 1881, he had urged Secretary Blaine to oppose Portuguese claims at the mouth of the Congo and to promote unrestricted trade in the area. In the spring of 1883 he urged Frelinghuysen to send a consul to the Congo, whose salary the Association would pay. By November, 1883, the campaign in Washington began in earnest. Sanford arrived from Brussels as Leopold's special envoy, loaded with arguments and documents designed to win friends for the Association. Colonel Strauch astutely directed the campaign from Brussels. Already Sanford personally had softened up Arthur and Frelinghuysen, and Leopold in personal correspondence had received cautious encouragement from Arthur.[4]

For the next six months Sanford entertained in Washington and buttonholed political leaders, even enlisting the support of the powerful New York Chamber of Commerce. Arthur, Frelinghuysen, and Secretary of Navy William E. Chandler were easy marks. In his message to Congress in December, 1883, Arthur used Sanford's words, transmitted by Frelinghuysen, to throw out the hint that the United States ought to cooperate with the Association. Frelinghusen, freely using Sanford's data and arguments summarized above, was fully convinced of American opportunities in the Congo, but he approached Leopold's plan cautiously because of the obvious departure in our recognition policy. Were Leopold's stations self sustaining? Only with the greatest imagination could they be considered as constituting an entity deserving recognition in the community of nations. Arthur and Frelinghuysen knew little about Central Africa and the Association other than information coming from Sanford. Something more than Sanford's prodding was needed.

Fate smiled kindly upon the Association, for at this point John Tyler Morgan of the Senate Foreign Relations Committee vociferously arose to the lure and succeeded in turning the committee into a pressure group for recognition of Leopold's Congo stations. Morgan, a pugnacious, blustering little man, was one of the few ex-Confederate brigadiers of the period who carried real weight in the Congress. Elected to the Senate in 1876 from Alabama, he had staked out foreign affairs as his bailiwick and boldly began demanding a spirited foreign policy. Enthusiastically joining, and at times leading, his Republican colleagues, he could always be counted on for support for the extension of diplomatic influence and trade, the perfection of hemispheric solidarity, the construction of an isthmian canal, and the annexation of territory anywhere, any time. In the Congo, Morgan foresaw through optimistic glasses a thriving transplanted American Negro and a teeming native population eagerly welcoming shiploads of cotton textiles manufactured in the New South. Thus, the Congo Valley, if left free and open to trade, and to Negro immigrants from the United States, would not only help solve the South's race problem, but it also would create a market for the wondrous industrial New South of the future which Henry W. Grady and his apostles were then hailing in a fervid, religious tone.

Working hand in glove with Sanford, Morgan seized the initiative in the Senate — to Frelinghuysen's delight. By May, 1884, while Frelinghuysen and Sanford drafted executive declarations to be exchanged, Morgan drove through a Senate resolution calling for the recognition of the Association's flag as that of a friendly power. With Senate backing, the cautious Secretary of State now felt safe, and he exchanged declarations with Sanford, according recognition in April, 1884. Senator Morgan next pushed through an appropriation for a consular mission to the Congo, and then succeeded in having his personal friend, Willard Tisdel, a former explorer of the Amazon Valley, appointed to fill the mission. Tisdel's later reports showed curiously that he had two masters — the Republican Secretary of State and the Democratic Senator from Alabama.

In the midst of Sanford's campaign, Portugal and Britain concluded (February, 1884) a treaty which, if ratified, would throw British power behind Portuguese claims to the area at the mouth of the Congo. American recognition of the Congo Free State, ignoring the Anglo-Portuguese treaty, set off a chain reaction which eventually would block the treaty, giving Leopold time to consolidate his position. France, preferring Leopold to Britain and Portugal as a rival, quickly came to terms with the Association and recognized it a few days following the American action.

With keen discernment, the Iron Chancellor in Berlin was also observing the doings in Washington. Now feverishly engaged in the quest for colonies himself, Bismarck, incensed at Britain over the disposition of barren Angra Pequena in Southwest Africa, saw further frustrations in the Anglo-Portuguese treaty which he strongly protested. In a temporary rapprochement with France he initiated discussion designed to isolate Britain in Africa and to bring about general recognition of Leopold's Association. His future opportunities in Africa were more promising with Central Africa under the control of the weak Association rather than under strong Britain. Americans felt the same way in respect to their interests.[5]

With American recognition the Congo Free State was born. It was a weak, strange child, now struggling for a place in the community of nations. The United States as godfather would yet have to discharge some of the obligations of paternity in order that it might survive.[6]

It came to pass therefore in the summer of 1884 that as John Kasson journeyed to Berlin, Germany and France were planning a conference to settle conflicting claims in Central Africa and to lay down rules for future acquisitions on the Dark Continent.

One of the first to congratulate Kasson upon his appointment as Minister to Berlin was Henry Sanford who wrote from Brussels that Kasson could do "a great work of civilization in respect to the Congo." Sanford planned to return to America to campaign for Blaine, but he wanted Kasson to visit him in Brussels. Sanford expected Germany to recognize the Association soon, and then there would be a "general following" from other nations.

When Kasson reached Brussels, Sanford was in England with Stanley. Kasson, however, had an interview with Leopold II, and then spent a day and night with Mrs. Sanford and the children in the countryside at "Gingelom." The Belgian King expressed the hope that Kasson "might favorably influence" the German government toward recognizing the Association. No evidence has been found to suggest that Kasson had been a subject of, or a party to, Sanford's campaign in Washington, although he had been for several years a personal acquaintance of the Sanfords.[7] Feeling as he did about expansion, Kasson naturally approved recognition of Leopold's stations; moreover, he would seize any and every opportunity to further the interest of the Association whose interest was also the American interest, he believed.

Kasson began to hear rumors of a conference shortly after reaching Berlin. To Frelinghuysen he at once expressed favor of American participation. Early in October, Frelinghuysen received an invitation, but he needed reassurance. What were Kasson's views? Would participation "comport with the American policy of non-interference"? Kasson of course jumped at this opportunity to extend American trade and influence beyond the seas. Hastening to the German Foreign Office, he ascertained that conference discussion would be confined to (1) freedom of trade in the Congo Basin, (2) freedom of trade and navigation on the waters of the Congo and Niger, (3) the formulation of rules to be observed in future African acquisitions. Not a word here about political and territorial arrangements, the real aims of the conference. Great commercial interests and the rights of natives were at stake, Kasson replied, and since no government was bound to adhere to conference conclusions, he urged participation as advisable and consistent with American precedents and policies. Frelinghuysen concurred and appointed Kasson conference delegate. Other governments also accredited their regular legation heads at Berlin to represent them in the conference.

Sanford, now back in Brussels, sent Kasson hearty congratulations and urged him to oppose Portuguese claims. To permit the Association to control the Congo's mouth "would be a matter of pride to us Americans."

When Kasson learned that each delegate was entitled to have an associate delegate and technical experts, he immediately, upon his own initiative, enlisted the aid of Stanley and Sanford, both of whom were by then in Scotland on Association business. Leopold, in reply to an inquiry, assured Kasson that the Association would have no experts at the conference; in other words, Stanley and Sanford were available as members of the official American delegation. Anticipating criticism because of the close connection of these men to the Association, Kasson requested and received assurance that they would be subordinate to himself and subject to instructions from Washington transmitted through himself. He then succeeded in having Sanford made associate delegate and Stanley, American expert — both without pay, for poor Frelinghuysen was always having trouble financing his special agents from limited State Department funds. Thus Sanford and Stanley were to play dual roles as official American representatives and as unofficial agents of the Association. As conference time approached, Willard Tisdel, Morgan's agent, showed up under instructions to attend the conference. But Kasson sent him on to the mouth of the Congo after allowing him time to familiarize himself with Sanford's data. Tisdel urged Kasson to take the lead in the conference and secure Association recognition from the other powers. So did Sanford. Kasson needed no urging.

Frelinghuysen's instructions were brief, allowing Kasson broad discretion. He was cautioned to avoid a course contrary to our well-known policy of noninterference and to support "neutral control of Central Africa as promised by the International Association." [8]

But how was one to avoid political and territorial questions? Kasson had to ponder. In securing freedom of commerce in the region, would it not be necessary to ascertain the ownership of the territory? What power on the Congo would be responsible for enforcing whatever regulations the conference set up? If Kasson supported "neutral control" would he not be "intervening" against the territorial and political claims of, say, Portugal? His task was a contradictory and impossible one, for American participation was intervention in the power politics of Europe — pure and simple.

In this dilemma, Kasson guardedly pursued the only line of action possible. Inside the conference he vigorously supported unrestricted trade and humanitarian policies, carefully avoiding political and territorial issues. "Outside preliminary discussions" dealing with the "elimination of territory" he left to Sanford and Stanley; and Sanford, as political negotiator, hopped from one European capital to another while the conference droned on in Berlin.[9]

The sessions opened November 15, 1884, and dragged on through February of the next year, awaiting territorial agreements, beyond the scope of the conference, between France, Portugal, and the Association. Fourteen nations participated, and the meetings were particularly noted for the imposing array of experts — geographers, international lawyers, and explorers.

At the opening session Kasson was, for the first time on this mission, introduced to Bismarck, who was serving as president of the conference. The Chancellor warmly greeted the American Minister and remarked that Kasson appeared "to be more a European with military training than an American," to which Kasson replied that he hoped a few years in Europe had not obscured his "'American qualities." The conference, Bismarck flatteringly added, had been called because of the action of the American government. "We have followed your example, and recognized the Flag of the Association," he revealed. This was fresh news to Kasson, for such German action had not been made public. Later in the day the Chancellor came to

Kasson in "a wholly cordial manner" and engaged him in "frank conversation" upon pending questions. Kasson henceforth regarded German-American relations as "altogether amicable and agreeable." Thereafter, he cooperated both openly and secretly with Bismarck and with the Association through Sanford and Stanley. When the conference ended he could take up the pork question, for then the touchy Chancellor would be purring in contentment at the turn in German-American relations.[10]

In conference proceedings, Kasson served on a subcommittee to handle proposals as they arose. Here he became better acquainted with Bismarck, whose aims coincided with those of the Americans and the Association. In committee and on the floor Kasson pushed hard for a broad definition of the Congo Basin, for its neutralization against war, and for complete freedom of trade for all nations within it. The commercial or conventional basin, as distinguished from the geographical basin, ought to include, he argued, the entire commercial delta of the Congo at its mouth, its headwaters in the interior, and the territory covered by the eastern feeders of the great lake country to the Indian Ocean. Both Bismarck and Stanley strongly supported this proposition, and in time the conference designated a broad belt of equatorial Africa roughly from ocean to ocean as a free trade belt.

Following up this point, Kasson next made a sweeping proposal for the powers to guarantee the neutrality of the entire conventional basin. Again he received strong backing from Bismarck and from Leopold's agents. Germany, a nonpossessory power on the Congo, naturally desired to neutralize the area to keep it from falling into the hands of a strong nation. Leopold's nonmilitary Association, moreover, welcomed an international guarantee of neutrality in a region which it hoped to administer. So much was the proposal in harmony with Leopold's aims that a Belgian representative later stated that Kasson introduced it at Leopold's request. Energetically opposed by France and Portugal, the proposal was postponed time after time until the *"Trustee* government" (as Kasson confidentially put it to Frelinghuysen) could be settled upon. At the last session, once the matter of who owned the territory was agreed upon, the signatories pledged themselves to respect the neutrality of any area declared neutral by the possessory power. The Association, it was believed, would declare itself perpetually neutral.

In order to fortify neutralization, Kasson championed advanced machinery to settle amicably any international disputes arising in the area. He proposed to prohibit the sale of contraband and to outlaw war by making it mandatory that all disputes be submitted to a court of arbitration of civilized nations. The compulsory arbitration of political disputes being an extreme step even in the mid-twentieth century, the most he could get was an article binding signatories to accept mediation from a third power before going to war. Even so this was one of the early instances where great powers pledged themselves to submit to the principle of peaceful intervention by third parties in international disputes.

On one matter Kasson refused to go along with his associate delegate Sanford, who was also Leopold's private agent. In the discussions leading to the prohibition of any commercial monopoly in the basin, Sanford requested an exception: he wanted a monopoly for the construction of a railroad along the Congo River between the upper and lower courses. Already a group of Belgian capitalists and other interested persons had been organized under Leopold's direction to carry on such a project. But Kasson, leary of railroad schemes from experience in America and probably expecting a storm of criticism at home, was quick to declare that Sanford's proposal did not represent the official position of the American government. It was merely a private proposition of Sanford's, he explained, with the object of bringing before the conference the problem of improving navigation along the river. The proposal was never included in the final agreement or General Act.

Of all the delegates, Kasson was loudest in behalf of the rights of the natives. When it was proposed that their "existing rights" be respected, he demanded a more emphatic declaration. But his proposal to recognize their rights to dispose freely of themselves and their hereditary territory was rejected. Nor did he succeed in prohibiting the traffic in spiritous liquors. To do so would interfere with important trade and involve the right of search by foreign vessels, it was maintained. Dutch and German producers whose liquor trade was heaviest in the area must have smiled with satisfaction at the innocuous statement that the natives *ought* to be protected and the powers *ought* to arrive at an understanding which would conciliate the legitimate interests of commerce with the rights of humanity.

Kasson was more successful with respect to the slave trade carried on primarily by Arab traders. He demanded and got a stronger declaration than the British proposal that it was the "duty" of all nations to suppress the trade as far as possible. Eventually each nation pledged to put on end to such activity and to punish those engaged in it. Although the conference had failed to live up to widespread expectations of great humanitarian achievement, Kasson received many letters from humanitarians lauding his support of them. Only three of the thirty-eight articles in the final treaty, called the General Act, dealt with such objectives.

Despite the fact that he was confined to economic and humanitarian interests within the conference, Kasson could not conceal his inner urgings for imperialism. When Germany, Italy, and Spain sent naval vessels to the Congo as the conference began, he urged Frelinghuysen to send a naval squadron there to linger, make soundings, and secure a "commercial resort . . . a depot and factorial establishment" for the exclusive use of American citizens, provided it was not too late to find a healthful unappropriated "point." The discoveries of an American citizen (Stanley) would justify "special influence" in the administration of the area.

Evidently Frelinghuysen was impressed. Two months later Admiral Earl English, Commander of the European squadron, under orders that used some of Kasson's identical terminology, was directed to proceed to the mouth of the Congo with two ships. English was to ascertain whether "a healthful point well situated for a commercial resort, not already appropriated . . . a concession from the natives . . . a depot and factorial establishment" for the exclusive use of Americans could be obtained. The Commander was to make a "prolonged stay," until studies were made of the area all the way up to Stanley Pool.

Frelinghuysen's reply to Kasson failed to make it clear that English was to explore the possibilities of a concession. So Kasson renewed his plea for a "coaling station . . . the best district on the lower Congo . . . the best stretch of river coast." Still later he urged that Commander English hurry on to the Congo; it might restrain France and Portugal if these powers undertook to enforce their territorial claims by the "strong arm." [11]

While Admiral English made "soundings," territorial disputes were worked out in separate treaties between France, Portugal, and the Association. The Anglo-Portuguese treaty had failed of ratification, and Britain had withheld her support of Portuguese claims, preferring free trade in the Congo under the Association. At the last meeting of the conference on February 25, 1885, the Association was formally welcomed into the family of nations as one power after another had extended recognition. The Congo Free State, thanks in part to the United States, now had a firm lease on life.

The main object of the conference and of the American government had been accomplished. At the moment convinced of their success, the American delegates readily signed the General Act. Sanford's "outside" work in Berlin, London, and Paris had been a main factor behind the territorial arrangements which led to the Association's success. Next to Bismarck, he was perhaps the most effective participant. Stanley's counsel had commanded great respect throughout. Although Germany and Britain were well satisfied with the results, Leopold II was the real winner.

The conclusion of the most recent historian of the conference — that its results were as empty as Pandora's box and that Kasson "appears to have been distinguished more by verbosity than by brains" — is carelessly sweeping. Despite the fact that Leopold II emerged as the real winner, Britain and Germany and most of the other powers were satisfied. The immediate goal to stabilize fluid developments in Central Africa was achieved, and later partitions did not lead to war, owing in part to precedents set at Berlin.[12]

Kasson, anxious for the United States to occupy a position of éclat and prestige, had thrown himself into the conference with enthusiasm. Restrained by attitudes at home and by his instructions, he had to confine his discussion to nonpolitical matters; and since political and nonpolitical affairs were inextricably interwoven, he may have seemed shallow and naive in his relentless advocacy of the widest application of every liberal principle that came up, including free trade and free navigation on the Congo and Niger, the abolition of the slave trade and liquor traffic, the arbitration and mediation of international disputes, the international regulation of colonial occupations in Africa, and complete religious tolerance. Loudest of all delegates in support of these principles, he also ably presented them; he was a good influence on the conference in the mid-eighties.

The mistake lay not in the support of an open door in the Congo, not in participation in the conference, not in the advocacy of liberal and humanitarian principles. All these were in keeping with sound national policy for America, whose industrial system was on the point of producing mountains of surpluses. The mistake lay in the failure of those backing participation to ascertain the facts and conditions themselves, to formulate policy based on them, and to assume the necessary responsibilities to carry them out regardless of tradition. Arthur, Frelinghuysen, Morgan, and Kasson had viewed the Congo through the rosy glasses of Sanford and Stanley and their patron, Leopold II, and had been taken in by their high sounding phrases, without fully understanding the personal relationships between Leopold and the Association, without recognizing the speculative motives behind the scheme, and without an adequate knowledge of the trade possibilities in the Congo, which Sanford, fountainhead of all knowledge on the area, had grossly exaggerated as the situation then existed. Both Commander English and Consul Tisdel were to render dismal reports on the trade possibilities, and the former was to advise that no "healthful spots" suitable for a "factorial establishment" existed.[13]

For a man who thought the American eagle a mere hen, Secretary Frelinghuysen was doing queer things. Caught up by the pulling and hauling of Stalwarts and Half Breeds, he had reversed Blaine's spirited policy. Beset with pressure from pork men, textile men, oil men, canal men, railroad men, navy men, ship building men, adventuring men, political men like Kasson, and members of the Senate Foreign Relations Committee — all demanding a more aggressive policy — he had reversed his own reversals. Among the cross currents, the American eagle, if not screaming and soaring, was zigzagging, dipping, but always rising in a manner unnatural to a hen.

From Washington came rumblings of discontent with America's participation in the conference long before the closing session. In the November election, while conference preliminaries were being worked out, Grover Cleveland had defeated James G. Blaine for the presidency. Only a few weeks after the conference ended, and for the first time since Buchanan, a Democrat would be installed in the White House. This not only meant that Kasson would soon be leaving Berlin, but that the Berlin General Act would have rough sledding under the new administration, for Grover Cleveland was ruggedly opposed to imperialism, protectorates, and any other activity suggesting entanglements.

The issue had been joined early in January. Prompted by news-paper rumors of a pending "alliance" and of a gigantic speculation on the part of Sanford and Leopold II, House Democrats on the Foreign Affairs Committee flushed a request for all correspondence relating to the matter. Frelinghuysen, now on the defensive, responded with alacrity. From the material, the committee submitted a majority and minority report, both reports criticizing American participation as a dangerous precedent and contrary to traditional policy. The minority report, a copy of which President-elect Cleveland requested for study, bluntly called the conference a "European broil." Among many objections raised was the fear that America's participation in a Euro-pean conference to settle African affairs would lead Europe to demand a conference to settle American affairs, especially the problem of an isthmian canal. Even Blaine opposed the conference on this ground.

Cleveland in his inaugural address warned against meddling in "foreign broils and ambitions in other continents." One of his first acts as President was to withdraw the conference protocols by that time submitted to the Senate. In his annual message, he declared that to share the obligation of enforcing neutrality in the remote Congo Valley meant "alliances." The United States would assume only a "friendly attitude" toward the conference declarations. Thereafter the General Act gathered dust in the State Department, but not without persistent efforts of the Senate Foreign Relations Committee in the future to resurrect it and confirm it, going so far at one time as to call in Kasson by resolution to correct alleged mistranslations in the conference protocols.[14]

Kasson bitterly resented the administration's action, taking it as a personal affront as well as a serious policy mistake. From the moment the House began its investigation until far into the year 1886 he bombarded Washington with reams of eloquent arguments in behalf of the General Act — a correspondence course in an aggressive for-eign policy. In tones of wounded pride and sarcasm he wrote long dispatches caviling against a negative foreign policy and shrilly warn-ing Frelinghuysen and Cleveland's Secretary of State, Thomas F. Bayard, against the designs of Old World powers, particularly France and Germany, in the Caribbean and the Pacific. Although his argu-ments in behalf of the General Act were cogent and designed to be persuasive, he could not explain away the fact that he and his col-leagues had been participating in the power politics of Europe. And that, in the middle eighteen eighties, was held by the American public to be a cardinal sin which no administration could transgress and stay in power for long.

Our true interest in the Congo after Stanley opened it up, Kasson insisted, was to secure equal rights for American citizens and commerce. Two courses lay open. First, to wait until the area was partitioned by strong powers and then try to achieve our aims through piecemeal bilateral treaties. This "waiting policy would have been simply an abdication of duty." For in the Congo Basin there were "elements of future international strife, of fatal conflicts," which might lead to complete control and trade exclusion by a strong power. The second alternative, to act at once and achieve our objective through common consent of all interested governments, was obviously preferable because it could be done with certainty at one stroke, while simultaneously establishing peace and stability in the area. As proof of the wisdom of this course, possessors of African territory in the conference had voluntarily conceded to nonpossessors like the United States freedom of trade in the Basin and freedom of navigation on the Congo and Niger rivers. Throughout the conference, Kasson declared, he had seen to it that all phrases anticipating guaranties and joint action to enforce decisions were stricken from the General Act. No such questions as the recognition of governments and the disposition of territory had come before the conference. The powers merely agreed to accept certain common rules as the basis of their future action in Africa. There were no responsibilities, only rights and privileges.

Repeating the same arguments to Secretary Bayard and trying to educate him for an aggressive policy, Kasson declared that "it would require timidity, even cowardice, rarely seen in America, to discover danger" in the conference declarations, where the United States would hold an equal veto over all action. "There are still faint, patriotic hopes . . . that we shall some time be able to export manufactured goods direct, under our own flag to foreign countries," he added sarcastically. "A sufficiently enthusiastic American — like the American minister at Berlin, for example, might hope some day to hear that an American commercial vessel, bearing the national flag, would enter these African rivers with American goods on board" not sent by way of England or Holland. In the General Act was neither "substance nor shadows of entanglement or alliance." It engaged the United States only to

observe the declarations; if others violated them, there was no obligation of the United States to enforce them.[15]

As his time ran out at Berlin, Kasson turned to his favorite themes
of an isthmian canal, expansion in the Pacific, and a large navy. His
dispatches glow with the fresh immediacy inspired by his direct contacts with the race for empire in Europe.

During Kasson's absence, Frelinghuysen, weary of trying to deal
with competing canal companies in America and fearful lest these
turn to Europe for capital, took matters into his own hands and negotiated a treaty (Frelinghuysen-Zavala) with Nicaragua by which the
United States government itself would build a canal across Nicaragua.
This of course was a reckless step and utterly contrary to the terms
of the Clayton-Bulwer treaty with Britain. It went far beyond
Blaine's spirited efforts merely to modify the Anglo-American treaty.
It could have been the cause for a diplomatic rupture with Britain.
But Kasson was unperturbed. The de Lesseps project in Panama was
"ripening fruit awaiting to be picked by an ambitious French govern-
ment." So forceful was Kasson's dispatch on behalf of the Nicaraguan
treaty that Frelinghuysen submitted it to the Senate Foreign Relations
Committee which was then considering the treaty.[16]

Although Kasson had great personal admiration for Bismarck, he
considered him a serious danger to the United States and gazed at his
colonial adventures with an envious eye. While in Berlin he concealed
his hostility to the Iron Chancellor's designs with discreet silence, but
he opened up freely to Frelinghuysen and Bayard. The occasion for
his most scathing criticism arose from German aggressiveness in faraway Samoa, where Germans, Americans, and British had settled
down to stay.

"Fair phrases about traditional friendships, the progress of liberty
and civilization, the brother hood of nations," Kasson declared, had no
more "practical significance" for Bismarck "than a blank sheet of state
paper." He was indeed the "honest broker," and as such always demanded a commission for every international transaction. Applying
the maxim "*beati possidentes* — if it be a fait accompli, 'let it stand
and seek something elsewhere' " — the Chancellor purposely moved
on to develop a completely unexpected complication which he would
unsnarl and exploit for a price. Eventually, Kasson feared, the "keen
sighted Chancellor" would come to an understanding with France
by which Germany would accept an equivalent on the Isthmus of

Panama for backing up French (de Lesseps) claims there. The "great man" would then repeat "a little favorite Latin *do et des* . . . and laugh at American 'brag' and helplessness on the seas."

European nations were acutely aware of America's naval weakness, he continued, and of her "culpable inaction and timidity on the Isthmus, where we do nothing decisive ourselves, and merely 'bark' at the foreigner who is disposed" to act decisively. "It is purely impossible," he prophetically declared, "that we remain in the future so completely isolated from foreign advances and aggressions as we have been in the past. It is the proper function of statesmanship to provide for this dangerous future, lest it shall become a ruinous past." And in the same vein, "Our *naked* American 'Declaration' [Monroe Doctrine] unsupported by possessions or long-range guns is mere vapour in the presence of European self interest, backed by Krupp cannon and a purely materialistic diplomacy." [17] Against German aggressions in Samoa and American weakness in the Pacific, Kasson urged Bayard to adopt strong measures, and added:

> I venture to add an expression of my sorrow, bordering upon a sense of shame, that the blindness, weakness and timidity of a long continuing so-called American policy has made our navy on the Pacific Ocean insignificant, and has led foreign nations to ask for our views, if asked at all, after the *fait accompli*, instead of before it. The Pacific Ocean should have been an American sea, traversed by American ships not only to Japan and China but to the new Australian world, touching at numerous islands having American plantations, and covered by the American flag. Instead of this, which would have signified peace, prosperity, and wealth, we have now everywhere the flag of the three embattled nations of Europe still grasping for the insular fragments left unappropriated, and exposing every American interest of the present and the future on the Pacific, to embroilment in their wars.
>
> The system of Protectorate, as now understood, if adopted by us for such islands as Samoa or for other weak govts. where we have special interests . . . would be of special advantage to the beneficiaries of it, as it would give to us the control of their foreign relations.
>
> It should not occasion surprise if we yet see these European govts. intriguing for the possession of the Sandwich Islands. Would it not be well to send a Quaker to be Minister there that Europe may have notice that our rights in such an emergency will be defended in our usual energetic manner?

On learning that Bismarck had successfully pushed through the German legislature a subsidy for new steamer lines, Kasson, with bitter reference to criticism of the American delegates in the conference, wrote Bayard:

The determined resolution of the Chancellor to provide this new opening to markets for the surplus manufactures of Germany, to open new spheres of employment to the enterprising German people, and to increase the influence of Germany in the world, enforced by his powerful and patriotic arguments in parliament, carried the day over the combination of opposing parties. Happy country, where intelligent and patriotic statesmanship is not howled down by the demagogue's cry of "jobbery"! [18]

While trying to educate Secretary Bayard for an aggressive foreign policy, Kasson proposed to take up the pork controversy. At the same time he tried to impress upon the new Secretary the importance of the Berlin legation and its personnel.

Near the end of the conference he had reported a seeming change of sentiment in Germany toward the United States. Newspapers had ceased unfriendly remarks and advocacy of trade discrimination. Businessmen seemed to be no longer hostile. On the eve of Cleveland's inauguration, Kasson talked with Bismarck who complimented him on having restored "mutual esteem and confidence." This was not only the Chancellor's "own sentiment," continued Bismarck, "but also that of his Majesty, of all of his Majesty's servants, and of all his subjects." Therefore, Kasson thought the time ripe for a reopening of the pork controversy. Since Bismarck had been denouncing Britain for making her Minister a mere messenger in Berlin, Kasson recommended that negotiations be carried on in "free conversation" between the American Minister and the Chancellor. He awaited instructions — which were never sent. The pork controversy remained dangling for five more years, until the United States passed laws requiring meat inspection and empowering her diplomats to retaliate against German discrimination. These steps Kasson had recommended at Vienna. Without them, it is doubtful that, if given instructions, he would have been any more successful in Germany than he had been in Austria in settling this controversy.

That Kasson was popular in Germany there is no doubt. In Berlin, even Bismarck's political opponents were complimentary. In Washington the German Minister in conversation with Secretary Bayard "confidentially mentioned that Prince Bismarck would be pleased to have Kasson remain at Berlin." Although Kasson would have liked to stay, he had no illusion about it, and as soon as he learned of Bayard's appointment as Secretary of State he submitted his resignation. His successor, he advised Bayard, should speak some German and French;

also "the *manners* of both the Minister and his *wife* would play a great part in the good or ill success of the legation." To give some continuity to legation affairs in Berlin he begged Bayard to retain the legation secretaries.

As his successor, Kasson was well satisfied with the selection of "Gentleman" George Pendleton of Ohio, whose civil service bill, two years back, had been accepted in the House instead of his own. The day before Pendleton's arrival Kasson sent Bayard a memorandum of work carried on in the legation during his eight and one-half months as Minister. Bayard would use the data, he hoped, to correct erroneous impressions in the House (in connection with appropriations for the diplomatic service) that "Legations are merely ornamental establishments, a sort of refuge for idle 'statesmen.' " The memorandum not only showed how busy Kasson had been, but it also showed how the business of the United States had expanded in recent years.[19]

Back in Washington, Kasson undertook to smoke the Congo Treaty out of the White House, to defend himself against the inference in the President's message that he had exceeded his instructions by signing the Act, and to convince the President and the public that the Act was neither an alliance nor entangling. In a clear and forceful article published in the *North American Review* he pleaded for America's adherence to the Act; at the same time, in a tone of hurt pride and condescension, he accused Secretary Bayard of putting into the President's mouth "a blunder so stupendous as to be incredible." He maintained in effect that the Secretary had mistranslated and misunderstood the Act and had misrepresented to the President the obligations it entailed. In defense of his signing it, he correctly stated that no multilateral convention is binding until ratified by the home government. As for the merits of the Act, we conceded nothing except those rights guaranteed to the United States under it, he declared.

While Kasson's article awaited publication, he turned to the Senate Foreign Relations Committee and found a warmer attitude among its members who, paced by Morgan, pressed Bayard to submit the Treaty for Senate consideration. Failing to budge the administration, the committee called in Kasson, who probably provided Morgan with a private copy of the Act and who, under a Senate resolution, corrected the mistranslations.

Once his article was published, Kasson hastened to Cleveland's private secretary with a copy of it for the President to read, in order that the latter might correct his "misjudgment of . . . my official action," and, as "a stronger motive," that he might recognize the great public interest involved in the question. Kasson next urged Hamilton Fish to read his article. The Act, he confided, was the "most liberal, the most advanced in the direction of American constitutional ideas ever signed by an assemblage of powers"; and he did not "wish it hid under a bushel."

Fish replied that Kasson's article was "wondrously able," and Bayard would probably feel that he had been "rubbed . . . hardly." Then, in a fatherly tone, Fish confidentially pointed out a weak point in his pupil's case. "I cannot divest myself of the idea," he said, "that it was a mistake to have the *second* plenipotentiary at the conference." There was a lurking, persisting suspicion that a "secret speculative commercial interest" existed between the Belgian King and Henry Sanford, "the diplomatic flea . . . the peripatetic vendor of sewing machines." "I think you may well afford to hold the account between you and Bayard as 'quits,'" Fish advised. "He laughs best who laughs last."

John Kasson ceased his efforts to persuade Bayard and Cleveland, but he never ceased regretting that the Congo Treaty was not ratified. The Senate Foreign Relations Committee, led by Morgan, vainly and repeatedly renewed the struggle. Although participation in the Congo Conference was the most serious deviation in our traditional policy since Monroe, Kasson had been drawn into the deeper current of American thinking — which would become the main current within fifteen years.

In time, shocking news leaked out from the Congo Basin. Under Leopold's management, it had become the scene of some of the worst brutalities in colonial history. To numerous letters of inquiry from interested Americans, Kasson replied with a stock answer which in principle refuted his previous arguments that the Congo Treaty required no obligations: "The signatories to every contract have the right to insist that the provisions of it shall be executed by the other party whose duty it is to execute them." The United States had "forfeited her right to bring reform to the Congo," he added, by failure to adhere to the General Act. Kasson now had spotted the rub in the whole matter. It would be difficult indeed for Americans to accept the cold fact that for rights and privileges abroad there would also be annoying duties and obligations to assume.[20]

☆ XVIII ☆

Harrison's Samoan Commissioner at Berlin

THE "REVOLUTION" which John Kasson had come all the way from Vienna on unauthorized leave to help avert in 1880 had taken place during his absence in Berlin. In the White House and on Capitol Hill, Democrats held a shaky grip on the government. It was a new experience to Kasson; for the first time in twenty-four years his party had not controlled the presidency. It was not a happy experience for a man who as the years ran along had become more and more partisan in his political outlook. So impelling was his party loyalty, in fact, that it was inextricably bound up with his intense feeling of patriotism.

To be called away from Berlin, to have the Congo Treaty shelved, and now to have to sit in Washington without political employment was disappointing and frustrating. In a reference to the services of Henry Wheaton, international lawyer and diplomat, Kasson showed disgust with spoilsmanship: "It is a sad reflection that even such a man was not spared . . . by the God of political spoils. May heaven grant that this unworthy deity be speedily dethroned!"

Kasson settled down in a house at 924 McPherson Square in Washington to wait out the "revolution." In the harsh winter of 1885-1886 the family of his sister Maria, six in all, moved in with him. When they left at midwinter, he hovered around the fire and complained of the cold; snow, sleet, and ice kept him inside. He was lonesome; his old restlessness returned; he had to be busy; he could not for long remain cooped up.

Turning to writing and feuding with the Cleveland administration, he published four magazine articles and topped these off with a full-length book on the evolution of the Constitution of the United States. The first article, on the Congo Treaty, has been noted above. In the second he painted a vivid and penetrating portrait of "Bismarck — Man and Minister." Finding in the Chancellor's life both romance and realism, Kasson made no attempt to conceal his admiration for his subject, whom he considered "the most illustrious figure of the nineteenth century." The third article, "The Hohenzollern Kaiser," written upon the death of the German Emperor, lacked the forcefulness and richness of texture which he had woven into his treatment of Bismarck. Primarily an historical sketch of the Emperor's role in the unification of Germany, it was nevertheless a flattering piece which elicited a warm note of appreciation from the Chancellor's son and German foreign minister, Herbert Bismarck.

The fourth was a partisan political essay on the tariff issue, which Cleveland had brought to a raging point of eruption. Written with the national election of 1888 in mind, it was reprinted and distributed by organized protectionist interests. Purporting to show that Western farmers favored a high tariff, it really showed that the tariff issue was clearly joined by the two major parties.[1]

At the end of his first year of Democratic-imposed waiting, Kasson assumed a responsibility whose importance in his life outweighs the space which can be given to it in this story of his life. In December, 1886, he was chosen chairman of the Constitutional Centennial Commission to stage a three-day celebration in Philadelphia of the one hundredth birthday of the Constitution. Initiated by the New Jersey legislature and organized at a joint meeting of the governors of the thirteen original states, the Centennial Commission included one representative appointed by the governor of each state desiring to participate in the celebration. At the first organizational meeting of the Commission, Kasson, upon the nomination of William Wirt Henry of Virginia, was elected, first, president of the Commission and, second, chairman of a committee of five to plan and put on the Centennial.

Combining robust patriotism with broad experience and driving energy, Kasson carried on his duties with abundant enthusiasm. Throughout the spring and summer of 1887 he helped line up the speakers, invite distinguished guests, and plan the exhibits. The first object, Kasson later explained, was to make the celebration national and unifying, to assemble representatives of "all orders and classes and from all parts of the country with a view to harmony of feeling and purpose . . . the North and East, the South and West, the common people, the rich and the poor, the religious and secular, scientific and artistic, politicians of all loyal colors, in a word every element of national progress."

A three-day program was put on in mid-September, 1887, including parades, displays, banquets, and oratory. The first day was taken up by the Industrial Display procession which included floats from as many representative groups as could be worked in within one day. The second day was devoted to military parades by the army, navy, state militias, the governors of the various states and their staffs; the third day, to special services of commemoration in Independence Square. The orator of the day was Associate Justice Samuel F. Miller, formerly of Iowa, whose appointment to the Supreme Court Kasson had urged upon Lincoln in 1862. In accepting Kasson's invitation to give the speech, Miller had commented upon the public career of himself and Kasson — parallel they were, and handled in a manner in which their friends would "not be ashamed."

Throughout the celebration Kasson hurried from one program to another, giving welcoming addresses, presiding over banquets, and working out seating arrangements for the nation's dignitaries. He was in his element, displaying (said a reporter) extraordinary suavity of manners, easy deportment, fluent speech, perfect self-possession. The secretary of the Commission, who worked closely with Kasson for months, praised him for his "kind, courteous, and considerate for-bearance" to the Commission staff. The Philadelphia *Press* lauded him for serving "without reward and teaching us all new reverence for the sacred charter of our liberty" — the Constitution.

At a final banquet given in appreciation of his services, Kasson indicated that he was writing a history of the Constitution to supple-ment the Centennial aims. This book, completed the next year, was published in the impressive illustrated two-volume history of the Cen-tennial. It was later to be published as a single book under the title of *The Evolution of the Constitution of the United States of America*.

Kasson's purpose in writing the book was to give busy public men and the general reader, with little or no time for research and study, a "clearer understanding and a more loyal devotion" to the "great charter of our American liberties." Written in a clear, simple, charm-ing style, the content was more sentimental than scholarly. Although he provided a wealth of historical information, little or none of it was original, nor were the interpretations profound. With reverence for the Founding Fathers and for a strong national government, he allowed himself in places to be carried away by a robust patriotism which approached a fine poetic frenzy. As a survey of the founding and development of the Constitution, as a work designed to fan up a lofty, patriotic exhalation of spirit and sentiment, as a sustained project requiring from Kasson self-discipline, industry, and time, it was a real achievement. A significant index to the thinking of the time is revealed in the fact that in neither Kasson's book nor in the Centen-nial oratory are to be found more than vague, passing references to Jefferson and that other greater charter of human liberties, the Declaration of Independence. Hamilton and the Constitution reigned supreme in this era.[2]

With his book finished Kasson went to Iowa for a visit, vacationed in California, and returned to Washington via Mexico City and Vera Cruz. In Mexico City he went to a bull fight but left in disgust be-fore the killing was over. All along, since he began to earn money at New Bedford forty years before, Kasson had been a frugal liver and a shrewd investor, and now a bachelor at the age of sixty-five, he could indulge his fondness for travel. He was back in Washington in time for the presidential campaign of 1888. There was talk of his running for Congress again, but he "discouraged the idea." In the spring of 1888 the LL.D. degree was conferred upon him by his alma mater, the University of Vermont. The next spring he was invited to give a series of six lectures on diplomacy for the Lowell Institute.

Meanwhile, death was taking a heavy toll of Kasson's friends and former associates. In the brief span of three years former President Arthur, former Secretary Frelinghuysen, and H. M. (Hub) Hoxie all passed away. Hoxie, since he and Kasson had parted ways twenty years before, had become one of the leading railroad men of the country as Jay Gould's first vice-president and general manager of the Southwestern System. His untimely death, according to General Dodge, was brought on by overwork in breaking the Southwestern Strike of 1886 on the Gould lines, and thus defeating the "menacing elements of socialism and anarchy." [3]

In the national election of 1888, in which Benjamin Harrison defeated Grover Cleveland for the presidency, Kasson's advice and support was solicited by a Harrison manager before the nomination. Through this manager Kasson maintained contact with the Harrison forces. After Harrison's nomination, Kasson campaigned in Connecticut, New York, and Iowa, and after the general election he urged Harrison to reside at his Washington home on "neutral ground" while awaiting inauguration. In reference to the Republican victory, Kasson wrote his sister: "The time approaches for a change 'when the King shall have his own again.' I mentally shout Glory hallelujah!" In a private memorandum he recorded that Cleveland, without manners, taste, or refinement, would leave office "with few if any personal friends in either party." [4]

March the Fourth, 1889, finally arrived. "Rain all day! Dripping multitudes marching in prolonged column, and thousands and thousands occupying windows and scaffolds, protected and unprotected, along Pennsylvania Avenue." As John Kasson watched the "King's" inauguration from a roofed gallery on Pennsylvania Avenue, opposite the White House, he must have pondered his own fate. He perhaps already had an inkling. The German Minister, Count d'Arco Valley, had called on him several times lately.

Again on the morning of March 9 Count d'Arco called with a letter from Herbert Bismarck, the German foreign secretary. Both the

Bismarcks wanted Kasson to come to Berlin as the new envoy — "they wanted someone they knew — they did not want in this affair a nervous man to deal with." Kasson answered that he had not applied for a place, that it took time for the President and Secretary of State to fill the different posts.[5]

"This affair" to which Count d'Arco referred was the long festering dispute, now come to a head, between Germany and the United States over rivalry in Samoa. Americans had demonstrated a real interest in these islands and the spacious harbor of Pago Pago during the years immediately following the Civil War. Completion of transcontinental railway lines and the anticipated construction of an isthmian canal promised a greatly enlarged trade in the Pacific. In 1878 a treaty had been concluded with a native chief, which gave the United States the *right* to a naval station at Pago Pago and the *obligation* to use her good offices to adjust differences arising between Samoa and foreign powers. This treaty, the base of American Samoan policy, led to prolonged entanglements with Britain and Germany. These powers negotiated treaties with Samoa the following year, each securing a harbor and commercial privileges. Thereafter, the Islands seethed with the intrigues of consuls, commercial agents, and naval officers. Germans, seeking annexation, clashed with Americans, bent on preserving for Samoans autonomy and for the United States a naval station at Pago Pago.

When after 1884 the mighty Bismarck toyed with the idea of annexing the Islands, he met the determined resistance of Cleveland's Secretary of State Bayard, whom, it will be remembered, Kasson had vigorously warned against the Chancellor's ambitions. By the summer of 1887 German-American rivalry became so threatening that Bayard called a conference of the three powers in Washington. Germany, because of her commercial superiority in Samoa, demanded superior political control, and Britain supported this position in return for territorial concessions elsewhere. Bayard stood firm for Samoan autonomy and equal control by the three powers, and the conference failed. The situation now became worse. The Germans declared war upon the hapless Samoan King Malietoa, deported him, and set up their own King, a puppet named Tamasese. Natives under the leadership of a third chief, Mataafa, encouraged locally by British and Americans, revolted. In December, 1888, Samoans ambushed a group of German sailors, killing twenty and wounding thirty. German, American, and British warships crowded ominously into Apia harbor.

During the election year of 1888, a wave of anti-German feeling swept the United States. Prominent American dailies called for a vigorous defense of our Samoan interests and soberly talked of war with Germany. Republican Senators condemned Bayard for his weak-kneed policy and called for an investigation. Secretary of the Navy William C. Whitney foresaw a "National disgrace" in a weak Samoan policy. Congress appropriated $600,000 to protect American interests and to improve the harbor of Pago Pago. And in January, 1889, President Cleveland submitted the Samoan problem to Congress for consideration.

The illustrious German Chancellor, under these circumstances, concluded that Samoa was not worth a possible conflict with the United States. Ascertaining that he could no longer count upon British support, he had no desire to bring about a united Anglo-American diplomatic front. Moreover, his political opponents in Germany were sniping at his colonial policies. So he suggested to Bayard a "resumption" in Berlin of the Washington Conference of 1887. Cleveland and his Secretary of State agreed to the conference but left the selection of American delegates to the incoming Harrison administration.[6]

In the negotiations Harrison and his Secretary of State James G. Blaine would have to adopt a firmer tone toward Germany; they would have to avoid Bayard's proposed joint three-power plan of control. Not only was it a Democratic proposal, but entangling and contrary to our historic policy; it was certain to ignite a general fire of criticism. Moreover, *party* diplomacy as well as *Samoan* diplomacy required care in the choice of the Commissioners. Numerous party faithfuls awaited diplomatic favors, and the magnetic Secretary's obligations alone were so great that the President would have to watch out else the diplomatic service be packed with zealous Half Breed Blainites. Also it would be advantageous if one or more of the delegates had previously adopted a strong anti-German tone. Finally, the complicated nature of the problem required appointees who had some understanding both of the Germans and the fury in Samoa. Mixed motives would determine the selections of the delegates.[7]

John Kasson meanwhile began to hear that he was to be one of the delegates. At midnight, March 12, he hastily pencilled a note to his sister, to beat the newspapers with the news. That evening Blaine had said: "Tomorrow I expect to tell you what we want you to do. But I will not anticipate. The President is inclined to be rather slow." Later that evening at a party, the German Minister informed Kasson that he was to go to Berlin. Kasson's note to his sister shows concern as to whether the appointment was to be permanent or merely to settle Samoan matters. Two days later Count d'Arco called again and congratulated Kasson on his appointment as *chairman* of the Samoan Commission. Of this the Count had just been advised by a note from Blaine. From the newspapers that evening Kasson learned that his colleagues were to be William Walter Phelps and George Handy Bates, commissioners; Harold M. Sewall, special disbursing agent; and two naval lieutenants, with previous duty either in Germany or Samoa, as secretaries.[8]

The choice of young Harold M. Sewall as disbursing agent was motivated by something more than his ability to keep books. As Cleveland's consul general at Apia in Samoa he had boldly and captiously opposed the Germans. Returning to Washington, this wealthy Democratic shipbuilder from Maine had persuaded Republican Senator Frye from Maine to investigate Democrat Bayard's Samoan policy, for which he was dismissed from his post. Now he was appointed to the Berlin Mission under Republican Secretary of State Blaine of Maine. John Sherman was said to consider Sewall a fool.

The junior commissioner, George Handy Bates, was also a Democrat with personal experience in Samoa. Bayard had sent him there to observe conditions preliminary to the Washington Conference. Back in America, he had written an article for *Century* magazine, blasting Bismarckian deceit and advocating war rather than dishonor. His article was so fiery that the *Century* editor urged him to be "a little more diplomatic and less rasping" when referring to foreigners. Having vigorously protested his appointment, Herbert Bismarck was to refuse to shake hands with him in Berlin.

The second commissioner, William Walter Phelps, was a social and political intimate of Blaine, whose presidential aspirations he had supported with unflagging loyalty. Blaine in turn had promoted Phelps's candidacy for the vice-presidency in 1888. Having lost the New Jersey senatorship in November, Phelps reminded Harrison that he was one of the "president makers" who supported the President-elect in the Convention. Blaine himself considered Phelps first for the French post, then *urged* him to join the Samoan Commission. "No friend," wrote Blaine, "should make you underrate the Samoan appointment . . . far the most important for many years." According to a newspaper reporter, Phelps was told *privately* that the *permanent* German post might be his.

In personality Phelps was cultivated, genial, and witty. In intimate Blaine circles he was popular. Under Garfield he had served as Minister at Vienna for about one year. As one-time member of the House Committee on Foreign Affairs, he had followed the Samoan question with interest.[9]

John Kasson, the first commissioner, like Phelps, desired something better than a temporary mission. The oldest member of the Commission and the most experienced diplomat, he liked the Germans and the Bismarcks, and they, him. Naturally he preferred to remain at Berlin after the Samoan matter was settled. Yet he distrusted the Secretary of State; his closest friends were among the former Stalwarts; in 1884, he had supported Arthur's nomination, not Blaine's; he considered Blaine "merely a manager of a rival theater in politics." On the other hand Blaine had opposed American participation in the Congo Conference as well as Kasson's bill to incorporate the Nicaraguan Canal Company.

Often bypassed over the years when the choice political plums were handed out, Kasson, now sixty-seven years old, was suspicious and crotchety. He would have to look into the matter a little more fully; on the day following the newspaper announcements of the appointment of the commissioners, he proceeded to the Department of State. Blaine's offices were so jammed with office seekers that he could not get in to see the Secretary. But he did confer briefly with George H. Bates, who also was trying to see Blaine.

Returning home, Kasson sent his servant with a note to the President, requesting an interview. He shows his distrust of Blaine clearly in a memorandum:

I doubt if Mr. Blaine is not trying to dispose of me on a shelf, while using my supposed diplomatic ability to remove the chief difficulty between the two governments. That done, any of his favorites can be sent to take care of the routine business of the Legation, and what the politicians call my "claim" would so far be satisfied by this honor that all the other great posts could be passed on to others. I must consider this.

The President saw him the next day. Kasson showed reluctance to accept a post which required two ocean voyages for only about three months' service. He had hoped the government might use him in some more permanent position, he explained. Harrison replied that there was honor in the Samoan appointment, that he personally had decided on Kasson. Very cautiously the President went on to say that appointees for none of the four great missions had been determined. Kasson left, feeling that Harrison wanted him to understand that the door was not closed to some other post. As he left he stepped into the room of the President's private secretary who volunteered interesting information: before leaving Indianapolis, Harrison had Kasson in mind for a mission, had considered him for London, and was averse to Blaine's desire to send there his "chief henchman," Whitelaw Reid. Kasson concludes his version of these talks: ". . . it seems my duty to undertake this German Duty, and let others work out their schemes."

There is evident disappointment in his next memorandum:

The last three weeks have been busy and anxious times for the politicians. The great places have been filled; Robert T. Lincoln goes to England; Whitelaw Reid to France; and A. Thorndike Rice to Russia. A third Editor, Murat Halstead . . . for the German Mission, but on two successive votes rejected by a decisive majority of the Senate. . . . Lincoln to England and Frederick Grant to Austria are largely made on account of public admiration and gratitude for the service of two eminent Presidents, their fathers. But Mr. Lincoln adds, as Grant does not, some personal qualification and experience. . . . Germany still remains unfilled. And there is a general impression that it will be offered me. But I so dread the winter climate of Berlin, that I could not take it except with the condition that I might reside in the South in the Winter.

In the same memo Kasson described his Democratic colleague Bates as in a "sea of trouble" because of his *Century* article berating the German government for its conduct in Samoa. In great excitement the German Minister came running to Kasson twice in one day, magazine in hand. He could not attend Kasson's diplomatic dinner in honor of Bismarck's birthday, he said, because Bates would be there. But Kasson explained that, inasmuch as he would first toast the President and then the Chancellor, it would seem awkward for the German Minister to be absent. "That shot brought him around," records Kasson; "but on the condition that Bates should not be present, or seated near him." The German envoys, observed Kasson, resembled "school boys in fear of a prompt whipping from their master" — the Chancellor.[10]

While these events took place Blaine studied up on Samoa and in mid-April submitted his instructions to the President, who approved them only after a careful reading. To Kasson the instructions left something to be desired. In retrospect he wrote: "Under Mr. Blaine's instructions it seemed that no agreement would be possible . . . unless it could be secured outside the Conference, as it were behind the curtain."

That the instructions were skimpy and vague, historians have agreed. On the critical plan of government the Secretary of State was in a quandary. Like Bayard he insisted on a stable government based on Samoan autonomy and the equal rights of the three powers. He did not, however, favor Bayard's three-power scheme of joint control because it was entangling and undoubtedly because it was a Democratic proposal. Not having any positive solution of the key problem, he placed the responsibility squarely upon the commissioners, who would have to report minutely on their work and stand by for additional instructions. In the absence of clearer and fuller instructions, the Commission would have to report extensively and daily on the course of the negotiations, sending long and detailed dispatches. Some member would need to assume this responsibility, act as spokesman for the three, reconcile their views if in disagreement, coordinate their activities, and generally act as chairman.[11]

Yet the Secretary of State left much room for misunderstanding on this point. There is no indication that he ever called in the commissioners jointly for consultation, though he did see them separately. Kasson claimed to have conferred with both the President and the Secretary, and later wrote that he was appointed "by the President to head the Commission." As he departed for Berlin he assumed this role, and there is some evidence that the Department of State so led him to assume it. In the press announcements, in the letters of credence, and in the instructions Kasson was first named. Subordinates in the State Department, arranging minor details for the Commission's departure, addressed their notes to Kasson. One of the naval lieutenants was instructed to report to Kasson. Most revealing, however, was Blaine's instruction to the disbursing agent, Sewall. "You will, of course," he wrote, "be governed by the directions of the chief of the Commission in the matter of your disbursement and will have all your vouchers bear his approval." Though Blaine was never to signify the name of the chief, most of these vouchers when recently located in the National Archives were signed by Kasson as "First Commissioner." [12]

Bismarck described squabbling in Samoa among consuls as *furor consularis*. To coin a phrase similarly descriptive of relations between the American commissioners at Berlin, one can safely choose *furor commissionaris*, for friction among the Americans was more acute than between the Germans and the Americans.

En route to Berlin the Commission stopped long enough in London for Kasson to have an extensive interview with the British foreign minister, Lord Salisbury. The commissioners arrived in Berlin late at night near the end of April. At the American Legation, Kasson found a note from Sir Edward Malet, a former diplomatic acquaintance now head of the British Samoan Commission. Malet wanted to explain German objections to Bates, who was under heavy attack from the German press. The Chancellor was demanding for publication some explanatory statement of the *Century* article. Kasson thereupon wrung from the junior commissioner the promise of a statement. Next day Herbert Bismarck, the German foreign minister, received the Commission and shook hands with Kasson and Phelps but ignored the outstretched hand of Bates. A little later Kasson alluded to the *Century* article and let Bates eat "humble pie." In German newspapers the next day Bates was reported to have explained that he wrote the article only as an "imperfectly informed private individual," then unaware that he was to be appointed commissioner; he had full regard for the German nation and no wish to offend its government.

In a long unofficial private letter to Blaine, Kasson reported the Bates incident as "happily closed." But it must have fallen far short of a happy experience for Bates, whose distrust of the Germans was already great. Nor did it likely increase his esteem for Kasson, whatever that may have been.[13]

From the outset Herbert Bismarck and Sir Edward Malet, First Commissioners, accepted Kasson as their equal. A Big Three thus emerged, meeting informally and reaching general agreements outside the conference sessions. With experience as delegate at two previous international conferences, Kasson took the position that broad principles of agreement must be reached outside. Inside, Bates and Phelps could help work out details in subcommittees.

From Salisbury in London and from Herbert Bismarck and Malet in Berlin, Kasson perceived that the Germans were prepared to make a general retreat if it could be done gracefully and without undue press criticism of the Chancellor's past Samoan policy. He also learned that the British, lukewarm on Samoa, would play the conference role of adjusting differences between Germans and Americans. He trusted Herbert Bismarck's candor and was willing to make minor concessions to save face for the Chancellor's government.[14]

With Kasson's "hands on the bellows," the first thirteen days of the Conference developed auspiciously. Germany renounced her previous demand for predominant control in Samoa and released the deported King. Plainly, she was preparing to accept with minor modifications whatever plan of government the Americans might propose. In Washington, Blaine's enthusiasm is clearly revealed in his correspondence with the President. Kasson, elated at what he considered his personal diplomatic successes, proposed on May 10 that armed factions in Samoa be disbanded. Blaine promptly wired the President's "hearty approval." But the next day Blaine suspended this instruction in a wire to the whole Commission. Something had gone wrong.[15]

Phelps and Bates were far from satisfied with Kasson's conduct. Several days previously they both had protested to Blaine in long unofficial private letters. According to Phelps the Conference was merely drifting along with "less directness and fewer signs of business, method and dispatch" than Blaine might have expected had Phelps's "hands been on the bellows." Kasson, suggesting "mysterious confidences" with Blaine and Harrison, had made himself chief both "to plan and report." As to the plan of government for Samoa, Phelps frankly admitted that "Bayard's three-fold representation" was the best; but because "it was his" (Bayard's) among other reasons, he was trying to think of some other plan but had not succeeded. These unofficial letters from Phelps and Bates were followed by official dispatches on the day Kasson proposed disbanding the Samoan factions. They opposed disbanding on the ground that the American-supported faction was stronger and might gain control of Samoa in the absence of Conference accord. Sewall and John F. Parker, one of the naval lieutenants, agreed. But Kasson, according to Bates, declined consultation with the rest of the Commission.

Two days later, Blaine reprimanded the Commission, aimed his

SAMOAN COMMISSIONERS, 1889

Leslie's Weekly, 1889

WILLIAM W. PHELPS

JOHN A. KASSON

GEORGE HANDY BATES

CANADIAN RECIPROCITY COMMISSION AT QUEBEC, 1898

(Kasson is third from left)

heavy darts at Kasson, stressed their equal power, and demanded that each should see all correspondence. The immediate reaction of Phelps was to send another unofficial personal letter to his political intimate. The thought of disbanding the Samoan natives made Phelps, Parker, Bates, and Sewall "nearly crazy." As for Kasson, he knew nothing about Samoan affairs and had refused to discuss the problem during the passage from America. However, confided Phelps, the air was now clear. He had just forced Kasson to agree to joint consultation.

But the air was not clear. Kasson affirmed by wire that all his correspondence was on file with the Secretary and accessible to all. He threatened to withdraw and "so escape tricephalous jealousies." Phelps denied seeing all Kasson's correspondence and affirmed that his was with the Secretary, accessible to all. As indicated above, each commissioner had already sent Blaine private letters, unseen by the others, and Phelps continued to do so until the conference was almost over.[16]

When Bates on May 15 followed with another long dispatch emphasizing American disunity and urging stronger demands upon Germany, Blaine shot back: the President "expressed chagrin and deep disappointment. . . . There is no justification . . . for personal differences on a subject which is official and patriotic; and he specially desires that the public should know nothing of disagreements." With these strong words the commissioners acted in concert and meekly wired back: "We think you have an exaggerated conception of differences existing here. We beg to relieve your own mind and that of the President." [17]

But the next day, Phelps confidentially proceeded to explain things to Blaine. It was a chummy, personal letter, unseen by the other commissioners. "Tell me: weren't you a little bit ashamed to send that despatch . . . about peace making." "Fiery" Bates and "sulky, impossible" Kasson were hard to handle. He *could* handle Bates, but no one could manage Kasson "except by humoring him into the belief that it is his way; and this is very painful and humiliating, as his manners are not always what they should be." Phelps ended his letter with this gentle hint for the permanent Berlin post: won't you intimate to the President "that I deserve something for humbling myself so often to be a peacemaker?" In another letter he urged Blaine to communicate with him secretly by code.[18]

Despite this internal squabbling, the conference proceeded rapidly and successfully. When for a time Phelps put his hand on the bellows, he, like Kasson, found the Germans conciliatory though careful to shield from criticism the Chancellor's previous Samoan policy. Phelps, again like Kasson, found the British useful to harmonize minor German-American differences. Therefore, it turned out that Kasson and Phelps, during the rest of the conference, tended to agree on main points. But Bates, sometimes supported by Sewall, continued to view German intentions with deep suspicion; he frequently so informed Blaine, who attached great importance to his reports. Bates suspected trickery from the British also, and his suspicions found fertile ground in the mind of the Secretary of State. Old, suffering from lumbago, distrustful of his own commissioners, and unable to suggest a positive program himself, Blaine cancelled and withdrew instructions, contradicted himself, and, seeking to manage minute details from Washington, frequently lost his temper and delayed the delegates in Berlin, already at odds with one another and eager to escape the oppressive heat. Moreover the Secretary of State chafed under the close supervision maintained by the President, who suspiciously scrutinized with a legal eye all correspondence, sometimes revising Blaine's instructions and frequently demanding minute changes of agreements reached by the commissioners.[19]

By the end of May the Treaty, providing for a three-power control of Samoa, was ready for the signatures of the delegates, eager to hurry from Berlin on their vacations. But for the next two weeks Blaine and Harrison held them there while they emasculated the Treaty with changes so numerous and minute that a complete renegotiation would be necessary. Phelps and Kasson defended the Treaty, pleading for only minor modifications. Bates, backed up by Sewall, found many fatal defects in it. He had not been able to express himself fully in the conference, he asserted, and he could sign "only as an agent under direct instructions."

Kasson's exasperation is clearly revealed in a rough dispatch, drafted at a boiling point, but sent to Washington only after it was toned down. "The product of many weeks of careful thought, discussion, and anxious work is totally disapproved," he fumed. "The same work is considered here on all sides as an unexpected American success. Your telegram seems to assume that three governments must necessarily follow the instructions of one. If the details as well as the principles could be regulated exclusively from Washington there was no need of a Conference. . . . A discredited envoy is not the proper person to initiate such radical change. . . . I . . . place my resignation in your hands . . . unusual prostration caused by hot weather, and hard work combined . . . make longer stay in this oppressive climate dangerous." A few days later in a "Personal Report" of some 3,000 words *to the President* he carefully explained the Treaty, section by section, in an effort to relieve some of the misapprehension in Washington.

Finally on June 9 the entire Commission tried to speed up Blaine and Harrison. "The President does not know the irritability of our associates," they wired, "who believe they have yielded already in all essentials to claims of the United States, nor the danger of asking now too many changes." Blaine fired back with a wire which has become legendary: "Irritability on the part of your English and German associates is not a determining factor with the Govt. of the U. S." For many years Blaine was given credit for rebuking the mighty German Chancellor rather than the American delegates.

Eventually the President and Secretary, deluged with explanations and entreaties from Kasson and Phelps, yielded most of their demands, although Bates stood firm to the last against such "abandonment." The Treaty was signed at the ninth session of the Conference on June 14. Four days later, as the delegates hurried away from Berlin, Kasson had the last word with Washington. In a long "Supplementary Personal Report to the President" he further defended the treaty and signed the dispatch, No. 108, "John A. Kasson, 1st Commissioner." [20]

Parker, the naval lieutenant, returned to Samoa under orders from the Navy and State Departments. Former Democrat Sewall, now a Republican and a staunch imperialist, returned to Samoa as Consul General. Bates returned to Delaware to practice law. After vacationing in Europe, Kasson returned to Washington to prepare a series of lectures on diplomacy to be given at the Johns Hopkins University and the Lowell Institute. Phelps left Berlin immediately with the Samoan Triumph — the treaty of Peace and Honor — in a "little yellow leather bag." Hastening to Washington, he and Blaine called on the President who took a commission from a drawer and handed it to Phelps, the new, permanent Minister to Germany. [21]

Blaine and Harrison, in an effort to please those who demanded a strong stand against Germany and striving to avoid the proposal of Bayard, the Democrat, had been unable to give their commissioners clear instructions. They had further paved the road for confusion and misunderstanding by failing to be straightforward in the choice of a commission head and the ministership at Berlin. Bates and Sewall, moreover, former Democrats with public records of hostility to Bismarck, were appointments hardly calculated to achieve conciliation and compromise at Berlin — the only course open. In short, the Secretary and the President had set up an ideal situation for friction — not harmony. On the other hand the commissioners had been less diplomatic in their relations with one another than with the German diplomats.

En route home, Kasson found Parisians expressing joy at the American success: "They said the U. States have humiliated them [Germans] — we can't do anything of that sort, but we are glad you have done it." He reported Sir Julian Pauncefote to have said, "No nation in Europe could make them do what your country have done; and I rejoice you have made them back down." From Berlin later Phelps wrote Blaine that "the American people never sufficiently appreciated the courage and magnanimity of the German Government in undoing a great wrong at a cost which seemed to impulsive Germans to put into their history a second Olmütz."

Yet, these expressions exaggerated the importance and scope of the American "victory." Germans, British, and Americans still remained in Samoa. The new tripartite arrangement proved to be no more satisfactory than the old ones, and *furor consularis* for another decade continued to characterize relations in Samoa. Until the United States was willing either to get out of the Samoan Islands and leave them in German hands, or to divide them up, there was no other solution than joint control. By 1899 American public opinion had moved far enough along the road toward imperialism to condone partitioning, and then it fell to the lot of John Kasson to draft the treaty of partition, which gave Pago Pago Bay to the United States with no strings attached. He would have been willing to partition them in 1889.[22]

☆ XIX ☆

McKinley's Reciprocity Minister

IN THE EARLY eighteen nineties John Kasson took a house in Washington near the White House, at 1726 I Street, disposed of his home in Des Moines, and settled down to live out his life at a more leisurely pace. "I am perfectly conscious inwardly that I am getting old, though I do not acknowledge it outwardly," he wrote his sister Mary. "I pray for cheerfulness and would fain grow old unconsciously and without observation, but with the inward eye looking heavenward with faith and Christian hope," he went on. "I feel it is better for me — and for you — and for all about us and under our influence, that we distribute more smiles than tears. Religion and philosophy alike recommend it. And in that way old age grows beloved and loving." [1]

Now at the age of seventy, Kasson had his portrait painted for the state capitol portrait gallery in Des Moines. It showed him to be an energetic man who would pass for fifty-five. To retire to a private and tranquil life would be difficult for an active, restless man like Kasson. Busy years yet lay ahead — of traveling, lecturing, writing, and participating in the activities of a number of religious, learned, and philanthropic organizations. If not as active in politics as usual, his interest in national affairs was as great as ever, and the lure of the lecture platform was too strong to resist. He made no effort to procure an additional appointment under the Harrison administration, and in 1892 the re-election of Democrat Grover Cleveland sealed him off for another four years.

Yet he filled in these years with a variety of activities which revealed remarkable physical and mental vigor. During the first three years of the decade he gave a series of lectures at the Lowell Institute on the evolution of diplomacy, and two series on the same subject at the Johns Hopkins University. These lectures, tracing the origin and development of diplomacy from ancient times to the present, were prepared, Kasson told his students, to prove "that behind all the lace and tinsel, the frippery and deceit" popularly associated with diplomacy was a profession which had made unsurpassed contributions to humanity during its slow progress from barbarism to Christian civilization. The lectures, emphasizing the development of international law, contained interesting pen portraits of such persons as Machiavelli, Grotius, and Bismarck. Although not profound, they were comprehensive, well organized, and always entertainingly delivered. Owing to Kasson's "eloquent and graceful manner," the lectures were "truly delightful," it was reported. Somewhat later Kasson was offered a lectureship on diplomacy at the Columbian University (now George Washington), but was too busy with other matters to accept it.[2]

Seldom a month passed in these years without an invitation to give an address somewhere. In 1892 he was elected to Phi Beta Kappa at the University of Vermont and spoke there on the "Permanent Forces [individual liberty and Christianity] Operating toward a Higher Civilization." Before women's clubs of Washington and Des Moines he discussed social womanhood, society, and etiquette at the European capitals. Before the Scotch Irish Society of Des Moines, he spoke against the immigration of peoples from southern and southeastern Europe. In a number of addresses and statements released to the press he continued to advocate a policy of overseas expansion including the annexation of Hawaii, and he railed against the lack of continuity in personnel and policy in the State Department.

One of the most effective addresses of his lifetime was given in 1895 at the new Naval War College at Newport, Rhode Island, on International Arbitration. The speech attracted nationwide attention. It was a subtle appeal for Senate ratification of the Anglo-American Treaty of Arbitration then pending. Kasson took a dry subject and pumped it full of sparkle. The speech was brief, crisp, clear, lofty, and optimistic but also solid and practical. Every word and sentence rang with pointedness. Only among nations with kindred ideals, aspirations, and institutions was arbitration practicable, he believed; only with Britain, France, and the other American nations could the United States expect in the present generation to work out satisfactory compulsory arbitration treaties; only questions not involving national honor could yet be successfully submitted to arbitration. Although optional arbitration and compulsory mediation (in accordance with his recommendations at the Congo Conference) were great gains for peace, the United States would still have to look "to the polished points of our bayonets" and to sleek new warships "to reflect on us the desired sunshine of Peace." [3]

In the national election of 1892 Kasson made at least one campaign speech — in Des Moines, where he appeared with "Czar" Reed, his former colleague in the House. After the Democratic victory, Kasson was more tolerant of Cleveland's second administration than he had been of the first. He had confidence in Cleveland's Secretary of State, Walter Q. Gresham, whom he had known for many years; and he admired Cleveland's conservative financial policies as well as the President's use of federal troops to quell labor disorders in Chicago during the railway strike of 1894.

Kasson also made at least one campaign appearance in the national election of 1896 — again in Des Moines. Previously he had mailed a long political exposition, presumably for publication, to his old friend Cole Noel of Dallas County. Written with apparent deep feeling, and aimed at the Iowa farmers, it was a typical conservative attack upon William Jennings Bryan and the silver forces. Free silver was a "moral sin and a crime" by which profit would be taken "from the people's pocket and put into the pocket of the owner of silver bullion." Bryan, the "voluble and theatrical talker," had never done more than defy law and order, excite "socialistic tendencies in the loyal and industrious North," and stir up sectional wrath in the South. The farmers, "the special guardians of our national Constitution," he urged, should stand solid behind William McKinley and the "conservative forces which were to defend law and order, and public and private honor and honesty, against riot and repudiation, against socialism and anarchy." [4]

Since 1873 Kasson had become less and less the spokesman of depressed agriculture and more and more the spokesman of the businessman, chiefly as an advocate of the expansion of foreign trade. There is little evidence to show that he had deep concern with, or understanding of, the growing chasm between capital and labor during the Gilded Age.

☆   ☆   ☆

In the national election of 1896 the "King" returned again in the person of William McKinley, a former colleague of Kasson in several sessions of the House of Representatives. Soon after the inauguration, Kasson was out riding with the President in his carriage, but he does not seem to have pressed for an appointment. James Wilson, McKinley's Secretary of Agriculture and Kasson's colleague in the Iowa House a quarter of a century before, urged Kasson to make his desires known. The mission to Madrid was still open, said Wilson, and McKinley had Kasson in mind for this post. Because Kasson had declined recently to take charge of an international postal congress held in Washington, it was rumored that his health was delicate. Therefore, Kasson had better speak up and assure the President of "sufficient vigor" for the Spanish position if he wanted it.

Early in October, 1897, the President called Kasson to the White House and offered him the position of Minister Plenipotentiary to negotiate reciprocity treaties in accordance with Republican platform pledges. It was McKinley's aim to set up a Reciprocity Commission with offices in the State Department. Kasson could be head of the Commission with a secretarial staff to help handle the details; salary, $10,000 a year; diplomatic rank of a minister. This was an important assignment requiring technical knowledge, concentrated and sustained effort, and the ability to shrug off disappointment if the party leadership in the Senate proved unwilling to redeem platform pledges. Although outwardly spry at seventy-five, Kasson would have to think it over.[5]

As has been seen, Kasson's real belief most of the time since the Civil War had led him to favor tariff revision downward. But his efforts in behalf of reduction boiled down to mild protestations which, as gentle taps on protectionist wrists, merely put them on guard. At election time, with the rhythmic chant of the dominant manufacturing interests in the party demanding solidarity on this issue, Kasson usually let himself be driven into line. Yet from firsthand observation, few people were more vividly aware than Kasson of the need for expanded overseas markets and the danger of losing those already secured. American goods continued to invade Europe while, at the same time, the government built up higher walls against European goods. In Vienna twenty years before, Kasson had advocated a tariff commission and reciprocity treaties as a means of circumventing tariff logrolling in Congress, which almost invariably led to revision upward. In the second Harrison campaign of 1892 he had recommended a tariff reduction in the platform. Then, and again in 1896, the platform-makers had included a reciprocity plank; now, under McKinley, party leadership in Congress had passed the Dingley Tariff Act, which gave the President a green light to proceed with reciprocity negotiations. Here was Kasson's chance to put into effect one of his favorite schemes. Here was a chance to cap his long public career with his most constructive achievement, to broaden the American trade base, and to ease trade tensions between the United States and such countries as Germany, France, Austria-Hungary, and Canada. Moreover, to open up trade channels between the United States and other nations would help promote the universal peace movement in which Kasson had demonstrated a growing interest in the nineties.

So, after three days' deliberation, Kasson took the job on the condition that he could choose his own secretary. McKinley concurred, and Kasson chose Chapman Coleman of Kentucky, former secretary of the Berlin Legation during Kasson's two missions there, a competent linguist with scholarly interests in economics. Young John Ball Osborne of Scranton, Pennsylvania, whose father was a personal friend of the President, was chosen second secretary. These three men constituted the Reciprocity Commission; the treaties they were to negotiate became known in history as the Kasson treaties — Mc-Kinley Reciprocity.[6]

Since the Civil War, reciprocity treaties had had rough treatment. They had elicited much talk and little concrete action. Blaine's Pan-American plans had included reciprocity, and under his successor, Frelinghuysen, some half dozen reciprocity treaties had been negotiated; but these treaties lay around in the Senate until Grover Cleveland in the late eighties withdrew them. The Democratic President wanted thoroughgoing tariff reform; reciprocity was a dodge, merely scratching the surface of a deeper problem, he implied. In the platforms of 1888, Democrats stood for tariff reduction, Republicans for protection. The issue was clearly joined, and the Republicans won. In the McKinley Act of 1890 tariff rates were upped all along the line, but Secretary Blaine managed to have inserted a section providing for backhanded or retaliatory reciprocity to be used as a lever against foreign discrimination. Under this section about a dozen treaties were put into operation with Latin American countries and with Germany and Austria.

Meantime the high rates of the McKinley Act aroused a storm of opposition in the United States and played a decisive part in bringing on a Democratic landslide in the mid-term elections of 1890. Two years later reciprocity received a prominent place in both major party platforms. Democrats called it a "time-honored doctrine of Democratic faith" and denounced Republican reciprocity as a sham and a juggle. Republicans lauded it as their doctrine, called it a practical business measure, and promised that it "would give us control of the trade of the world." Popular reaction against the McKinley Act was a major factor in the second election of Grover Cleveland in 1892, but his efforts for tariff reform as usual were blunted in the Senate. The resulting Wilson-Gorman Act was little if any better than the McKinley Act. The new act contained no reciprocity features. The Blaine treaties were automatically ended. From Germany and Austria-Hungary came stiff protests and threats of retaliation. Latin American states saw in such abrupt termination an act of bad faith. In the United States, tariff reformers and distressed agrarians were stunned, especially after an income tax clause of the Wilson Act was declared unconstitutional. Anger welled up in the land under a smothering blanket of economic depression.

Republicans could now hold Democrats responsible for the tariff mess at home, for repudiation of reciprocity, and for aggravated trade relations abroad. The Republican platform of 1896 consequently castigated the Democrats and laid down a ringing and clear plank in favor of reciprocity. There was no political evasion in these words:

We believe the repeal of the reciprocity arrangements negotiated by the last Republican Administration was a national calamity, and demand their renewal and extension on such terms as will equalize our trade with other nations, remove the restrictions which now obstruct the sale of American products in the ports of other countries and secure enlarged markets for the products of our farms, forests and factories.

Protection and reciprocity are twin measures of American policy and go hand in hand. Democratic rule has recklessly struck down both, and both must be re-established. . . . Protection builds up domestic industry and trade and secures our own market for ourselves; reciprocity builds up foreign trade and finds an outlet for surplus.

Republicans hoped to make the tariff the main issue in the campaign of 1896, but the combined Democratic-Populist stampede to silver and William Jennings Bryan focused the spotlight on the money question. In their platform Democrats merely reaffirmed the party's "historic doctrine of tariff for revenue only." [7]

Upon McKinley's election the road was clear for a new tariff measure that would include reciprocity. Faced with a federal deficit, the new President at once summoned a special session of Congress to revise the tariff in order (1) to raise desperately-sought revenue, and (2) to restore the rates reduced by the Wilson Act.

Already the House Ways and Means Committee had conducted an investigation which showed that in addition to the manufacturers' demand for a higher tariff, a large bloc of businessmen also demanded reciprocity; more in fact requested reciprocity than opposed it. During the summer of 1897, the Dingley Tariff Act, carrying reciprocity sections, emerged from Congress and was signed by the President. With rates higher on the average than in the old McKinley Act of 1890, it was later maintained that the rates had been deliberately upped in order to make reciprocity more palatable to foreign countries. Another strong reason for adding reciprocity was to make at least a gesture toward the clear, unequivocating platform pledge. Neither in the committees nor on the floor of either house, however, did reciprocity create much interest. At best the concessions to be made were narrow in scope, and there was an undercurrent of feeling in Congress that reciprocity, ostensibly designed to aid the consumer, especially the farmer, was a mere blind for the manufacturing interests which helped write the Dingley Act.

The Act provided for three kinds of reciprocity: (1) With European nations the President could negotiate and directly put into effect treaties granting concessions on such articles as argols, crude tartar, brandies, still wines, paintings, and statuary. (2) With Hispanic-American countries he could negotiate and proclaim treaties based on concessions on tea, tonka, and vanilla beans. (3) With any country he could negotiate reciprocity treaties, bargaining for the most favorable terms possible, without limitation to an enumerated list of articles; he was permitted, for suitable equivalents, to reduce Dingley tariff rates on foreign goods as much as 20 per cent; the treaties were to be effective for at least five years.

This third category, introduced as an amendment by Senator Allison, looked good on paper. Its potential for tariff reduction and freer trade relations was great. In reality, however, it conferred upon the President little power that he did not already possess, for all of the treaties negotiated would have to be confirmed not only by the Senate but also by the House. This section then might be considered as a hint from Congress to the President to go ahead, negotiate the treaties, fulfill the party commitments, and we shall stand behind you. On the other hand, it might be strategy, arrived at consciously or unconsciously, by which party leaders in Congress could say, "Well, we provided for reciprocity in the Dingley Act," and the President could say, "Well, we negotiated the treaties." But if special interests crowded in and defeated the treaties in the Senate, what then? Somebody would be deceiving somebody.

In the absence of successful reciprocity promised by the Dingley Act, the high rates of the same Act would require much explaining to foreign countries whose markets our products were invading. France had already taken the defensive in her system of maximum-minimum tariff schedules. Maximum rates were applied to the goods of those countries that discriminated against French goods. Of western nations only Portugal and the United States suffered from French maximum rates. Germany, Austria, Belgium, and Switzerland, moreover, had worked out an arrangement which lowered their tariff walls only to nations willing to make reciprocal concessions by treaty.[8]

To American exporters the reciprocity features of the Dingley Act looked good, as European nations girded themselves for a trade war.

The appointment by the President of a Reciprocity Commission only a few weeks after the Act was signed seemed to indicate that he meant to see the program through. By mid-October, 1897, Kasson and his secretaries had moved into the State Department, and negotiations with a number of countries were quickly under way.

John Ball Osborne, second secretary, recalled many years later that as Kasson took hold of this work he was dignified in bearing, reserved, and suave. He took pride in his keen, quick memory and was sensitive as to his advanced age. He was a master of the English language, Osborne thought. A tireless worker and extremely meticulous as to details, he guarded his prerogatives as head of the Commission, especially as to his signature on official correspondence. Young Osborne looked upon him then as a wealthy man who was "close" with his money.[9]

In addition to his reciprocity work, Kasson was called upon by the McKinley administration to draft other treaties, to determine matters of protocol and precedence at official dinners and receptions, and to perform other miscellaneous functions for the State Department, playing somewhat the role of a senior diplomat, suggesting, advising, drafting.

Kasson barely had time to get his office organized when he was called into a series of discussions with Canadian representatives — discussions which led to his appointment as one of six American High Commissioners to settle a half-century backlog of Canadian-American disputes.

Throughout the nineteenth century Canadian-American relations had been plagued by the tariff and fisheries problems. Again and again, beset with economic depression from lack of trade, Canadians had tried to use the American liberty to take fish in Canadian territorial waters as a lever to wrest trade concessions. From the end of the Civil War down to 1897 Canada suffered intermittently from serious economic depressions. Repeatedly her representatives trekked to Washington, begging for a renewal of trade favors through a reciprocity arrangement, such as had been tried for an eleven-year period before and during the war with a great deal of success. The idea of a customs union flourished on both sides of the boundary. Several Americans considered reciprocity or a customs union as a means to eventual annexation. Both countries nevertheless maintained their protective systems. But despite frequent discussions in Washington, Canadian-American problems remained unsolved and piled up. By 1897 the great depression in Canada had lifted; Canadians, rebuffed by the United States, were turning to the mother country for relief; British capital began to pour in; in the Klondike region of the Far West gold was discovered, and immigrants were swarming into the area; and Canadian goods were finding a ready market in England under the protection of the British imperial system.[10]

Although Canadians no longer felt dependent upon the United States, they still hoped to break through the Dingley tariff wall by means of reciprocity. More pressing, however, as points of friction were the fur seals and Alaskan boundary disputes. For more than two decades Americans and Canadians had wrangled over Canadian pelagic sealing around the American-owned Pribilof Islands in the North Pacific. While the wrangling went on, eventual decimation of the great seal herd by indiscriminate killing was clearly in sight. The Alaskan boundary dispute arose from the discovery of gold in the Klondike region. Canadians desired an outlet from the gold mines to the Pacific Ocean; but in accordance with treaty arrangements between the United States and Russia, and earlier between Russia and Great Britain, the United States owned, as a part of Alaska, a thirty-mile strip along the western coast of Canada, tightly sealing off Canadians from the sea. Now the Canadians were trumping up a claim to one or more of the natural canals or indentations leading to the open sea. In addition to these major points of friction — trade, the fur seals, the Alaskan boundary — a dozen other problems such as mining rights, alien labor laws, extradition, and the North Atlantic fisheries compounded the difficulty of normal diplomatic relations.

Before McKinley's inauguration, the Canadian Prime Minister, Sir Wilfred Laurier, talked over mutual problems with the President-elect at the latter's Ohio home. McKinley held out the prospect of trade concessions under the Dingley Act then being drafted. During the summer and early autumn of 1897 Canadian and American representatives carried on inconclusive negotiations on the fur seals dispute. As winter came on, Kasson was in frequent conference with the British Ambassador, Sir Julian Pauncefote, on reciprocity matters. In the spring Kasson and John W. Foster, former Secretary of State and negotiator of the Blaine reciprocity treaties, were designated to meet two Canadian diplomats in Washington to discuss the whole array of problems and prepare the agenda for a conference of a Joint High Commission to be composed of six High Commissioners on each side.

Five conferences took place in Washington between Kasson, Foster, and the two Canadians. As a result, Kasson drafted a protocol setting forth twelve issues to be ironed out, if possible. In the summer McKinley appointed the six American commissioners. In addition to Kasson and Foster, they were Senator Charles Fairbanks of Indiana, chairman; Nelson Dingley of Maine, chairman of the House Ways and Means committee, who had given his name to the tariff act; George W. Gray, Democratic Senator from Delaware; and T. Jefferson Coolidge of Massachusetts, a great-grandson of Thomas Jefferson. Before Commission sessions ended Dingley died and Gray was sent to Paris to help negotiate the treaty ending the Spanish-American War. They were replaced respectively by Senator Charles J. Faulkner of West Virginia and Representative Sereno Payne of Ohio. Of the six Anglo-Canadian commissioners, there was only one Briton — Baron Herschell, the English Lord High Chancellor.[11]

The Joint High Commission met in Quebec at the Chateau Frontenac, and sessions were scattered over August, September, and October of 1898. After two weeks of meetings the Commission recessed for three weeks and then returned for another two weeks of meetings. At Canadian request, no records were kept of daily proceedings, making it difficult to pinpoint the activities of any given individual. Thirteen committees were set up to handle the same number of specific problems. Logically, Kasson was named to the reciprocity committee, and he served as a kind of unofficial secretary for it. When the Commission recessed, he remained at his own request in Quebec where it was cool and quiet, arranging data for the reciprocity committee, answering correspondence, and enjoying the lively social activities which continued even during the recess.

Although the Quebec meetings were inconclusive, much exploratory work was done, and the basic points of disagreement were high-lighted. Clearly, Canadian enthusiasm for reciprocity had declined from that of previous years. Now prosperous and protected by the British imperial preference system, they were in no mood to make far-reaching trade concessions unless they could receive concessions on some of the other points in dispute, such as the Alaskan boundary. Moreover, they were vigilant against having their aims sacrificed at the expense of Anglo-American accord. Most of all they wanted access to the Pacific through the thirty-mile Alaskan strip claimed by the United States. This issue led to stormy sessions at Quebec, clouding all other issues, and on October 10, 1898, the Commission adjourned.

In Washington the sessions were resumed in early November and continued until late February, 1899. For a time optimism prevailed, as real headway was made in most of the committees. But news soon began to trickle out that Lord Herschell, the British member, was wrecking general accord. Cantankerous and with excessive lawyer-like zeal, he was making extreme claims. Nevertheless, by early February all minor disputes had been agreed upon and incorporated in a draft treaty. The key to the eventual solution of the fur seals problem had been settled upon, the existing *modus vivendi* governing the Northeast fisheries extended, a general approach on the Alaskan boundary worked out, and a number of concessions accepted for a reciprocity treaty.

Reciprocity discussions revealed a host of problems peculiar to such bargaining. While Kasson was in Canada, American lumber interests and agriculturists made it clear that they did not want to have anything to do with similar Canadian products. Even in prairie Iowa lumbermen made their opposition clear to Kasson and Senator Allison. Keep out any Canadian goods which will compete against us, they demanded. Canadian manufacturers, just beginning to feel their power, also had their views. Keep out American sewing machines, typewriters, bicycles, furniture, shoes, and cotton goods. In the Canadian and American legislatures the interests in the nineties were better represented than the average consumer who hoped to buy the goods at a price he could afford.

Despite these obvious handicaps, reciprocity negotiations proceeded apace. Kasson and his American colleagues agreed to put minerals, stone, marble, and slate upon the free list, to reduce the duty on articles manufactured from steel and iron, on coal, even lumber. At the same time cautious Canadians were lifting barriers to the entry of American products.

And then with sudden finality Lord Herschell demanded a Canadian waterway through Alaskan territory. The British government, leaning over backward to offend neither Canada nor the United States, backed him up; and all the agreements and all the potential agreements were wrecked by Canadian demands in connection with the

PAINTING OF JOHN A. KASSON, 1892

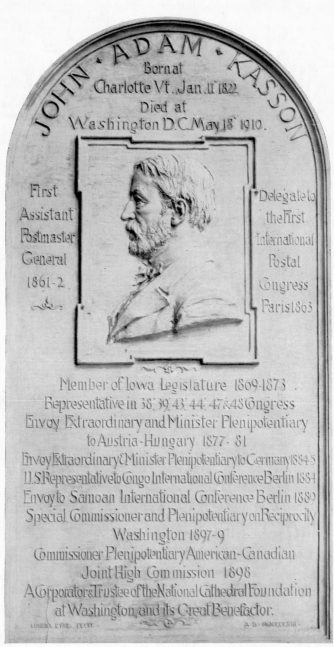

JOHN · ADAM · KASSON

Born at
Charlotte Vt., Jan. 11, 1822
Died at
Washington D.C. May 18, 1910.

First
Assistant
Postmaster
General
1861-2

Delegate to
the First
International
Postal
Congress
Paris 1863

Member of Iowa Legislature 1869-1873
Representative in 38, 39, 43, 44, 47 & 48 Congress
Envoy Extraordinary and Minister Plenipotentiary
to Austria-Hungary 1877- 81
Envoy Extraordinary & Minister Plenipotentiary to Germany 1884-5
U.S. Representative to Congo International Conference Berlin 1884
Envoy to Samoan International Conference Berlin 1889
Special Commissioner and Plenipotentiary on Reciprocity
Washington 1897-9
Commissioner Plenipotentiary American-Canadian
Joint High Commission 1898
A Corporator & Trustee of the National Cathedral Foundation
at Washington, and its Great Benefactor.

LOUISA EYRE FECIT
A. D. MDCCCCXII

Historical Dept., Des Moines
BRONZE PLAQUE IN CASADY VAULT AT
WOODLAND CEMETERY, DES MOINES

Alaskan boundary. On February 20 the Commission adjourned with the expectation of reassembling again sometime. The conduct of the Canadian Commissioners at this time, Kasson recorded, "impressed us as in some way influenced by the conditions of party politics in the Dominion, and not by a conviction that an adjustment was impracticable. We were the more surprised by this sudden termination of negotiations because they had previously indicated to us that the question of reciprocity was the hinge upon which success or failure of negotiations would turn." [12]

Within a year Lord Herschell was dead; T. J. Coolidge resigned. Coolidge thought the Commission too large and filled with too many hairsplitting lawyers like Lord Herschell and Senator Fairbanks; diplomats, not lawyers, had a better chance to succeed, he averred. Kasson, who had developed a close friendship with Coolidge, concurred and also resigned. The Commission was never assembled again; all the thirteen problems would have to be taken up one by one in the future.

Kasson was just too busy with the total problems of reciprocity to get bogged down any further in dozens of grinding sessions where twelve men, representing hundreds of special interests, plus the national interests of Britain, Canada, and the United States, spun out endless discussions. Besides, he was getting old and the rheumatic pains in his joints required that he take a little rest now and then. Actually he had rendered an effective service in the negotiations if for no other reason than that he had helped distill, and finally had drafted, the proposal which later unlocked the Alaskan boundary deadlock which had tied up all the other agreements. [13]

In all these negotiations reciprocity had been sacrificed to extreme Canadian claims on the Alaskan boundary. But in a broader sense Canadian-American disputes were submerged by the more important Anglo-American accord on problems arising from the Spanish-American War, on an isthmian canal, and on events shaping up in the Far East, as the United States made the transition at the turn of the century to a world power and to active participation in power politics. In comparison with these developments, Canadian-American points of friction were minor and could work themselves out one by one later. The Joint High Commission, groping somewhat blindly behind a maze of larger issues, had only succeeded in defining and pointing up the problems.

☆ ☆ ☆

Throughout the Canadian negotiations, Kasson and his secretaries with admirable dispatch moved toward completion of several reciprocity treaties with other countries. In all, seventeen such treaties were concluded. Those requiring executive approval only — with France, Portugal, Germany, and Italy — created no opposition and were immediately put into effect. They not only provided tariff concessions on certain enumerated articles, but also the French treaty was designed to head off pending retaliation and to pave the way for a more far-reaching agreement under the third category envisioned by the Dingley Act. No great trade increase can be attributed to these treaties simply because the number of articles was so narrowly limited and the products themselves relatively unimportant in the stream of trade.

Under the third category, where 20 per cent reductions below the Dingley rates could be made without limitation to specified products, thirteen treaties were negotiated. Although all of these were in time submitted to the Senate, only four — with France, Jamaica (Britain), Argentina, and Ecuador — made serious inroads upon the protective system. The other nine were with Caribbean countries or with Caribbean possessions of Britain and Denmark. Kasson had hurried up the negotiations with France, first, because France had imposed her maximum tariff rates against American products, and, second, the French treaty could be made a trial balloon in the Senate. If it failed, there was hardly any need to go on interminably negotiating treaties. It was a good chance to find out whether party leaders would back up their commitments in their platforms and in the Dingley Act.

In the French treaty Kasson limited his concessions to goods peculiarly French and kept the reductions on those items in most cases to 5 or 10 per cent, or an average of about 8 per cent. With a few exceptions, France conceded her minimum tariff schedules to all American products, or an average rate of reduction of about 26 per cent. In the Caribbean and South American treaties, rates on sugar and fruit were reduced in return for concessions on American products such as canned meat, liquor, tobacco, and a number of manufactured articles. The treaty with Argentina boldly reduced the rates on Argentine sugar, hides, and wool the full 20 per cent allowed under the Dingley Act. The treaty with Ecuador put hides, skins, coffee, wool, and a few other items on the free list and reduced the rates by 20 per cent on raw sugar and leaf tobacco. In return, such American articles as machinery, manufactures, locomotives, and coal were admitted free.[14]

Most of the treaties were submitted to the Senate immediately following the President's annual message, December 6, 1899. During the first two or three months of 1900, the Foreign Relations Committee conducted elaborate hearings on them. Although the French treaty was to be the test case, persons favoring and opposing the other treaties also were heard.

Letters and petitions poured into the committee, and representatives of the various interests appeared in person. Representatives of agricultural machinery, iron and steel, and smelting and refining strongly backed the treaties. Greatest support geographically lay in the South and in the Upper Mississippi Valley, where most reciprocity organizations were located.

The opposition forces were far better organized and more vociferous. In addition to specific industries, such organizations as the Boston Home Market Club and the American Protective League ground out a steady stream of opposition literature. Against the French treaty were arrayed such industries as cotton knit-goods, braids, paper, brushes, perfumes, spectacle and optical instruments, decorated tiles and bricks, electric and gas fixtures; against the Caribbean treaties (especially Jamaica), California fruit growers led by Senator George C. Perkins; against the Argentine treaty, the powerful wool growers of Ohio. The knit-goods industry was centered in New England, braids in New York and Pennsylvania, brushes in Massachusetts, electric and gas fixtures in New York, Massachusetts, and Pennsylvania, paper in Massachusetts, perfumes in New York. Thus it could be seen as the hearings developed that the opposition would rest its case with a small bloc of Eastern Senators, among whom the voice of Nelson Aldrich, protectionist watchdog from Rhode Island, would carry the most weight.

Kasson appeared at least twice before the Committee. In the French treaty he pointed out that the United States had made concessions on only 126 of her 705 tariff items, while France had made reductions on all but 19 of her 654 tariff items. Our average reduction amounted to only about 7 per cent while that of France amounted to more than 26 per cent. Kasson pointed up the growing hostility in Europe toward our trade, stressed the future importance of new trade opened by the treaties, and reiterated the commonly expressed view that the rates in the Dingley Act had been upped with the explicit intent to lower them by reciprocity. On a second appearance before the Committee, in refutation of Senator Perkins' attack upon the Jamaica treaty, Kasson maintained that Jamaican fruits would not seriously compete with American fruits because they were inferior in quality and would be marketed in America during the slack season of American production.

Late in February, 1900, the French treaty was reported favorably by the Senate Foreign Relations Committee, but on the floor in executive session Senator Aldrich immediately moved that the treaties be referred to the Finance Committee of which he was chairman. Here, the New York *Times* predicted, they would have been sealed up forever. Although the Aldrich motion was not voted upon, neither were the treaties. Had they been brought to a vote at this time Kasson had reason to believe they would have been confirmed in accordance with a poll of the Senate submitted by Robert P. Porter, a McKinley trouble shooter. Porter listed fifty Senators as favoring the French treaty, eleven against, and the position of twenty-six not known. All of those definitely opposed were Republicans; most of those unknown were Democrats. Several of those listed as favorable would probably have voted against the treaty, but there is a fair possibility at least that enough Democrats would have voted for it to muster the fifty-eight votes required for confirmation.[15]

Apparently after the hassle on the Senate floor over referring the treaties to the Finance Committee, the treaties remained in the hands of the Foreign Relations Committee, where they languished for the rest of the year. Significantly, in their platform of 1900, a few months later, Republicans hedged on the reciprocity plank. They still favored reciprocity as an "associated policy" with protection, but only on goods which "we do not ourselves produce, in return for free foreign markets."

In his annual message to Congress in December, 1900, in his inaugural address, and again a few days after his second inauguration, McKinley urged favorable consideration of the treaties. These expressions brought forth a reply from Senator Perkins that he thought the treaties in the last session of Congress had been abandoned to sleep forever. Nevertheless, Senator Shelby M. Cullom, Illinois chairman of the Foreign Relations Committee, renewed consideration of the treaties. Kasson was called in and, in his last appearance before the committee, defended the Jamaican treaty against Perkins' attacks. But Cullom found little interest in the Senate for the treaties and bitter opposition from a small coterie of Senators like Aldrich and Hanna.[16]

With no hope of future action, Kasson submitted his resignation on March 9, 1901. His salary was a waste of government funds, he said. Businessmen in the future would bring enough pressure on individual Senators to assure action, he hoped. But for a personal reason also one can understand why he resigned. Having just passed his eightieth birthday, the work of the Commission was too heavy and frustrating to continue. His body required a slower pace; his nervous system, less exasperation.[17]

As partial proof that McKinley had not abandoned reciprocity, he accepted Kasson's resignation only reluctantly and promised to call him back if prospects for the treaties brightened. Late that summer the President journeyed to Buffalo and made a speech before the Pan-American Exposition. "The time of exclusiveness is past," he said. "We cannot repose in fancied security that we can forever sell everything and buy little or nothing." Reciprocity treaties were in "harmony with the spirit of the times." These were prophetic words and can be construed as a strong endorsement of reciprocity. But the President's plans to save the treaties were never divulged; at the end of his speech he was struck down by an assassin's bullet. For the third time John Kasson had lived through a presidential assassination, each in one way or another vitally affecting his career.

In his speech McKinley had somewhat weakened his endorsement of reciprocity with such expressions as "arrangements which will not interrupt our home production" or "if perchance some of our tariffs are no longer needed." The President's biographer states that Mc-Kinley planned to take the issue to the people and quotes the President's private secretary as saying, "I never saw him more determined on anything than this." But the same private secretary later authorized a satement to the effect that McKinley was merely counting on the *future* adoption of reciprocity — not in his own time. In his speech he was not throwing "the gauntlet down to recalcitrant" Senators like Aldrich; he did not expect the treaties to be ratified.

To push the Kasson treaties through, McKinley would have had to exert strong executive pressure on about a dozen Senators who were his close friends and who in effect controlled the Senate in the nineties, represented the dominant wealthy protectionist elements of the country, operated behind closed doors, and were little responsive to popular demands. At the head of this powerful coterie were the famous "Four" — Aldrich of Rhode Island, Platt of Connecticut, Spooner of Wisconsin, and Allison of Iowa. The President would probably not have taken on a fight with the protectionist Senators had he lived.[18]

Nor was his vigorous successor willing to do so. Theodore Roosevelt committed himself to McKinley's policies and for a time assumed that the Kasson treaties would be acted upon. But after corresponding and consulting with a few industrialists and Senators, including the "Four," in reference to his annual message, he adopted a policy of caution. At this point Senator Allison began to find his position among the "Four" uncomfortable. In Iowa, tariff revision demands had rumbled out from the state Republican convention in the form of the famous "Iowa Idea." Reciprocity was the "natural complement" to protection, declared convention resolutions. Tariffs should be no higher than absolutely necessary to give protection when foreign competition would otherwise destroy the home industry. The consumer interest in the price of goods would have to be considered too, it was inferred. Here was a potential, dangerous political issue growing hot in the state. Senator Allison, the moderate protectionist, now spoke out for reciprocity at Tama, Iowa, and wrote Roosevelt that he thought it the "duty" of the Senate to take up the Kasson treaties and "act upon them." If they were not satisfactory, they could be amended or rejected, but "good faith" under the Dingley Act commitments and to foreign nations with whom the treaties had been made required some kind of action. But Roosevelt instead took the advice of Aldrich, and in his first annual message of December, 1901, threw out the usual bouquets to reciprocity — it was the handmaiden of protection; but he hurried on over the Kasson treaties with a wave, asking the "attention of the Senate" to them. This attention the President never expected, and they never got.

Although Secretary of State John Hay had little or no interest in the treaties, he was sympathetic with Kasson in his struggle with the Senate, which also had wrecked many of the Secretary's well-laid plans. "What a lot of fine things we could do," Hay longingly wrote to Kasson, "if it were not for the Senate!" There had never been "a period in our history so pregnant with opportunity." Yet a third of the Senate, "ignorant or malignant, or merely desirous of a sensation," stood ready to kill everything put before them. But the Secretary misjudged the handful of Senators who held back the treaties. They were not ignorant; they knew precisely what they were doing. They were shrewd men; and as spokesmen of powerful industrialists who did not want *any* foreign competition, they did not intend for reciprocity to become an entering wedge into the ironbound protective system. These gentlemen had the power but not much foresight. Already their comfortable ascendency had begun to recede. In effect, then, reciprocity, which had cropped up in so many Republican platforms and tariff acts in the past, was but a sop to the agrarians, exporters, and dissatisfied consumers in the party.[19]

For the next few years reciprocity continued to be a lively issue. Kasson joined up with reciprocity leagues, worked with political science and economic associations, wrote letters, made speeches, and helped keep flowing a stream of favorable information. But as the first decade of the twentieth century sped on, reciprocity was finally snowed under by a host of other issues embraced within the progressive movement and America's new foreign policies as an active world power. In Iowa, Kasson watched with admiration the rise of a young progressive politician named Albert B. Cummins, provided him with information respecting reciprocity, and took consolation from the fact that Cummins in time was elected to the United States Senate, in part because of his liberal stand on the tariff.

In Washington the Kasson treaties continued to gather dust in a pigeonhole of the Senate Foreign Relations Committee. The failure of reciprocity was naturally a disappointment to Kasson, but he need not have been bitterly disappointed. His negotiations had defined the terms, crystallized the problems, and provided a background of experience for a future generation to use. These treaties proved that reciprocity could not succeed where every concession in a treaty had to undergo the close scrutiny of each Senator and of whatever special interest he might represent. Reciprocity was an administrative function which could best be handled by the executive under authority delegated by the Congress. Kasson had started out on a track which had not yet been laid down all the way through the wilderness of conflicting self-interests. As in so many other cases in his past, he was ahead of his time — this time, three and a half decades.[20]

☆ ☆ ☆

During the four years Kasson was engaged in reciprocity and Canadian negotiations he fell into a pattern of activities which extended far into the first decade of the twentieth century. Outwardly spry and mentally agile, he responded to numerous requests, which increased as he grew older, to make speeches, write mottoes, contribute to learned and historical societies, give opinions on public issues, donate funds to charitable and religious institutions, attend private and social functions, and always, always to participate in political campaigns. But as the years swiftly moved along, he observed that the rheumatic pains in his joints got sharper and the colds of winter lasted longer. He did not snap back quickly at home or in the Reciprocity offices at the State Department, and he frequently left the business of the office to secretaries, or later, the management of his house to his servants, and traveled or took rest cures. Trips to Des Moines, to Burlington, and to New Bedford broke the monotony and pressure of life and quenched his thirst for old friends but did not quite fill up a yearning, a nostalgia, a mellow mood for reminiscence. Other trips seemed to make him forget the passing years — those to Los Angeles, Saratoga Springs, Richfield Springs, the Virginia Springs, Lenox and Nahant, Massachusetts, Bar Harbor, Palm Beach, St. Augustine, and an excursion through the Everglades of Florida.

In a speech in 1899 Kasson dedicated the new historical building at Des Moines. For the past fifteen years he had been turning over some of his private papers to Charles Aldrich, curator of state archives. As plans for the new historical building developed, Kasson advised the procuring of plenty of land, a competent architect, and a handsome building. Even a cheap building ought to be given a pretty face, he insisted. In Washington he also showed an interest in history. He joined the Columbia Historical Society, became its president, solicited members, and provided reminiscences of the Lincoln and Blair administration.[21]

He made one political appearance in the national campaign of 1900 — in Des Moines where he was reported to have been wildly received. Previously he had written a long political speech backing McKinley and imperialism — a speech which was said to have been published in twenty Iowa newspapers. Quoting Bismarck, he declared that a nation which had ceased to grow had begun to decay. Growth meant territorial expansion, and Kasson defended retention of the Philippines, not only in this treatise but in a number of other speeches before commercial organizations near the turn of the century. He had also heartily approved of the annexation of Hawaii and the partition of Samoa, immediately following the Spanish-American War.[22]

In 1901 he gave the dedicatory address upon the unveiling of the Floyd monument at Sioux City, Iowa. The monument was in honor of Sergeant Charles Floyd, a member of the Lewis and Clark expedition, who had died and been buried on a bluff at Sioux City overlooking the Missouri River, as the expedition headed off to the Pacific Coast. Kasson's speech — "The Expansion of the Republic West of the Mississippi" — blended the history of the Louisiana Purchase with the thesis that the hand of Providence had guided the nation in its breath-taking expansion across the continent, in its fulfillment of an age-old dream of human and personal liberty. The speech inferred, as did many other of Kasson's pronouncements during this era, that the ultimate destiny of the Republic lay in further overseas expansion, in extending to less privileged people the benefits of our republican institutions. Hearing this speech was a professor, James Davie Butler, who many years before in the pulpit had preached to Kasson in Burlington, Vermont. Butler, now representing the University of Wisconsin, was exhibiting to the audience materials from the famous Draper Collection of Western History, rich in data on the Lewis and Clark Expedition.[23]

Kasson again appeared in Des Moines in 1904 in behalf of Theodore Roosevelt for president. In the same year he had delivered an address on "The Advance in International Relations" at the University of Vermont. At eighty-two he was reported to be "as straight as a Lombardy Poplar," with a "simple quiet elegance of bearing, fine height and exquisitely cut features." [24]

After 1904 he had to stay at home in Washington more and more. In this year his sister Mary passed away. Already most of his political associates of former years had died. But younger Iowans called frequently at the old-fashioned yellow house at 1726 I Street to see the lonely old-fashioned man whose ideas on the tariff and an aggressive foreign policy were completely up-to-date. Two young grandnieces, Eunice and Katharine Wead, were frequent callers upon their Uncle John who advised them on their dress, manners, and the ways of the world. Although becoming enfeebled physically, he loved to reminisce on the era of Lincoln, about General Grant and Bismarck. His eye was bright and his memory keen. He still held membership in the Cosmos Club and the Metropolitan Club, participated in the Columbia Historical Society, attended church at St. John's, the church of the Presidents, and was making plans for, and contributions to, the National Cathedral of Washington and a National University in Washington.

Since 1890 representatives of learned societies — political science, economic, history, metrological, geographic, postal, and several others — had become interested in his public career and kept up a stream of correspondence for information. The Episcopal Church in Iowa as in Washington looked after his personal welfare and sought his support. It was not until the 1890's that his contributions in postal and metric affairs were fully recognized.

Kasson made his will in 1906.[25] The estate, mostly in railroad stocks and bonds, amounted to more than $100,000. Most of this amount was divided among a number of nephews and nieces, grandnephews and grandnieces. But from his estate also, he contributed $10,000 in bonds to the Church Orphanage Association of St. John's Episcopal Parish, Washington; made a liberal allowance for the National Cathedral building; and gave $10,000 to Simon Casady, his old Democratic friend of Des Moines, for the sick and poor of that city. This fund was augmented in 1909 by another $5,000 from Kasson to the Episcopalian Church in East Des Moines to build a Memorial Neighborhood House in which charitable, recreational, and social services could be carried on without reference to any given religious denomination. The building was to be known as the Kasson Building. In 1909, at the cornerstone ceremonies, Henry C. Wallace, editor of *Wallaces' Farmer,* was one of the speakers. An usher exclaimed that Mr. Wallace looked very much like Mr. Kasson — a real likeness. The Kasson Building was to be finished on June 1, 1910, and John Kasson, it was hoped, would be at the formal opening.[26]

But Kasson had grown weaker and weaker since 1907. On May 18, 1910, he died at the age of eighty-eight. For the last three years he had been confined to his house in Washington as an invalid under the care of his relatives and his doctor. Mentally alert to the last, he had died of a common cold that had developed into a strangling throat disorder. He would have enjoyed speaking at the opening of the Kasson Building, and more particularly so, had he known it was eventually to become an archive for the manuscript collections of notable Iowans. He had great fondness for the history of state and nation.

By 1910 the name of John A. Kasson had been eclipsed by the events of a new era which he had helped to bring on. Only a few white-haired men and women attended the funeral. He was buried in the Casady vault in the Woodland Cemetery of Des Moines in accordance with a request he had made a decade before. Only General Dodge and Ret Clarkson still lived to retell the stories of the political combats of olden times.

On the day of his funeral an Iowa bard paid final tribute to Kasson as the "tallest tree"

> That stood upon our level plain
> So strong, so straight that all could see. . . .
>
> Firm and erect in peace, or strife
> He was the courteous gentleman.[27]

If not the "tallest tree" among his political contemporaries in Iowa, Kasson was the peer of all of them. In constructive effort he surpassed many in both state and nation who held higher office than he. His place in American politics and diplomacy rests firmly upon his cumulative record as a constructive conservative. The concentrated work of such secondary figures accounts for much of the general competence and historical achievement of Kasson's era.

I Am Indebted

To Stull Holt of the University of Washington for the suggestion which led to this study; to Howard Merriman of George Washington University for directing it in its early stages; and to Wood Gray of George Washington for his wise counsel and encouragement throughout; to my colleague, Bernard Mayo, for early, helpful criticism.

To M. L. Williams and May Foote of the Charlotte (Vermont) Town Hall; to Gladys Flint and Doris J. Harvey of the University of Vermont Library; to William T. O'Rourke and Gertrude Wilcox of the Public Library of New Bedford, Massachusetts; to Ralph Bieber and John Francis McDermott of Washington University, St. Louis; to Harry E. Pratt of the Illinois State Historical Library; to W. D. Lewis of the University of Delaware Library.

To Willard Webb, Bob Land, Percy Powell, and Stuart Dickson of the Library of Congress; to the late Mrs. Natalie Summers of the National Archives; to Harry Clemons, Jack Dalton, Roy Land, Louise Savage, and Betty Hoskins of the Alderman Library, University of Virginia.

To Curators Ora Williams and Claude R. Cook of the Iowa State Department of History and Archives, Des Moines, and particularly to Emory H. English, editor of the *Annals of Iowa,* for his patient and warm response to my many requests for aid; to Mrs. Frank I.

Herriott, Henry H. Griffiths, John Sherman, Bishop Thomas Casady, Mary B. Kasson, and John Ball Osborne for their memories.

To my colleague, Thomas Perkins Abernethy, for reading parts of the manuscript, for his encouragement, and for his example of work; to Watt Stuart, New York State College for Teachers (Albany), Kenneth C. Crosby, Juniata College (Pennsylvania), Paul A. Varg, Ohio State University, Frank Berkeley and John Wyllie, Alderman Library, University of Virginia, for reading parts of the manuscript; to my students whose works are cited herein, and to Larry Burnette, Bill Runge, and Jack Large for research assistance.

To Eunice and Katharine Wead of Hartford, Connecticut, and Frederick W. Wead of Boston, Massachusetts, who generously and without restriction made available to me the Wead Collection containing much rich material on their great-uncle, John A. Kasson.

To William J. Petersen, superintendent of the State Historical Society of Iowa, whose generous shouldering of the heavy responsibilities of publication has enabled me to complete this work; and to a fine editor and scholar, Mildred Throne, associate editor of the State Historical Society of Iowa, who has kept me from making numerous errors of fact, rhetoric, and interpretation.

To the University of Virginia Committee on Faculty Research for two grants; to the Richmond Area University Research Center for one Summer Grant; and, most of all, to the University of Virginia Institute for Research in the Social Sciences without whose six Summer Grants and splendid clerical assistance this book would not have been written.

To Leland Sage of the Iowa State Teachers College at Cedar Falls, for serving in many respects as co-author without getting credit for it. Soon to publish a biography of William Boyd Allison, whose life parallels Kasson's, Mr. Sage has given me leads, provided me with materials, permitted me to read his manuscript biography of Allison, has read and criticized my entire manuscript, and has been a constant source of encouragement.

To my wife, Barbara Ellen Younger, for her typing, research assistance, criticism, patience, and even more important, her judgment.

EDWARD YOUNGER

Corcoran Department of History,
   University of Virginia

Bibliography:
Manuscript Materials

The most extensive collection of John A. Kasson papers, including the Proceedings of the Paris Postal Conference, 1863, in French, is in the Iowa State Department of History and Archives, Des Moines. This collection, containing much unimportant material, has been supplemented by: (1) the bound volumes of Kasson correspondence in the Charles Aldrich Collection, located at the same place; (2) the valuable private and political correspondence of Kasson in the possession of his relatives, Eunice and Katharine Wead of Hartford, Connecticut, and Frederick W. Wead of Boston; (3) Kasson letters written while a tutor at Charlottesville, Virginia, in the Alderman Library, University of Virginia.

For Kasson's political activities, the Grenville M. Dodge, Samuel J. Kirkwood, and James S. Clarkson collections have been invaluable. The Dodge collection contains Dodge's private correspondence, typescripts of much of his correspondence, a typescript Personal Biography, several diaries, and other materials. It is the best single source on Kasson's political career during the Civil War and Reconstruction. The Kirkwood collection of private correspondence contains fewer Kasson letters, but it is rich in material on state and national politics. The Dodge and Kirkwood collections are in the Iowa State Department of History and Archives. Some of the Clarkson papers are located at the same place, but another collection is in the Manuscripts Division, Library of Congress. Although less extensive than the Dodge and Kirkwood collections, the Clarkson papers have helped clarify Kasson's political ups and downs.

Other collections of Kasson's contemporaries have thrown much light on his life — both political and diplomatic. *Iowa State Department of History and Archives, Des Moines*: papers of William Boyd Allison, P. M. Casady, William Penn Clarke, and Frank I. Herriott. *State Historical Society of Iowa, Iowa City*: Cyrus Clay Carpenter papers, including his diary. *Wilbur Library, University of Vermont*: Alumni Records, A. D. Barber manuscript diary, L. E. Chittenden manuscript diary, Student Letters. *University of Delaware Library*: George Handy Bates papers. *Rutherford B. Hayes Memorial Library, Fremont, Ohio*: Rutherford B. Hayes papers. *Smith College Women's Collection, Northampton, Massachusetts*: letters of Kasson's sister, Maria. *Manuscripts Division, Library of Congress*: papers of Thomas F. Bayard, James G. Blaine, the Blairs (Francis P., Montgomery, and Francis P., Jr.), Salmon P. Chase, Grover Cleveland, Hamilton Fish, James A. Garfield (including his manuscript diary), Robert Garrett, Benjamin Harrison, Andrew Johnson, Robert T. Lincoln, William McKinley, John Tyler Morgan, James K. Polk, Edwin M. Stanton, Elihu B. Washburne, and John Russell Young.

Of the voluminous manuscript material in the National Archives, bearing on Kasson's diplomatic career, his Diplomatic Despatches, including rough drafts, in the *Department of State Archives*, have been of greatest value. Other Department of State series used in this book include Appointment Papers; Credences; Consular Despatches; Instructions — Consular and Diplomatic; John A. Kasson Samoan Conference Papers, 1889; John A. Kasson Reciprocity Papers, 1897-1901; Legation Notes; Miscellaneous Letters; Special Agents and Special Missions. *Interior Department*: Applications. *Navy Department*: European Squadron Letters. *Post Office Department*: Journal and Letterbooks of the Postmaster General.

Footnotes

CHAPTER I — AT LINCOLN'S FIRST INAUGURATION

[1] Grenville M. Dodge to Annie Dodge, March 4, 17, 1861, *Grenville M. Dodge Papers* (Iowa State Dept. of History and Archives, Des Moines); Dodge manuscript biography, *ibid.*, 1:33-5.

[2] Charles Aldrich, "At Lincoln's First Inauguration," *Annals of Iowa* (third series), 8:43-50 (April, 1907).

[3] Dodge to his wife, March 12, 1861, *Dodge Papers.*

[4] Aldrich, "At Lincoln's First Inauguration," 43-50; Albert G. Riddle, *Recollections of War Times . . . 1861-1865* (New York, 1895), 15.

[5] Kasson to Dodge, Feb. 8, 1861, *Dodge Papers.*

[6] To be elaborated upon and documented in Chapters VII and VIII.

[7] Dubuque *Herald,* Nov. 24, 1895.

[8] Sioux City *Journal,* June 9, 1907.

CHAPTER II — ANCESTRY, BOYHOOD, AND EDUCATION

[1] G. M. Kasson, *Genealogy of a Part of the Kasson Family* (Woodbury, Conn., 1882), 4, 50; H. J. Ford, *The Scotch-Irish in America* (New York, 1941), 165-229; C. K. Bolton, *Scotch Irish Pioneers in Ulster and America* (Boston, 1910), 37ff.; C. A. Hanna, *The Scotch Irish* (2 vols., New York, 1902), 2:16-23.

2 G. L. Clark, *A History of Connecticut* . . . (New York, 1914), 198; Dorothy Deming, *The Settlement of the Connecticut Towns* (New Haven, 1933), 73-4, and *The Settlement of Litchfield County* (New Haven, 1933), 15-16; E. L. Heermance (comp.), *The Connecticut Guide* (Hartford, 1935), 265-8; E. D. Larned, *History of Windham County* (2 vols., Worcester, Mass., 1874, 1880), 1: 239-302, 391-5, 454-8; Oscar Zeichner, *Connecticut's Years of Controversy, 1750-1756* (Chapel Hill, N. C., 1949), 3-28; S. A. Peters, *General History of Connecticut* (London, 1781), 158-9.

3 Speech at Des Moines before the Scotch-Irish Society of America, June, 1894, typed manuscript in *Wead Collection* (The *Wead Collection* of Kasson papers is in the possession of Kasson's relatives, the Misses Eunice and Katharine Wead of Hartford, Conn., and Mr. Frederick W. Wead of Boston, Mass.), and in *Proceedings*, Scotch-Irish Society, Vol. 6; "John A. Kasson," an undated biographical sketch prepared by a University of Vermont alumnus, *Wead Collection*; Kasson's own biographical sketch, a typed manuscript in File 9 of the *Kasson Papers* (State Dept. of History and Archives, Des Moines); Kasson, *Genealogy*, 5-8, 50-51; Heermance (comp.), *Connecticut Guide*, 104-108; Larned, *Windham County*, 1: 540-56; Zeichner, *Years of Controversy*, 30-31; William Cothren, *History of Ancient Woodbury* . . . (2 vols., Woodbury, Conn., 1854-72), 1: 248-57, 779-94; 2: 603; C. P. Smith, *The Housatonic* (New York, 1946), 7-12, 74-6, 92-3, 97, 152; H. P. Johnson (ed.), *Record of Connecticut Men in the Military and Naval Service, 1775-1848* (Hartford, 1889), 75, 480, 611.

4 D. S. Durrie, *The Steele Family: A Genealogical History* (Albany, 1859), 7, 8, 10, 13, 18; Samuel Orcutt and Ambrose Beardsley, *History of . . . Derby* (Springfield, Mass., 1886), 249-59; Samuel Orcutt, *History of . . . Bridgeport and . . . Stratford* (2 vols., New Haven, 1886), 2: 958-9, 997-1004; Heermance (comp.), *Connecticut Guide*, 117-18; Smith, *Housatonic*, 59, 73-6, 84-5; Kasson family gravestones, Barber Cemetery, Charlotte, Vermont; Kasson family deeds, letter to writer from Frederick W. Wead, who has given invaluable assistance on Kasson genealogy.

5 Lois K. Mathews, *The Expansion of New England* . . . (Boston, 1909), 108ff; Lois K. Mathews Rosenberry, *Migrations from Connecticut Prior to 1800* (New Haven, 1934) and *Migrations from Connecticut After 1800* (New Haven, 1936); H. L. Morrow, *Connecticut Influences in Western Massachusetts and Vermont* (New Haven, 1936); Smith, *Housatonic*, 149-209; Orcutt and Beardsley, *Derby*, 249-59.

6 The purchase price was $3,500; the mortgage of $1,900 with interest was paid off in 1824. Charlotte Land Records (Charlotte Townhall, Charlotte, Vermont), 6: 289, 300; 7: 201; 8: 12, 20.

7 W. S. Rann (ed.), *History of Chittenden County, Vermont* (Syracuse, 1886), 311, 325; A. M. Hemenway (ed.), *Vermont Historical Gazetteer* (Burlington, 1868), 1: 693-7; Lewis D. Stillwell, *Migrations from Vermont* (Montpelier, 1948), 64, 154, 176, 200; Chilton Williamson, *Vermont in Quandry, 1763-1825* (Montpelier, 1949), 283, 288.

8 Stillwell, *Migrations from Vermont*, 98; in 1823 Charlotte contained three sawmills (one sawing marble), four gristmills, five taverns, five tanneries, eight blacksmiths, and one distillery producing 2,400 gallons of cider brandy and 3,000 gallons of whisky. Zadock Thompson, *A Gazeteer of the State of Vermont* (Montpelier, 1824), 100. The old Kasson home was still standing in 1954.

9 Rann (ed.), *Chittenden County*, 536; Charlotte Land Records, 10: 375.

10 From Kasson's own account of his boyhood in *Wead Collection*. This manuscript of about 2,500 words in Kasson's longhand, written when he was eighty, will be cited hereafter as "Memoirs of Boyhood."

11 Kasson, St. Louis, to his sister Mary and his mother, May 4, 1851, *Wead Collection*.

12 Kasson, Fryston Hall, Femjbridge, England, to his sisters, June 12, 1867, *ibid.*

[13] Kasson, "Memoirs of Boyhood," *ibid.*

[14] Stillwell, *Migrations from Vermont*, 134, 160.

[15] M. E. Gates (ed.), *Men of Mark in America* (2 vols., Washington, 1906), 2:82. In this biographical sketch, Kasson is frequently quoted.

[16] Kasson, "Memoirs of Boyhood," *Wead Collection*.

[17] D. M. Ludlum, *Social Ferment in Vermont, 1791-1850* (New York, 1939), 24-62; W. H. Crockett, *Vermont, The Green Mountain State* (4 vols., New York, 1921), 3:154; Hemenway (ed.), *Vermont Gazeteer*, 1:737; Stillwell, *Migrations from Vermont*, 137, 179, 203.

[18] Kasson, "Memoirs of Boyhood," *Wead Collection*.

[19] Stillwell, *Migrations from Vermont*, 112-14.

[20] The Charlotte Kassons were Democrats and subscribed to William Cullen Bryant's New York *Evening Post*, poisoned "with the gall of Jacksonism." Kasson to the *Post*, Oct. 10, 1901, *Kasson Papers*; Kasson autobiographical sketch, *ibid.*, File 9.

[21] Hemenway (ed.), *Vermont Gazeteer*, 1:737; Thompson, *Gazeteer of Vermont*, 36-100.

[22] Hemenway (ed.), *Vermont Gazeteer*, 1:737-8.

[23] Charlotte Land Records, 8:20.

[24] Stillwell, *Migrations from Vermont*, 100, 159; Gates (ed.), *Men of Mark*, 2:82.

[25] Stillwell, *Migrations from Vermont*, 132, 157, 172, 198, 221.

[26] Kasson, "Memoirs of Boyhood," *Wead Collection*.

[27] Thompson, *Gazeteer of Vermont*, 39.

[28] Kasson, "Memoirs of Boyhood," *Wead Collection*.

[29] Stillwell, *Migrations from Vermont*, 107-108, 128-9, 202.

[30] Gates (ed.), *Men of Mark*, 2:82; Kasson, "Memoirs of Boyhood," *Wead Collection*; Charlotte Gravestone Inscriptions, Barber Cemetery, Charlotte.

[31] Undated letter to Kasson from his sister Mary, *Wead Collection*.

[32] Gates (ed.), *Men of Mark*, 2:82.

[33] Kasson, "Memoirs of Boyhood," *Wead Collection*.

[34] Kasson, Washington, to his sister Mary, Oct. 13, 1892, *ibid.*

[35] Kasson, "Memoirs of Boyhood," *ibid.*; Charlotte Gravestone Inscriptions, Barber Cemetery, Charlotte.

[36] Williamson, *Vermont in Quandry*, 284; Stillwell, *Migrations from Vermont*, 155, 184, 195, 211; Hannah Josephson, *The Gold Threads: New England's Mill Girls and Magnates* (New York, 1949), 78; Larned, *Windham County*, 2:429-31; Orcutt and Beardsley, *Derby*, 259; Hemenway (ed.), *Vermont Gazeteer*, 1:734-7.

[37] Charlotte Land Records, 10:138.

[38] Kasson, "Memoirs of Boyhood," *Wead Collection*. The farm was sold for $3,800, or $300 above what Adam Kasson had paid for it. It is probable that some of its proceeds were divided among the older children, for about two years later Charles De Forest borrowed $1,000 from his two sisters to apply to the debt on the farm he had purchased at Charlotte.

Also, the deeds of sale indicate division except for the minors, Chester and John. John's share was undoubtedly used to send him to the University. Charlotte Land Records, 10: 375-7; 11: 62.

[39] University of Vermont Wilbur Library, *Student Letters*, Oscar F. Dana, Jr., to G. D. Dana, June 26, 1836.

[40] Kasson, "Memoirs of Boyhood," *Wead Collection*; [An Octogenarian Alumnus], "University Life in the Forties," *Vermont Cynic and Monthly*, 26: 288ff (May, 1905).

[41] Kasson, "Memoirs of Boyhood," *Wead Collection*; Crockett, *Vermont*, 4: 13-19; L. E. Chittenden, *Personal Reminiscences, 1840-1890* (New York, 1893), 4-10; Charlotte Land Records, 10: 62; 11: 7, 62, 442.

[42] Sketch by Walter L. Wright, Jr., in *Dictionary of American Biography*, 12: 297-8; Merle Curti, *The Growth of American Thought* (New York, 1943), 399, 403, 411; Kasson, "Memoirs of Boyhood," *Wead Collection*.

[43] Frederick Tupper, *A Notable Chapter* (Paper read before Phi Beta Kappa, Burlington, 1923), 6.

[44] Charles A. Huntington, *The University of Vermont Fifty Years Ago* (Burlington, 1892), 15-46. Sketch of Marsh by Henry H. Parkes, *Dictionary of American Biography*, 12: 299-300; Marjorie H. Nicolson, "James Marsh and the Vermont Transcendentalists," *Philosophical Review*, 34: 31-4 (January, 1925); William Maxwell, *A Memoir of Reverend John H. Rice* (Richmond, 1835), 2-23; sketch of Rice by E. T. Thompson, *Dict. of Amer. Biog.*, 15: 541-2; A. J. Morrison, *The College of Hampden-Sidney: Calendar of Board Minutes, 1776-1876* (Richmond, 1912), 92, 93, 95n; *Dictionary of Biography, 1776-1825* (Hampden-Sidney, 1921), 253-9.

[45] T. P. Abernethy, *Historical Sketch of the University of Virginia* (Richmond, 1948), 1-9; Roy J. Honeywell, *The Educational Work of Thomas Jefferson* (Cambridge, Mass., 1931), 54ff; S. G. Brown, *The Life of Rufus Choate* (Boston, 1891), 34; Morrison, *College of Hampden-Sidney*, 95n; A. J. Morrison, *Addresses . . . Before Literary and Philosophical Society* (Roanoke, Va., 1917), 4-5.

[46] Nicolson, "Vermont Transcendentalists," 29, 34-50; J. I. Lindsay, "Coleridge and the University of Vermont," *Alumni Weekly*, 15: 8-13 (January-February, 1936); Alice D. Snyder, "American Comments on Coleridge a Century Ago," in Edmund Blunden and E. L. Griggs (eds.), *Coleridge: Studies by Several Hands . . .* (London, 1934), 214ff; Curti, *American Thought*, 215, 217, 226, 243, 354; Huntington, *University of Vermont*, 6-8; J. E. Goodrich, *A Sketch of the History of the University of Vermont* (Burlington, 1899), Part II, 159-61; Kasson, "Memoirs of Boyhood," *Wead Collection*; Gates (ed.), *Men of Mark*, 2: 85-6.

[47] J. W. Dana to his family, Sept. 29, 1839, U. V. M. *Student Letters*; Kasson, St. Louis, to his brother Charles, June 13, 1851, *Wead Collection*; Huntington, *University of Vermont*, 6-12.

[48] J. W. Dana to his family, Sept. 29, 1839, U. V. M. *Student Letters*; Kasson, New Bedford, Mass., to his brother Charles, Feb. 18, 1849, *Wead Collection*; "University Life in the Forties," 288ff.

[49] Tupper, *Notable Chapter*, 6-10; U. V. M. *Calendars and Student Records*, 1838-1842.

[50] Sketch of Wheeler by E. C. Smith in *Dict. of Amer. Biog.*, 20: 57-8; of Hale by A. S. McDaniel, *ibid.*, 8: 110-11; of Billings by J. D. Hicks, *ibid.*, 2: 265-6; of Raymond by Elmer Davis, *ibid.*, 15: 408-412; Frank Luther Mott, *American Journalism . . .* (New York, 1941), 269-70, 278; Rann (ed.), *Chittenden County*, 205; Lindsay, "Coleridge and the University of Vermont," 9-10; J. B. Hedges, "The Colonization Work of the Northern Pacific Railroad," *Mississippi Valley Historical Review*, 13: 311-42 (December, 1926).

⁵¹ Kasson's University of Vermont record, 1840, *Wead Collection*; Goodrich, *University of Vermont*, 176; "University Life in the Forties," 288ff.

⁵² New York *Evening World*, Aug. 1, 1860.

⁵³ Augustus Maverick, *Henry J. Raymond and the New York Press* (Hartford, 1870), 26-7; Burlington *Weekly Free Press and Times*, Jan. 10, 1900.

⁵⁴ Kasson, Charlottesville, Va., to his brother Charles, Dec. 27, 1842, *Wead Collection*; U. V. M. *Catalogues*, 1838-1842; Gates (ed.), *Men of Mark*, 2: 80.

⁵⁵ U. V. M. *Records of Examinations*, 1834-1848.

⁵⁶ Kasson, "Memoirs of Boyhood," *Wead Collection*.

⁵⁷ *Ibid.*

⁵⁸ Kasson, New Bedford, to his brother Charles, Feb. 18, 1849, *ibid.*; Manuscript Diary of A. D. Barber, Aug. 2, 1842 (University of Vermont Wilbur Library).

⁵⁹ Kasson, "Memoirs of Boyhood," *Wead Collection*.

⁶⁰ Stillwell, *Migrations from Vermont*, 65-6, 132, 231.

⁶¹ *Ibid.*, 144, 146, 165, 166, 191, 195.

⁶² Kasson, Worcester, Mass., to his brother Charles, April 19, May 31, 1844, and from Charlottesville, Va., Feb. 4, 1843, *Wead Collection*. For a fuller treatment of Kasson's early life and education, see Edward Younger, "The Education of John A. Kasson," *Iowa Journal of History*, 49: 289-310 (October, 1951).

CHAPTER III — CONTRASTS IN VIRGINIA AND MASSACHUSETTS

¹ Kasson, Hagley near Fredericksburg, to his mother, Sept. 27, 1842. This is the first of six letters upon which the story of Kasson's Virginia experience is primarily based. The originals are in the Alderman Library, University of Virginia, as gifts from the Misses Eunice and Katherine Wead and Mr. Frederick W. Wead. See also the same letters with editorial notes and a few deletions, in Edward Younger (ed.), "A Yankee Reports on Virginia, 1842-1843," *Virginia Magazine of History and Biography*, 56: 408-430 (October, 1948). See also S. J. Quinn, *History of Fredericksburg, Virginia* (Richmond, 1908), 67.

² Kasson, Hagley near Fredericksburg, to his brother Charles, Oct. 21, 1842, Alderman Library Collection.

³ *Ibid.*; Mary Rawlings (ed.), *Early Charlottesville . . . 1828-1874* (Charlottesville, 1942), *passim*.

⁴ P. A. Bruce, *History of the University of Virginia, 1819-1919* (5 vols., New York, 1928), 1: 103-104, 110-15.

⁵ Kasson, Keelona near Charlottesville, to his sister Maria, Nov. 22, 1842, Alderman Library Collection; sketch of Tucker by Broadus Mitchell, *Dictionary of American Biography*, 19: 28-30; Malcolm Lester, "George Tucker: His Early Life and Public Service, 1775-1825" (M. A. thesis, University of Virginia, 1946), *passim*; Gates (ed.), *Men of Mark*, 2: 86.

⁶ Abernethy, *University of Virginia*, 9-12; Bruce, *University of Virginia*, 2: 246-336.

⁷ Kasson, Keelona near Charlottesville, to his brother Charles, Feb. 4, 1843, Alderman Library Collection.

⁸ Bruce, *University of Virginia*, 2: 70.

[9] Mary Rawlings, *Albemarle of Other Days* (Charlottesville, Va., 1925), 109-140, and *Ante-Bellum Albemarle* (Charlottesville, Va., 1935), *passim*; Edgar Woods, *Albemarle County in Virginia* (Charlottesville, 1901), *passim*; Alexander Brown, *The Cabells and Their Kin* (Richmond, 1939), 479-80; A. B. Coles, *The Coles Family of Virginia* (New York, 1931), 641ff.

[10] Kasson, Keelona near Charlottesville, to his sister Maria, Nov. 22, 1842, Alderman Library Collection; Albemarle County Records, Deed Books, Vols. 28, 29, 31, 38, 42, 44.

[11] Kasson, Keelona, to his brother Charles, Dec. 27, 1842, Feb. 4, 1843, Alderman Library Collection; A. R. Burr, *Weir Mitchell* . . . (New York, 1929), 33, 161, 227-30; Earnest Earnest, S. *Weir Mitchell* . . . (Philadelphia, 1950), 11, 65-8; Weir Mitchell to Kasson, Dec. 25, 1895, *Wead Collection.*

[12] Kasson to his brother Charles, Oct. 21, 1842, Feb. 4, 1843, Alderman Library Collection; Rawlings, *Albemarle of Other Days*, 133-6.

[13] Kasson to his brother Charles, Nov. 22, Dec. 27, 1842; Feb. 4, June 12, 1843, Alderman Library Collection.

[14] *Ibid.* See also letter for Oct. 21, 1842.

[15] *Ibid.*, Dec. 27, 1842, Feb. 4, 1843.

[16] Maria H. Kasson, Mt. Holyoke, to her mother and sister, Apr. 13, May 2, 1843, in *Smith College Women's Collection.*

[17] Kasson's own biographical sketch (typed manuscript) in *Kasson Papers*; Des Moines *Iowa State Weekly Register*, Aug. 27, 1862.

[18] Charles Dickens, *American Notes* . . . (London, 1842), 78-9; George F. Hoar, *Autobiography of Seventy Years* (2 vols., New York, 1903), 1:160-68; J. McM. Shafter, Secy. of State of Vermont, "To Whom It May Concern," Jan. 19, 1844, *Charles Aldrich Collection* (Iowa State Dept. of Hist. and Archives, Des Moines), Vol. 2.

[19] Sketch of Washburn by Zechariah Chafee, Jr., *Dictionary of American Biography*, 19: 499; Hoar, *Autobiography*, 1: 160-68; *The Western Life-Boat: A Monthly Magazine of Biography, History and Geography*, Vol. 14 (Des Moines, 1872); Kasson, Worcester, to his brother Charles, Jan. 30, 1844, *Wead Collection.*

[20] Kasson, Worcester, to his brother Charles, Apr. 19, 1844, *Wead Collection.*

[21] *Ibid.*, May 31, 1844.

[22] W. G. Bean, "Party Transformation in Massachusetts . . . 1848-1860" (Ph.D. thesis, Harvard, 1934), 8ff.

[23] Charles Northend, *Elihu Burritt* . . . (New York, 1879), 13-33.

[24] Kasson, Worcester, to his brother Charles, May 31, 1844, *Wead Collection.*

[25] *Western Life-Boat*, Vol. 14 (1872); Sioux City *Journal*, June 9, 1907; Kasson, New Bedford, to his brother Charles, Sept. 25, 1844, *Wead Collection.* For a more detailed treatment of this phase of Kasson's life, see Edward Younger, "John A. Kasson: Early Contrasting Environments," *Annals of Iowa* (third series), 31:241-62 (April, 1952).

CHAPTER IV — LAW AND POLITICS IN NEW BEDFORD

[1] Herman Melville, *Moby Dick* (Modern Library ed., 1926), 31-3, 59, 457; Samuel E. Morison, *The Maritime History of Massachusetts, 1783-1860* (Boston, 1921), 314-26; G. L. Prentiss, *The Life of Elizabeth Prentiss* (2 vols., New York, 1898), 1:95-6, and *Memoir of S. S. Prentiss* (2 vols., New York, 1883), 2:531-2.

² Z. W. Pease, *History of New Bedford* (3 vols., New York, 1918), 1:37ff; L. B. Ellis, *History of New Bedford* . . . (Syracuse, 1892), 418ff; "New Bedford in 1845," *National Magazine*, Sept., 1845, pp. 328-43; Kasson to Z. W. Pease, June, 1907, *Wead Collection*.

³ Kasson to brother Charles, Sept. 25, 1844, and to mother, Dec. 19, 1845, *Wead Collection*; Kasson's Pocket Memorandum, Autumn, 1844, *Kasson Papers*, File 11; New Bedford *Standard Times*, Jan. 2, 1944.

⁴ Kasson to his mother, Dec. 19, 1845, *Wead Collection*.

⁵ Kasson to sister Mary, May 1, 1846, *ibid.*

⁶ Nancy (Blackman) Kasson, Burlington, to her daughter Mary, quoting extensively from John's letters, undated but probably in 1846, *ibid.*

⁷ *Aldrich Collection*: Thomas Barstow to Kasson, Dec. 2, 1849, Vol. 2; Longfellow to Kasson, March 28, 1849, Vol. 1; Mrs. Pierce Butler to Kasson, June 8, 1849, Vol. 1; Park Benjamin to Kasson, Sept. 7, 1849, Vol. 2. *Kasson Papers*, File 6: James C. Briggs, Clerk Trinitarian Church, to Kasson, Jan. 20, 1908. *Wead Collection*: G. L. Prentiss to Kasson, Oct. 15, 1897; Chas. Sumner to Kasson, Feb. 25, 1849. New Bedford *Mercury*, July 4, Oct. 24, Nov. 3, 9, 1846; Feb. 9, March 9, June 26, 1848; Ellis, *New Bedford*, 29, 293-4, 303.

⁸ Kasson to his family, Oct. 13, 1845, and to sister Mary, June 29, 1847, *Wead Collection*; U. V. M. *Alumni Records*, Charles Kasson Wead; Kasson, *Genealogy*, 47.

⁹ W. Lyman, Washington, to Chas. D. Kasson, March 10, 1845; June 1, 16, 1846; and T. B. Ransom, Norwich University, to C. D. Kasson, March 16, 1846, *Wead Collection*; Chas. D. Kasson to James K. Polk (confidential), Jan. 5, 1845, *James K. Polk Papers* (Library of Congress).

¹⁰ D. H. Hurd, *History of Bristol County, Massachusetts* (Philadelphia, 1883), 10; New Bedford *Standard Times*, Dec. 26, 1943; C. C. Eliot, *William Greenleaf Eliot* . . . (New York, 1904), xix.

¹¹ Kasson to sister Mary, May 1, 1846, *Wead Collection*.

¹² Kasson to sister Mary, June 29, 1847, *ibid.*; Ellis, *New Bedford*, 293-4; New Bedford *Mercury*, March 9, July 31, 1848; C. T. Congdon, *Reminiscences of a Journalist* (Boston, 1880), 75.

¹³ Kasson to brother Charles, Jan. 29, 1848; Feb. 18, 1849, *Wead Collection*.

¹⁴ John A. Kasson, "Law Reform — Practice," *The Monthly Law Reporter* (Boston), 12:61-81 (June, 1849); Sumner to Kasson, July 12, 1849, *Aldrich Collection*, Vol. 1; E. L. Pierce, *Memoirs and Letters of Charles Sumner* (4 vols., Boston, 1877-93), 3:15, 38-43; *The Works of Charles Sumner* (15 vols., Boston, 1875-95), 2:185, 206, 393-7.

¹⁵ Kasson to brother Charles, May 31, 1844, *Wead Collection*.

¹⁶ W. Lyman to C. D. Kasson, June 1, 16, 1846, *ibid.*

¹⁷ Bernard DeVoto, *The Year of Decision: 1846* (Boston, 1943), 5-29; T. A. Bailey, *Diplomatic History of the American People* (New York, 1950), 262-79.

¹⁸ Howard Robinson, *The British Post Office* . . . (Princeton, 1948), 394-8.

¹⁹ Allan Nevins, *Ordeal of the Union* (2 vols., New York, 1947), 1:3-26; Arthur M. Schlesinger, Jr., *Age of Jackson* (Boston, 1945), 450-64.

²⁰ Kasson to brother Charles, Jan. 29, 1848, *Wead Collection*; Ludlum, *Social Ferment in Vermont*, 189-93; Chittenden, *Reminiscences*, 4-8; Chittenden's Manuscript Diary (Wilbur Library, University of Vermont).

[21] Kasson to Lewis Cass, Sept. 14, 1847, *Aldrich Collection*, Vol. 2; Nevins, *Ordeal of the Union*, 1:190-202; Bean, "Party Transformation in Massachusetts . . . 1848-1860," 25.

[22] Kasson to Z. W. Pease, June, 1907, *Wead Collection*.

[23] Ludlum, *Social Ferment in Vermont*, 189-93; Chittenden, *Reminiscences*, 4-8; Chittenden's Manuscript Diary; Burlington *Free Press and Times*, Jan. 10, 1900.

[24] Schlesinger, *Age of Jackson*, 463-5; Nevins, *Ordeal of the Union*, 1:202-206; Chittenden, *Reminiscences*, 11-17.

[25] Pierce, *Charles Sumner*, 3:165-6; Hoar, *Autobiography*, 1:146-53; *Free Soilers of 1848-1852; Reunion at Boston* . . . (Cambridge, 1888); New Bedford *Daily Mercury*, June 30, 1848.

[26] New Bedford *Daily Mercury*, July 27, 31, Aug. 4, 1848.

[27] Kasson to his mother, Aug. 27, 1848, *Wead Collection*; J. P. Wood (ed.), *One Hundred Years Ago, Writings* . . . (New York, 1947), 11.

[28] John Hubbell, "The National Free Soil Convention of '48," *Buffalo Historical Society Publications*, 4:147-62 (1896).

[29] Kasson to his mother, Aug. 27, 1848, *Wead Collection*.

[30] *Idem*; Kasson to Hampton Moore, Feb. 14, 1906, *ibid.*; Nevins, *Ordeal of the Union*, 2:206-211; Pierce, *Sumner*, 3:171-3.

[31] Carl Sandburg, *Abraham Lincoln: The Prairie Years* (2 vols., New York, 1926), 1:399.

[32] New Bedford *Morning Mercury*, Sept. 7, 9, 1848; Stephen Pitter, North Dartmouth, to Kasson, Oct. 12, 1848, *Aldrich Collection*, Vol. 1.

[33] Kasson's own biographical sketch, manuscript, in *Kasson Papers*.

[34] Kasson to his mother, Dec. 19, 1845, and to sister Mary, June 29, 1847, *Wead Collection*.

[35] Kasson to brother Charles, Jan. 29, 1848, *ibid.*

[36] *Ibid.*, Feb. 18, 1849.

[37] *Idem.*

[38] Morison, *Maritime History of Massachusetts*, 331-3.

[39] Kasson to brother Charles, Feb. 18, 1849, *Wead Collection*.

[40] Kasson to Z. W. Pease, June, 1907, *ibid.*

[41] Kasson's own biographical sketch, manuscript, *Kasson Papers*; Sioux City *Journal*, June 9, 1907.

[42] Eliot, *W. G. Eliot*, 52-8.

[43] Thomas Barstow, committee chairman, to Kasson, Dec. 2, 1849, *Aldrich Collection*, Vol. 2.

[44] Washington *National Intelligencer*, May 3, 4, 1850.

CHAPTER V — BECOMING WESTERNIZED IN ST. LOUIS

[1] Kasson to his brother Charles, June 13, 1851, *Wead Collection*.

[2] John Hogan, "Thoughts about the City of St. Louis, 1854," *Glimpses of the Past*, 3:151-76 (October-December, 1936).

³ Some of the more useful works on the St. Louis background are: L. C. Hunter, *Steamboats on the Western Waters* . . . (Cambridge, 1949); W. W. Belcher, *Economic Rivalry Between St. Louis and Chicago, 1850-1880* (New York, 1947); Nevins, *Ordeal of the Union*, Vol. 2; Floyd C. Shoemaker, *Missouri and Missourians* (5 vols., Chicago, 1943), Vol. I; C. G. Rosenberg, *Jenny Lind in America* (New York, 1851); J. Thomas Scharf, *History of Saint Louis City and County* . . . (2 vols., Philadelphia, 1883). In *Missouri Historical Review*: R. H. Luthin, "Organizing the Republican Party in the 'Border-Slave' Regions: Edward Bates's Presidential Candidacy in 1860," 38:138-61 (January, 1944): Helen D. Williams, "Social Life in St. Louis from 1840 to 1860," 31:10-24 (October, 1936); Laura Langehennig, "The Steamboat, a Playground for St. Louis in the Fifties," 40:205-214 (January, 1946); Russell M. Nolen, "The Labor Movement in St. Louis Prior to the Civil War," 34:18-37 (October, 1939); William O. Lynch, "The Influence of Population Movements on Missouri Before 1861," 16:506-516 (July, 1922). In *Glimpses of the Past*: "St. Louis in Patches," 6:14-30 (January-March, 1939); Thomas L. Rodgers, "Recollections of St. Louis — 1857-1860," 9:111-21 (October-December, 1942).

⁴ Kasson to brother Charles, Dec. 28, 1851, *Wead Collection*; Kasson's own biographical sketch, *Kasson Papers*; *National Cyclopedia of American Biography*, 8:33.

⁵ Lucy L. Tasker, "The *Missouri Democrat* and the Civil War," *Missouri Historical Review*, 31:402-419 (July, 1937).

⁶ On Brown, the Blairs, and Kasson's relationship with them, see sketch of Brown by P. O. Ray, *Dictionary of American Biography*, 3:105-107; Daniel M. Grissom, "Personal Recollections . . . Frank P. Blair," *Missouri Historical Review*, 20:397-8 (April, 1926); W. E. Smith, *The Francis Preston Blair Family in Politics* (2 vols., New York, 1933), 1:101-292; Kasson's biographical sketch, *Kasson Papers*; Kasson's speech at the Opera House, Des Moines, Oct. 3, 1874, in an unidentified newspaper supplement, *Wead Collection*; St. Louis Directories: Green's, 1851; Morrison's, 1852; and Montague's, 1854-1855.

⁷ F. A. McNeil, "Lincoln's Attorney General: Edward Bates" (Ph.D. dissertation, University of Iowa, 1930), 22, 34-5, 129, 132.

⁸ Sketch of Kasson in *Western Life-Boat* (1872).

⁹ Kasson to Washburne, June 5, 1850, and Sept. 18, 1854, *Elihu B. Washburne Papers* (Library of Congress); Thomas J. McCormack (ed.), *Memoirs of Gustave Koerner, 1809-1896* . . . (2 vols., Cedar Rapids, 1909), 1:591-5.

¹⁰ *Western Life-Boat* (1872); Scharf, *Saint Louis*, 1:614-17.

¹¹ Kasson to his brother Charles, Dec. 13, 28, 1851, *Wead Collection*.

¹² Belcher, *Rivalry Between St. Louis and Chicago*, 78.

¹³ Kasson to brother Charles, Dec. 28, 1851, *Wead Collection*; Crockett, *Vermont*, 4:13-19.

¹⁴ St. Louis *Intelligencer*, Dec. 3, 5, 11, 17, 20, 1851; Kasson to brother Charles, Dec. 28, 1851, *Wead Collection*.

¹⁵ McCormack (ed.), *Memoirs of Gustave Koerner*, 1:610-13.

¹⁶ Kasson's speech in St. Louis *Missouri Republican*, March 13, 1852, and typed copy in *Wead Collection*; Scharf, *Saint Louis*, 2:1832; M. E. Curti, " 'Young America,' " *American Historical Review*, 32:34-55 (October, 1926); John W. Oliver, "Louis Kossuth's Appeal to the Middle West — 1852," *Mississippi Valley Historical Review*, 14:481-95 (March, 1928); Nevins, *Ordeal of the Union*, 1:547-9.

¹⁷ St. Louis *Intelligencer*, June 3, 28, 1850.

[18] C. H. McClure, *Opposition in Missouri to Thomas Hart Benton* (Nashville, 1927), *passim*; P. O. Ray, "The Retirement of Thomas H. Benton from the Senate and Its Significance," *Missouri Historical Review*, 2: 1-14, 97-111 (October, 1907; January, 1908); Smith, *Blair Family*, 1: 291ff; Benjamin C. Merkel, "The Slavery Issue and the Political Decline of Thomas Hart Benton, 1846-1856," *Missouri Historical Review*, 38: 388-407 (July, 1944).

[19] Kasson to his brother Charles, June 13, 1851, *Wead Collection*.

[20] Roy F. Nichols, *Disruption of American Democracy* (New York, 1948), 20-40.

[21] Before Pierce's nomination, the Blairs and Benton had vainly groomed good-natured and tractable General William O. Butler of Kentucky as the Democratic standard-bearer. Kasson observed that the "supposed favor" of Free Soilers "depressed" Butler's "interests with old Hunky." Kasson to brother Charles, Dec. 28, 1851, *Wead Collection*; Smith, *Blair Family*, 1: 272-4.

[22] R. R. Russel, *Improvement of Communication with the Pacific Coast as an Issue in American Politics, 1783-1864* (Cedar Rapids, 1948), 43-50; P. Orman Ray, *The Repeal of the Missouri Compromise: Its Origin and Authorship* (Cleveland, 1909), 72-6.

[23] *Proceedings of the Southern and Western Commercial Convention* . . . 1853 (Memphis, 1854), 15-19; Russel, *Communication with Pacific Coast*, 86-109, 130-49.

[24] *Proceedings . . . of the Convention*, 15.

[25] Herbert Wender, *Southern Commercial Conventions, 1837-1859* (Baltimore, 1930), and Glyndon G. Van Deusen, *Ante-Bellum Southern Commercial Conventions* (Durham, N. C., 1926).

[26] Ray, *Repeal of Missouri Compromise*, 102ff.

[27] *Ibid.*, 173, 260-61; P. O. Ray to Kasson, Aug. 2, 13, 1904, *Kasson Papers*; Merkel, "Slavery Issue and . . . Thomas Hart Benton," 388-407.

[28] P. Orman Ray, "The Genesis of the Kansas-Nebraska Act," *Report*, American Historical Association, 1: 261ff (1914); for a convenient and convincing analysis of Douglas' motives, see Nevins, *Ordeal of the Union*, 2: 105ff.

[29] Nevins, *Ordeal of the Union*, 2: 107-135, 307-322; Smith, *Blair Family*, 1: 299ff; in *Missouri Historical Review*: Walter H. Ryle, "Slavery and Party Realignment in Missouri in the State Election of 1856," 39: 320-32 (April, 1945); and Luthin, "Organizing the Republican Party in the 'Border-Slave' Regions . . . ," 138-61.

[30] S. W. Swisher, *History of the Church of the Messiah* [W. G. Eliot's church] (St. Louis, 1934), 25; George W. Smith, "New England Business Interests in Missouri During the Civil War," *Missouri Historical Review*, 41: 1-18 (October, 1946); McNeil, "Edward Bates," 151; Lloyd Lewis, *Captain Sam Grant* (Boston, 1950), 333-58.

[31] Des Moines *Iowa State Register*, Nov. 4, 9, 1864. Copy of deed of manumission from St. Louis Circuit Court, dated Dec. 8, 1855.

[32] Kasson to mother and sister Mary, May 4, 1851, *Wead Collection*.

[33] Letter dated Sept. 10, in middle 1850's, *ibid.*

[34] Caroline Kasson to John's mother, March 2, 1852 [?], *ibid.*

[35] Letter of Sept. 10, middle 1850's, *ibid.*

[36] Caroline Kasson to John's mother, March 2, 1852 [?], *ibid.*

[37] *Idem.*

[38] Burlington *Free Press*, July 10, 1853; Eliot, *W. G. Eliot*, xix.

[39] Kasson, probably to sister Mary, undated, but sometime in the 1850's; for John's earlier aid to Chester, see Kasson, New Bedford, to his sister Mary, June 29, 1847, *Wead Collection*.

[40] Kasson to sister Mary, middle 1850's, *Wead Collection*.

[41] Kasson's own biographical sketch, *Kasson Papers*; Sioux City *Journal*, June 9, 1907.

[42] Smith, *Blair Family*, 1: 331ff; Nevins, *Ordeal of the Union*, 2: 460ff.

[43] Kasson, New Bedford, to Frank P. Blair, Jr., Aug. 6, 1856, *Frank P. Blair Papers* (Library of Congress).

[44] Kasson's biographical sketch, *Kasson Papers*.

[45] In *Kasson Papers*.

[46] Kasson to Blair, Aug. 6, 1856, *Blair Papers*.

[47] Sioux City *Journal*, June 9, 1907.

CHAPTER VI — WINNING REPUBLICAN SPURS IN IOWA

[1] John J. Halloran, "Pioneer Bench and Bar," *Annals of Iowa* (third series), 25: 43-58 (July, 1943); and "Men of a Frontier Town," *ibid.*, 28: 248 (January, 1946). H. C. Evans, "At Washington," Dubuque *Herald*, Nov. 24, 1925, and "Iowa's '57 Variety," Iowa Magazine Section, Oskaloosa *Times-Globe*, March 27, 1924; C. C. Cole in Des Moines *Register and Leader*, April 9, 1911; Edward Younger, "The Rise of John A. Kasson in Iowa Politics," *Iowa Journal of History*, 50: 289-314 (October, 1952).

[2] F. I. Herriott in *Annals of Iowa* (third series): "Whence Came the Pioneers of Iowa?" 7: 367-79, 446-65 (April, July, 1906); and "Iowa and the First Nomination of Abraham Lincoln," 8: 195-202, 444-66 (October, 1907, July, 1908). Henry C. Hubbart, " 'Pro-Southern' Influences in the Free West, 1840-1865," *Mississippi Valley Historical Review*, 20: 45-62 (June, 1933); D. S. Sparks, "The Republican Party in Iowa, 1848-1860" (Ph.D. thesis, University of Chicago, 1951), 59-109, 178. In *Iowa Journal of History and Politics*: Cardinal Goodwin, "The American Occupation of Iowa, 1833 to 1860," 17: 83-102 (January, 1919); William J. Petersen, "Population Advance to the Upper Mississippi Valley, 1830-1860," 32: 312-53 (October, 1934). Dan E. Clark, "The Westward Movement in the Upper Mississippi Valley During the Fifties," *Proceedings*, Mississippi Valley Historical Association, 7: 212-19 (1913-1914).

[3] William Salter, *The Life of James W. Grimes . . .* (New York, 1876); sketch of Grimes by B. F. Shambaugh, *Dictionary of American Biography*, 7: 631-2; Sparks, "Republican Party," 42-72.

[4] On the origin and early history of the Republican party in Iowa: B. F. Gue, *History of Iowa . . .* (4 vols., New York, 1903), 1: 224ff; six articles in *Iowa Journal of History and Politics*: Louis Pelzer, "The Origin and Organization of the Republican Party in Iowa," 4: 487-525 (October, 1906); and "The History and Principles of the Democratic Party of Iowa, 1846-1857," 6: 163-246 (April, 1908); and "The History of Political Parties in Iowa from 1857 to 1860," 7: 179-229 (April, 1909); John W. Gannaway, "The Development of Party Organization in Iowa," 1: 491-524 (October, 1903); Charles Roll, "Political Trends in Iowa History," 26: 499-519 (October, 1928); Dan E. Clark, "The History of Liquor Legislation in Iowa, 1846-1861," 6: 55-87 (January, 1908). See also F. I. Herriott, "James W. Grimes versus the Southrons," *Annals of Iowa* (third series), 15: 323-57, 403-432 (July, October, 1926); Sparks, "Republican Party," 72-150. Leland Sage, in his biog-

raphy of William B. Allison, soon to be published by the State Historical Society of Iowa, has the most recent and discerning summary. (Hereafter referred to as Sage, "Allison.")

[5] Johnson Brigham, *James Harlan* (Iowa City, 1913); sketch by E. D. Ross, *Dictionary of American Biography*, 8: 268-9.

[6] James W. Grimes to C. C. Carpenter, Nov. 30, 1857, "Letters of James W. Grimes," *Annals of Iowa* (third series), 22: 489 (October, 1940). Sage, "Allison."

[7] Dan E. Clark, *Samuel Jordan Kirkwood* (Iowa City, 1917).

[8] New York *Tribune Almanac* (1858), 2: 62; Gue, *History of Iowa*, 1: 351-5; Carl H. Erbe, "Constitutional Provisions for the Suffrage in Iowa," *Iowa Journal of History and Politics*, 22: 163-216 (April, 1924); Sparks, "Republican Party," 154ff.

[9] "Grimes Letters," 477, 481; Herriott, "First Nomination of Lincoln," 202-203; Pelzer, "Political Parties in Iowa," 179-229.

[10] Kasson's own biographical sketch, *Kasson Papers*. "Kasson's Word Pictures," Des Moines *Daily Capitol*, Magazine Section, World's Fair Edition (1904); Kenneth E. Colton, "Stagecoach Travel in Iowa," *Annals of Iowa* (third series), 22: 175-200 (January, 1940).

[11] Kasson's speech before Old Settlers Reunion, unidentified clipping in *Kasson Papers*; Josiah B. Grinnell, *Men and Events of Forty Years* . . . (Boston, 1891), 120-27; R. H. Patchin, "An Old Fashioned Man from Iowa," Sioux City *Journal*, June 9, 1907.

[12] Other works used on the Des Moines background: Howard J. Nelson, "The Economic Development of Des Moines," *Iowa Journal of History*, 48: 193-220 (July, 1950); J. M. Dixon, *Centennial History of Polk County, Iowa* (Des Moines, 1876), 138-9; Frank M. Mills, "Early Commercial Traveling in Iowa," *Annals of Iowa* (third series), 11: 328-35 (April, 1914); Tacitus Hussey, "History of Steamboating on the Des Moines from 1837 to 1862," *ibid.*, 4: 323-82 (April, 1900).

[13] Des Moines *Iowa State Journal*, Jan. 9, 1858; Des Moines *Iowa Citizen*, Jan. 14, 16, 1858; Johnson Brigham, *History of Des Moines and Polk County, Iowa* . . . (2 vols., Chicago, 1911), 1: 162.

[14] Des Moines *Iowa Citizen*, Feb. 25, 1858; Des Moines *Iowa State Journal*, Feb. 24, 1858; Brigham, *Des Moines*, 1: 162.

[15] Cole, *Iowa Reports*, Vols. VI-VIII and Withrow, *ibid.*, Vols. IX-XII. Associated with Kasson in law cases from time to time were J. E. Jewett, a brother-in-law and later law partner of Samuel J. Kirkwood; D. O. Finch, life-long Democrat and later political adversary of Kasson; Thomas Withrow, young Republican lawyer and politician from Virginia and Wisconsin; and C. C. Cole, another prominent Democrat. Other Des Moines colleagues were P. M. Casady, C. C. Nourse, and M. M. Crocker.

[16] Des Moines *Campaign State Journal*, Aug. 18, 1859, quoting the Sioux City *Register*; for more details on this case, in which Judge Test of Indiana was Kasson's opponent, see F. I. Herriott, "Judge Orlando C. Howe . . . ," *Annals of Iowa* (third series), 19: 172, 308 (January, April, 1934).

[17] Withrow, *Reports*, X, 594-603. The deceased member of the state supreme court was Judge L. D. Stockton.

[18] Kasson's own biographical sketch, *Kasson Papers*. Among the young law students was George W. Bassett of Fort Dodge, later a state senator, *Annals of Iowa* (third series), 2: 405 (April, 1895). The child adoption law was drafted for Ira Cook of Des Moines, *ibid.*, 4: 550-51 (October, 1900). On the courthouse case and the M. & M. railroad meeting, see Des Moines *Iowa Statesman*, Aug. 12, Dec. 2, 1858.

[19] Mills, "Commercial Traveling," 328-35, and "F. M. Mills Writes of Kasson," *Annals of Iowa* (third series), 12: 610-13 (April, 1921).

[20] Grimes to Kirkwood, March 11, 1858, "Grimes Letters," 494; Herriott, "First Nomination of Lincoln," 213; Ivan L. Pollock, "State Finances in Iowa During the Civil War," *Iowa Journal of History and Politics*, 16: 53-107 (January, 1918).

[21] Jacob A. Swisher, "The Capitols at Des Moines," *Iowa Journal of History and Politics*, 39: 52-87 (January, 1941); L. F. Andrews, *Pioneers of Polk County, Iowa* . . . (2 vols., Des Moines, 1908), 1: 217-26.

[22] F. I. Herriott, "The Republican State Convention, Des Moines, January 18, 1860," *Annals of Iowa* (third series), 9: 433 (July-October, 1910); and "The Preservation of Iowa's Public Documents," *ibid.*, 5: 293-306 (January, 1902); Thomas Teakle, "The Defalcation of Superintendent James D. Eads," *Iowa Journal of History and Politics*, 12: 205-244 (April, 1914).

[23] Des Moines *Iowa State Journal*, Nov. 11, Dec. 26, 1857; Des Moines *Iowa Citizen*, Feb. 10, 1858.

[24] Grimes to Kirkwood, Dec. 15, 1857, "Grimes Letters," 491; Pelzer, "Political Parties in Iowa," 179-229; Gue, *History of Iowa*, 1: 362-9.

[25] Grimes to Kirkwood, March 6, 11, 1858, "Grimes Letters," 493-4.

[26] Gue, *History of Iowa*, 4: 292.

[27] Pelzer, "Political Parties in Iowa," 179-229.

[28] Grimes to Kirkwood, Apr. 28, 1859, "Grimes Letters," 497-8. Compare Iowa election results, 1856 and 1858, in New York *Tribune Almanac*, Vol. 2; Herriott, "First Nomination of Lincoln," 202-207, 213-15, 452-61; Sparks, "Republican Party," 193-7.

[29] Herriott, "First Nomination of Lincoln," *passim*. William E. Dodd, "The Fight for the Northwest, 1860," *American Historical Review*, 16: 781-4 (July, 1911).

[30] Sells to Dodge, Feb. 28, 1859, *Dodge Papers*.

[31] Clark, *Kirkwood*, 128.

[32] Hamilton to Kirkwood, Apr. 12, 1859, *Samuel J. Kirkwood Papers* (Iowa State Dept. of History and Archives, Des Moines). A Democratic editor described Lowe as a "mild, pleasant looking old gentleman" with "a whining and stammering delivery . . . not forcible in word or gesture." Des Moines *Iowa State Journal*, Oct. 3, 1857. George G. Wright remembered him as a "most credulous man." "Chief Justice Caleb Baldwin," *Annals of Iowa* (third series), 1: 211 (October, 1893). Charles Aldrich thought he combined "gentle graciousness with high dignity" — putting everyone at ease in his presence — "a reliable and abiding friend." "Governor Kirkwood's First Nomination," *ibid.*, 4: 547 (October, 1900).

[33] John W. Thompson to C. C. Carpenter, Feb. 26, 1859, *Cyrus Clay Carpenter Papers* (State Historical Society of Iowa, Iowa City).

[34] Clark, *Kirkwood*, 2-122; Sage, "Allison."

[35] "Grimes Letters," 476-501, esp. 478, 482, 484; Platt Smith to Charles Aldrich, May 21, 1859, *Kirkwood Papers*.

[36] Kasson to Kirkwood, confidential, May 1, 1859, *Kirkwood Papers*; Sparks, "Republican Party," 209.

[37] Kasson to Kirkwood, May 17, 1859, *Kirkwood Papers*; also printed in Edgar R.

Harlan, " 'Private Archives' of Governor Kirkwood," *Annals of Iowa* (third series), 11: 454-9 (July, 1914).

[38] *Ibid*. Rusch to Kirkwood, Apr. 20, 1859, *Kirkwood Papers*. Herriott, "First Nomination of Lincoln," 208. See also Elijah Sells, May [n. d.], and W. H. Hamilton, May 17, 1859, to Kirkwood, *Kirkwood Papers*; Clark, *Kirkwood*, 124-6.

[39] Sells to Kirkwood, July 22, 1859, *Kirkwood Papers*.

[40] Kasson to Kirkwood, July 18, 20, 1859, *ibid*.

[41] Kasson to Kirkwood, July 23, Aug. 15, 23, 24, 1859; Hoxie to Kirkwood, July 31, 1859, *ibid*.

[42] Louis Pelzer, *Augustus Caesar Dodge* (Iowa City, 1908), 247; Clark, *Kirkwood*, 127; Sage, "Allison." Though Kasson had invited Abraham Lincoln to speak during the campaign, the Railsplitter's surprise appearance at Council Bluffs, on his return from Kansas, was motivated by personal affairs, not politics. R. T. Lincoln to F. I. Herriott, Feb. 1, 1909; *R. T. Lincoln Papers* (Library of Congress); Jacob A. Swisher, "Lincoln in Iowa," *Iowa Journal of History and Politics*, 43: 69-84 (January, 1945). For their budding newspapers, editors did not hesitate to solicit funds from the candidates and committee. Frank Palmer of the Dubuque *Times* sought a "loan of $400" from Kirkwood, and W. H. Bigelow of Sioux City requested $40 of Kasson and Rice and $65 of Kirkwood and his friends for a "Republican Press." William Vandever, July 5, 1859, and W. H. Bigelow, Oct. 24, 1859, to Kirkwood, *Kirkwood Papers*. Kasson had invited Lincoln to speak at the Oskaloosa State Fair, Sept. 28, but Lincoln declined, presumably because he was then preparing for an Ohio speaking tour. Kasson to Lincoln, Sept. 13, 1859, *Frank I. Herriott Papers* (Iowa State Dept. of History and Archives, Des Moines).

[43] Grimes to Kirkwood, Aug. 2, and to C. C. Carpenter, July 15, 1859, in "Grimes Letters," 503, 557.

[44] Clark, *Kirkwood*, 123-43; Pelzer, *Dodge*, 235-48; Herriott, "First Nomination of Lincoln," 213-17.

[45] Grimes to Kirkwood, June 25, July 14, 29, 1859, "Grimes Letters," 501, 502, 556-7; Kasson to Kirkwood, July 18, Oct. 12, 1859, *Kirkwood Papers*; New York *Tribune Almanac*, 2: 62 (1858), 2: 60 (1859). Four of the counties specifically mentioned by Kasson — Appanoose, Davis, Decatur, and Wayne — and many other southern, western, and eastern counties, fell to Dodge.

[46] F. I. Herriott, "Germans in the Gubernatorial Campaign of Iowa in 1859," German-American Historical Society of Illinois, *Year-Book* (1915), sections 23-9.

[47] Clark, *Kirkwood*, 127; Stevens and Grimes to Kirkwood, July 9, Aug. 30, 1859, *Kirkwood Papers*; Cole on Kasson, Des Moines *Register and Leader*, Apr. 9, 1911.

[48] Herriott, "First Nomination of Lincoln," 208-210; Edwards, July 15, and Teesdale, June 7, July 9, 1859, to Kirkwood, *Kirkwood Papers*.

[49] Savery, July 3, and Sells, July 22, 1859, to Kirkwood, *Kirkwood Papers*.

[50] Patchin, "Old Fashioned Man," Sioux City *Journal*, June 9, 1907.

[51] Savery to Kirkwood, Nov. 26, 1859, *Kirkwood Papers*.

[52] New York *Tribune Almanac*, 2: 60 (1859); Herriott, "First Nomination of Lincoln," 217.

CHAPTER VII — IN THE FIRST LINCOLN CAMPAIGN

[1] Madison Kuhn, "Economic Issues and the Rise of the Republican Party in the Northwest" (Ph.D. dissertation, University of Chicago, 1940), ii, 133-49.

[2] *Ibid.*, 156-63; T. E. Strevey, "Joseph Medill and the Chicago *Tribune* During the Civil War" (Ph.D. dissertation, University of Chicago, 1950), 57-62.

[3] Des Moines *Iowa State Register* (daily), Jan. 9, 10, 1860. This was the first issue of the daily *Register*. For the preceding week, during the editor's illness, Kasson had given "timely aid to the editorial column."

[4] For the details of this convention, I have relied heavily upon F. I. Herriott, "Republican State Convention," and "Republican Presidential Preliminaries in Iowa, 1859-1860," *Annals of Iowa* (third series), 9: 241-83, 401-446 (January, July-October, 1910). Unless otherwise cited, this section is based on these articles.

[5] Kirkwood followed his remarks on Brown's raid with a sincere plea for a Pacific railroad bill and homestead act. As a risky sop to the radicals, he then, on a technicality, barred the extradition to Virginia of two of Brown's raiders. Sparks, "Republican Party in Iowa," 232-5.

[6] Dan E. Clark, *History of Senatorial Elections in Iowa* (Iowa City, 1912), 126-7; Herriott, "Republican Preliminaries of 1860," 251-64.

[7] Grimes to Kirkwood, Dec. 26, 1859, "Grimes Letters," 562-3.

[8] Henry O'Connor, radical member of the central committee, to Harlan, Jan. 15, 1860, quoted in Herriott, "Republican Preliminaries of 1860," 282. Though O'Connor disliked the "availability element," he would still support the party nominee.

[9] Fitz Henry Warren in Springfield (Mass.) *Republican*, Feb. 4, 1860, quoted in Herriott, "Republican State Convention," 438.

[10] Des Moines *Iowa State Register*, Jan. 20, 1860. (This paper will hereafter be referred to as Des Moines *Register*.)

[11] Herriott, "Republican State Convention," 422-3.

[12] William Richards, quoted in Herriott, *ibid.*, 423; and in "First Nomination of Lincoln," 105.

[13] Fitz Henry Warren, quoted in Herriott, "Republican State Convention," 438.

[14] Hawkins Taylor, after a hog-buying trip through southern Iowa, wrote: "I tell you there is [*sic*] no *Seward or Chase men there*. . . . We have men that can be elected *but we can not elect anybody*." Pennsylvania had to "be carried and the question is who can do it." Quoted in Herriott, "Republican Preliminaries in Iowa," 283.

[15] Kasson to Herriott, Aug. 28, 1906, *Herriott Papers*; Herriott, "First Nomination of Lincoln," 213-15; Luthin, "Organizing the Republican Party in the 'Border-Slave Regions,'" 138-61.

[16] Des Moines *Register*, March 29, 1860.

[17] Kasson to Kirkwood, Apr. 17, 1860, *Kirkwood Papers*.

[18] Charles Aldrich to Kasson, Oct. 6, 1906, *Kasson Papers*, File 6.

[19] All the literature used on the Chicago convention and the Lincoln campaign is too extensive to cite. Among the most valuable works for background are William E. Baringer, *Lincoln's Rise to Power* (Boston, 1937); Reinhard H. Luthin, *The First Lincoln Campaign*

(Cambridge, Mass., 1944); E. D. Fite, *The Presidential Campaign of 1860* (New York, 1911); P. Orman Ray, *The Convention That Nominated Lincoln* . . . (Chicago, 1916); Allan Nevins, *The Emergence of Lincoln* (2 vols., New York, 1950), Vol. 2; Jeter A. Isely, *Horace Greeley and the Republican Party* (Princeton, 1947); Frederic Bancroft, *The Life of William H. Seward* (2 vols., New York, 1900), Vol. 1; and the memoirs and biographies of a number of other participants.

[20] Charles W. Johnson, *Proceedings of the First Three Republican National Conventions* (Minneapolis, 1893), 83-105. Greeley, elbowed from the New York delegation by the Seward faction, turned up at the convention as a proxy from Oregon.

[21] Kasson to Hampton Moore, Feb. 14, 1906, *Wead Collection*; Kasson to Henry H. Smith, quoted in Henry H. Smith, *All Republican National Conventions* . . . (Washington, 1896), 18-20; Kasson to Smith, Apr. 22, 1896, and to B. F. Gue, Apr. 20, 1901, *Kasson Papers*; *Sioux City Journal*, June 9, 1907; May 19, 1910.

[22] Contemporaries and historians have disagreed on who served on the subcommittee. Close investigation shows that it was originally to consist of five men, but that eight actually participated. These were, in addition to Kasson and Greeley, Austin Blair of Michigan, William Jessup of Pennsylvania, Gustave Koerner of Illinois, William T. Otto of Indiana, Carl Schurz of Wisconsin, and F. P. Tracy of California. Thus, all the doubtful states, the Far West, the Lakes region, and the foreign-born were represented. Johnson, *Republican Conventions*, 105, 134; McCormack (ed.), *Memoirs of Gustave Koerner*, 2: 86-90; Schurz to Kasson, Aug. 21, 1904, *Wead Collection*.

[23] Thomas M. Pitkin, "The Tariff and the Early Republican Party" (Ph.D. dissertation, Western Reserve University, 1935), 130-92; George F. Hunsberger, "Development of Tariff Policy in the Republican Party" (Ph.D. dissertation, University of Virginia, 1934), 44-56; Thomas M. Pitkin, "Western Republicans and the Tariff in 1860," *Mississippi Valley Historical Review*, 27: 401-420 (December, 1940); Reinhard H. Luthin, "Abraham Lincoln and the Tariff," *American Historical Review*, 49: 609-629 (July, 1944).

[24] *Sioux City Journal*, June 9, 1907; the New Jersey delegate was Thomas H. Dudley. W. J. Potts, "Biographical sketch of . . . Dudley," *Proceedings*, American Philosophical Society, 34: 102-134 (January, 1895).

[25] Henry H. Smith to Kasson, Apr. 22, 1896, *Kasson Papers*, File 3; Kasson to Smith in Smith, *All Republican Conventions*, 18-20; *Sioux City Journal*, June 9, 1907. The tariff plank carefully avoided the word "protection" : ". . . while providing revenues for the support of the general government by duties upon imports, sound policy requires such an adjustment of these imposts as to encourage the development of the industrial interests of the whole country." Johnson, *Republican National Conventions*, 132. A rough draft of the platform, mostly in Kasson's handwriting, appears in Kasson materials from Simon Casady Collection, *Kasson Papers*, File 14.

[26] Eli Thayer, another proxy delegate from Oregon, also took credit for this plank, saying that he urged Greeley to abandon his stand on the Wilmot Proviso. Franklin P. Rice, "Life of Eli Thayer" (unpublished manuscript in Harvard University Library), 3-7. McCormack (ed.), *Memoirs of Gustave Koerner*, 2: 86-90, says Greeley did not want a direct repudiation of Douglas' popular sovereignty doctrine.

[27] Kasson to Smith in Smith, *All Republican Conventions*, 18-20; Nevins, *Emergence of Lincoln*, 2: 253. Schurz considered the "Dutch Planks" as "moderate but unequivocal." Frederic Bancroft and Archibald Dunning (eds.), *Reminiscences of Carl Schurz* (3 vols., New York, 1900), 2: 179-82.

[28] Johnson, *Republican National Conventions*, 133.

[29] Murat Halstead, *Caucuses of 1860* . . . (Columbus, 1860), 135.

30 Thayer was one of the "spotters." Rice, "Life of Eli Thayer," 3-7.

31 According to the convention proceedings, Frank Blair of Missouri and George W. Curtis of New York took the lead in supporting Giddings. But there comes to this writer an interesting letter plausibly showing that Judge Milton Sutliff, a delegate from Ohio, personally placated Giddings and persuaded him to return to his place in the convention hall. O. D. Wheeler, Council Bluffs, Iowa, to writer, Apr. 17, 1947.

32 Johnson, *Republican National Conventions,* 142.

33 New York *Tribune,* May 22, 1860; Henry H. Smith to Kasson, Apr. 22, 1896, *Kasson Papers,* File 3.

34 The platform, as officially adopted, is printed in Johnson, *Republican National Conventions,* 131-3.

35 *Ibid.,* 149-55; Herriott, "First Nomination of Lincoln," 186-288.

36 Nevins, *Emergence of Lincoln,* 2: 240, 257-8; Luthin, *First Lincoln Campaign,* 220-27; J. R. Perkins, *Trails, Rails and War: The Life of General G. M. Dodge* (Indianapolis, 1929), 54-67. (Hereafter referred to as Perkins, *Dodge.*)

37 Sparks, "Republican Party in Iowa," 252.

38 C. Baldwin to G. M. Dodge, Apr. 19, June 27, 1860, *Dodge Papers;* E. Sells, June 12, 1860, and H. M. Hoxie, Sept. 26, 1860, to Kirkwood, *Kirkwood Papers;* sketch of C. C. Nourse in *Annals of Iowa* (third series), 12: 632 (April, 1921).

39 Sparks, "Republican Party in Iowa," 250-58.

40 Luella M. Wright, "Henry A. and George D. Perkins in the Campaign of 1860," *Iowa Journal of History and Politics,* 42: 162-91 (April, 1944); Charles Fairman, *Mr. Justice Miller and the Supreme Court, 1862-1890* (Cambridge, Mass., 1939), 33-5; Charles J. Fulton, "Jefferson County at the Beginning of the Civil War," *Annals of Iowa* (third series), 11: 81-95 (July-October, 1913). In the middle of this campaign, Kasson's mother, Nancy (Blackman) Kasson, died.

41 Hoxie to Dodge, Oct. 3, 10, 26, Nov. 16, 25, 1860, and Farnam to Dodge, Oct. 11, 1860, *Dodge Papers.*

42 Curtis' margin of victory in '56 had been 1,817, and in '58, 600. New York *Tribune Almanac,* 57, 62.

43 For basic details on Dodge, but not for interpretations, I have relied on Perkins, *Dodge,* 1-67. Only by reading the *Dodge Papers,* and between the lines of Perkins' book, does one obtain a realistic picture of Dodge.

44 Sparks, "Republican Party in Iowa," 179-90; Dwight L. Agnew, "Iowa's First Railroad," *Iowa Journal of History,* 48: 1-26 (January, 1950).

45 See above, p. 83.

46 Wright, "Baldwin," 209-214; Baldwin to Dodge, March 13, 1861, *Dodge Papers.*

47 James S. ("Ret") Clarkson in Des Moines *Register,* Oct. 19, 1879; Elijah Sells to Kirkwood, March 22, 1861, *Kirkwood Papers;* Kasson to Salmon P. Chase, *Salmon P. Chase Papers* (Library of Congress); "Men of a Frontier Town," *Annals of Iowa* (third series), 27: 247-8 (January, 1946); *Harper's Weekly,* 30: 784 (December, 1886).

48 Perkins, *Dodge,* 57; see above, p. 82; Hoxie, Oct. 3, 1860, and Kasson, Jan. 3, 1861, to Dodge, *Dodge Papers.*

49 Reed to Dodge, Nov. 12, 1860, *Dodge Papers.* For some of the letters herewith cited,

I am indebted to Leland L. Sage. In his manuscript biography of William B. Allison, Professor Sage quotes these letters more fully than I am here doing.

[50] Hoxie to Dodge, Nov. 16, 1860, *Dodge Papers.*

[51] Reed to Dodge, Nov. 19, 1860, *ibid.*

[52] Hoxie to Dodge, Nov. 25, 1860, *ibid.*

[53] Baldwin to Dodge, Dec. 9, 1860, *ibid.*

[54] Reed to Dodge, Dec. 14, 1860, *ibid.*

[55] Kasson to Dodge, Jan. 3, 1861, *ibid.*

[56] Hoxie to Dodge, Jan. 5, 1861, *ibid.*

[57] Kasson to Dodge, Jan. 10, 1860, *ibid.*

[58] Kenneth M. Stampp, *And the War Came* (Baton Rouge, 1950), 89-96; S. H. M. Byers, *Iowa in War Times* (Des Moines, 1888), 36-7.

[59] Kasson to W. P. Clarke, Jan. 25, 1861, *William Penn Clarke Papers* (Iowa State Dept. of History and Archives, Des Moines), Vol. 2.

[60] Kasson to Dodge, Feb. 8, 1861, *Dodge Papers.*

[61] Dodge to his wife, Feb. 17, 1861, *ibid.*

CHAPTER VIII — POLITICS AND PATRONAGE UNDER LINCOLN

[1] Letters of S. R. Curtis to his wife, Jan. 19 to March 4, 1861, in Kenneth E. Colton (ed.), " 'The Irrepressible Conflict of 1861,' The Letters of Samuel Ryan Curtis," *Annals of Iowa* (third series), 24: 19-37 (July, 1942). Other Curtis letters appear in the same volume, pp. 105-167 (October, 1942), 298-315 (April, 1943). Sage, "Allison."

[2] Sage, "Allison"; Perkins, *Dodge,* 63-6. See above, pp. 1-3. Hoxie frequently used the expression quoted in the first sentence of this paragraph.

[3] Dodge Personal Biography, 1: 33-5, *Dodge Papers.*

[4] Dodge to his wife, March 8, 1861, *ibid.* See above, p. 4. Since Lincoln, for the most part, permitted his Cabinet heads to choose their chief aides, it is likely that Blair also had something to do with it. See Harry J. Carman and Reinhard H. Luthin, *Lincoln and the Patronage* (New York, 1943), 54.

[5] Elijah Sells considered Hoxie's appointment as an "outrage," maintaining that Hoxie went to Washington to support Stewart Goodrell for the same position. Sells characterized Hoxie in most unflattering terms. Sells to Kirkwood, March 22, 1861, *Kirkwood Papers.* (See above, p. 113). Aspiring to the governorship, Sells hoped to boost Kirkwood to the Senate, and he warned Kirkwood that the "Hoxie clique" was "out to thwart" Kirkwood as future Senator. *Ibid.,* Apr. 4, 1861.

[6] Dodge to his wife, March 1, 4, 12, 17, and to Kasson, Apr. 2, 1861, in Dodge Personal Biography, 2: 2-13, 190-91, *Dodge Papers.* Perkins, *Dodge,* 63-7.

[7] Stampp, *And the War Came,* 125, 275-86.

[8] Allison to Dodge, Apr. 2, 1861, *Dodge Papers,* cited in Sage, "Allison."

[9] Hoxie wanted to know whether Platt Smith was "perfectly reliable"; Watt J. Smith also wanted "to enter into some speculation." Hoxie to Dodge, Apr. 12, 1861, *Dodge Papers.*

[10] Apr. 16, 1861, *ibid.*

[11] Allison to Dodge, Apr. 19, 1861, *ibid.*

[12] Hoxie to Dodge, Apr. 20, 1861, *ibid.*

[13] Baldwin regretted that Dodge had not sent Judge Wright passes also; court had adjourned and the railroad "Bond cases" had not yet been decided. Baldwin to Dodge, Apr. 16, 1861, *ibid.* Hoxie had been conferring with Judge Lowe but feared he would "make a decision against us." Hoxie to Dodge, Apr. 9, 12, 1861, *ibid.*

[14] See also Reed to Dodge, May 20, 1861, *ibid.*

[15] Perkins, *Dodge*, 68.

[16] Kasson to Dodge, June 7, 1861, *Dodge Papers.*

[17] Perkins, *Dodge*, 10, 16, 68.

[18] See "Gen. G. M. Dodge's Historical Address," *Annals of Iowa* (third series), 4: 580 (January, 1901), for Dodge's own version.

[19] Mrs. Kasson ("Miriam") in Des Moines *Register*, July 3, 1861; Dodge to his wife, June 11, 1861, in Dodge Personal Biography, 2: 26-8, *Dodge Papers.*

[20] Dodge Personal Biography, June 18, 1861, 2: 28-9, *Dodge Papers*; Perkins, *Dodge*, 69-73. Rankin was in Washington to procure equipment for troops commanded by S. R. Curtis, who was soon to resign from Congress. Colton (ed.), "Curtis Letters," 53-4.

[21] Kasson, July 23, 1861, and Grimes, July 27, 1861, to Dodge, *Dodge Papers*; Byers, *Iowa in War Times*, 605.

[22] Margaret Leech, *Reveille in Washington, 1860-1865* (New York, 1941), 5-6, map of Washington, 1861, inside covers.

[23] This characterization is based upon more than fifty "Miriam" letters appearing in the weekly Des Moines *Register* (1861-1865); and upon personal letters and references later to be cited. For the quoted material, see the Des Moines *Register* for March 5, 19, 26, June 11, Dec. 24, 1862; Feb. 18, 25, 1863.

[24] Kasson interview, Sioux City *Journal*, June 9, 1907.

[25] "Miriam" and "Charley" letters, Des Moines *Register*, July 31, 1861; Kasson's autobiographical sketch, *Kasson Papers*; Leech, *Reveille in Washington*, 94-105. Senator Grimes, a Centreville spectator of the horrible details, barely escaped capture. Salter, *Grimes*, 146.

[26] "Miriam" and "Linkensale" (L. D. Ingersoll) letters, the latter quoting Washington *Republican*, in Des Moines *Register*, Jan. 15, 1862.

[27] From *Dodge Papers*: Kasson to Dodge, Aug. 8, 14, Nov. 13, Dec. 7, 17, 1861; Palmer to Dodge, Nov. 6, 1861; M. P. Small to Dodge, Nov. 23, 1861; Baldwin to Dodge, Dec. 1, 1861; Withrow to Dodge, Nov. 2, 1861. Grimes was probably holding back for another reason, also. A little later he told the Senate there were too many brigadiers — 180 volunteers, and only eight from the regular army. No person, said he, should be commissioned brigadier without demonstrated competence in command or gallantry in action. Carman and Luthin, *Lincoln and the Patronage*, 157-8.

[28] Kasson to Dodge, June 3, 5, 1862; Dodge's Diary, Apr. 30, 1862, *Dodge Papers*; Dodge had also been wounded at Rolla, "by a shot from his pocket pistol." Colton (ed.), "Curtis Letters," 309. For Kasson's efforts in behalf of Dodge's friends and relatives, see Kasson to Dodge, June 21, 1861; Nathan Dodge to Dodge, Apr. 30, 1862; and Dodge Diary, May 7, 1862, *Dodge Papers.*

[29] Cara E. Kasson to Dodge, Apr. 9, 1862, *ibid.*

[30] Kasson to Whittier, March 18, 1862; Whittier and Longfellow to Kasson, March 22, 25, 1862; S. T. Pickard to Charles Aldrich, Apr. 24, 1893, *Aldrich Collection*, Vol. 1.

[31] The staff consisted of Blair, three assistant postmaster generals, a chief clerk, four messengers, and several nightwatchmen and laborers. Kasson's annual salary was $3,000. Smith, *Blair Family*, 2:100-101; Des Moines *Register*, May 16, 1861; Hoxie to Dodge, late 1861, *Dodge Papers*.

[32] Smith, *Blair Family*, 2:90-111; Robinson, *The British Post Office*, 378-81.

[33] Smith, *Blair Family*, 2:90-111; Dorothy G. Fowler, *The Cabinet Politician: Postmasters General, 1829-1909* (New York, 1943), 103-110.

[34] Smith, *Blair Family*, 2:90-111.

[35] Kasson's autobiographical sketch, *Kasson Papers*; Kasson to S. P. Chase, and to Asst. Sec. of Treas., July 6, Sept. 7, 1861, Postmaster General's Letter Book (National Archives).

[36] Cleveland *Herald*; Mead (Pa.) *Journal*; "J. B." in Erie (Pa.) *Gazette*, cited respectively in Des Moines *Register*, Oct. 15, June 25, Aug. 7, Feb. 26, 1862; Riddle, *Recollections*, 21-2.

[37] Draft of letter for Young Citizens for American Institute of Civics, *Kasson Papers*, 1890.

[38] Carman and Luthin, *Lincoln and the Patronage*, 70-71, 112, 118, 129, 331ff; Fowler, *Cabinet Politician*, 103-110; Montgomery Blair to S. S. Blair, Apr. 26, 1861, Postmaster General's Letter Book.

[39] Dubuque *Herald*, Nov. 24, 1895.

[40] Iowans Frank Hatton and James S. Clarkson, as First Assistant Postmaster Generals, were later to perform the functions of "cabinet politicians." Fowler, *Cabinet Politician*, 166, 212.

[41] Kirkwood resented Kasson's interference in Washington in organizing and officering independent regiments, thus depriving Kirkwood of certain appointments. John E. Briggs, "The Enlistment of Iowa Troops During the Civil War," *Iowa Journal of History and Politics*, 15:323-92 (July, 1917). The scope of Kasson's activities as head of the appointment office is indicated in the private papers of Dodge, Kasson, Kirkwood, Aldrich, W. P. Clarke, E. B. Washburne, S. P. Chase, John G. Nicolay (Library of Congress), Robert T. Lincoln, A. H. Markland (Library of Congress), and Andrew Johnson (Library of Congress); in the Interior Department, Applications (National Archives); in Theodore C. Pease and James G. Randall (eds.), *Diary of Oliver Hickman Browning* (Collections of the Illinois State Historical Library, Vol. XX, Springfield, 1925); in the Des Moines *Register*, May 22, June 5, July 31, Aug. 7, Sept. 11, Dec. 25, 1861; in Carman and Luthin, *Lincoln and the Patronage, passim*. In all probability the towns of Kasson, located in Iowa, Indiana, and Minnesota, may have been named by postmasters appointed by the First Assistant Postmaster General.

[42] "Miriam," Des Moines *Register*, March 26, June 11, July 16, 1862.

[43] James G. Randall, *The Civil War and Reconstruction* (Boston, 1937), 594-9.

[44] Paul S. Peirce, "Congressional Districting in Iowa," *Iowa Journal of History and Politics*, 1:334-54 (July, 1903); Sage, "Allison." James W. Grimes confided: "My political friends . . . in their greediness to secure all the six representatives in Congress . . . managed to make them doubtful districts. . . ." Grimes to G. V. Fox, Sept. 15, 1862, in R. M. Thompson and Richard Wainwright, *Confidential Correspondence of Gustavus Vasa Fox* (2 vols., New York, 1919), 2:377.

[45] Balloting of the convention, meeting at Winterset: informal ballot, Kasson 34, Benton 33, E. H. Sears 31, M. L. McPherson 17, Lawrence 1; first formal ballot, Kasson 50, Benton 33, Sears 31, McPherson 9; second formal ballot, Kasson 56, Benton 31, Sears 27, McPherson 9, Lawrence 1; third formal ballot, Kasson 61, Benton 31, Sears 27, McPherson 1, Lawrence 1. Kasson then received unanimous vote. Des Moines *Register*, July 23, 1862; Johnson Brigham, *Iowa, Its History and Its Foremost Citizens* (3 vols., Chicago, 1915), 1: 364.

[46] Biographical sketch of Benton in Gue, *History of Iowa*, 4: 18-19; Baldwin to Dodge, Sept. 24, 1862, *Dodge Papers*.

[47] "H" in Des Moines *Register*, Aug. 13, 1862.

[48] *R. T. Lincoln Collection.*

[49] Leland L. Sage, "William B. Allison's First Term in Congress, 1863-1865," *Iowa Journal of History*, 50: 330 (October, 1952); Gue, *History of Iowa*, 2: 71-8; Sage, "Allison." See also Wood Gray, *The Hidden Civil War, The Story of the Copperheads* (New York, 1942), 83-104. Kasson, writing of Mahony's arrest, observed that there had been recently "many wonderful conversions" of the "loyal Democracy" to the Republican party. Kasson to Dodge, Aug. 25, 1862, *Dodge Papers*.

[50] Obituary of Finch in *Annals of Iowa* (third series), 7: 639 (January, 1907); M. M. Crocker to Dodge, Aug. 23, 1862, Dodge Personal Biography, 1: 69, *Dodge Papers*.

[51] Kasson to Kirkwood [Aug. 17], 1862, in undated file, *Kirkwood Papers*; Des Moines *Register*, Aug. 20, Oct. 1, 1862.

[52] Grimes to Fox, Sept. 15, Oct. 6, 24, 1862, in Thompson and Wainwright, *Fox Correspondence*, 2: 377, 399, 499.

[53] For Kasson's main arguments, see text of his keynote speech in Des Moines *Register*, Oct. 1, 1862; also see same newspaper for Aug. 2, 23, Sept. 10, 17, 24, Oct. 8, 15, 1862. For evidence that Kasson "used up" Finch on the stump, see Baldwin, Dodge's brother, and mother, to Dodge, Sept. 8, 9, 24, 1862, Dodge Personal Biography, 2: 770, 773, 813, *Dodge Papers*. Baldwin constantly urged a more radical stand against the South. Baldwin to Dodge, July 25, Sept. 24, 1862, Dodge Personal Biography, 2: 719, *ibid.*

[54] Kasson, Aug. 25; Hoxie, Sept. 18; Williamson, Sept. 20, 1862, to Dodge, *Dodge Papers*. Williamson said Capt. Taylor could carry his company for Republicans, but Ankeny, popular with his men, was a Democrat, *ibid.*, Oct. 9. Lieut. W. Tracy promised Dodge to give the entire vote of Co. C to Kasson, *ibid.*, Sept. 30, 1862.

[55] Des Moines *Register*, Oct. 1, 8, 1862.

[56] *Ibid.*, Nov. 19, 1862; New York *Tribune Almanac* (1863), 61; Sage, "Allison."

[57] Nathan Dodge, Oct. 11, and Baldwin, Oct. 12, 1862, to Dodge, Dodge Personal Biography, 2: 857-9, *Dodge Papers*. Baldwin had previously written that Kirkwood had not wanted Kasson nominated, that Kirkwood believed Kasson to be "an arm of the Grimes Dynasty." Baldwin criticized some of Kirkwood's military appointees as being "drunkards and cowards." Baldwin to Dodge, Sept. 24, 1862, *ibid.*, 2: 813-19.

[58] Kasson to Dodge, Oct. 16, 1862, *ibid.*, 2: 869.

[59] Salary as special agent, $1,600 per annum and $2.00 per diem for travel and subsistence. Postmaster General Journal (Orderbook), National Archives. The Democratic Des Moines *Times*, referring to Kasson's resignation *after* election, quipped: "Unlike General Pope he was able to appreciate a 'strong position' and had an eye to 'lines of retreat.' Whatever he may do or not do in Congress, we regard him the better General of the two." Oct.

29, 1862. Lincoln's selection of Governor Alexander W. Randall of Wisconsin to succeed Kasson was a disappointment to Iowa Republicans, who had settled upon Elijah Sells, disgruntled gubernatorial candidate, for the position; the recent state convention had "unanimously" agreed upon Sells. Des Moines *Register*, Oct. 29, 1862.

60 Baldwin, Oct. 21; Hoxie, Oct. 24; J. M. Tuttle, Nov. 22, 1862, Dodge Personal Biography, 2: 876, 882, 917, *Dodge Papers*.

61 Kasson to Dodge, Nov. 12, 1862, *ibid.*, 2: 911.

62 Extract, Dodge to Kasson, Nov. 22, 1862, *R. T. Lincoln Papers*; Kasson to Dodge, Dec. 9, 1862, Dodge Personal Biography, 2: 958, *Dodge Papers*.

63 Kasson to Dodge, Feb. 3, 1863, Dodge Personal Biography, 3: 90, *Dodge Papers*.

64 Kasson, Feb. 17, March 2, and Crocker, March 19, 1863, to Dodge, *ibid.*, 3: 55, 129, 148.

65 Postmaster General Journal (Orderbook), March 6, 1863, National Archives; Des Moines *Register*, Jan. 7, 1863; Kasson to his sister, March 6, 1863, *Wead Collection*.

66 "Linkensale" in Des Moines *Register*, Apr. 22, 1863; Kasson to Chase, March 31, 1863, *Chase Papers*.

CHAPTER IX — A VENTURE IN INTERNATIONAL COOPERATION

1 L. S. Woolf, *International Government* (New York, 1916), 118-19; Hugo Weithase, *Geschichte des Weltpostvereins* (Strassburg, 1895), 17; Hubert Krains, *L'Union Postale universelle; sa fondation et son developpment* (Berne, 1908), 9-23; R. W. Hatswell, "The Foundation and Development of the Universal Postal Union," *St. Martin's-Le-Grand*, 11: 150 (January, 1901); John F. Sly, "The Genesis of the Universal Postal Union," in *International Conciliation* (Worcester, 1927), No. 233, pp. 397ff.

2 *Annual Report of the Postmaster General, 1862*, 26-7, 121, 159; *ibid.*, 1895, 448-9; "A Hundred Years of Postal Statistics," *Union Postale*, 14: 145-9 (September 1, 1889).

3 Kasson's role in the Paris Postal Conference has been worked out in detail and more fully documented in Edward Younger, "John Adam Kasson and the Beginnings of the Universal Postal Union, 1863, 1867," *Annals of Iowa* (third series), 28: 3-35 (July, 1946). See also John E. Briggs, "Kasson and the First International Postal Conference," *Iowa Journal of History and Politics*, 19: 366-88 (July, 1921); Madison Davis, "Public Career of Montgomery Blair," *Records of the Columbia Historical Society*, 13: 132-7 (1910); R. A. McReynolds, *United States Postal Development: Summary and Interpretation* (Chicago, 1937), 19, 24, 55; Clyde Kelly, *United States Postal Policy* (New York, 1931), 19.

4 *Annual Report of the Postmaster General, 1862*, 165-8; U. S. Dept. of State Archives, *Miscellaneous Letters*, Blair to Seward, Sept. 3, 1863; *Instructions. France*, Seward to Dayton, Jan. 5, 1863; *Despatches. France*, Dayton to Seward, May 1, 8, 1863. U. S. P. O. Archives, *Journal of the Postmaster General*, Nov. 1, 1862, March 6, Apr. 1, 1863.

5 S. A. Wallace and F. E. Gillespie (eds.), *The Journal of Benjamin Moran, 1857-1865* (2 vols., Chicago, 1949), 2: 1150.

6 Kasson to Blair, Apr. 24, 1863, *Blair Papers*; Margaret Clapp, *Forgotten First Citizen: John Bigelow* (Boston, 1947), 191-4, 209-210.

7 Kasson to Blair, Apr. 26, 1863, *Blair Papers*; Wallace and Gillespie (eds.), *Journal of Benjamin Moran*, 2: 1432 and *passim*.

[8] Kasson to Blair, May 28, 1863, *Blair Papers.* Kasson's "Journal" here mentioned has not been located.

[9] Countries represented were: Austria, Belgium, Costa Rica, Denmark, the Hanseatic Cities, Spain, France, Great Britain, Italy, Holland, Portugal, Prussia, the Sandwich Islands, Switzerland, and the United States. Russia and Turkey approved of the meeting but were unable to send delegates at the time. Ecuador was represented by the American delegate. The foregoing account of conference proceedings is based upon "Proceedings of the Paris Postal Conference of 1863," in *Report of the Postmaster General, 1863,* Post Office Department Library, Washington, D. C. Another copy in French is deposited with the *Kasson Papers* at Des Moines.

[10] *Ibid.,* 110-24.

[11] *Ibid.,* 137.

[12] *Ibid.,* 163-4.

[13] State Department Archives, *Despatches. France,* Dayton to Drouyn de Lhuys, June 22, Sept. 10, 1863; *Report of Postmaster General, 1866,* 57-61.

[14] Wallace and Gillespie (eds.), *Journal of Benjamin Moran,* 2: 1185, 1195.

[15] S. E. Baldwin, "List of Memorable International Conferences, or Associations of Official Representatives of Governments, Exclusive of Those Mainly Concerned with the Results of a Particular War, 1826-1907," *American Journal of International Law,* Vol. 1 (July, 1907).

[16] Clark E. Persinger, "Internationalism in the '60's," *The Historical Outlook,* 20: 324-7 (November, 1929).

[17] Raoul Blayac, *Origine, evolution, et organization de L'Union Postale Universelle* (Montpellier, 1932), *passim;* Hans Buhler, *Der Weltpostverein . . .* (Berlin, 1930), *passim;* P. S. Reinsch, "International Unions and Their Administrations," *American Journal of International Law,* 1: 581 (July, 1907).

[18] "Report of Postmaster General, 1863," *House Ex. Doc. No. 1,* 38 Cong., 1 Sess., 5: 9.

[19] *Report of Postmaster General, 1894,* 38-41.

[20] Sioux City *Journal,* June 9, 1907.

CHAPTER X — A LINCOLN MODERATE IN CONGRESS

[1] From Corydon, Wayne County, correspondent in Des Moines *Register,* Oct. 14, 1863. Also see *Register* for Sept. 9, 16, Oct. 2, 14, 1863.

[2] *Ibid.,* Aug. 12, 1863; Tichenor to Dodge, Sept. 5, 11, 14, 1863, Dodge Personal Biography, 3: 538, 555, 584, *Dodge Papers;* Dillon to Kirkwood, Aug. 28, 1863, *Kirkwood Papers.*

[3] Des Moines *Register,* Oct. 14, 1863; Dodge's sister to Dodge, Sept. 18, 1863, *Dodge Papers.* She thought Mrs. Kasson the "finest lady I ever met. Do you wonder that Lt. Tichenor spoke in such exalted terms of her?"

[4] Kasson to Blair, Sept. 22, 1863, *Gist Blair Collection* (Library of Congress).

[5] Kasson to Dodge, Oct. 29 [?], 1863, Dodge Personal Biography, 3: 584, *Dodge Papers;* Gue, *History of Iowa,* 2; 96,

[6] Hoxie to Dodge, July 25, 1863; Cara Eliot Kasson to Dodge, July 28, 1863, Dodge Personal Biography, 3: 467-8, *Dodge Papers.*

[7] Kasson to Dodge, Aug. 26, 1863, *ibid.*, 3: 516. On the strength of Grant's backing Kasson "hoped for Dodge's success" but much would depend on Halleck.

[8] Perkins, *Dodge,* 121-3.

[9] Russel, *Communication with the Pacific Coast,* 294-308.

[10] *Ibid.*, 309-313; Jack T. Johnson, *Peter Anthony Dey* (Iowa City, 1939), 85-8; Perkins, *Dodge,* 123-6; Baldwin to Dodge, Oct. 21, 1862, Dodge Personal Biography, 2: 876, *Dodge Papers.*

[11] Kasson to Lincoln, Sept. 22, 1863, *R. T. Lincoln Collection*; Kasson to Blair, Sept. 22, 1863, *Gist Blair Collection.*

[12] Kasson to Dodge, Sept. 29, 1863, Dodge Personal Biography, 3: 570, *Dodge Papers.* Also see *ibid.*, 1: 120; Kasson (Sept. 13, 1863), Dodge's brother (Sept. 26, 1863), Dodge's sister (Sept. 27, 1863) to Dodge, *ibid.*, 3: 550, 563, 564.

[13] Kasson to Dodge, Oct. 29 [?], 1863, *ibid.*, 3: 584. In the meantime, Judge Baldwin had assured Dodge that he could control railroad matters in the Iowa legislature. Baldwin to Dodge, Oct. 8, 10, 1863, *ibid.*, 3: 573-4.

[14] Johnson, *Peter A. Dey,* 85-116; Russel, *Communication with the Pacific Coast,* 311. Many years later Kasson recorded that he had gone "to Washington to secure an order" from Lincoln fixing the initial point of the Union Pacific in the river between Council Bluffs and Omaha. Kasson's "Iowa of '46 and '04," Des Moines *Daily Capitol*, World's Fair Edition, Magazine Section, *Wead Collection.* This is plausible, for Kasson was in Washington a great part of 1863. But his call upon Lincoln cannot be confirmed. Nor can the more famous "before Vicksburg" trip by Dodge be confirmed. It is odd that there is no reference in Dodge's papers to his celebrated call upon Lincoln, described by Dodge himself. See F. I. Herriott, "Memories of the Chicago Convention of 1860," *Annals of Iowa* (third series), 12: 453 (October, 1920), and Perkins, *Dodge,* 127-32. Peter A. Dey and Durant also are reported to have pressed Lincoln to designate Council Bluffs, *idem.*, and Johnson, *Peter A. Dey,* 89.

[15] Kasson to Dodge, Dec. 6, 1863, *Dodge Papers.*

[16] "Miriam" in Des Moines *Register,* Dec. 23, 30, 1863; Jan. 13, Feb. 3, 1864.

[17] T. Harry Williams, *Lincoln and the Radicals* (Madison, Wisc., 1941), 293-6; Richard N. Current, *Old Thad Stevens: A Story of Ambition* (Madison, Wisc., 1942), 188-200; J. G. Randall, *Lincoln the President, Springfield to Gettysburg* (2 vols., New York, 1945), 2: 207-237; Des Moines *Register,* July 13, 1864.

[18] *Cong. Globe,* 38 Cong., 1 Sess. (1863-1864), 18, 39, 310, 552.

[19] *Ibid.*, 21, 39, 45, 112, 258, 519, 598-9, 738, 829, 895, 991, 1325, 1532, 2286, 2995.

[20] *Ibid.*, 21, 495, 659, 707, 738, 1836, 2265.

[21] *Ibid.*, 1733, 2743.

[22] *Ibid.*, 168-70, 1763, 2138, 2216; Current, *Old Thad Stevens,* 192.

[23] *Cong. Globe,* 38 Cong., 1 Sess., 2107-2108, and Appendix, 46-51.

[24] Leland Sage, "Iowa Politics and Politicians During the Era of Reconstruction," unpublished ms. read at Chicago meeting of Mississippi Valley Historical Association, April, 1952; Williams, *Lincoln and the Radicals,* 307, 316.

[25] Samuel Wilkeson, Washington correspondent of the New York *Tribune*, in Des Moines *Register,* July 13, 1864; Sage, "Allison." Also see Des Moines *Register,* Dec. 8, 1863; Apr. 13, 29, July 20, 1864. Kasson's photograph appears among the twelve "Eminent Upholders in Congress of the War for the Union" in Horace Greeley, *The American Conflict* . . . (2 vols., Hartford, 1866), 2: 256.

[26] *Cong. Globe,* 38 Cong., 1 Sess., 2292, 2297.

[27] Sage, "Allison." Hoxie (Jan. 30, Feb. 27, 1864), Wilson (Feb. 15, 1864), Tichenor (March 18, 1864) to Dodge, *Dodge Papers.*

[28] *Cong. Globe,* 38 Cong., 1 Sess., 1886-7.

[29] Johnson, *Peter A. Dey,* 121; Hoxie to Dodge, Apr. 5, 1864, *Dodge Papers.*

[30] *Cong. Globe,* 38 Cong., 1 Sess., 3050, 3051, 3226; *ibid.,* 40 Cong., 2 Sess. (1867-1868), 2135; Russel, *Communication with the Pacific Coast,* 309-322.

[31] For the quotes: Oglesby (March 15, 1864), Hoxie (Apr. 5, 1864), Kasson (June 4, 1864) to Dodge, *Dodge Papers.* On Dodge's promotion at this time, see also Kasson to Dodge, Dec. 9, 20, 26, 1863; Jan. 8, 29, Feb. 5, March 25, 1864, Dodge Personal Biography, 3: 770, 818, 836; 4: 18, 160, 209, 425; Hoxie (Feb. 21, March 24, 1864), and Colonel Elliot Rice (Dec. 27, 1863, Jan. 20, 1864) to Dodge, *ibid.,* 3: 846; 4: 272, 428, 742. Kasson also at this time checked on certain accounts Dodge had with the Ordnance Department.

[32] N. P. Dodge to Dodge, Feb. 14, 20, 1864, *Dodge Papers.* It will be remembered that Dodge's business firm had been heavily in debt in 1861 and that Dodge, as he entered the service, had written his mother that "pecuniarily" the war would ruin him. See above, pp. 112, 122.

[33] Carman and Luthin, *Lincoln and the Patronage,* 228-41; Fowler, *Cabinet Politician,* 119-21; *Cong. Globe,* 38 Cong., 1 Sess., 738.

[34] Hoxie had planned his trip East for December, 1863, but Kasson, evidently with coming political events in mind, told him to hold up until February. Hoxie to Dodge, Jan. 10, 1864, Dodge Personal Biography, 4: 170, *Dodge Papers.* See also Des Moines *Register,* Feb. 2, 14, 1864.

[35] Des Moines *Register,* Feb. 23, 1864; Carman and Luthin, *Lincoln and the Patronage,* 239-60.

[36] Kasson to Lincoln, March 1, Apr. 26, 1864, *R. T. Lincoln Collection.* One of the officers Kasson wanted to appoint was "either governor, judge, secretary, or marshall" for the new Territory of Montana. The other was an assistant judge advocate "under the Bill establishing a Bureau of Military Justice." This position was evidently for George Tichenor who took credit for suggesting to Kasson and Grimes a bill providing additional judge advocates for divisions and corps. Tichenor to Dodge, March 18, 1864, Dodge Personal Biography, 4: 1527, *Dodge Papers.*

[37] Sage, "Iowa Politics and Politicians During Reconstruction"; "Linkensale" [L. D. Ingersoll] in Des Moines *Register,* June 8, 1864; Francis Brown, *Raymond of the Times* (New York, 1951), 249-51. See above, p. 113. In Washington, Iowa Delegate Peter Melendy conferred with Grimes, Hubbard, Allison, and Grinnell and then toured army hospitals with Secretary Chase. Luella M. Wright, *Peter Melendy, The Mind and the Soil* (Iowa City, 1943), 262.

[38] "Linkensale," in Des Moines *Register,* June 7, 1864. "Outside pressure against the Blairs was 'terrific.' " On Kasson's illness, see *Cong. Globe,* 38 Cong., 1 Sess., 2743; Des Moines *Register,* June 18, July 12, Aug. 2, 1864.

[39] "Linkensale" in Des Moines *Register*, June 30, 1864; Brown, *Raymond*, 252-5; Johnson, *Proceedings . . . Republican Conventions*, 225ff; Carman and Luthin, *Lincoln and the Patronage*, 260.

[40] Radicals had already nominated Fremont at Cleveland, May 31, 1864. Democrats were to nominate McClellan at Chicago, Aug. 30, 1864.

[41] Carman and Luthin, *Lincoln and the Patronage*, 286-7; Fowler, *Cabinet Politician*, 121-4; "Linkensale" in Des Moines *Register*, July 3, Sept. 9, 1864.

[42] Crocker to Dodge, June 24, 1864, in "Gen. G. M. Dodge's Historical Address," 590. General Crocker was suffering from tuberculosis. Due in part to Kasson's efforts, he was to be given a Pacific command for his health, but within a year he was dead from "bronchitis" — another casualty of the war. See also Bell to Kasson, June 9, 1864, *R. T. Lincoln Collection*; Hoxie to Dodge, June 28, 1864, Dodge Personal Biography, 4: 909, *Dodge Papers*.

[43] Des Moines *Register*, June 12, July 5, 6, 8, 9, 1864.

[44] Hoxie to Dodge, July 18, 1864, Dodge Personal Biography, 4: 994, *Dodge Papers*. Kasson pointed out that Williamson, "an old and influential Democrat," had changed his "relation" and that he had been chosen as delegate to Baltimore but had remained with Sherman's army at Atlanta. Williamson himself had been in Washington in December, 1863. Kasson to Lincoln, July 25, 1864, *R. T. Lincoln Collection*; Kasson to Dodge, Dec. 20, 1863, Dodge Personal Biography, 3: 818, *Dodge Papers*. Years later Kasson wrote that the pressure for Williamson had been so great that it was intimated that he (Kasson) would lose the soldiers' vote if he failed. "Heaven grant a speedy end" to such duties of Congressmen, he prayed. Allen Thorndike Rice, *Reminiscences of Abraham Lincoln by Distinguished Men of His Time* (New York, 1889), 380.

[45] Hoxie to Dodge, Aug. 12, 1864, Dodge Personal Biography, 4: 1345, *Dodge Papers*. Dodge had contributed $100 to the campaign fund. Des Moines *Register*, Aug. 3, 27, Sept. 3, 9, 14, 1864; Pegram to Dodge, Sept. 7, 1864, Dodge Personal Biography, 4: 1412, *Dodge Papers*. Behind the armies, Pegram, Dodge's former business associate, had been speculating in cotton. Perkins, *Dodge*, 97. Dodge to his brother, Sept. 5, 1864, Dodge Personal Biography, 4: 1413; Dodge Diary, Sept. 10, 1864, *Dodge Papers*.

[46] Perkins, *Dodge*, 150-52; Hoxie to Dodge, Sept. 6, 1864, *Dodge Papers*.

[47] John P. Davis, *The Union Pacific Railway* (Chicago, 1894), 163-4, 177; Nelson Trottman, *History of the Union Pacific* (New York, 1923), 25-44; Johnson, *Peter A. Dey*, 129.

[48] Des Moines *Register*, Sept. 2, Nov. 8, 1864.

[49] New York *Tribune Almanac* (1865), 62.

[50] Williams, *Lincoln and the Radicals*, 329-33.

[51] "Miriam" in Des Moines *Register*, Jan. 25, March 11, 1865.

[52] Williams, *Lincoln and the Radicals*, 350-52; Current, *Old Thad Stevens*, 206.

[53] "Miriam" in Des Moines *Register*, Feb. 15, 1865; *Cong. Globe*, 38 Cong., 2 Sess., 39, 189-93; J. K. Hosmer, *Outcome of the Civil War, 1863-1865* (New York, 1927), 221-2; "T. S. D." and "Mack" in Des Moines *Register*, Jan. 25, 1865.

[54] *Cong. Globe*, 38 Cong., 1 Sess., 1002.

[55] *Ibid.*, 26, 33, 67, 300, 303, 694.

[56] *Ibid.*, 257; Williams, *Lincoln and the Radicals*, 363-8. Previously, Wilkeson had written up Kasson favorably, though not flatteringly, in the New York *Tribune*. Des Moines *Register*, July 13, 1864.

57 Des Moines *Register*, Feb. 1, 1865.

58 *Cong. Globe*, 38 Cong., 1 Sess., 316-21; Rice, *Reminiscences of Lincoln*, 379-84; Alonzo Rothschild, *Lincoln, Master of Men* (Boston, 1906), 242-4; *Edwin M. Stanton Papers* (Library of Congress), Jan. 26, 1865; Rothschild to Kasson, March 8, 1901, *Kasson Papers*; Army chaplain, Alton, Ill., to Kasson (n. d.), *Aldrich Collection*, Vol. 2; Medill to Washburne, Apr. 12, 1864, *Washburne Papers*; Des Moines *Register*, Feb. 1, 1865.

59 Rice, *Reminiscences of Lincoln*, 383-4.

60 "T. S. D." in Des Moines *Register*, Jan. 25, 1865. Also see *Register* for July 9, 1864. Obituary sketch of Knox in *Annals of Iowa* (third series), 5: 400 (April, 1902); sketch of Todhunter in Gue, *History of Iowa*, 4:265.

61 Kasson to Dodge, Dec. 18, 1864, Dodge Personal Biography, 1: 302-303, *Dodge Papers*.

62 *Ibid.*, Apr. 4, July 10, 1862, 2: 518, 597; Dodge Diary, Apr. 30, May 7, 1862, 2: 995-6.

63 Perkins, *Dodge*, 152-5, 171.

64 Hoxie to Dodge, Dec. 8, 1864, Dodge Personal Biography, 5: 15, *Dodge Papers*.

65 Kasson to Dodge, Dec. 18, 1864, *ibid.*, 1: 302-303. Dodge "immediately formed the acquaintance" of Eliot and Yeatman.

66 Hoxie to Dodge, Dec. 8, 1864, *ibid.*, 5: 15. Unobtrusively behind the scenes, Eliot had fostered the Radical movement by opposing Lincoln's Missouri policies and commanders. Constantly in touch with Radical New England capitalists, he would be riding the crest of the Radical storm when it broke in full fury over Missouri. Smith, "New England Business Interests in Missouri During the Civil War," 18; McNeil, "Lincoln's Attorney General," 330; Howard K. Beale (ed.), *The Diary of Edward Bates, 1859-1866* (*Report*, American Historical Association, 1930, Vol. 4, Washington, D. C., 1933), 198; Kasson to Lincoln, Dec. 22, 1863, inclosing Eliot to Lincoln, Dec. 16, 1863, *R. T. Lincoln Collection*.

67 Kasson to Dodge, Jan. 6, 1865, Dodge Personal Biography, 5: 84, *Dodge Papers*.

68 Des Moines *Register*, Feb. 1, 1865.

69 "Quixote" in *ibid.*, March 8, 1865; Hoxie to Dodge, March 3, 1865, Dodge Personal Biography, 5: 269-70, *Dodge Papers*; Washington *Post*, May 19, 1910.

70 "Miriam" in Des Moines *Register*, March 15, 1865.

CHAPTER XI — JOHNSONIZED, SCANDALIZED, DEFEATED

1 Dodge Diary, Apr. 1, 1865, *Dodge Papers*; Rice, *Reminiscences*, 384-5; Des Moines *Register and Leader*, Nov. 12, 1904; J. S. Clarkson to Frank W. Palmer, Sept. 15, 1874, *James S. Clarkson Papers* (Library of Congress).

2 May 4, 1865, *Andrew Johnson Papers*.

3 Nathan Dodge to Dodge, March 17, 21, May 26, 1865; Tichenor to Dodge, Apr. 8, 1865, Dodge MSS., 5: 328, 384, 469, 809, *Dodge Papers*.

4 Rich, April 10, 1865, and Nourse, April 27, 1865, to Kirkwood, *Kirkwood Papers*.

5 Kasson to Dodge, May 4, 1865, Dodge MSS., 5: 437; Dodge Personal Biography, 2: 349, *Dodge Papers*. Kasson to Seward, June 8, 1865, *Aldrich Collection*, Vol. 1.

[6] George Fort Milton, *The Age of Hate: Andrew Johnson and the Radicals* (New York, 1930), 160ff; Randall, *Civil War and Reconstruction*, 694ff; Howard K. Beale, *The Critical Year: A Study of Andrew Johnson and Reconstruction* (New York, 1939), 47ff.

[7] Gue, *History of Iowa*, 3: 102; M. B. Hoxie to Dodge, June 16, 1865, Dodge Personal Biography, 2: 550-51, *Dodge Papers*.

[8] Des Moines *Register*, June 21, 24, July 12, 19, 26, Aug. 9, 1865; Kasson to Dodge, July 27, 1865, Dodge MSS., 5: 901, *Dodge Papers*.

[9] Des Moines *Register*, Aug. 18, 1865.

[10] Dodge to James S. Clarkson (1874), *Clarkson Papers* (Library of Congress). The historian, Annie Heloise Abel, in her *The American Indian Under Reconstruction* (Cleveland, 1925), 125, holds that Dodge was relentless and precipitate in his operations against the Indians.

[11] Dodge Personal Biography, 2: 390-418, and Dodge MSS., 5: 1007, 1031, *Dodge Papers*.

[12] Des Moines *Register*, Aug. 13, 16, 21, 30, Sept. 6, Oct. 4, 18, Nov. 8, 1865; Tichenor to Dodge, Aug. 24, 25, 26, 30, Sept. 23, 1865, *Dodge Papers*; Tichenor to Kirkwood, Aug. 29, Sept. 23, and other letters during the summer and autumn, 1865, *Kirkwood Papers*; Kasson to Johnson, Aug. 30, 1865, *Johnson Papers*.

[13] Oct. 21, 1865, *Kirkwood Papers*.

[14] Oct. 24, 1865, *ibid.*

[15] Des Moines *Register*, Nov. 22, 1865; Tichenor (Nov. 20), Kasson (Nov. 13), and Baldwin (Nov. 24), 1865, to Dodge, Dodge MSS., 5: 1275-6, 1305, 1314, *Dodge Papers*.

[16] Dodge Personal Biography, 2: 445, *Dodge Papers*; Tuttle to P. M. Casady, June 7, 1861, *P. M. Casady Papers* (Iowa State Dept. of History and Archives, Des Moines).

[17] Tichenor to C. C. Carpenter, May 10, 1865, *Carpenter Papers*. For this letter I am indebted to Dr. Mildred Throne.

[18] Tichenor, Nov. 13, 29, 1865, to Dodge; Nathan Dodge to Dodge, Dec. 1, 1865, Dodge MSS., 5: 1355, *Dodge Papers*.

[19] Des Moines *Register*, Dec. 13, 1865; Dodge Personal Biography, 2: 442-3, *Dodge Papers*.

[20] Current, *Old Thad Stevens*, 213-25; Beale, *Critical Year*, 227ff, makes the most thorough analysis of the connection between Radicalism and economic policy; Brown, *Raymond of the Times*, 281-6; *Cong. Globe*, 39 Cong., 1 Sess. (1865-1866), 6.

[21] Tichenor to Dodge, Dec. 5, 1865, Dodge MSS., 5: 1367, *Dodge Papers*.

[22] *Cong. Globe*, 39 Cong., 1 Sess., 21, 235, 325-7, 720-24, 725-6, 751, 838-9, 854, 855; Ruth Painter Randall, *Mary Lincoln: Biography of a Marriage* (Boston, 1953), 388.

[23] *Cong. Globe*, 39 Cong., 1 Sess., 33, 61-2, 507, 712-13, 920.

[24] *Ibid.*, 235-42, 310-11, 457-8, 688; Current, *Old Thad Stevens*, 231; Beale, *Bates Diary*, 535.

[25] *Cong. Globe*, 39 Cong., 1 Sess., 20, 31, 224, 607, 719, 848.

[26] *Ibid.*, 101-104.

[27] Des Moines *Register*, Dec. 20, 1865; Tichenor (Dec. 7, 1865), Kasson (Dec. 23,

1865, Jan. 12, 1866), Sherman (Jan. 16, 1866) to Dodge, and Dodge to Kasson, Jan. 4, 1866, Dodge MSS., 5: 1369, 1407, 1453, 1461-2, and Box 12, *Dodge Papers*; Leland L. Sage, "William B. Allison and Iowa Senatorial Politics, 1865-1870," *Iowa Journal of History*, 52: 114 (April, 1954).

[28] Tichenor (Dec. 6, 18, 21), Hoxie (Dec. 21), and Kasson (Dec. 23), 1865, to Dodge, Dodge MSS., 5: 1397-1407, *Dodge Papers*.

[29] Dodge MSS., 5: 1413, *ibid.*

[30] Dodge MSS., 1: 631; 5: 1439, *ibid.*

[31] Box 12, *ibid.*

[32] Clark, *Senatorial Elections in Iowa*, 249n, 286; Tichenor to Dodge, Jan. 14, 1866, *Dodge Papers*; Dodge to Kirkwood, Feb. 9, 1866, *Kirkwood Papers*.

[33] *Kirkwood Papers.*

[34] See Dubuque *Herald*, Feb. 19, 27, March 1, 9, 14, 1866, which ran excerpts on the case from numerous other newspapers; St. Louis *Missouri Democrat*, March 13, 28, 1866; Des Moines *Register* opened up on May 30, 1866, and ran a story from a Chariton, Iowa, correspondent, ostensibly a friend of Kasson's, who nevertheless connected him with the Nashville Convention; Beale, *Bates Diary*, 553.

[35] District Court, Warren County, February Term, Box 134. During the war, Orwig had moved from Pennsylvania to Des Moines, where he became Governor Stone's private secretary. He was soon to be sued for missing swamp land funds, in whose transfer to the state treasury Kasson had been instrumental the previous Congress. Des Moines *Register*, Feb. 22, 1865; May 30, 1866.

[36] To Kirkwood, March 5, 1866, *Kirkwood Papers*; Peter A. Dey, "Robert S. Finkbine and His Associates in the Erection of the Iowa Capitol," *Annals of Iowa* (third series), 5: 209-218 (October, 1901); Finkbine obituary notice, *ibid.*, 235-6; March 6, 1866, Dodge MSS., 5: 1727, *Dodge Papers*.

[37] Tichenor (March 10), Hoxie (March 2), Baldwin (March 16), Nathan Dodge (March 18), 1866, to Dodge, Dodge MSS., 5: 1712, 1752, 1758; 6: 387, *Dodge Papers*.

[38] Quoted in Dubuque *Herald*, March 14, 1866.

[39] *Cong. Globe*, 39 Cong., 1 Sess., 2318, 2373-8.

[40] *Idem.*; Kasson to Dodge, Apr. 9, 1866, *Dodge Papers*; Dewey to Kirkwood, Feb. 16, 1866, *Kirkwood Papers*.

[41] Tichenor to Dodge, March 31, Apr. 6, 1866, Box 12, *Dodge Papers*; Tichenor to C. C. Carpenter, May 20, 1866, *Carpenter Papers*.

[42] To Dodge, Apr. 16, 1866, Dodge Personal Biography, 2: 479, and Box 12, *Dodge Papers*.

[43] May 1, 1866, Dodge Personal Biography, 2: 1113-16, *ibid.*

[44] Box 12, *ibid.*

[45] Perkins, *Dodge*, 196-7; Dodge Personal Biography, 4: 1118-19; Palmer to Hoxie, Apr. 25, 1866, Dodge MSS., 5: 1893, *Dodge Papers*.

[46] May, 1866, Dodge MSS., 5: 1892, *Dodge Papers*.

[47] Box 12, *ibid.*

[48] Des Moines *Register*, May 28, 1866.

[49] Apr. 29, 1866, *Wead Collection.*

[50] E. L. Blackmar (May 11), A. Barnett (May 23), Charles Linderman (May 30), Hoxie (May 30), 1866, to Dodge, and Dr. Cory Lewis to L. W. Ross, May 19, 1866, Box 12, *Dodge Papers.*

[51] May 30, June 7, 10, 1866, Box 12, *ibid.*

[52] May 30, 1866, Box 12; Dodge Personal Biography, 4: 1117, *ibid.*

[53] May 26, 29, 30, 1866, Box 12, *ibid.*

[54] Eliot (May 29), and L. Lingenfetler (June 7), 1866, to Dodge, Box 12; Dodge Personal Biography, 4: 1119, *ibid.*; McNeil, "Edward Bates," 322-3; Beale, *Bates Diary,* 540.

[55] Circular, and Eliot to Dodge, June 1, 7, 1866, Box 12, *Dodge Papers.*

[56] For McPherson, see Herriott, "First Nomination of Lincoln," 192, 198. McPherson to Dodge, June 4, 1866, Dodge Personal Biography, 4: 112ff; Dodge MSS., 1: 406-411, *Dodge Papers*; McPherson to Kirkwood, June 20, 1866, *Kirkwood Papers.*

[57] June 20, 1866, *Kirkwood Papers*; June 26, 1866, Box 12, *Dodge Papers.*

[58] July 16, 1866, *Kirkwood Papers.*

[59] July 8, 1866, *ibid.*

[60] Italics at this point are the author's.

[61] June 22, 30, 1866, Box 12, *Dodge Papers.*

[62] July 3, 1866, Dodge MSS., 6: 114, *ibid.*

[63] Dodge Personal Biography, 2: 445; 4: 1113-19; I. D. Blanchard (May 20), and S. R. Stockton (May 31), 1866, to L. W. Ross; A. Barnett (May 23), and G. W. Harlan (June 8), 1866, to Dodge, Box 12, *ibid.*

[64] Frank M. Mills to E. R. Harlan, Jan. 27, 1921, *Edgar R. Harlan Papers* (State Dept. of History and Archives, Des Moines); and from interview with H. H. Griffiths, Des Moines, 1946.

[65] William Hyde and Howard L. Conrad, *History of St. Louis* (4 vols., St. Louis, 1899), 2: 1205; Scharf, *History of Saint Louis,* 2: 1402; Walter B. Stevens, "The New Journalism in Missouri," *Missouri Historical Review,* 9: 336-7 (January, 1925).

CHAPTER XII — POLITICAL RETREAT AND FOREIGN MISSION

[1] *Cong. Globe,* 39 Cong., 1 Sess., 2653; *Report of Committee on Coinage, Weights, and Measures, 17 May 1866* (Washington, 1866).

[2] *Cong. Globe,* 39 Cong., 1 Sess., 3850, 3881, 3975-81.

[3] Kasson (Nov. 13, Dec. 23, 1865; Jan. 12, 1866), Baldwin (Nov. 24, 1865), Tichenor (Dec. 7, 1865) to Dodge, Dodge MSS., 5: 1275, 1314, 1369, 1407, *Dodge Papers.* Kasson to John W. Garrett, *Robert Garrett Papers* (Library of Congress). Des Moines *Register,* Dec. 20, 1865. F. W. Palmer to J. S. Clarkson, Sept. 13, 1874, and another undated letter of 1874, Boxes 2, 4, *Clarkson Papers* (Library of Congress). *Cong. Globe,* 39 Cong., 1 Sess., 607, 719, 2376, 3268, 3299, 3421-4.

[4] Chester McArthur Destler, *American Radicalism, 1865-1901* (New London, Conn., 1946), 5; Current, *Old Thad Stevens,* 237; *Cong. Globe,* 39 Cong., 1 Sess., 224, 920, 3240, 3471-2, 3518, 3688, 3694, 3717-18.

[5] From Executive Committee to Kasson, June 19, 1866, in unidentified newspaper *Supplement*, Oct. 3, 1874, *Wead Collection*; Palmer to Dodge, July 19, 30, 1866, Box 13, *Dodge Papers*.

[6] Dewey to Kirkwood, Aug. 21, 1866, *Kirkwood Papers*; Des Moines *Register*, Aug. 15, 22, Sept. 5, 1866; Brigham, *Des Moines*, 1: 243; Tacitus Hussey, "How the Des Moines Valley Railroad Came to Des Moines," *Annals of Iowa* (third series), 8: 125-34 (July, 1907); *History of Polk County, Iowa* . . . (Des Moines, 1880), 705.

[7] Palmer to Dodge, June 25, July 30, 1866, Boxes 12, 13; Tichenor to Dodge, Aug. 17, 1866, Dodge Personal Biography, 4: 1131, *Dodge Papers*.

[8] To Dodge, Aug. 13, 1866, Dodge Personal Biography, 4: 1130, *ibid*.

[9] Palmer (undated) and Withrow (Aug. 23, 1866) to Dodge, Dodge Personal Biography, 4: 1131-2, *ibid*.

[10] Sept. 8, 1866, Dodge Personal Biography, 4: 1133, *ibid*.

[11] Des Moines *Register*, Aug. 22, 29, 1866; Dewey to Kirkwood, Aug. 21, 1866, *Kirkwood Papers*; Withrow to Dodge, Aug. 23, 1866, Box 13, *Dodge Papers*.

[12] Cutts to Kirkwood, Aug. 24, 1866, *Kirkwood Papers*; Dubuque *Herald*, Oct. 5, 1866; Des Moines *Register*, Oct. 8, 1866.

[13] Dubuque *Herald*, June 26, Aug. 26, 1866.

[14] Kasson to Blair, Aug. 28, 1866, *Johnson Papers*; Blair to Kasson, Sept. 12, 1866, *Aldrich Collection*, Vol. 1; Des Moines *Register*, Aug. 29, Sept. 5, 1866.

[15] Des Moines *Register*, Nov. 21, 1866; Dodge Personal Biography, 2: 584; Tichenor to Dodge, Oct. 12, 1866, Box 13, *Dodge Papers*; Sage, "Allison."

[16] Stampp, *And the War Came*, 297-8.

[17] Current, *Old Thad Stevens*, 262-75; Brown, *Raymond of the Times*, 310-14.

[18] *Cong. Globe*, 39 Cong., 2 Sess. (1866-1867), 4, 24, 50, 91-4, 321, 324, 344, 481-2, 806, 810-12, 1105, 1215, 1321, 1340, 1659, 1733; James G. Blaine, *Twenty Years of Congress* . . . (2 vols., Norwich, Conn., 1884), 2: 255.

[19] Dodge to his family, Dodge Personal Biography, 4: 1142-3; Dodge MSS., 6: 789, *Dodge Papers*.

[20] Dodge to his wife, March 6, 1867, Dodge Personal Biography, 4: 1138; March 8, 10, Apr. 5, 1867, Dodge MSS., 6: 381-91, 461, *ibid*.

[21] Tichenor to Dodge, Jan. 9, 17, Feb. 3, March 1, 12, 14, Apr. 7, 14, 1867; Palmer to Dodge, Jan. 25, March 7, 15, 19, Apr. 2, 4, 1867; Withrow to Dodge, Apr. 9, 1867, Box 14, *ibid*. See also in same file, letters of L. W. Ross, John A. Williamson, N. B. Baker, Josiah B. Grinnell, C. C. Cole, and Kirkwood. Tichenor to Kirkwood, Jan. 10, 24, Feb. 2, 1867, *Kirkwood Papers*; Tichenor to C. C. Carpenter, Dec. 11, 1866, *Carpenter Papers*.

[22] McPherson (March 7, 19, Nov. 15) and Palmer (March 22), 1867, to Dodge, Box 14, *Dodge Papers*.

[23] Dodge Personal Biography, 4: 1139-41; Iowa Congressional Delegation (March 25), and Tichenor (Apr. 18, May 3), 1867, to Dodge, Box 14, *ibid*.

[24] Des Moines *Register*, July 2, 1862. Spencer to Dodge, Jan. 28, 1866; Dodge MSS., 5: 1532; Tichenor to Dodge, Jan. 9, Feb. 9, 1867, Box 14, *Dodge Papers*. For Spencer, see Cyrus C. Carpenter, "Major-General G. M. Dodge," *Annals of Iowa* (third series),

1: 175, 305 (October, 1893; January, 1894); and Charles Aldrich, "Journalism of North-west Iowa," *ibid.*, 13: 517 (January, 1923); W. L. Fleming, *Civil War and Reconstruction in Alabama* (New York, 1905), 737, 755, 766; John W. Dubose and James K. Greer, *Alabama's Tragic Decade* (Birmingham, Ala., 1940), 291.

25 This postal mission has been worked out in detail and fully documented in Younger, "Kasson and the Universal Postal Union, 1863, 1867," 27-33.

26 Journal of Postmaster General (Order Book), Apr. 5, 10, 1867 (National Archives); "The Postal Convention with France," *House Ex. Doc. No. 40*, 41 Cong., 2 Sess. (1870-1871), 5: 3-5. Kasson to his sister, Apr. 3, 1867, *Wead Collection.*

27 Kasson to his sisters (London, May 29, June 19; Fryston Hall, June 12; Paris, July 5, 19, 26; Brussels, Aug. 25), 1867, *Wead Collection.* Clapp, *John Bigelow*, 251.

28 "Correspondence with France Relative to the Postal Convention of 1867," *Senate Ex. Doc. No. 14*, 41 Cong., 2 Sess., 1: 1-20.

29 *House Ex. Doc. No. 40*, 41 Cong., 2 Sess., 5: 3-5.

30 Sherman (June 7), Spencer (July 1, Oct. 22), Tichenor (Aug. 28, Oct. 19), 1867, to Dodge, Box 14, *Dodge Papers.* T. C. Smith, *Life and Letters of James A. Garfield* (2 vols., New Haven, 1925), 1: 414; Sage, "Allison."

CHAPTER XIII — THE FIGHT BACK: IN THE IOWA LEGISLATURE

1 Brigham, *History of Iowa*, 1: 414.

2 *House Journal, 1868*, 78, 125, 133, 194, 214-15; Des Moines *Register*, Jan. 4, 18, March 15, 1868; Brigham, *Des Moines*, 1: 553, 591-6; Earl S. Beard, "The Background of State Railroad Regulation in Iowa," *Iowa Journal of History*, 51: 21-4 (January, 1953). Literature on the capitol affair is extensive. Kasson, in his "The Fight for the New Capitol," *Annals of Iowa* (third series), 4: 241-62 (January, 1900), gives the most detail, which, when checked wherever possible in the *House Journal*, proves accurate. See also Johnson Brigham, "Kasson's Long Fight for the New Capitol," *Annals of Iowa* (third series), 10: 81-9 (July, 1911); Brigham, *History of Iowa*, 1: 480ff; Swisher, "Capitols at Des Moines," 52ff.

3 This summary of Iowa politics is based upon numerous letters from Tichenor, Palmer, Hoxie, Wilson, and Allison to Dodge, January, 1868, through March, 1870; on Dodge Personal Biography, Vol. 4; and Dodge MSS., Vol. 7, *Dodge Papers.* See also Des Moines *Register*, March 22, May 7, July 11, 12, Aug. 30, Oct. 22, Nov. 6, 1868; May 20, June 6, 9, 1869; Sage, "Allison."

4 Clark, *Senatorial Elections in Iowa*, 148. The most detailed and realistic account of this senatorial contest is in Sage, "Allison."

5 Dubuque *Times*, Jan. 27, 1870; Tichenor (Jan. 17, Feb. 10, 12), and Palmer (Feb. 8), 1870, to Dodge, Box 17, *Dodge Papers.*

6 Kasson, "The Fight for the New Capitol," 249ff.

7 Tichenor to Dodge, Feb. 10, 1870, Box 17, *Dodge Papers.*

8 Kasson, "The Fight for the New Capitol," 249ff; Constant R. Marks, "Reminiscences," *Annals of Iowa* (third series), 16: 595ff (April, 1929), and "Something Additional on Kasson's Fight for the Capitol," *ibid.*, 10: 552-3 (October, 1912); Dubuque *Times*, Apr. 13, 1870; *House Journal, 1870, passim*, Senate File, 72; Aldrich to Carpenter, Dec. 22, 1869, *Carpenter Papers.*

[9] Kasson to his sister Mary, Apr. 16, 1870, *Wead Collection*; Aldrich to Des Moines *Register*, Apr. 24, 1891; Dubuque *Times*, Apr. 26, 1870; Kasson, "The Fight for the New Capitol," 252, 261.

[10] Tichenor (Apr. 17), Hoxie (Apr. 13), and Palmer (Apr. 18), 1870, to Dodge, Box 17, *Dodge Papers*; Kasson, "The Fight for the New Capitol," 257; Swisher, "The Capitols at Des Moines," 69; *House Journal, 1870*, 316, 564.

[11] Dubuque *Times*, Apr. 26, 1870; Withrow (Apr. 22, 23, May 9), William Maxwell (May 3), Palmer (May 8), W. F. Sapp (May 10), Tichenor (June 10), 1870, to Dodge, Box 17, *Dodge Papers*; Broadside, "Attempted Fraud Upon the Republican Voters of the Fifth Congressional District," Box 130, *ibid.*; Chicago *Tribune*, May 27, June 1, 1870.

[12] Sage, "Allison"; Box 17, *Dodge Papers, passim.*

[13] Kasson to his sisters, Sept. 27, Oct. 16, 1870; Jan. 14, Apr. 23, May 4, 1871, *Wead Collection*; Reverdy Johnson to Kasson, Jan. 25, 1869, *Aldrich Collection*, Vol. 1.

[14] *Wead Collection.*

[15] Box 18, *Dodge Papers, passim*; Swisher, "Capitols at Des Moines," 70-72; Peter A. Dey, "Recollections of the Old Capitol and the New," *Annals of Iowa* (third series), 7: 81-101 (July, 1905); and "Robert S. Finkbine and . . . the Erection of the Iowa Capitol," 209-218.

[16] Mildred Throne, "Electing an Iowa Governor, 1871: Cyrus Clay Carpenter," *Iowa Journal of History*, 48: 335-70 (October, 1950), is a thorough treatment of Iowa politics at the time of Kasson's absence. To Dr. Throne, who is writing a biography of Carpenter, I am deeply indebted for certain Kasson materials from the *Carpenter Papers*. See also Sage, "Allison."

[17] James S. (Ret) Clarkson to F. H. Whitney, Apr. 3, 1907, *James S. Clarkson Papers* (Iowa State Dept. of History and Archives, Des Moines); George Mills, "The Fighting Clarksons," *The Palimpsest*, 30: 283-9 (September, 1949); Sage, "Allison"; Dubuque *Times*, Aug. 4, 1871.

[18] Kasson to Tichenor, Aug. 22, 1871, in Dubuque *Times*, Sept. 22, 1871; Sioux City *Journal*, Oct. 13, 1871.

[19] Dey, "Recollections of the Old Capitol and the New," 89; *History of Polk County*, 704-705; Dewey to Clarkson, Nov. 16, 1871, *Clarkson Papers* (Library of Congress); Box 18, *Dodge Papers, passim*; Brigham, *Des Moines*, 1: 268.

[20] Dewey to Dodge, Aug. 13, 1866, Dodge Personal Biography, 4: 1130-31, *Dodge Papers*; Dewey to Ret Clarkson, Dec. 16, 1871, *Clarkson Papers* (Library of Congress). For an exhaustive treatment, rich in manuscript materials, of this senatorial contest, see Sage, "Allison." An obituary sketch of Taylor appears in *Annals of Iowa* (third series), 1: 343-4 (January, 1894). The Sioux City *Journal's* charge of Jan. 23, 1872, that Clarkson got the state printership in return for his support of Allison is doubtless correct.

[21] *House Journal, 1872*, 77, 89-91, and *passim*; for a biographical sketch of Wilson, see *Annals of Iowa* (third series), 14: 233-4 (January, 1924).

[22] *House Journal, 1870*, 241; *1872*, 425, 485, and *passim*, House Files 12, 166, 279; Beard, "Background of State Railroad Regulation in Iowa," 21-9; Throne, "Electing an Iowa Governor," 362-3. William H. Fleming, "Gov. John Henry Gear," *Annals of Iowa* (third series), 5: 585-7 (January, 1903).

[23] *House Journal, 1870*, 580-87, and *passim*, House File 265; Kasson, "Fight for the New Capitol," 258-61; Dey, "Recollections of the Old Capitol and the New," 90-91; Swisher, "Capitols at Des Moines," 72-9.

[24] *House Journal, 1872,* 689, and *passim,* Senate File 223; Peirce, "Congressional Districting in Iowa," 343-7. Dubuque *Times,* Feb. 23, 1872; Tichenor (June 20) and Wilson (June 23), 1870, to Dodge, Box 17, *Dodge Papers.*

[25] *House Journal, 1872,* 318, House File 49; Dubuque *Times,* March 12, 1872; Clifford Powell, "History of the Codes of Iowa Law: Code of 1873," *Iowa Journal of History and Politics,* 11: 166-220 (April, 1913).

[26] Sioux City *Journal,* May 19, June 18, 1872; Dubuque *Times,* July 19, 1872; Chicago *Tribune,* Aug. 12, 1872; Clarkson to Dodge, July 24, 1872, Box 19, *Dodge Papers;* Taylor to Clarkson, May 29, 1866, *Clarkson Papers* (Des Moines). In 1886 Taylor, then angry at Clarkson, promised to write his recollections — "all that I know." In a letter dated Apr. 24, 1891, to the Des Moines *Register,* Charles Aldrich stated that he had seen a typed copy, ready for the press, of Taylor's recollections (*My Book*) of men and events in Iowa — Aldrich letter printed in an undated clipping from the Des Moines *Register* in *Wead Collection.* Both Taylor's manuscript and letters would throw much light on Iowa politics in the Gilded Age.

[27] Des Moines *Daily Republican,* July 19, 1872.

[28] Earle D. Ross, *The Liberal Republican Movement* (New York, 1919), *passim;* Fred E. Haynes, *Third Party Movements Since the Civil War* . . . (Iowa City, 1916), 22ff; Kasson to S. C. Wead, June 30, 1871, *Wead Collection;* Maxwell to Dodge, May 3, 1870, Box 17, *Dodge Papers.* Maxwell had been Kasson's colleague in the Fourteenth Assembly. In 1877 he was murdered in New Mexico, *Annals of Iowa* (third series), 6: 640 (January, 1905). Dubuque *Times,* Aug. 15, Oct. 8, 11, Nov. 6, 1872; *Western Life-Boat* (1872), 4; unidentified newspaper clipping quoting Clinton *Bee* in *Wead Collection;* Kasson to his sister Mary, Nov. 7, 1872, *ibid.*

[29] Unidentified newspaper clipping in *Wead Collection;* Dubuque *Times,* Apr. 28, 1872.

[30] Mildred Throne, "The Grange in Iowa, 1868-1875," *Iowa Journal of History,* 47: 313-17 (October, 1949); Haynes, *Third Party Movements,* 68-71.

[31] Box 19, *Dodge Papers, passim.* Tichenor (Jan. 7, 1873, March 28, 1880), Michener (July 21, Aug. 2, Nov. 21, 25, 1905, Dec. 27, 1907) to Clarkson, and Clarkson to Dodge, Aug. 26, 1902, Files D & Q, *Clarkson Papers* (Library of Congress). For biographical sketch of Palmer, see *Annals of Iowa* (third series), 8: 316-17 (January, 1908); and *Leslie's Illustrated Weekly* (May 25, 1889), 272; for Tichenor, Dodge Personal Biography, 2: 445, *Dodge Papers.*

[32] William H. Fleming, "The Autobiography of a Private Secretary," *Annals of Iowa* (third series), 15: 19-20 (July, 1925). Fleming, as private secretary to seven Iowa governors, beginning with Merrill, and as a member of the inner circle of Republican politicians, became a "walking encyclopedia" of Iowa political history. His casual reference in this article to the efforts of anti-Kassonites to organize a bloc of angry farmers against Kasson is perplexing. The position and objectives of the Clarksons in the agrarian movement of the 1870's need further study. As long as they could control the movement along conservative lines within the Republican party, they seem to have promoted it. But for the farmers boldly to strike out to help themselves through independent politics was something approaching treason. For a nontraditional appraisal of the Clarksons, see Herbert Quick, *One Man's Life* (Indianapolis, 1925), 218-29, and *The Hawkeye* (Indianapolis, 1923), 96-105. Both these books yield insight into state machine politics of the Gilded Age. For Anti-Monopoly Movement, see Mildred Throne, "The Anti-Monopoly Party in Iowa, 1873-1874," *Iowa Journal of History,* 52: 289-325 (October, 1954).

[33] Des Moines *Register and Leader,* Apr. 25, 1909; *Western Life-Boat* (1872), *passim.*

CHAPTER XIV — HALF WAY WITH GRANT: IN CONGRESS

[1] James A. Garfield Manuscript Diary, Dec. 5, 1873-March 11, 1874, *James A. Garfield Papers* (Library of Congress); *Cong. Record*, 43 Cong., 1 Sess. (1873-1874), 74, 92-7, 135, 157-8, 285.

[2] Kasson's "Reminiscences" in New York *Tribune*, Sept. 20, 1885; *Cong. Record*, 43 Cong., 1 Sess., 3971.

[3] *Cong. Record*, 43 Cong., 1 Sess., 487-90.

[4] *Ibid.*, 67, 450, 1134, 1862, 2108, 2193; Appendix, 163, 1202, 2377, 3078, 4318.

[5] *Ibid.*, 4043-6.

[6] *Ibid.*, 1607-11, 1645-56, 1994, 4108-09.

[7] *Ibid.*, 5439-40.

[8] Palmer to Clarkson, Jan. 29, 1870, *Clarkson Papers* (Library of Congress); sketch of Clarkson in Andrews, *Pioneers of Polk County*, 1: 325.

[9] Palmer to Clarkson, Dec. 23, 1873, Box 4, *Clarkson Papers* (Library of Congress); Sage, "Allison"; Kasson's rival in the general election of 1872 was O. W. Palmer. See Herbert S. Fairall, *Manual of Iowa Politics* . . . (Iowa City, 1884), 38. Ret's brother Richard had been made state printer.

[10] Dewey to Clarkson, Feb. 14, 1873, *Clarkson Papers* (Library of Congress).

[11] Withrow to Clarkson, Dec. 25, 1873, Jan. 12, 1874, File Y, *ibid.*

[12] Kasson's letters are reprinted in the Des Moines *Register*, Aug. 27, 1874. Italics are the author's.

[13] Palmer (June 28, Sept. 13, 15), Dodge (n. d.), Allen (July 17), 1874, Box 4 and Files P. Q. Y., *Clarkson Papers* (Library of Congress); Des Moines *Register*, July 11 to Oct. 15, 1874, *passim*, esp. Oct. 10, 11, 1874; Fleming "Autobiography," 19-20.

[14] File Y, *Clarkson Papers* (Library of Congress).

[15] Carpenter Diary, July 26, 1874, *Carpenter Papers*; Tyner to Palmer (July 29, Aug. 10), and to Clarkson (July 30, Aug. 3, 10), 1874, File Y; Palmer to Clarkson, July 31, 1874, File Q, *Clarkson Papers* (Library of Congress); Des Moines *Register*, Aug. 2, 8, Sept. 2, Oct. 10, 11, 1874; for defense of Kasson, see National Archives, *Journal* and *Letterbooks* of Postmaster General, Nov. 1, 1862; March 6, Apr. 1, Oct. 10, 1863; Apr. 5, Dec. 31, 1867; Feb. 13, 24, 1869; statement from auditor and superintendent of foreign mails in Kasson's "Supplement," *Wead Collection*. See also above, Chaps. VIII, IX, and XII.

[16] Des Moines *Register*, Aug. 6, 1874; Carpenter Diary, July 10, Aug. 5, 1874, *Carpenter Papers*.

[17] Des Moines *Register*, Sept. 4, 13, 18, 25, 26, Oct. 7, 1874.

[18] *Ibid.*, Sept. 17, 27, Oct. 4, 10, 11, 1874; "Supplement," Kasson's Opera House Speech, *Wead Collection*.

[19] Des Moines *Register*, Oct. 14, 15, 21, 1874.

[20] Tyner to Clarkson, Jan. 15, 1875, inclosing Kasson-Tyner correspondence, File Y, *Clarkson Papers* (Library of Congress); Fowler, *Cabinet Politician*, *passim*.

[21] *Cong. Record*, 43 Cong., 2 Sess. (1874-1875), 319, 377, 793, 891-902, 1011, 1875; Des Moines *Register*, Jan. 22, 28, 29, 30, Feb. 16, 28, 1875.

[22] *Cong. Record*, 43 Cong., 2 Sess., 293, 475, 757-61, 1600, 1801; Des Moines *Register*, Jan. 23, Feb. 23, March 2, Sept. 9, 1875.

[23] Des Moines *Register*, March 5, Apr. 10, Sept. 28, 1875; Burlington *Hawk-Eye*, May 30, 1875; Kasson to John W. Garrett, May 7, 1875, *Garrett Papers*; Leland L. Sage, "Weaver in Allison's Way . . . ," *Annals of Iowa* (third series), 31: 485-507 (January, 1953).

[24] The following summary of the trial is based primarily on the Des Moines *Register*, Nov. 11 to 28, 1875, in which the day-to-day court proceedings are published, with the exception of several apparently important deletions. The official records have been destroyed by a courthouse fire.

[25] *Cong. Record*, 39 Cong., 1 Sess. (1865-1866), 3421-4.

[26] Garfield Diary, Dec. 20, 1875, to Feb. 24, 1876, *Garfield Papers*; Kasson to his sister, Mrs. M. K. Wead, June 18, 1876, *Wead Collection*; *Cong. Record*, 44 Cong., 1 Sess. (1875-1876), 920, 1392, 5227, 5633, 5684.

[27] Kasson's "Reminiscences" in New York *Tribune*, Sept. 20, 1885; Garfield Diary, March 2, 1876, *Garfield Papers*; *Cong. Record*, 44 Cong., 1 Sess., 1525-6; Belknap Trial, 269; Des Moines *Register*, March 3, 1876.

[28] Sage, "Allison."

[29] *Cong. Record*, 44 Cong., 1 Sess., 5636-40; Des Moines *Register*, Aug. 16, 1876; see also issues of March 23, 25, May 25, 1876, for politics in the Seventh District.

[30] Des Moines *Register*, Oct. 17, 18, 19, 1876.

[31] W. W. Davis, *Civil War and Reconstruction in Florida* (New York, 1913), 687-738; P. L. Haworth, *The Hayes-Tilden Election* (Indianapolis, 1927), *passim*; Des Moines *Register*, Dec. 5, 1876; Fowler, *Cabinet Politician,* 161.

[32] *Cong. Record*, 44 Cong., 2 Sess. (1876-1877), 1050; Kasson to Hayes, Dec. 17, 27, 1876, and Hayes to Kasson, Dec. 31, 1876, *Rutherford B. Hayes Papers* (Hayes Memorial Library, Fremont, Ohio).

[33] C. Vann Woodward has pieced together the whole story in his gripping *Reunion and Reaction: The Compromise of 1877 and the End of Reconstruction* (Baton Rouge, La., 1951).

[34] *Cong. Record*, 44 Cong., 1 Sess., 250; Kasson, Autobiographical Sketch, *Kasson Papers*; Dodge to Scott, quoted in Perkins, *Dodge,* 257.

[35] *Cong. Record*, 44 Cong., 1 Sess., "Proceedings of the Electoral Commission," 4-14, 1501; Garfield Diary, Feb. 2, 1877, *Garfield Papers*.

[36] Perkins to Manning F. Force, Feb. 23, 1877; Force (Feb. 26) and Hubbell (March 3), 1877, to Hayes, *Hayes Papers*; Sage, "Allison"; Des Moines *Register*, Feb. 27, 1877; Fowler, *Cabinet Politician,* 161; *Cong. Record*, 44 Cong., 2 Sess., 176-7.

[37] Allison, John J. Ingalls, A. B. Anthony, O. P. Morton, A. A. Sargent, Newton Booth to Hayes, March 26, 1877; J. C. Stone, Rush Clark, Addison Oliver (Apr. 4); S. C. Deering (Apr. 11), W. F. Sapp (Apr. 13), H. J. B. Cummings (n. d.), 1877, to Hayes, *Department of State Appointment Papers* (National Archives); Lowell to Kasson, March 14, 1877, typescript, *Wead Collection*; L. N. Richardson, "Men of Letters and the Hayes Administration," *New England Quarterly*, 15: 110-41 (March, 1942).

CHAPTER XV — HAYES'S MINISTER TO AUSTRIA-HUNGARY

[1] Kasson, San Francisco, to Frederick W. Seward, May 22, 1877, *Despatches. Spain* (National Archives); Fish and Curtis to Kasson, June 28, 1877, *Aldrich Collection*, Vol. 2.

[2] Kasson to his sisters Mary (July 22) and Maria (Nov. 20), 1877, *Wead Collection*; *Despatches. Austria*, No. 2: Kasson to Evarts, Aug. 30, 1877; Keyes manuscript, *Kasson Papers*.

[3] Kasson's typescript speech, "Observations on Social Womanhood — Going from West to East," delivered before the Washington Woman's Club, Apr. 5, 1897, *Kasson Papers*.

[4] Nov. 20, 1877, *Wead Collection*.

[5] Kasson to Fish, Feb. 13, 1878, *Hamilton Fish Papers* (Library of Congress); Fish (Mar. 4, May 1), Garfield (Feb. 20), Sherman (Nov. 29), Noyes (May 16, Sept. 17), 1878, and Marsh, July 26, 1877, to Kasson, *Aldrich Collection*, Vols. 1, 3.

[6] *Despatches. Austria*, No. 109: Kasson to Evarts, Aug. 27, 1878; Kasson to sister Mary, Aug. 27, 1878, *Wead Collection*; John Russell Young to J. G. Bennett, Sept. 7, 1878, *John Russell Young Papers* (Library of Congress); Kasson's "Reminiscences," New York *Tribune*, Sept. 20, 1885.

[7] Hay to Kasson (unofficial), Mar. 16, 1880, *Aldrich Collection*, Vol. 3.

[8] New York *Herald*, Nov. 14, 1892; *Public Opinion*, Feb. 9, 1889; Tyner to L. T. Michener, Dec. 24, 1888, *Benjamin Harrison Papers* (Library of Congress).

[9] Robert Seager II, "Ten Years Before Mahan: The Unofficial Case for the New Navy, 1880-1890," *Mississippi Valley Historical Review*, 40: 497 (December, 1953).

[10] *Despatches. Austria*, No. 140: March 25, 1881; see also Nos. 4, 40, 121, 156: Sept. 4, 1877, to Jan. 24, 1879; Chester L. Barrows, *William M. Evarts* (Chapel Hill, N. C., 1942), *passim*.

[11] *Despatches. Austria*, No. 56: March 21, 1878; L. I. Strakhovsky, "Russia's Privateering Projects of 1878," *Journal of Modern History*, 7: 22-40 (March, 1935); Kasson to Fish, Apr. 14, May 18, 1878, *Fish Papers*.

[12] F. A. Golder, "The Russian Fleet and the Civil War," *American Historical Review*, 20: 802ff (July, 1915); see above, Chap. X.

[13] *Despatches. Austria*, No. 58: March 27, 1878. See also Nos. 76, 87: May 19, June 18, 1878.

[14] *Ibid.*, Nos. 82, 105, 126, 167, 179, 247, 255, 256, 258, 261, 271, 314, 315, 426: June 5, 1878-Feb. 23, 1881; *Instructions. Austria*, Nos. 42, 116, 121, 122, 158, 179: June 22, 1878-June 29, 1880; *Despatches. Rumania*, No. 32: Jan. 31, 1881.

[15] *Despatches. Austria*, Nos. 5, 24, 51, 133: Sept. 5 to Nov. 30, 1877.

[16] *Ibid.*, No. 434: March 12, 1881.

[17] *Ibid.*, Nos. 230, 428, 430, 434, 438, 453: Sept. 2, 1879, to Apr. 1, 1881; Nos. 133, 187, 198: Jan. 1 to Oct. 31, 1891; *Consular Despatches. Vienna*, Nos. 4, 114, 119, 122: June 24, 1878, to March 22, 1881; *Instructions. Austria*, Nos. 217, 223: Feb. 24, March 21, 1881. Brainerd Dyer, *The Public Career of William M. Evarts* (Berkeley, Calif., 1933), *passim*; Agnes Felt Tyler, *Foreign Policy of James G. Blaine* (Minneapolis, 1927), 292-3; Otto zu Stolberg-Wernigerode, *Germany and the United States During the Era of Bismarck* (Reading, Pa., 1937), 150; Jeanette Keim, *Forty Years of German-American Political Relations* (Philadelphia, 1919), 70.

[18] *Despatches. Austria*, No. 300: March 18, 1880.

[19] *Ibid.*, No. 319: April 30, 1880.

[20] John A. Kasson, "The Monroe Doctrine in 1881," *North American Review*, 133: 527,

528-9, 533 (December, 1881); and "The Monroe Declaration," *ibid.*, 133: 247-9 (September, 1881).

[21] Seager, "Ten Years Before Mahan," 491-512.

CHAPTER XVI — ALL THE WAY WITH ARTHUR: IN CONGRESS

[1] Woodward, *Reunion and Reaction*, 216-46.

[2] "Linkensale" (L. D. Ingersoll) to Clarkson, Feb. 2, 1878, File Q, *Clarkson Papers* (Library of Congress); Des Moines *Register*, June 6, 13, 15, 21, Aug. 6, 24, Oct. 1, 8, 1878; Fairall, *Manual of Iowa Politics*, 49-52.

[3] Garfield (Jan. 8, Feb. 20), Fish (March 4, May 1), 1878, to Kasson, *Aldrich Collection*, Vol. 3; Noyes to Kasson, Sept. 17, 1877, May 16, 1878, *Kasson Papers*, Box 1; Kasson to Garfield, Jan. 27, 1878, *Garfield Papers*; Kasson to Fish, Feb. 13, 1878, *Fish Papers*; Kasson to George William Curtis, Jan. 16, 1879, *Aldrich Collection*, Vol. 3.

[4] Des Moines *Register*, June 21, 26, July 2, 1879; Chicago *Times*, June 26, 1879; Charles Aldrich to Kirkwood, July 19, 1880, *Kirkwood Papers*: "Ret, I hear is inclined to bury the hatchet with Kasson, but Dick, I am told, is vindictive and totally opposed to him."

[5] Kasson to sister Mary, Mar. 5, 1880, *Wead Collection*.

[6] Kasson to S. J. Loughran, May 28, 1880, printed in Des Moines *Capitol*, May 23, 1910.

[7] Des Moines *Register*, Feb. 28, Mar. 18, 19, Apr. 15, June 29, 30, 1880.

[8] Kasson to Garfield, June 10, Aug. 7, 1880, *Garfield Papers*; Kasson to Evarts, June 26, Aug. 1, 5, and Evarts to Kasson, Aug. 4, 1880, *Despatches. Austria*, Nos. 183, 334, 472; Evarts to Kasson, Aug. 3, 1880, *Aldrich Collection*, Vol. 3.

[9] Des Moines *Register*, Sept. 17, Oct. 27, 29, Nov. 4, 1880; Brigham, *Des Moines*, 289.

[10] Clarkson to Kasson, Nov. 5, 1880, *Wead Collection*.

[11] Kasson to Garfield, Nov. 9 (telegram), 11, 1880, *Garfield Papers*. Italics the author's.

[12] Kasson to sister Mary, Nov. 18, Dec. 5, 1880, *Wead Collection*.

[13] Kasson to sister Mary, June 5, 1881, *ibid.*; Sage, "Allison." President Garfield's Cabinet included James G. Blaine, state; William Windom, treasury; Robert T. Lincoln, war; W. H. Hunt, navy; S. J. Kirkwood, interior; Wayne McVeagh, attorney general; Thomas L. James, post office.

[14] Kasson to Garfield, July 2, 1881, *Garfield Papers*; Des Moines *Register*, Sept. 20, 1881.

[15] This portrait and the following account of the speakership contest is based primarily upon information from the following newspapers: Des Moines *Register*, Burlington *Hawk-Eye*, Davenport *Gazette*, Chicago *Tribune*, Chicago *Times*, New York *Herald*, New York *Tribune*, New York *Times*, Boston *Traveller*, Boston *Evening Star*, *Harper's Weekly*, Washington *Post*, Washington *Republican*, Washington *Capitol*, Pittsburgh *Telegraph*, St. Louis *Republican*. The Des Moines *Register*, Washington *Post*, and Washington *Republican* have been checked systematically, the others from newspaper clippings in the *Kasson Papers* and *Wead Collection*.

[16] Des Moines *Register*, Nov. 6, 8, 30, 1880; Nov. 15, 16, 27, Dec. 2, 1881; Washington *Post*, Nov. 22, 25, 29, Dec. 1, 2, 1881; Washington *Republican*, Nov. 23, 28, 30, Dec. 2, 1881; Washington *Capitol*, Nov. 27, 1881.

[17] For balloting figures, see Washington *Post*, Dec. 4, 1881.

[18] Des Moines *Register*, Dec. 6, 1881.

[19] *Ibid.*, Dec. 8, 9, 1881; Gath's letter, an unidentified clipping, *Kasson Papers*, Box 12; Washington *Republican*, Dec. 5, 1881; Washington *Post*, Dec. 23, 1881; William A. Robinson, *T. B. Reed, Parliamentarian* (New York, 1930), 81-2; Albert V. House, Jr., "The Political Career of Samuel J. Randall" (Ph.D. dissertation, University of Wisconsin, 1934), 153. Former Governor C. C. Carpenter, then in the House, recorded that Keifer's election was brought about by "the fellows calling themselves *Stalwarts* & skillful playing upon the sectional issue." Carpenter was disappointed with the results. Carpenter Diary, Dec. 3, 1881, *Carpenter Papers.*

[20] Jacob Rich to Kirkwood, June 17, 1880, Feb. 20, 1881, *Kirkwood Papers*; Sage, "Allison"; Brigham, *Des Moines*, 293.

[21] Washington *Post*, Dec. 22, 1881; Jan. 5, 8, 1882; Des Moines *Register*, Dec. 24, 1881; *Cong. Record*, 47 Cong., 1 Sess. (1881-1882), 238, 461-2; G. F. Howe, *Chester A. Arthur* (New York, 1934), *passim.*

[22] *Cong. Record*, 47 Cong., 1 Sess., 280, 2687; House, "S. J. Randall," 226-8; Ida M. Tarbell, *The Tariff in Our Times* (New York, 1911), 86-101.

[23] *Cong. Record*, 47 Cong., 1 Sess., 4859; Washington *Post*, June 14, Aug. 3, 1882.

[24] Fish to Davis, Dec. 15, 16, 1881; Davis to Fish, Jan. 1, 1882, *Fish Papers*. For an original and penetrating approach to the diplomacy of the period, see Ollen L. Burnette, Jr., "The Senate Foreign Relations Committee and the Diplomacy of Garfield, Arthur, and Cleveland" (Ph.D. dissertation, University of Virginia, 1952). Kenneth W. Crosby, "The Diplomacy of the United States in Relation to the War of the Pacific, 1879-1884" (Ph.D. dissertation, George Washington University, 1949) is the best study on this subject.

[25] Indianapolis *Journal*, Feb. 2, 1882; Washington *Post*, March 3, 1882; Chicago *Tribune*, March 4, 1882; *Cong. Record*, 47 Cong., 1 Sess., 1555, 1564-5, 1882.

[26] *Cong. Record*, 47 Cong., 1 Sess., 2170, 2225-7, 2972, 3777; Washington *Post*, March 24, Apr. 7, 1882.

[27] *Cong. Record*, 47 Cong., 2 Sess. (1882-1883), 35, 318, 2133, 6316; Sarah G. Walton has produced a detailed treatment of Frelinghuysen's canal policy in "The Frelinghuysen-Zavala Treaty, 1884-1885" (M. A. thesis, University of Virginia, 1953).

[28] Mrs. E. M. Chapin, *American Court Gossip or Life at the National Capital* (Marshalltown, Iowa, 1887), 69-73; Edward Thoron (ed.), *The Letters of Mrs. Henry Adams, 1865-1883* (Boston, 1936), *passim*; Keyes Manuscript, *Kasson Papers.*

[29] D. S. Muzzey, *James G. Blaine* (New York, 1934), 250; Brigham, *Des Moines*, 295; Haynes, *Third Party Movements*, 187; Kasson to Clarkson, July 10, 1882, *Clarkson Papers* (Des Moines).

[30] Thoron (ed.), *Letters of Mrs. Henry Adams*, 414; Worthington C. Ford (ed.), *Letters of Henry Adams, 1858-1891* (Boston, 1930), 345; *Cong. Record*, 47 Cong., 2 Sess., 16, 19-21, 862-7; D. B. Eaton (Dec. 9), G. W. Curtis (Dec. 9), A. D. White (Dec. 29), 1882, to Kasson, *Kasson Papers*, Box 2.

[31] *Cong. Record*, 47 Cong., 2 Sess., 2338-50, 2957, 3740; Washington *Republican*, Dec. 4, 1882; Washington *Post*, Feb. 1, 10, 1883; Medill to Kasson, Dec. 8, 1882, *Kasson Papers*, Box 2; Tarbell, *Tariff in Our Times*, 100-132; James A. Barnes, *John G. Carlisle* (New York, 1931), 57-63; Kasson to sister Mary, Mar. 4, 1883, *Wead Collection.*

[32] McCormack (ed.), *Koerner Memoirs*, 673ff; David C. Mott, "The Pivotal Convention

of 1883," *Annals of Iowa* (third series), 26: 254-60 (April, 1945); reprint of dedicatory address, *Wead Collection*; Edward Russell to Kasson, Jan. 17, 1884, *Kasson Papers*, Box 2; John A. Kasson, "Municipal Reform," *North American Review* (September, 1883).

[33] Kasson to Charles K. Wead, Dec. 15, 1883, *Wead Collection*; Washington *Post*, Dec. 2, 4, 20, 1883; *Cong. Record*, 48 Cong., 1 Sess. (1883-1884), 223, 1601, 3193; "Free Trade Not the International Law of the Almighty," speech before Brooklyn Reform Club, Feb. 6, 1883, published by the American Iron and Steel Association, *Wead Collection.*

[34] Kasson (Jan. 31), G. F. Boulton (May 3), 1884, to Clarkson, *Clarkson Papers* (Des Moines); Muzzey, *Blaine*, 269-70, 295-6; Des Moines *Register*, June 12, 1884.

[35] *Cong. Record*, 48 Cong., 1 Sess., Feb. 28, March 10, 19, 1884; *House Ex. Doc. No. 113*, Vol. 26; *House Report No. 988*, Vol. 4; Stolberg-Wernigerode, *Germany and the United States*, 163ff; undated clipping from the Des Moines *Leader, Kasson Papers*, Box 12.

CHAPTER XVII — ARTHUR'S MINISTER TO GERMANY: THE CONGO

[1] Sister Mary (Sept. 3, 25) and Eugene Schuyler (Sept. 8, Oct. 7), 1884, to Kasson, *Wead Collection*; Nicholas Fish (July 7), Henry White (July 8), John Jay (Aug. 3), 1884, to Kasson, *Kasson Papers*, Box 2; *Despatches. Germany*, No. 5: Sept. 11, 1884.

[2] For general treatment of the Congo Conference, I have used Stolberg-Wernigerode, *Germany and the United States*; R. S. Thomson, *Foundation de l'Etat indépendant du Congo* . . . (Brussels, 1933); S. E. Crowe, *The Berlin West African Conference* . . . (London, 1942); J. S. Reeves, *The International Beginnings of the Congo Free State* (Baltimore, 1894); A. B. Keith, *The Belgian Congo and the Berlin Act* (London, 1919); George Königk, *Die Berliner Kongo-konferenz* . . . (Essen, 1938); H. E. Yarnall, *The Great Powers and the Congo Conference* (Göttingen, 1934); Geoffroy de Courcel, *L'influence de la Conférence* . . . *sur le droit, colonial, international* (Paris, 1936); H. M. Stanley, *The Congo and the Founding of its Free State* (2 vols., New York, 1885); W. O. Aydelotte, *Bismarck and British Colonial Policy* (Philadelphia, 1937).

[3] Dorothy Stanley (ed.), *Autobiography of Sir Henry M. Stanley* (London, 1909); A. J. A. Symons, *H. M. Stanley* (London, 1933); Jakob Wassermann, *H. M. Stanley — Bula Matari* (New York, 1933); sketch of Stanley by Constance L. Skinner in *Dict. of Amer. Biog.*, 18: 509; Demetrius C. Boulger, *The Reign of Leopold II* . . . (2 vols., London, 1925).

[4] I have been unable to obtain access to the Henry S. Sanford Papers in the Connecticut Historical Society Archives, Hartford, Conn. These papers, it is reported, will in time be moved to Sanford, Florida, and opened to the public. Fortunately, Robert Stanley Thomson has examined these papers and from them has published the correspondence pertinent to the Congo question in three important articles in *Le Congo, Revue générale de la Colonie belge* (Brussels, 1930-1931): "Leopold II et Henry S. Sanford," 11: 2: 295-331 (October, 1930); "Leopold II et la Conférence de Berlin," 12: 2: 325-52 (October, 1931); "Leopold II et le Congo révélés par les nottes privées de Henry S. Sanford," 12: 1: 167-96 (February, 1931). See also *Some Account of Belair; also of the City of Sanford with a Brief Sketch of Their Founder* (Sanford, Fla., 1889), and sketch of Sanford by M. B. Giffen in *Dict. of Amer. Biog.*, 16: 348. See *The Diary of Gideon Welles* . . . (3 vols., Boston, 1911), 3: 39, for a pen portrait of Sanford.

[5] For further background on the diplomacy of colonialism, see M. E. Townsend, *Origin of Modern German Colonialism* . . . (New York, 1921); R. J. Sontag, *Germany and England* . . . (New York, 1938); A. J. P. Taylor, *Germany's First Bid for Colonies* . . . (New York, 1938).

[6] O. L. Burnette, Jr., in his "The Senate Foreign Relations Committee and the Diplo-

macy of Garfield, Arthur, and Cleveland," and in a private mss. in his possession has given the best account of Morgan; William H. Halligan, Jr., uses some new material in his systematic, "The Berlin West African Conference . . . from the Viewpoint of American Participation" (M. A. thesis, University of Virginia, 1949); Morgan's role in the Congo affair is partly revealed in his personal correspondence (Library of Congress).

7 Sanford to Kasson, Aug. 25, 1884, *Kasson Papers*, Box 2; *Despatches. Germany*, Nos. 20, 30: Sept. 27, Oct. 10, 1884.

8 *Despatches. Germany*, Nos. 34-72: Oct. 13 to Nov. 17, 1884; *Instructions*, Nos. 37-44: Oct. 17 to Nov. 6, 1884; *Miscellaneous Letters*, Fish (Oct. 22), Sanford (Oct. 23, 30), 1884, to Kasson; Tisdel to Frelinghuysen (Nov. 23) and to Morgan (Nov. 25), 1884, *Morgan Papers*.

9 In addition to the works already cited, the following summary of conference proceedings is based upon *Protocols and General Acts of the West African Conference* (London, 1885); Kasson's extensive day-to-day reports in *Despatches. Germany*; Emile Banning, *Memoires Politiques et Diplomatiques; Comment Fut Fonde le Congo Belge* (Brussels, 1927); *Senate Ex. Doc. Nos. 68, 196*, 49 Cong., 1 Sess. (1885-1886), Vols. 2, 3.

10 *Despatches. Germany*, Nos. 70-71: Nov. 17, 1884.

11 *Ibid.*, Nos. 60, 109, 115: Nov. 3, Dec. 22, 29, 1884; *Instructions*, No. 66: Dec. 5, 1884.

12 Crowe, *Berlin West African Conference*, 4, 97.

13 U. S. Navy Dept., *European Squadron Letters*, Rear Admiral English to W. C. Whitney, May 2, 1885 (Navy Bldg., Arlington, Va.); Tisdel to Bayard, Apr. 25, June 29, Aug. 10, 25, 1885, *Special Agents* (U. S. Dept. of State Archives).

14 *House Ex. Docs. Nos. 156, 247*, 48 Cong., 2 Sess. (1884-1885), Vols. 27, 29; *House Report No. 2655, ibid.*, Vol. 2; Perry Belmont, *An American Democrat* (New York, 1941), *passim*; New York *Herald*, Nov. 15, Dec. 27, 1884; Jan. 6, 11, 17, 21, Feb. 27, 1885; New York *Times*, Nov. 30, 1884; Jan. 8, 25, 1885; Muzzey, *Blaine*, 425, note 1; *Cong. Record*, 50 Cong., 1 Sess. (1887-1888), 5671-2; Burnette, "Senate Foreign Relations Committee," 346ff; J. D. Richardson (ed.), *Compilation of the Messages and Papers of the Presidents* (20 vols., published by the Bureau of National Literature, Inc., New York, from the 1897 edition, 1911-1927), 10: 4886, 4915.

15 *Despatches. Germany*, Nos. 125, 131, 205, 233: Jan. 7 to Apr. 13, 1885.

16 *Ibid.*, No. 120: Jan. 5, 1885.

17 *Ibid.*, Nos. 251, 255: Apr. 30, 1885.

18 *Ibid.*, Nos. 215, 230: March 30, Apr. 13, 1885.

19 *Ibid.*, Nos. 158, 191, 194, 197, 213, 266: Feb. 7, March 2, 5, 9, 26, May 20, 1885; Kasson to Bayard (March 5) and Henry White to Kasson (March 20), 1885, *Kasson Papers*, Box 2; Memorandum of Secretary Bayard, March 13, 1885, *Thomas F. Bayard Papers* (Library of Congress); Hatzfeld to Kasson, March 29, 1885, *Legation Notes. Berlin* (National Archives); L. L. Snyder, "German-American Pork Dispute," *Journal of Modern History*, 17: 16-28 (November, 1945).

20 John A. Kasson, "The Congo Conference and the President's Message," *North American Review*, 142: 119-33 (February, 1886); Burnette, "Senate Foreign Relations Committee," 346-53, 471-3; *Cong. Record*, 49 Cong., 1 Sess. (1885-1886), 643-4; 50 Cong., 1 Sess., 5671-2; Kasson to Daniel S. Lamont, Feb. 1, 1886, *Grover Cleveland Papers* (Library of Congress); Kasson to Hamilton Fish, March 13, 1886, *Fish Papers*; Fish to Kasson, March 23, 1886, *Aldrich Collection*, Vol. 1; H. E. Mitchell to Kasson, Apr. 2, 1906, *Kasson Papers*, Box 6.

CHAPTER XVIII — HARRISON'S SAMOAN COMMISSIONER AT BERLIN

[1] Kasson to sister Mary, Nov. 27, 1885; Feb. 5, 1886, *Wead Collection*; C. W. Ernst to Kasson, Dec. 19, 1885, *Kasson Papers*, Box 2; H. Bismarck to Kasson, June 4, 1888, *Aldrich Collection*, Vol. 1; John A. Kasson, "Bismarck — Man and Minister," and "The Hohenzollern Kaiser," *North American Review*, Aug. 1886, Apr. 1888; John A. Kasson, "The Western View of the Tariff," *Forum*, December, 1887.

[2] Some of Kasson's correspondence in connection with the Centennial may be found in the *Kasson Papers*, Box 2; *Aldrich Collection*, Vol. 1; and *Wead Collection, passim*; Philadelphia *Press*, Oct. 14, 1887. For his activity during the Celebration, see Hampton L. Carson (ed.), *History of the Celebration of the One Hundredth Anniversary . . . of the Constitution* (2 vols., Philadelphia, 1889), 1: 272, 275; 2: 255, 406, 415, 421, and *passim*; for Kasson's book, see *ibid.*, 1: 1-133 and John A. Kasson, *The Evolution of the Constitution . . . and History of the Monroe Doctrine* (Boston, 1904).

[3] Kasson to sister Mary, Feb. 6, Apr. 25, 1888, *Wead Collection*; G. G. Benedict, Burlington, Vt., to Kasson, June 29, 1889, *Aldrich Collection*, Vol. 3; Augustus Lowell to Kasson, Feb. 7, 1889, *Kasson Papers*, Box 3; Kasson to Fish, Dec. 23, 1887, *Fish Papers*; General Dodge wrote Hoxie's obituary for the Des Moines *Register*, Dodge, New York, to Clarkson, Nov. 24, 1887, *Clarkson Papers* (Library of Congress); Des Moines *Register*, Nov. 24, 27, 1886.

[4] Stanton J. Peele, Indianapolis, to Kasson, Apr. 4, 18, July 11, 1888, *Kasson Papers*, Box 3; Frank L. Smith (Nov. 10), Levi P. Morton (Nov. 15), Benjamin Harrison (Dec. 7), 1888, to Kasson, *Aldrich Collection*, Vols. 1, 2, 3; Charles Beardsley to Ret Clarkson, Aug. 24, Sept. 21, 1888, *Clarkson Papers* (Des Moines); Kasson to Allison, Oct. 28, 1888, *William B. Allison Papers* (Iowa State Dept. of Hist. & Archives, Des Moines); Kasson to sister Mary, Oct. 19, 1888; Feb. 17, 1889, *Wead Collection*, and to Benjamin Harrison, Dec. 3, 1888, *Harrison Papers*; Kasson Memorandum, Jan. 1, 1889, *Wead Collection*.

[5] Kasson Memorandum, March 9, 1889, *Wead Collection*.

[6] The standard monograph on the subject is G. H. Ryden, *The Foreign Policy of the United States in Relation to Samoa* (New Haven, 1933), 367-429; see also C. E. Schieber, *Transformation of American Sentiment Toward Germany* (Boston, 1923), 54-79; C. C. Tansill, *Foreign Policy of Thomas F. Bayard* (New York, 1940), 75, 88, 99-100; Alfred Vagts, *Deutschland und die Vereinigten Staaten in der Weltpolitik* (2 vols., New York, 1934), 1: 659-69.

[7] A. T. Volwiler (ed.), *Correspondence between Benjamin Harrison and James G. Blaine* (Philadelphia, 1940), 17, 301-302; D. M. Dozer, "Benjamin Harrison and the Presidential Campaign of 1892," *American Historical Review*, 44: 50-52 (October, 1948).

[8] Kasson to sister Mary, March 11-12, 1889, and Kasson Memorandum, March 14, 1889, *Wead Collection*.

[9] For Sewall, see *Dict. of Amer. Biog.*, 16: 606; Tansill, *Foreign Policy of Thomas F. Bayard*, 100, 115. For Bates, see *Dict. of Amer. Biog.*, 2: 50; George H. Bates, "Some Aspects of the Samoan Question," *Century*, 37: 25-35 (April, 1889); R. W. Gilder to Bates, Feb. 6, 1889, *George Handy Bates Papers* (University of Delaware): New York *Herald*, Jan. 22, 1889. For Phelps, see Muzzey, *Blaine*, 229, 231; H. S. Beale (ed.), *Letters of Mrs. James G. Blaine* (2 vols., New York, 1908), *passim*; H. M. Herrick, *William Walter Phelps . . .* (New York, 1904), 43, 209-210; Phelps to Harrison, Nov. 7, 1888, *Harrison Papers*, and to Blaine, Dec. 6, 1888, *James G. Blaine Papers* (Library of Congress); Washington *Evening News*, Jan. 21, 1893.

[10] Kasson Memorandum, March 15, 16, 1889, *Wead Collection*.

[11] *Samoan Conference. Kasson Drafts*, Blaine's Instructions, April 11, 1889 (National

Archives); Beale (ed.), *Letters of Mrs. James G. Blaine*, 2: 243, 245; Volwiler (ed.), *Correspondence between Harrison and Blaine*, 57-9; Kasson's biog. sketch, *Wead Collection*; Ryden, *Foreign Policy of U. S. in Relation to Samoa*, 438-41; Muzzey, *Blaine*, 401-402.

12 Kasson Memorandum, March 15, 1889, and biog. sketch, *Wead Collection*; *English and American Register* (London), Apr. 27, 1889; Washington *Evening News*, Jan. 21, 1893; Herrick, *Phelps*, 206. In National Archives the following: *Credences*, Apr. 3, 1889; *Instructions. Germany*, Apr. 3, 1889; *Samoan Conference. Kasson Drafts*, Adee (Apr. 11), Howell (Apr. 6), 1889, to Kasson; Walker to Blaine, Apr. 13, 1889; *Special Missions. Instructions*, Blaine to Sewall, Apr. 9, 1889; *Bureau of Accounts*, "American Interests in Samoa," incorrectly filed under year 1899.

13 *Samoan Conference. Despatches and Protocols*, Kasson to Blaine, Apr. 24, 29, 1889; Henry White to Randolph P. Churchill, Apr. 23, 1889, *Aldrich Collection*, Vol. 1; Anonymous note, Florence, Italy, to Bates, Apr. 30, 1889, *Bates Papers*; Tyler, *Foreign Policy of J. G. Blaine*, 233-4; *Norddeutsche Allegemine Zeitung*, Apr. 28, 1889, in *Despatches. Germany*, No. 777: Apr. 29, 1889.

14 H. Bismarck (May 1) and Malet (June 20), 1889, to Kasson, *Aldrich Collection*, Vol. 1; Malet (Apr. 29, May 2, 14) and Holstein (May 23, 26), 1889, to Kasson, *Kasson Papers*, Box 3; H. Bismarck, June 12, 1889, to Kasson, *Wead Collection*; Ryden, *Foreign Policy of U. S. in Relation to Samoa*, 472-3; *Despatches and Protocols*, Nos. 4, 29, 31: Apr. 28, May 12, 13, June 5, 1889.

15 *Despatches and Protocols*, Nos. 24, 27: May 2, 1889; Blaine to Harrison, May 2, 1889, *Harrison Papers*.

16 *Kasson Drafts*, Blaine to Kasson, May 12, 1889, and Kasson, Phelps, and Bates to Blaine, May 13, 1889; *Despatches and Protocols*, Nos. 34, 35, 37, 41: May 12, 13, 1889; Bates to Blaine, May 7, 1889, *Bates Papers*; Phelps to Blaine, May 6, 31, 1889, *Blaine Papers*. I am indebted to Professor A. T. Volwiler for copies of Phelps's private letters, which have been checked against the originals in the *Blaine Papers*.

17 *Despatches and Protocols*, Nos. 45, 49: May 14, 16, 1889; *Kasson Drafts*, Blaine to the Commission, May 16, 1889.

18 Phelps to Blaine, May 17, 24, 1889, *Blaine Papers*.

19 *Despatches and Protocols*, Nos. 43, 44, 51, 52, 78, 79, 91: May 14-June 12, 1889; *Kasson Drafts*, Blaine to Commission (telegrams), May 21, 27, 30, June 7, 8, 11, 1889; Blaine to Harrison, May 2, and Harrison Memorandum, June 14, 1889, *Blaine Papers*; Volwiler (ed.), *Correspondence between Harrison and Blaine*, 1, 2, 5, 16, 17, 57, 58, 59, 61, 63, 65, 301-302; Beale (ed.), *Letters of Mrs. James G. Blaine*, 262-3, 269; Muzzey, *Blaine*, 401-402, 425; Herrick, *Phelps*, 216-17.

20 *Despatches and Protocols*, Nos. 78, 84, 86, 95: June 6-13, 1889; "Personal Reports," Kasson to Harrison, June 5, 18, 1889; *Kasson Drafts*, Kasson to Harrison ("not sent"), June 8, 1889; Blaine to Commission, June 9, 1889; Muzzey, *Blaine*, 402.

21 "American Interests in Samoa," *Bureau of Accounts*, May 28, 1890; *Dict. of Amer. Biog.*, 2: 50; 16: 606; *Leslie's Illustrated Weekly*, July 27, 1889; Herrick, *Phelps*, 219-29; Phelps to Blaine, Sept. 4, 1889, *Blaine Papers*; *Despatches and Protocols*, No. 104: June 15, 1889.

22 Kasson to Burns (J. P. Morgan & Co.), Aug. 17, 1889, and Kasson's biog. sketch, *Wead Collection; Despatches. Germany*, No. 92; Phelps to Blaine, March 31, 1890; rough draft of Samoan Treaty of 1889 in Kasson's handwriting, *Kasson Papers*, Box 4, dated June 14, 1899; Joseph W. Ellison, "The Partition of Samoa . . . ," *Pacific Historical Review*, 8: 260-61 (September, 1939).

CHAPTER XIX — McKINLEY'S RECIPROCITY MINISTER

[1] Kasson to sister Mary, Oct. 13, 1892, *Wead Collection.*

[2] J. R. Lowell (Nov. 6, 1890) and D. C. Gilmore (May 15, 1891) to Kasson, *Aldrich Collection*, Vol. 1; H. B. Adams (May 28, Dec. 21, 30, 1892; Apr. 27, 1893) and H. J. Hutchins (Oct. 5, 1903) to Kasson, *Kasson Papers*, Boxes 3, 6. Boston *Transcript*, Nov. 8, 1890.

[3] See drafts of several speeches and correspondence concerning them in *Kasson Papers*, Box 3; John A. Kasson, *International Arbitration* (Washington, 1896); Des Moines *Daily Capitol*, June 16, 1894.

[4] Brigham, *Des Moines*, 326; Kasson to Charles Aldrich, Feb. 12, Mar. 1, 1893; to W. Q. Gresham, March 1, 1893, *Aldrich Collection*, Vols. 1, 2; Kasson to Cole Noel, Aug. 25, 1896, *Kasson Papers*, Box 3.

[5] James Boyle (Apr. 14), James Wilson (May 26), John A. Porter (Oct. 4), 1897, to Kasson, *Kasson Papers*, Box 3.

[6] Davis S. Berry, "Men and Affairs at Washington," *New England Magazine*, 36: 407 (June, 1907); *Who Was Who in America*, Vol. 1, p. 243; *Who's Who in America*, Vol. 27, p. 1854.

[7] For background on reciprocity see *passim*: Frank W. Taussig, *The Tariff History of the United States* (New York, 1923); Muzzey, *Blaine*; Tyler, *Foreign Policy of Blaine*; James L. Laughlin and H. Parker Willis, *Reciprocity* (New York, 1903); Edward Stanwood, *American Tariff Controversies* (2 vols., Boston, 1903), Vol. 2; Tarbell, *Tariff in Our Time*; United States Tariff Commission, *Reciprocity and Commercial Treaties* (Washington, 1919); Kirk H. Porter (ed.), *National Party Platforms* (New York, 1924). Lilyan Sydenham in "McKinley Reciprocity, 1897-1903" (M. A. thesis, University of Virginia, 1953) renders a fresh and able treatment of the subject.

[8] Laughlin and Willis, *Reciprocity*, 270-310; Taussig, *Tariff History*, 323-31; U. S. Tariff Comm., *Reciprocity and Commercial Treaties*, 197-203; E. N. Dingley, *Nelson Dingley, Jr.* (Kalamazoo, Mich., 1902), 414-47; Nathaniel W. Stephenson, *Nelson W. Aldrich* (New York, 1930), 141; *Cong. Record*, 55 Cong., 1 Sess. (1897-1898), 133, 418, 2230.

[9] Interview with Osborne, Washington, D. C., 1946.

[10] This summary of Canadian-American relations and the work of the Joint High Commission is based, *passim*, upon: C. C. Tansill, *Canadian-American Relations, 1875-1911* (New Haven, 1943), which exhausts the basic manuscript material; H. L. Keenleyside and G. S. Brown, *Canada and the United States* (New York, 1952); L. M. Gelber, *The Rise of Anglo-American Friendship* (London, 1938); Tyler Dennett, *John Hay* (New York, 1933); Allan Nevins, *Henry White* (New York, 1930); Sydenham, "McKinley Reciprocity"; U. S. Tariff Commission, *Reciprocity with Canada* (Washington, 1920); *Kasson Papers*, Box 5; *Kasson Reciprocity Papers* (National Archives).

[11] A. H. U. Colquhoun, "Reciprocity Trips to Washington," *Canadian Magazine of Politics*, 8: 427 (March, 1897); Edward Farrer, "The Anglo-American Commission," *Forum*, 35: 654-5 (August, 1898); Protocol No. 2, *Kasson Reciprocity Papers*.

[12] Undated Kasson memorandum; Allison to Kasson, Oct. 7, 1898; Fairbanks to McKinley, Feb. 3, 1899, *Kasson Reciprocity Papers*.

[13] Coolidge to Kasson, Mar. 21, 1899; June 14, 1900; *ibid*.; Joseph S. McCoy to Kasson, Nov. 21, 1903, *Kasson Papers*, Box 6.

[14] Laughlin and Willis, *Reciprocity*, 311-44; U. S. Tariff Comm., *Reciprocity and Commercial Treaties, passim*.

[15] "Reciprocity Convention with France," *Senate Ex. Doc. No. 225*, 56 Cong., 1 Sess. (1899-1900), 66-122; *Manufacturers' Record*, 37: 2-3, 37-8 (Feb. 8, 1900); *Senate Ex. Journal*, 56 Cong., 1 Sess., 399; New York *Times*, Feb. 27, 1900; Porter to Kasson, March 4, 1900, and undated Senate Canvass, *Kasson Papers*, Box 4.

[16] Porter (ed.), *Party Platforms*, 231; Richardson, *Messages and Papers of the Presidents*, 13: 6435, 6465; Kasson's reply to Perkins, *Kasson Papers*, Box 4.

[17] U. S. Tariff Comm., *Reciprocity and Commercial Treaties*, 30; Washington *Mirror*, March 16, 1901; Kasson to McKinley, Apr. 26, 1900, *Kasson Papers*, Box 5; Kasson to Aldrich, March 30, 1901, *Aldrich Collection*, Vol. 3.

[18] Richardson, *Messages and Papers of the Presidents*, 13: 6621; Charles S. Olcott, *Life of William McKinley* (2 vols., New York, 1916), 2: 300; Stephenson, *Aldrich*, 450, note 10, 134, and *passim*.

[19] Stephenson, *Aldrich*, 175-80; George E. Roberts, "The Origin and History of the Iowa Idea," *Iowa Journal of History and Politics*, 2: 68-82 (January, 1904); Roosevelt to Allison (Oct. 5) and Allison to Roosevelt (Nov. 2), 1901, *Allison Papers*, Boxes 341, 344; Henry F. Pringle, *Theodore Roosevelt* (New York, 1931), 244; W. S. Holt, *Treaties Defeated by the Senate* (Baltimore, 1933), 197-8; Hay to Kasson, Aug. 11, 1900, *Aldrich Collection*, Vol. 3. Sydenham, "McKinley Reciprocity," 144-74, has the most comprehensive analysis of the causes for defeat of the treaties.

[20] Abundant evidence of Kasson's continuing work in behalf of reciprocity, including the correspondence with Cummins, is found in *Kasson Papers*, Boxes 5, 6.

[21] Kasson-Aldrich correspondence and that connected with the Columbia Historical Society in *Kasson Papers*, Boxes 3, 4, 6, and *Aldrich Collection*, Vols. 1, 2; "Laying of Cornerstone," *Annals of Iowa* (third series), 4: 90-99 (July, 1899); Des Moines *Leader*, May 18, 1899; Ora Williams, "The Iowa Historical Department," *Annals of Iowa* (third series), 22: 283 (April, 1942).

[22] Kasson to H. O. Weaver, Oct. 1, 1900, *Kasson Papers*, Box 4; Des Moines *Leader*, Oct. 11, Nov. 6, 1900.

[23] Printed speech in *Kasson Papers* and *Wead Collection*; obituary of Butler in *Annals of Iowa* (third series), 7: 475-6 (July, 1906); correspondence relating to Floyd Monument dedication, *Kasson Papers*, Boxes 3, 4.

[24] Des Moines *Register and Leader*, Nov. 7, 1904; Boston *Transcript*, July 20, 1904.

[25] U. S. Court, Dist. of Columbia, Register of Deeds, March 3, 1906.

[26] Thomas Casady to Kasson, June 18, Sept. 30, Dec. 1, 1909, *Kasson Papers*, Box 6; "Historical Activities," *Iowa Journal of History and Politics*, 41: 330 (October, 1943).

[27] From a six-stanza poem by S. H. M. Byers in Des Moines *Register and Leader*, May 22, 1910.

Index

Index

437